SELECTIONS FOR CONTRACTS

UNIFORM COMMERCIAL CODE,
UNIFORM ELECTRONIC TRANSACTIONS ACT,
ELECTRONIC SIGNATURES IN GLOBAL AND
NATIONAL COMMERCE ACT,
RESTATEMENT SECOND,
UN SALES CONVENTION,
UNIDROIT PRINCIPLES,
FORMS

Compiled by

E. ALLAN FARNSWORTH
Late Alfred McCormack Professor of Law
Columbia University

WILLIAM F. YOUNG
James L. Dohr Professor of Law Emeritus
Columbia University

CAROL SANGER
Barbara Aronstein Black Professor of Law
Columbia University

NEIL B. COHEN
Jeffrey D. Forchelli Professor of Law
Brooklyn Law School

RICHARD BROOKS
Professor of Law
Yale Law School

FOUNDATION PRESS
2007

© 1980, 1988, 1992, 1998, 2001, 2003 FOUNDATION PRESS

———————————

© 2007
By
FOUNDATION PRESS
395 Hudson Street
New York, NY 10014
Phone Toll Free 1–877–888–1330
Fax (212) 367–6799
foundation–press.com

ISBN 978-1-59941-023-4

 *TEXT IS PRINTED ON 10% POST CONSUMER RECYCLED PAPER*

TABLE OF CONTENTS

*

SELECTIONS FOR CONTRACTS

UNIFORM COMMERCIAL CODE,
UNIFORM ELECTRONIC TRANSACTIONS ACT,
ELECTRONIC SIGNATURES IN GLOBAL AND
NATIONAL COMMERCE ACT,
RESTATEMENT SECOND,
UN SALES CONVENTION,
UNIDROIT PRINCIPLES,
FORMS

*

UNIFORM COMMERCIAL CODE

(Articles 1 and 2)

COMPILERS' NOTE

The Uniform Commercial Code (UCC), a joint project of the National Conference of Commissioners on Uniform State Laws and the American Law Institute, was originally promulgated in 1951 and has been amended a number of times in succeeding years. By the 1960s, it had been enacted in every state (although some Articles, including Article 2, were not enacted in Louisiana). Topics covered include sales of goods (Article 2), leases of goods (Article 2A), negotiable instruments (Article 3), bank deposits and collections (Article 4), funds transfers (Article 4A), letters of credit (Article 5), documents of title (Article 7), investment securities (Article 8), and secured transactions (Article 9). In addition, Article 1 contains general provisions (including extensive definitions) that apply to all transactions within the scope of the UCC. Another Article (Article 6) dealt with bulk sales, but this Article has been repealed in all but a few states.

For purposes of the law of contracts, the two most important Articles of the UCC are Articles 1 and 2, the former containing general provisions that apply to all transactions within the scope of the UCC and the latter governing sales of goods. Both Articles were widely enacted by the 1960s (Article 1 was enacted in every state and Article 2 was enacted in every state except Louisiana), and remained quite stable until very recently, with the only amendments being minor changes to conform to revisions to other Articles. In the last decade, though, both Articles have been the subject of much change. In 2001, a revised text of Article 1 was promulgated by the National Conference of Commissioners on Uniform State Laws and the American Law Institute, and in 2003 those organizations promulgated substantial amendments to Article 2. As of the publication of this volume, 29 states and the U.S. Virgin Islands had enacted revised Article 1, and other states seem poised to do so in the near future. No states, however, have enacted the amendments to Article 2, and it does not appear that enactments will be forthcoming in the near future.

For purposes of understanding the UCC as it is today, this volume presents both the former version of Article 1 (often referred to as the 2000 text) and the revised version (often referred to as the 2001 text), as well as the current version of Article 2. Because Article 1 contains a number of provisions (including definitions) that are not relevant to

1

Article 2 and contract law, both versions of Article 1 in this volume are abridged by the omission of those provisions. While the amendments to Article 2 have not been enacted, they can nonetheless provide a useful basis of comparison and, accordingly, have been included as well.

Sections of the Uniform Commercial Code are typically accompanied by "Official Comments" supplied by the drafters. These Comments, although not enacted by the legislature, have proven to be quite helpful and are often cited by judges. This volume contains a selection of those Comments.

UNIFORM COMMERCIAL CODE[1]

ARTICLE 1. GENERAL PROVISIONS
(2001 Official Text)*
(Abridged)

Table of Contents

PART 1. GENERAL PROVISIONS

---

1. The original and revised texts of the Code are copyrighted by the American Law Institute and the National Conference of Commissioners on Uniform State Laws. Reprinted with permission of the Permanent Editorial Board of the Uniform Commercial Code.

* As of July 13, 2007, the 2001 text of Article 1 had been enacted in the following 29 states: Alabama, Arizona, Arkansas, California, Colorado, Connecticut, Delaware, Florida, Hawaii, Idaho, Indiana, Iowa, Kansas, Kentucky, Louisiana, Minnesota, Montana, Nebraska, Nevada, New Hampshire, New Mexico, North Carolina, North Dakota, Oklahoma, Rhode Island, Texas, Utah, Virginia, West Virginia.

PART 1

GENERAL PROVISIONS

§ 1–101. Short Titles

(a) This [Act] may be cited as the Uniform Commercial Code.

(b) This article may be cited as Uniform Commercial Code–General Provisions.

§ 1–102. Scope of Article

This article applies to a transaction to the extent that it is governed by another article of [the Uniform Commercial Code].

§ 1–103. Construction of [Uniform Commercial Code] to Promote Its Purposes and Policies; Applicability of Supplemental Principles of Law.

(a) [The Uniform Commercial Code] must be liberally construed and applied to promote its underlying purposes and policies, which are:

　　(1) to simplify, clarify, and modernize the law governing commercial transactions;

　　(2) to permit the continued expansion of commercial practices through custom, usage, and agreement of the parties; and

　　(3) to make uniform the law among the various jurisdictions.

(b) Unless displaced by the particular provisions of [the Uniform Commercial Code], the principles of law and equity, including the law merchant and the law relative to capacity to contract, principal and agent, estoppel, fraud, misrepresentation, duress, coercion, mistake, bankruptcy, and other validating or invalidating cause supplement its provisions.

Official Comments

Source: Former Section 1–102 (1)–(2); Former Section 1–103.

Changes from former law: This section is derived from subsections (1) and (2) of former Section 1–102 and from former Section 1–103. Subsection (a) of this section combines subsections (1) and (2) of former Section 1–102. Except for changing the form of reference to the Uniform Commercial Code and minor stylistic changes, its language is the same as subsections (1) and (2) of former Section 1–102. Except for changing the form of reference to the Uniform Commercial Code and minor stylistic changes, subsection (b) of this section is identical to former Section 1–103. The provisions have been combined in this section to reflect the interrelationship between them.

1. The Uniform Commercial Code is drawn to provide flexibility so that, since it is intended to be a semi-permanent and infrequently-amended piece of legislation, it will provide its own machinery for expansion of commercial practices. It is intended to make it possible for the law embodied in the Uniform Commercial Code to be applied by the courts in the light of un-

foreseen and new circumstances and practices. The proper construction of the Uniform Commercial Code requires, of course, that its interpretation and application be limited to its reason.

Even prior to the enactment of the Uniform Commercial Code, courts were careful to keep broad acts from being hampered in their effects by later acts of limited scope. See *Pacific Wool Growers v. Draper & Co.*, 158 Or. 1, 73 P.2d 1391 (1937), and compare Section 1–104. The courts have often recognized that the policies embodied in an act are applicable in reason to subject-matter that was not expressly included in the language of the act, *Commercial Nat. Bank of New Orleans v. Canal–Louisiana Bank & Trust Co.*, 239 U.S. 520, 36 S.Ct. 194, 60 L.Ed. 417 (1916) (bona fide purchase policy of Uniform Warehouse Receipts Act extended to case not covered but of equivalent nature), and did the same where reason and policy so required, even where the subject-matter had been intentionally excluded from the act in general. *Agar v. Orda*, 264 N.Y. 248, 190 N.E. 479 (1934) (Uniform Sales Act change in seller's remedies applied to contract for sale of choses in action even though the general coverage of that Act was intentionally limited to goods "other than things in action.") They implemented a statutory policy with liberal and useful remedies not provided in the statutory text. They disregarded a statutory limitation of remedy where the reason of the limitation did not apply. *Fiterman v. J. N. Johnson & Co.*, 156 Minn. 201, 194 N.W. 399 (1923) (requirement of return of the goods as a condition to rescission for breach of warranty; also, partial rescission allowed). Nothing in the Uniform Commercial Code stands in the way of the continuance of such action by the courts.

The Uniform Commercial Code should be construed in accordance with its underlying purposes and policies. The text of each section should be read in the light of the purpose and policy of the rule or principle in question, as also of the Uniform Commercial Code as a whole, and the application of the language should be construed narrowly or broadly, as the case may be, in conformity with the purposes and policies involved.

2. **Applicability of supplemental principles of law.** Subsection (b) states the basic relationship of the Uniform Commercial Code to supplemental bodies of law. The Uniform Commercial Code was drafted against the backdrop of existing bodies of law, including the common law and equity, and relies on those bodies of law to supplement it provisions in many important ways. At the same time, the Uniform Commercial Code is the primary source of commercial law rules in areas that it governs, and its rules represent choices made by its drafters and the enacting legislatures about the appropriate policies to be furthered in the transactions it covers. Therefore, while principles of common law and equity may *supplement* provisions of the Uniform Commercial Code, they may not be used to *supplant* its provisions, or the purposes and policies those provisions reflect, unless a specific provision of the Uniform Commercial Code provides otherwise. In the absence of such a provision, the Uniform Commercial Code preempts principles of common law and equity that are inconsistent with either its provisions or its purposes and policies.

The language of subsection (b) is intended to reflect both the concept of supplementation and the concept of preemption. Some courts, however, had difficulty in applying the identical language of former Section 1–103 to determine when other law appropriately may be applied to supplement the Uniform Commercial Code, and when that law has been displaced by the Code. Some decisions applied other law in situations in which that application, while not inconsistent with the text of any particular provision of the Uniform Commercial Code, clearly was inconsistent with the underlying purposes and policies reflected in the relevant provisions of the Code. *See, e.g., Sheerbonnet, Ltd. v. American Express Bank, Ltd.*, 951 F. Supp. 403 (S.D.N.Y. 1995). In part, this difficulty arose from Comment 1 to former Section 1–103, which stated that "this section indicates the continued applicability to commercial contracts of all supplemental bodies of law except insofar as they are explicitly displaced by this Act." The "explicitly displaced" language of that Comment did not accurately reflect the proper scope of Uniform Commercial Code preemption, which extends to displacement of other law that is inconsistent with the purposes and policies of the Uniform Commercial Code, as well as with its text.

3. **Application of subsection (b) to statutes.** The primary focus of Section 1–103 is on the relationship between the Uniform Commercial Code and principles of common law and equity as developed by the courts. State law, however, increasingly is statutory. Not only are there a growing number of state statutes addressing specific issues that come within the scope of the Uniform Commercial Code, but in some States many general principles of common law and equity have been codified. When the other law relating to a matter within the scope of the Uniform Commercial Code is a statute, the principles of subsection (b) remain relevant to the court's analysis of the relationship between that statute and the Uniform Commercial Code, but other principles of statutory interpretation that specifically address the interrelationship between statutes will

be relevant as well. In some situations, the principles of subsection (b) still will be determinative. For example, the mere fact that an equitable principle is stated in statutory form rather than in judicial decisions should not change the court's analysis of whether the principle can be used to supplement the Uniform Commercial Code–under subsection (b), equitable principles may supplement provisions of the Uniform Commercial Code only if they are consistent with the purposes and policies of the Uniform Commercial Code as well as its text. In other situations, however, other interpretive principles addressing the interrelationship between statutes may lead the court to conclude that the other statute is controlling, even though it conflicts with the Uniform Commercial Code. This, for example, would be the result in a situation where the other statute was specifically intended to provide additional protection to a class of individuals engaging in transactions covered by the Uniform Commercial Code.

4. **Listing not exclusive.** The list of sources of supplemental law in subsection (b) is intended to be merely illustrative of the other law that may supplement the Uniform Commercial Code, and is not exclusive. No listing could be exhaustive. Further, the fact that a particular section of the Uniform Commercial Code makes express reference to other law is not intended to suggest the negation of the general application of the principles of subsection (b). Note also that the word "bankruptcy" in subsection (b), continuing the use of that word from former Section 1–103, should be understood not as a specific reference to federal bankruptcy law but, rather as a reference to general principles of insolvency, whether under federal or state law.

§ 1–106. Use of Singular and Plural; Gender

In [the Uniform Commercial Code], unless the statutory context otherwise requires:

> (1) words in the singular number include the plural, and those in the plural include the singular; and

> (2) words of any gender also refer to any other gender.

§ 1–107. Section Captions

Section captions are part of [the Uniform Commercial Code].

§ 1–108. Relation to Electronic Signatures in Global and National Commerce Act

This article modifies, limits, and supersedes the federal Electronic Signatures in Global and National Commerce Act, 15 U.S.C. Section 7001 *et seq.*, except that nothing in this article modifies, limits, or supersedes Section 7001(C) of that Act or authorizes electronic delivery of any of the notices described in Section 7003(B) of that Act.

PART 2

GENERAL DEFINITIONS AND PRINCIPLES OF INTERPRETATION

§ 1–201. General Definitions

(a) Unless the context otherwise requires, words or phrases defined in this section, or in the additional definitions contained in other articles of [the Uniform Commercial Code] that apply to particular articles or parts thereof, have the meanings stated.

(b) Subject to definitions contained in other articles of [the Uniform Commercial Code] that apply to particular articles or parts thereof:

> (1) "Action", in the sense of a judicial proceeding, includes recoupment, counterclaim, set-off, suit in equity, and any other proceeding in which rights are determined.

> (2) "Aggrieved party" means a party entitled to pursue a remedy.

> (3) "Agreement", as distinguished from "contract", means the bargain of the parties in fact, as found in their language or inferred from other circumstances, including course of performance, course of dealing, or usage of trade as provided in Section 1–303.

> (4) "Bank" means a person engaged in the business of banking and includes a savings bank, savings and loan association, credit union, and trust company.

(6) "Bill of lading" means a document of title evidencing the receipt of goods for shipment issued by a person engaged in the business of directly or indirectly transporting or forwarding goods. The term does not include a warehouse receipt.

(8) "Burden of establishing" a fact means the burden of persuading the trier of fact that the existence of the fact is more probable than its nonexistence.

(9) "Buyer in ordinary course of business" means a person that buys goods in good faith, without knowledge that the sale violates the rights of another person in the goods, and in the ordinary course from a person, other than a pawnbroker, in the business of selling goods of that kind. A person buys goods in the ordinary course if the sale to the person comports with the usual or customary practices in the kind of business in which the seller is engaged or with the seller's own usual or customary practices. A person that sells oil, gas, or other minerals at the wellhead or minehead is a person in the business of selling goods of that kind. A buyer in ordinary course of business may buy for cash, by exchange of other property, or on secured or unsecured credit, and may acquire goods or documents of title under a preexisting contract for sale. Only a buyer that takes possession of the goods or has a right to recover the goods from the seller under Article 2 may be a buyer in ordinary course of business. "Buyer in ordinary course of business" does not include a person that acquires goods in a transfer in bulk or as security for or in total or partial satisfaction of a money debt.

(10) "Conspicuous", with reference to a term, means so written, displayed, or presented that a reasonable person against which it is to operate ought to have noticed it. Whether a term is "conspicuous" or not is a decision for the court. Conspicuous terms include the following:

(A) a heading in capitals equal to or greater in size than the surrounding text, or in contrasting type, font, or color to the surrounding text of the same or lesser size; and

(B) language in the body of a record or display in larger type than the surrounding text, or in contrasting type, font, or color to the surrounding text of the same size, or set off from surrounding text of the same size by symbols or other marks that call attention to the language.

(11) "Consumer" means an individual who enters into a transaction primarily for personal, family, or household purposes

(12) "Contract", as distinguished from "agreement", means the total legal obligation that results from the parties' agreement as determined by [the Uniform Commercial Code] as supplemented by any other applicable laws.

(13) "Creditor" includes a general creditor, a secured creditor, a lien creditor, and any representative of creditors, including an assignee for the benefit of creditors, a trustee in bankruptcy, a receiver in equity, and an executor or administrator of an insolvent debtor's or assignor's estate.

(15) "Delivery", with respect to an electronic document of title means voluntary transfer of control and with respect to an instrument, a tangible document of title, or chattel paper, means voluntary transfer of possession.

(16) "Document of title" means a record (i) that in the regular course of business or financing is treated as adequately evidencing that the person in possession or control of the record is entitled to receive, control, hold, and dispose of the record and the goods the record covers and (ii) that purports to be issued by or addressed to a bailee and to cover goods in the bailee's possession which are either identified or are fungible portions of an identified mass. The term includes a bill of lading, transport document, dock warrant, dock receipt, warehouse receipt, and order for delivery of goods. An electronic document of title is evidenced by a record consisting of information stored in an electronic medium. A tangible document of title is evidenced by a record consisting of information that is inscribed on a tangible medium.

(17) "Fault" means a default, breach, or wrongful act or omission.

(18) "Fungible goods" means:

(A) goods of which any unit, by nature or usage of trade, is the equivalent of any other like unit; or

(B) goods that by agreement are treated as equivalent.

(20) "Good faith," except as otherwise provided in Article 5, means honesty in fact and the observance of reasonable commercial standards of fair dealing.[a]

a. Of the 29 states that had enacted the 2001 text of Article 1 by June 8, 2007, 20 had enacted this provision, while nine retained the definition in the 2000 text that did not refer to the observance of reasonable commercial standards of fair dealing.

(21) "Holder" means:

    (A) the person in possession of a negotiable instrument that is payable either to bearer or to an identified person that is the person in possession;

    (B) the person in possession of a negotiable tangible document of title if the goods are deliverable either to bearer or to the order of the person in possession; or

    (C) a person in control of a negotiable electronic document of title

(23) "Insolvent" means:

    (A) having generally ceased to pay debts in the ordinary course of business other than as a result of bona fide dispute;

    (B) being unable to pay debts as they become due; or

    (C) being insolvent within the meaning of federal bankruptcy law.

(24) "Money" means a medium of exchange currently authorized or adopted by a domestic or foreign government. The term includes a monetary unit of account established by an intergovernmental organization or by agreement between two or more countries.

(26) "Party", as distinguished from "third party", means a person that has engaged in a transaction or made an agreement subject to [the Uniform Commercial Code].

(27) "Person" means an individual, corporation, business trust, estate, trust, partnership, limited liability company, association, joint venture, government, governmental subdivision, agency, or instrumentality, public corporation, or any other legal or commercial entity.

(29) "Purchase" means taking by sale, lease, discount, negotiation, mortgage, pledge, lien, security interest, issue or reissue, gift, or any other voluntary transaction creating an interest in property.

(30) "Purchaser" means a person that takes by purchase.

(31) "Record" means information that is inscribed on a tangible medium or that is stored in an electronic or other medium and is retrievable in perceivable form.

(32) "Remedy" means any remedial right to which an aggrieved party is entitled with or without resort to a tribunal.

(34) "Right" includes remedy.

(35) "Security interest" means an interest in personal property or fixtures which secures payment or performance of an obligation. "Security interest" includes any interest of a consignor and a buyer of accounts, chattel paper, a payment intangible, or a promissory note in a transaction that is subject to Article 9. "Security interest" does not include the special property interest of a buyer of goods on identification of those goods to a contract for sale under Section 2–401, but a buyer may also acquire a "security interest" by complying with Article 9. Except as otherwise provided in Section 2–505, the right of a seller or lessor of goods under Article 2 or 2A to retain or acquire possession of the goods is not a "security interest", but a seller or lessor may also acquire a "security interest" by complying with Article 9. The retention or reservation of title by a seller of goods notwithstanding shipment or delivery to the buyer under Section 2–401 is limited in effect to a reservation of a "security interest." Whether a transaction in the form of a lease creates a "security interest" is determined pursuant to Section 1–203.

(36) "Send" in connection with a writing, record, or notice means:

(A) to deposit in the mail or deliver for transmission by any other usual means of communication with postage or cost of transmission provided for and properly addressed and, in the case of an instrument, to an address specified thereon or otherwise agreed, or if there be none to any address reasonable under the circumstances; or

(B) in any other way to cause to be received any record or notice within the time it would have arrived if properly sent.

(37) "Signed" includes using any symbol executed or adopted with present intention to adopt or accept a writing.

(40) "Term" means a portion of an agreement that relates to a particular matter.

(43) "Writing" includes printing, typewriting, or any other intentional reduction to tangible form. "Written" has a corresponding meaning.

§ 1–202. Notice; Knowledge

(a) Subject to subsection (f), a person has "notice" of a fact if the person:

(1) has actual knowledge of it;

11

(2) has received a notice or notification of it; or

(3) from all the facts and circumstances known to the person at the time in question, has reason to know that it exists.

(b) "Knowledge" means actual knowledge. "Knows" has a corresponding meaning.

(c) "Discover", "learn", or words of similar import refer to knowledge rather than to reason to know.

(d) A person "notifies" or "gives" a notice or notification to another person by taking such steps as may be reasonably required to inform the other person in ordinary course, whether or not the other person actually comes to know of it.

(e) Subject to subsection (f), a person "receives" a notice or notification when:

(1) it comes to that person's attention; or

(2) it is duly delivered in a form reasonable under the circumstances at the place of business through which the contract was made or at another location held out by that person as the place for receipt of such communications.

(f) Notice, knowledge, or a notice or notification received by an organization is effective for a particular transaction from the time it is brought to the attention of the individual conducting that transaction and, in any event, from the time it would have been brought to the individual's attention if the organization had exercised due diligence. An organization exercises due diligence if it maintains reasonable routines for communicating significant information to the person conducting the transaction and there is reasonable compliance with the routines. Due diligence does not require an individual acting for the organization to communicate information unless the communication is part of the individual's regular duties or the individual has reason to know of the transaction and that the transaction would be materially affected by the information.

§ 1–204. Value

Except as otherwise provided in Articles 3, 4, [and] 5, [and 6], a person gives value for rights if the person acquires them:

(1) in return for a binding commitment to extend credit or for the extension of immediately available credit, whether or not drawn upon and whether or not a charge-back is provided for in the event of difficulties in collection;

(2) as security for, or in total or partial satisfaction of, a preexisting claim;

(3) by accepting delivery under a preexisting contract for purchase; or

(4) in return for any consideration sufficient to support a simple contract.

§ 1–205. Reasonable Time; Seasonableness

(a) Whether a time for taking an action required by [the Uniform Commercial Code] is reasonable depends on the nature, purpose, and circumstances of the action.

(b) An action is taken seasonably if it is taken at or within the time agreed or, if no time is agreed, at or within a reasonable time.

PART 3

TERRITORIAL APPLICABILITY AND GENERAL RULES

§ 1–302. Variation By Agreement

(a) Except as otherwise provided in subsection (b) or elsewhere in [the Uniform Commercial Code], the effect of provisions of [the Uniform Commercial Code] may be varied by agreement.

(b) The obligations of good faith, diligence, reasonableness, and care prescribed by [the Uniform Commercial Code] may not be disclaimed by agreement. The parties, by agreement, may determine the standards by which the performance of those obligations is to be measured if those standards are not manifestly unreasonable. Whenever [the Uniform Commercial Code] requires an action to be taken within a reasonable time, a time that is not manifestly unreasonable may be fixed by agreement.

(c) The presence in certain provisions of [the Uniform Commercial Code] of the phrase "unless otherwise agreed", or words of similar import, does not imply that the effect of other provisions may not be varied by agreement under this section.

Official Comments

Source: Former Sections 1–102(3)–(4) and 1–204(1).

Changes: This section combines the rules from subsections (3) and (4) of former Section 1–102 and subsection (1) of former Section 1–204. No substantive changes are made.

1. Subsection (a) states affirmatively at the outset that freedom of contract is a principle of the Uniform Commercial Code: "the effect" of its provisions may be varied by "agreement." The meaning of the statute itself must be found in its text, including its definitions, and in appropriate extrinsic aids; it cannot be varied by agreement. But the Uniform Commercial Code seeks to avoid the type of interference with evolutionary growth found in pre-Code cases such as *Manhattan Co. v. Morgan*, 242 N.Y. 38, 150 N.E. 594 (1926). Thus, private parties cannot make an instrument negotiable within the meaning of Article 3 except as provided in Section 3–104; nor can they change the meaning of such terms as "bona fide purchaser," "holder in due course," or "due negotiation," as used in the Uniform Commercial Code.

13

But an agreement can change the legal consequences that would otherwise flow from the provisions of the Uniform Commercial Code. "Agreement" here includes the effect given to course of dealing, usage of trade and course of performance by Sections 1–201 and 1–303; the effect of an agreement on the rights of third parties is left to specific provisions of the Uniform Commercial Code and to supplementary principles applicable under Section 1–103. The rights of third parties under Section 9–317 when a security interest is unperfected, for example, cannot be destroyed by a clause in the security agreement.

This principle of freedom of contract is subject to specific exceptions found elsewhere in the Uniform Commercial Code and to the general exception stated here. The specific exceptions vary in explicitness: the statute of frauds found in Section 2–201, for example, does not explicitly preclude oral waiver of the requirement of a writing, but a fair reading denies enforcement to such a waiver as part of the "contract" made unenforceable; Section 9–602, on the other hand, is a quite explicit limitation on freedom of contract. Under the exception for "the obligations of good faith, diligence, reasonableness and care prescribed by [the Uniform Commercial Code]," provisions of the Uniform Commercial Code prescribing such obligations are not to be disclaimed. However, the section also recognizes the prevailing practice of having agreements set forth standards by which due diligence is measured and explicitly provides that, in the absence of a showing that the standards manifestly are unreasonable, the agreement controls. In this connection, Section 1–303 incorporating into the agreement prior course of dealing and usages of trade is of particular importance.

Subsection (b) also recognizes that nothing is stronger evidence of a reasonable time than the fixing of such time by a fair agreement between the parties. However, provision is made for disregarding a clause which whether by inadvertence or overreaching fixes a time so unreasonable that it amounts to eliminating all remedy under the contract. The parties are not required to fix the most reasonable time but may fix any time which is not obviously unfair as judged by the time of contracting.

2. An agreement that varies the effect of provisions of the Uniform Commercial Code may do so by stating the rules that will govern in lieu of the provisions varied. Alternatively, the parties may vary the effect of such provisions by stating that their relationship will be governed by recognized bodies of rules or principles applicable to commercial transactions. Such bodies of rules or principles may include, for example, those that are promulgated by intergovernmental authorities such as UNCITRAL or Unidroit (*see, e.g.,* Unidroit Principles of International Commercial Contracts), or non-legal codes such as trade codes.

3. Subsection (c) is intended to make it clear that, as a matter of drafting, phrases such as "unless otherwise agreed" have been used to avoid controversy as to whether the subject matter of a particular section does or does not fall within the exceptions to subsection (b), but absence of such words contains no negative implication since under subsection (b) the general and residual rule is that the effect of all provisions of the Uniform Commercial Code may be varied by agreement.

§ 1–303. Course of Performance, Course of Dealing, and Usage of Trade

(a) A "course of performance" is a sequence of conduct between the parties to a particular transaction that exists if:

14

(1) the agreement of the parties with respect to the transaction involves repeated occasions for performance by a party; and

(2) the other party, with knowledge of the nature of the performance and opportunity for objection to it, accepts the performance or acquiesces in it without objection.

(b) A "course of dealing" is a sequence of conduct concerning previous transactions between the parties to a particular transaction that is fairly to be regarded as establishing a common basis of understanding for interpreting their expressions and other conduct.

(c) A "usage of trade" is any practice or method of dealing having such regularity of observance in a place, vocation, or trade as to justify an expectation that it will be observed with respect to the transaction in question. The existence and scope of such a usage must be proved as facts. If it is established that such a usage is embodied in a trade code or similar record, the interpretation of the record is a question of law.

(d) A course of performance or course of dealing between the parties or usage of trade in the vocation or trade in which they are engaged or of which they are or should be aware is relevant in ascertaining the meaning of the parties' agreement, may give particular meaning to specific terms of the agreement, and may supplement or qualify the terms of the agreement. A usage of trade applicable in the place in which part of the performance under the agreement is to occur may be so utilized as to that part of the performance.

(e) Except as otherwise provided in subsection (f), the express terms of an agreement and any applicable course of performance, course of dealing, or usage of trade must be construed whenever reasonable as consistent with each other. If such a construction is unreasonable:

(1) express terms prevail over course of performance, course of dealing, and usage of trade;

(2) course of performance prevails over course of dealing and usage of trade; and

(3) course of dealing prevails over usage of trade.

(f) Subject to Section 2–209, a course of performance is relevant to show a waiver or modification of any term inconsistent with the course of performance.

(g) Evidence of a relevant usage of trade offered by one party is not admissible unless that party has given the other party notice that the court finds sufficient to prevent unfair surprise to the other party.

Official Comments

Source: Former Sections 1–205, 2–208, and Section 2A–207.

Changes from former law: This section integrates the "course of performance" concept from Articles 2 and 2A into the principles of former Section 1–

205, which deals with course of dealing and usage of trade. In so doing, the section slightly modifies the articulation of the course of performance rules to fit more comfortably with the approach and structure of former Section 1–205. There are also slight modifications to be more consistent with the definition of "agreement" in former Section 1–201(3). It should be noted that a course of performance that might otherwise establish a defense to the obligation of a party to a negotiable instrument is not available as a defense against a holder in due course who took the instrument without notice of that course of performance.

1. The Uniform Commercial Code rejects both the "lay-dictionary" and the "conveyancer's" reading of a commercial agreement. Instead the meaning of the agreement of the parties is to be determined by the language used by them and by their action, read and interpreted in the light of commercial practices and other surrounding circumstances. The measure and background for interpretation are set by the commercial context, which may explain and supplement even the language of a formal or final writing.

2. "Course of dealing," as defined in subsection (b), is restricted, literally, to a sequence of conduct between the parties previous to the agreement. A sequence of conduct after or under the agreement, however, is a "course of performance." "Course of dealing" may enter the agreement either by explicit provisions of the agreement or by tacit recognition.

3. The Uniform Commercial Code deals with "usage of trade" as a factor in reaching the commercial meaning of the agreement that the parties have made. The language used is to be interpreted as meaning what it may fairly be expected to mean to parties involved in the particular commercial transaction in a given locality or in a given vocation or trade. By adopting in this context the term "usage of trade," the Uniform Commercial Code expresses its intent to reject those cases which see evidence of "custom" as representing an effort to displace or negate "established rules of law." A distinction is to be drawn between mandatory rules of law such as the Statute of Frauds provisions of Article 2 on Sales whose very office is to control and restrict the actions of the parties, and which cannot be abrogated by agreement, or by a usage of trade, and those rules of law (such as those in Part 3 of Article 2 on Sales) which fill in points which the parties have not considered and in fact agreed upon. The latter rules hold "unless otherwise agreed" but yield to the contrary agreement of the parties. Part of the agreement of the parties to which such rules yield is to be sought for in the usages of trade which furnish the background and give particular meaning to the language used, and are the framework of common understanding controlling any general rules of law which hold only when there is no such understanding.

4. A usage of trade under subsection (c) must have the "regularity of observance" specified. The ancient English tests for "custom" are abandoned in this connection. Therefore, it is not required that a usage of trade be "ancient or immemorial," "universal," or the like. Under the requirement of subsection (c) full recognition is thus available for new usages and for usages currently observed by the great majority of decent dealers, even though dissidents ready to cut corners do not agree. There is room also for proper recognition of usage agreed upon by merchants in trade codes.

5. The policies of the Uniform Commercial Code controlling explicit unconscionable contracts and clauses (Sections 1–304, 2–302) apply to im-

plicit clauses that rest on usage of trade and carry forward the policy underlying the ancient requirement that a custom or usage must be "reasonable." However, the emphasis is shifted. The very fact of commercial acceptance makes out a *prima facie* case that the usage is reasonable, and the burden is no longer on the usage to establish itself as being reasonable. But the anciently established policing of usage by the courts is continued to the extent necessary to cope with the situation arising if an unconscionable or dishonest practice should become standard.

6. Subsection (d), giving the prescribed effect to usages of which the parties "are or should be aware," reinforces the provision of subsection (c) requiring not universality but only the described "regularity of observance" of the practice or method. This subsection also reinforces the point of subsection (c) that such usages may be either general to trade or particular to a special branch of trade.

7. Although the definition of "agreement" in Section 1–201 includes the elements of course of performance, course of dealing, and usage of trade, the fact that express reference is made in some sections to those elements is not to be construed as carrying a contrary intent or implication elsewhere. Compare Section 1–302(c).

8. In cases of a well established line of usage varying from the general rules of the Uniform Commercial Code where the precise amount of the variation has not been worked out into a single standard, the party relying on the usage is entitled, in any event, to the minimum variation demonstrated. The whole is not to be disregarded because no particular line of detail has been established. In case a dominant pattern has been fairly evidenced, the party relying on the usage is entitled under this section to go to the trier of fact on the question of whether such dominant pattern has been incorporated into the agreement.

9. Subsection (g) is intended to insure that this Act's liberal recognition of the needs of commerce in regard to usage of trade shall not be made into an instrument of abuse.

§ 1–304. Obligation of Good Faith

Every contract or duty within [the Uniform Commercial Code] imposes an obligation of good faith in its performance and enforcement.

Official Comments

Source: Former Section 1–203.

Changes from former law: Except for changing the form of reference to the Uniform Commercial Code, this section is identical to former Section 1–203.

1. This section sets forth a basic principle running throughout the Uniform Commercial Code. The principle is that in commercial transactions good faith is required in the performance and enforcement of all agreements or duties. While this duty is explicitly stated in some provisions of the Uniform Commercial Code, the applicability of the duty is broader than merely these situations and applies generally, as stated in this section, to the performance or enforcement of every contract or duty within this Act. It is further implemented by Section 1–303 on course of dealing, course of performance, and usage of trade. This section does not support an independent cause of action for failure to perform or enforce in good faith. Rather, this section means that a failure to perform or enforce, in good faith, a specific duty or obligation under the

contract, constitutes a breach of that contract or makes unavailable, under the particular circumstances, a remedial right or power. This distinction makes it clear that the doctrine of good faith merely directs a court towards interpreting contracts within the commercial context in which they are created, performed, and enforced, and does not create a separate duty of fairness and reasonableness which can be independently breached.

2. "Performance and enforcement" of contracts and duties within the Uniform Commercial Code include the exercise of rights created by the Uniform Commercial Code.

§ 1–305. Remedies to Be Liberally Administered

(a) The remedies provided by [the Uniform Commercial Code] must be liberally administered to the end that the aggrieved party may be put in as good a position as if the other party had fully performed but neither consequential or special damages nor penal damages may be had except as specifically provided in [the Uniform Commercial Code] or by other rule of law.

(b) Any right or obligation declared by [the Uniform Commercial Code] is enforceable by action unless the provision declaring it specifies a different and limited effect.

Official Comments

Source: Former Section 1–106.

Changes from former law: Other than changes in the form of reference to the Uniform Commercial Code, this section is identical to former Section 1–106.

1. Subsection (a) is intended to effect three propositions. The first is to negate the possibility of unduly narrow or technical interpretation of remedial provisions by providing that the remedies in the Uniform Commercial Code are to be liberally administered to the end stated in this section. The second is to make it clear that compensatory damages are limited to compensation. They do not include consequential or special damages, or penal damages; and the Uniform Commercial Code elsewhere makes it clear that damages must be minimized. Cf. Sections 1–304, 2–706(1), and 2–712(2). The third purpose of subsection (a) is to reject any doctrine that damages must be calcula-ble with mathematical accuracy. Compensatory damages are often at best approximate: they have to be proved with whatever definiteness and accuracy the facts permit, but no more. Cf. Section 2–204(3).

2. Under subsection (b), any right or obligation described in the Uniform Commercial Code is enforceable by action, even though no remedy may be expressly provided, unless a particular provision specifies a different and limited effect. Whether specific performance or other equitable relief is available is determined not by this section but by specific provisions and by supplementary principles. Cf. Sections 1–103, 2–716.

3. "Consequential" or "special" damages and "penal" damages are not defined in the Uniform Commercial Code; rather, these terms are used in the sense in which they are used outside the Uniform Commercial Code.

§ 1–306. Waiver or Renunciation of Claim or Right After Breach

A claim or right arising out of an alleged breach may be discharged in whole or in part without consideration by agreement of the aggrieved party in an authenticated record.

Official Comments

Source: Former Section 1–107.

Changes from former law: This section changes former law in two respects. First, former Section 1–107, requiring the "delivery" of a "written waiver or renunciation" merges the separate concepts of the aggrieved party's agreement to forego rights and the manifestation of that agreement. This section separates those concepts, and explicitly requires *agreement* of the aggrieved party. Second, the revised section reflects developments in electronic commerce by providing for memorialization in an authenticated record. In this context, a party may "authenticate" a record by (i) signing a record that is a writing or (ii) attaching to or logically associating with a record that is not a writing an electronic sound, symbol or process with the present intent to adopt or accept the record. See Sections 1–201(b)(37) and 9–102(a)(7).

1. This section makes consideration unnecessary to the effective renunciation or waiver of rights or claims arising out of an alleged breach of a commercial contract where the agreement effecting such renunciation is memorialized in a record authenticated by the aggrieved party. Its provisions, however, must be read in conjunction with the section imposing an obligation of good faith. (Section 1–304).

§ 1–308. Performance or Acceptance Under Reservation of Rights

(a) A party that with explicit reservation of rights performs or promises performance or assents to performance in a manner demanded or offered by the other party does not thereby prejudice the rights reserved. Such words as "without prejudice," "under protest," or the like are sufficient.

(b) Subsection (a) does not apply to an accord and satisfaction.

Official Comments

Source: Former Section 1–207.

Changes from former law: This section is identical to former Section 1–207.

1. This section provides machinery for the continuation of performance along the lines contemplated by the contract despite a pending dispute, by adopting the mercantile device of going ahead with delivery, acceptance, or payment "without prejudice," "under protest," "under reserve," "with reservation of all our rights," and the like. All of these phrases completely reserve all rights within the meaning of this section. The section therefore contemplates that limited as well as general reservations and acceptance by a party may be made "subject to satisfaction of our purchaser," "subject to acceptance by our customers," or the like.

2. This section does not add any new requirement of language of reservation where not already required by law, but merely provides a specific measure on which a party can rely as

that party makes or concurs in any interim adjustment in the course of performance. It does not affect or impair the provisions of this Act such as those under which the buyer's remedies for defect survive acceptance without being expressly claimed if notice of the defects is given within a reasonable time. Nor does it disturb the policy of those cases which restrict the effect of a waiver of a defect to reasonable limits under the circumstances, even though no such reservation is expressed.

The section is not addressed to the creation or loss of remedies in the ordinary course of performance but rather to a method of procedure where one party is claiming as of right something which the other believes to be unwarranted.

3. Subsection (b) states that this section does not apply to an accord and satisfaction. Section 3–311 governs if an accord and satisfaction is attempted by tender of a negotiable instrument as stated in that section. If Section 3–311 does not apply, the issue of whether an accord and satisfaction has been effected is determined by the law of contract. Whether or not Section 3–311 applies, this section has no application to an accord and satisfaction.

ARTICLE 1.   GENERAL PROVISIONS
(2000 Official Text)
(Abridged)

Table of Contents

PART 1.   SHORT TITLE, CONSTRUCTION, APPLICATION AND SUBJECT MATTER OF THE ACT

PART 1

SHORT TITLE, CONSTRUCTION, APPLICATION AND SUBJECT MATTER OF THE ACT

§ 1–101.   Short Title

This Act shall be known and may be cited as Uniform Commercial Code.

§ 1–102.   Purposes; Rules of Construction; Variation by Agreement

(1) This Act shall be liberally construed and applied to promote its underlying purposes and policies.

(2) Underlying purposes and policies of this Act are

    (a) to simplify, clarify and modernize the law governing commercial transactions;

    (b) to permit the continued expansion of commercial practices through custom, usage and agreement of the parties;

21

(c) to make uniform the law among the various jurisdictions.

(3) The effect of provisions of this Act may be varied by agreement, except as otherwise provided in this Act and except that the obligations of good faith, diligence, reasonableness and care prescribed by this Act may not be disclaimed by agreement but the parties may by agreement determine the standards by which the performance of such obligations is to be measured if such standards are not manifestly unreasonable.

(4) The presence in certain provisions of this Act of the words "unless otherwise agreed" or words of similar import does not imply that the effect of other provisions may not be varied by agreement under subsection (3).

(5) In this Act unless the context otherwise requires

(a) words in the singular number include the plural, and in the plural include the singular;

(b) words of the masculine gender include the feminine and the neuter, and when the sense so indicates words of the neuter gender may refer to any gender.

§ 1–103. Supplementary General Principles of Law Applicable

Unless displaced by the particular provisions of this Act, the principles of law and equity, including the law merchant and the law relative to capacity to contract, principal and agent, estoppel, fraud, misrepresentation, duress, coercion, mistake, bankruptcy, or other validating or invalidating cause shall supplement its provisions.

§ 1–106. Remedies to Be Liberally Administered

(1) The remedies provided by this Act shall be liberally administered to the end that the aggrieved party may be put in as good a position as if the other party had fully performed but neither consequential or special nor penal damages may be had except as specifically provided in this Act or by other rule of law.

(2) Any right or obligation declared by this Act is enforceable by action unless the provision declaring it specifies a different and limited effect.

§ 1–107. Waiver or Renunciation of Claim or Right After Breach

Any claim or right arising out of an alleged breach can be discharged in whole or in part without consideration by a written waiver or renunciation signed and delivered by the aggrieved party.

§ 1–109. Section Captions

Section captions are parts of this Act.

PART 2

GENERAL DEFINITIONS AND PRINCIPLES OF INTERPRETATION

§ 1–201. General Definitions

Subject to additional definitions contained in the subsequent Articles of this Act which are applicable to specific Articles or Parts thereof, and unless the context otherwise requires, in this Act:

(1) "Action" in the sense of a judicial proceeding includes recoupment, counterclaim, set-off, suit in equity and any other proceedings in which rights are determined.

(2) "Aggrieved party" means a party entitled to resort to a remedy.

(3) "Agreement" means the bargain of the parties in fact as found in their language or by implication from other circumstances including course of dealing or usage of trade or course of performance as provided in this Act (Sections 1–205 and 2–208). Whether an agreement has legal consequences is determined by the provisions of this Act, if applicable; otherwise by the law of contracts (Section 1–103). (Compare "Contract".)

(4) "Bank" means any person engaged in the business of banking.

(5) "Bearer" means the person in possession of an instrument, document of title, or certificated security payable to bearer or indorsed in blank.

(6) "Bill of lading" means a document evidencing the receipt of goods for shipment issued by a person engaged in the business of transporting or forwarding goods, and includes an airbill. "Airbill" means a document serving for air transportation as a bill of lading does for marine or rail transportation, and includes an air consignment note or air waybill.

(8) "Burden of establishing" a fact means the burden of persuading the triers of fact that the existence of the fact is more probable than its non-existence.

(9) "Buyer in ordinary course of business" means a person who in good faith and without knowledge that the sale to him is in violation of the ownership rights or security interest of a third party in the goods buys in ordinary course from a person in the business of selling goods of that kind but does not include a pawnbroker. All persons who sell minerals or the like (including oil and gas) at wellhead or minehead shall be deemed to be persons in the business of selling goods of that kind. "Buying" may be for cash or by exchange of other property or on

secured or unsecured credit and includes receiving goods or documents of title under a preexisting contract for sale but does not include a transfer in bulk or as security for or in total or partial satisfaction of a money debt.

(10) "Conspicuous": A term or clause is conspicuous when it is so written that a reasonable person against whom it is to operate ought to have noticed it. A printed heading in capitals (as: NON–NEGOTIABLE BILL OF LADING) is conspicuous. Language in the body of a form is "conspicuous" if it is in larger or other contrasting type or color. But in a telegram any stated term is "conspicuous". Whether a term or clause is "conspicuous" or not is for decision by the court.

(11) "Contract" means the total legal obligation which results from the parties' agreement as affected by this Act and any other applicable rules of law. (Compare "Agreement".)

(12) "Creditor" includes a general creditor, a secured creditor, a lien creditor and any representative of creditors, including an assignee for the benefit of creditors, a trustee in bankruptcy, a receiver in equity and an executor or administrator of an insolvent debtor's or assignor's estate.

(14) "Delivery" with respect to instruments, documents of title, chattel paper, or certificated securities means voluntary transfer of possession.

(15) "Document of title" includes bill of lading, dock warrant, dock receipt, warehouse receipt or order for the delivery of goods, and also any other document which in the regular course of business or financing is treated as adequately evidencing that the person in possession of it is entitled to receive, hold and dispose of the document and the goods it covers. To be a document of title a document must purport to be issued by or addressed to a bailee and purport to cover goods in the bailee's possession which are either identified or are fungible portions of an identified mass.

(16) "Fault" means wrongful act, omission or breach.

(17) "Fungible" with respect to goods or securities means goods or securities of which any unit is, by nature or usage of trade, the equivalent of any other like unit. Goods which are not fungible shall be deemed fungible for the purposes of this Act to the extent that under a particular agreement or document unlike units are treated as equivalents.

(18) "Genuine" means free of forgery or counterfeiting.

(19) "Good faith" means honesty in fact in the conduct or transaction concerned.

(20) "Holder," with respect to a negotiable instrument, means the person in possession if the instrument is payable to bearer or, in the case of an instrument payable to an identified person, if the identified person

is in possession. "Holder" with respect to a document of title means the person in possession if the goods are deliverable to bearer or to the order of the person in possession.

(22) "Insolvency proceedings" includes any assignment for the benefit of creditors or other proceedings intended to liquidate or rehabilitate the estate of the person involved.

(23) A person is "insolvent" who either has ceased to pay his debts in the ordinary course of business or cannot pay his debts as they become due or is insolvent within the meaning of the federal bankruptcy law.

(24) "Money" means a medium of exchange authorized or adopted by a domestic or foreign government and includes a monetary unit of account established by an intergovernmental organization or by agreement between two or more nations.

(25) A person has "notice" of a fact when

(a) he has actual knowledge of it; or

(b) he has received a notice or notification of it; or

(c) from all the facts and circumstances known to him at the time in question he has reason to know that it exists.

A person "knows" or has "knowledge" of a fact when he has actual knowledge of it. "Discover" or "learn" or a word or phrase of similar import refers to knowledge rather than to reason to know. The time and circumstances under which a notice or notification may cease to be effective are not determined by this Act.

(26) A person "notifies" or "gives" a notice or notification to another by taking such steps as may be reasonably required to inform the other in ordinary course whether or not such other actually comes to know of it. A person "receives" a notice or notification when

(a) it comes to his attention; or

(b) it is duly delivered at the place of business through which the contract was made or at any other place held out by him as the place for receipt of such communications.

(27) Notice, knowledge or a notice or notification received by an organization is effective for a particular transaction from the time when it is brought to the attention of the individual conducting that transaction, and in any event from the time when it would have been brought to his attention if the organization had exercised due diligence. An organization exercises due diligence if it maintains reasonable routines for communicating significant information to the person conducting the transaction and there is reasonable compliance with the routines. Due diligence does not require an individual acting for the organization to communicate information unless such communication is part of his

regular duties or unless he has reason to know of the transaction and that the transaction would be materially affected by the information.

(29) "Party", as distinct from "third party", means a person who has engaged in a transaction or made an agreement within this Act.

(30) "Person" includes an individual or an organization (See Section 1–102).

(32) "Purchase" includes taking by sale, discount, negotiation, mortgage, pledge, lien, issue or re-issue, gift or any other voluntary transaction creating an interest in property.

(33) "Purchaser" means a person who takes by purchase.

(34) "Remedy" means any remedial right to which an aggrieved party is entitled with or without resort to a tribunal.

(35) "Representative" includes an agent, an officer of a corporation or association, and a trustee, executor or administrator of an estate, or any other person empowered to act for another.

(36) "Rights" includes remedies.

(37) "Security interest" means an interest in personal property or fixtures which secures payment or performance of an obligation. The term also includes any interest of a consignor and a buyer of accounts, chattel paper, a payment intangible, or a promissory note in a transaction that is subject to Article 9. . . . Whether a transaction creates a lease or security interest is determined by the facts of each case. . . .[a]

(38) "Send" in connection with any writing or notice means to deposit in the mail or deliver for transmission by any other usual means of communication with postage or cost of transmission provided for and properly addressed and in the case of an instrument to an address specified thereon or otherwise agreed, or if there be none to any address reasonable under the circumstances. The receipt of any writing or notice within the time at which it would have arrived if properly sent has the effect of a proper sending.

(39) "Signed" includes any symbol executed or adopted by a party with present intention to authenticate a writing.

(41) "Telegram" includes a message transmitted by radio, teletype, cable, any mechanical method of transmission, or the like.

(42) "Term" means that portion of an agreement which relates to a particular matter.

(44) "Value". Except as otherwise provided with respect to negotiable instruments and bank collections (Sections 3–303, 4–208 and 4–209) a person gives "value" for rights if he acquires them

---

a. The remainder of this definition, not reprinted here, contains extensive rules for distinguishing "true leases" from security interests.

(a) in return for a binding commitment to extend credit or for the extension of immediately available credit whether or not drawn upon and whether or not a charge-back is provided for in the event of difficulties in collection; or

(b) as security for or in total or partial satisfaction of a pre-existing claim; or

(c) by accepting delivery pursuant to a pre-existing contract for purchase; or

(d) generally, in return for any consideration sufficient to support a simple contract.

(46) "Written" or "writing" includes printing, typewriting or any other intentional reduction to tangible form.

§ 1–203. Obligation of Good Faith

Every contract or duty within this Act imposes an obligation of good faith in its performance or enforcement.

§ 1–204. Time; Reasonable Time; "Seasonably"

(1) Whenever this Act requires any action to be taken within a reasonable time, any time which is not manifestly unreasonable may be fixed by agreement.

(2) What is a reasonable time for taking any action depends on the nature, purpose and circumstances of such action.

(3) An action is taken "seasonably" when it is taken at or within the time agreed or if no time is agreed at or within a reasonable time.

§ 1–205. Course of Dealing and Usage of Trade

(1) A course of dealing is a sequence of previous conduct between the parties to a particular transaction which is fairly to be regarded as establishing a common basis of understanding for interpreting their expressions and other conduct.

(2) A usage of trade is any practice or method of dealing having such regularity of observance in a place, vocation or trade as to justify an expectation that it will be observed with respect to the transaction in question. The existence and scope of such a usage are to be proved as facts. If it is established that such a usage is embodied in a written trade code or similar writing the interpretation of the writing is for the court.

(3) A course of dealing between parties and any usage of trade in the vocation or trade in which they are engaged or of which they are or should be aware give particular meaning to and supplement or qualify terms of an agreement.

(4) The express terms of an agreement and an applicable course of dealing or usage of trade shall be construed wherever reasonable as

consistent with each other; but when such construction is unreasonable express terms control both course of dealing and usage of trade and course of dealing controls usage of trade.

(5) An applicable usage of trade in the place where any part of performance is to occur shall be used in interpreting the agreement as to that part of the performance.

(6) Evidence of a relevant usage of trade offered by one party is not admissible unless and until he has given the other party such notice as the court finds sufficient to prevent unfair surprise to the latter.

§ 1–206. Statute of Frauds for Kinds of Personal Property Not Otherwise Covered

(1) Except in the cases described in subsection (2) of this section a contract for the sale of personal property is not enforceable by way of action or defense beyond five thousand dollars in amount or value of remedy unless there is some writing which indicates that a contract for sale has been made between the parties at a defined or stated price, reasonably identifies the subject matter, and is signed by the party against whom enforcement is sought or by his authorized agent.

(2) Subsection (1) of this section does not apply to contracts for the sale of goods (Section 2–201) nor of securities (Section 8–319) nor to security agreements (Section 9–203).

§ 1–207. Performance or Acceptance Under Reservation of Rights

(1) A party who with explicit reservation of rights performs or promises performance or assents to performance in a manner demanded or offered by the other party does not thereby prejudice the rights reserved. Such words as "without prejudice", "under protest" or the like are sufficient.

(2) Subsection (1) does not apply to an accord and satisfaction.

ARTICLE 2.   SALES (Current Text)

Table of Contents

PART 1.   SHORT TITLE, GENERAL CONSTRUCTION AND SUBJECT MATTER

PART 2.   FORM, FORMATION AND READJUSTMENT OF CONTRACT

PART 3.   GENERAL OBLIGATION AND CONSTRUCTION OF CONTRACT

PART 1

SHORT TITLE, GENERAL CONSTRUCTION AND SUBJECT MATTER

§ 2–101. Short Title

This Article shall be known and may be cited as Uniform Commercial Code—Sales.

§ 2–102. Scope; Certain Security and Other Transactions Excluded From This Article

Unless the context otherwise requires, this Article applies to transactions in goods; it does not apply to any transaction which although in the form of an unconditional contract to sell or present sale is intended to operate only as a security transaction nor does this Article impair or repeal any statute regulating sales to consumers, farmers or other specified classes of buyers.

Definitional Cross References:

"Contract". Section 1–201.

"Contract for sale". Section 2–106.

"Present sale". Section 2–106.

"Sale". Section 2–106.

§ 2–103. Definitions and Index of Definitions

(1) In this Article unless the context otherwise requires

    (a) "Buyer" means a person who buys or contracts to buy goods.

    (b) "Good faith" in the case of a merchant means honesty in fact and the observance of reasonable commercial standards of fair dealing in the trade.[a]

    (c) "Receipt" of goods means taking physical possession of them.

    (d) "Seller" means a person who sells or contracts to sell goods.

(2) Other definitions applying to this Article or to specified Parts thereof, and the sections in which they appear are:

"Acceptance". Section 2–606.

"Banker's credit". Section 2–325.

"Between merchants". Section 2–104.

"Cancellation". Section 2–106(4).

"Commercial unit". Section 2–105.

"Confirmed credit". Section 2–325.

"Conforming to contract". Section 2–106.

"Contract for sale". Section 2–106.

"Cover". Section 2–712.

"Entrusting". Section 2–403.

"Financing agency". Section 2–104.

"Future goods". Section 2–105.

"Goods". Section 2–105.

"Identification". Section 2–501.

"Installment contract". Section 2–612.

"Letter of Credit". Section 2–325.

"Lot". Section 2–105.

"Merchant". Section 2–104.

"Overseas". Section 2–323.

"Person in position of seller". Section 2–707.

---

a. As of June 8, 2007, this definition has been deleted in the 20 states that have enacted the 2001 text of UCC § 1–201(b)(20).

"Present sale". Section 2–106.

"Sale". Section 2–106.

"Sale on approval". Section 2–326.

"Sale or return". Section 2–326.

"Termination". Section 2–106.

(3) The following definitions in other Articles apply to this Article:

"Check". Section 3–104.

"Consignee". Section 7–102.

"Consignor". Section 7–102.

"Consumer goods". Section 9–102.

"Dishonor". Section 3–502.

"Draft". Section 3–104.

(4) In addition Article 1 contains general definitions and principles of construction and interpretation applicable throughout this Article.

Definitional Cross Reference:

"Person". Section 1–201.

§ 2–104. Definitions; "Merchant"; "Between Merchants"; "Financing Agency"

(1) "Merchant" means a person who deals in goods of the kind or otherwise by his occupation holds himself out as having knowledge or skill peculiar to the practices or goods involved in the transaction or to whom such knowledge or skill may be attributed by his employment of an agent or broker or other intermediary who by his occupation holds himself out as having such knowledge or skill.

(2) "Financing agency" means a bank, finance company or other person who in the ordinary course of business makes advances against goods or documents of title or who by arrangement with either the seller or the buyer intervenes in ordinary course to make or collect payment due or claimed under the contract for sale, as by purchasing or paying the seller's draft or making advances against it or by merely taking it for collection whether or not documents of title accompany the draft. "Financing agency" includes also a bank or other person who similarly intervenes between persons who are in the position of seller and buyer in respect to the goods (Section 2–707).

(3) "Between merchants" means in any transaction with respect to which both parties are chargeable with the knowledge or skill of merchants.

Definitional Cross References: "Buyer". Section 2–103.

"Bank". Section 1–201.

§ 2-105. Definitions: Transferability; "Goods"; "Future" Goods; "Lot"; "Commercial Unit"

(1) "Goods" means all things (including specially manufactured goods) which are movable at the time of identification to the contract for sale other than the money in which the price is to be paid, investment securities (Article 8) and things in action. "Goods" also includes the unborn young of animals and growing crops and other identified things attached to realty as described in the section on goods to be severed from realty (Section 2–107).

(2) Goods must be both existing and identified before any interest in them can pass. Goods which are not both existing and identified are "future" goods. A purported present sale of future goods or of any interest therein operates as a contract to sell.

(3) There may be a sale of a part interest in existing identified goods.

(4) An undivided share in an identified bulk of fungible goods is sufficiently identified to be sold although the quantity of the bulk is not determined. Any agreed proportion of such a bulk or any quantity thereof agreed upon by number, weight or other measure may to the extent of the seller's interest in the bulk be sold to the buyer who then becomes an owner in common.

(5) "Lot" means a parcel or a single article which is the subject matter of a separate sale or delivery, whether or not it is sufficient to perform the contract.

(6) "Commercial unit" means such a unit of goods as by commercial usage is a single whole for purposes of sale and division of which materially impairs its character or value on the market or in use. A commercial unit may be a single article (as a machine) or a set of articles (as a suite of furniture or an assortment of sizes) or a quantity (as a bale, gross, or carload) or any other unit treated in use or in the relevant market as a single whole.

Definitional Cross References:
    "Buyer". Section 2–103.
    "Contract". Section 1–201.
"Contract for sale". Section 2–106.

§ 2-106. Definitions: "Contract"; "Agreement"; "Contract for Sale"; "Sale"; "Present Sale"; "Conforming" to Contract; "Termination"; "Cancellation"

(1) In this Article unless the context otherwise requires "contract" and "agreement" are limited to those relating to the present or future sale of goods. "Contract for sale" includes both a present sale of goods and a contract to sell goods at a future time. A "sale" consists in the

passing of title from the seller to the buyer for a price (Section 2–401). A "present sale" means a sale which is accomplished by the making of the contract.

(2) Goods or conduct including any part of a performance are "conforming" or conform to the contract when they are in accordance with the obligations under the contract.

(3) "Termination" occurs when either party pursuant to a power created by agreement or law puts an end to the contract otherwise than for its breach. On "termination" all obligations which are still executory on both sides are discharged but any right based on prior breach or performance survives.

(4) "Cancellation" occurs when either party puts an end to the contract for breach by the other and its effect is the same as that of "termination" except that the cancelling party also retains any remedy for breach of the whole contract or any unperformed balance.

Definitional Cross References:

"Agreement". Section 1–201.

"Buyer". Section 2–103.

"Contract". Section 1–201.

"Goods". Section 2–105.

"Party". Section 1–201.

"Remedy". Section 1–201.

"Rights". Section 1–201.

"Seller". Section 2–103.

§ 2–107. Goods to Be Severed From Realty: Recording

(1) A contract for the sale of minerals or the like (including oil and gas) or a structure or its materials to be removed from realty is a contract for the sale of goods within this Article if they are to be severed by the seller but until severance a purported present sale thereof which is not effective as a transfer of an interest in land is effective only as a contract to sell.

(2) A contract for the sale apart from the land of growing crops or other things attached to realty and capable of severance without material harm thereto but not described in subsection (1) or of timber to be cut is a contract for the sale of goods within this Article whether the subject matter is to be severed by the buyer or by the seller even though it forms part of the realty at the time of contracting, and the parties can by identification effect a present sale before severance.

(3) The provisions of this section are subject to any third party rights provided by the law relating to realty records, and the contract for sale may be executed and recorded as a document transferring an interest in land and shall then constitute notice to third parties of the buyer's rights under the contract for sale.

Definitional Cross References:

"Buyer". Section 2–103.

"Contract". Section 1–201.

"Contract for sale". Section 2–106.

"Goods". Section 2–105.

"Party". Section 1–201.

"Present sale". Section 2–106.

"Rights". Section 1–201.

"Seller". Section 2–103.

PART 2

FORM, FORMATION AND READJUSTMENT OF CONTRACT

§ 2–201. Formal Requirements; Statute of Frauds

(1) Except as otherwise provided in this section a contract for the sale of goods for the price of $500 or more is not enforceable by way of action or defense unless there is some writing sufficient to indicate that a contract for sale has been made between the parties and signed by the party against whom enforcement is sought or by his authorized agent or broker. A writing is not insufficient because it omits or incorrectly states a term agreed upon but the contract is not enforceable under this paragraph beyond the quantity of goods shown in such writing.

(2) Between merchants if within a reasonable time a writing in confirmation of the contract and sufficient against the sender is received and the party receiving it has reason to know its contents, it satisfies the requirements of subsection (1) against such party unless written notice of objection to its contents is given within ten days after it is received.

(3) A contract which does not satisfy the requirements of subsection (1) but which is valid in other respects is enforceable

    (a) if the goods are to be specially manufactured for the buyer and are not suitable for sale to others in the ordinary course of the seller's business and the seller, before notice of repudiation is received and under circumstances which reasonably indicate that the goods are for the buyer, has made either a substantial beginning of their manufacture or commitments for their procurement; or

    (b) if the party against whom enforcement is sought admits in his pleading, testimony or otherwise in court that a contract for sale was made, but the contract is not enforceable under this provision beyond the quantity of goods admitted; or

    (c) with respect to goods for which payment has been made and accepted or which have been received and accepted (Sec. 2–606).

Official Comment

Prior Uniform Statutory Provision: Section 4, Uniform Sales Act (which was based on Section 17 of the Statute of 29 Charles II).

Changes: Completely rephrased; restricted to sale of goods. See also Sections 1–206, 8–319 and 9–203.

Purposes of Changes: The changed phraseology of this section is intended to make it clear that:

1. The required writing need not contain all the material terms of the contract and such material terms as are stated need not be precisely stated. All that is required is that the writing afford a basis for believing that the offered oral evidence rests on a real transaction. It may be written in lead pencil on a scratch pad. It need not indicate which party is the buyer and which the seller. The only term which must appear is the quantity term which need not be accurately stated but recovery is limited to the amount stated. The price, time and place of payment or delivery, the general quality of the goods, or any particular warranties may all be omitted.

Special emphasis must be placed on the permissibility of omitting the price term in view of the insistence of some courts on the express inclusion of this term even where the parties have contracted on the basis of a published price list. In many valid contracts for sale the parties do not mention the price in express terms, the buyer being bound to pay and the seller to accept a reasonable price which the trier of the fact may well be trusted to determine. Again, frequently the price is not mentioned since the parties have based their agreement on a price list or catalogue known to both of them and this list serves as an efficient safeguard against perjury. Finally, "market" prices and valuations that are current in the vicinity constitute a similar check. Thus if the price is not stated in the memorandum it can normally be supplied without danger of fraud. Of course if the "price" consists of goods rather than money the quantity of goods must be stated.

Only three definite and invariable requirements as to the memorandum are made by this subsection. First, it must evidence a contract for the sale of goods; second, it must be "signed", a word which includes any authentication which identifies the party to be charged; and third, it must specify a quantity.

2. "Partial performance" as a substitute for the required memorandum can validate the contract only for the goods which have been accepted or for which payment has been made and accepted.

Receipt and acceptance either of goods or of the price constitutes an unambiguous overt admission by both parties that a contract actually exists. If the court can make a just apportionment, therefore, the agreed price of any goods actually delivered can be recovered without a writing or, if the price has been paid, the seller can be forced to deliver an apportionable part of the goods. The overt actions of the parties make admissible evidence of the other terms of the contract necessary to a just apportionment. This is true even though the actions of the parties are not in themselves inconsistent with a different transaction such as a consignment for resale or a mere loan of money.

Part performance by the buyer requires the delivery of something by him that is accepted by the seller as such performance. Thus, part payment may be made by money or check, accepted by the seller. If the agreed price consists of goods or services, then they must also have been delivered and accepted.

3. Between merchants, failure to answer a written confirmation of a contract within ten days of receipt is tantamount to a writing under subsection (2) and is sufficient against both parties under subsection (1). The only effect, however, is to take away from the party who fails to answer the defense of the Statute of Frauds; the

burden of persuading the trier of fact that a contract was in fact made orally prior to the written confirmation is unaffected. Compare the effect of a failure to reply under Section 2–207.

4. Failure to satisfy the requirements of this section does not render the contract void for all purposes, but merely prevents it from being judicially enforced in favor of a party to the contract. For example, a buyer who takes possession of goods as provided in an oral contract which the seller has not meanwhile repudiated, is not a trespasser. Nor would the Statute of Frauds provisions of this section be a defense to a third person who wrongfully induces a party to refuse to perform an oral contract, even though the injured party cannot maintain an action for damages against the party so refusing to perform.

5. The requirement of "signing" is discussed in the comment to Section 1–201.

6. It is not necessary that the writing be delivered to anybody. It need not be signed or authenticated by both parties but it is, of course, not sufficient against one who has not signed it. Prior to a dispute no one can determine which party's signing of the memorandum may be necessary but from the time of contracting each party should be aware that to him it is signing by the other which is important.

7. If the making of a contract is admitted in court, either in a written pleading, by stipulation or by oral statement before the court, no additional writing is necessary for protection against fraud. Under this section it is no longer possible to admit the contract in court and still treat the Statute as a defense. However, the contract is not thus conclusively established. The admission so made by a party is itself evidential against him of the truth of the facts so admitted and of nothing more; as against the other party, it is not evidential at all.

Cross References:

See Sections 1–201, 2–202, 2–207, 2–209 and 2–304.

Definitional Cross References:

"Action". Section 1–201.

"Between merchants". Section 2–104.

"Buyer". Section 2–103.

"Contract". Section 1–201.

"Contract for sale". Section 2–106.

"Goods". Section 2–105.

"Notice". Section 1–201.

"Party". Section 1–201.

"Reasonable time". Section 1–204.

"Sale". Section 2–106.

"Seller". Section 2–103.

§ 2–202. Final Written Expression: Parol or Extrinsic Evidence

Terms with respect to which the confirmatory memoranda of the parties agree or which are otherwise set forth in a writing intended by the parties as a final expression of their agreement with respect to such terms as are included therein may not be contradicted by evidence of any prior agreement or of a contemporaneous oral agreement but may be explained or supplemented

> (a) by course of dealing or usage of trade (Section 1–205) or by course of performance (Section 2–208); and

(b) by evidence of consistent additional terms unless the court finds the writing to have been intended also as a complete and exclusive statement of the terms of the agreement.

Definitional Cross References:

"Agreed" and "agreement". Section 1–201.

"Course of dealing". Section 1–205.

"Parties". Section 1–201.

"Term". Section 1–201.

"Usage of trade". Section 1–205.

"Written" and "writing". Section 1–201.

§ 2–203. Seals Inoperative

The affixing of a seal to a writing evidencing a contract for sale or an offer to buy or sell goods does not constitute the writing a sealed instrument and the law with respect to sealed instruments does not apply to such a contract or offer.

Definitional Cross References:

"Contract for sale". Section 2–106.

"Goods". Section 2–105.

"Writing". Section 1–201.

§ 2–204. Formation in General

(1) A contract for sale of goods may be made in any manner sufficient to show agreement, including conduct by both parties which recognizes the existence of such a contract.

(2) An agreement sufficient to constitute a contract for sale may be found even though the moment of its making is undetermined.

(3) Even though one or more terms are left open a contract for sale does not fail for indefiniteness if the parties have intended to make a contract and there is a reasonably certain basis for giving an appropriate remedy.

Definitional Cross References:

"Agreement". Section 1–201.

"Contract". Section 1–201.

"Contract for sale". Section 2–106.

"Goods". Section 2–105.

"Party". Section 1–201.

"Remedy". Section 1–201.

"Term". Section 1–201.

§ 2–205. Firm Offers

An offer by a merchant to buy or sell goods in a signed writing which by its terms gives assurance that it will be held open is not revocable, for lack of consideration, during the time stated or if no time is stated for a reasonable time, but in no event may such period of irrevocability exceed three months; but any such term of assurance on a form supplied by the offeree must be separately signed by the offeror.

Definitional Cross References:

"Goods". Section 2–105.

"Merchant". Section 2–104.

"Signed". Section 1–201.

"Writing". Section 1–201.

§ 2–206. Offer and Acceptance in Formation of Contract

(1) Unless otherwise unambiguously indicated by the language or circumstances

> (a) an offer to make a contract shall be construed as inviting acceptance in any manner and by any medium reasonable in the circumstances;

> (b) an order or other offer to buy goods for prompt or current shipment shall be construed as inviting acceptance either by a prompt promise to ship or by the prompt or current shipment of conforming or non-conforming goods, but such a shipment of non-conforming goods does not constitute an acceptance if the seller seasonably notifies the buyer that the shipment is offered only as an accommodation to the buyer.

(2) Where the beginning of a requested performance is a reasonable mode of acceptance an offeror who is not notified of acceptance within a reasonable time may treat the offer as having lapsed before acceptance.

Definitional Cross References:

"Buyer". Section 2–103.
"Conforming". Section 2–106.
"Contract". Section 1–201.

"Goods". Section 2–105.
"Notifies". Section 1–201.
"Reasonable time". Section 1–204.

§ 2–207. Additional Terms in Acceptance or Confirmation

(1) A definite and seasonable expression of acceptance or a written confirmation which is sent within a reasonable time operates as an acceptance even though it states terms additional to or different from those offered or agreed upon, unless acceptance is expressly made conditional on assent to the additional or different terms.

(2) The additional terms are to be construed as proposals for addition to the contract. Between merchants such terms become part of the contract unless:

> (a) the offer expressly limits acceptance to the terms of the offer;

> (b) they materially alter it; or

> (c) notification of objection to them has already been given or is given within a reasonable time after notice of them is received.

(3) Conduct by both parties which recognizes the existence of a contract is sufficient to establish a contract for sale although the writings of the parties do not otherwise establish a contract. In such case the terms of the particular contract consist of those terms on which the

writings of the parties agree, together with any supplementary terms incorporated under any other provisions of this Act.

Official Comment

Prior Uniform Statutory Provision: Sections 1 and 3, Uniform Sales Act.

Changes: Completely rewritten by this and other sections of this Article.

Purposes of Changes:

1. This section is intended to deal with two typical situations. The one is the written confirmation, where an agreement has been reached either orally or by informal correspondence between the parties and is followed by one or both of the parties sending formal memoranda embodying the terms so far as agreed upon and adding terms not discussed. The other situation is offer and acceptance, in which a wire or letter expressed and intended as an acceptance or the closing of an agreement adds further minor suggestions or proposals such as "ship by Tuesday," "rush," "ship draft against bill of lading inspection allowed," or the like. A frequent example of the second situation is the exchange of printed purchase order and acceptance (sometimes called "acknowledgment") forms. Because the forms are oriented to the thinking of the respective drafting parties, the terms contained in them often do not correspond. Often the seller's form contains terms different from or additional to those set forth in the buyer's form. Nevertheless, the parties proceed with the transaction. [Comment 1 was amended in 1966.]

2. Under this Article a proposed deal which in commercial understanding has in fact been closed is recognized as a contract. Therefore, any additional matter contained in the confirmation or in the acceptance falls within subsection (2) and must be regarded as a proposal for an added term unless the acceptance is made conditional on the acceptance of the additional or different terms. [Comment 2 was amended in 1966.]

3. Whether or not additional or different terms will become part of the agreement depends upon the provisions of subsection (2). If they are such as materially to alter the original bargain, they will not be included unless expressly agreed to by the other party. If, however, they are terms which would not so change the bargain they will be incorporated unless notice of objection to them has already been given or is given within a reasonable time.

4. Examples of typical clauses which would normally "materially alter" the contract and so result in surprise or hardship if incorporated without express awareness by the other party are: a clause negating such standard warranties as that of merchantability or fitness for a particular purpose in circumstances in which either warranty normally attaches; a clause requiring a guaranty of 90% or 100% deliveries in a case such as a contract by cannery, where the usage of the trade allows greater quantity leeways; a clause reserving to the seller the power to cancel upon the buyer's failure to meet any invoice when due; a clause requiring that complaints be made in a time materially shorter than customary or reasonable.

5. Examples of clauses which involve no element of unreasonable surprise and which therefore are to be incorporated in the contract unless notice of objection is seasonably given are: a clause setting forth and perhaps enlarging slightly upon the seller's exemption due to supervening causes beyond his control, similar to those covered by the provision of this Article on

merchant's excuse by failure of presupposed conditions or a clause fixing in advance any reasonable formula of proration under such circumstances; a clause fixing a reasonable time for complaints within customary limits, or in the case of a purchase for sub-sale, providing for inspection by the sub-purchaser; a clause providing for interest on overdue invoices or fixing the seller's standard credit terms where they are within the range of trade practice and do not limit any credit bargained for; a clause limiting the right of rejection for defects which fall within the customary trade tolerances for acceptance "with adjustment" or otherwise limiting remedy in a reasonable manner (see Sections 2–718 and 2–719).

6. If no answer is received within a reasonable time after additional terms are proposed, it is both fair and commercially sound to assume that their inclusion has been assented to. Where clauses on confirming forms sent by both parties conflict each party must be assumed to object to a clause of the other conflicting with one on the confirmation sent by himself. As a result the requirement that there be notice of objection which is found in subsection (2) is satisfied and the conflicting terms do not become a part of the contract. The contract then consists of the terms originally expressly agreed to, terms on which the confirmations agree, and terms supplied by his Act, including subsection (2). The written confirmation is also subject to Section 2–201. Under that section a failure to respond permits enforcement of a prior oral agreement; under this section a failure to respond permits additional terms to become part of the agreement. [Comment 6 was amended in 1966.]

7. In many cases, as where goods are shipped, accepted and paid for before any dispute arises, there is no question whether a contract has been made. In such cases, where the writings of the parties do not establish a contract, it is not necessary to determine which act or document constituted the offer and which the acceptance. See Section 2–204. The only question is what terms are included in the contract, and subsection (3) furnishes the governing rule. [Comment 7 was added in 1966.]

Cross References:

See generally Section 2–302.

Point 5: Sections 2–513, 2–602, 2–607, 2–609, 2–612, 2–614, 2–615, 2–616, 2–718 and 2–719.

Point 6: Sections 1–102 and 2–104.

Definitional Cross References:

"Between merchants". Section 2–104.

"Contract". Section 1–201.

"Notification". Section 1–201.

"Reasonable time". Section 1–204.

"Seasonably". Section 1–204.

"Send". Section 1–201.

"Term". Section 1–201.

"Written". Section 1–201.

§ 2–208. Course of Performance or Practical Construction[b]

(1) Where the contract for sale involves repeated occasions for performance by either party with knowledge of the nature of the performance and opportunity for objection to it by the other, any course

---

b. This section has been repealed in the 29 states that, as of July 13, 2007, have enacted the 2001 text of Article 1.

of performance accepted or acquiesced in without objection shall be relevant to determine the meaning of the agreement.

(2) The express terms of the agreement and any such course of performance, as well as any course of dealing and usage of trade, shall be construed whenever reasonable as consistent with each other; but when such construction is unreasonable, express terms shall control course of performance and course of performance shall control both course of dealing and usage of trade (Section 1–205).

(3) Subject to the provisions of the next section on modification and waiver, such course of performance shall be relevant to show a waiver or modification of any term inconsistent with such course of performance.

Prior Uniform Statutory Provision: No such general provision but concept of this section recognized by terms such as "course of dealing", "the circumstances of the case," "the conduct of the parties," etc., in Uniform Sales Act.

§ 2–209. Modification, Rescission and Waiver

(1) An agreement modifying a contract within this Article needs no consideration to be binding.

(2) A signed agreement which excludes modification or rescission except by a signed writing cannot be otherwise modified or rescinded, but except as between merchants such a requirement on a form supplied by the merchant must be separately signed by the other party.

(3) The requirements of the statute of frauds section of this Article (Section 2–201) must be satisfied if the contract as modified is within its provisions.

(4) Although an attempt at modification or rescission does not satisfy the requirements of subsection (2) or (3) it can operate as a waiver.

(5) A party who has made a waiver affecting an executory portion of the contract may retract the waiver by reasonable notification received by the other party that strict performance will be required of any term waived, unless the retraction would be unjust in view of a material change of position in reliance on the waiver.

Definitional Cross References:

"Agreement". Section 1–201.

"Between merchants". Section 2–104.

"Contract". Section 1–201.

"Notification". Section 1–201.

"Signed". Section 1–201.

"Term". Section 1–201.

"Writing". Section 1–201.

§ 2–210. Delegation of Performance; Assignment of Rights

(1) A party may perform his duty through a delegate unless otherwise agreed or unless the other party has a substantial interest in having

his original promisor perform or control the acts required by the contract. No delegation of performance relieves the party delegating of any duty to perform or any liability for breach.

(2) Except as otherwise provided in Section 9–406, unless otherwise agreed all rights of either seller or buyer can be assigned except where the assignment would materially change the duty of the other party, or increase materially the burden or risk imposed on him by his contract, or impair materially his chance of obtaining return performance. A right to damages for breach of the whole contract or a right arising out of the assignor's due performance of his entire obligation can be assigned despite agreement otherwise.

(3) The creation, attachment, perfection, or enforcement of a security interest in the seller's interest under a contract is not a transfer that materially changes the duty of or increases materially the burden or risk imposed on the buyer or impairs materially the buyer's chance of obtaining return performance within the purview of subsection (2) unless, and then only to the extent that, enforcement actually results in a delegation of material performance of the seller. Even in that event, the creation, attachment, perfection, and enforcement of the security interest remains effective, but (i) the seller is liable to the buyer for damages caused by the delegation to the extent that the damages could not reasonably be prevented by the buyer, and (ii) a court having jurisdiction may grant other appropriate relief, including cancellation of the contract for sale or an injunction against enforcement of the security interest or consummation of the enforcement.

(4) Unless the circumstances indicate the contrary a prohibition of assignment of "the contract" is to be construed as barring only the delegation to the assignee of the assignor's performance.

(5) An assignment of "the contract" or of "all my rights under the contract" or an assignment in similar general terms is an assignment of rights and unless the language or the circumstances (as in an assignment for security) indicate the contrary, it is a delegation of performance of the duties of the assignor and its acceptance by the assignee constitutes a promise by him to perform those duties. This promise is enforceable by either the assignor or the other party to the original contract.

(6) The other party may treat any assignment which delegates performance as creating reasonable grounds for insecurity and may without prejudice to his rights against the assignor demand assurances from the assignee (Section 2–609).

Definitional Cross References:

"Agreement". Section 1–201.

"Buyer". Section 2–103.

"Contract". Section 1–201.

"Party". Section 1–201.

"Rights". Section 1–201.

"Seller". Section 2–103.

"Term". Section 1–201.

PART 3

GENERAL OBLIGATION AND CONSTRUCTION OF CONTRACT

§ 2–301. General Obligations of Parties

The obligation of the seller is to transfer and deliver and that of the buyer is to accept and pay in accordance with the contract.

Definitional Cross References:

"Buyer". Section 2–103.

"Contract". Section 1–201.

"Party". Section 1–201.

"Seller". Section 2–103.

§ 2–302. Unconscionable Contract or Clause

(1) If the court as a matter of law finds the contract or any clause of the contract to have been unconscionable at the time it was made the court may refuse to enforce the contract, or it may enforce the remainder of the contract without the unconscionable clause, or it may so limit the application of any unconscionable clause as to avoid any unconscionable result.

(2) When it is claimed or appears to the court that the contract or any clause thereof may be unconscionable the parties shall be afforded a reasonable opportunity to present evidence as to its commercial setting, purpose and effect to aid the court in making the determination.

Official Comment

Prior Uniform Statutory Provision: None.

Purposes:

1. This section is intended to make it possible for the courts to police explicitly against the contracts or clauses which they find to be unconscionable. In the past such policing has been accomplished by adverse construction of language, by manipulation of the rules of offer and acceptance or by determinations that the clause is contrary to public policy or to the dominant purpose of the contract. This section is intended to allow the court to pass directly on the unconscionability of the contract or particular clause therein and to make a conclusion of law as to its unconscionability. The basic test is whether, in the light of the general commercial background and the commercial needs of the particular trade or case, the clauses involved are so one-sided as to be unconscionable under the circumstances existing at the time of the making of the contract. Subsection (2) makes it clear that it is proper for the court to hear evidence upon these questions. The principle is one of the prevention of oppression and unfair surprise (Cf. Campbell Soup Co. v. Wentz, 172 F.2d 80, 3d Cir.1948) and not of disturbance of allocation of risks because of superior bargaining power. The underlying basis of this section is illustrated by the results in cases such as the following:

Kansas City Wholesale Grocery Co. v. Weber Packing Corporation, 93 Utah 414, 73 P.2d 1272 (1937), where a clause limiting time for complaints was held inapplicable to latent defects in a shipment of catsup which could be discovered only by microscopic analysis; Hardy v. General Motors Acceptance Corporation, 38 Ga.App. 463, 144 S.E. 327 (1928), holding that a disclaimer of warranty clause applied only to express warranties, thus letting in a fair implied warranty; Andrews Bros. v. Singer & Co. (1934 CA) 1 K.B. 17, holding that where a car with substantial mileage was delivered instead of a "new" car, a disclaimer of warranties, including those "implied," left unaffected an "express obligation" on the description, even though the Sale of Goods Act called such an implied warranty; New Prague Flouring Mill Co. v. G.A. Spears, 194 Iowa 417, 189 N.W. 815 (1922), holding that a clause permitting the seller, upon the buyer's failure to supply shipping instructions, to cancel, ship, or allow delivery date to be indefinitely postponed 30 days at a time by the inaction, does not indefinitely postpone the date of measuring damages for the buyer's breach, to the seller's advantage; and Kansas Flour Mills Co. v. Dirks, 100 Kan. 376, 164 P. 273 (1917), where under a similar clause in a rising market the court permitted the buyer to measure his damages for non-delivery at the end of only one 30 day postponement; Green v. Arcos, Ltd. (1931 CA) 47 T.L.R. 336, where a blanket clause prohibiting rejection of shipments by the buyer was restricted to apply to shipments where discrepancies represented merely mercantile variations; Meyer v. Packard Cleveland Motor Co., 106 Ohio St. 328, 140 N.E. 118 (1922), in which the court held that a "waiver" of all agreements not specified did not preclude implied warranty of fitness of a rebuilt dump truck for ordinary use as a dump truck; Austin Co. v. J.H. Tillman Co., 104 Or. 541, 209 P. 131 (1922), where a clause limiting the buyer's remedy to return was held to be applicable only if the seller had delivered a machine needed for a construction job which reasonably met the contract description; Bekkevold v. Potts, 173 Minn. 87, 216 N.W. 790, 59 A.L.R. 1164 (1927), refusing to allow warranty of fitness for purpose imposed by law to be negated by clause excluding all warranties "made" by the seller; Robert A. Munroe & Co. v. Meyer (1930) 2 K.B. 312, holding that the warranty of description overrides a clause reading "with all faults and defects" where adulterated meat not up to the contract description was delivered.

2. Under this section the court, in its discretion, may refuse to enforce the contract as a whole if it is permeated by the unconscionability, or it may strike any single clause or group of clauses which are so tainted or which are contrary to the essential purpose of the agreement, or it may simply limit unconscionable clauses so as to avoid unconscionable results.

3. The present section is addressed to the court, and the decision is to be made by it. The commercial evidence referred to in subsection (2) is for the court's consideration, not the jury's. Only the agreement which results from the court's action on these matters is to be submitted to the general triers of the facts.

Definitional Cross Reference:

"Contract". Section 1–201.

§ 2–303. Allocation or Division of Risks

Where this Article allocates a risk or a burden as between the parties "unless otherwise agreed", the agreement may not only shift the allocation but may also divide the risk or burden.

Definitional Cross References:

"Agreement". Section 1–201.

"Party". Section 1–201.

§ 2–304. Price Payable in Money, Goods, Realty, or Otherwise

(1) The price can be made payable in money or otherwise. If it is payable in whole or in part in goods each party is a seller of the goods which he is to transfer.

(2) Even though all or part of the price is payable in an interest in realty the transfer of the goods and the seller's obligations with reference to them are subject to this Article, but not the transfer of the interest in realty or the transferor's obligations in connection therewith.

§ 2–305. Open Price Term

(1) The parties if they so intend can conclude a contract for sale even though the price is not settled. In such a case the price is a reasonable price at the time for delivery if

> (a) nothing is said as to price; or
>
> (b) the price is left to be agreed by the parties and they fail to agree; or
>
> (c) the price is to be fixed in terms of some agreed market or other standard as set or recorded by a third person or agency and it is not so set or recorded.

(2) A price to be fixed by the seller or by the buyer means a price for him to fix in good faith.

(3) When a price left to be fixed otherwise than by agreement of the parties fails to be fixed through fault of one party the other may at his option treat the contract as cancelled or himself fix a reasonable price.

(4) Where, however, the parties intend not to be bound unless the price be fixed or agreed and it is not fixed or agreed there is no contract. In such a case the buyer must return any goods already received or if unable so to do must pay their reasonable value at the time of delivery and the seller must return any portion of the price paid on account.

Definitional Cross References:

"Agreement". Section 1–201.

"Burden of establishing". Section 1–201.

"Buyer". Section 2–103.

"Cancellation". Section 2–106.

"Contract". Section 1–201.

"Contract for sale". Section 2–106.

"Fault". Section 1–201.

"Goods". Section 2–105.

"Party". Section 1–201.

"Receipt of goods". Section 2–103.

"Seller". Section 2–103.

"Term". Section 1–201.

§ 2-306. Output, Requirements and Exclusive Dealings

(1) A term which measures the quantity by the output of the seller or the requirements of the buyer means such actual output or requirements as may occur in good faith, except that no quantity unreasonably disproportionate to any stated estimate or in the absence of a stated estimate to any normal or otherwise comparable prior output or requirements may be tendered or demanded.

(2) A lawful agreement by either the seller or the buyer for exclusive dealing in the kind of goods concerned imposes unless otherwise agreed an obligation by the seller to use best efforts to supply the goods and by the buyer to use best efforts to promote their sale.

Definitional Cross References:

"Agreement". Section 1-201.

"Buyer". Section 2-103.

"Contract for sale". Section 2-106.

"Good faith". Section 1-201.

"Goods". Section 2-105.

"Party". Section 1-201.

"Term". Section 1-201.

"Seller". Section 2-103.

§ 2-307. Delivery in Single Lot or Several Lots

Unless otherwise agreed all goods called for by a contract for sale must be tendered in a single delivery and payment is due only on such tender but where the circumstances give either party the right to make or demand delivery in lots the price if it can be apportioned may be demanded for each lot.

Definitional Cross References:

"Contract for sale". Section 2-106.

"Goods". Section 2-105.

"Lot". Section 2-105.

"Party". Section 1-201.

"Rights". Section 1-201.

§ 2-308. Absence of Specified Place for Delivery

Unless otherwise agreed

    (a) the place for delivery of goods is the seller's place of business or if he has none his residence; but

    (b) in a contract for sale of identified goods which to the knowledge of the parties at the time of contracting are in some other place, that place is the place for their delivery; and

    (c) documents of title may be delivered through customary banking channels.

Definitional Cross References:

"Contract for sale". Section 2-106.

"Delivery". Section 1-201.

"Document of title". Section 1-201.

"Goods". Section 2-105.

"Party". Section 1-201.

"Seller". Section 2-103.

§ 2–309. Absence of Specific Time Provisions; Notice of Termination

(1) The time for shipment or delivery or any other action under a contract if not provided in this Article or agreed upon shall be a reasonable time.

(2) Where the contract provides for successive performances but is indefinite in duration it is valid for a reasonable time but unless otherwise agreed may be terminated at any time by either party.

(3) Termination of a contract by one party except on the happening of an agreed event requires that reasonable notification be received by the other party and an agreement dispensing with notification is invalid if its operation would be unconscionable.

Definitional Cross References:

"Agreement". Section 1–201.

"Contract". Section 1–201.

"Notification". Section 1–201.

"Party". Section 1–201.

"Reasonable time". Section 1–204.

"Termination". Section 2–106.

§ 2–310. Open Time for Payment or Running of Credit; Authority to Ship Under Reservation

Unless otherwise agreed

(a) payment is due at the time and place at which the buyer is to receive the goods even though the place of shipment is the place of delivery; and

(b) if the seller is authorized to send the goods he may ship them under reservation, and may tender the documents of title, but the buyer may inspect the goods after their arrival before payment is due unless such inspection is inconsistent with the terms of the contract (Section 2–513); and

(c) if delivery is authorized and made by way of documents of title otherwise than by subsection (b) then payment is due at the time and place at which the buyer is to receive the documents regardless of where the goods are to be received; and

(d) where the seller is required or authorized to ship the goods on credit the credit period runs from the time of shipment but post-dating the invoice or delaying its dispatch will correspondingly delay the starting of the credit period.

Definitional Cross References:

"Buyer". Section 2–103.

"Delivery". Section 1–201.

"Document of title". Section 1–201.

"Goods". Section 2–105.

"Receipt of goods". Section 2–103.

"Seller". Section 2–103.

"Send". Section 1–201.

"Term". Section 1–201.

§ 2–311. Options and Cooperation Respecting Performance

(1) An agreement for sale which is otherwise sufficiently definite (subsection (3) of Section 2–204) to be a contract is not made invalid by the fact that it leaves particulars of performance to be specified by one of the parties. Any such specification must be made in good faith and within limits set by commercial reasonableness.

(2) Unless otherwise agreed specifications relating to assortment of the goods are at the buyer's option and except as otherwise provided in subsections (1)(c) and (3) of Section 2–319 specifications or arrangements relating to shipment are at the seller's option.

(3) Where such specification would materially affect the other party's performance but is not seasonably made or where one party's cooperation is necessary to the agreed performance of the other but is not seasonably forthcoming, the other party in addition to all other remedies

> (a) is excused for any resulting delay in his own performance; and
>
> (b) may also either proceed to perform in any reasonable manner or after the time for a material part of his own performance treat the failure to specify or to cooperate as a breach by failure to deliver or accept the goods.

Definitional Cross References:

"Agreement". Section 1–201.

"Buyer". Section 2–103.

"Contract for sale". Section 2–106.

"Goods". Section 2–105.

"Party". Section 1–201.

"Remedy". Section 1–201.

"Seasonably". Section 1–204.

"Seller". Section 2–103.

§ 2–312. Warranty of Title and Against Infringement; Buyer's Obligation Against Infringement

(1) Subject to subsection (2) there is in a contract for sale a warranty by the seller that

> (a) the title conveyed shall be good, and its transfer rightful; and
>
> (b) the goods shall be delivered free from any security interest or other lien or encumbrance of which the buyer at the time of contracting has no knowledge.

(2) A warranty under subsection (1) will be excluded or modified only by specific language or by circumstances which give the buyer reason to know that the person selling does not claim title in himself or that he is purporting to sell only such right or title as he or a third person may have.

(3) Unless otherwise agreed a seller who is a merchant regularly dealing in goods of the kind warrants that the goods shall be delivered

free of the rightful claim of any third person by way of infringement or the like but a buyer who furnishes specifications to the seller must hold the seller harmless against any such claim which arises out of compliance with the specifications.

Definitional Cross References:

"Buyer". Section 2–103.

"Contract for sale". Section 2–106.

"Goods". Section 2–105.

"Person". Section 1–201.

"Right". Section 1–201.

"Seller". Section 2–103.

§ 2–313. Express Warranties by Affirmation, Promise, Description, Sample

(1) Express warranties by the seller are created as follows:

(a) Any affirmation of fact or promise made by the seller to the buyer which relates to the goods and becomes part of the basis of the bargain creates an express warranty that the goods shall conform to the affirmation or promise.

(b) Any description of the goods which is made part of the basis of the bargain creates an express warranty that the goods shall conform to the description.

(c) Any sample or model which is made part of the basis of the bargain creates an express warranty that the whole of the goods shall conform to the sample or model.

(2) It is not necessary to the creation of an express warranty that the seller use formal words such as "warrant" or "guarantee" or that he have a specific intention to make a warranty, but an affirmation merely of the value of the goods or a statement purporting to be merely the seller's opinion or commendation of the goods does not create a warranty.

Definitional Cross References:

"Buyer". Section 2–103.

"Conforming". Section 2–106.

"Goods". Section 2–105.

"Seller". Section 2–103.

§ 2–314. Implied Warranty: Merchantability; Usage of Trade

(1) Unless excluded or modified (Section 2–316), a warranty that the goods shall be merchantable is implied in a contract for their sale if the seller is a merchant with respect to goods of that kind. Under this section the serving for value of food or drink to be consumed either on the premises or elsewhere is a sale.

(2) Goods to be merchantable must be at least such as

(a) pass without objection in the trade under the contract description; and

(b) in the case of fungible goods, are of fair average quality within the description; and

51

(c) are fit for the ordinary purposes for which such goods are used; and

(d) run, within the variations permitted by the agreement, of even kind, quality and quantity within each unit and among all units involved; and

(e) are adequately contained, packaged, and labeled as the agreement may require; and

(f) conform to the promises or affirmations of fact made on the container or label if any.

(3) Unless excluded or modified (Section 2–316) other implied warranties may arise from course of dealing or usage of trade.

Definitional Cross References:

"Agreement". Section 1–201.

"Contract". Section 1–201.

"Contract for sale". Section 2–106.

"Goods". Section 2–105.

"Merchant". Section 2–104.

"Seller". Section 2–103.

§ 2–315. Implied Warranty: Fitness for Particular Purpose

Where the seller at the time of contracting has reason to know any particular purpose for which the goods are required and that the buyer is relying on the seller's skill or judgment to select or furnish suitable goods, there is unless excluded or modified under the next section an implied warranty that the goods shall be fit for such purpose.

Definitional Cross References:

"Buyer". Section 2–103.

"Goods". Section 2–105.

"Seller". Section 2–103.

§ 2–316. Exclusion or Modification of Warranties

(1) Words or conduct relevant to the creation of an express warranty and words or conduct tending to negate or limit warranty shall be construed wherever reasonable as consistent with each other; but subject to the provisions of this Article on parol or extrinsic evidence (Section 2–202) negation or limitation is inoperative to the extent that such construction is unreasonable.

(2) Subject to subsection (3), to exclude or modify the implied warranty of merchantability or any part of it the language must mention merchantability and in case of a writing must be conspicuous, and to exclude or modify any implied warranty of fitness the exclusion must be by a writing and conspicuous. Language to exclude all implied warranties of fitness is sufficient if it states, for example, that "There are no warranties which extend beyond the description on the face hereof."

(3) Notwithstanding subsection (2)

(a) unless the circumstances indicate otherwise, all implied warranties are excluded by expressions like "as is", "with all faults" or other language which in common understanding calls the buyer's attention to the exclusion of warranties and makes plain that there is no implied warranty; and

(b) when the buyer before entering into the contract has examined the goods or the sample or model as fully as he desired or has refused to examine the goods there is no implied warranty with regard to defects which an examination ought in the circumstances to have revealed to him; and

(c) an implied warranty can also be excluded or modified by course of dealing or course of performance or usage of trade.

(4) Remedies for breach of warranty can be limited in accordance with the provisions of this Article on liquidation or limitation of damages and on contractual modification of remedy (Sections 2–718 and 2–719).

Definitional Cross References:

"Agreement". Section 1–201.

"Buyer". Section 2–103.

"Contract". Section 1–201.

"Course of dealing". Section 1–205.

"Goods". Section 2–105.

"Remedy". Section 1–201.

"Seller". Section 2–103.

"Usage of trade". Section 1–205.

§ 2–317. Cumulation and Conflict of Warranties Express or Implied

Warranties whether express or implied shall be construed as consistent with each other and as cumulative, but if such construction is unreasonable the intention of the parties shall determine which warranty is dominant. In ascertaining that intention the following rules apply:

(a) Exact or technical specifications displace an inconsistent sample or model or general language of description.

(b) A sample from an existing bulk displaces inconsistent general language of description.

(c) Express warranties displace inconsistent implied warranties other than an implied warranty of fitness for a particular purpose.

Definitional Cross Reference:

"Party". Section 1–201.

§ 2–318. Third Party Beneficiaries of Warranties Express or Implied

Note: *If this Act is introduced in the Congress of the United States this section should be omitted. (States to select one alternative.)*

Alternative A

A seller's warranty whether express or implied extends to any natural person who is in the family or household of his buyer or who is a guest in his home if it is reasonable to expect that such person may use, consume or be affected by the goods and who is injured in person by breach of the warranty. A seller may not exclude or limit the operation of this section.

Alternative B

A seller's warranty whether express or implied extends to any natural person who may reasonably be expected to use, consume or be affected by the goods and who is injured in person by breach of the warranty. A seller may not exclude or limit the operation of this section.

Alternative C

A seller's warranty whether express or implied extends to any person who may reasonably be expected to use, consume or be affected by the goods and who is injured by breach of the warranty.

A seller may not exclude or limit the operation of this section with respect to injury to the person of an individual to whom the warranty extends.

§ 2–319. F.O.B. and F.A.S. Terms

(1) Unless otherwise agreed the term F.O.B. (which means "free on board") at a named place, even though used only in connection with the stated price, is a delivery term under which

    (a) when the term is F.O.B. the place of shipment, the seller must at that place ship the goods in the manner provided in this Article (Section 2–504) and bear the expense and risk of putting them into the possession of the carrier; or

    (b) when the term is F.O.B. the place of destination, the seller must at his own expense and risk transport the goods to that place and there tender delivery of them in the manner provided in this Article (Section 2–503);

    (c) when under either (a) or (b) the term is also F.O.B. vessel, car or other vehicle, the seller must in addition at his own expense and risk load the goods on board. If the term is F.O.B. vessel the buyer must name the vessel and in an appropriate case the seller must comply with the provisions of this Article on the form of bill of lading (Section 2–323).

(2) Unless otherwise agreed the term F.A.S. vessel (which means "free alongside") at a named port, even though used only in connection with the stated price, is a delivery term under which the seller must

    (a) at his own expense and risk deliver the goods alongside the vessel in the manner usual in that port or on a dock designated and provided by the buyer; and

(b) obtain and tender a receipt for the goods in exchange for which the carrier is under a duty to issue a bill of lading.

(3) Unless otherwise agreed in any case falling within subsection (1)(a) or (c) or subsection (2) the buyer must seasonably give any needed instructions for making delivery, including when the term is F.A.S. or F.O.B. the loading berth of the vessel and in an appropriate case its name and sailing date. The seller may treat the failure of needed instructions as a failure of cooperation under this Article (Section 2–311). He may also at his option move the goods in any reasonable manner preparatory to delivery or shipment.

(4) Under the term F.O.B. vessel or F.A.S. unless otherwise agreed the buyer must make payment against tender of the required documents and the seller may not tender nor the buyer demand delivery of the goods in substitution for the documents.

Definitional Cross References:

"Agreed". Section 1–201.

"Bill of lading". Section 1–201.

"Buyer". Section 2–103.

"Goods". Section 2–105.

"Seasonably". Section 1–204.

"Seller". Section 2–103.

"Term". Section 1–201.

§ **2–320.** C.I.F. and C. & F. Terms

(1) The term C.I.F. means that the price includes in a lump sum the cost of the goods and the insurance and freight to the named destination. The term C. & F. or C.F. means that the price so includes cost and freight to the named destination.

(2) Unless otherwise agreed and even though used only in connection with the stated price and destination, the term C.I.F. destination or its equivalent requires the seller at his own expense and risk to

(a) put the goods into the possession of a carrier at the port for shipment and obtain a negotiable bill or bills of lading covering the entire transportation to the named destination; and

(b) load the goods and obtain a receipt from the carrier (which may be contained in the bill of lading) showing that the freight has been paid or provided for; and

(c) obtain a policy or certificate of insurance, including any war risk insurance, of a kind and on terms then current at the port of shipment in the usual amount, in the currency of the contract, shown to cover the same goods covered by the bill of lading and providing for payment of loss to the order of the buyer or for the account of whom it may concern; but the seller may add to the price the amount of the premium for any such war risk insurance; and

(d) prepare an invoice of the goods and procure any other documents required to effect shipment or to comply with the contract; and

(e) forward and tender with commercial promptness all the documents in due form and with any indorsement necessary to perfect the buyer's rights.

(3) Unless otherwise agreed the term C. & F. or its equivalent has the same effect and imposes upon the seller the same obligations and risks as a C.I.F. term except the obligation as to insurance.

(4) Under the term C.I.F. or C. & F. unless otherwise agreed the buyer must make payment against tender of the required documents and the seller may not tender nor the buyer demand delivery of the goods in substitution for the documents.

Definitional Cross References:

"Bill of lading". Section 1–201.

"Buyer". Section 2–103.

"Contract". Section 1–201.

"Goods". Section 2–105.

"Rights". Section 1–201.

"Seller". Section 2–103.

"Term". Section 1–201.

§ 2–321.   C.I.F. or C. & F.: "Net Landed Weights"; "Payment on Arrival"; Warranty of Condition on Arrival

Under a contract containing a term C.I.F. or C. & F.

(1) Where the price is based on or is to be adjusted according to "net landed weights", "delivered weights", "out turn" quantity or quality or the like, unless otherwise agreed the seller must reasonably estimate the price. The payment due on tender of the documents called for by the contract is the amount so estimated, but after final adjustment of the price a settlement must be made with commercial promptness.

(2) An agreement described in subsection (1) or any warranty of quality or condition of the goods on arrival places upon the seller the risk of ordinary deterioration, shrinkage and the like in transportation but has no effect on the place or time of identification to the contract for sale or delivery or on the passing of the risk of loss.

(3) Unless otherwise agreed where the contract provides for payment on or after arrival of the goods the seller must before payment allow such preliminary inspection as is feasible; but if the goods are lost delivery of the documents and payment are due when the goods should have arrived.

Definitional Cross References:

"Agreement". Section 1–201.

"Contract". Section 1–201.

"Delivery". Section 1–201.

"Goods". Section 2–105.

"Seller". Section 2–103.

"Term". Section 1–201.

§ 2–322. Delivery "Ex–Ship"

(1) Unless otherwise agreed a term for delivery of goods "ex-ship" (which means from the carrying vessel) or in equivalent language is not restricted to a particular ship and requires delivery from a ship which has reached a place at the named port of destination where goods of the kind are usually discharged.

(2) Under such a term unless otherwise agreed

(a) the seller must discharge all liens arising out of the carriage and furnish the buyer with a direction which puts the carrier under a duty to delivery the goods; and

(b) the risk of loss does not pass to the buyer until the goods leave the ship's tackle or are otherwise properly unloaded.

Definitional Cross References:

"Buyer". Section 1–103.

"Goods". Section 2–105.

"Seller". Section 2–103.

"Term". Section 1–201.

§ 2–323. Form of Bill of Lading Required in Overseas Shipment; "Overseas"

(1) Where the contract contemplates overseas shipment and contains a term C.I.F. or C. & F. or F.O.B. vessel, the seller unless otherwise agreed must obtain a negotiable bill of lading stating that the goods have been loaded on board or, in the case of a term C.I.F. or C. & F., received for shipment.

(2) Where in a case within subsection (1) a bill of lading has been issued in a set of parts, unless otherwise agreed if the documents are not to be sent from abroad the buyer may demand tender of the full set; otherwise only one part of the bill of lading need be tendered. Even if the agreement expressly requires a full set

(a) due tender of a single part is acceptable within the provisions of this Article on cure of improper delivery (subsection (1) of Section 2–508); and

(b) even though the full set is demanded, if the documents are sent from abroad the person tendering an incomplete set may nevertheless require payment upon furnishing an indemnity which the buyer in good faith deems adequate.

(3) A shipment by water or by air or a contract contemplating such shipment is "overseas" insofar as by usage of trade or agreement it is subject to the commercial, financing or shipping practices characteristic of international deep water commerce.

Definitional Cross References:

"Bill of lading". Section 1–201.

"Buyer". Section 2–103.

"Contract". Section 1–201.

"Delivery". Section 1–201.

"Financing agency". Section 2–104.

"Person". Section 1–201.

"Seller". Section 2–103.

"Send". Section 1–201.

"Term". Section 1–201.

§ 2–324. "No Arrival, No Sale" Term

Under a term "no arrival, no sale" or terms of like meaning, unless otherwise agreed,

    (a) the seller must properly ship conforming goods and if they arrive by any means he must tender them on arrival but he assumes no obligation that the goods will arrive unless he has caused the non-arrival; and

    (b) where without fault of the seller the goods are in part lost or have so deteriorated as no longer to conform to the contract or arrive after the contract time, the buyer may proceed as if there had been casualty to identified goods (Section 2–613).

Definitional Cross References:

"Buyer". Section 2–103.

"Conforming". Section 2–106.

"Contract". Section 1–201.

"Fault". Section 1–201.

"Goods". Section 2–105.

"Sale". Section 2–106.

"Seller". Section 2–103.

"Term". Section 1–201.

§ 2–325. "Letter of Credit" Term; "Confirmed Credit"

(1) Failure of the buyer seasonably to furnish an agreed letter of credit is a breach of the contract for sale.

(2) The delivery to seller of a proper letter of credit suspends the buyer's obligation to pay. If the letter of credit is dishonored, the seller may on seasonable notification to the buyer require payment directly from him.

(3) Unless otherwise agreed the term "letter of credit" or "banker's credit" in a contract for sale means an irrevocable credit issued by a financing agency of good repute and, where the shipment is overseas, of good international repute. The term "confirmed credit" means that the credit must also carry the direct obligation of such an agency which does business in the seller's financial market.

Definitional Cross References:

"Buyer". Section 2–103.

"Contract for sale". Section 2–106.

"Draft". Section 3–104.

"Financing agency". Section 2–104.

"Notifies". Section 1–201.

"Overseas". Section 2–323.

"Purchaser". Section 1–201.

"Seasonably". Section 1–204.

"Seller". Section 2–103.

"Term". Section 1–201.

§ 2–326. Sale on Approval and Sale or Return; Rights of Creditors

(1) Unless otherwise agreed, if delivered goods may be returned by the buyer even though they conform to the contract, the transaction is

(a) a "sale on approval" if the goods are delivered primarily for use, and

(b) a "sale or return" if the goods are delivered primarily for resale.

(2) Goods held on approval are not subject to the claims of the buyer's creditors until acceptance; goods held on sale or return are subject to such claims while in the buyer's possession.

(3) Any "or return" term of a contract for sale is to be treated as a separate contract for sale within the statute of frauds section of this Article (Section 2–201) and as contradicting the sale aspect of the contract within the provisions of this Article on parol or extrinsic evidence (Section 2–202).

Definitional Cross References:

"Between merchants". Section 2–104.

"Buyer". Section 2–103.

"Conform". Section 2–106.

"Contract for sale". Section 2–106.

"Creditor". Section 1–201.

"Goods". Section 2–105.

"Sale". Section 2–106.

"Seller". Section 2–103.

§ 2–327. Special Incidents of Sale on Approval and Sale or Return

(1) Under a sale on approval unless otherwise agreed

(a) although the goods are identified to the contract the risk of loss and the title do not pass to the buyer until acceptance; and

(b) use of the goods consistent with the purpose of trial is not acceptance but failure seasonably to notify the seller of election to return the goods is acceptance, and if the goods conform to the contract acceptance of any part is acceptance of the whole; and

(c) after due notification of election to return, the return is at the seller's risk and expense but a merchant buyer must follow any reasonable instructions.

(2) Under a sale or return unless otherwise agreed

(a) the option to return extends to the whole or any commercial unit of the goods while in substantially their original condition, but must be exercised seasonably; and

(b) the return is at the buyer's risk and expense.

Definitional Cross References:

"Agreed". Section 1–201.

"Buyer". Section 2–103.

"Commercial unit". Section 2–105.

"Conform". Section 2–106.

"Contract". Section 1–201.

"Goods". Section 2–105.

"Merchant". Section 2–104.

"Notifies". Section 1–201.

"Notification". Section 1–201.

"Sale on approval". Section 2–326.

"Sale or return". Section 2–326.

"Seasonably". Section 1–204.

"Seller". Section 2–103.

§ 2–328. Sale by Auction

(1) In a sale by auction if goods are put up in lots each lot is the subject of a separate sale.

(2) A sale by auction is complete when the auctioneer so announces by the fall of the hammer or in other customary manner. Where a bid is made while the hammer is falling in acceptance of a prior bid the auctioneer may in his discretion reopen the bidding or declare the goods sold under the bid on which the hammer was falling.

(3) Such a sale is with reserve unless the goods are in explicit terms put up without reserve. In an auction with reserve the auctioneer may withdraw the goods at any time until he announces completion of the sale. In an auction without reserve, after the auctioneer calls for bids on an article or lot, that article or lot cannot be withdrawn unless no bid is made within a reasonable time. In either case a bidder may retract his bid until the auctioneer's announcement of completion of the sale, but a bidder's retraction does not revive any previous bid.

(4) If the auctioneer knowingly receives a bid on the seller's behalf or the seller makes or procures such a bid, and notice has not been given that liberty for such bidding is reserved, the buyer may at his option avoid the sale or take the goods at the price of the last good faith bid prior to the completion of the sale. This subsection shall not apply to any bid at a forced sale.

Definitional Cross References:

"Buyer". Section 2–103.

"Good faith". Section 1–201.

"Goods". Section 2–105.

"Lot". Section 2–105.

"Notice". Section 1–201.

"Sale". Section 2–106.

"Seller". Section 2–103.

PART 4

TITLE, CREDITORS AND GOOD FAITH PURCHASERS

§ 2–401. Passing of Title; Reservation for Security; Limited Application of This Section

Each provision of this Article with regard to the rights, obligations and remedies of the seller, the buyer, purchasers or other third parties applies irrespective of title to the goods except where the provision refers to such title. Insofar as situations are not covered by the other provisions of this Article and matters concerning title become material the following rules apply:

(1) Title to goods cannot pass under a contract for sale prior to their identification to the contract (Section 2–501), and unless otherwise explicitly agreed the buyer acquires by their identification a special property as limited by this Act. Any retention or reservation by the seller of the title (property) in goods shipped or delivered to the buyer is limited in effect to a reservation of a security interest. Subject to these provisions and to the provisions of the Article on Secured Transactions (Article 9), title to goods passes from the seller to the buyer in any manner and on any conditions explicitly agreed on by the parties.

(2) Unless otherwise explicitly agreed title passes to the buyer at the time and place at which the seller completes his performance with reference to the physical delivery of the goods, despite any reservation of a security interest and even though a document of title is to be delivered at a different time or place; and in particular and despite any reservation of a security interest by the bill of lading

    (a) if the contract requires or authorizes the seller to send the goods to the buyer but does not require him to deliver them at destination, title passes to the buyer at the time and place of shipment; but

    (b) if the contract requires delivery at destination, title passes on tender there.

(3) Unless otherwise explicitly agreed where delivery is to be made without moving the goods,

    (a) if the seller is to deliver a document of title, title passes at the time when and the place where he delivers such documents; or

    (b) if the goods are at the time of contracting already identified and no documents are to be delivered, title passes at the time and place of contracting.

(4) A rejection or other refusal by the buyer to receive or retain the goods, whether or not justified, or a justified revocation of acceptance revests title to the goods in the seller. Such revesting occurs by operation of law and is not a "sale".

Definitional Cross References:

"Agreement". Section 1–201.

"Bill of lading". Section 1–201.

"Buyer". Section 2–103.

"Contract". Section 1–201.

"Contract for sale". Section 2–106.

"Delivery". Section 1–201.

"Document of title". Section 1–201.

"Good faith". Section 2–103.

"Goods". Section 2–105.

"Party". Section 1–201.

"Purchaser". Section 1–201.

"Receipt" of goods. Section 2–103.

"Remedy". Section 1–201.

"Rights". Section 1–201.

"Sale". Section 2–106.

"Security interest". Section 1–201.

"Seller". Section 2–103.

"Send". Section 1–201.

§ 2–402. Rights of Seller's Creditors Against Sold Goods

(1) Except as provided in subsections (2) and (3), rights of unsecured creditors of the seller with respect to goods which have been identified to a contract for sale are subject to the buyer's rights to recover the goods under this Article (Sections 2–502 and 2–716).

(2) A creditor of the seller may treat a sale or an identification of goods to a contract for sale as void if as against him a retention of possession by the seller is fraudulent under any rule of law of the state where the goods are situated, except that retention of possession in good faith and current course of trade by a merchant-seller for a commercially reasonable time after a sale or identification is not fraudulent.

(3) Nothing in this Article shall be deemed to impair the rights of creditors of the seller

(a) under the provisions of the Article on Secured Transactions (Article 9); or

(b) where identification to the contract or delivery is made not in current course of trade but in satisfaction of or as security for a pre-existing claim for money, security or the like and is made under circumstances which under any rule of law of the state where the goods are situated would apart from this Article constitute the transaction a fraudulent transfer or voidable preference.

Definitional Cross References:

"Contract for sale". Section 2–106.

"Creditor". Section 1–201.

"Good faith". Section 2–103.

"Goods". Section 2–105.

"Merchant". Section 2–104.

"Money". Section 1–201.

"Reasonable time". Section 1–204.

"Rights". Section 1–201.

"Sale". Section 2–106.

"Seller". Section 2–103.

§ 2–403. Power to Transfer; Good Faith Purchase of Goods; "Entrusting"

(1) A purchaser of goods acquires all title which his transferor had or had power to transfer except that a purchaser of a limited interest acquires rights only to the extent of the interest purchased. A person with voidable title has power to transfer a good title to a good faith purchaser for value. When goods have been delivered under a transaction of purchase the purchaser has such power even though

(a) the transferor was deceived as to the identity of the purchaser, or

(b) the delivery was in exchange for a check which is later dishonored, or

(c) it was agreed that the transaction was to be a "cash sale", or

(d) the delivery was procured through fraud punishable as larcenous under the criminal law.

(2) Any entrusting of possession of goods to a merchant who deals in goods of that kind gives him power to transfer all rights of the entruster to a buyer in ordinary course of business.

(3) "Entrusting" includes any delivery and any acquiescence in retention of possession regardless of any condition expressed between the parties to the delivery or acquiescence and regardless of whether the procurement of the entrusting or the possessor's disposition of the goods have been such as to be larcenous under the criminal law.

(4) The rights of other purchasers of goods and of lien creditors are governed by the Articles on Secured Transactions (Article 9), Bulk Transfers (Article 6) and Documents of Title (Article 7).

Definitional Cross References:

"Buyer in ordinary course of business". Section 1–201.

"Good faith". Sections 1–201 and 2–103.

"Goods". Section 2–105.

"Person". Section 1–201.

"Purchaser". Section 1–201.

"Signed". Section 1–201.

"Term". Section 1–201.

"Value". Section 1–201.

PART 5

PERFORMANCE

§ 2–501. Insurable Interest in Goods; Manner of Identification of Goods

(1) The buyer obtains a special property and an insurable interest in goods by identification of existing goods as goods to which the contract refers even though the goods so identified are non-conforming and he has an option to return or reject them. Such identification can be made at any time and in any manner explicitly agreed to by the parties. In the absence of explicit agreement identification occurs

(a) when the contract is made if it is for the sale of goods already existing and identified;

(b) if the contract is for the sale of future goods other than those described in paragraph (c), when goods are shipped, marked or otherwise designated by the seller as goods to which the contract refers;

(c) when the crops are planted or otherwise become growing crops or the young are conceived if the contract is for the sale of unborn young to be born within twelve months after contracting or for the sale of crops to be harvested within twelve months or the next normal harvest season after contracting whichever is longer.

(2) The seller retains an insurable interest in goods so long as title to or any security interest in the goods remains in him and where the identification is by the seller alone he may until default or insolvency or notification to the buyer that the identification is final substitute other goods for those identified.

(3) Nothing in this section impairs any insurable interest recognized under any other statute or rule of law.

Definitional Cross References:

"Agreement". Section 1–201.

"Contract". Section 1–201.

"Contract for sale". Section 2–106.

"Future goods". Section 2–105.

"Goods". Section 2–105.

"Notification". Section 1–201.

"Party". Section 1–201.

"Sale". Section 2–106.

"Security interest". Section 1–201.

"Seller". Section 2–103.

§ 2–502. Buyer's Right to Goods on Seller's Repudiation, Failure to Deliver, or Insolvency

(1) Subject to subsections (2) and (3) and even though the goods have not been shipped a buyer who has paid a part or all of the price of goods in which he has a special property under the provisions of the immediately preceding section may on making and keeping good a tender of any unpaid portion of their price recover them from the seller if:

(a) in the case of goods bought for personal, family, or household purposes, the seller repudiates or fails to deliver as required by the contract; or

(b) in all cases, the seller becomes insolvent within ten days after receipt of the first installment on their price.

(2) The buyer's right to recover the goods under subsection (1)(a) vests upon acquisition of a special property, even if the seller had not then repudiated or failed to deliver.

(3) If the identification creating his special property has been made by the buyer he acquires the right to recover the goods only if they conform to the contract for sale.

Definitional Cross References:

"Buyer". Section 2–103.

"Conform". Section 2–106.

"Contract for sale". Section 2–106.

"Goods". Section 2–105.

"Insolvent". Section 1–201.

"Right". Section 1–201.

"Seller". Section 2–103.

§ 2–503. Manner of Seller's Tender of Delivery

(1) Tender of delivery requires that the seller put and hold conforming goods at the buyer's disposition and give the buyer any notification reasonably necessary to enable him to take delivery. The manner, time and place for tender are determined by the agreement and this Article, and in particular

> (a) tender must be at a reasonable hour, and if it is of goods they must be kept available for the period reasonably necessary to enable the buyer to take possession; but

> (b) unless otherwise agreed the buyer must furnish facilities reasonably suited to the receipt of the goods.

(2) Where the case is within the next section respecting shipment tender requires that the seller comply with its provisions.

(3) Where the seller is required to deliver at a particular destination tender requires that he comply with subsection (1) and also in any appropriate case tender documents as described in subsections (4) and (5) of this section.

(4) Where goods are in the possession of a bailee and are to be delivered without being moved

> (a) tender requires that the seller either tender a negotiable document of title covering such goods or procure acknowledgment by the bailee of the buyer's right to possession of the goods; but

> (b) tender to the buyer of a non-negotiable document of title or of a written direction to the bailee to deliver is sufficient tender unless the buyer seasonably objects, and receipt by the bailee of notification of the buyer's rights fixes those rights as against the bailee and all third persons; but risk of loss of the goods and of any failure by the bailee to honor the non-negotiable document of title or to obey the direction remains on the seller until the buyer has had a reasonable time to present the document or direction, and a refusal by the bailee to honor the document or to obey the direction defeats the tender.

(5) Where the contract requires the seller to deliver documents

> (a) he must tender all such documents in correct form, except as provided in this Article with respect to bills of lading in a set (subsection (2) of Section 2–323); and

> (b) tender through customary banking channels is sufficient and dishonor of a draft accompanying the documents constitutes non-acceptance or rejection.

Definitional Cross References:

"Agreement". Section 1–201.

"Bill of lading". Section 1–201.

"Buyer". Section 2–103.

"Conforming". Section 2–106.

"Contract". Section 1–201.

"Delivery". Section 1–201.

"Dishonor". Section 3–508.

"Document of title". Section 1–201.

"Draft". Section 3–104.

"Goods". Section 2–105.

"Notification". Section 1–201.

"Reasonable time". Section 1–204.

"Receipt of goods". Section 2–103.

"Rights". Section 1–201.

"Seasonably". Section 1–204.

"Seller". Section 2–103.

"Written". Section 1–201.

§ 2–504. Shipment by Seller

Where the seller is required or authorized to send the goods to the buyer and the contract does not require him to deliver them at a particular destination, then unless otherwise agreed he must

(a) put the goods in the possession of such a carrier and make such a contract for their transportation as may be reasonable having regard to the nature of the goods and other circumstances of the case; and

(b) obtain and promptly deliver or tender in due form any document necessary to enable the buyer to obtain possession of the goods or otherwise required by the agreement or by usage of trade; and

(c) promptly notify the buyer of the shipment.

Failure to notify the buyer under paragraph (c) or to make a proper contract under paragraph (a) is a ground for rejection only if material delay or loss ensues.

Definitional Cross References:

"Agreement". Section 1–201.

"Buyer". Section 2–103.

"Contract". Section 1–201.

"Delivery". Section 1–201.

"Goods". Section 2–105.

"Notifies". Section 1–201.

"Seller". Section 2–103.

"Send". Section 1–201.

"Usage of trade". Section 1–205.

§ 2–505. Seller's Shipment Under Reservation

(1) Where the seller has identified goods to the contract by or before shipment:

(a) his procurement of a negotiable bill of lading to his own order or otherwise reserves in him a security interest in the goods. His procurement of the bill to the order of a financing agency or of the buyer indicates in addition only the seller's expectation of transferring that interest to the person named.

(b) a non-negotiable bill of lading to himself or his nominee reserves possession of the goods as security but except in a case of conditional delivery (subsection (2) of Section 2–507) a non-negotiable bill of lading naming the buyer as consignee reserves no security interest even though the seller retains possession of the bill of lading.

(2) When shipment by the seller with reservation of a security interest is in violation of the contract for sale it constitutes an improper contract for transportation within the preceding section but impairs neither the rights given to the buyer by shipment and identification of the goods to the contract nor the seller's powers as a holder of a negotiable document.

Definitional Cross References:

"Bill of lading". Section 1–201.

"Buyer". Section 2–103.

"Consignee". Section 7–102.

"Contract". Section 1–201.

"Contract for sale". Section 2–106.

"Delivery". Section 1–201.

"Financing agency". Section 2–104.

"Goods". Section 2–105.

"Holder". Section 1–201.

"Person". Section 1–201.

"Security interest". Section 1–201.

"Seller". Section 2–103.

§ 2–506. Rights of Financing Agency

(1) A financing agency by paying or purchasing for value a draft which relates to a shipment of goods acquires to the extent of the payment or purchase and in addition to its own rights under the draft and any document of title securing it any rights of the shipper in the goods including the right to stop delivery and the shipper's right to have the draft honored by the buyer.

(2) The right to reimbursement of a financing agency which has in good faith honored or purchased the draft under commitment to or authority from the buyer is not impaired by subsequent discovery of defects with reference to any relevant document which was apparently regular on its face.

Definitional Cross References:

"Buyer". Section 2–103.

"Document of title". Section 1–201.

"Draft". Section 3–104.

"Financing agency". Section 2–104.

"Good faith". Section 2–103.

"Goods". Section 2–105.

"Honor". Section 1–201.

"Purchase". Section 1–201.

"Rights". Section 1–201.

"Value". Section 1–201.

§ 2–507. Effect of Seller's Tender; Delivery on Condition

(1) Tender of delivery is a condition to the buyer's duty to accept the goods and, unless otherwise agreed, to his duty to pay for them. Tender entitles the seller to acceptance of the goods and to payment according to the contract.

(2) Where payment is due and demanded on the delivery to the buyer of goods or documents of title, his right as against the seller to

retain or dispose of them is conditional upon his making the payment due.

Definitional Cross References:

"Buyer". Section 2–103.

"Contract". Section 1–201.

"Delivery". Section 1–201.

"Document of title". Section 1–201.

"Goods". Section 2–105.

"Rights". Section 1–201.

"Seller". Section 2–103.

§ 2–508. Cure by Seller of Improper Tender or Delivery; Replacement

(1) Where any tender or delivery by the seller is rejected because non-conforming and the time for performance has not yet expired, the seller may seasonably notify the buyer of his intention to cure and may then within the contract time make a conforming delivery.

(2) Where the buyer rejects a non-conforming tender which the seller had reasonable grounds to believe would be acceptable with or without money allowance the seller may if he seasonably notifies the buyer have a further reasonable time to substitute a conforming tender.

Definitional Cross References:

"Buyer". Section 2–103.

"Conforming". Section 2–106.

"Contract". Section 1–201.

"Money". Section 1–201.

"Notifies". Section 1–201.

"Reasonable time". Section 1–204.

"Seasonably". Section 1–204.

"Seller". Section 2–103.

§ 2–509. Risk of Loss in the Absence of Breach

(1) Where the contract requires or authorizes the seller to ship the goods by carrier

    (a) if it does not require him to deliver them at a particular destination, the risk of loss passes to the buyer when the goods are duly delivered to the carrier even though the shipment is under reservation (Section 2–505); but

    (b) if it does require him to deliver them at a particular destination and the goods are there duly tendered while in the possession of the carrier, the risk of loss passes to the buyer when the goods are there duly so tendered as to enable the buyer to take delivery.

(2) Where the goods are held by a bailee to be delivered without being moved, the risk of loss passes to the buyer

    (a) on his receipt of a negotiable document of title covering the goods; or

    (b) on acknowledgment by the bailee of the buyer's right to possession of the goods; or

(c) after his receipt of a non-negotiable document of title or other written direction to deliver, as provided in subsection (4)(b) of Section 2–503.

(3) In any case not within subsection (1) or (2), the risk of loss passes to the buyer on his receipt of the goods if the seller is a merchant; otherwise the risk passes to the buyer on tender of delivery.

(4) The provisions of this section are subject to contrary agreement of the parties and to the provisions of this Article on sale on approval (Section 2–327) and on effect of breach on risk of loss (Section 2–510).

Definitional Cross References:

"Agreement". Section 1–201.	"Goods". Section 2–105.
"Buyer". Section 2–103.	"Merchant". Section 2–104.
"Contract". Section 1–201.	"Party". Section 1–201.
"Delivery". Section 1–201.	"Receipt" of goods. Section 2–103.
"Document of title". Section 1–201.	"Sale on approval". Section 2–326.
	"Seller". Section 2–103.

§ 2–510. Effect of Breach on Risk of Loss

(1) Where a tender or delivery of goods so fails to conform to the contract as to give a right of rejection the risk of their loss remains on the seller until cure or acceptance.

(2) Where the buyer rightfully revokes acceptance he may to the extent of any deficiency in his effective insurance coverage treat the risk of loss as having rested on the seller from the beginning.

(3) Where the buyer as to conforming goods already identified to the contract for sale repudiates or is otherwise in breach before risk of their loss has passed to him, the seller may to the extent of any deficiency in his effective insurance coverage treat the risk of loss as resting on the buyer for a commercially reasonable time.

Definitional Cross References:

"Buyer". Section 2–103.	"Contract for sale". Section 2–106.
"Conform". Section 2–106.	"Goods". Section 2–105.
	"Seller". Section 2–103.

§ 2–511. Tender of Payment by Buyer; Payment by Check

(1) Unless otherwise agreed tender of payment is a condition to the seller's duty to tender and complete any delivery.

(2) Tender of payment is sufficient when made by any means or in any manner current in the ordinary course of business unless the seller demands payment in legal tender and gives any extension of time reasonably necessary to procure it.

(3) Subject to the provisions of this Act on the effect of an instrument on an obligation (Section 3–802), payment by check is conditional

and is defeated as between the parties by dishonor of the check on due presentment.

Definitional Cross References:

"Buyer". Section 2–103.

"Check". Section 3–104.

"Dishonor". Section 3–508.

"Party". Section 1–201.

"Reasonable time". Section 1–204.

"Seller". Section 2–103.

§ 2–512. Payment by Buyer Before Inspection

(1) Where the contract requires payment before inspection non-conformity of the goods does not excuse the buyer from so making payment unless

> (a) the non-conformity appears without inspection; or
>
> (b) despite tender of the required documents the circumstances would justify injunction against honor under the provisions of this Act (Section 5–114).

(2) Payment pursuant to subsection (1) does not constitute an acceptance of goods or impair the buyer's right to inspect or any of his remedies.

Definitional Cross References:

"Buyer". Section 2–103.

"Conform". Section 2–106.

"Contract". Section 1–201.

"Financing agency". Section 2–104.

"Goods". Section 2–105.

"Remedy". Section 1–201.

"Rights". Section 1–201.

§ 2–513. Buyer's Right to Inspection of Goods

(1) Unless otherwise agreed and subject to subsection (3), where goods are tendered or delivered or identified to the contract for sale, the buyer has a right before payment or acceptance to inspect them at any reasonable place and time and in any reasonable manner. When the seller is required or authorized to send the goods to the buyer, the inspection may be after their arrival.

(2) Expenses of inspection must be borne by the buyer but may be recovered from the seller if the goods do not conform and are rejected.

(3) Unless otherwise agreed and subject to the provisions of this Article on C.I.F. contracts (subsection (3) of Section 2–321), the buyer is not entitled to inspect the goods before payment of the price when the contract provides

> (a) for delivery "C.O.D." or on other like terms; or
>
> (b) for payment against documents of title, except where such payment is due only after the goods are to become available for inspection.

(4) A place or method of inspection fixed by the parties is presumed to be exclusive but unless otherwise expressly agreed it does not post-

pone identification or shift the place for delivery or for passing the risk of loss. If compliance becomes impossible, inspection shall be as provided in this section unless the place or method fixed was clearly intended as an indispensable condition failure of which avoids the contract.

Definitional Cross References:

"Buyer". Section 2–103.

"Conform". Section 2–106.

"Contract". Section 1–201.

"Contract for sale". Section 2–106.

"Document of title". Section 1–201.

"Goods". Section 2–105.

"Party". Section 1–201.

"Presumed". Section 1–201.

"Reasonable time". Section 1–204.

"Rights". Section 1–201.

"Seller". Section 2–103.

"Send". Section 1–201.

"Term". Section 1–201.

§ 2–514. When Documents Deliverable on Acceptance; When on Payment

Unless otherwise agreed documents against which a draft is drawn are to be delivered to the drawee on acceptance of the draft if it is payable more than three days after presentment; otherwise, only on payment.

Definitional Cross References:

"Delivery". Section 1–201.

"Draft". Section 3–104.

§ 2–515. Preserving Evidence of Goods in Dispute

In furtherance of the adjustment of any claim or dispute

(a) either party on reasonable notification to the other and for the purpose of ascertaining the facts and preserving evidence has the right to inspect, test and sample the goods including such of them as may be in the possession or control of the other; and

(b) the parties may agree to a third party inspection or survey to determine the conformity or condition of the goods and may agree that the findings shall be binding upon them in any subsequent litigation or adjustment.

Definitional Cross References:

"Conform". Section 2–106.

"Goods". Section 2–105.

"Notification". Section 1–201.

"Party". Section 1–201.

PART 6

BREACH, REPUDIATION AND EXCUSE

§ 2–601. Buyer's Rights on Improper Delivery

Subject to the provisions of this Article on breach in installment contracts (Section 2–612) and unless otherwise agreed under the sections on contractual limitations of remedy (Sections 2–718 and 2–719), if the goods or the tender of delivery fail in any respect to conform to the contract, the buyer may

    (a) reject the whole; or

    (b) accept the whole; or

    (c) accept any commercial unit or units and reject the rest.

Definitional Cross References:

"Buyer". Section 2–103.
"Commercial unit". Section 2–105.
"Conform". Section 2–106.
"Contract". Section 1–201.

"Goods". Section 2–105.
"Installment contract". Section 2–612.
"Rights". Section 1–201.

§ 2–602. Manner and Effect of Rightful Rejection

(1) Rejection of goods must be within a reasonable time after their delivery or tender. It is ineffective unless the buyer seasonably notifies the seller.

(2) Subject to the provisions of the two following sections on rejected goods (Sections 2–603 and 2–604),

    (a) after rejection any exercise of ownership by the buyer with respect to any commercial unit is wrongful as against the seller; and

    (b) if the buyer has before rejection taken physical possession of goods in which he does not have a security interest under the provisions of this Article (subsection (3) of Section 2–711), he is under a duty after rejection to hold them with reasonable care at the seller's disposition for a time sufficient to permit the seller to remove them; but

    (c) the buyer has no further obligations with regard to goods rightfully rejected.

(3) The seller's rights with respect to goods wrongfully rejected are governed by the provisions of this Article on Seller's remedies in general (Section 2–703).

Definitional Cross References:

"Buyer". Section 2–103.
"Commercial unit". Section 2–105.

"Goods". Section 2–105.
"Merchant". Section 2–104.

"Notifies". Section 1–201.

"Reasonable time". Section 1–204.

"Remedy". Section 1–201.

"Rights". Section 1–201.

"Seasonably". Section 1–204.

"Security interest". Section 1–201.

"Seller". Section 2–103.

§ 2–603. Merchant Buyer's Duties as to Rightfully Rejected Goods

(1) Subject to any security interest in the buyer (subsection (3) of Section 2–711), when the seller has no agent or place of business at the market of rejection a merchant buyer is under a duty after rejection of goods in his possession or control to follow any reasonable instructions received from the seller with respect to the goods and in the absence of such instructions to make reasonable efforts to sell them for the seller's account if they are perishable or threaten to decline in value speedily. Instructions are not reasonable if on demand indemnity for expenses is not forthcoming.

(2) When the buyer sells goods under subsection (1), he is entitled to reimbursement from the seller or out of the proceeds for reasonable expenses of caring for and selling them, and if the expenses include no selling commission then to such commission as is usual in the trade or if there is none to a reasonable sum not exceeding ten per cent on the gross proceeds.

(3) In complying with this section the buyer is held only to good faith and good faith conduct hereunder is neither acceptance nor conversion nor the basis of an action for damages.

Definitional Cross References:

"Buyer". Section 2–103.

"Good faith". Section 1–201.

"Goods". Section 2–105.

"Merchant". Section 2–104.

"Security interest". Section 1–201.

"Seller". Section 2–102.

§ 2–604. Buyer's Options as to Salvage of Rightfully Rejected Goods

Subject to the provisions of the immediately preceding section on perishables if the seller gives no instructions within a reasonable time after notification of rejection the buyer may store the rejected goods for the seller's account or reship them to him or resell them for the seller's account with reimbursement as provided in the preceding section. Such action is not acceptance or conversion.

Definitional Cross References:

"Buyer". Section 2–103.

"Notification". Section 1–201.

"Reasonable time". Section 1–204.

"Seller". Section 2–103.

§ 2–605. Waiver of Buyer's Objections by Failure to Particularize

(1) The buyer's failure to state in connection with rejection a particular defect which is ascertainable by reasonable inspection precludes him from relying on the unstated defect to justify rejection or to establish breach

> (a) where the seller could have cured it if stated seasonably; or
>
> (b) between merchants when the seller has after rejection made a request in writing for a full and final written statement of all defects on which the buyer proposes to rely.

(2) Payment against documents made without reservation of rights precludes recovery of the payment for defects apparent on the face of the documents.

Definitional Cross References:

"Between merchants". Section 2–104.

"Buyer". Section 2–103.

"Seasonably". Section 1–204.

"Seller". Section 2–103.

"Writing" and "written". Section 1–201.

§ 2–606. What Constitutes Acceptance of Goods

(1) Acceptance of goods occurs when the buyer

> (a) after a reasonable opportunity to inspect the goods signifies to the seller that the goods are conforming or that he will take or retain them in spite of their nonconformity; or
>
> (b) fails to make an effective rejection (subsection (1) of Section 2–602), but such acceptance does not occur until the buyer has had a reasonable opportunity to inspect them; or
>
> (c) does any act inconsistent with the seller's ownership; but if such act is wrongful as against the seller it is an acceptance only if ratified by him.

(2) Acceptance of a part of any commercial unit is acceptance of that entire unit.

Definitional Cross References:

"Buyer". Section 2–103.

"Commercial unit". Section 2–105.

"Goods". Section 2–105.

"Seller". Section 2–103.

§ 2–607. Effect of Acceptance; Notice of Breach; Burden of Establishing Breach After Acceptance; Notice of Claim or Litigation to Person Answerable Over

(1) The buyer must pay at the contract rate for any goods accepted.

(2) Acceptance of goods by the buyer precludes rejection of the goods accepted and if made with knowledge of a non-conformity cannot

be revoked because of it unless the acceptance was on the reasonable assumption that the non-conformity would be seasonably cured but acceptance does not of itself impair any other remedy provided by this Article for non-conformity.

(3) Where a tender has been accepted.

(a) the buyer must within a reasonable time after he discovers or should have discovered any breach notify the seller of breach or be barred from any remedy; and

(b) if the claim is one for infringement or the like (subsection (3) of Section 2–312) and the buyer is sued as a result of such a breach he must so notify the seller within a reasonable time after he receives notice of the litigation or be barred from any remedy over for liability established by the litigation.

(4) The burden is on the buyer to establish any breach with respect to the goods accepted.

(5) Where the buyer is sued for breach of a warranty or other obligation for which his seller is answerable over

(a) he may give his seller written notice of the litigation. If the notice states that the seller may come in and defend and that if the seller does not do so he will be bound in any action against him by his buyer by any determination of fact common to the two litigations, then unless the seller after seasonable receipt of the notice does come in and defend he is so bound.

(b) if the claim is one for infringement or the like (subsection (3) of Section 2–312) the original seller may demand in writing that his buyer turn over to him control of the litigation including settlement or else be barred from any remedy over and if he also agrees to bear all expense and to satisfy any adverse judgment, then unless the buyer after seasonable receipt of the demand does turn over control the buyer is so barred.

(6) The provisions of subsection (3), (4) and (5) apply to any obligation of a buyer to hold the seller harmless against infringement or the like (subsection (3) of Section 2–312).

Definitional Cross References:

"Burden of establishing". Section 1–201.

"Buyer". Section 2–103.

"Conform". Section 2–106.

"Contract". Section 1–201.

"Goods". Section 2–105.

"Notifies". Section 1–201.

"Reasonable time". Section 1–204.

"Remedy". Section 1–201.

"Seasonably". Section 1–204.

§ 2–608.   Revocation of Acceptance in Whole or in Part

(1) The buyer may revoke his acceptance of a lot or commercial unit whose non-conformity substantially impairs its value to him if he has accepted it

    (a) on the reasonable assumption that its non-conformity would be cured and it has not been seasonably cured; or

    (b) without discovery of such non-conformity if his acceptance was reasonably induced either by the difficulty of discovery before acceptance or by the seller's assurances.

(2) Revocation of acceptance must occur within a reasonable time after the buyer discovers or should have discovered the ground for it and before any substantial change in condition of the goods which is not caused by their own defects. It is not effective until the buyer notifies the seller of it.

(3) A buyer who so revokes has the same rights and duties with regard to the goods involved as if he had rejected them.

Definitional Cross References:

"Buyer". Section 2–103.

"Commercial unit". Section 2–105.

"Conform". Section 2–106.

"Goods". Section 2–105.

"Lot". Section 2–105.

"Notifies". Section 1–201.

"Reasonable time". Section 1–204.

"Rights". Section 1–201.

"Seasonably". Section 1–204.

"Seller". Section 2–103.

§ 2–609.   Right to Adequate Assurance of Performance

(1) A contract for sale imposes an obligation on each party that the other's expectation of receiving due performance will not be impaired. When reasonable grounds for insecurity arise with respect to the performance of either party the other may in writing demand adequate assurance of due performance and until he receives such assurance may if commercially reasonable suspend any performance for which he has not already received the agreed return.

(2) Between merchants the reasonableness of grounds for insecurity and the adequacy of any assurance offered shall be determined according to commercial standards.

(3) Acceptance of any improper delivery or payment does not prejudice the aggrieved party's right to demand adequate assurance of future performance.

(4) After receipt of a justified demand failure to provide within a reasonable time not exceeding thirty days such assurance of due performance as is adequate under the circumstances of the particular case is a repudiation of the contract.

Official Comment

Prior Uniform Statutory Provision: See Sections 53, 54(1)(b), 55 and 63(2), Uniform Sales Act.

Purposes:

1. The section rests on the recognition of the fact that the essential purpose of a contract between commercial men is actual performance and they do not bargain merely for a promise, or for a promise plus the right to win a lawsuit and that a continuing sense of reliance and security that the promised performance will be forthcoming when due, is an important feature of the bargain. If either the willingness or the ability of a party to perform declines materially between the time of contracting and the time for performance, the other party is threatened with the loss of a substantial part of what he has bargained for. A seller needs protection not merely against having to deliver on credit to a shaky buyer, but also against having to procure and manufacture the goods, perhaps turning down other customers. Once he has been given reason to believe that the buyer's performance has become uncertain, it is an undue hardship to force him to continue his own performance. Similarly, a buyer who believes that the seller's deliveries have become uncertain cannot safely wait for the due date of performance when he has been buying to assure himself of materials for his current manufacturing or to replenish his stock of merchandise.

2. Three measures have been adopted to meet the needs of commercial men in such situations. First, the aggrieved party is permitted to suspend his own performance and any preparation therefor, with excuse for any resulting necessary delay, until the situation has been clarified. "Suspend performance" under this section means to hold up performance pending the outcome of the demand, and includes also the holding up of any preparatory action. This is the same principle which governs the ancient law of stoppage and seller's lien, and also of excuse of a buyer from prepayment if the seller's actions manifest that he cannot or will not perform. (Original Act, Section 63(2).)

Secondly, the aggrieved party is given the right to require adequate assurance that the other party's performance will be duly forthcoming. This principle is reflected in the familiar clauses permitting the seller to curtail deliveries if the buyer's credit becomes impaired, which when held within the limits of reasonableness and good faith actually express no more than the fair business meaning of any commercial contract.

Third, and finally, this section provides the means by which the aggrieved party may treat the contract as broken if his reasonable grounds for insecurity are not cleared up within a reasonable time. This is the principle underlying the law of anticipatory breach, whether by way of defective part performance or by repudiation. The present section merges these three principles of law and commercial practice into a single theory of general application to all sales agreements looking to future performance.

3. Subsection (2) of the present section requires that "reasonable" grounds and "adequate" assurance as used in subsection (1) be defined by commercial rather than legal standards. The express reference to commercial standards carries no connotation that the obligation of good faith is not equally applicable here.

Under commercial standards and in accord with commercial practice, a ground for insecurity need not arise from or be directly related to the contract in question. The law as to "dependence" or "independence" of promises within a single contract does not control the application of the present section.

Thus a buyer who falls behind in "his account" with the seller, even though the items involved have to do with separate and legally distinct contracts, impairs the seller's expectation of due performance. Again, under the same test, a buyer who requires precision parts which he intends to use immediately upon delivery, may have reasonable grounds for insecurity if he discovers that his seller is making defective deliveries of such parts to other buyers with similar needs. Thus, too, in a situation such as arose in Jay Dreher Corporation v. Delco Appliance Corporation, 93 F.2d 275 (C.C.A. 2, 1937), where a manufacturer gave a dealer an exclusive franchise for the sale of his product but on two or three occasions breached the exclusive dealing clause, although there was no default in orders, deliveries or payments under the separate sales contract between the parties, the aggrieved dealer would be entitled to suspend his performance of the contract for sale under the present section and to demand assurance that the exclusive dealing contract would be lived up to. There is no need for an explicit clause tying the exclusive franchise into the contract for the sale of goods since the situation itself ties the agreements together.

The nature of the sales contract enters also into the question of reasonableness. For example, a report from an apparently trustworthy source that the seller had shipped defective goods or was planning to ship them would normally give the buyer reasonable grounds for insecurity. But when the buyer has assumed the risk of payment before inspection of the goods, as in a sales contract on C.I.F. or similar cash against documents terms, that risk is not to be evaded by a demand for

assurance. Therefore no ground for insecurity would exist under this section unless the report went to a ground which would excuse payment by the buyer.

4. What constitutes "adequate" assurance of due performance is subject to the same test of factual conditions. For example, where the buyer can make use of a defective delivery, a mere promise by a seller of good repute that he is giving the matter his attention and that the defect will not be repeated, is normally sufficient. Under the same circumstances, however, a similar statement by a known corner-cutter might well be considered insufficient without the posting of a guaranty or, if so demanded by the buyer, a speedy replacement of the delivery involved. By the same token where a delivery has defects, even though easily curable, which interfere with easy use by the buyer, no verbal assurance can be deemed adequate which is not accompanied by replacement, repair, money-allowance, or other commercially reasonable cure.

A fact situation such as arose in Corn Products Refining Co. v. Fasola, 94 N.J.L. 181, 109 A. 505 (1920) offers illustration both of reasonable grounds for insecurity and "adequate" assurance. In that case a contract for the sale of oils on 30 days' credit, 2% off for payment within–10 days, provided that credit was to be extended to the buyer only if his financial responsibility was satisfactory to the seller. The buyer had been in the habit of taking advantage of the discount but at the same time that he failed to make his customary 10 day payment, the seller heard rumors, in fact false, that the buyer's financial condition was shaky. Thereupon, the seller demanded cash before shipment or security satisfactory to him. The buyer sent a good credit report from his banker, expressed willingness to make payments when due on the 30 day terms and insisted on further deliveries under the contract. Under this Article the rumors, although false, were enough to make the buyer's financial condition "unsatisfactory" to the seller under the contract clause. Moreover, the buyer's practice of taking the cash discounts is enough, apart from the contract clause, to lay a commercial foundation for suspicion when the practice is suddenly stopped. These matters, however, go only to the justification of the seller's demand for security, or his "reasonable grounds for insecurity".

The adequacy of the assurance given is not measured as in the type of "satisfaction" situation affected with intangibles, such as in personal service cases, cases involving a third party's judgment as final, or cases in which the whole contract is dependent on one party's satisfaction, as in a sale on approval. Here, the seller must exercise good faith and observe commercial standards. This Article thus approves the statement of the court in James B. Berry's Sons Co. of Illinois v. Monark Gasoline & Oil Co., Inc., 32 F.2d 74 (C.C.A.8, 1929), that the seller's satisfaction under such a clause must be based upon reason and must not be arbitrary or capricious; and rejects the purely personal "good faith" test of the Corn Products Refining Co. case, which held that in the seller's sole judgment, if for any reason he was dissatisfied, he was entitled to revoke the credit. In the absence of the buyer's failure to take the 2% discount as was his custom, the banker's report given in that case would have been "adequate" assurance under this Act, regardless of the language of the "satisfaction" clause. However, the seller is reasonably entitled to feel insecure at a sudden expansion of the buyer's use of a credit term, and should be entitled either to security or to a satisfactory explanation.

The entire foregoing discussion as to adequacy of assurance by way of explanation is subject to qualification when repeated occasions for the application of this section arise. This Act recognizes that repeated delinquencies must be viewed as cumulative. On the other hand, commercial sense also requires that if repeated claims for assurance are made under this section, the basis for these claims must be increasingly obvious.

5. A failure to provide adequate assurance of performance and thereby to re-establish the security of expectation, results in a breach only "by repudiation" under subsection (4). Therefore, the possibility is continued of retraction of the repudiation under the section dealing with that problem, unless the aggrieved party has acted on the breach in some manner.

The thirty day limit on the time to provide assurance is laid down to free the question of reasonable time from uncertainty in later litigation.

6. Clauses seeking to give the protected party exceedingly wide powers to cancel or readjust the contract when ground for insecurity arises must be read against the fact that good faith is a part of the obligation of the contract and not subject to modification by agreement and includes, in the case of a merchant, the reasonable observance of commercial standards of fair dealing in the trade. Such clauses can thus be effective to enlarge the protection given by the present section to a certain extent, to fix the reasonable time within which requested assurance must be given, or to define adequacy of the assurance in any commercially reasonable fashion. But any clause seeking to set up arbitrary standards for action is ineffective under this Article. Acceleration clauses are treated similarly in the Articles on Commercial Paper and Secured Transactions.

Cross References:

Point 3: Section 1–203.

Point 5: Section 2–611.

Point 6: Sections 1–203 and 1–208 and Articles 3 and 9.

Definitional Cross References:

"Aggrieved party". Section 1–201.

"Between merchants". Section 2–104.

"Contract". Section 1–201.

"Contract for sale". Section 2–106.

"Party". Section 1–201.

"Reasonable time". Section 1–204.

"Rights". Section 1–201.

"Writing". Section 1–201.

§ 2–610. Anticipatory Repudiation

When either party repudiates the contract with respect to a performance not yet due the loss of which will substantially impair the value of the contract to the other, the aggrieved party may

> (a) for a commercially reasonable time await performance by the repudiating party; or
>
> (b) resort to any remedy for breach (Section 2–703 or Section 2–711), even though he has notified the repudiating party that he would await the latter's performance and has urged retraction; and
>
> (c) in either case suspend his own performance or proceed in accordance with the provisions of this Article on the seller's right to identify goods to the contract notwithstanding breach or to salvage unfinished goods (Section 2–704).

Definitional Cross References:

"Aggrieved party". Section 1–201.

"Contract". Section 1–201.

"Party". Section 1–201.

"Remedy". Section 1–201.

§ 2–611. Retraction of Anticipatory Repudiation

(1) Until the repudiating party's next performance is due he can retract his repudiation unless the aggrieved party has since the repudiation cancelled or materially changed his position or otherwise indicated that he considers the repudiation final.

(2) Retraction may be by any method which clearly indicates to the aggrieved party that the repudiating party intends to perform, but must include any assurance justifiably demanded under the provisions of this Article (Section 2–609).

(3) Retraction reinstates the repudiating party's rights under the contract with due excuse and allowance to the aggrieved party for any delay occasioned by the repudiation.

Definitional Cross References:

"Aggrieved party". Section 1–201.

"Cancellation". Section 2–106.

"Contract". Section 1–201.

"Party". Section 1–201.

"Rights". Section 1–201.

§ 2–612. "Installment Contract"; Breach

(1) An "installment contract" is one which requires or authorizes the delivery of goods in separate lots to be separately accepted, even though the contract contains a clause "each delivery is a separate contract" or its equivalent.

(2) The buyer may reject any installment which is non-conforming if the non-conformity substantially impairs the value of that installment and cannot be cured or if the non-conformity is a defect in the required documents; but if the non-conformity does not fall within subsection (3) and the seller gives adequate assurance of its cure the buyer must accept that installment.

(3) Whenever non-conformity or default with respect to one or more installments substantially impairs the value of the whole contract there is a breach of the whole. But the aggrieved party reinstates the contract if he accepts a non-conforming installment without seasonably notifying of cancellation or if he brings an action with respect only to past installments or demands performance as to future installments.

Definitional Cross References:

"Action". Section 1–201.

"Aggrieved party". Section 1–201.

"Buyer". Section 2–103.

"Cancellation". Section 2–106.

"Conform". Section 2–106.

"Contract". Section 1–201.

"Lot". Section 2–105.

"Notifies". Section 1–201.

"Seasonably". Section 1–204.

"Seller". Section 2–103.

§ 2–613. Casualty to Identified Goods

Where the contract requires for its performance goods identified when the contract is made, and the goods suffer casualty without fault of either party before the risk of loss passes to the buyer, or in a proper case under a "no arrival, no sale" term (Section 2–324) then

(a) if the loss is total the contract is avoided; and

(b) if the loss is partial or the goods have so deteriorated as no longer to conform to the contract the buyer may nevertheless demand inspection and at his option either treat the contract as avoided or accept the goods with due allowance from the contract price for the deterioration or the deficiency in quantity but without further right against the seller.

Definitional Cross References:

"Buyer". Section 2–103.

"Conform". Section 2–106.

"Contract". Section 1–201.

"Fault". Section 1–201.

"Goods". Section 2–105.

"Party". Section 1–201.

"Rights". Section 1–201.

"Seller". Section 2–103.

§ 2–614. Substituted Performance

(1) Where without fault of either party the agreed berthing, loading, or unloading facilities fail or an agreed type of carrier becomes unavailable or the agreed manner of delivery otherwise becomes commercially impracticable but a commercially reasonable substitute is available, such substitute performance must be tendered and accepted.

(2) If the agreed means or manner of payment fails because of domestic or foreign governmental regulation, the seller may withhold or stop delivery unless the buyer provides a means or manner of payment which is commercially a substantial equivalent. If delivery has already been taken, payment by the means or in the manner provided by the regulation discharges the buyer's obligation unless the regulation is discriminatory, oppressive or predatory.

Definitional Cross References: "Party". Section 1–201.
  "Buyer". Section 2–103.
  "Seller". Section 2–103.
  "Fault". Section 1–201.

§ 2–615. Excuse by Failure of Presupposed Conditions

Except so far as a seller may have assumed a greater obligation and subject to the preceding section on substituted performance:

    (a) Delay in delivery or non-delivery in whole or in part by a seller who complies with paragraphs (b) and (c) is not a breach of his duty under a contract for sale if performance as agreed has been made impracticable by the occurrence of a contingency the non-occurrence of which was a basic assumption on which the contract was made or by compliance in good faith with any applicable foreign or domestic governmental regulation or order whether or not it later proves to be invalid.

    (b) Where the causes mentioned in paragraph (a) affect only a part of the seller's capacity to perform, he must allocate production and deliveries among his customers but may at his option include regular customers not then under contract as well as his own requirements for further manufacture. He may so allocate in any manner which is fair and reasonable.

    (c) The seller must notify the buyer seasonably that there will be delay or non-delivery and, when allocation is required under paragraph (b), of the estimated quota thus made available for the buyer.

Official Comment

Prior Uniform Statutory Provision: None.

Purposes:

1. This section excuses a seller from timely delivery of goods contracted for, where his performance has become commercially impracticable because of unforeseen supervening circumstances not within the contemplation of the parties at the time of contracting. The destruction of specific goods and the problem of the use of substituted performance on points other than delay or quantity, treated elsewhere in this Article, must be distinguished from the matter covered by this section.

2. The present section deliberately refrains from any effort at an exhaustive expression of contingencies and is to be interpreted in all cases sought to be brought within its scope in terms of its underlying reason and purpose.

3. The first test for excuse under this Article in terms of basic assumption is a familiar one. The additional test of commercial impracticability (as contrasted with "impossibility," "frustration of performance" or "frustration of the venture") has been adopted in order to call attention to the commercial character of the criterion chosen by this Article.

4. Increased cost alone does not excuse performance unless the rise in cost is due to some unforeseen contingency which alters the essential nature of the performance. Neither is a rise or a collapse in the market in itself a justification, for that is exactly the type of business risk which business contracts made at fixed prices are intended to cover. But a severe shortage of raw materials or of supplies due to a contingency such as war, embargo, local crop failure unforeseen shutdown of major sources of supply or the like, which either causes a marked increase in cost or altogether prevents the seller from securing supplies necessary to his performance, is within the contemplation of this section. (See Ford & Sons, Ltd. v. Henry Leetham & Sons, Ltd., 21 Com.Cas. 55 (1915, K.B.D.).)

5. Where a particular source of supply is exclusive under the agreement and fails through casualty, the present section applies rather than the provision on destruction or deterioration of specific goods. The same holds true where a particular source of supply is shown by the circumstances to have been contemplated or assumed by the parties at the time of contracting. (See Davis Co. v. Hoffmann–LaRoche Chemical Works, 178 App.Div. 855, 166 N.Y.S. 179 (1917) and International Paper Co. v. Rockefeller, 161 App. Div. 180, 146 N.Y.S. 371 (1914).) There is no excuse under this section, however, unless the seller has employed all due measures to assure himself that his source will not fail. (See Canadian Industrial Alcohol Co., Ltd. v. Dunbar Molasses Co., 258 N.Y. 194, 179 N.E. 383, 80 A.L.R. 1173 (1932) and Washington Mfg. Co. v. Midland Lumber Co., 113 Wash. 593, 194 P. 777 (1921).)

In the case of failure of production by an agreed source for causes beyond the seller's control, the seller should, if possible, be excused since production by an agreed source is without more a basic assumption of the contract. Such excuse should not result in relieving the defaulting supplier from liability nor in dropping into the seller's lap an unearned bonus of damages over. The flexible adjustment machinery of this Article provides the solution under the provision on the obligation of good faith. A condition to his making good the claim of excuse is the turning over to the buyer of his rights against the defaulting source of supply to the extent of the buyer's contract in relation to which excuse is being claimed.

6. In situations in which neither sense nor justice is served by either answer when the issue is posed in flat terms of "excuse" or "no excuse," adjustment under the various provisions of this Article is necessary, especially the sections on good faith, on insecurity and assurance and on the reading of all provisions in the light of their purposes, and the general policy of this Act to use equitable principles in furtherance of commercial standards and good faith.

7. The failure of conditions which go to convenience or collateral values rather than to the commercial practicability of the main performance does not amount to a complete excuse. However, good faith and the reason of the present section and of the preceding one may properly be held to justify and even to require any needed delay involved in a good faith inquiry seeking a readjustment of the contract terms to meet the new conditions.

8. The provisions of this section are made subject to assumption of greater liability by agreement and such agreement is to be found not only in the expressed terms of the contract but in the circumstances surrounding the contracting, in trade usage and the like. Thus the exemptions of this section do not apply when the contingency in question is sufficiently foreshadowed at the time of contracting to be included among the business risks which are fairly to be regarded as part of the dickered terms, either consciously or as a matter of reasonable, commercial interpretation from the circumstances. (See Madeirense Do Brasil, S.A. v. Stulman–Emrick Lumber Co., 147 F.2d 399 (C.C.A., 2 Cir., 1945).) The exemption otherwise present through usage of trade under the present section may also be expressly negated by the language of the agreement. Generally, express agreements as to exemptions designed to enlarge upon or supplant the provisions of this section are to be read in the light of mercantile sense and reason, for this section itself sets up the commercial standard for normal and reasonable interpretation and provides a minimum beyond which agreement may not go.

Agreement can also be made in regard to the consequences of exemption as laid down in paragraphs (b) and (c) and the next section on procedure on notice claiming excuse.

9. The case of a farmer who has contracted to sell crops to be grown on designated land may be regarded as falling either within the section on casualty to identified goods or this section, and he may be excused, when there is a failure of the specific crop, either on the basis of the destruction of identified goods or because of the failure of a basic assumption of the contract.

Exemption of the buyer in the case of a "requirements" contract is covered by the "Output and Requirements" section both as to assumption and allocation of the relevant risks. But when a contract by a manufacturer to buy fuel or raw material makes no specific reference to a particular venture and no such reference may be drawn from the circumstances, commercial understanding views it as a general deal in the general market and not conditioned on any assumption of the continuing operation of the buyer's plant. Even when notice is given by the buyer that the supplies are needed to fill a specific contract of a normal commercial kind, commercial understanding does not see such a supply contract as conditioned on the continuance of the buyer's further contract for outlet. On the other hand, where the buyer's contract is in reasonable commercial understanding conditioned on a definite and specific venture or assumption as, for instance, a war procurement subcontract known to be based on a prime contract which is subject to termination, or a supply contract for a particular construction venture, the reason of the present section may well apply and entitle the buyer to the exemption.

10. Following its basic policy of using commercial practicability as a test for excuse, this section recognizes as of equal significance either a foreign or domestic regulation and disregards any technical distinctions between "law," "regulation," "order" and the like. Nor does it make the present action of the seller depend upon the eventual judicial determination of the legality of the particular governmental action. The seller's good faith belief in the validity of the regulation is the test under this Article and the best evidence of his good faith is the general commercial acceptance of the regulation. However, governmental interference cannot excuse unless it truly "supervenes" in such a manner as to be beyond the seller's assumption of risk. And any action by the party claiming excuse which causes or colludes in inducing the governmental action preventing his performance would be in breach of good faith and would destroy his exemption.

11. An excused seller must fulfill his contract to the extent which the supervening contingency permits, and if the situation is such that his customers are generally affected he must take account of all in supplying one. Subsections (a) and (b), therefore, explicitly permit in any proration a fair and reasonable attention to the needs of regular customers who are probably relying on spot orders for supplies. Customers at different stages of the manufacturing process may be fairly treated by including the seller's manufacturing requirements. A fortiori, the seller may also take account of contracts later in date than the one in question. The fact that such spot orders may be closed at an advanced price causes no difficulty, since any allocation which exceeds normal past requirements will not be reasonable. However, good faith requires, when prices have advanced, that the seller exercise real care in making his allocations, and in case of doubt his contract customers should be favored and supplies prorated evenly among them regardless of price. Save for the extra care thus required by changes in the market, this section seeks to leave every reasonable business leeway to the seller.

Cross References:

Point 1: Sections 2–613 and 2–614.

Point 2: Section 1–102.

Point 5: Sections 1–203 and 2–613.

Point 6: Sections 1–102, 1–203 and 2–609.

Point 7: Section 2–614.

Point 8: Sections 1–201, 2–302 and 2–616.

Point 9: Sections 1–102, 2–306 and 2–613.

Definitional Cross References:

"Between merchants". Section 2–104.

"Buyer". Section 2–103.

"Contract". Section 1–201.

"Contract for sale". Section 2–106.

"Good faith". Section 1–201.

"Merchant". Section 2–104.

"Notifies". Section 1–201.

"Seasonably". Section 1–204.

"Seller". Section 2–103.

§ 2–616. Procedure on Notice Claiming Excuse

(1) Where the buyer receives notification of a material or indefinite delay or an allocation justified under the preceding section he may by written notification to the seller as to any delivery concerned, and where the prospective deficiency substantially impairs the value of the whole contract under the provisions of this Article relating to breach of installment contracts (Section 2–612), then also as to the whole,

> (a) terminate and thereby discharge any unexecuted portion of the contract; or

> (b) modify the contract by agreeing to take his available quota in substitution.

(2) If after receipt of such notification from the seller the buyer fails so to modify the contract within a reasonable time not exceeding thirty days the contract lapses with respect to any deliveries affected.

(3) The provisions of this section may not be negated by agreement except in so far as the seller has assumed a greater obligation under the preceding section.

Definitional Cross References:

"Buyer". Section 2–103.

"Contract". Section 1–201.

"Installment contract". Section 2–612.

"Notification". Section 1–201.

"Reasonable time". Section 1–204.

"Seller". Section 2–103.

"Termination". Section 2–106.

"Written". Section 1–201.

PART 7

REMEDIES

§ 2–701. Remedies for Breach of Collateral Contracts Not Impaired

Remedies for breach of any obligation or promise collateral or ancillary to a contract for sale are not impaired by the provisions of this Article.

Definitional Cross References:

"Contract for sale". Section 2–106.

"Remedy". Section 1–201.

§ 2–702. Seller's Remedies on Discovery of Buyer's Insolvency

(1) Where the seller discovers the buyer to be insolvent he may refuse delivery except for cash including payment for all goods theretofore delivered under the contract, and stop delivery under this Article (Section 2–705).

(2) Where the seller discovers that the buyer has received goods on credit while insolvent he may reclaim the goods upon demand made within ten days after the receipt, but if misrepresentation of solvency has been made to the particular seller in writing within three months before delivery the ten day limitation does not apply. Except as provided in this subsection the seller may not base a right to reclaim goods on the buyer's fraudulent or innocent misrepresentation of solvency or of intent to pay.

(3) The seller's right to reclaim under subsection (2) is subject to the rights of a buyer in ordinary course or other good faith purchaser under this Article (Section 2-403). Successful reclamation of goods excludes all other remedies with respect to them.

Definitional Cross References:

"Buyer". Section 2-103.

"Buyer in ordinary course of business". Section 1-201.

"Contract". Section 1-201.

"Good faith". Section 1-201.

"Goods". Section 2-105.

"Insolvent". Section 1-201.

"Person". Section 1-201.

"Purchaser". Section 1-201.

"Receipt" of goods. Section 2-103.

"Remedy". Section 1-201.

"Rights". Section 1-201.

"Seller". Section 2-103.

"Writing". Section 1-201.

§ 2-703. Seller's Remedies in General

Where the buyer wrongfully rejects or revokes acceptance of goods or fails to make a payment due on or before delivery or repudiates with respect to a part or the whole, then with respect to any goods directly affected and, if the breach is of the whole contract (Section 2-612), then also with respect to the whole undelivered balance, the aggrieved seller may

    (a) withhold delivery of such goods;

    (b) stop delivery by any bailee as hereafter provided (Section 2-705);

    (c) proceed under the next section respecting goods still unidentified to the contract;

    (d) resell and recover damages as hereafter provided (Section 2-706);

    (e) recover damages for non-acceptance (Section 2-708) or in a proper case the price (Section 2-709);

    (f) cancel.

Definitional Cross References:

"Aggrieved party". Section 1-201.

"Buyer". Section 2-103.

"Cancellation". Section 2-106.

"Contract". Section 1-201.

"Goods". Section 2-105.

"Remedy". Section 1-201.

"Seller". Section 2-103.

§ 2–704. Seller's Right to Identify Goods to the Contract Notwithstanding Breach or to Salvage Unfinished Goods

(1) An aggrieved seller under the preceding section may

    (a) identify to the contract conforming goods not already identified if at the time he learned of the breach they are in his possession or control;

    (b) treat as the subject of resale goods which have demonstrably been intended for the particular contract even though those goods are unfinished.

(2) Where the goods are unfinished an aggrieved seller may in the exercise of reasonable commercial judgment for the purposes of avoiding loss and of effective realization either complete the manufacture and wholly identify the goods to the contract or cease manufacture and resell for scrap or salvage value or proceed in any other reasonable manner.

Definitional Cross References:

"Aggrieved party". Section 1–201.
"Conforming". Section 2–106.
"Contract". Section 1–201.

"Goods". Section 2–105.
"Rights". Section 1–201.
"Seller". Section 2–103.

§ 2–705. Seller's Stoppage of Delivery in Transit or Otherwise

(1) The seller may stop delivery of goods in the possession of a carrier or other bailee when he discovers the buyer to be insolvent (Section 2–702) and may stop delivery of carload, truckload, planeload or larger shipments of express or freight when the buyer repudiates or fails to make a payment due before delivery or if for any other reason the seller has a right to withhold or reclaim the goods.

(2) As against such buyer the seller may stop delivery until

    (a) receipt of the goods by the buyer; or

    (b) acknowledgment to the buyer by any bailee of the goods except a carrier that the bailee holds the goods for the buyer; or

    (c) such acknowledgment to the buyer by a carrier by reshipment or as warehouseman; or

    (d) negotiation to the buyer of any negotiable document of title covering the goods.

(3)(a) To stop delivery the seller must so notify as to enable the bailee by reasonable diligence to prevent delivery of the goods.

(b) After such notification the bailee must hold and deliver the goods according to the directions of the seller but the seller is liable to the bailee for any ensuing charges or damages.

(c) If a negotiable document of title has been issued for goods the bailee is not obliged to obey a notification to stop until surrender of the document.

(d) A carrier who has issued a non-negotiable bill of lading is not obliged to obey a notification to stop received from a person other than the consignor.

Definitional Cross References:

"Buyer". Section 2–103.

"Contract for sale". Section 2–106.

"Document of title". Section 1–201.

"Goods". Section 2–105.

"Insolvent". Section 1–201.

"Notification". Section 1–201.

"Receipt" of goods. Section 2–103.

"Rights". Section 1–201.

"Seller". Section 2–103.

§ 2–706. Seller's Resale Including Contract for Resale

(1) Under the conditions stated in Section 2–703 on seller's remedies, the seller may resell the goods concerned or the undelivered balance thereof. Where the resale is made in good faith and in a commercially reasonable manner the seller may recover the difference between the resale price and the contract price together with any incidental damages allowed under the provisions of this Article (Section 2–710), but less expenses saved in consequence of the buyer's breach.

(2) Except as otherwise provided in subsection (3) or unless otherwise agreed resale may be at public or private sale including sale by way of one or more contracts to sell or of identification to an existing contract of the seller. Sale may be as a unit or in parcels and at any time and place and on any terms but every aspect of the sale including the method, manner, time, place and terms must be commercially reasonable. The resale must be reasonably identified as referring to the broken contract, but it is not necessary that the goods be in existence or that any or all of them have been identified to the contract before the breach.

(3) Where the resale is at private sale the seller must give the buyer reasonable notification of his intention to resell.

(4) Where the resale is at public sale

(a) only identified goods can be sold except where there is a recognized market for a public sale of futures in goods of the kind; and

(b) it must be made at a usual place or market for public sale if one is reasonably available and except in the case of goods which are perishable or threaten to decline in value speedily the seller must give the buyer reasonable notice of the time and place of the resale; and

(c) if the goods are not to be within the view of those attending the sale the notification of sale must state the place where the goods are located and provide for their reasonable inspection by prospective bidders; and

(d) the seller may buy.

(5) A purchaser who buys in good faith at a resale takes the goods free of any rights of the original buyer even though the seller fails to comply with one or more of the requirements of this section.

(6) The seller is not accountable to the buyer for any profit made on any resale. A person in the position of a seller (Section 2–707) or a buyer who has rightfully rejected or justifiably revoked acceptance must account for any excess over the amount of his security interest, as hereinafter defined (subsection (3) of Section 2–711).

Definitional Cross References:

"Buyer". Section 2–103.

"Contract". Section 1–201.

"Contract for sale". Section 2–106.

"Good faith". Section 2–103.

"Goods". Section 2–105.

"Merchant". Section 2–104.

"Notification". Section 1–201.

"Person in position of seller". Section 2–707.

"Purchase". Section 1–201.

"Rights". Section 1–201.

"Sale". Section 2–106.

"Security interest". Section 1–201.

"Seller". Section 2–103.

§ 2–707. "Person in the Position of a Seller"

(1) A "person in the position of a seller" includes as against a principal an agent who has paid or become responsible for the price of goods on behalf of his principal or anyone who otherwise holds a security interest or other right in goods similar to that of a seller.

(2) A person in the position of a seller may as provided in this Article withhold or stop delivery (Section 2–705) and resell (Section 2–706) and recover incidental damages (Section 2–710).

Definitional Cross References:

"Consignee". Section 7–102.

"Consignor". Section 7–102.

"Goods". Section 2–105.

"Security interest". Section 1–201.

"Seller". Section 2–103.

§ 2–708. Seller's Damages for Non-acceptance or Repudiation

(1) Subject to subsection (2) and to the provisions of this Article with respect to proof of market price (Section 2–723), the measure of damages for non-acceptance or repudiation by the buyer is the difference between the market price at the time and place for tender and the unpaid contract price together with any incidental damages provided in this Article (Section 2–710), but less expenses saved in consequence of the buyer's breach.

(2) If the measure of damages provided in subsection (1) is inadequate to put the seller in as good a position as performance would have done then the measure of damages is the profit (including reasonable overhead) which the seller would have made from full performance by the buyer, together with any incidental damages provided in this Article (Section 2–710), due allowance for costs reasonably incurred and due credit for payments or proceeds of resale.

Definitional Cross References:

"Buyer". Section 2–103.

"Contract". Section 1–201.

"Seller". Section 2–103.

§ 2–709. Action for the Price

(1) When the buyer fails to pay the price as it becomes due the seller may recover, together with any incidental damages under the next section, the price

> (a) of goods accepted or of conforming goods lost or damaged within a commercially reasonable time after risk of their loss has passed to the buyer; and
>
> (b) of goods identified to the contract if the seller is unable after reasonable effort to resell them at a reasonable price or the circumstances reasonably indicate that such effort will be unavailing.

(2) Where the seller sues for the price he must hold for the buyer any goods which have been identified to the contract and are still in his control except that if resale becomes possible he may resell them at any time prior to the collection of the judgment. The net proceeds of any such resale must be credited to the buyer and payment of the judgment entitles him to any goods not resold.

(3) After the buyer has wrongfully rejected or revoked acceptance of the goods or has failed to make a payment due or has repudiated (Section 2–610), a seller who is held not entitled to the price under this section shall nevertheless be awarded damages for non-acceptance under the preceding section.

Definitional Cross References:

"Action". Section 1–201.

"Buyer". Section 2–103.

"Conforming". Section 2–106.

"Contract". Section 1–201.

"Goods". Section 2–105.

"Seller". Section 2–103.

§ 2–710. Seller's Incidental Damages

Incidental damages to an aggrieved seller include any commercially reasonable charges, expenses or commissions incurred in stopping delivery, in the transportation, care and custody of goods after the buyer's breach, in connection with return or resale of the goods or otherwise resulting from the breach.

Definitional Cross References:

"Aggrieved party". Section 1–201.

"Buyer". Section 2–103.

"Goods". Section 2–105.

"Seller". Section 2–103.

§ 2–711. Buyer's Remedies in General; Buyer's Security Interest in Rejected Goods

(1) Where the seller fails to make delivery or repudiates or the buyer rightfully rejects or justifiably revokes acceptance then with respect to any goods involved, and with respect to the whole if the breach goes to the whole contract (Section 2–612), the buyer may cancel and whether or not he has done so may in addition to recovering so much of the price as has been paid

> (a) "cover" and have damages under the next section as to all the goods affected whether or not they have been identified to the contract; or

> (b) recover damages for non-delivery as provided in this Article (Section 2–713).

(2) Where the seller fails to deliver or repudiates the buyer may also

> (a) if the goods have been identified recover them as provided in this Article (Section 2–502); or

> (b) in a proper case obtain specific performance or replevy the goods as provided in this Article (Section 2–716).

(3) On rightful rejection or justifiable revocation of acceptance a buyer has a security interest in goods in his possession or control for any payments made on their price and any expenses reasonably incurred in their inspection, receipt, transportation, care and custody and may hold such goods and resell them in like manner as an aggrieved seller (Section 2–706).

Definitional Cross References:

"Aggrieved party". Section 1–201.

"Buyer". Section 2–103.

"Cancellation". Section 2–106.

"Contract". Section 1–201.

"Cover". Section 2–712.

"Goods". Section 2–105.

"Notifies". Section 1–201.

"Receipt" of goods. Section 2–103.

"Remedy". Section 1–201.

"Security interest". Section 1–201.

"Seller". Section 2–103.

§ 2–712. "Cover"; Buyer's Procurement of Substitute Goods

(1) After a breach within the preceding section the buyer may "cover" by making in good faith and without unreasonable delay any reasonable purchase of or contract to purchase goods in substitution for those due from the seller.

(2) The buyer may recover from the seller as damages the difference between the cost of cover and the contract price together with any

incidental or consequential damages as hereinafter defined (Section 2–715), but less expenses saved in consequence of the seller's breach.

(3) Failure of the buyer to effect cover within this section does not bar him from any other remedy.

Definitional Cross References:

"Buyer". Section 2–103.

"Contract". Section 1–201.

"Good faith". Section 2–103.

"Goods". Section 2–105.

"Purchase". Section 1–201.

"Remedy". Section 1–201.

"Seller". Section 2–103.

§ 2–713. Buyer's Damages for Non-delivery or Repudiation

(1) Subject to the provisions of this Article with respect to proof of market price (Section 2–723), the measure of damages for non-delivery or repudiation by the seller is the difference between the market price at the time when the buyer learned of the breach and the contract price together with any incidental and consequential damages provided in this Article (Section 2–715), but less expenses saved in consequence of the seller's breach.

(2) Market price is to be determined as of the place for tender or, in cases of rejection after arrival or revocation of acceptance, as of the place of arrival.

Definitional Cross References:

"Buyer". Section 2–103.

"Contract". Section 1–201.

"Seller". Section 2–103.

§ 2–714. Buyer's Damages for Breach in Regard to Accepted Goods

(1) Where the buyer has accepted goods and given notification (subsection (3) of Section 2–607) he may recover as damages for any non-conformity of tender the loss resulting in the ordinary course of events from the seller's breach as determined in any manner which is reasonable.

(2) The measure of damages for breach of warranty is the difference at the time and place of acceptance between the value of the goods accepted and the value they would have had if they had been as warranted, unless special circumstances show proximate damages of a different amount.

(3) In a proper case any incidental and consequential damages under the next section may also be recovered.

Definitional Cross References:

"Buyer". Section 2–103.

"Conform". Section 2–106.

"Goods". Section 1–201.

"Notification". Section 1–201.

"Seller". Section 2–103.

§ 2–715. Buyer's Incidental and Consequential Damages

(1) Incidental damages resulting from the seller's breach include expenses reasonably incurred in inspection, receipt, transportation and care and custody of goods rightfully rejected, any commercially reasonable charges, expenses or commissions in connection with effecting cover and any other reasonable expense incident to the delay or other breach.

(2) Consequential damages resulting from the seller's breach include

(a) any loss resulting from general or particular requirements and needs of which the seller at the time of contracting had reason to know and which could not reasonably be prevented by cover or otherwise; and

(b) injury to person or property proximately resulting from any breach of warranty.

Definitional Cross References:　　"Person". Section 1–201.

"Cover". Section 2–712.　　"Receipt" of goods. Section 2–103.

"Goods". Section 1–201.　　"Seller". Section 2–103.

§ 2–716. Buyer's Right to Specific Performance or Replevin

(1) Specific performance may be decreed where the goods are unique or in other proper circumstances.

(2) The decree for specific performance may include such terms and conditions as to payment of the price, damages, or other relief as the court may deem just.

(3) The buyer has a right of replevin for goods identified to the contract if after reasonable effort he is unable to effect cover for such goods or the circumstances reasonably indicate that such effort will be unavailing or if the goods have been shipped under reservation and satisfaction of the security interest in them has been made or tendered. In the case of goods bought for personal, family, or household purposes, the buyer's right of replevin vests upon acquisition of a special property, even if the seller had not then repudiated or failed to deliver.

Definitional Cross References:　　"Goods". Section 1–201.

"Buyer". Section 2–103.　　"Rights". Section 1–201.

§ 2–717. Deduction of Damages From the Price

The buyer on notifying the seller of his intention to do so may deduct all or any part of the damages resulting from any breach of the contract from any part of the price still due under the same contract.

Definitional Cross References:　　"Notifies". Section 1–201.

"Buyer". Section 2–103.

§ 2–718. Liquidation or Limitation of Damages; Deposits

(1) Damages for breach by either party may be liquidated in the agreement but only at an amount which is reasonable in the light of the anticipated or actual harm caused by the breach, the difficulties of proof of loss, and the inconvenience or non-feasibility of otherwise obtaining an adequate remedy. A term fixing unreasonably large liquidated damages is void as a penalty.

(2) Where the seller justifiably withholds delivery of goods because of the buyer's breach, the buyer is entitled to restitution of any amount by which the sum of his payments exceeds

> (a) the amount to which the seller is entitled by virtue of terms liquidating the seller's damages in accordance with subsection (1), or

> (b) in the absence of such terms, twenty per cent of the value of the total performance for which the buyer is obligated under the contract or $500, whichever is smaller.

(3) The buyer's right to restitution under subsection (2) is subject to offset to the extent that the seller establishes

> (a) a right to recover damages under the provisions of this Article other than subsection (1), and

> (b) the amount or value of any benefits received by the buyer directly or indirectly by reason of the contract.

(4) Where a seller has received payment in goods their reasonable value or the proceeds of their resale shall be treated as payments for the purposes of subsection (2); but if the seller has notice of the buyer's breach before reselling goods received in part performance, his resale is subject to the conditions laid down in this Article on resale by an aggrieved seller (Section 2–706).

Definitional Cross References:

"Aggrieved party". Section 1–201.	"Goods". Section 2–105.
"Agreement". Section 1–201.	"Action". 1–201.
"Buyer". Section 2–103.	"Seller". Section 2–103.
	"Term". Section 1–201.

§ 2–719. Contractual Modification or Limitation of Remedy

(1) Subject to the provisions of subsections (2) and (3) of this section and of the preceding section on liquidation and limitation of damages,

> (a) the agreement may provide for remedies in addition to or in substitution for those provided in this Article and may limit or alter the measure of damages recoverable under this Article, as by limiting the buyer's remedies to return of the goods and repayment of the price or to repair and replacement of non-conforming goods or parts; and

95

(b) resort to a remedy as provided is optional unless the remedy is expressly agreed to be exclusive, in which case it is the sole remedy.

(2) Where circumstances cause an exclusive or limited remedy to fail of its essential purpose, remedy may be had as provided in this Act.

(3) Consequential damages may be limited or excluded unless the limitation or exclusion is unconscionable. Limitation of consequential damages for injury to the person in the case of consumer goods is prima facie unconscionable but limitation of damages where the loss is commercial is not.

Definitional Cross References:

"Agreement". Section 1–201.

"Buyer". Section 2–103.

"Conforming". Section 2–106.

"Contract". Section 1–201.

"Goods". Section 2–105.

"Remedy". Section 1–201.

"Seller". Section 2–103.

§ 2–720. Effect of "Cancellation" or "Rescission" on Claims for Antecedent Breach

Unless the contrary intention clearly appears, expressions of "cancellation" or "rescission" of the contract or the like shall not be construed as a renunciation or discharge of any claim in damages for an antecedent breach.

Definitional Cross References:

"Cancellation". Section 2–106.

"Contract". Section 1–201.

§ 2–721. Remedies for Fraud

Remedies for material misrepresentation or fraud include all remedies available under this Article for non-fraudulent breach. Neither rescission or a claim for rescission of the contract for sale nor rejection or return of the goods shall bar or be deemed inconsistent with a claim for damages or other remedy.

Definitional Cross References:

"Contract for sale". Section 2–106.

"Goods". Section 1–201.

"Remedy". Section 1–201.

§ 2–722. Who Can Sue Third Parties for Injury to Goods

Where a third party so deals with goods which have been identified to a contract for sale as to cause actionable injury to a party to that contract

(a) a right of action against the third party is in either party to the contract for sale who has title to or a security interest or a special property or an insurable interest in the goods; and if the goods have been destroyed or converted a right of action is also in the party who either bore the risk of loss under the contract for sale or has since the injury assumed that risk as against the other;

(b) if at the time of the injury the party plaintiff did not bear the risk of loss as against the other party to the contract for sale and there is no arrangement between them for disposition of the recovery, his suit or settlement is, subject to his own interest, as a fiduciary for the other party to the contract;

(c) either party may with the consent of the other sue for the benefit of whom it may concern.

Definitional Cross References:

"Action". Section 1–201.

"Buyer". Section 2–103.

"Contract for sale". Section 2–106.

"Goods". Section 2–105.

"Party". Section 1–201.

"Rights". Section 1–201.

"Security interest". Section 1–201.

§ 2–723. Proof of Market Price: Time and Place

(1) If an action based on anticipatory repudiation comes to trial before the time for performance with respect to some or all of the goods, any damages based on market price (Section 2–708 or Section 2–713) shall be determined according to the price of such goods prevailing at the time when the aggrieved party learned of the repudiation.

(2) If evidence of a price prevailing at the times or places described in this Article is not readily available the price prevailing within any reasonable time before or after the time described or at any other place which in commercial judgment or under usage of trade would serve as a reasonable substitute for the one described may be used, making any proper allowance for the cost of transporting the goods to or from such other place.

(3) Evidence of a relevant price prevailing at a time or place other than the one described in this Article offered by one party is not admissible unless and until he has given the other party such notice as the court finds sufficient to prevent unfair surprise.

Definitional Cross References:

"Action". Section 1–201.

"Aggrieved party". Section 1–201.

"Goods". Section 2–105.

"Notifies". Section 1–201.

"Party". Section 1–201.

"Reasonable time". Section 1–204.

"Usage of trade". Section 1–205.

§ 2–724. Admissibility of Market Quotations

Whenever the prevailing price or value of any goods regularly bought and sold in any established commodity market is in issue, reports in official publications or trade journals or in newspapers or periodicals of general circulation published as the reports of such market shall be admissible in evidence. The circumstances of the preparation of such a report may be shown to affect its weight but not its admissibility.

Definitional Cross Reference:

"Goods". Section 2–105.

§ 2–725. Statute of Limitations in Contracts for Sale

(1) An action for breach of any contract for sale must be commenced within four years after the cause of action has accrued. By the original agreement the parties may reduce the period of limitation to not less than one year but may not extend it.

(2) A cause of action accrues when the breach occurs, regardless of the aggrieved party's lack of knowledge of the breach. A breach of warranty occurs when tender of delivery is made, except that where a warranty explicitly extends to future performance of the goods and discovery of the breach must await the time of such performance the cause of action accrues when the breach is or should have been discovered.

(3) Where an action commenced within the time limited by subsection (1) is so terminated as to leave available a remedy by another action for the same breach such other action may be commenced after the expiration of the time limited and within six months after the termination of the first action unless the termination resulted from voluntary discontinuance or from dismissal for failure or neglect to prosecute.

(4) This section does not alter the law on tolling of the statute of limitations nor does it apply to causes of action which have accrued before this Act becomes effective.

Definitional Cross References:

"Action". Section 1–201.

"Aggrieved party". Section 1–201.

"Agreement". Section 1–201.

"Contract for sale". Section 2–106.

"Goods". Section 2–105.

"Party". Section 1–201.

"Remedy". Section 1–201.

"Term". Section 1–201.

"Termination". Section 2–106.

PROPOSED AMENDMENTS TO UNIFORM COMMERCIAL CODE ARTICLE 2— SALES*

Table of Contents

Prefatory Note

PART 1. SHORT TITLE, GENERAL CONSTRUCTION AND SUBJECT MATTER

PART 2. FORM, FORMATION, TERMS AND READJUSTMENT OF CONTRACT; ELECTRONIC CONTRACTING

PART 3. GENERAL OBLIGATION AND CONSTRUCTION OF CONTRACT

* Material to be added to current Article 2 is indicated by underlining. Material to be deleted is indicated by ~~strikeouts~~. Only comments that explain proposed changes from current law have been included.

PREFATORY NOTE

After over a decade of analysis and discussion, a set of amendments to Article 2 has been adopted. For the most part, the changes update the article to accommodate electronic commerce, which is desirable to avoid questions of interrelation with federal law, and also to reflect the development of business practices, changes in other law, and to resolve some interpretive difficulties of practical significance. The amendments reflect the fact that, overall, Article 2 continues to serve well. This is largely a result of the approach of the Article, which relies to a large extent on the ability of the parties to adapt its provisions by agreement, including course of performance, course of dealing and usage of trade, and on the courts to apply the provisions sensibly. A summary of the amendments includes:

Good Faith

Consistent with the other articles of the Uniform Commercial Code, other than Article 5, the definition of good faith, which is in Section 2–103(1)(j), is amended to cover both "honesty in fact and observance of reasonable commercial standards of fair dealing".

Scope

Although the scope of Article 2 remains unchanged, three amendments affect its application. First, "information," which is an undefined term, is excluded from the definition of "goods" in Section 2–103(1)(k). Second, the subject matter of "foreign exchange transactions," a term defined in Section 2–103(1)(i) in a manner that distinguishes transactions crediting and debiting trading balances from transactions for the physical exchange of money, is also excluded from the definition of "goods." Finally, Section 2–108 addresses the relationship between Article 2 and other laws relating to transactions in goods.

Electronic Commerce

There are a number of changes designed to accommodate electronic commerce. These include the change of the term "writing" to "record" throughout the article, a redefinition of the terms "sign" and "conspicuous", and definitions and use of the new terms "electronic," "electronic agent," and "electronic record."

Section 2–204, which is concerned with formation generally, has been amended to provide that a contract may be formed by the interaction of electronic agents or the interaction of an individual and an electronic agent. New Section 2–211 provides that a record, signature, or contract cannot be denied legal effect and enforceability merely because it is electronic in form. New Section 2–212 provides a rule to determine whether an electronic record or electronic signature is attributable to a person. New Section 2–213 provides that if receipt of an electronic communication has a legal effect, that effect is not changed merely because no individual is aware of the receipt. This section also provides that receipt of an electronic communication does not establish the content of the communication.

Formation and Terms

The statute-of-frauds provision, contained in Section 2–201, has been amended to change the jurisdictional amount from $500 to $5,000 to reflect over 50 years of inflation. The exception for admissions in court has been broadened to include out-of-court admissions "under oath." The amended section also implicitly recognizes the application of nonstatutory exceptions such as promissory estoppel. The section also expressly excludes application of a statute-of-frauds provision from other law which is predicated on the passage of time.

Section 2–202, which sets out the rules on parol or extrinsic evidence, has been amended to clarify that a finding of ambiguity is not a prerequisite to an admission of evidence of a course of dealing, course of performance, or usage of trade for the purpose of explaining a term.

Section 2–207 has been thoroughly revised. The section no longer addresses issues of offer and acceptance. The principle that a definite and seasonable expression of acceptance on terms other than those of the offer may operate as an acceptance, which was contained previously in Section 2–207(1), has been moved to Section 2–206(3), and Section 2–207 is now only concerned with the terms of the contract. Section 2–207 applies to all contracts, not just those formed by a "battle of the forms". The amended section now provides that terms that appear in the records of both parties, terms to which both parties agree, and supplemental terms under the UCC constitute the contract.

Former Sections 2–319 through 2–324 that dealt with shipping and delivery have been deleted. Those sections dealt with standard shipping terms in a manner inconsistent with modern commercial usage.

Clarifying what was unclear in the prior law, Section 2–503 now provides that, when goods are in the bailee's possession and are to be delivered without movement by tender of delivery, a bailee's acknowledgment must be to the buyer. This section now explicitly provides that the effect of a bailee's receipt of notice on third-party rights is subject to Article 9. Section 2–504 has also been changed to clarify that compliance with the requirements for a shipping contract requires a seller to put "conforming" goods in the carrier's possession.

Section 2–513 now provides explicitly that the parties may by agreement fix a standard of inspection, and Section 2–309 now provides explicitly that the parties may by agreement specify a standard for the nature and timing of a notice of termination.

Sections 2–325, 2–506, and 2–514 have been amended to coordinate with Article 5.

Warranties

Section 2–312 has been amended to bring into the text what was formerly in the comments; that is, the warranty of title is breached if the sale "unreasonably exposes the buyer to litigation because of a colorable claim or interest in the goods."

Section 2–313, which is subject to Section 2–318, has been amended to make it clear that the section applies only to parties in privity. The section has also been amended to provide that a "remedial promise," which is defined in Section 2–103(1)(n) as a promise by a seller to repair, replace, or refund upon the happening of an agreed event, is enforceable without reference to the basis-of-the-bargain test. "Remedial promise" as a distinct category of promise was created to deal with a statute-of-limitations problem. New Section 2–725(2)(c) provides that a cause of action accrues if a remedial promise is not performed when performance is due.

New Sections 2–313A and 2–313B, which are also subject to Section 2–318, create statutory obligations in the nature of express warranties that run directly from a seller to a remote purchaser that is not in privity. Each section applies only to "new goods or goods sold or leased as new goods in a transaction of purchase in the normal chain of distribution," excludes liability for statements that are mere opinion, permits the seller to modify or limit remedies as long as the modification or limitation is provided to the remote purchaser at or before the time of purchase, and excludes recovery for consequential damages in the form of lost profits. Liability under Section 2–313A arises only if the seller "makes an affirmation of fact or promise that relates to the goods, provides a description that relates to the goods, or makes a remedial promise," the affirmation, promise, description or remedial promise is "in a record packaged with or accompanying the goods," and the seller "reasonably expects the record to be, and the record is, furnished to the remote purchaser." Section 2–313B differs from Section 2–313A in that it is predicated on an affirmation of fact, promise, description or remedial promise made "in advertising or a similar communication to the public." In addition to the tests for liability set forth in Section 2–313A, under Section 2–313B the remote purchaser must also enter into the transaction "with knowledge of and with the expectation that the goods will conform to the affirmation of fact, promise, or description, or that the seller will perform the remedial promise."

Section 2–316, which deals with the exclusion or modification of warranties, has been amended to provide that a disclaimer of the implied warranty of merchantability in a consumer contract, which is defined in Section 2–103(1)(d) as a contract between a merchant seller and a consumer, must be in a record, must be conspicuous, and must use understandable language that states "[T]he seller undertakes no responsibility for the quality of the goods except as otherwise provided in this contract." The section as amended also provides that a disclaimer of the implied warranty of fitness for a particular purpose in a consumer contract must be in a record, be conspicuous, and use understandable language that states "[T]he seller assumes no responsibility that the goods will be fit for any particular purpose for which you may be buying these goods, except as otherwise provided in this contract." The amendments also now provide that an "as is" or "with all faults" disclaimer in a consumer contract must be conspicuously set forth in a record if the consumer contract is evidenced by a record. The amended section also clarifies that a buyer's refusal to inspect must be predicated on a demand by the seller.

Section 2–318 retains the three alternatives of the former article but is revised to extend to the class of persons designated in each alternative the benefits of remedial promises and statutory obligations in the nature of express warranties under Sections 2–313A and 2–313B.

Performance and Breach

Several provisions on acceptance, rejection, and revocation of acceptance have been amended. The test for rejection of a single installment in Section 2–612 is now consistent with the test for revocation of acceptance under Section 2–608. The test is that the installment may be rejected if the installment's value to the buyer is substantially impaired. Section 2–602 has been amended to clarify that the buyer must take reasonable care of the goods in both rightful and wrongful rejection cases. Sections 2–602 and 2–608 have been amended in light of many cases to provide that a buyer's reasonable use of goods after rejection or revocation of acceptance is not an acceptance of the goods, but the buyer may be obligated to pay for the value of the use to the buyer. Unreasonable use remains wrongful against the seller and is an acceptance if ratified.

Section 2–508 has been revised to provide that, in a nonconsumer contract, the seller has a right to cure if the buyer justifiably revokes acceptance under Section 2–608(2). The section now predicates the right to cure on good-faith performance by the seller and, when the time for performance has expired, on the cure being appropriate and timely under the circumstances. Another amendment to this section imposes liability on the seller for the buyer's reasonable expenses caused by the breach and subsequent cure.

Section 2–605 has been amended to provide that a buyer that fails to state with particularity a defect ascertainable by reasonable inspection that justifies revocation of acceptance suffers the same consequences as a buyer that similarly fails to particularize a defect in connection with a rejection. The particularity requirement applies only if the seller has a right to cure the defect, not merely the ability to cure. Failure to state a defect with particularity bars the buyer from predicating a rightful rejection or justifiable revocation of acceptance on the defect but no longer bars the buyer from using the defect to establish breach. Section 2–607 has been amended to provide that failure to give timely notice of breach in the case of accepted goods bars a remedy only to the extent the seller is prejudiced by the untimely notice.

Section 2–509, which governs risk of loss, has been amended to provide that if the goods are to be delivered through a bailee and tender is based on notification to the bailee, for risk of loss to pass, the bailee must acknowledge to the buyer that the buyer has a right to possess the goods. In the case of a noncarrier, nonbailee delivery, the section has been amended so that risk of loss for both merchant and nonmerchant passes upon the buyer's receipt of the goods.

The terminology in the excuse provisions; Sections 2–614 through 2–616, has been changed to govern all performance issues and not just delivery issues.

Remedies

Sections 2–703 and 2–711 contain a comprehensive indexing, respectively, of seller's and buyer's remedies.

A credit seller's right to reclaim the goods under Section 2–702 has been changed to provide that demand must be made within a "reasonable time" based on the circumstances instead of the former fixed period of 10 days after delivery or a longer reasonable time if there has been a misrepresentation of solvency. A cash seller's right to reclaim goods under Section 2–507 is now parallel to the credit seller's right under Section 2–702.

For a stoppage in transit in cases other than insolvency, Section 2–705 has been broadened by eliminating the requirement that the goods be by the "carload, truckload, planeload or larger shipments of express or freight" as this is no longer necessary due to modern tracking technology.

The amendments incorporate the change to Section 2–502(1) that were promulgated as part of the revision of Article 9 which provide a consumer buyer with a right to possession if the seller repudiates or fails to deliver the goods as required by the contract. The vesting rule of subsection (2) has been broadened to cover all rights of buyer under the section. The change to Section 2–716 promulgated as part of the revision of Article 9 is also included in the amendments with the vesting rule in this section broadened so that it applies to all buyers that seek replevin. In addition, Section 2–716 has been expanded to give courts discretion in nonconsumer contracts to enforce the parties' agreement for specific performance unless the sole remaining obligation is the payment of money.

Several provisions governing sellers' damages have been clarified or amended. Section 2–706 now explicitly provides that a seller's failure to resell in accordance with the section does not bar the seller from other remedies. Under Section 2–707, the remedies available to a person in the position of a seller include all remedies available to sellers generally. Under Section 2–708, the market price of goods in the case of an anticipatory repudiation is measured at the "expiration of a commercially reasonable time after the seller learned of the repudiation" and Section 2–723 has been amended to be consistent. Section 2–708(2) now explicitly provides that the lost-profit measure of damages is available when the resale remedy is not adequate and the troublesome language in former 2–708(2) that provided for "due allowance for costs reasonably incurred and due credit for payments or proceeds of resale" has been deleted. Moreover, sellers may now recover consequential damages in nonconsumer contracts subject to a test set out in Section 2–710(2) that parallels the test for buyers' consequential damages in Section 2–715(2)(a). Sellers may not recover consequential damages in consumer contracts.

Consistent with Section 2–708(1), Section 2–713 on buyers' market damages has been amended to provide that the market price in the case of an anticipatory repudiation is measured at the "expiration of a commercially reasonable time after the seller learned of the repudiation." The market price in cases other than anticipatory repudiation is now measured at the time for tender.

Section 2–718 has been amended to provide that, in a nonconsumer contract, the test for enforceability of a liquidated damage clause is limited to the reasonableness of the clause in light of the actual or anticipated harm. The former language that indicated that a clause that provided for an unreasonably large amount of liquidated damages was void as a penalty has been deleted because it might cause some to infer, incorrectly, that a clause setting an unreasonably small amount of liquidated damages cannot constitute a penalty. Language has also been added to clarify that the enforceability of a clause that limits remedies is to be determined under Section 2–719.

Section 2–718(3) has been amended to expand a buyer's right to restitution of the price paid to all circumstances in which the seller stops performance because of the buyer's breach or insolvency. The statutory liquidated-damages deduction from the breaching buyer's restitution remedy has also been eliminated.

The general limitations period of Section 2–725(1) has been amended from a flat four years to "one year after the breach was or should have been discovered, but no longer than five years after the right of action accrued." The limitation period may not be reduced in a consumer contract. In addition to retaining the accrual rules from current law, the section now provides specific accrual rules for breach by repudiation, breach of a remedial promise, a claim over (indemnity), breach of a warranty of title, breach of a warranty against infringement, and breach of a statutory obligation arising under Section 2–313A or Section 2–313B.

A Note Regarding the CISG

When parties enter into an agreement for the international sale of goods, because the United States is a party to the United Nations Convention on Contracts for the International Sale of Goods (CISG), the Convention may be the applicable law. Since many of the provisions of the CISG appear similar to provisions of Article 2, the committee drafting the amendments considered making references in the Official Comments to provisions in the CISG. However, upon reflection, it was decided that this would not be done because the inclusion of such references might suggest a greater similarity between Article 2 and the CISG than in fact exists.

The principle concern was the possibility of an inappropriate use of cases decided under one law to interpret provisions of the other law. This type of interpretation is contrary to the mandate of both the Uniform Commercial Code and the CISG. Specifically, Section 1–103(b) of the Code directs courts to interpret it in light of its common-law history. This was an underlying principle in original Article 2, and these amendments do not change this in any way. On the other hand, the CISG specifically directs courts to interpret its provisions in light of international practice with the goal of achieving international uniformity. *See* CISG Art. 7. This approach specifically eschews the use of domestic law, such as Article 2, as a basis for interpretation.

PART 1

SHORT TITLE, GENERAL CONSTRUCTION AND SUBJECT MATTER

§ 2–101. Short Title

This Article shall be known and may be cited as Uniform Commercial Code—Sales.

§ 2–102. Scope; Certain Security and Other Transactions Excluded from This Article

Unless the context otherwise requires, this Article applies to transactions in goods; it does not apply to any transaction which although in the form of an unconditional contract to sell or present sale is intended to operate only as a security transaction nor does this Article impair or repeal any statute regulating sales to consumers, farmers or other specified classes of buyers.

§ 2–103. Definitions and Index of Definitions

(1) In this article unless the context otherwise requires:

(a) "Buyer" means a person ~~who~~ that buys or contracts to buy goods.

(b) "Conspicuous", with reference to a term, means so written, displayed, or presented that a reasonable person against which it is to operate ought to have noticed it. A term in an electronic record intended to evoke a response by an electronic agent is conspicuous if it is presented in a form that would enable a reasonably configured electronic agent to take it into account or react to it without review of the record by an individual. Whether a term is "conspicuous" or not is a decision for the court. Conspicuous terms include the following:

(i) for a person:

(A) a heading in capitals equal to or greater in size than the surrounding text, or in contrasting type, font, or color to the surrounding text of the same or lesser size; and

(B) language in the body of a record or display in larger type than the surrounding text, or in contrasting type, font, or color to the surrounding text of the same size, or set off from surrounding text of the same size by symbols or other marks that call attention to the language; and

(ii) for a person or an electronic agent, a term that is so placed in a record or display that the person or electronic agent may not proceed without taking action with respect to the particular term.

(c) "Consumer" means an individual who buys or contracts to buy goods that, at the time of contracting, are intended by the individual to be used primarily for personal, family, or household purposes.

(d) "Consumer contract" means a contract between a merchant seller and a consumer.

(e) "Delivery" means, with respect to goods, the voluntary transfer of physical possession or control of goods.

(f) "Electronic" means relating to technology having electrical, digital, magnetic, wireless, optical, electromagnetic, or similar capabilities.

(g) "Electronic agent" means a computer program or an electronic or other automated means used independently to initiate an action or respond to electronic records or performances in whole or in part, without review or action by an individual.

(h) "Electronic record" means a record created, generated, sent, communicated, received, or stored by electronic means.

(i) "Foreign exchange transaction" means a transaction in which one party agrees to deliver a quantity of a specified money or unit of account in consideration of the other party's agreement to deliver another quantity of a different money or unit of account either currently or at a future date, and in which delivery is to be through funds transfer, book entry accounting, or other form of payment order, or other agreed means to transfer a credit balance. The term includes a transaction of this type involving two or more moneys and spot, forward, option, or other products derived from underlying moneys and any combination of these transactions. The term does not include a transaction involving two or more moneys in which one or both of the parties is obligated to make physical delivery, at the time of contracting or in the future, of banknotes, coins, or other form of legal tender or specie.

[(j) Reserved]

[(j) "Good faith" means honesty in fact and the observance of reasonable commercial standards of fair dealing.]

Legislative Note: The definition of "good faith" should not be adopted if the jurisdiction has enacted this definition as part of Article 1.

(k) "Goods" means all things that are movable at the time of identification to a contract for sale. The term includes future goods, specially manufactured goods, the unborn young of animals, growing crops, and other identified things attached to realty as described in Section 2–107. The term does not include information, the money in which the price is to be paid, investment securities under Article 8, the subject matter of foreign exchange transactions, or choses in action.

(*l*) "Receipt of goods" means taking physical possession of goods.

(m) "Record" means information that is inscribed on a tangible medium or that is stored in an electronic or other medium and is retrievable in perceivable form.

Legislative Note: The definition of "record" should not be adopted if the jurisdiction has enacted revised Article 1.

(n) "Remedial promise" means a promise by the seller to repair or replace goods or to refund all or part of the price of goods upon the happening of a specified event.

~~(d)~~ (*o*) "Seller" means a person ~~who~~ that sells or contracts to sell goods.

(p) "Sign" means, with present intent to authenticate or adopt a record:

    (i) to execute or adopt a tangible symbol; or

    (ii) to attach to or logically associate with the record an electronic sound, symbol, or process.

(2) Other definitions applying to this Article or to specified Parts thereof, and the sections in which they appear are:

"Acceptance". Section 2–606.

~~"Banker's credit". Section 2–325~~

"Between merchants". Section 2–104.

"Cancellation". Section 2–106(4).

"Commercial unit". Section 2–105.

~~"Confirmed credit". Section 2–325~~

"Conforming to contract". Section 2–106.

"Contract for sale". Section 2–106.

"Cover". Section 2–712.

"Entrusting". Section 2–403.

"Financing agency". Section 2–104.

"Future goods". Section 2–105.

"Identification". Section 2–501.

"Installment contract". Section 2–612.

~~"Letter of credit". Section 2–325~~

"Lot". Section 2–105.

"Merchant". Section 2–104.

~~"Overseas". Section 2–323~~

"Person in position of seller". Section 2–707.

"Present sale". Section 2–106.

"Sale". Section 2–106.

"Sale on approval". Section 2–326.

"Sale or return". Section 2–326.

"Termination". Section 2–106.

(3) "Control" as provided in Section 7–106 ~~The~~ and the following definitions in other Articles apply to this Article:

"Check". Section 3–104(f).

"Consignee". Section 7–102(3)

"Consignor". Section 7–102(4)

"Consumer goods". Section 9–102(a)(23).

"Dishonor". Section 3–502.

"Draft". Section 3–104(e).

"Honor". Section 5–102(a)(8).

"Injunction against honor". Section 5–109(b).

"Letter of credit". Section 5–102(a)(10).

(4) In addition Article 1 contains general definitions and principles of construction and interpretation applicable throughout this Article.

Official Comment

1. The first sentence of the definition of "conspicuous" is based on Section 1–201(10) but the concept is expanded to include terms in electronic records. The general standard is, that to be conspicuous, a term ought to be noticed by a reasonable person. The second sentence states a special rule for situations where the sender of an electronic record intends to evoke a response from an electronic agent. In that case, the presentation of the term must be capable of evoking a response from a reasonably configured electronic agent. Whether a term is conspicuous is an issue for the court.

Paragraphs (i) and (ii) set out several methods for making a term conspicuous. The requirement that a term be conspicuous functions both as notice (the term ought to be noticed) and as a basis for planning (giving guidance to the party that relies on the term about how that result can be achieved).

Paragraph (i), which relates to the general standard for conspicuousness, is based on original Section 1–201(10) but it is intended to give more guidance than was given in the prior version of this definition. Paragraph (ii) is new and it relates to the special standard for electronic records that are intended to evoke a response from an electronic agent. Although these paragraphs indicate some of the methods for calling attention to a term, the test is whether notice of the term can reasonably be expected. The statutory language should not be construed to permit a result that is inconsistent with that test.

2. A "consumer" is a natural person (*cf.* Section 1–201(27)) who enters into a transaction for a purpose typically associated with consumers–*i.e.*, a personal, family or household purpose. The requirement that the buyer intend that the goods be used "primarily" for personal, family or household purposes is generally consistent with the defini-

tion of consumer goods in revised Article 9. *See* Section 9–102(a)(23).

3. The term "consumer contract" is limited to a contract for sale between a seller that is a "merchant" and a buyer that is a "consumer". Thus, neither a sale by a consumer to a consumer nor a sale by a merchant to an individual who intends that the goods be used primarily in a home business qualify as a consumer contract.

4. "Delivery" with respect to documents of title is defined in Section 1–201(15) as the voluntary transfer of possession of the document. This Article defines "delivery" with respect to goods to mean the voluntary transfer of physical possession or control of the goods.

5. The electronic contracting provisions, including the definitions of "electronic," "electronic agent," "electronic record," and "record" are based on the provisions of the Uniform Electronic Transactions Act and are consistent with the federal Electronic Signatures in Global and National Commerce Act (15 U.S.C. § 7001 *et seq.*).

6. The term "foreign exchange transaction" is used in the definition of goods in Section 2–103(1)(k). That definition excludes "the subject matter of foreign exchange transactions."

7. The definition of "goods" in this article has been amended to exclude information not associated with goods. Thus, this article does not directly apply to an electronic transfer of information, such as the transaction involved in *Specht v. Netscape*, 150 F. Supp. 2d 585 (S.D.N.Y. 2001), *aff'd*, 306 F.3d 17 (2d. Cir. 2002). However, transactions often include both goods and information: some are transactions in goods as that term is used in Section 2–102, and some are not. For example, the sale of "smart goods"

such as an automobile is a transaction in goods fully within this article even though the automobile contains many computer programs. On the other hand, an architect's provision of architectural plans on a computer disk would not be a transaction in goods. When a transaction includes both the sale of goods and the transfer of rights in information, it is up to the courts to determine whether the transaction is entirely within or outside of this article, or whether or to what extent this article should be applied to a portion of the transaction. While this article may apply to a transaction including information, nothing in this Article alters, creates, or diminishes intellectual property rights.

The definition has also been amended to exclude the subject matter of "foreign exchange transactions." *See* Section 2–103(1)(i). Although a contract in which currency in the commodity exchanged is a sale of goods, an exchange in which delivery is "through funds transfer, book entry accounting, or other form of payment order, or other agreed means to transfer a credit balance" is not a sale of goods and is not governed by this article. In the latter case, Article 4A or other law applies. On the other hand, if the parties agree to a forward transaction where dollars are to be physically delivered in exchange for the delivery of another currency, the transaction is not within the "foreign exchange" exclusion and this article applies.

8. Section 1–202(e) provides rules for determining whether a notice or notification has been received. This Article by contrast defines "receipt of goods" to mean the taking of physical possession of the goods.

9. A "remedial promise" is a promise by the seller to take a certain remedial action upon the happening of a specified event. The types of remedies contemplated by this term as used in

this Article are specified in the definition–repair or replacement of the goods, or refund of all or part of the price. No other promise by a seller qualifies as a remedial promise. Furthermore, the seller is entitled to specify precisely the event that will precipitate the obligation. Typical examples include a commitment to repair any parts of the goods that are defective, or a commitment to refund the purchase price if the goods fail to perform in a certain manner. A post-sale promise to correct a problem with the goods that the seller is not obligated to correct that is made to placate a dissatisfied customer is not within the definition of remedial promise. Whether the promised remedy is exclusive, and if so whether it has failed its essential purpose, is determined under Section 2–719.

The distinction between a remedial promise and a warranty that is made in this Article resolves a statute-of-limitations problem. Under original Section 2–725, a right of action for breach of an express warranty accrued at the time the goods were tendered unless the warranty explicitly extended to the future performance of the goods. In that case, the statute of limitations began to run at the time of the discovery of the breach. By contrast, a right of action for breach of an ordinary (non-warranty) promise accrued when the promise was breached. A number of courts held that commitments by sellers to take remedial action in the event the goods proved to be defective during a specified period of time constituted a warranty, and in theses cases the courts determined that the statute of limitations began to run at the time that the goods were tendered. Other courts used strained reasoning that allowed them to apply the discovery rule even though the promise referred to the future performance of the seller and not the future performance of the goods.

Under this Article, a promise by the seller to take remedial action is not a warranty at all and therefore the statute of limitations for a breach of a remedial promise does not begin to run at either the time the goods are tendered or at the time the breach is discovered. Section 2–725(2)(c) separately addresses the accrual of a right of action for a remedial promise. *See* Official Comment 3 to Section 2–725.

10. The definition of "sign" is broad enough to cover any record that is signed within the meaning of Article 1 or that contains an electronic signature within the meaning of the Uniform Electronic Transactions Act. It is consistent with the federal Electronic Signatures in Global and National Commerce Act (15 U.S.C. § 7001 *et seq.*).

§ 2–104. Definitions: "Merchant"; "Between Merchants"; "Financing Agency"

(1) "Merchant" means a person ~~who~~ that deals in goods of the kind or otherwise ~~by his occupation holds himself out~~ holds itself out by occupation as having knowledge or skill peculiar to the practices or goods involved in the transaction or to ~~whom~~ which ~~such~~ the knowledge or skill may be attributed by ~~his~~ the person's employment of an agent or broker or other intermediary ~~who by his occupation holds himself out~~ that holds itself out by occupation as having ~~such~~ the knowledge or skill.

(2) "Financing agency" means a bank, finance company, or other person ~~who~~ that in the ordinary course of business makes advances

against goods or documents of title or ~~who~~ that by arrangement with either the seller or the buyer intervenes in ordinary course to make or collect payment due or claimed under the contract for sale, as by purchasing or paying the seller's draft or making advances against it or by merely taking it for collection whether or not documents of title accompany or are associated with the draft. ~~"Financing agency"~~ The term includes also a bank or other person ~~who~~ that similarly intervenes between persons ~~who~~ that are in the position of seller and buyer in respect to the goods (Section 2–707).

(3) "Between merchants" means in any transaction with respect to which both parties are chargeable with the knowledge or skill of merchants.

§ 2–105. Definitions: Transferability; ~~"Goods";~~ "Future" Goods; "Lot"; "Commercial Unit"

~~(1) "Goods" means all things (including specially manufactured goods) which are movable at the time of identification to the contract for sale other than the money in which the price is to be paid, investment securities (Article 8) and things in action. "Goods" also includes the unborn young of animals and growing crops and other identified things attached to realty as described in the section on goods to be severed from realty (Section 2–107).~~

~~(2)~~ (1) Goods must be both existing and identified before any interest in them ~~can~~ may pass. Goods ~~which~~ that are not both existing and identified are "future" goods. A purported present sale of future goods or of any interest therein operates as a contract to sell.

~~(3)~~ (2) There may be a sale of a part interest in existing identified goods.

~~(4)~~ (3) An undivided share in an identified bulk of fungible goods is sufficiently identified to be sold although the quantity of the bulk is not determined. Any agreed proportion of ~~such a~~ the bulk or any quantity thereof agreed upon by number, weight, or other measure may to the extent of the seller's interest in the bulk be sold to the buyer ~~who~~ that then becomes an owner in common.

~~(5)~~ (4) "Lot" means a parcel or a single article which is the subject matter of a separate sale or delivery, whether or not it is sufficient to perform the contract.

~~(6)~~ (5) "Commercial unit" means such a unit of goods as by commercial usage is a single whole for purposes of sale and division of which materially impairs its character or value on the market or in use. A commercial unit may be a single article (as a machine) or a set of articles (as a suite of furniture or an assortment of sizes) or a quantity (as a bale, gross, or carload) or any other unit treated in use or in the relevant market as a single whole.

§ 2–106. Definitions: "Contract"; "Agreement"; "Contract for Sale"; "Sale"; "Present Sale"; "Conforming" to Contract; "Termination"; "Cancellation"

(1) In this Article unless the context otherwise requires "contract" and "agreement" are limited to those relating to the present or future sale of goods. "Contract for sale" includes both a present sale of goods and a contract to sell goods at a future time. A "sale" consists in the passing of title from the seller to the buyer for a price (Section 2–401). A "present sale" means a sale which is accomplished by the making of the contract.

(2) Goods or conduct including any part of a performance are "conforming" or conform to the contract when they are in accordance with the obligations under the contract.

(3) "Termination" occurs when either party pursuant to a power created by agreement or law puts an end to the contract otherwise than for its breach. On "termination" all obligations which are still executory on both sides are discharged but any right based on prior breach or performance survives.

(4) "Cancellation" occurs when either party puts an end to the contract for breach by the other and its effect is the same as that of "termination" except that the cancelling party also retains any remedy for breach of the whole contract or any unperformed balance.

§ 2–107. Goods to Be Severed from Realty: Recording

(1) A contract for the sale of minerals or the like (including oil and gas) or a structure or its materials to be removed from realty is a contract for the sale of goods within this Article if they are to be severed by the seller but until severance a purported present sale thereof which is not effective as a transfer of an interest in land is effective only as a contract to sell.

(2) A contract for the sale apart from the land of growing crops or other things attached to realty and capable of severance without material harm thereto but not described in subsection (1) or of timber to be cut is a contract for the sale of goods within this Article whether the subject matter is to be severed by the buyer or by the seller even though it forms part of the realty at the time of contracting, and the parties can by identification effect a present sale before severance.

(3) The provisions of this section are subject to any third party rights provided by the law relating to realty records, and the contract for sale may be executed and recorded as a document transferring an interest in land and shall then constitute notice to third parties of the buyer's rights under the contract for sale.

§ 2–108. Transactions Subject to Other Law

(1) A transaction subject to this article is also subject to any applicable:

(a) [list any certificate of title statutes of this State covering automobiles, trailers, mobile homes, boats, farm tractors, or the like], except with respect to the rights of a buyer in ordinary course of business under Section 2–403(2) which arise before a certificate of title covering the goods is effective in the name of any other buyer;

(b) rule of law that establishes a different rule for consumers; or

(c) statute of this state applicable to the transaction, such as a statute dealing with:

(i) the sale or lease of agricultural products;

(ii) the transfer of human blood, blood products, tissues, or parts;

(iii) the consignment or transfer by artists of works of art or fine prints;

(iv) distribution agreements, franchises, and other relationships through which goods are sold;

(v) the misbranding or adulteration of food products or drugs; and

(vi) dealers in particular products, such as automobiles, motorized wheelchairs, agricultural equipment, and hearing aids.

(2) Except for the rights of a buyer in ordinary course of business under subsection (1)(a), in the event of a conflict between this article and a law referred to in subsection (1), that law governs.

(3) For purposes of this article, failure to comply with a law referred to in subsection (1) has only the effect specified in that law.

(4) This article modifies, limits, and supersedes the federal Electronic Signatures in Global and National Commerce Act, 15 U.S.C. Section 7001 et seq., except that nothing in this article modifies, limits, or supersedes Section 7001(c) of that Act or authorizes electronic delivery of any of the notices described in Section 7003(b) of that Act.

Official Comment

1. Section 2–108, which was not in the prior version of this Article, follows the form of Section 2A–104(1).

2. In subsection (1), it is assumed that this article is subject to any applicable federal law, such as the United Nations Convention on Contracts for the International Sale of Goods, 15 U.S.C. App., or the Magnuson–Moss Warranty Act, 15 U.S.C. Sections 2301–2312.

3. Subsection (1)(a) permits the states to list any applicable certificate-of-title statutes. It also provides that Article 2 is subject to their provisions on the transfer and effect of title except for the rights of a buyer in ordinary course of business in certain limited situations. In entrustment situations, the exception in subsection (1)(a) overrides those certificate-of-title statutes that provide that a person cannot qualify as an owner unless a certificate has been issued in the person's name. In those cases where an owner in whose name a certificate has been issued entrusts a titled asset to a dealer that then sells it to a buyer in ordinary course of business, this section provides that the priority issue between the owner and the buyer is to be resolved by reference to the certificate-of-title statute.

Illustration #1. A used car is stolen from the owner by a thief and the thief, by fraud, is able to obtain a clean certificate of title from State X. The thief sells the car to the buyer, a good faith purchaser for value but not a buyer in ordinary course of business, and the thief transfers the certificate of title to the buyer. The exception in subsection (1)(a) does not apply to protect the buyer. Furthermore, under Section 2–403(1), the buyer does not get good title from the thief, regardless of the certificate. The same result follows if the applicable state certificate of title law makes the certificate prima facie evidence of ownership. The buyer will prevail, however, if the applicable certificate of title law conflicts with the result obtained under this Article by making issuance of the certificate conclusive on title.

Illustration #2. The dealer sells a new car to buyer #1 and the dealer signs a form permitting buyer #1 to apply for a certificate of title. Buyer #1 leaves the car with the dealer so that the dealer can finish the preparation work on the car. While the car remains in the dealer's possession and before the state issues a certificate of title in buyer #1's name, buyer #2 makes the dealer a better offer on the car, which the dealer accepts. Buyer #1 entrusted the car to the dealer, and if buyer #2 qualifies as a buyer in ordinary course of business, buyer #2's title to the car will be superior to that of buyer #1.

Illustration #3. An owner in whose name a certificate of title has been issued leaves a car with a dealer for repair. The dealer sells the car to a buyer, who qualifies as a buyer in ordinary course of business. If the certificate-of-title law in the state resolves the priority contest between the owner and the buyer, that solution should be implemented. Otherwise, the buyer prevails under Section 2–403(2).

4. This section also deals with the effect of a conflict or failure to comply with any other state law that might apply to a transaction governed by this Article. Subsection (1) provides that a transaction subject to this Article is also subject to other applicable law, and subsection (2) provides that in the event of a conflict the other law governs (except for the rights of a buyer in ordinary course of business under subsection (1)(a)).

Subsection (1)(b) provides that this Article is also subject to any rule of law that establishes a different rule for consumers. "Rule of law" includes a statute, an administrative rule properly promulgated under the statute, and a final court decision.

The relationship between Article 2 and federal and state consumer laws will vary from transaction to transaction and from State to State. For example, the Magnuson–Moss Warranty Act, 15 U.S.C.A. §§ 2301 *et seq.*, may or may not apply to the consumer dispute in question and the applicable state "lemon law" may provide more or less protection than Magnuson–Moss. To the extent that the other law applies and there is a conflict with this Article, that law controls.

Subsection (1)(c) provides an illustrative but not exhaustive list of other applicable state statutes that may preempt all or part of Article 2. For example, franchise contracts may be regulated by state franchise acts, the seller of unmerchantable blood or human tissue may be insulated from warranty liability and disclaimers of the implied warranty of merchantability may be invalidated by non-uniform amendments to Article 2. The existence, scope, and effect of these statutes must be assessed from State to State.

Assuming that there is a conflict, subsection (3) deals with the failure of parties to the contract to comply with the applicable law. The failure has the "effect specified" in the law. Thus, the failure to obtain a required license may make the contract illegal, and therefore unenforceable, while the nonnegligent supply of unmerchantable blood under a "blood shield" statute may mean only that the supplier is insulated from liability for injury to person or property.

5. Subsection (4) takes advantage of a provision of the federal Electronic Signatures in Global and National Commerce Act (E–Sign). E–Sign permits state law to modify, limit or supersede its provisions if the state law is consistent with Titles I and II of E–Sign, gives no special legal effect or validity to and does not require the implementation or application of specific technologies or technical specifications, and if enacted subsequent to E–Sign makes specific reference to E–Sign. Subsection (4) does not apply to section 101(c) of E–Sign, nor does it authorize electronic delivery of the notices described in section 103(b) of E–Sign.

PART 2

FORM, FORMATION, <u>TERMS</u> AND READJUSTMENT OF CONTRACT; <u>ELECTRONIC CONTRACTING</u>

§ 2–201. Formal Requirements; Statute of Frauds

(1) ~~Except as otherwise provided in this section a~~ A contract for the sale of goods for the price of ~~$500~~ $5,000 or more is not enforceable by way of action or defense unless there is some ~~writing~~ record sufficient to indicate that a contract for sale has been made between the parties and signed by the party against ~~whom~~ which enforcement is sought or by ~~his~~ the party's authorized agent or broker. A ~~writing~~ record is not insufficient because it omits or incorrectly states a term agreed upon, but the contract is not enforceable under this ~~paragraph~~ subsection beyond the quantity of goods shown in ~~such~~ the ~~writing~~ record.

(2) Between merchants if within a reasonable time a ~~writing~~ record in confirmation of the contract and sufficient against the sender is received and the party receiving it has reason to know its contents, it satisfies the requirements of subsection (1) against ~~such party~~ the

recipient unless ~~written~~ notice of objection to its contents is given <u>in a record</u> within 10 days after it is received.

(3) A contract ~~which~~ <u>that</u> does not satisfy the requirements of subsection (1) but which is valid in other respects is enforceable<u>:</u>

    (a) if the goods are to be specially manufactured for the buyer and are not suitable for sale to others in the ordinary course of the seller's business and the seller, before notice of repudiation is received and under circumstances ~~which~~ <u>that</u> reasonably indicate that the goods are for the buyer, has made either a substantial beginning of their manufacture or commitments for their procurement; ~~or~~

    (b) if the party against ~~whom~~ <u>which</u> enforcement is sought admits in ~~his~~ <u>the party's</u> pleading, <u>or in the party's</u> testimony or otherwise ~~in court~~ <u>under oath</u> that a contract for sale was made, but the contract is not enforceable under this ~~provision~~ <u>paragraph</u> beyond the quantity of goods admitted; or

    (c) with respect to goods for which payment has been made and accepted or which have been received and accepted (Sec. 2–606).

<u>(4) A contract that is enforceable under this section is not unenforceable merely because it is not capable of being performed within one year or any other period after its making.</u>

Official Comment

1. The record required by subsection (1) need not contain all of the material terms of the contract, and the material terms that are stated need not be precise or accurate. All that is required is that the record afford a reasonable basis to determine that the offered oral evidence rests on a real transaction. The record may be written on a piece of paper or entered into a computer. It need not indicate which party is the buyer and which party is the seller. The only term which must appear is the quantity term. A term indicating the manner by which the quantity is determined is sufficient. Thus, for example, a term indicating that the quantity is based on the output of the seller or the requirements of the buyer satisfies the requirement. *See e.g., Advent Systems v. Unisys*, 925 F.2d 670 (3d Cir. 1991); *Gestetner*

Corp. v. Case Equip. Co., 815 F.2d 806 (1st Cir. 1987). The same reasoning can be extended to a term that indicates that the contract is similar to, but does not qualify as, an output or requirement contract. *See e.g., PMC Corp. v. Houston Wire and Cable Co.* 797 A.2d 125 (N.H. 2002). Similarly, a term that refers to a master contract that provides a basis for determining a quantity satisfies this requirement. *See e.g., Reigel Fiber Corp. v. Anderson Gin Co.*, 512 F.2d 784 (5th Cir.1975). If a specific amount is stated in the record, even if not accurately stated, recovery is limited to the stated amount. However, the price, time and place of payment or delivery, the general quality of the goods, or any particular warranties need not be included.

Special emphasis must be placed on the permissibility of omitting the price term. In many valid contracts for sale the parties do not mention the price in express terms. The buyer is bound to pay and the seller to accept a reasonable price, which the trier of the fact will determine. Frequently the price is not mentioned at all since the parties have based their agreement on a price list or catalogue known to both of them, and the list or catalogue serves as an efficient safeguard against perjury. Also, "market" prices and valuations that are current in the vicinity constitute a similar check. Of course, if the "price" consists of goods rather than money, the quantity of goods must be stated.

There are only three definite and invariable requirements for the memorandum made by subsection (1). First, the memorandum must evidence a contract for the sale of goods; second, the memorandum must be signed; and third, the memorandum must have a quantity term or a method to determine the quantity.

2. The prior version of subsection (1) began with the phrase "Except as otherwise provided in this section." This language has been deleted. This change was made to provide that the statement of the three statutory exceptions in subsection (3) should not be read as limiting under subsection (1) the possibility that a promisor will be estopped to raise the statute-of-frauds defense in appropriate cases.

3. "Partial performance" as a substitute for the required record can validate the contract only for the goods which have been accepted or for which payment has been made and accepted.

Receipt and acceptance either of goods or of the price constitutes an unambiguous overt admission by both parties that a contract exists. If the court can make a just apportionment, therefore, the agreed price of any goods actually delivered can be recovered without a writing or, if the price has been paid, the seller can be forced to deliver an apportionable part of the goods. The overt actions of the parties make admissible evidence of the other terms of the contract necessary to a just apportionment. This is true even though the actions of the parties are not in themselves inconsistent with a different transaction such as a consignment for resale or a mere loan of money.

Part performance by the buyer requires that the buyer deliver something that is accepted by the seller as the performance. Thus, part payment may be made by money or check accepted by the seller. If the agreed price consists of goods or services, then they must also have been delivered and accepted. When the seller accepts partial payment for a single item the statute is satisfied as to that item. *See Lockwood v. Smigel*, 18 Cal App.3d 800, 99 Cal Rept. 289 (1971).

4. Between merchants, failure to answer a confirmation of a contract in a record that satisfies the requirements of subsection (1) against the sender within ten days of receipt renders the record sufficient against the recipient. The only effect, however, is to take away from the party that fails to answer the defense of the Statute of Frauds. The burden of persuading the trier of fact that a contract was in fact made orally prior to the record confirmation is unaffected.

A merchant includes a person "that by occupation purports to have knowledge or skill peculiar to the *practices* or goods involved in the transaction." Section 2–104(1) (emphasis supplied). Thus, a professional or a farmer should be considered a merchant because the practice of objecting to an improper confirmation ought to be familiar to any person in business.

5. Failure to satisfy the requirements of this section does not render the contract void for all purposes, but

merely prevents it from being judicially enforced in favor of a party to the contract. For example, a buyer that takes possession of goods provided for in an oral contract which the seller has not meanwhile repudiated is not a trespasser. Nor would the statute-of-frauds provisions of this section be a defense to a third person that wrongfully induces a party to refuse to perform an oral contract, even though the injured party cannot maintain an action for damages against the party that refuses to perform.

6. It is not necessary that the record be delivered to anybody, nor is this section intended to displace decisions that have given effect to lost records. It need not be signed by both parties, but except as stated in subsection (2), it is not sufficient against a party that has not signed it. Prior to a dispute, no one can determine which party's signature may be necessary, but from the time of contracting each party should be aware that it is the signature of the other which is important.

7. If the making of a contract is admitted in court, either in a written pleading, by stipulation or by oral statement before the court, or is admitted under oath but not in court, as by testimony in a deposition or an affidavit filed with a motion, no additional record is necessary. Subsection (3)(b) makes it impossible to admit the contract in these contexts, and assert that the Statute of Frauds is still a defense. However, in these circumstances, the contract is not conclusively established. The admission is evidential only against the maker and only for the facts admitted. As against the other party, it is not evidential at all.

8. Subsection (4), which was not in prior versions of this Article, repeals the "one year" provision of the Statute of Frauds for contracts for the sale of goods. The phrase "any other applicable period" recognizes that some state statutes apply to periods longer than one year. The confused and contradictory interpretations under the so-called "one year" clause are illustrated by *C.R. Klewin, Inc. v. Flagship Properties, Inc.*, 600 A.2d 772 (Conn. 1991).

§ 2–202. Final ~~Written~~ Expression in a Record: Parol or Extrinsic Evidence

(1) Terms with respect to which the confirmatory ~~memoranda~~ records of the parties agree or which are otherwise set forth in a ~~writing~~ record intended by the parties as a final expression of their agreement with respect to such terms as are included therein may not be contradicted by evidence of any prior agreement or of a contemporaneous oral agreement but may be ~~explained or~~ supplemented by evidence of:

(a) ~~by course of dealing or usage of trade (Section 1–205) or by course of performance (Section 2–208)~~ course of performance, course of dealing, or usage of trade (Section 1–303); and

(b) ~~by evidence of~~ consistent additional terms unless the court finds the ~~writing~~ record to have been intended also as a complete and exclusive statement of the terms of the agreement.

(2) Terms in a record may be explained by evidence of course of performance, course of dealing, or usage of trade without a preliminary determination by the court that the language used is ambiguous.

Official Comment

1. Subsection (1) codifies the parol evidence rule. The operation of this rule depends on the intention of both parties that the terms in a record are the "final expression of their agreement with respect to the included terms." Without this mutual intention to integrate the record, the parol evidence rule does not apply to exclude evidence of other terms allegedly agreed to prior to or contemporaneously with the record. Unless there is a final record, these alleged terms are provable as part of the agreement by relevant evidence from any credible source. When each party sends a confirmatory record, mutual intention to integrate the agreement is presumed for terms "with respect to which the confirmatory records of the parties agree."

2. Because a record is final for the included terms (an integration), this does not mean that the parties intended that the record contain all the terms of their agreement (a total integration). If a record is final but not complete and exclusive, it cannot be contradicted by evidence of prior agreements reflected in a record or prior or contemporaneous oral agreements, but it can be supplemented by other evidence, drawn from any source, of consistent additional terms. Even if the record is final, complete and exclusive, it can be supplemented by evidence of noncontradictory terms drawn from an applicable course of performance, course of dealing, or usage of trade unless those sources are carefully negated by a term in the record. If the record is final, complete and exclusive it cannot be supplemented by evidence of terms drawn from other sources, even terms that are consistent with the record.

3. Whether a writing is final, and whether a final writing is also complete, are issues for the court. This section rejects any assumption that because a record has been worked out which is final on some matters, it is to be taken as including all the matters agreed upon. If the additional terms are those that, if agreed upon, would certainly have been included in the document in the view of the court, then evidence of their alleged making must be kept from the trier of fact. This section is not intended to suggest what should be the evidentiary strength of a merger clause as evidence of the mutual intent that the record be final and complete. That determination depends upon the particular circumstances of each case.

4. This section does not exclude evidence introduced to show that the contract is avoidable for misrepresentation, mistake, or duress, or that the contract or a term is unenforceable because of unconscionability. This section also does not operate to exclude evidence of a subsequent modification or evidence that, for the purpose of claiming excuse, both parties assumed that a certain event would not occur.

5. Issues of interpretation are generally left to the courts. In interpreting terms in a record, subsection (2) permits either party to introduce evidence drawn from a course of performance, a course of dealing, or a usage of trade without any preliminary determination by the court that the term at issue is ambiguous. This article takes no position on whether a preliminary determination of ambiguity is a condition to the admissibility of evidence drawn from any other source or on whether a contract clause can exclude an otherwise applicable implied-in-fact source.

§ 2–203. Seals Inoperative

The affixing of a seal to a ~~writing~~ <u>record</u> evidencing a contract for sale or an offer to buy or sell goods does not constitute the ~~writing~~

record a sealed ~~instrument and the~~ instrument. The law with respect to sealed instruments does not apply to such a contract or offer.

§ 2–204. Formation in General

(1) A contract for sale of goods may be made in any manner sufficient to show agreement, including offer and acceptance, conduct by both parties which recognizes the existence of ~~such~~ a contract, the interaction of electronic agents, and the interaction of an electronic agent and an individual.

(2) An agreement sufficient to constitute a contract for sale may be found even ~~though~~ if the moment of its making is undetermined.

(3) Even ~~though~~ if one or more terms are left open, a contract for sale does not fail for indefiniteness if the parties have intended to make a contract and there is a reasonably certain basis for giving an appropriate remedy.

(4) Except as otherwise provided in Sections 2–211 through 2–213, the following rules apply:

> (a) A contract may be formed by the interaction of electronic agents of the parties, even if no individual was aware of or reviewed the electronic agents' actions or the resulting terms and agreements.

> (b) A contract may be formed by the interaction of an electronic agent and an individual acting on the individual's own behalf or for another person. A contract is formed if the individual takes actions that the individual is free to refuse to take or makes a statement, and the individual has reason to know that the actions or statement will:

>> (i) cause the electronic agent to complete the transaction or performance; or

>> (ii) indicate acceptance of an offer, regardless of other expressions or actions by the individual to which the electronic agent cannot react.

Official Comment

1. Subsection (1) sets forth the basic policy to recognize any manner of expression of agreement. In addition to traditional contract formation by oral or written agreement, or by performance, subsection (1) provides that an agreement may be made by electronic means. Regardless of how the agreement is formed under this section, the legal effect of the agreement is subject to the other provisions of this Article.

2. Under subsection (1), appropriate conduct by the parties may be sufficient to establish an agreement. Subsection (2) is directed primarily when the correspondence does not disclose the exact point at which the agreement was formed, but the conduct of the parties indicate that a binding obligation has been undertaken.

3. Subsection (3) states the principle for "open terms" which underlies later sections of this Article. If the

parties intend to enter into a binding agreement, this subsection recognizes the agreement as valid in law, despite missing terms, if there is any reasonably certain basis for granting a remedy based on commercial standards of indefiniteness. Neither certainty for what the parties were to do nor a finding of the exact amount of damages is required. Neither is the fact that one or more terms are left to be agreed upon enough by itself to defeat an otherwise adequate agreement. This Act makes provision elsewhere for missing terms needed for performance, open price, remedies and the like.

The more terms the parties leave open, the less likely it is that the parties have intended to conclude a binding agreement, but their actions may be conclusive on the matter despite the omissions.

4. Subsections (4)(a) and (b) are derived from Sections 14(a) and (b) of the Uniform Electronic Transactions Act. Subsection (4)(a) confirms that contracts may be formed by machines functioning as electronic agents for the parties to a transaction. This subsection is intended to negate any claim that lack of human intent, at the time of contract formation, prevents contract formation. When machines are involved, the requisite intention to contract flows from the programing and use of the machine. This provision, along with sections 2–211, 2–212, and 2–213, is intended to remove barriers to electronic contract formation.

5. When the requisite intent to enter into a contract exists, subsection (4)(b) validates contracts formed by an individual and an electronic agent. This subsection validates an anonymous click-through transaction. As with subsection (4)(a), the intent to

contract by means of an electronic agent comes from the programing and use of the machine. The requisite intent to contract by the individual is found by the acts of the individual that the individual has reason to know will be interpreted by the machine as allowing the machine to complete the transaction or performance, or that will be interpreted by the machine as signifying acceptance on the part of the individual. This intent is only found, though, when the individual is free to refuse to take the actions that the machine will interpret as acceptance or allowance to complete the transaction. For example, if A goes to a website that provides for purchasing goods over the Internet, and after choosing items to be purchased is confronted by a screen which advises her that the transaction will be completed if A clicks "I agree," then A will be bound by the click if A knew or had reason to know that the click would be interpreted as signifying acceptance and A was also free to refuse to take the final action. This provision does not, however, provide for a determination of what terms exist in the agreement. That question is governed by Section 2–207.

6. Nothing in this section is intended to restrict equitable defenses, such as fraud or mistake, in electronic contract formation. However, because the law of electronic mistake is not well developed, and because factual issues may arise that are not easily resolved by legal standards developed for nonelectronic transactions, courts should not automatically apply standards developed in other contexts. The specific differences between electronic and nonelectronic transactions should also be factored in to resolve equitable claims in electronic contracts.

§ 2–205. Firm Offers

An offer by a merchant to buy or sell goods in a signed ~~writing which~~ record that by its terms gives assurance that it will be held open is not revocable, for lack of consideration, during the time stated or if no time is stated for a reasonable time, but in no event may ~~such~~ the period of irrevocability exceed three ~~months, but any~~ months. Any such term of assurance ~~on a form~~ in a form supplied by the offeree must be separately signed by the offeror.

§ 2–206. Offer and Acceptance in Formation of Contract

(1) Unless otherwise unambiguously indicated by the language or circumstances:

  (a) an offer to make a contract shall be construed as inviting acceptance in any manner and by any medium reasonable in the circumstances;

  (b) an order or other offer to buy goods for prompt or current shipment shall be construed as inviting acceptance either by a prompt promise to ship or by the prompt or current shipment of conforming or ~~non-conforming~~ nonconforming goods, but ~~such a~~ the shipment of ~~non-conforming~~ nonconforming goods ~~does not constitute~~ is not an acceptance if the seller seasonably notifies the buyer that the shipment is offered only as an accommodation to the buyer.

(2) ~~Where~~ If the beginning of a requested performance is a reasonable mode of acceptance, an offeror ~~who~~ that is not notified of acceptance within a reasonable time may treat the offer as having lapsed before acceptance.

(3) A definite and seasonable expression of acceptance in a record operates as an acceptance even if it contains terms additional to or different from the offer.

Official Comment

1. Subsection (1)(b) deals with a shipment that contains defective goods which is made following an order for the goods. The nonconforming shipment is normally understood as intended to close the bargain even though it constitutes a breach. However, the seller by stating that the shipment is nonconforming and is offered only as an accommodation to the buyer keeps the shipment of from operating as an acceptance.

2. The mirror image rule is rejected in subsection (3), but any responsive record must still be reasonably understood as an "acceptance" and not as a proposal for a different transaction.

See Official Comment 2 to Section 2–207.

3. Subsection (3) makes it clear that an expression of acceptance can operate as an acceptance (i.e., create a contract) even though it contains terms that are not identical to those in the offer. This rule applies, however, only to an expression of acceptance that is not only seasonable but also "definite." A purported expression of acceptance containing additional or different terms would not be a "definite" acceptance when the offeree's expression clearly communicates to the offeror the offeree's unwillingness to do business unless the offeror assents to those additional or different terms.

This is not a definite acceptance since the offeree's expression makes it clear that the offeree is not "accepting" anything; but rather that the offeree is indicating a willingness to do business only on the offeree's terms and that the offeree is awaiting the offeror's assent to those terms. (This result is consistent with the final clause of former Section 2–207(1).) In a situation in which the offer clearly indicates that the offeror is unwilling to do business on any terms other than those contained in the offer, and the offeree responds with an expression of acceptance that contains additional or different terms, a court could also conclude that the offeree's response does not constitute a definite expression of acceptance.

§ 2–207. ~~Additional Terms in Acceptance or~~ Terms of Contract; Effect of Confirmation

~~(1) A definite and seasonable expression of acceptance or a written confirmation which is sent within a reasonable time operates as an acceptance even though it states terms additional to or different from those offered or agreed upon, unless acceptance is expressly made conditional on assent to the additional or different terms.~~

~~(2) The additional terms are to be construed as proposals for addition to the contract. Between merchants such terms become part of the contract unless:~~

> ~~(a) the offer expressly limits acceptance to the terms of the offer;~~
>
> ~~(b) they materially alter it; or~~
>
> ~~(c) notification of objection to them has already been given or is given within a reasonable time after notice of them is received.~~

~~(3) Conduct by both parties which recognizes the existence of a contract is sufficient to establish a contract for sale although the writings of the parties do not otherwise establish a contract. In such case the terms of the particular contract consist of those terms on which the writings of the parties agree, together with any supplementary terms incorporated under any other provisions of this Act.~~

Subject to Section 2–202, if (i) conduct by both parties recognizes the existence of a contract although their records do not otherwise establish a contract, (ii) a contract is formed by an offer and acceptance, or (iii) a contract formed in any manner is confirmed by a record that contains terms additional to or different from those in the contract being confirmed, the terms of the contract are:

> (a) terms that appear in the records of both parties;
>
> (b) terms, whether in a record or not, to which both parties agree; and
>
> (c) terms supplied or incorporated under any provision of this Act.

127

Official Comment

1. This section applies to all contracts for the sale of goods, and it is not limited only to those contracts where there has been a "battle of the forms."

2. This section applies only when a contract has been created under another section of this Article. The purpose of this section is solely to determine the terms of the contract. When forms are exchanged before or during performance, the result from the application of this section differs from the prior Section 2–207 of this Article and the common law in that this section gives no preference to either the first or the last form; the same test is applied to the terms in each. Terms in a record that insist on all of that record's terms and no other terms as a condition of contract formation have no effect on the operation of this section. When one party insists in that party's record that its own terms are a condition to contract formation, if that party does not subsequently perform or otherwise acknowledge the existence of a contract, if the other party does not agree to those terms, the record's insistence on its own terms will keep a contract from being formed under Sections 2–204 or 2–206, and this section is not applicable. As with original Section 2–207, the courts will have to distinguish between "confirmations" that are addressed in this section and "modifications" that are addressed in Section 2–209.

3. Terms of a contract may be found not only in the consistent terms of records of the parties but also from a straightforward acceptance of an offer, and an expression of acceptance accompanied by one or more additional terms might demonstrate the offeree's agreement to the terms of the offer. If, for example, a buyer sent a purchase order with technical specifications and the seller responded with a record stating "Thank you for your order. We will fill it promptly. Note that we do not make deliveries after 3:00 p.m. on Fridays." it might be reasonable to conclude that both parties agreed to the technical specifications.

Similarly, an offeree's performance is sometimes the acceptance of an offer. If, for example, a buyer sends a purchase order, there is no oral or other agreement, and the seller delivers the goods in response to the purchase order–but the seller does not send the seller's own acknowledgment or acceptance–the seller should normally be treated as having agreed to the terms of the purchase order.

If, however, parties exchange records with conflicting or inconsistent terms, but conduct by both parties recognizes the existence of a contract, subsection (a) provides that the terms of the contract are terms that appear in the records of both parties. But even when both parties send records, there could be nonverbal agreement to additional or different terms that appear in only one of two records. If, for example, both parties' forms called for the sale of 700,000 nuts and bolts but the purchase order or another record of the buyer conditioned the sale on a test of a sample to see if the nuts and bolts would perform properly, the seller's sending a small sample to the buyer might be construed to be an agreement to the buyer's condition. It might also be found that the contract called for arbitration when both forms provided for arbitration but each contained immaterially different arbitration provisions.

In a rare case the terms in the records of both parties might not become part of the contract. This could be the case, for example, when the parties contemplated an agreement to a single negotiated record, and each party submitted to the other party similar proposals and then commenced performance, but the parties never reached a negotiated agreement because of the differences over crucial terms. There is a variety of verbal and nonverbal behavior that may be suggest agreement to another's record. This section leaves the interpretation of that behavior to the discretion of the courts.

4. An "agreement" may include terms derived from a course of performance, a course of dealing, and usage of trade. *See* Sections 1–201(a)(2) and 1–303. If the members of a trade, or if the contracting parties, expect to be bound by a term that appears in the record of only one of the contracting parties, that term is part of the agreement. However, repeated use of a particular term or repeated failure to object to a term on another's record is not normally sufficient in itself to establish a course of performance, a course of dealing or a trade usage.

5. The section omits any specific treatment of terms attached to the goods, or in or on the container in which the goods are delivered. This article takes no position on whether a court should follow the reasoning in Step–Saver Data Systems, Inc. v. Wyse Technology, 939 F.2d 91 (3d Cir. 1991) and Klocek v. Gateway, Inc. 104 F. Supp. 2d 1332 (D. Kan. 2000) (original 2–207 governs) or the contrary reasoning in Hill v. Gateway 2000, 105 F. 3d 1147(7th Cir. 1997) (original 2–207 inapplicable).

§ 2–208. ~~Course of Performance on Practical Construction~~ Reserved

~~(1) Where the contract for sale involves repeated occasions for performance by either party with knowledge of the nature of the performance and opportunity for objection to it by the other, any course of performance accepted or acquiesced in without objection shall be relevant to determine the meaning of the agreement.~~

~~(2) The express terms of the agreement and any such course of performance, as well as any course of dealing and usage of trade, shall be construed whenever reasonable as consistent with each other; but when such construction is unreasonable, express terms shall control course of performance and course of performance shall control both course of dealing and usage of trade (Section 1–205).~~

~~(3) Subject to the provisions of the next section on modification and waiver, such course of performance shall be relevant to show a waiver or modification of any term inconsistent with such course of performance.~~

Legislative Note: This section should not be repealed if the jurisdiction has not adopted revised Article 1.

§ 2–209. Modification; Rescission and Waiver

(1) An agreement modifying a contract within this Article needs no consideration to be binding.

(2) ~~A signed agreement~~ An agreement in a signed record which excludes modification or rescission except by a signed ~~writing cannot~~ record may not be otherwise modified or rescinded, but except as

between merchants such a requirement ~~on a form~~ in a form supplied by the merchant must be separately signed by the other party.

(3) The requirements of ~~the statute of frauds section of this Article (Section 2-201)~~ Section 2–201 must be satisfied if the contract as modified is within its provisions.

(4) Although an attempt at modification or rescission does not satisfy the requirements of subsection (2) or (3), it ~~can~~ may operate as a waiver.

(5) A party ~~who~~ that has made a waiver affecting an executory portion of ~~the~~ a contract may retract the waiver by reasonable notification received by the other party that strict performance will be required of any term waived, unless the retraction would be unjust in view of a material change of position in reliance on the waiver.

§ 2–210. Delegation of Performance; Assignment of Rights

~~(1) A party may perform his duty through a delegate unless otherwise agreed or unless the other party has a substantial interest in having his original promisor perform or control the acts required by the contract. No delegation of performance relieves the party delegating of any duty to perform or any liability for breach.~~

~~(2) Except as otherwise provided in Section 9–406, unless otherwise agreed, all rights of either seller or buyer can be assigned except where the assignment would materially change the duty of the other party, or increase materially the burden or risk imposed on him by his contract, or impair materially his chance of obtaining return performance. A right to damages for breach of the whole contract or a right arising out of the assignor's due performance of his entire obligation can be assigned despite agreement otherwise.~~

~~(3) The creation, attachment, perfection, or enforcement of a security interest in the seller's interest under a contract is not a transfer that materially changes the duty of or increases materially the burden or risk imposed on the buyer or impairs materially the buyer's chance of obtaining return performance within the purview of subsection (2) unless, and then only to the extent that, enforcement actually results in a delegation of material performance of the seller. Even in that event, the creation, attachment, perfection, and enforcement of the security interest remain effective, but (i) the seller is liable to the buyer for damages caused by the delegation to the extent that the damages could not reasonably be prevented by the buyer, and (ii) a court having jurisdiction may grant other appropriate relief, including cancellation of the contract for sale or an injunction against enforcement of the security interest or consummation of the enforcement.~~

~~(4) An assignment of "the contract" or of "all my rights under the contract" or an assignment in similar general terms is an assignment of~~

~~rights and unless the language or the circumstances (as in an assignment for security) indicate the contrary, it is a delegation of performance of the duties of the assignor and its acceptance by the assignee constitutes a promise by him to perform those duties. This promise is enforceable by either the assignor or the other party to the original contract.~~

~~(5) The other party may treat any assignment which delegates performance as creating reasonable grounds for insecurity and may without prejudice to his rights against the assignor demand assurances from the assignee (Section 2–609).~~

(1) If the seller or buyer assigns rights under a contract, the following rules apply:

    (a) Subject to paragraph (b) and except as otherwise provided in Section 9–406 or as otherwise agreed, all rights of the seller or the buyer may be assigned unless the assignment would materially change the duty of the other party, increase materially the burden or risk imposed on that party by the contract, or impair materially that party's chance of obtaining return performance. A right to damages for breach of the whole contract or a right arising out of the assignor's due performance of its entire obligation may be assigned despite an agreement otherwise.

    (b) The creation, attachment, perfection, or enforcement of a security interest in the seller's interest under a contract is not an assignment that materially changes the duty of or materially increases the burden or risk imposed on the buyer or materially impairs the buyer's chance of obtaining return performance under paragraph (a) unless, and only to the extent that, enforcement of the security interest results in a delegation of a material performance of the seller. Even in that event, the creation, attachment, perfection, and enforcement of the security interest remain effective. However, the seller is liable to the buyer for damages caused by the delegation to the extent that the damages could not reasonably be prevented by the buyer, and a court may grant other appropriate relief, including cancellation of the contract or an injunction against enforcement of the security interest or consummation of the enforcement.

(2) If the seller or buyer delegates performance of its duties under a contract, the following rules apply:

    (a) A party may perform its duties through a delegate unless otherwise agreed or unless the other party has a substantial interest in having the original promisor perform or control the acts required by the contract. Delegation of performance does not relieve the delegating party of any duty to perform or liability for breach.

(b) Acceptance of a delegation of duties by the assignee constitutes a promise to perform those duties. The promise is enforceable by either the assignor or the other party to the original contract.

(c) The other party may treat any delegation of duties as creating reasonable grounds for insecurity and may without prejudice to its rights against the assignor demand assurances from the assignee under Section 2–609.

(d) A contractual term prohibiting the delegation of duties otherwise delegable under paragraph (a) is enforceable, and an attempted delegation is not effective.

(3) An assignment of "the contract" or of "all my rights under the contract" or an assignment in similar general terms is an assignment of rights and unless the language or the circumstances, as in an assignment for security, indicate the contrary, it is also a delegation of performance of the duties of the assignor.

(4) Unless the circumstances indicate the contrary, a prohibition of assignment of "the contract" is to be construed as barring only the delegation to the assignee of the assignor's performance.

Official Comment

1. This section conforms with revised Article 9.

2. The principles in this section are consistent with the recognition that both the assignment of rights and the delegation of duties are generally normal and permissible incidents of a contract for the sale of goods.

3. Subsection (1)(a) sets out the effect of an assignment by either the seller or the buyer of the rights but not the duties arising under the contract for sale. These rights may effectively be assigned to a third party unless the assignment materially increases the duty, burden or risk, or materially impairs expected performance to the other party, or, subject to subsection (1)(b) and Section 9–406, unless the parties have agreed otherwise. Even then, a right to damages for breach of the whole contract or a right arising out of the assignor's due performance of the assignor's entire obligation can be assigned despite contrary agreement.

An assignment, however, is not effective if it would "materially change the duty of the other party, increase materially the burden or risk imposed on that party by the contract, or increase materially that party's likelihood of obtaining return performance." Subsection (1)(a). The cases where these limitations apply are rare. For example, a seller that has fully performed the contract should always be able to assign the right to payment. This is the basis for most accounts receivable financing. If, however, the contract is still executory, the assignment of the right to payment to a third person might decrease the seller's incentive to perform and, thus, increase the buyer's risk. Similarly, the buyer's assignment of the right to receive a fixed quantity of goods should not usually be objectionable but if the parties have a "requirements" contract, the assignment could increase materially the seller's risk.

Subsection (1)(a) is subject to Section 9–406 of revised Article 9. That provision makes rights to payment for goods sold ("accounts"), whether or not earned, freely alienable notwithstanding a contrary agreement or rule of law.

4. Subsection (1)(a) is subject to subsection (1)(b), which conforms with revised Article 9. If an assignment of rights creates a security interest in the seller's interest under the contract, including a right to future payments, subsection (1)(b) states that there is no material impairment under subsection (1)(a) unless the creation, attachment, perfection and enforcement "results in a delegation of material performance of the seller." This is unlikely in most assignments, and the buyer's basic protection is to demand adequate assurance of due performance from the seller if the assignment creates reasonable grounds for insecurity.

5. Occasionally a seller or buyer will delegate duties under the contract without also assigning rights. For example, a dealer might delegate its duty to procure and deliver a fixed quantity of goods to the buyer to a third party. In these cases, subsection (2) sets the limitations on that power. A contract term prohibiting the delegation of duties renders an attempted delegation ineffective. Subsection (2)(d).

If the third person accepts the delegation, an enforceable promise is made both to the delegator and the person entitled under the contract to perform those duties. Subsection (2)(b). In short, as to the person entitled under the contract a third party beneficiary contract is created. However, the delegator's duty to perform under the contract is not discharged unless the person entitled to performance agrees to substitute the delegatee for the delegator (a novation). *See* subsection (2)(a), last sentence.

The person entitled under the contract may treat any delegation of duties as reasonable grounds for insecurity and may demand adequate assurance of due performance for the assignee-delegatee. Subsection (2)(c).

In any event, a delegation of duties is not effective if the person entitled under the contract has a "substantial interest in having the original promisor perform or control the performance required by the contract." Subsection (2)(a).

6. In the case of ambiguity, subsection (3) provides a rule of interpretation to determine when an assignment of rights should also be considered a delegation of duties. The preference is to construe the language as both a delegation of duties as well as an assignment of rights.

7. This section is not intended as a complete statement of the law of delegation and assignment but is limited to clarifying a few points doubtful under the case law. In particular, neither this section nor this Article touches directly on the questions as the need or effect of notice of the assignment, the rights of successive assignees, or any question of the form of an assignment, either as between the parties or as against any third parties. Some of these questions are dealt with in Article 9.

§ 2–211. Legal Recognition of Electronic Contracts, Records, and Signatures

(1) A record or signature may not be denied legal effect or enforceability solely because it is in electronic form.

(2) A contract may not be denied legal effect or enforceability solely because an electronic record was used in its formation.

(3) This article does not require a record or signature to be created, generated, sent, communicated, received, stored, or otherwise processed by electronic means or in electronic form.

(4) A contract formed by the interaction of an individual and an electronic agent under Section 2–204(4)(b) does not include terms provided by the individual if the individual had reason to know that the agent could not react to the terms as provided.

Official Comment

1. Subsections (1) and (2) are derived from Section 7(a) and (b) of the Uniform Electronic Transactions Act (UETA), and subsection (3) is derived from Section 5(b) of UETA. Subsection (4) is based on Section 206(c) of the Uniform Computer Information Transactions Act (UCITA). Each subsection conforms to the federal Electronic Signatures in Global and National Commerce Act (15 U.S.C. § 7001 *et seq.*).

2. This section sets forth the premise that the medium in which a record, signature, or contract is created, presented or retained does not affect its legal significance. Subsections (1) and (2) are designed to eliminate the single element of medium as a reason to deny effect or enforceability to a record, signature, or contract. The fact that the information is set forth in an electronic, as opposed to paper, medium is irrelevant.

3. A contract may have legal effect and yet be unenforceable. *See* Restatement 2d Contracts Section 8. To the extent that a contract in electronic form may have legal effect but be un-

enforceable, because it is in electronic form, subsection (2) validates its legality. Likewise, to the extent that a record or signature in electronic form may have legal effect but be unenforceable, because it is in electronic form, subsection (1) validates the legality of the record or signature.

For example, though a contract may be unenforceable, the parties' electronic records may have collateral effects, as in the case of a buyer that insures goods purchased under a contract that is unenforceable under Section 2–201. The insurance company may not deny a claim on the ground that the buyer is not the owner, though the buyer may have no direct remedy against the seller for failure to deliver. *See* Restatement 2d Contracts, Section 8, Illustration 4. Whether an electronic record or signature is valid under other law is not addressed by this Act.

4. While subsection (2) validates the legality of an electronic contract, it does not in any way diminish the requirements for the formation of contracts under Sections 2–204 and 2–206.

§ 2–212. Attribution

An electronic record or electronic signature is attributable to a person if it was the act of the person or the person's electronic agent or the person is otherwise legally bound by the act.

Official Comment

1. This section is based on Section 9 of the Uniform Electronic Transactions Act (UETA).

2. As long as an electronic record is created by a person or the electronic

signature results from a person's action it is attributed to that person. The legal effect of the attribution is derived from other provisions of this Act or from other law. This section simply assures that these rules will be applied in the electronic environment. A person's actions include actions taken by a human agent of the person as well as actions taken by an electronic agent, of the person. Although this section may appear to state the obvious, it assures that the record or signature is not ascribed to a machine, as opposed to the person operating or programming the machine.

3. In each of the following cases, both the electronic record and electronic signature would be attributable to a person under this section:

    A. The person types his or her name as part of an e-mail purchase order;

    B. The person's employee, pursuant to authority, types the person's name as part of an e-mail purchase order;

    C. The person's computer, programmed to order goods upon receipt of inventory information within particular parameters, issues a purchase order which includes the person's name, or other identifying information, as part of the order.

In each of these cases, law other than this Act would ascribe both the signature and the action to the person if done in a paper medium. This section provides that the same result will occur when an electronic medium is used.

4. Nothing in this section affects the use of an electronic signature as a means of attributing a record to a person. Once an electronic signature is attributed to the person, the electronic record with which it is associated would also be attributed to the person unless the person established fraud, forgery, or other invalidating cause. However, an electronic signature is not the only method for attribution of a record.

5. In the context of attribution of records, normally the content of the record will provide the necessary information for a finding of attribution. It is also possible that an established course of dealing between parties may result in a finding of attribution. Just as with a paper record, evidence of forgery or counterfeiting may be introduced to rebut the evidence of attribution. The use of facsimile transmissions provides a number of examples of attribution using information other than a signature. A facsimile may be attributed to a person because of the information printed across the top of the page that indicates the machine from which it was sent. Similarly, the transmission may contain a letterhead which identifies the sender. Some cases have held that the letterhead actually constituted a signature because it was a symbol adopted by the sender with intent to sign the record. *See Cox Engineering v. Funston Mach. & Supply*, 749 S.W.2d 508, 511 (Tex. App. 1988) (plaintiff's letterhead, including address, appearing at top of invoice, provides authentication that identifies the party to be charged and thus satisfies the statute of frauds' signature requirement); *Owen v. Kroger Co.*, 936 F. Supp. 579 (S.D. Ind. 1996) (determining that a letterhead satisfies the signature requirement of the UCC). However, the signature determination resulted from the necessary finding of intention in that case. Other cases have found letterheads not to be signatures because the requisite intention was not present. *See First National Bank in Alamosa v. Ford Motor Credit Co.*, 748 F. Supp 1464 (D. Colo, 1990) (determining that a pre-printed name on a draft was not a signature for the purpose of accepting a draft). The critical point is that with or without a signature, information within the electronic record may well suffice to provide the facts resulting in attribution

of an electronic record to a particular party.

6. Certain information may be present in an electronic environment that does not appear to attribute but which clearly links a person to a particular record. Numerical codes, personal identification numbers, public and private key combinations, all serve to establish the party to which an electronic record should be attributed. Security procedures will be another piece of evidence available to establish attribution.

7. Once it is established that a record or signature is attributable to a particular person, the legal significance of the record or signature is determined by the context and surrounding circumstances in which the recorder signature is created, including the parties' agreement, if any. This will primarily be governed by other sections of this article. *See, e.g.,* Sections 2–201, 2–202, 2–204, 2–206, 2–207, and 2–209.

§ 2–213. Electronic Communication

(1) If the receipt of an electronic communication has a legal effect, it has that effect even if no individual is aware of its receipt.

(2) Receipt of an electronic acknowledgment of an electronic communication establishes that the communication was received but, in itself, does not establish that the content sent corresponds to the content received.

Official Comment

1. This section is adapted from Sections 15(e) and (f) of the Uniform Electronic Transactions Act (UETA).

2. This section deals with electronic communications generally, and it is not limited to electronic records which must be retrievable in perceivable form. The section does not resolve the questions of when or where electronic communications are determined to be sent or received, nor does it indicate that a communication has any particular substantive legal effect.

3. Under subsection (1), receipt is not dependent on a person having notice of the communication. An analogy in a paper based transaction is the recipient that does not read a notice received in the mail. Although "receipt" as defined in Article 1 applies by its terms only to notices, the same concept would apply equally to a communication that is not a notice.

4. Subsection (2) provides legal certainty about the effect of an electronic acknowledgment. This subsection only addresses the fact of the receipt, and it does not set forth the legal significance of the quality of the content, nor whether the electronic communication was read or "opened."

5. This section does not address the question of whether the exchange of electronic communications constitutes the formation of a contract. Those questions are addressed by Sections 2–204 and 2–206.

PART 3

GENERAL OBLIGATION AND CONSTRUCTION OF CONTRACT

§ 2–301. General Obligations of Parties

The obligation of the seller is to transfer and deliver and that of the buyer is to accept and pay in accordance with the contract.

§ 2–302. Unconscionable Contract or ~~Clause~~ Term

(1) If the court as a matter of law finds the contract or any ~~clause~~ term of the contract to have been unconscionable at the time it was made, the court may refuse to enforce the contract, or it may enforce the remainder of the contract without the unconscionable ~~clause~~ term, or it may so limit the application of any unconscionable ~~clause~~ term as to avoid any unconscionable result.

(2) ~~When~~ If it is claimed or appears to the court that the contract or any ~~clause~~ term thereof may be unconscionable, the parties shall be afforded a reasonable opportunity to present evidence as to its commercial setting, purpose, and effect to aid the court in making the determination.

Official Comment

1. This section makes it possible for a court to police explicitly against the contracts or terms which the court finds to be unconscionable instead of attempting to achieve the result by an adverse construction of language, by manipulation of the rules of offer and acceptance, or by a determination that the term is contrary to public policy or to the dominant purpose of the contract. The section allows a court to pass directly on the unconscionability of the contract or a particular term of the contract and to make a conclusion of law as to its unconscionability. Courts have been particularly vigilant when the contract at issue is set forth in a standard form. The principle is one of prevention of oppression and unfair surprise and not of disturbance of allocation of risks because of superior bargaining power. The basic test is whether, in the light of the general commercial background and the commercial needs of the particular trade or case, the term or contract involved is so one-sided as to be unconscionable under the circumstances existing at the time of the making of the contract.

2. Under this section, the court, in its discretion, may refuse to enforce the contract as a whole if the whole contract is determined to be unconscionable, or the court may strike any single term or group of terms which are unconscionable or which are contrary to the essential purpose of the agreement or to material terms to which the parties have expressly agreed, or the court may simply limits the unconscionable results.

3. This section is addressed to the court, and the decision is to be made by the court. The evidence referred to in subsection (2) is for the court's consideration, not the trier of fact. Only the agreement which results from the court's action on these matters is to be submitted to the general trier of the facts.

§ 2–303. Allocation or Division of Risks

Where this Article allocates a risk or a burden as between the parties "unless otherwise agreed", the agreement may not only shift the allocation but may also divide the risk or burden.

§ 2–304. Price Payable in Money, Goods, Realty, or Otherwise

(1) The price ~~can~~ may be made payable in money or otherwise. If it is payable in whole or in part in goods, each party is a seller of the goods ~~which he~~ that the party is to transfer.

(2) Even ~~though~~ if all or part of the price is payable in an interest in ~~realty~~ real property the transfer of the goods, and the seller's obligations with reference to them are subject to this Article, but not the transfer of the interest in ~~realty~~ real property or the transferor's obligations in connection therewith.

§ 2–305. Open Price Term

(1) The parties if they so intend ~~can~~ may conclude a contract for sale even ~~though~~ if the price is not settled. In such a case the price is a reasonable price at the time for delivery if:

    (a) nothing is said as to price; ~~or~~

    (b) the price is left to be agreed by the parties and they fail to agree; or

    (c) the price is to be fixed in terms of some agreed market or other standard as set or recorded by a third person or agency and it is not so set or recorded.

(2) A price to be fixed by the seller or by the buyer means a price ~~for him to fix~~ to be fixed in good faith.

(3) ~~When~~ If a price left to be fixed otherwise than by agreement of the parties fails to be fixed through fault of one party, the other may at ~~his~~ the party's option treat the contract as canceled or ~~himself~~ the party may fix a reasonable price.

(4) ~~Where~~ If, however, the parties intend not to be bound unless the price ~~be~~ is fixed or agreed and it is not fixed or agreed, there is no contract. In such a case the buyer must return any goods already received or if unable ~~so~~ to do so must pay their reasonable value at the time of delivery and the seller must return any portion of the price paid on account.

§ 2–306. Output, Requirements and Exclusive Dealings

(1) A term which measures the quantity by the output of the seller or the requirements of the buyer means such actual output or requirements as may occur in good faith, except that no quantity unreasonably disproportionate to any stated estimate or in the absence of a stated estimate to any normal or otherwise comparable prior output or requirements may be tendered or demanded.

(2) A lawful agreement by either the seller or the buyer for exclusive dealing in the kind of goods concerned imposes unless otherwise

agreed an obligation by the seller to use best efforts to supply the goods and by the buyer to use best efforts to promote their sale.

§ 2–307. Delivery in Single Lot or Several Lots

Unless otherwise agreed all goods called for by a contract for sale must be tendered in a single delivery and payment is due only on such tender but where the circumstances give either party the right to make or demand delivery in lots the price if it can be apportioned may be demanded for each lot.

§ 2–308. Absence of Specified Place for Delivery

Unless otherwise agreed:

(a) the place for delivery of goods is the seller's place of business or if ~~he has~~ none, ~~his~~ the seller's residence; but

(b) in a contract for sale of identified goods ~~which~~ that to the knowledge of the parties at the time of contracting are in some other place, that place is the place for their delivery; and

(c) documents of title may be delivered through customary banking channels.

§ 2–309. Absence of Specific Time Provisions; Notice of Termination

(1) The time for shipment or delivery or any other action under a contract if not provided in this Article or agreed upon shall be a reasonable time.

(2) ~~Where~~ If the contract provides for successive performances but is indefinite in duration, it is valid for a reasonable time but unless otherwise agreed may be terminated at any time by either party.

(3) Termination of a contract by one party except on the happening of an agreed event requires that reasonable notification be received by the other party and an agreement dispensing with notification is invalid if its operation would be unconscionable. A term specifying standards for the nature and timing of notice is enforceable if the standards are not manifestly unreasonable.

Official Comment

11. The last sentence of subsection (3) is new and is based on Section 1–302(b). It provides for greater party autonomy. In an appropriate circumstance, the parties may agree that the standard for notice is no notice at all.

§ 2–310. Open Time for Payment or Running of Credit; Authority to Ship Under Reservation

Unless otherwise agreed:

(a) payment is due at the time and place at which the buyer is to receive the goods even though the place of shipment is the place of delivery; ~~and~~

(b) if the seller is <u>required or</u> authorized to send the goods, ~~he~~ <u>the seller</u> may ship them under reservation, and may tender the documents of title, but the buyer may inspect the goods after their arrival before payment is due unless ~~such~~ <u>the</u> inspection is inconsistent with the terms of the contract (Section 2–513); ~~and~~

(c) if <u>tender of</u> delivery is ~~authorized and~~ <u>agreed to be</u> made by way of documents of title otherwise than by ~~subsection~~ <u>paragraph</u> (b)<u>,</u> then payment is due <u>regardless of where the goods are to be received (i)</u> at the time and place at which the buyer is to receive <u>delivery of</u> the <u>tangible</u> documents, <u>or (ii) at the time the buyer is to receive delivery of the electronic documents and at the seller's place of business or if none, the seller's residence</u> ~~regardless of where the goods are to be received~~; and

(d) ~~where~~ <u>if</u> the seller is required or authorized to ship the goods on credit<u>,</u> the credit period runs from the time of shipment but ~~post-dating~~ <u>postdating</u> the invoice or delaying its dispatch will correspondingly delay the starting of the credit period.

§ 2–311. Options and Cooperation Respecting Performance

(1) An agreement for sale which is otherwise sufficiently definite ~~(Subsection (3) of Section 2–204)~~ <u>(Section 2–204(3))</u> to be a contract is not made invalid by the fact that it leaves particulars of performance to be specified by one of the parties. Any such specification must be made in good faith and within limits set by commercial reasonableness.

(2) Unless otherwise agreed<u>,</u> specifications relating to assortment of the goods are at the buyer's option and ~~except as otherwise provided in subsections (1)(c) and (3) of Section 2–319~~ specifications or arrangements relating to shipment are at the seller's option.

(3) ~~Where such~~ <u>If the</u> specification would materially affect the other party's performance but is not seasonably made or ~~where~~ <u>if</u> one party's cooperation is necessary to the agreed performance of the other but is not seasonably forthcoming, the other party in addition to all other remedies<u>:</u>

(a) is excused for any resulting delay in ~~his own~~ <u>that party's</u> performance; and

(b) may also either proceed to perform in any reasonable manner or after the time for a material part of ~~his~~ <u>that party's</u>

~~own~~ performance treat the failure to specify or to cooperate as a breach by failure to deliver or accept the goods.

§ 2–312. Warranty of Title and Against Infringement; Buyer's Obligation Against Infringement

(1) Subject to subsection ~~(2)~~(3), there is in a contract for sale a warranty by the seller that:

    (a) the title conveyed shall be ~~good,~~ good and its transfer rightful <u>and shall not unreasonably expose the buyer to litigation because of any colorable claim to or interest in the goods</u>; and

    (b) the goods shall be delivered free from any security interest or other lien or encumbrance of which the buyer at the time of contracting has no knowledge.

~~(2) A warranty under subsection (1) will be excluded or modified only by specific language or by circumstances which give the buyer reason to know that the person selling does not claim title in himself or that it is purporting to sell only such right or title as it or a third person may have.~~

~~(3) Unless otherwise agreed a seller who is a merchant regularly dealing in goods of the kind warrants that the goods shall be delivered free of the rightful claim of any third person by way of infringement or the like but a buyer who furnishes specifications to the seller must hold the seller harmless against any such claim which arises out of compliance with the specifications.~~

(2) <u>Unless otherwise agreed, a seller that is a merchant regularly dealing in goods of the kind warrants that the goods shall be delivered free of the rightful claim of any third person by way of infringement or the like but a buyer that furnishes specifications to the seller must hold the seller harmless against any such claim that arises out of compliance with the specifications.</u>

(3) <u>A warranty under this section may be disclaimed or modified only by specific language or by circumstances that give the buyer reason to know that the seller does not claim title, that the seller is purporting to sell only the right or title as the seller or a third person may have, or that the seller is selling subject to any claims of infringement or the like.</u>

Official Comment

1. Subsection (1) provides for a buyer's basic needs for a title which the buyer in good faith expects to acquire by the purchase, namely, that the buyer receive a good, clean title transferred also in a rightful manner so that the buyer will not be exposed to a lawsuit to protect the title. Under subsection (1), the seller warrants that (1) the title conveyed is good, (2) the transfer is rightful, and (3) the transfer does not unreasonably expose the buyer to litigation because a third person has or asserts a "colorable claim" to or interest in the goods.

In addition to sales in which there is an actual cloud on the title, a warranty that the "title conveyed is good and its transfer rightful" also covers cases when the title is good but the transfer is not rightful. For example, a wrongful transfer with good title occurs where a merchant bailee to which goods are entrusted for repair sells them without authority to a buyer in the ordinary course of business. *See* Section 2–403(2); *Sumner v. Fel–Air, Inc.*, 680 P.2d 1109 (Alaska 1984).

The subsection now expressly states what the courts have long recognized; further protection for the buyer is needed when the title is burdened by colorable claims that affect the value of the goods. *See Frank Arnold KRS, Inc. v. L.S. Meier Auction Co., Inc.*, 806 F.2d 462 (3d Cir. 1986) (two lawsuits contest title); *Jeanneret v. Vichey*, 693 F.2d 259 (2d Cir. 1982) (export restrictions in country from which painting was taken affect value); Colton v. Decker, 540 N.W.2d 172 (S.D. 1995) (conflicting vehicle identification numbers). Therefore, not only is the buyer entitled to a good title, but the buyer is also entitled to a marketable title, and until the colorable claim is resolved the market for the goods is impaired. *See Wright v. Vickaryous*, 611 P.2d 20 (Alaska 1980).

The justification for this rule is that the buyer of goods that are warranted for title has a right to rely on the fact that there will be no need later to have to contest ownership. The mere casting of a substantial shadow over the buyer's title, regardless of the ultimate outcome, violates the warranty of good title. *See American Container Corp. v. Hanley Trucking Corp.*, 111 N.J. Super. 322, 268 A.2d 313,318 (1970). It should be noted that not any assertion of a claim by a third party will constitute a breach of the warranty of title. The claim must be reasonable and col-

orable. *See C.F. Sales, Inc. v. Amfert*, 344 N.W.2d 543 (Iowa 1983).

The warranty of title extends to a buyer whether or not the seller was in possession of the goods at the time the sale or contract to sell was made.

Consistent with original Article 2, this section does not provide for a separate warranty of quiet possession in addition to the warranty of title. Disturbance of quiet possession, although not mentioned specifically, is one way, among many, in which the breach of the warranty of title might be established.

2. "Knowledge" as referred to in subsection (1)(b) is actual knowledge as distinct from notice.

3. The provisions of this Article that require notification to the seller within a reasonable time after the buyer's discovery of a breach (Section 2–607(3)(a)) apply to notice of a breach of the warranty of title when the seller's breach was innocent. However, if the seller's breach were in bad faith, the seller cannot claim prejudice by the delay in giving notice.

4. Subsection (2) provides the warranty against infringement. Unlike the warranty of title, this warranty is limited to sellers that are merchants that "regularly dealing in goods of the kind" sold.

When the goods are part of the seller's normal stock, and are sold in the normal course of business, it is the seller's duty to see that no claim of infringement of a patent or trademark by a third party will impair the buyer's title. A sale by a person other than a dealer, however, raises no implication in its circumstances of the warranty. Nor is there an implication when the buyer orders goods to be assembled, prepared or manufactured on the buyer's own specifications. If, in such a case, the resulting product infringes a patent or trademark, the liability will run from buyer to seller. There is, under these circumstances, a tacit representation on the part of the buyer that the seller will be safe in manufacturing according to the specifications, and the buyer is under an obligation in good faith to indemnify the seller for any loss suffered.

5. Under this section, the cases which recognize the principle that infringements violate the warranty of title but deny the buyer a remedy unless he has been expressly prevented from using the goods are rejected. Under this Article "eviction" is not a necessary condition to the buyer's remedy since the buyer's remedy arises immediately upon receipt of notice of infringement; it is merely one way of establishing the fact of breach.

6. Subsection (3) is concerned with the disclaimer or modification of the warranties of title or against infringement. This is a self-contained provision that govern the modification or disclaimer of warranties under this section. The warranties in this section are not designated as "implied" warranties, and hence these warranties are not subject to the modification and disclaimer provisions of Section 2–316(2) and (3). Unlike Section 2–316, subsection (3) of this section does not create any specific requirements that the disclaimer or modification be contained in a record or be conspicuous.

Under subsection (3), sales by sheriffs, executors, certain foreclosing lienors and persons similarly situated are recognized as possibly being so out of the ordinary commercial course that their peculiar character is immediately apparent to the buyer, and therefore no personal obligation is imposed upon the seller that is purporting to sell only an unknown or limited right. This subsection is not intended to touch upon, and it leaves open, all questions of restitution that arise in these cases, such as when a unique article that is sold is reclaimed by a third party as the rightful owner.

For a foreclosure sale under Article 9, Section 9–610 of revised Article 9 provides that a disposition of collateral under that section includes warranties such as those imposed by this section on a voluntary disposition of property. Consequently, unless properly excluded under subsection (3) or under the special provisions for exclusion in Section 9–610, a disposition under that section of collateral consisting of goods includes the warranties imposed by subsection (1) and, if applicable, subsection (2).

7. The statute of limitations for a breach of warranty under this section is determined under the provisions set out in Section 2–725(1) and (3)(c).

§ 2–313. Express Warranties By Affirmation, Promise, Description, Sample; Remedial Promise

(1) In this section, "immediate buyer" means a buyer that enters into a contract with the seller.

(1) (2) Express warranties by the seller to the immediate buyer are created as follows:

(a) Any affirmation of fact or promise made by the seller to the buyer which relates to the goods and becomes part of the basis of the bargain creates an express warranty that the goods shall conform to the affirmation or promise.

143

(b) Any description of the goods which is made part of the basis of the bargain creates an express warranty that the goods shall conform to the description.

(c) Any sample or model ~~which~~ <u>that</u> is made part of the basis of the bargain creates an express warranty that the whole of the goods shall conform to the sample or model.

~~(2)~~ <u>(3)</u> It is not necessary to the creation of an express warranty that the seller use formal words such as "warrant" or "guarantee" or that ~~he~~ <u>the seller</u> have a specific intention to make a warranty, but an affirmation merely of the value of the goods or a statement purporting to be merely the seller's opinion or commendation of the goods does not create a warranty.

<u>(4) Any remedial promise made by the seller to the immediate buyer creates an obligation that the promise will be performed upon the happening of the specified event.</u>

Official Comment

1. In subsections (2) and (4) the term "immediate buyer" is used to make clear that the section is limited to express warranties and remedial promises made by a seller to a buyer with which the seller has a contractual relationship. Sections 2–313A and 2–313B address obligations that run directly from a seller to a remote purchaser.

2. Subsection (4) uses the term "remedial promise," which was not used in original Article 2. This section deals with remedial promises to immediate buyers. Sections 2–313A and 2–313B deal with remedial promises running directly from a seller to a remote purchaser. Remedial promise is defined in Section 2–103(1)(n).

3. "Express" warranties rest on "dickered" aspects of the individual bargain, and go so clearly to the essence of that bargain that words of disclaimer in a form are repugnant to the basic dickered terms. "Implied" warranties rest so clearly on a common factual situation or set of conditions that no particular language or action is necessary to evidence them and they will arise in such a situation unless unmistakably negated. As with original Article 2, warranties of description and sample are designated "express" rather than "implied."

4. This section is limited in its scope and direct purpose to express warranties and remedial promises made by the seller to the immediate buyer as part of a contract for sale. It is not designed in any way to disturb those lines of case law which have recognized that warranties need not be confined to contracts within the scope of this Article.

Under Section 2–313B, a seller may incur an obligation to a remote purchaser through a medium for communication to the public such as advertising. An express warranty to an immediate buyer may also arise through a medium for communication to the public if the elements of this section are satisfied.

The fact that a buyer has rights against an immediate seller under this section does not preclude the buyer from also asserting rights against a remote seller under Section 2–313A or 2–313B.

5. The present section deals with affirmations of fact or promises made by the seller, descriptions of the goods,

or exhibitions of samples or models, exactly as it deals with any other part of a negotiation which ends in a contract. No specific intention to make a warranty is necessary if any of these factors is made part of the basis of the bargain. In actual practice affirmations of fact and promises made by the seller about the goods during a bargain are regarded as part of the description of those goods; hence no particular reliance on these statements need be shown in order to weave them into the fabric of the agreement. Rather, any fact which is to take these affirmations or promises, once made, out of the agreement requires clear affirmative proof. The issue normally is one of fact.

6. In view of the principle that the whole purpose of the law of warranty is to determine what it is that the seller has in essence agreed to sell, the policy is adopted of those cases which refuse except in unusual circumstances to recognize a material deletion of the seller's obligation. Thus, a contract is normally a contract for a sale of something describable and described. A clause generally disclaiming "all warranties, express or implied" cannot reduce the seller's obligation for the description and therefore cannot be given literal effect under Section 2–316(1).

This is not intended to mean that the parties, if they consciously desire, cannot make their own bargain as they wish. But in determining what they have agreed upon good faith is a factor and consideration should be given to the fact that the probability is small that a real price is intended to be exchanged for a pseudo-obligation.

7. Subsection (2)(b) makes specific some of the principles set forth above when a description of the goods is given by the seller.

A description need not be by words. Technical specifications, blueprints and the like can afford more exact description than mere language and if made part of the basis of the bargain goods must conform with them. Past deliveries may set the description of quality, either expressly or impliedly by course of dealing. Of course, all descriptions by merchants must be read against the applicable trade usages with the general rules as to merchantability resolving any doubts.

8. The basic situation as to statements affecting the true essence of the bargain is no different when a sample or model is involved in the transaction. This section includes both a "sample" actually drawn from the bulk of goods which is the subject matter of the sale, and a "model" which is offered for inspection when the subject matter is not at hand and which has not been drawn from the bulk of the goods.

Although the underlying principles are unchanged, the facts are often ambiguous when something is shown as illustrative, rather than as a straight sample. In general, the presumption is that any sample or model, just as any affirmation of fact, is intended to become a basis of the bargain. But there is no escape from the question of fact. When the seller exhibits a sample purporting to be drawn from an existing bulk, good faith of course requires that the sample be fairly drawn. But in mercantile experience the mere exhibition of a "sample" does not of itself show whether it is merely intended to "suggest" or to "be" the character of the subject-matter of the contract. The question is whether the seller has so acted with reference to the sample as to become responsible that the whole shall have at least the values shown by it. The circumstances aid in answering this question. If the sample has been drawn from an existing bulk, it must be regarded as describing values of the goods contracted for unless it is accompanied by an unmistakable denial of

145

responsibility. If, on the other hand, a model of merchandise not on hand is offered, the mercantile presumption that it has become a literal description of the subject matter is not so strong, and particularly so if modification on the buyer's initiative impairs any feature of the model.

9. The precise time when words of description or affirmation are made or samples are shown is not material. The sole question is whether the language or samples or models are fairly to be regarded as part of the contract. If language that would otherwise create an obligation under this section is used after the closing of the deal (as when the buyer when taking delivery asks and receives an additional assurance), an obligation will arise if the requirements for a modification are satisfied. *See Downie v. Abex Corp.*, 741 F.2d 1235 (10th Cir. 1984).

10. Concerning affirmations of value or a seller's opinion or commendation under subsection (3), the basic question remains the same: What statements of the seller have in the circumstances and in objective judgment become part of the basis of the bargain? As indicated above, all of the statements of the seller do so unless good reason is shown to the contrary. The provisions of subsection (3) are included, however, since common experience discloses that some statements or predictions cannot fairly be viewed as entering into the bargain. Even as to false statements of value, however, the possibility is left open that a remedy may be provided by the law relating to fraud or misrepresentation.

There are a number of factors relevant to determine whether an expression creates a warranty under this section or is merely puffing. For example, the relevant factors may include whether the seller's representations taken in context, (1) were general rather than specific, (2) related to the consequences of buying rather than the goods themselves, (3) were "hedged" in some way, (4) were related to experimental rather than standard goods, (5) were concerned with some aspects of the goods but not a hidden or unexpected nonconformity, (6) were informal statements made in a formal contracting process, (7) were phrased in terms of opinion rather than fact, or (8) were not capable of objective measurement.

11. The use of the word "promise" in subsection (2)(a) refers to statements about the quality or performance characteristics of the goods. For example, a seller might make an affirmation of fact to the buyer that the goods are of a certain quality, or may promise that the goods when delivered will be of a certain quality, or may promise that the goods will perform in a certain manner after delivery. In normal usage, "promise" refers to a what a person, not goods, will do; that is, a promise is a commitment to act, or refrain from acting, in a certain manner in the future. A promise about the quality or performance characteristics of the goods creates an express warranty if the other elements of a warranty are present whereas a promise by which the seller commits itself to take remedial action upon the happening of a specified event is a remedial promise. The distinction has meaning in the context of the statute of limitations. A right of action for breach of an express warranty accrues when the goods are tendered to the immediate buyer (Section 2–725(3)(a)) unless the warranty consists of a promise that explicitly extends to the future performance of the goods and discovery must await the time for performance, in which case accrual occurs when the immediate buyer discovers or should have discovered the breach (Section 2–725(3)(d)). Section 2–725(2)(c) separately addresses the accrual of a right

of action for breach of a remedial promise.

The concept of remedial promise is dealt with in a separate subsection to make clear that it is a concept separate and apart from express warranty and that the elements of an express warranty, such as basis of the bargain, are not applicable.

§ 2–313A. Obligation to Remote Purchaser Created By Record Packaged With or Accompanying Goods

(1) In this section:

(a) "Immediate buyer" means a buyer that enters into a contract with the seller.

(b) "Remote purchaser" means a person that buys or leases goods from an immediate buyer or other person in the normal chain of distribution.

(2) This section applies only to new goods and goods sold or leased as new goods in a transaction of purchase in the normal chain of distribution.

(3) If in a record packaged with or accompanying the goods the seller makes an affirmation of fact or promise that relates to the goods, provides a description that relates to the goods, or makes a remedial promise, and the seller reasonably expects the record to be, and the record is, furnished to the remote purchaser, the seller has an obligation to the remote purchaser that:

(a) the goods will conform to the affirmation of fact, promise, or description unless a reasonable person in the position of the remote purchaser would not believe that the affirmation of fact, promise, or description created an obligation; and

(b) the seller will perform the remedial promise.

(4) It is not necessary to the creation of an obligation under this section that the seller use formal words such as "warrant" or "guarantee" or that the seller have a specific intention to undertake an obligation, but an affirmation merely of the value of the goods or a statement purporting to be merely the seller's opinion or commendation of the goods does not create an obligation.

(5) The following rules apply to the remedies for breach of an obligation created under this section:

(a) The seller may modify or limit the remedies available to the remote purchaser if the modification or limitation is furnished to the remote purchaser no later than the time of purchase or if the modification or limitation is contained in the record that contains the affirmation of fact, promise, or description.

(b) Subject to a modification or limitation of remedy, a seller in breach is liable for incidental or consequential damages under Section 2–715, but not for lost profits.

(c) The remote purchaser may recover as damages for breach of a seller's obligation arising under subsection (3) the loss resulting in the ordinary course of events as determined in any reasonable manner.

(6) An obligation that is not a remedial promise is breached if the goods did not conform to the affirmation of fact, promise, or description creating the obligation when the goods left the seller's control.

Official Comment

1. Sections 2–313A and 2–313B are new, and they follow case law and practice in extending a seller's obligations regarding new goods to remote purchasers. Section 2–313A deals with what are commonly called "pass-through warranties". The usual transaction in which this obligation arises is when a manufacturer sells goods in a package to a retailer and include in the package a record that sets forth the obligations that the manufacturer is willing to undertake in favor of the final party in the distributive chain, who is the person that buys or leases the goods from the retailer. If the manufacturer had sold the goods directly to the final party in the distributive chain, whether the manufacturer would incur liability is determined by Section 2–313 and this section is inapplicable.

No direct contract exists between the seller and the remote purchaser, and thus the seller's obligation under this section is not referred to as an "express warranty." Use of "obligation" rather than "express warranty" avoids any inference that the obligation arises as part of the basis of the bargain as would be required to create an express warranty under section 2–313. The test for whether an obligation other than a remedial promise arises is similar in some respects to the basis of the bargain requirement in section 2–313, but the test set forth in this section is exclusive. Because "remedial promise" in Section 2–313 is not subject to the requirement that it arise as part of the basis of the bargain, the term is used in this section.

2. The party to which an obligation runs under this section may either buy or lease the goods, and thus the term "remote purchaser" is used. The term is more limited than "purchaser" in Article 1, however, and does not include a donee or any voluntary transferee who is not a buyer or lessee. Moreover, the remote purchaser must be part of the normal chain of distribution for the particular product. That chain will, by definition, include at least three parties and may well include more. For example, the manufacturer might sell first to a wholesaler that would then resell the goods to a retailer for sale or lease to the public. A buyer or lessee from the retailer would qualify as a remote purchaser and could invoke this section against either the manufacturer or the wholesaler (if the wholesaler provided a record to the retailer to be furnished to the final party in the distribution chain), but no subsequent transferee, such as a used-goods buyer or sublessee, would qualify. The law governing assignment and third-party beneficiary, including Section 2–318, should be consulted to determine whether a party other than the remote purchaser can enforce an obligation created under this section.

3. The application of this section is limited to new goods and goods sold or leased as new goods within the normal chain of distribution. It does not apply to goods that are sold outside the normal chain, such as "gray" goods or salvaged goods, nor does it apply if the goods are unused but sold as seconds. The concept is flexible, and to determine whether goods have been sold or leased in the normal chain of distribution requires consideration of the seller's expectations for the manner in which its goods will reach the remote purchaser. For example, a car manufacturer may be aware that certain of its dealers transfer cars among themselves, and under the particular circumstances of the case a court might find that a new car sold initially to one dealer but leased to the remote purchaser by another dealer was leased in the normal chain of distribution. The concept may also include such practices as door-to-door sales and distribution through a nonprofit organization.

The phrase "goods sold or leased as new goods" refers to goods that in the normal course of business would be considered new. There are many instances in which goods might be used for a limited purpose yet be sold or leased in the normal chain of distribution as new goods. For example, goods that have been returned to a dealer by a purchaser and placed back into the dealer's inventory might be sold or leased as new goods in the normal chain of distribution. Other examples might include goods that have been used for the purpose of inspection (*e.g.*, a car that has been test-driven) and goods that have been returned by a sale-or-return buyer (Section 2–326).

4. This section applies only to obligations set forth in a record that is packaged with the goods or otherwise accompanies them (subsection (2)). Examples include a label affixed to the outside of a container, a card inside a container, or a booklet handed to the remote purchaser at the time of purchase. In addition, the seller must be able to anticipate that the remote purchaser will acquire the record, and therefore this section is limited to records that the seller reasonably expects to be furnished, and that are in fact furnished, to the remote purchaser.

Neither this section nor Section 2–313B are intended to overrule cases that impose liability on facts outside the direct scope of one of the sections. For example, the sections are not intended to overrule a decision imposing liability on a seller that distributes a sample to a remote purchaser.

5. Obligations other than remedial promises created under this section are analogous to express warranties and are subject to a test that is akin to the basis of the bargain test of Section 2–313(2). The seller is entitled to shape the scope of the obligation, and the seller's language tending to create an obligation must be considered in context. If a reasonable person in the position of the remote purchaser, reading the seller's language in its entirety, would not believe that an affirmation of fact, promise or description created an obligation, there is no liability under this section.

6. There is no difference between remedial promise as used in this section (and Section 2–313B) and the same term as used in Section 2–313.

7. Subsection (5)(a) makes clear that the seller may employ the provisions of Section 2–719 to modify or limit the remedies available to the remote purchaser for breach of the seller's obligation in this section. The modification or limitation may appear on the same record as the one which creates the obligation, or it may be provided to the remote purchaser separately, but in no event may it be fur-

nished to the remote purchaser any later than the time of purchase.

The requirements and limitations set forth in Section 2–719, such as the requirement of an express statement of exclusivity and the tests for failure of essential purpose (Section 2–719(2)) and unconscionability (Section 2–719(3)) are applicable to a modification or limitation of remedy under this section.

8. As with express warranties, no specific language or intention is necessary to create an obligation, and whether an obligation exists is normally an issue of fact. Subsection (3) is virtually identical to Section 2–313(3), and the tests developed under the common law and under that section to determine whether a statement creates an obligation or is mere puffing are applicable to this section.

Just as a seller can limit the extent to which its language creates an express warranty under Section 2–313 by placing that language in a broader context, a seller under this section or Section 2–313B can limit the extent of its liability to a remote purchaser (subsection(4)(a)). In other words, the seller, in undertaking an obligation under these sections, can control the scope and limits of that obligation.

9. As a rule, a remote purchaser may recover monetary damages measured in the same manner as in the case of an aggrieved buyer under Section 2–714 as well as incidental and consequential damages under Section 2–715 to the extent they would be available to an aggrieved buyer. Subsection (5)(c) parallels Section 2–714(1) in allowing the buyer to recover for loss resulting in the ordinary course of events as determined in any manner which is reasonable. In the case of an obligation that is not a remedial promise, the normal measure of damages would be the difference between the value of the goods if they had conformed to the seller's statements and their actual value, and the normal measure of damages for breach of a remedial promise would be the difference between the value of the promised remedial performance and the value of the actual performance received.

Subsection (5)(b) precludes a remote purchaser from recovering consequential damages in the form of lost profits.

§ 2–313B. Obligation to Remote Purchaser Created By Communication to the Public

(1) In this section:

    (a) "Immediate buyer" means a buyer that enters into a contract with the seller.

    (b) "Remote purchaser" means a person that buys or leases goods from an immediate buyer or other person in the normal chain of distribution.

(2) This section applies only to new goods and goods sold or leased as new goods in a transaction of purchase in the normal chain of distribution.

(3) If in an advertisement or a similar communication to the public a seller makes an affirmation of fact or promise that relates to the goods, provides a description that relates to the goods, or makes a remedial promise, and the remote purchaser enters into a transaction of purchase with knowledge of and with the expectation that the goods will conform

to the affirmation of fact, promise, or description, or that the seller will perform the remedial promise, the seller has an obligation to the remote purchaser that:

(a) the goods will conform to the affirmation of fact, promise, or description unless a reasonable person in the position of the remote purchaser would not believe that the affirmation of fact, promise, or description created an obligation; and

(b) the seller will perform the remedial promise.

(4) It is not necessary to the creation of an obligation under this section that the seller use formal words such as "warrant" or "guarantee" or that the seller have a specific intention to undertake an obligation, but an affirmation merely of the value of the goods or a statement purporting to be merely the seller's opinion or commendation of the goods does not create an obligation.

(5) The following rules apply to the remedies for breach of an obligation created under this section:

(a) The seller may modify or limit the remedies available to the remote purchaser if the modification or limitation is furnished to the remote purchaser no later than the time of purchase. The modification or limitation may be furnished as part of the communication that contains the affirmation of fact, promise, or description.

(b) Subject to a modification or limitation of remedy, a seller in breach is liable for incidental or consequential damages under Section 2–715, but not for lost profits.

(c) The remote purchaser may recover as damages for breach of a seller's obligation arising under subsection (3) the loss resulting in the ordinary course of events as determined in any reasonable manner.

(6) An obligation that is not a remedial promise is breached if the goods did not conform to the affirmation of fact, promise, or description creating the obligation when the goods left the seller's control.

Official Comment

1. Sections 2–313B and 2–313A are new, and they follow case law and practice in extending a seller's obligations for new goods to remote purchasers. This section deals with obligations to a remote purchaser created by advertising or a similar communication to the public. The normal situation where this obligation will arise is when a manufacturer engages in an advertising campaign directed towards all or part of the market for its product and will make statements that if made to an immediate buyer would amount to an express warranty or remedial promise under Section 2–313. The goods, however, are sold to someone other than the recipient of the advertising and are then resold or leased to the recipient. By imposing liability on the seller, this section adopts the approach of cases such as *Randy Knitwear, Inc. v. American Cyanamid Co.*,

11 N.Y.2d 5, 226 N.Y.S.2d 363, 181 N.E.2d 399 (Ct. App. 1962).

If the seller's advertisement is made to an immediate buyer, whether the seller incurs liability is determined by Section 2–313 and this section is inapplicable.

2. This section parallels Section 2–313A in most respects, and the Official Comments to that section should be consulted. In particular, the reasoning of Comment 1 (scope and terminology), Comment 2 (definition of remote purchaser), Comment 3 (new goods and goods sold as new goods in the normal chain of distribution), Comment 4 (reasonable person in the position of the remote purchaser), Comment 7 (modification or limitation of remedy), Comment 8 (puffing and limitations on extent of obligation) and Comment 9 (damages) is adopted here.

3. This section provides an additional test for enforceability not found in Section 2–313A. For the obligation to be created the remote purchaser must, at the time of purchase, have knowledge of the affirmation of fact, promise, description or remedial promise and must also have an expectation that the goods will conform or that the seller will comply. This test is entirely subjective, while the reasonable person test in subsection (3)(a) is objective in nature. Both tests must be met.

Thus, the seller will incur no liability to the remote purchaser if: i) the purchaser did not have knowledge of the seller's statement at the time of purchase; ii) the remote purchaser knew of the seller's statement at the time of purchase but did not expect the goods to conform or the seller to comply; iii) a reasonable person in the position of the remote purchaser would not believe that the seller's statement created an obligation (this test does not apply to remedial promises), or iv) the seller's statement is puffing.

4. To determine whether the tests set forth in this section are satisfied the temporal relationship between the communication and the purchase should be considered by the court. For example, the remote purchaser may acquire the goods years after the seller's advertising campaign. In this circumstance, it would be highly unusual for the advertisement to have created the level of expectation in the remote purchaser or belief in the reasonable person in the position of the remote person necessary for the creation of an obligation under this section.

5. To determine whether an obligation arises under this Section, all information known to the remote purchaser at the time of contracting must be considered. For example, a news release by a manufacturer limiting the statements made in its advertising and which are known by the remote purchaser, or a communication to the remote purchaser by the immediate seller limiting the statements made in the manufacturer's advertising must be considered to determine whether the expectation requirement applicable to the remote purchaser and the belief requirement applicable to the reasonable person in the position of the remote purchaser are satisfied.

6. The remedies for breach of an obligation arising under this section may be modified or limited as set forth in Section 2–719. The modification or limitation may be contained in the advertisement that creates the obligation, or it may be separately furnished to the remote purchaser no later than the time of purchase.

7. Section 2–318 deals with the extension of obligations to certain third-party beneficiaries. Of course, no extension is necessary if the goods are purchased by an agent. In this case, the knowledge and expectation of the principal, not the agent, are relevant in determining whether an obligation

arises under this section. Nothing in this Act precludes a court from deter-   mining that a household operates as a buying unit under the law of agency.

§ 2–314. Implied Warranty: Merchantability; Usage of Trade

(1) Unless excluded or modified (Section 2–316), a warranty that the goods shall be merchantable is implied in a contract for their sale if the seller is a merchant with respect to goods of that kind. Under this section the serving for value of food or drink to be consumed either on the premises or elsewhere is a sale.

(2) Goods to be merchantable must be at least such as:

    (a) pass without objection in the trade under the contract description; ~~and~~

    (b) in the case of fungible goods, are of fair average quality within the description; ~~and~~

    (c) are fit for the ordinary purposes for which ~~such~~ goods of that description are used; ~~and~~

    (d) run, within the variations permitted by the agreement, of even kind, quality and quantity within each unit and among all units involved; ~~and~~

    (e) are adequately contained, packaged, and labeled as the agreement may require; and

    (f) conform to the promise or affirmations of fact made on the container or label if any.

(3) Unless excluded or modified (Section 2–316) other implied warranties may arise from course of dealing or usage of trade.

Official Comment

1. The phrase "goods of that description" rather than the language from the original Article 2 "for which such goods are used" is used in subsection (2)(c). This change emphasizes the importance of the agreed description in determining fitness for ordinary purposes.

2. The seller's obligation applies to present sales as well as to contracts to sell subject to the effects of any examination of specific goods. *See* Section 2–316(3)(b). The warranty of merchantability also applies to sales for use as well as to sales for resale.

3. The question when the warranty is imposed turns basically on the meaning of the terms of the agreement as recognized in the trade. Goods delivered under an agreement made by a merchant in a given line of trade must be of a quality comparable to that generally acceptable in that line of trade under the description or other designation of the goods used in the agreement. The responsibility imposed rests on any merchant-seller.

4. A specific designation of goods by the buyer does not exclude the seller's obligation that they be fit for the general purposes appropriate to the goods. A contract for the sale of second-hand goods, however, involves only an obligation as is appropriate to the goods according to their contract description. A person making an isolated sale of goods is not a "merchant"

within the meaning of the full scope of this section and, thus, no warranty of merchantability would apply. The seller's knowledge of any defects not apparent on inspection would, however, without need for express agreement and in keeping with the underlying reason of the present section and the provisions on good faith, impose an obligation that known material but hidden defects be fully disclosed.

5. Although a seller may not be a "merchant" for the goods in question, if the seller states generally that the goods are "guaranteed," the provisions of this section may furnish a guide to the content of the resulting express warranty. This has particular significance in the case of second-hand sales, and has further significance in limiting the effect of fine-print disclaimer clauses where their effect would be inconsistent with large-print assertions of "guarantee."

6. The second sentence of subsection (1) covers the warranty for food and drink. The serving for value of food or drink for consumption on the premises or elsewhere is treated as a sale.

7. Suppose that an unmerchantable lawn mower causes personal injury to the buyer, who is operating the mower. Without more, the buyer can sue the seller for breach of the implied warranty of merchantability and recover for injury to person "proximately resulting" from the breach. Section 2–715(2)(b).

This opportunity does not resolve the tension between warranty law and tort law where goods cause personal injury or property damage. The primary source of that tension arises from disagreement over whether the concept of defect in tort and the concept of merchantability in Article 2 are coextensive where personal injuries are involved, *i.e.*, if goods are merchantable under warranty law, can they still

be defective under tort law, and if goods are not defective under tort law, can they be unmerchantable under warranty law? The answer to both questions should be no, and the tension between merchantability in warranty and defect in tort where personal injury or property damage is involved should be resolved as follows:

> When recovery is sought for injury to person or property, whether goods are merchantable is to be determined by applicable state products liability law. When, however, a claim for injury to person or property is based on an implied warranty of fitness under Section 2–315 or an express warranty under Section 2–313 or an obligation arising under Section 2–313A or 2–313B, this Article determines whether an implied warranty of fitness or an express warranty was made and breached, as well as what damages are recoverable under Section 2–715.

To illustrate, suppose that the seller makes a representation about the safety of a lawn mower that becomes part of the basis of the buyer's bargain. The buyer is injured when the gas tank cracks and a fire breaks out. If the lawnmower without the representation is not defective under applicable tort law, it is not unmerchantable under this section. On the other hand, if the lawnmower did not conform to the representation about safety, the seller made and breached an express warranty and the buyer may sue under Article 2.

8. Subsection (2) does not purport to exhaust the meaning of "merchantable" nor to negate any of its attributes not specifically mentioned in the text of the statute but that arise by usage of trade or through case law. The language used is "must be at least such as ...," and the intention is to

leave open other possible attributes of merchantability.

9. Paragraphs (a) and (b) of subsection (2) are to be read together. Both refer to the standards of that line of the trade which fits the transaction and the seller's business. "Fair average" is a term directly appropriate to agricultural bulk products and means goods centering around the middle belt of quality, not the least or the worst that can be understood in the particular trade by the designation, but such as can pass "without objection." Of course a fair percentage of the least is permissible but the goods are not "fair average" if they are all of the least or worst quality possible under the description. In cases of doubt about what quality is intended, the price at which a merchant closes a contract is an excellent indication of the nature and scope of the merchant's obligation under the present section.

10. Fitness for the ordinary purposes for which goods of the type are used is a fundamental concept of the present section and is covered in paragraph (2)(c). As stated above, merchantability is also a part of the obligation owing to the buyer for use. Correspondingly, protection, under this aspect of the warranty, of the person buying for resale to the ultimate consumer is equally necessary, and merchantable goods must therefore be "honestly" resalable in the normal course of business because they are what they purport to be.

11. Paragraph (2)(d) on evenness of kind, quality and quantity follows case law. But precautionary language has been added as a remainder of the frequent usages of trade which permit substantial variations both with and without an allowance or an obligation to replace the varying units.

12. Paragraph (2)(e) applies only where the nature of the goods and of the transaction require a certain type of container, package or label. Paragraph (2)(f) applies, on the other hand, wherever there is a label or container on which representations are made, even though the original contract, either by express terms or usage of trade, may not have required either the labeling or the representation. This follows from the general obligation of good faith which requires that a buyer should not be placed in the position of reselling or using goods delivered under false representations appearing on the package or container. No problem of extra consideration arises in this connection since, under this Article, an obligation is imposed by the original contract not to deliver mislabeled articles, and the obligation is imposed where mercantile good faith so requires and without reference to the doctrine of consideration.

13. Exclusion or modification of the warranty of merchantability, or of any part of it, is dealt with in Section 2–316. That section must be read with particular reference to subsection (4) on limitation of remedies. The warranty of merchantability, wherever it is normal, is so commonly taken for granted that its exclusion from the contract is a matter threatening surprise and therefore requiring special precaution.

14. Subsection (3) is to make explicit that usage of trade and course of dealing can create warranties and that they are implied rather than express warranties and thus subject to exclusion or modification under Section 2–316. A typical instance would be the obligation to provide pedigree papers to evidence conformity of the animal to the contract in the case of a pedigreed dog or blooded bull.

15. In an action based on breach of warranty, it is of course necessary to show not only the existence of the warranty but the fact that the warranty

was broken and that the breach of the warranty was the proximate cause of the loss sustained. An affirmative showing by the seller that the loss resulted from some action or event following the seller's delivery of the goods can operate as a defense. Equally, evidence indicating that the seller exercised care in the manufacture, processing or selection of the goods is relevant to the issue of whether the warranty was in fact broken. An action by the buyer following an examination of the goods which ought to have indicated the defect complained of can be shown as matter bearing on whether the breach itself was the cause of the injury.

§ 2–315. Implied Warranty: Fitness for Particular Purpose

Where the seller at the time of contracting has reason to know any particular purpose for which the goods are required and that the buyer is relying on the seller's skill or judgment to select or furnish suitable goods, there is unless excluded or modified under the next section an implied warranty that the goods shall be fit for such purpose.

§ 2–316. Exclusion or Modification of Warranties

(1) Words or conduct relevant to the creation of an express warranty and words or conduct tending to negate or limit warranty shall be construed wherever reasonable as consistent with each other; but subject to ~~the provisions of this Article on parol or extrinsic evidence (Section 2–202)~~ Section 2–202, negation or limitation is inoperative to the extent that such construction is unreasonable.

(2) Subject to subsection (3), to exclude or modify the implied warranty of merchantability or any part of it in a consumer contract the language must be in a record, be conspicuous, and state "The seller undertakes no responsibility for the quality of the goods except as otherwise provided in this contract," and in any other contract the language must mention merchantability and in case of a ~~writing~~ record must be conspicuous~~, and to~~. Subject to subsection (3), to exclude or modify the implied warranty of fitness, the exclusion must be ~~by a writing~~ in a record and be conspicuous. Language to exclude all implied warranties of fitness in a consumer contract must state "The seller assumes no responsibility that the goods will be fit for any particular purpose for which you may be buying these goods, except as otherwise provided in the contract," and in any other contract the language is sufficient if it states, for example, that "There are no warranties ~~which~~ that extend beyond the description on the face hereof." Language that satisfies the requirements of this subsection for the exclusion or modification of a warranty in a consumer contract also satisfies the requirements for any other contract.

(3) Notwithstanding subsection (2):

(a) unless the circumstances indicate otherwise, all implied warranties are excluded by expressions like "as is", "with all faults" or other language ~~which~~ that in common understanding calls the buyer's attention to the exclusion of warranties ~~and~~, makes plain that there is no implied warranty, <u>and, in a consumer contract evidenced by a record, is set forth conspicuously in the record</u>; ~~and~~

(b) ~~when~~ <u>if</u> the buyer before entering into the contract has examined the goods or the sample or model as fully as ~~he~~ desired or has refused to examine the goods <u>after a demand by the seller</u> there is no implied warranty with regard to defects ~~which~~ <u>that</u> an examination ~~ought~~ in the circumstances ~~to~~ <u>should</u> have revealed to ~~him~~ <u>the buyer</u>; and

(c) an implied warranty ~~can~~ <u>may</u> also be excluded or modified by course of dealing or course of performance or usage of trade.

(4) Remedies for breach of warranty ~~can~~ <u>may</u> be limited in accordance with ~~the provisions of this article on liquidation or limitation of damages and on contractual modification of remedy (Sections 2–718 and 2–719)~~ <u>Sections 2–718 and 2–719</u>.

Official Comment

1. Subsection (1) is designed principally to deal with those frequent clauses in sales contracts which seek to exclude "all warranties, express or implied." It seeks to protect a buyer from unexpected and unbargained language of disclaimer by denying effect to this language when inconsistent with language of express warranty and permitting the exclusion of implied warranties only by language or other circumstances which protect the buyer from surprise.

The seller is protected against false allegations of oral warranties by this Article's provisions on parol and extrinsic evidence and against unauthorized representations by the customary "lack of authority" clauses. This Article treats the limitation or avoidance of consequential damages as a matter of limiting remedies for breach, separate from the matter of creation of liability under a warranty. If no warranty exists, there is of course no problem of limiting remedies for breach of warranty. Under subsection (4), the question of limitation of remedy is governed by the sections referred to rather than by this section.

2. The general test for disclaimers of implied warranties remains in subsection (3)(a), and the more specific tests are in subsection (2). A disclaimer that satisfies the requirements of subsection (3)(a) need not also satisfy any of the requirements of subsection (2).

3. Subsection (2) distinguishes between commercial and consumer contracts. In a commercial contract, language that disclaims the implied warranty of merchantability need not be in a record, but if it is in a record it must be conspicuous. Under this subsection, a conspicuous record is required to disclaim the implied warranty of merchantability in a consumer contract and to disclaim the implied warranty of fitness in any contract. Use of the language required by this subsection for consumer contracts satisfies the language requirements for other contracts governed by this subsection.

4. Subsection (2) presupposes that the implied warranty in question exists unless excluded or modified. Whether

or not language of disclaimer satisfies the requirements of this section, the language may be relevant under other sections to the question of whether the warranty was ever in fact created. Thus, unless the provisions of this Article on parol and extrinsic evidence prevent its introduction, oral language of a disclaimer may raise issues of fact about whether reliance by the buyer occurred and whether the seller had "reason to know" under the section on implied warranty of fitness for a particular purpose.

5. Subsection (3)(a) deals with general terms such as "as is," "as they stand," "with all faults," and the like. These terms in ordinary commercial usage are understood to mean that the buyer takes the entire risk as to the quality of the goods involved. The terms covered by the subsection are in fact merely a particularization of subsection (3)(c), which provides for exclusion or modification of implied warranties by usage of trade. Nothing in subsection (3)(a) prevents a term such as "there are no implied warranties" from being effective in appropriate circumstances, as when the term is a negotiated term between commercial parties.

Satisfaction of subsection (3)(a) does not require that the language be set forth in a record, but if there is a record the language must be conspicuous if the contract is a consumer contract.

6. The exceptions to the general rule set forth in subsections (3)(b) and (3)(c) are common factual situations in which the circumstances surrounding the transaction are in themselves sufficient to call the buyer's attention to the fact that no implied warranties are made or that a certain implied warranty is being excluded.

Under subsection (3)(b), warranties may be excluded or modified by the circumstances when the buyer exam-

ines the goods or a sample or model of them before entering into the contract. "Examination" as used in this paragraph is not synonymous with inspection before acceptance or at any other time after the contract has been made. Of course if the buyer discovers the defect and uses the goods anyway, or if the buyer unreasonably fails to examine the goods before using them, the resulting injuries may be found to have resulted from the buyer's own action rather than have been proximately caused by a breach of warranty. *See* Sections 2–314 and 2–715.

To bring the transaction within the scope of "refused to examine" in subsection (3)(b), it is not sufficient that the goods are available for inspection. There must in addition be an actual examination by the buyer or a demand by the seller that the buyer examine the goods fully. The seller's demand must place the buyer on notice that the buyer is assuming the risk of defects which the examination ought to reveal.

Application of the doctrine of "caveat emptor" in all cases where the buyer examines the goods regardless of statements made by the seller is, however, rejected by this Article. Thus, if the offer of examination is accompanied by words about their merchantability or specific attributes, and the buyer indicates clearly a reliance on those words rather than on the buyer's examination, the words give rise to an "express" warranty. In these cases, the question is one of fact about whether a warranty of merchantability has been expressly incorporated in the agreement.

The particular buyer's skill and the normal method of examining goods in the circumstances determine what defects are excluded by the examination. A failure to notice defects which are obvious cannot excuse the buyer because of the lack of notice. However, an examination under circumstances which do not permit chemical or other testing of the goods does not exclude defects which could be ascertained only by testing. Nor can latent defects be excluded by a simple examination. A professional buyer examining a product in the buyer's field will be held to have assumed the risk for all defects which a professional in the field ought to observe, while a nonprofessional buyer will be held to have assumed the risk only for the defects as a layperson might be expected to observe.

7. The situation in which the buyer gives precise and complete specifications to the seller is not explicitly covered in this section, but this is a frequent circumstance by which the implied warranties may be excluded. The warranty of fitness for a particular purpose would not normally arise since in this situation there is usually no reliance on the seller by the buyer. The warranty of merchantability in a transaction of this type, however, must be considered in connection with the next section on the cumulation and conflict of warranties. Under paragraph(c) of that section in case of an inconsistency the implied warranty of merchantability is displaced by the express warranty that the goods will comply with the specifications. Thus, where the buyer gives detailed specifications as to the goods, neither of the implied warranties as to quality will normally apply to the transaction unless consistent with the specifications.

§ 2–317. Cumulation and Conflict of Warranties Express or Implied

Warranties whether express or implied shall be construed as consistent with each other and as cumulative, but if such construction is unreasonable the intention of the parties shall determine which warranty is dominant. In ascertaining that intention the following rules apply:

 (a) Exact or technical specifications displace an inconsistent sample or model or general language of description.

 (b) A sample from an existing bulk displaces inconsistent general language of description.

 (c) Express warranties displace inconsistent implied warranties other than an implied warranty of fitness for a particular purpose.

§ 2–318. ~~Third Party~~ Third–Party Beneficiaries of Warranties ~~Express or Implied~~ and Obligations

(1) In this section:

 (a) "Immediate buyer" means a buyer that enters into a contract with the seller.

 (b) "Remote purchaser" means a person that buys or leases goods from an immediate buyer or other person in the normal chain of distribution.

Alternative A to subsection (2)

(2) A seller's warranty whether express or implied extends to any natural person who is in the family or household of his buyer or who is a

~~guest in his home if it is reasonable to expect that such person may use, consume or be affected by the goods and who is injured in person by breach of the warranty.~~ A seller's warranty to an immediate buyer, whether express or implied, a seller's remedial promise to an immediate buyer, or a seller's obligation to a remote purchaser under Section 2–313A or 2–313B extends to any individual who is in the family or household of the immediate buyer or the remote purchaser or who is a guest in the home of either if it is reasonable to expect that the person may use, consume, or be affected by the goods and who is injured in person by breach of the warranty, remedial promise, or obligation. A seller may not exclude or limit the operation of this section.

Alternative B to subsection (2)

(2) ~~A seller's warranty whether express or implied extends to any natural person who may reasonably be expected to use, consume or be affected by the goods and who is injured in person by breach of the warranty.~~ A seller's warranty to an immediate buyer, whether express or implied, a seller's remedial promise to an immediate buyer, or a seller's obligation to a remote purchaser under Section 2–313A or 2–313B extends to any individual who may reasonably be expected to use, consume, or be affected by the goods and who is injured in person by breach of the warranty, remedial promise, or obligation. A seller may not exclude or limit the operation of this section.

Alternative C to subsection (2)

(2) ~~A seller's warranty whether express or implied extends to any person who may reasonably be expected to use, consume or be affected by the goods and who is injured by breach of the warranty.~~ A seller's warranty to an immediate buyer, whether express or implied, a seller's remedial promise to an immediate buyer, or a seller's obligation to a remote purchaser under Section 2–313A or 2–313B extends to any person that may reasonably be expected to use, consume, or be affected by the goods and that is injured by breach of the warranty, remedial promise, or obligation. A seller may not exclude or limit the operation of this section with respect to injury to the person of an individual to whom the warranty, remedial promise, or obligation extends.

Official Comment

1. This section retains original Article 2's alternative approaches but expands each alternative to cover obligations arising under Sections 2–313A and 2–313B and remedial promises.

2. The last sentence of each alternative to subsection (2) is not meant to suggest that a seller is precluded from excluding or disclaiming a warranty which might otherwise arise in connection with the sale provided the exclusion or modification is permitted by Section 2–316. Nor is it intended to suggest that the seller is precluded from limiting the remedies of the immediate buyer or remote purchaser in any manner provided in Sections 2–718 or 2–719. *See also* Section 2–313A(4) and Section 2–313B(4). To

the extent that the contract of sale contains provisions under which warranties are excluded or modified, or remedies for breach are limited, the provisions are equally operative against beneficiaries of warranties under this section. What this last sentence forbids is exclusion of liability by the seller to the persons to whom the warranties, obligations and remedial promises accruing to the immediate buyer or remote purchaser would extend under this section.

Alternative A extends protection to a third party beneficiaries who is a guest in the home of the immediate buyer or remoter purchaser. The status of "guest in the home" describes the category of beneficiaries covered by this provision, and it does not limit the situs of the breach. Thus, a guest in the home that would otherwise have rights under this section could be injured in the automobile of the immediate buyer or remote purchaser. Beyond this, the section is neutral and is not intended to enlarge or restrict the developed or developing case law on whether the seller's warranties, given to his buyer who resells, extend to other persons in the distributive chain.

The last sentence of Alternative C permits a seller to reduce its obligations to third-party beneficiaries to a level commensurate with that imposed on the seller under Alternative B–that

is, to eliminate liability to persons that are not individuals and to eliminate liability for damages other than personal injury.

3. As used in this section, the term "remote purchaser" refers to the party to whom an obligation initially runs under Section 2–313A or 2–313B. It does not refer to any subsequent purchaser of the goods.

4. As applied to warranties and remedial promises arising under Sections 2–313, 2–314 and 2–315, the purpose of this section is to give certain beneficiaries the benefit of the warranties and remedial promises which the immediate buyer received in the contract of sale, thereby freeing any beneficiaries from any technical rules as to "privity." It seeks to accomplish this purpose without any derogation of any right or remedy arising under the law of torts. Implicit in the section is that any beneficiary of a warranty may bring a direct action for breach of warranty against the seller whose warranty extends to the beneficiary.

Obligations and remedial promises under Sections 2–313A and 2–313B arise initially in a non-privity context but are extended under this section to the same extent as warranties and remedial promises running to a buyer in privity.

§ 2–319. F.O.B. and F.A.S. Terms Reserved

(1) Unless otherwise agreed the term F.O.B. (which means "free on board") at a named place, even though used only in connection with the stated price, is a delivery term under which

    (a) when the term is F.O.B. the place of shipment, the seller must at that place ship the goods in the manner provided in this Article (Section 2–504) and bear the expense and risk of putting them into the possession of the carrier; or

    (b) when the term is F.O.B. the place of destination, the seller must at his own expense and risk transport the goods to that place and there tender delivery of them in the manner provided in this Article (Section 2–503);

(c) when under either (a) or (b) the term is also F.O.B. vessel, car or other vehicle, the seller must in addition at his own expense and risk load the goods on board. If the term is F.O.B. vessel the buyer must name the vessel and in an appropriate case the seller must comply with the provisions of this Article on the form of bill of lading (Section 2–323).

(2) Unless otherwise agreed the term F.A.S. vessel (which means "free alongside") at a named port, even though used only in connection with the stated price, is a delivery term under which the seller must

(a) at his own expense and risk deliver the goods alongside the vessel in the manner usual in that port or on a dock designated and provided by the buyer; and

(b) obtain and tender a receipt for the goods in exchange for which the carrier is under a duty to issue a bill of lading.

(3) Unless otherwise agreed in any case falling within subsection (1)(a) or(c) or subsection (2) the buyer must seasonably give any needed instructions for making delivery, including when the term is F.A.S. or F.O.B. the loading berth of the vessel and in an appropriate case its name and sailing date. The seller may treat the failure of needed instructions as a failure of cooperation under this Article (Section 2–311). He may also at his option move the goods in any reasonable manner preparatory to delivery or shipment.

(4) Under the term F.O.B. vessel or F.A.S. unless otherwise agreed the buyer must make payment against tender of the required documents and the seller may not tender nor the buyer demand delivery of the goods in substitution for the documents.

Legislative Note: Sections 2–319 through 2–324 have been eliminated because they are inconsistent with modern commercial practices.

Official Comment

Sections 2–319 through 2–324 have been repealed. The effect of a party's use of shipping terms such as "FOB," "CIF," or the like, absent any express agreement to the meaning of the terms, must be interpreted in light of any applicable usage of trade and any course of performance or course of dealing between the parties.

§ 2–320. C.I.F. and C. & F. Terms Reserved

(1) The term C.I.F. means that the price includes in a lump sum the cost of the goods and the insurance and freight to the named destination. The term C. & F. or C.F. means that the price so includes cost and freight to the named destination.

(2) Unless otherwise agreed and even though used only in connection with the stated price and destination, the term C.I.F. destination or its equivalent requires the seller at his own expense and risk to

(a) put the goods into the possession of a carrier at the port for shipment and obtain a negotiable bill or bills of lading

162

covering the entire transportation to the named destination; and

(b) load the goods and obtain a receipt from the carrier (which may be contained in the bill of lading) showing that the freight has been paid or provided for; and

(c) obtain a policy or certificate of insurance, including any war risk insurance, of a kind and on terms then current at the port of shipment in the usual amount, in the currency of the contract, shown to cover the same goods covered by the bill of lading and providing for payment of loss to the order of the buyer or for the account of whom it may concern; but the seller may add to the price the amount of the premium for any such war risk insurance; and

(d) prepare an invoice of the goods and procure any other documents required to effect shipment or to comply with the contract; and

(e) forward and tender with commercial promptness all the documents in due form and with any indorsement necessary to perfect the buyer's rights.

(3) Unless otherwise agreed the term C. & F. or its equivalent has the same effect and imposes upon the seller the same obligations and risks as a C.I.F. term except the obligation as to insurance.

(4) Under the term C.I.F. or C. & F. unless otherwise agreed the buyer must make payment against tender of the required documents and the seller may not tender nor the buyer demand delivery of the goods in substitution for the documents.

§ 2–321. C.I.F. or C. & F.: "Net Landed Weights"; "Payment on Arrival"; Warranty of Condition on Arrival Reserved

Under a contract containing a term C.I.F. or C. & F.

(1) Where the price is based on or is to be adjusted according to "net landed weights", "delivered weights", "out turn" quantity or quality or the like, unless otherwise agreed the seller must reasonably estimate the price. The payment due on tender of the documents called for by the contract is the amount so estimated, but after final adjustment of the price a settlement must be made with commercial promptness.

(2) An agreement described in subsection (1) or any warranty of quality or condition of the goods on arrival places upon the seller the risk of ordinary deterioration, shrinkage and the like in transportation but has no effect on the place or time of identification to the contract for sale or delivery or on the passing of the risk of loss.

(3) Unless otherwise agreed where the contract provides for payment on or after arrival of the goods the seller must before payment allow such preliminary inspection as is feasible; but if the goods are lost delivery of the documents and payment are due when the goods should have arrived.

§ 2–322. ~~Delivery "Ex–Ship"~~ Reserved

(1) Unless otherwise agreed a term for delivery of goods "ex-ship" (which means from the carrying vessel) or in equivalent language is not restricted to a particular ship and requires delivery from a ship which has reached a place at the named port of destination where goods of the kind are usually discharged.

(2) Under such a term unless otherwise agreed

    (a) the seller must discharge all liens arising out of the carriage and furnish the buyer with a direction which puts the carrier under a duty to deliver the goods; and

    (b) the risk of loss does not pass to the buyer until the goods leave the ship's tackle or are otherwise properly unloaded.

§ 2–323. ~~Form of Bill of Lading Required in Overseas Shipment; "Overseas"~~ Reserved

(1) Where the contract contemplates overseas shipment and contains a term C.I.F. or C. & F. or F.O.B. vessel, the seller unless otherwise agreed must obtain a negotiable bill of lading stating that the goods have been loaded in board or, in the case of a term C.I.F. or C. & F., received for shipment.

(2) Where in a case within subsection (1) a bill of lading has been issued in a set of parts, unless otherwise agreed if the documents are not to be sent from abroad the buyer may demand tender of the full set; otherwise only one part of the bill of lading need be tendered. Even if the agreement expressly requires a full set

    (a) due tender of a single part is acceptable within the provisions of this Article on cure of improper delivery (subsection (1) of Section 2–508); and

    (b) even though the full set is demanded, if the documents are sent from abroad the person tendering an incomplete set may nevertheless require payment upon furnishing an indemnity which the buyer in good faith deems adequate.

(3) A shipment by water or by air or a contract contemplating such shipment is "overseas" insofar as by usage of trade or agreement it is subject to the commercial, financing or shipping practices characteristic of international deep water commerce.

§ 2-324. ~~"No Arrival, No Sale" Term~~ Reserved

~~Under a term "no arrival, no sale" or terms of like meaning, unless otherwise agreed,~~

> ~~(a) the seller must properly ship conforming goods and if they arrive by any means he must tender them on arrival but he assumes no obligation that the goods will arrive unless he has caused the non-arrival; and~~

> ~~(b) where without fault of the seller the goods are in part lost or have so deteriorated as no longer to conform to the contract or arrive after the contract time, the buyer may proceed as if there had been casualty to identified goods (Section 2-613).~~

§ 2-325. ~~"Letter of Credit" Term; "Confirmed Credit"~~ Failure to Pay By Agreed Letter of Credit

~~(1) Failure of the buyer seasonably to furnish an agreed letter of credit is a breach of the contract for sale.~~

~~(2) The delivery to seller of a proper letter of credit suspends the buyer's obligation to pay. If the letter of credit is dishonored, the seller may on seasonable notification to the buyer require payment directly from him.~~

~~(3) Unless otherwise agreed the term "letter of credit" or "banker's credit" in a contract for sale means an irrevocable credit issued by a financing agency of good repute and, where the shipment is overseas, of good international repute. The term "confirmed credit" means that the credit must also carry the direct obligation of such an agency which does business in the seller's financial market.~~

If the parties agree that the primary method of payment will be by letter of credit, the following rules apply:

> (a) The buyer's obligation to pay is suspended by seasonable delivery to the seller of a letter of credit issued or confirmed by a financing agency of good repute in which the issuer and any confirmer undertake to pay against presentation of documents that evidence delivery of the goods.

> (b) Failure of a party seasonably to furnish a letter of credit as agreed is a breach of the contract for sale.

> (c) If the letter of credit is dishonored or repudiated, the seller, on seasonable notification, may require payment directly from the buyer.

Official Comment

1. This section conforms to revised Article 5.

2. Subsection (c) follows the general policy of this Article and Article 3 (Section 3-310) on conditional pay-

ment, under which payment by check or other short-term instrument is not ordinarily final between the parties if the recipient presents the instrument and it is not paid. Thus the furnishing of a letter of credit does not substitute the financing agency's obligation for the buyer's, but the seller must first give the buyer reasonable notice of his intention to demand direct payment from the buyer.

§ 2–326. Sale on Approval and Sale or Return; ~~Consignment Sales and Rights of Creditors~~

(1) Unless otherwise agreed, if delivered goods may be returned by the buyer even ~~though~~ if they conform to the contract, the transaction is<u>:</u>

    (a) a "sale on approval" if the goods are delivered primarily for ~~use,~~ <u>use</u>; and

    (b) a "sale or return" if the goods are delivered primarily for resale.

(2) Goods held on approval are not subject to the claims of the buyer's creditors until acceptance; goods held on sale or return are subject to such claims while in the buyer's possession.

(3) Any "or return" term of a contract for sale is to be treated as a separate contract for sale ~~within the statute of frauds section of this Article (Section 2–201)~~ <u>under Section 2–201</u> and as contradicting the sale aspect of the contract ~~within the provisions of this Article on parol or extrinsic evidence (Section 2–202)~~ <u>under Section 2–202</u>.

Official Comment

1. Both a "sale on approval" and a "sale or return" should be distinguished from other types of transactions with which they frequently have been confused. A "sale on approval," sometimes also called a "sale on trial" or "on satisfaction," deals with a contract under which the seller undertakes a risk in order to satisfy its prospective buyer with the appearance or performance of the goods that are sold. The goods are delivered to the prospective purchaser but they remain the property of the seller until the buyer accepts them. The price has already been agreed. The buyer's willingness to receive and test the goods is the consideration for the seller's engagement to deliver and sell. A "sale or return," on the other hand, typically is a sale to a merchant whose unwillingness to buy is overcome by the seller's engagement to take back the goods (or any commercial unit of goods) in lieu of payment if they fail to be resold. A "sale or return" is a present sale of goods which may be undone at the buyer's option. Accordingly, subsection (2) provides that goods delivered on approval are not subject to the prospective buyer's creditors until acceptance, and goods delivered in a sale or return are subject to the buyer's creditors while in the buyer's possession.

These two transactions are so strongly delineated in practice and in general understanding that every presumption runs against a delivery to a consumer being a "sale or return" and against a delivery to a merchant for resale being a "sale on approval."

2. The right to return goods for failure to conform to the contract of sale does not make the transaction a "sale on approval" or "sale or return" and has nothing to do with this section or Section 2–327. This section is not

concerned with remedies for breach of contract. It deals instead with a power given by the contract to turn back the goods even though they are wholly as warranted. This section nevertheless presupposes that a contract for sale is contemplated by the parties, although that contract may be of the particular character that this section addresses (*i.e.*, a sale on approval or a sale or return).

If a buyer's obligation as a buyer is conditioned not on its personal approval but on the article's passing a described objective test, the risk of loss by casualty pending the test is properly the seller's and proper return is at its expense. On the point of "satisfaction" as meaning "reasonable satisfaction" when an industrial machine is involved, this Article takes no position.

3. Subsection (3) resolves a conflict in the pre-UCC case law by recognizing that an "or return" provision is so definitely at odds with any ordinary contract for sale of goods that if written agreement is involved the "return" term must be contained in a written memorandum. The "or return" aspect of a sales contract must be treated as a separate contract under the statute of frauds section and as contradicting the sale insofar as questions of parol or extrinsic evidence are concerned.

4. Certain true consignments transactions were dealt with in former Sections 2–326(3) and 9–114. These provisions have been deleted and have been replaced by new provisions of Article 9. *See e.g.*, Sections 9–109(a)(4); 9–103(d); 9–319.

§ 2–327. Special Incidents of Sale on Approval and Sale or Return

(1) Under a sale on approval unless otherwise agreed

    (a) although the goods are identified to the contract the risk of loss and the title do not pass to the buyer until acceptance; and

    (b) use of the goods consistent with the purpose of trial is not acceptance but failure seasonably to notify the seller of election to return the goods is acceptance, and if the goods conform to the contract acceptance of any part is acceptance of the whole; and

    (c) after due notification of election to return, the return is at the seller's risk and expense but a merchant buyer must follow any reasonable instructions.

(2) Under a sale or return unless otherwise agreed

    (a) the option to return extends to the whole or any commercial unit of the goods while in substantially their original condition, but must be exercised seasonably; and

    (b) the return is at the buyer's risk and expense.

§ 2–328. Sale By Auction

(1) In a sale by auction, if goods are put up in lots, each lot is the subject of a separate sale.

(2) A sale by auction is complete when the auctioneer so announces by the fall of the hammer or in other customary manner. ~~Where~~ If a bid is made ~~while the hammer is falling in acceptance of~~ during the process of completing the sale but before a prior bid is accepted, the auctioneer ~~may in his~~ has discretion to reopen the bidding or to declare the goods sold under the prior bid ~~on which the hammer was falling~~.

(3) ~~Such a sale is with reserve unless the goods are in explicit terms put up without reserve. In an auction with reserve the auctioneer may withdraw the goods at any time until he announces completion of the sale. In an auction without reserve, after the auctioneer calls for bids on an article or lot, that article or lot cannot be withdrawn unless no bid is made within a reasonable time. In either case a bidder may retract his bid until the auctioneer's announcement of completion of the sale, but a bidder's retraction does not revive any previous bid.~~ A sale by auction is subject to the seller's right to withdraw the goods unless at the time the goods are put up or during the course of the auction it is announced in express terms that the right to withdraw the goods is not reserved. In an auction in which the right to withdraw the goods is reserved, the auctioneer may withdraw the goods at any time until completion of the sale is announced by the auctioneer. In an auction in which the right to withdraw the goods is not reserved, after the auctioneer calls for bids on an article or lot, the article or lot may not be withdrawn unless no bid is made within a reasonable time. In either case a bidder may retract a bid until the auctioneer's announcement of completion of the sale, but a bidder's retraction does not revive any previous bid.

(4) If the auctioneer knowingly receives a bid on the seller's behalf or the seller makes or procures such a bid, and notice has not been given that liberty for such bidding is reserved, the buyer may at ~~his~~ the buyer's option avoid the sale or take the goods at the price of the last ~~good faith~~ good-faith bid prior to the completion of the sale. This subsection shall not apply to any bid at ~~a forced sale~~ an auction required by law.

Official Comment

1. The auctioneer may use discretion either in reopening the bidding or closing the sale on a bid made during the process of completing the sale when a bid is made at that moment. The recognition of a bid of this kind by the auctioneer does not mean a closing in favor of the bidder, but only that the bid has been accepted as a continuation of the bidding. If recognized, this bid discharges the bid made during the process of completing the sale.

2. An auction with the right to withdraw the goods is the normal procedure. Because of different usage, the phrases "with reserve" and "without reserve" are no longer used in this section. Nevertheless, auction sales subject to the seller's power to withdraw the goods are known as sales "with reserve," while auction sales where the seller has no power to withdraw the goods are known as sales "without reserve" or "absolute" sales.

3. Suppose, during the course of an auction where the seller reserves pow-

er to withdraw the goods, the auctioneer expressly announces that the seller no longer reserves power to withdraw the goods. Original Section 2–328(3) did not recognize this possibility, which exists in practice. Such a conversion, in effect, announces a "re- serve bid" in that the goods will not be sold below the last bid before the conversion. A sale "without reserve" can also be converted to a sale "with reserve" during the course of the auction.

PART 4

TITLE, CREDITORS, AND GOOD–FAITH PURCHASERS

§ 2–401. Passing of Title; Reservation for Security; Limited Application of This Section

Each provision of this Article with regard to the rights, obligations, and remedies of the seller, the buyer, purchasers, or other third parties applies irrespective of title to the goods except where the provision refers to such title. Insofar as situations are not covered by the other provisions of this Article and matters concerning title become material, the following rules apply:

(1) Title to goods cannot pass under a contract for sale prior to their identification to the contract (Section 2–501), and unless otherwise explicitly agreed, the buyer acquires by their identification a special property as limited by this Act. Any retention or reservation by the seller of the title (property) in goods shipped or delivered to the buyer is limited in effect to a reservation of a security interest. Subject to these provisions and to ~~the provisions of the Article on Secured Transactions (Article 9)~~ Article 9, title to goods passes from the seller to the buyer in any manner and on any conditions explicitly agreed on by the parties.

(2) Unless otherwise explicitly agreed title passes to the buyer at the time and place at which the seller completes ~~his~~ performance with reference to the ~~physical~~ delivery of the goods, despite any reservation of a security interest and even ~~though~~ if a document of title is to be delivered at a different time or place; and in particular and despite any reservation of a security interest by the bill of lading:

    (a) if the contract requires or authorizes the seller to send the goods to the buyer but does not require ~~him~~ the seller to deliver them at destination, title passes to the buyer at the time and place of shipment; but

    (b) if the contract requires delivery at destination, title passes on tender there.

(3) Unless otherwise explicitly agreed, ~~where~~ if delivery is to be made without moving the ~~goods,~~ goods:

    (a) if the seller is to deliver a tangible document of title, title passes at the time when and the place where ~~he~~ the seller delivers ~~such documents~~ the document, and if the seller is to

169

deliver an electronic document of title, title passes when the seller delivers the document; or

   (b) if the goods are at the time of contracting already identified and no documents of title are to be delivered, title passes at the time and place of contracting.

(4) A rejection or other refusal by the buyer to receive or retain the goods, whether or not justified, or a justified revocation of acceptance revests title to the goods in the seller. Such revesting occurs by operation of law and is not a "sale".

§ 2–402. Rights of Seller's Creditors Against Sold Goods

(1) Except as provided in subsections (2) and (3), rights of unsecured creditors of the seller with respect to goods which that have been identified to a contract for sale are subject to the buyer's rights to recover the goods under this Article (Sections 2–502 and 2–716) Sections 2–502 and 2–716.

(2) A creditor of the seller may treat a sale or an identification of goods to a contract for sale as void if as against him the creditor a retention of possession by the seller is fraudulent under any rule of law of the state where the goods are situated, except that situated. However, retention of possession in good faith and current course of trade by a merchant-seller for a commercially reasonable time after a sale or identification is not fraudulent.

(3) Nothing Except as otherwise provided in Section 2–403(2), nothing in this Article shall be deemed to impair the rights of creditors of the seller:

   (a) under the provisions of the Article on Secured Transactions (Article 9) Article 9; or

   (b) where if identification to the contract or delivery is made not in current course of trade but in satisfaction of or as security for a pre-existing preexisting claim for money, security, or the like and is made under circumstances which that under any rule of law of the state where the goods are situated would apart from this Article constitute the transaction a fraudulent transfer or voidable preference.

§ 2–403. Power to Transfer; Good Faith Purchase of Goods; "Entrusting"

(1) A purchaser of goods acquires all title which his that the purchaser's transferor had or had power to transfer except that a purchaser of a limited interest acquires rights only to the extent of the interest purchased. A person with voidable title has power to transfer a good title to a good faith good-faith purchaser for value. When If goods

have been delivered under a transaction of purchase, the purchaser has such power even ~~though~~ if:

(a) the transferor was deceived as to the identity of the ~~purchaser, or~~ purchaser;

(b) the delivery was in exchange for a check ~~which~~ that is later ~~dishonored, or~~ dishonored;

(c) it was agreed that the transaction was to be a "cash ~~sale",~~ "sale"; or

(d) the delivery was procured through criminal fraud ~~punishable as larcenous under the criminal law~~.

(2) Any entrusting ~~of possession~~ of goods to a merchant ~~who~~ that deals in goods of that kind gives ~~him~~ the merchant power to transfer ~~all rights of the entruster~~ all of the entruster's rights to the goods and to transfer the goods free of any interest of the entruster to a buyer in ordinary course of business.

(3) "Entrusting" includes any delivery and any acquiescence in retention of possession regardless of any condition expressed between the parties to the delivery or acquiescence and regardless of whether the procurement of the entrusting or the possessor's disposition of the goods ~~have been such as to be larcenous~~ was punishable under the criminal law.

[*Legislative Note: If a state adopts the repealer of Article 6—Bulk Transfers (Alternative A), subsection (4) should read as follows:*]

(4) The rights of other purchasers of goods and of lien creditors are governed by ~~the Articles on Secured Transactions (Article 9) and Documents of Title (Article 7)~~ Articles 7 and 9.

[*Legislative Note: If a state adopts revised Article 6—Bulk Sales (Alternative B), subsection (4) should read as follows:*]

(4) The rights of other purchasers of goods and of lien creditors are governed by ~~the Articles on Secured Transactions (Article 9), Bulk Sales (Article 6) and Documents of Title (Article 7)~~ Articles 6, 7, and 9.

Official Comment

1. The basic policy that allows the transfer of such title as the transferor has is recognized under subsection (1). In this respect, the provisions of the section are applicable to a person taking by any form of "purchase" as defined by this Act. (Section 1-201(a)(29)). Moreover the policy of this Act expressly providing for the application of supplementary general principles of law to sales transactions wherever appropriate (Section 1-103) joins with the present section to continue unimpaired all rights acquired under the law of agency or of apparent agency or ownership or other estoppel, whether based on statutory provisions or on case law. The section also leaves unimpaired the powers given to selling factors under the earlier Factors Acts. In addition, subsection (1) provides specifically for the protection of the good faith purchaser for value in a

number of specific situations which were troublesome under prior law.

On the other hand, the contract of purchase is of course limited by its own terms, as in a case of pledge for a limited amount, or of sale of a fractional interest in goods.

2. The many particular situations in which a buyer in ordinary course of business has been protected against a reservation of a property right or other interest are gathered by subsections (2) and (3) into a single principle protecting persons that buy in ordinary course of business. Consignors have no reason to complain, nor have lenders who hold a security interest in the inventory, since the very purpose of goods in inventory is to be turned into cash by sale. (Section 9–109, which provides that a consignment is within the scope of Article 9; Section 9–315(a), which provides that Article 9 security interests are defeated by the rights of a buyer in ordinary course of business under Section 2–403(2).).

The principle is extended in subsection (3) to fit with the abolition of the old law of "cash sale" by subsection (1)(c). It is freed from any local or specific technicalities, and it extends law to any criminal fraud or conduct punishable under criminal law. The policy is extended, in the interest of simplicity and sense, to any entrusting by a bailor. This is in consonance with the explicit provisions of Section 7–205 on the powers of a warehouse that is also in the business of buying and selling goods of the kind that are warehoused. As to entrusting by a secured party, subsection (2) provides that a buyer in ordinary course of business takes free of the security interest. (*See* Section 9–315(a)).

3. Except as provided in subsection (1), the rights of purchasers other than buyers in ordinary course are left to the Articles on Secured Transactions (Article 9) and Documents of Title (Article 7).

PART 5

PERFORMANCE

§ 2–501. Insurable Interest in Goods; Manner of Identification of Goods

(1) The buyer obtains a special property and an insurable interest in goods by identification of existing goods as goods to which the contract refers even ~~though~~ if the goods so identified are ~~non-conforming~~ nonconforming and ~~he~~ the buyer has an option to return or reject them. Such identification ~~can~~ may be made at any time and in any manner explicitly agreed to by the parties. In the absence of explicit agreement identification occurs:

(a) when the contract is made if it is for the sale of goods already existing and identified;

(b) if the contract is for the sale of future goods other than those described in paragraph (c), when goods are shipped, marked, or otherwise designated by the seller as goods to which the contract refers;

(c) when the crops are planted or otherwise become growing crops or the young are conceived if the contract is for the sale of unborn young to be born within ~~twelve~~ 12 months after contracting or for the sale of crops to be harvested within ~~twelve~~ 12 months or the next normal harvest season after contracting whichever is longer.

(2) The seller retains an insurable interest in goods so long as title to or any security interest in the goods remains in ~~him and where~~ the seller. If the identification is by the seller alone, ~~he~~ the seller may until default or insolvency or notification to the buyer that the identification is final substitute other goods for those identified.

(3) Nothing in this section impairs any insurable interest recognized under any other statute or rule of law.

§ 2–502. Buyer's Right to Goods on Seller's Insolvency, Repudiation, or Failure to Deliver

(1) Subject to subsections (2) and (3) and even ~~though~~ if the goods have not been shipped, a buyer ~~who~~ that has paid a part or all of the price of goods in which ~~he~~ the buyer has a special property under ~~the provisions of the immediately preceding section~~ Section 2–501 may on making and keeping good a tender of any unpaid portion of their price recover them from the seller if:

(a) in the case of goods bought ~~for personal, family, or household purposes~~ by a consumer, the seller repudiates or fails to deliver as required by the contract; or

(b) in all cases, the seller becomes insolvent within 10 days after receipt of the first installment on their price.

(2) The buyer's right to recover the goods under subsection (1) vests upon acquisition of a special property, even if the seller had not then repudiated or failed to deliver.

(3) If the identification creating ~~his~~ a special property has been made by ~~the buyer he~~ the buyer, the buyer acquires the right to recover the goods only if they conform to the contract for sale.

Official Comment

1. This section gives an additional right to the buyer as a result of identification of the goods to the contract in the manner provided in Section 2–501. The buyer is given a right to recover the goods, conditioned upon making and keeping good a tender of any unpaid portion of the price, in two limited circumstances. First, a consumer buyer may recover the goods if the seller repudiates the contract or fails to deliver the goods. Second, in any case, the buyer may recover the goods if the seller becomes insolvent within 10 days after the seller receives the first installment on their price. The buyer's right to recover the goods under this section is an exception to the usual rule, under which the disappointed buyer must resort to an action to recover damages.

2. The question of whether the buyer also acquires a security interest in identified goods and has rights to the goods when insolvency takes place

173

after the ten day period provided in this section depends upon compliance with the provisions of the Article on Secured Transactions (Article 9).

3. Under subsection (2), the buyer's right to recover goods under subsection (1) vests upon acquisition of a special property, which occurs upon identification of the goods to the contract. *See* Section 2–501. Inasmuch as a secured party normally acquires no greater rights in its collateral than its debtor had or had power to convey, *see* Section 2–403(1) (first sentence), a buyer who acquires a right to recover under this section will take free of a security interest created by the seller if

it attaches to the goods after the goods have been identified to the contract. The buyer will take free, even if the buyer does not buy in ordinary course and even if the security interest is perfected. Of course, to the extent that the buyer pays the price after the security interest attaches, the payments will constitute proceeds of the security interest.

4. Subsection (3) is included to preclude the possibility of unjust enrichment which would exist if the buyer were permitted to recover goods even though they were greatly superior in quality or quantity to that called for by the contract for sale.

§ 2–503. Manner of Seller's Tender of Delivery

(1) Tender of delivery requires that the seller put and hold conforming goods at the buyer's disposition and give the buyer any notification reasonably necessary to enable ~~him~~ the buyer to take delivery. The manner, time, and place for tender are determined by the agreement and this Article, and in particular:

> (a) tender must be at a reasonable hour, and if it is of goods they must be kept available for the period reasonably necessary to enable the buyer to take possession; but
>
> (b) unless otherwise agreed the buyer must furnish facilities reasonably suited to the receipt of the goods.

(2) ~~Where~~ If the case is within ~~the next section respecting shipment~~ Section 2–504, tender requires that the seller comply with its provisions.

(3) ~~Where~~ If the seller is required to deliver at a particular destination, tender requires that ~~he~~ the seller comply with subsection (1) and also in any appropriate case tender documents as described in subsections (4) and (5) of this section.

(4) ~~Where~~ If goods are in the possession of a bailee and are to be delivered without being moved:

> (a) tender requires that the seller either tender a negotiable document of title covering such goods or procure acknowledgment by the bailee to the buyer of the buyer's right to possession of the goods; but
>
> (b) tender to the buyer of a ~~non-negotiable~~ nonnegotiable document of title or of ~~a written direction to~~ a record directing the bailee to deliver is sufficient tender unless the buyer seasonably objects, and except as otherwise provided in

Article 9 receipt by the bailee of notification of the buyer's rights fixes those rights as against the bailee and all third persons; but risk of loss of the goods and of any failure by the bailee to honor the ~~non-negotiable~~ nonnegotiable document of title or to obey the direction remains on the seller until the buyer has had a reasonable time to present the document or ~~direction, and a refusal~~ direction. Refusal by the bailee to honor the document or to obey the direction defeats the tender.

(5) ~~Where~~ If the contract requires the seller to deliver documents:

    (a) ~~he~~ the seller must tender all such documents in correct form~~, except as provided in this Article with respect to bills of lading in a set (subsection (2) of Section 2–323)~~; and

    (b) tender through customary banking channels is sufficient and dishonor of a draft accompanying or associated with the documents constitutes ~~non-acceptance~~ nonacceptance or rejection.

Official Comment

1. The major general rules governing the manner of proper or due tender of delivery are gathered in this section. The term "tender" is used in this Article in two different senses. In one sense it refers to "due tender," which contemplates an offer coupled with a present ability to fulfill all the conditions that rest on the tendering party, and it must be followed by actual performance if the other party shows readiness to proceed. Unless the context unmistakably indicates otherwise this is the meaning of "tender" in this Article, and the occasional addition of the word "due" is only for clarity and emphasis. At other times it is used to refer to an offer of goods or documents under a contract as if in fulfillment of its conditions even though there is a defect when measured against the contract obligation. Used in either sense, however, "tender" connotes performance by the tendering party that the other party in default if the other party fails to proceed in some manner. These concepts of tender would apply to tender of either tangible or electronic documents of title.

2. The seller's general duty to tender and deliver is set out in Section 2–301 and more particularly in Section 2–507. The seller's right to a receipt if the seller demands one, if receipts are customary, is governed by Section 1–303.

Subsection (1) of this section sets forth two primary requirements of tender: first, that the seller "put and hold conforming goods at the buyer's disposition" and, second, that the seller "give the buyer any notice reasonably necessary to enable the buyer to take delivery."

In cases in which payment is due and demanded upon delivery, the "buyer's disposition" is qualified by the seller's right to reclaim the goods under Section 2–507(2). However, where the seller is demanding payment on delivery the seller must first allow the buyer to inspect the goods to avoid impairing the tender unless the contract contains standard shipping terms or other terms that would negate the right of inspection before payment. (*See* Section 2–513(3)).

In the case of contracts of sale involving documents, the seller can "put and hold conforming goods at the buyer's disposition" under subsection (1) by tendering documents which give the buyer complete control of the goods under the provisions of Article 7.

3. Under paragraph (a) of subsection (1) usage of the trade and the circumstances of the particular case determine what is a reasonable hour for tender and what constitutes a reasonable period of holding the goods available.

4. The buyer must furnish reasonable facilities for the receipt of the goods tendered by the seller under subsection (1), paragraph (b). This obligation of the buyer is not part of the seller's tender.

5. For the purposes of subsections (2) and (3) there is omitted from this Article the rule under prior uniform legislation that a term requiring the seller to pay the freight or cost of transportation to the buyer is equivalent to an agreement by the seller to deliver to the buyer or at an agreed destination. This omission is with the specific intention of negating the rule, for under this Article a "shipment" contract is regarded as the normal one and a "destination" contract as the variant type. The seller is not obligated to deliver at a named destination and bear the concurrent risk of loss until arrival unless the seller has specifically agreed to deliver or the commercial understanding of the terms used by the parties contemplates a destination contract.

6. Under Subsection (4)(a) the bailee's acknowledgment must be made to the buyer. *See Jason's Foods, Inc. V. Peter Eckrick & Sons, Inc.*, 774 F.2d 214 (7th Cir. 1985) Paragraph (b) of

subsection (4) adopts the rule, subject to Article 9, that between the buyer and the seller the risk of loss remains on the seller during a period reasonable for securing acknowledgment of the transfer from the bailee while as against all other parties the buyer's rights are fixed as of the time the bailee receives notice of the transfer.

7. Under subsection (5) documents are never "required" except where there is an express contract term or it is plainly implicit in the peculiar circumstances of the case or in a usage of trade. Documents may, of course, be "authorized" although not required, but these cases are not within the scope of this subsection. When documents are required, there are three main requirements of this subsection: (1) "All": each required document is essential to a proper tender; (2) "Such": the documents must be the ones actually required by the contract in terms of source and substance; (3) "Correct form": All documents must be in correct form. These requirements apply to both tangible and electronic documents of title. When tender is made through customary banking channels, a draft may accompany or be associated with a document of title. The language has been broadened to allow for drafts to be associated with an electronic document of title. Compare Section 2–104(2) definition of financing agency.

When a prescribed document cannot be procured, a question of fact arises under the provision of this Article on substituted performance about whether the agreed manner of delivery is actually commercially impracticable and whether the substitute is commercially reasonable.

§ 2–504. Shipment By Seller

~~Where~~ If the seller is required or authorized to send the goods to the buyer and the contract does not require ~~him~~ the seller to deliver them at a particular destination, then unless otherwise agreed ~~he~~ the seller must:

    (a) put ~~the~~ conforming goods in the possession of ~~such~~ a carrier and make ~~such a~~ proper contract for their transportation, ~~as may be reasonable~~ having regard to the nature of the goods and other circumstances of the case; ~~and~~

    (b) obtain and promptly deliver or tender in due form any document necessary to enable the buyer to obtain possession of the goods or otherwise required by the agreement or by usage of trade; and

    (c) promptly notify the buyer of the shipment.

Failure to notify the buyer under paragraph (c) or to make a proper contract under paragraph (a) is a ground for rejection only if material delay or loss ensues.

§ 2–505. Seller's Shipment Under Reservation

(1) ~~Where~~ If the seller has identified goods to the contract by or before shipment:

    (a) ~~his~~ The seller's procurement of a negotiable bill of lading to ~~his~~ the seller's own order or otherwise reserves in ~~him~~ the seller a security interest in the goods. ~~His~~ The seller's procurement of the bill to the order of a financing agency or of the buyer indicates in addition only the seller's expectation of transferring that interest to the person named.

    (b) ~~a non-negotiable~~ A nonnegotiable bill of lading to ~~himself~~ the seller or ~~his~~ the seller's nominee reserves possession of the goods as ~~security but~~ security. However, ~~except in a case of conditional delivery~~ unless a seller has a right to reclaim the goods under ~~(subsection (2) of Section 2–507)~~ Section 2–507(2) a ~~non-negotiable~~ nonnegotiable bill of lading naming the buyer as consignee reserves no security interest even ~~though~~ if the seller retains possession or control of the bill of lading.

(2) ~~When~~ If shipment by the seller with reservation of a security interest is in violation of the contract for sale, it constitutes an improper contract for transportation ~~within the preceding section~~ under Section 2–504 but impairs neither the rights given to the buyer by shipment and identification of the goods to the contract nor the seller's powers as a holder of a negotiable document of title.

Official Comment

1. The security interest reserved to the seller under subsection (1) is restricted to securing payment or performance by the buyer and the seller is strictly limited in the seller's disposition and control of the goods as against the buyer and third parties. Under this Article, the provision as to the passing of a property interest expressly applies "despite any reservation of security title" and also provides that the "rights, obligations and remedies" of the parties are not altered by the incidence of

177

title generally. The security interest, therefore, must be regarded as a means given to the seller to enforce the seller's rights against the buyer which is unaffected by and in turn does not affect the location of title generally. The rules set forth in subsection (1) are not to be altered by any apparent "contrary intent" of the parties as to passing of title, since the rights and remedies of the parties to the contract of sale, as defined in this Article, rest on the contract and its performance or breach and not on presumptions about the location of title.

This Article does not attempt to regulate local procedure for the effective maintenance of the seller's security interest when the action is in replevin by the buyer against the carrier.

2. Every shipment of identified goods under a negotiable bill of lading reserves a security interest in the seller under subsection (1) paragraph (a).

It is frequently convenient for the seller to make the bill of lading to the order of a nominee such as the seller's agent at destination, the financing agency to which the seller expects to negotiate the document or the bank issuing a credit to the seller. In many instances, also, the buyer is made the order party. This Article does not deal directly with the question as to whether a bill of lading made out by the seller to the order of a nominee gives the carrier notice of any rights which the nominee may have so as to limit the carrier's freedom or obligation to honor the bill of lading in the hands of the seller as the original shipper if the expected negotiation fails. This is dealt with in the Article on Documents of Title (Article 7).

3. A non-negotiable bill of lading taken to a party other than the buyer under subsection (1) paragraph (b) reserves possession of the goods as security in the seller but if the seller seeks to withhold the goods improperly the buyer can tender payment and recover them.

4. In the case of a shipment by non-negotiable bill of lading taken to a buyer, the seller, under subsection (1) retains no security interest or possession as against the buyer and by the shipment the seller *de facto* loses control as against the carrier except where he rightfully and effectively stops delivery in transit. (Section 2–705) In cases in which the contract gives the seller the right to payment against delivery, the seller, in appropriate cases, has a right to reclaim the goods under Section 2–507(2), although this right is subject to the claims of a good faith purchaser for value under Section 2–403.

5. Under subsection (2) an improper reservation by the seller which would constitute a breach in no way impairs such of the buyer's rights as result from identification of the goods. The security interest reserved by the seller under subsection (1) does not protect the seller from retaining possession or control of the document or the goods for the purpose of extracting more than is due him under the contract.

§ 2–506. Rights of Financing Agency

(1) A̶ Except as otherwise provided in Article 5, a financing agency by paying or purchasing for value a draft w̶h̶i̶c̶h̶ that relates to a shipment of goods acquires to the extent of the payment or purchase and in addition to its own rights under the draft and any document of title securing it any rights of the shipper in the goods including the right to stop delivery and the shipper's right to have the draft honored by the buyer.

(2) The right to reimbursement of a financing agency ~~which~~ that has in good faith honored or purchased the draft under commitment to or authority from the buyer is not impaired by subsequent discovery of defects with reference to any relevant document ~~which~~ that was apparently regular ~~on its face~~.

§ 2–507. Effect of Seller's Tender; Delivery on Condition

(1) Tender of delivery is a condition to the buyer's duty to accept the goods and, unless otherwise agreed, to ~~his~~ the buyer's duty to pay for them. Tender entitles the seller to acceptance of the goods and to payment according to the contract.

(2) ~~Where~~ If payment is due and demanded on the delivery to the buyer of goods or documents of title, ~~his right as against the seller to retain or dispose of them is conditional upon his making the payment due~~ the seller may reclaim the goods delivered upon a demand made within a reasonable time after the seller discovers or should have discovered that payment was not made.

(3) The seller's right to reclaim under subsection (2) is subject to the rights of a buyer in ordinary course of business or other good-faith purchaser for value under Section 2–403.

Official Comment

1.   The provisions of subsection(1), must be read within the framework of the other sections of this Article which bear upon the question of delivery and payment.

2.   The "unless otherwise agreed" provision of subsection (1) is directed primarily to cases in which payment in advance has been promised or a letter of credit term has been included. Payment "according to the contract" contemplates immediate payment, payment at the end of an agreed credit term, payment by a time acceptance or the like. Under this Act, "contract" means the total obligation in law which results from the parties' agreement including the effect of this Article. In this context, therefore, there must be considered the effect in law of provisions such as those on means and manner of payment and on the failure of the agreed means and manner of payment.

3.   Subsection (2) provides that the seller has a right to reclamation to recover the goods from the buyer in a cash-sale transaction when the sellers discovers payment has not been made. The phrase "due and demanded" refers to when the seller takes a check that is later dishonored. *See* Section 2–511. This subsection, and subsection (3), make the seller's rights parallel in credit-sale and cash-sale transactions. *See* Section 2–702.

4.   Subsection (3) clarifies the rule that the seller's right to reclaim goods under subsection (2) is subject to the right of the buyer in the ordinary course of business or other good faith purchaser.

§ 2–508. Cure By Seller of Improper Tender or Delivery; Replacement

~~(1) Where any tender or delivery by the seller is rejected because non-conforming and the time for performance has not yet expired, the seller may seasonably notify the buyer of his intention to cure and may then within the contract time make a conforming delivery.~~

~~(2) Where the buyer rejects a non-conforming tender which the seller had reasonable grounds to believe would be acceptable with or without money allowance the seller may if he seasonably notifies the buyer have a further reasonable time to substitute a conforming tender.~~

(1) If the buyer rejects goods or a tender of delivery under Section 2–601 or 2–612 or, except in a consumer contract, justifiably revokes acceptance under Section 2–608(1)(b) and the agreed time for performance has not expired, a seller that has performed in good faith, upon seasonable notice to the buyer and at the seller's own expense, may cure the breach of contract by making a conforming tender of delivery within the agreed time. The seller shall compensate the buyer for all of the buyer's reasonable expenses caused by the seller's breach of contract and subsequent cure.

(2) If the buyer rejects goods or a tender of delivery under Section 2–601 or 2–612 or, except in a consumer contract, justifiably revokes acceptance under Section 2–608(1)(b) and the agreed time for performance has expired, a seller that has performed in good faith, upon seasonable notice to the buyer and at the seller's own expense, may cure the breach of contract, if the cure is appropriate and timely under the circumstances, by making a tender of conforming goods. The seller shall compensate the buyer for all of the buyer's reasonable expenses caused by the seller's breach of contract and subsequent cure.

Official Comment

1. Subsection (1) permits a seller that has made a nonconforming tender in any case to make a conforming tender within the contract time upon seasonable notification to the buyer. It presumes that the buyer has rightfully rejected or justifiably revoked acceptance under Section 2–608(1)(b) through timely notification to the seller and has complied with any particularization requirements imposed by Section 2–605(1). This subsection also applies where the seller has taken back the nonconforming goods and refunded the purchase price. The seller may still make a good tender within the contract period. The closer, however, it is to the contract date, the greater is the necessity for extreme promptness on the seller's part in notifying of the intention to cure, if the notification is to be "seasonable" under this subsection.

The rule of this subsection, moreover, is qualified by its underlying reasons. Thus if, after contracting for June delivery, a buyer later makes known to the seller a need for shipment early in the month and the seller ships accordingly, the "contract time" has been cut down by the supervening modification and the time for cure of tender must reflect this modified time term.

2. Cure after a justifiable revocation of acceptance is not available as a matter of right in a consumer contract. Furthermore, even in a nonconsumer contract, cure is not available if the revocation is predicated on Section 2–608(1)(a). If the buyer is revoking because of a known defect that the seller has not been willing or able to cure, there is no justification for giving the seller a second chance to cure.

3. Subsection (2) expands the seller's right to cure after the time for performance has expired. As under subsection (1), the buyer's rightful rejection or in a nonconsumer contract justifiable revocation of acceptance under Section 2–608(1)(b) trigger the seller's right to cure. Original Section 2–508(2) was designed to prevent surprise rejections by requiring the seller to have "reasonable grounds to believe" the nonconforming tender was acceptable. Although this test has been abandoned, the requirement that the initial tender be made in good faith prevents a seller from deliberately tendering goods that the seller knows the buyer cannot use in order to save the contract and then, upon rejection, insisting on a second right to cure. The good faith standard applies under both subsection (1) and subsection (2).

4. The seller's cure under both subsection (1) and subsection (2) must be of conforming goods. Conforming goods includes not only conformity to the contracted-for quality but also as to quantity or assortment or other similar obligations under the contract. Since the time for performance has expired in a case governed by subsection (2), however, the seller's tender of conforming goods required to effect a cure under this section could not conform to the contracted time for performance. Thus, subsection (1) requires that cure be tendered "within the agreed time" while subsection (2) requires that the tender be "appropri-ate and timely under the circumstances."

The requirement that the cure be "appropriate and timely under the circumstances" provides important protection for the buyer. If the buyer is acquiring inventory on a just-in-time basis and needs to procure substitute goods from another supplier to keep the buyer's process moving, the cure would not be timely. If the seller knows from the circumstances that strict compliance with the contract obligations is expected, the seller's cure would not be appropriate. If the seller attempts to cure by repair, the cure would not be appropriate if the attempted cure resulted in goods that did not conform in every respect to the requirements of the contract. The standard for quality on the second tender is governed by Section 2–601. Whether a cure is appropriate and timely is based upon the circumstances and needs of the buyer. A seasonable notice to the buyer and timely cure are predicated on the requirement that the notice and offered cure would be untimely if the buyer has reasonably changed its position in good faith reliance on the nonconforming tender.

5. Cure is at the seller's expense, and the seller is obligated to compensate the buyer for all of the buyer's reasonable expenses caused by the breach and the cure. The term "reasonable expenses" is not limited to expenses that would qualify as incidental damages.

The seller's compensation of the buyer's expenses provided in both subsections (1) and (2) is not controlled by remedy limitations that the parties may have agreed to as provided in Section 2–719. A remedy limitation under Section 2–719 is based upon compensation to the aggrieved party for a breach. The reasonable expenses contemplated under this section are designed to cure the breach in conjunction with the seller's provision of a conforming tender or conforming goods. If the seller is not attempting to cure its breach, a remedy limitation agreed to by the parties under Section 2–719 is an effective way to provide compensation for breach.

§ 2–509. Risk of Loss in the Absence of Breach

(1) ~~Where~~ If the contract requires or authorizes the seller to ship the goods by carrier~~:~~

    (a) if it does not require ~~him~~ the seller to deliver them at a particular destination, the risk of loss passes to the buyer when the goods are ~~duly~~ delivered to the carrier even ~~though~~ if the shipment is under reservation (Section 2–505); but

    (b) if it does require ~~him~~ the seller to deliver them at a particular destination and the goods are there ~~duly~~ tendered while in the possession of the carrier, the risk of loss passes to the buyer when the goods are there ~~duly~~ so tendered as to enable the buyer to take delivery.

(2) ~~Where~~ If the goods are held by a bailee to be delivered without being moved, the risk of loss passes to the buyer~~:~~

    (a) on ~~his~~ the buyer's receipt of possession or control of a negotiable document of title covering the goods; ~~or~~

    (b) on acknowledgment by the bailee to the buyer of the buyer's right to possession of the goods; or

    (c) after ~~his~~ the buyer's receipt of possession or control of a ~~non-negotiable~~ nonnegotiable document of title or other ~~written~~ direction to deliver in a record, as provided in ~~subsection (4)(b) of~~ Section 2–503(4)(b).

(3) In any case not within subsection (1) or (2), the risk of loss passes to the buyer on ~~his~~ the buyer's receipt of the goods ~~if the seller is a merchant; otherwise the risk passes to the buyer on tender of delivery~~.

(4) The provisions of this section are subject to contrary agreement of the parties and to ~~the provisions of this Article on sale on approval (Section 2–327) and on effect of breach on risk of loss (Section 2–510)~~ Sections 2–327 and 2–510.

Official Comment

1. The underlying theory of this section on risk of loss is in conformity with common commercial and insurance practice, to base the risk of loss on the physical location of the goods and not by shifting of the risk with the "property" in the goods.

The scope of the section is limited to those cases where there has been no breach by the seller. When there has been a breach by either party, the risk of loss may be shifted to the breaching party under Section 2–510 if the breaching party did not already bear the risk for any reason the party's delivery or tender fails to conform to the contract, the present section does not apply and the situation is governed by the provisions on effect of breach on risk of loss.

2. In a shipment contract, the risk of loss shifts to the buyer when the goods are delivered to the carrier as required by Section 2–504; in a destination contract, the risk of loss shifts when the goods are tendered to the buyer as required by Section 2–503(3).

3. Unlike prior law, subsection (3) makes no distinction between merchant and non-merchant sellers. In a case not governed by subsection (1) or subsection (2) and not subject to a contrary result under subsection (4), the risk of loss passes to the buyer upon the buyer's receipt of the goods. Receipt requires taking the physical possession of the goods, Section 2–103(1)(*l*).

4. When the agreement provides for delivery of the goods from seller to the buyer without removal from the physical possession of a bailee, risk of loss passes to the buyer upon receipt of possession or control of the negotiable document of title, acknowledgment made by the bailee of the buyer's right of possession or the buyer's receipt of possession or control of a non-negotiable document of title or other direction to deliver in a record as provided in Section 2–503. See the definition of control in Article 7, 7–106.

5. Subsections (1) through (3) are subject to subsection (4) which provides for a "contrary agreement" of the parties. This language is intended as the equivalent of the phrase "unless otherwise agreed" used more frequently throughout this Act. "Contrary" is in no way used as a word of limitation, and the buyer and seller are left free to readjust their rights and risks in any manner agreeable to them. Contrary agreement can also be found in the circumstances of the case, a trade usage or practice, or a course of dealing or course of performance.

§ 2–510. Effect of Breach on Risk of Loss

(1) ~~Where~~ If a tender or delivery of goods so fails to conform to the contract as to give a right of rejection, the risk of their loss remains on the seller until cure or acceptance.

(2) ~~Where~~ If the buyer rightfully revokes acceptance, ~~he~~ the buyer may to the extent of any deficiency in ~~his~~ the buyer's effective insurance coverage treat the risk of loss as having rested on the seller from the beginning.

(3) ~~Where~~ If the buyer as to conforming goods already identified to the contract for sale repudiates or is otherwise in breach before risk of their loss has passed to ~~him~~ the buyer, the seller may to the extent of any deficiency in ~~his~~ the seller's effective insurance coverage treat the risk of loss as resting on the buyer for a commercially reasonable time.

§ 2–511. Tender of Payment By Buyer; Payment By Check

(1) Unless otherwise agreed tender of payment is a condition to the seller's duty to tender and complete any delivery.

(2) Tender of payment is sufficient when made by any means or in any manner current in the ordinary course of business unless the seller

demands payment in legal tender and gives any extension of time reasonably necessary to procure it.

(3) Subject to the provisions of this Act on the effect of an instrument on an obligation (Section 3–310), payment by check is conditional and is defeated as between the parties by dishonor of the check on due presentment.

As amended in 1994.

§ 2–512. Payment By Buyer Before Inspection

(1) ~~Where~~ If the contract requires payment before inspection, ~~non-conformity~~ nonconformity of the goods does not excuse the buyer from so making payment unless:

> (a) the ~~non-conformity~~ nonconformity appears without inspection; or
>
> (b) despite tender of the required documents the circumstances would justify injunction against honor under this Act (Section 5–109(b)).

(2) Payment pursuant to subsection (1) does not constitute an acceptance of goods or impair the buyer's right to inspect or any of ~~his~~ the buyer's remedies.

§ 2–513. Buyer's Right to Inspection of Goods

(1) Unless otherwise agreed and subject to subsection (3), ~~where~~ if goods are tendered or delivered or identified to the contract for sale, the buyer has a right before payment or acceptance to inspect them at any reasonable place and time and in any reasonable manner. ~~When~~ If the seller is required or authorized to send the goods to the buyer, the inspection may be after their arrival.

(2) Expenses of inspection must be borne by the buyer but may be recovered from the seller if the goods do not conform and are rejected.

(3) Unless otherwise agreed ~~and subject to the provisions of this Article on C.I.F. contracts (subsection (3) of Section 2–321)~~, the buyer is not entitled to inspect the goods before payment of the price ~~when~~ if the contract provides:

> (a) for delivery ~~"C.O.D." or on other like terms~~ on terms that under applicable course of performance, course of dealing, or usage of trade are interpreted to preclude inspection before payment; or
>
> (b) for payment against documents of title, except where ~~such~~ the payment is due only after the goods are to become available for inspection.

(4) A place ~~or method~~ , method, or standard of inspection fixed by the parties is presumed to be exclusive, but unless otherwise expressly

agreed it does not postpone identification or shift the place for delivery or for passing the risk of loss. If compliance becomes impossible, inspection shall be as provided in this section unless the place ~~or method~~ , method, or standard fixed was clearly intended as an indispensable condition failure of which avoids the contract.

§ 2–514. When Documents Deliverable on Acceptance; When on Payment

Unless otherwise agreed and except as otherwise provided in Article 5, documents against which a draft is drawn are to be delivered to the drawee on acceptance of the draft if it is payable more than three days after presentment; otherwise, only on payment.

Official Comment

This section, which is consistent with Section 4–503, is subject to Article 5. Under Article 5, because an issuer may have up to seven days to determine compliance of documents (Section 5–108), the delay beyond three days does not necessarily indicate that the draft should be treated as a time draft.

§ 2–515. Preserving Evidence of Goods in Dispute

In furtherance of the adjustment of any claim or dispute

(a) either party on reasonable notification to the other and for the purpose of ascertaining the facts and preserving evidence has the right to inspect, test and sample the goods including such of them as may be in the possession or control of the other; and

(b) the parties may agree to a third party inspection or survey to determine the conformity or condition of the goods and may agree that the findings shall be binding upon them in any subsequent litigation or adjustment.

PART 6

BREACH, REPUDIATION, AND EXCUSE

§ 2–601. Buyer's Rights on Improper Delivery

Subject to ~~the provisions of this Article on breach in installment contracts (Section 2–612)~~ Sections 2–504 and 2–612, and unless otherwise agreed under ~~the sections on contractual limitations of remedy (Sections 2–718 and 2–719)~~ Sections 2–718 and 2–719, if the goods or the tender of delivery fail in any respect to conform to the contract, the buyer may:

(a) reject the whole; ~~or~~

(b) accept the whole; or

(c) accept any commercial unit or units and reject the rest.

§ 2–602. Manner and Effect of ~~Rightful~~ Rejection

(1) Rejection of goods must be within a reasonable time after their delivery or tender. It is ineffective unless the buyer seasonably notifies the seller.

(2) Subject to ~~the provisions of the two following sections on reject-ed goods (Sections 2–603 and 2–604),~~ Sections 2–603, 2–604, and Section 2–608(4):

> (a) after rejection any exercise of ownership by the buyer with respect to any commercial unit is wrongful as against the seller; and

> (b) if the buyer has before rejection taken physical possession of goods in which ~~he~~ the buyer does not have a security interest under ~~the provisions of this Article (subsection (3) of Section 2–711)~~ Section 2–711(3), ~~he~~ the buyer is under a duty after rejection to hold them with reasonable care at the seller's disposition for a time sufficient to permit the seller to remove them; but

> (c) the buyer has no further obligations with regard to goods rightfully rejected.

(3) The seller's rights with respect to goods wrongfully rejected are governed by the provisions of this Article on Seller's remedies in general (Section 2–703).

Official Comment

2. Subsection (2) sets forth the duties of the buyer upon rejection. In addition to the duty to hold the goods with reasonable care for the seller's disposition, the buyer also has those duties specified in Sections 2–603, 2–604 and 2–608(4).

3. Elimination of the word "rightful" in the title makes it clear that a buyer can effectively reject goods even though the rejection is wrongful and constitutes a breach. *See* Section 2–703(1). The word "rightful" has also been deleted from the titles to Section 2–603 and 2–604. *See* Official Comments to those sections.

§ 2–603. Merchant Buyer's Duties as to ~~Rightfully~~ Rejected Goods

(1) Subject to any security interest in the buyer ~~(subsection (3) of Section 2–711)~~ under Section 2–711(3), ~~when~~ if the seller has no agent or place of business at the market of rejection, a merchant buyer is under a duty after rejection of goods in ~~his~~ the buyer's possession or control to follow any reasonable instructions received from the seller with respect to the goods and in the absence of such instructions to make reasonable efforts to sell them for the seller's account if they are perishable or threaten to decline in value speedily. ~~Instructions~~ In the case of a rightful rejection, instructions are not reasonable if on demand indemnity for expenses is not forthcoming.

(2) ~~When~~ If the buyer sells goods under subsection (1) <u>following a rightful rejection,</u> ~~he~~ <u>the buyer</u> is entitled to reimbursement from the seller or out of the proceeds for reasonable expenses of caring for and selling them, and if the expenses include no selling commission then to such commission as is usual in the trade or if there is none to a reasonable sum not exceeding ~~ten~~ <u>10</u> per cent on the gross proceeds.

(3) In complying with this section the buyer is held only to good faith and ~~good faith~~ <u>good-faith</u> conduct ~~hereunder~~ <u>under this section</u> is neither acceptance nor conversion nor the basis of an action for damages.

Official Comment

6. Except as otherwise stated in this section, its provisions apply to all effective rejections, including rejections that are wrongful. Thus, any merchant buyer whose rejection is effective is subject to the duties set forth in the first sentence of subsection (1), and a merchant buyer that complies with those duties is entitled to the protection provided by subsection (3). However, the right to indemnity for expenses on demand under the second sentence of subsection (1) and the right to reimbursement for expenses and a commission under subsection (2) are limited to buyers whose rejections are rightful.

§ 2–604. Buyer's Options as to Salvage of ~~Rightfully~~ Rejected Goods

Subject to the provisions of ~~the immediately preceding section~~ <u>Section 2–603</u> on perishables, if the seller gives no instructions within a reasonable time after notification of rejection, the buyer may store the rejected goods for the seller's account or reship them to ~~him~~ <u>the seller</u> or resell them for the seller's account with reimbursement as provided in ~~the preceding section~~ <u>Section 2–603</u>. Such action is not acceptance or conversion.

Official Comment

2. This section no longer refers to "rightful" rejections. Accordingly, its provisions apply to any buyer whose rejection is effective. However, this section is subject to Section 2–603, and the provisions of that section differentiate between rightful and wrongful rejections.

§ 2–605. Waiver of Buyer's Objections By Failure to Particularize

(1) ~~The~~ <u>A</u> buyer's failure to state in connection with rejection a particular defect <u>or in connection with revocation of acceptance a defect that justifies revocation</u> ~~which is ascertainable by reasonable inspection~~ precludes ~~him~~ <u>the buyer</u> from relying on the unstated defect to justify rejection or ~~to establish breach~~ <u>revocation of acceptance if the defect is ascertainable by reasonable inspection</u>:

    (a) ~~where~~ <u>if</u> the seller <u>had a right to cure the defect and</u> could have cured it if stated seasonably; or

187

(b) between merchants~~,~~ ~~when~~ if the seller has after rejection <u>or</u> <u>revocation of acceptance</u> made a request in ~~writing~~ <u>a record</u> ~~and~~ <u>for a full and</u> final ~~written~~ statement <u>in a record</u> of all defects on which the buyer proposes to rely.

(2) ~~Payment~~ <u>A buyer's payment</u> against documents <u>tendered to the</u> <u>buyer</u> made without reservation of rights precludes recovery of the payment for defects apparent ~~on the face of~~ <u>in</u> the documents.

Official Comment

1. This section rests upon a policy of permitting the buyer to give a quick and informal notice of defects in a tender without penalizing the buyer for omissions, while at the same time protecting a seller that is reasonably misled by the buyer's failure to state curable defects. When the defect in a tender is one which could have been cured by the seller, a buyer that merely rejects the delivery without stating any objections to the tender is probably acting in commercial bad faith and is seeking to get out of a agreement which has become unprofitable. Following the general policy of this Article to preserve the deal wherever possible, subsection (1)(a) requires that the seller's right to correct the tender in the circumstances be protected.

Subsection (1) as amended makes three substantive changes. First, the failure to particularize affects only the buyer's right to reject or revoke acceptance. It does not affect the buyer's right to establish a breach of the agreement. Waiver of a right to damages for breach because of a failure properly to notify the seller is governed by Section 2–607(3).

Second, subsection (1) now requires the seller to have had a right to cure under Section 2–508 in addition to having the ability to cure. This point was perhaps implicit in the original provision, but it is now expressly stated to avoid any question of whether this section creates a seller's right to cure independent of the right enumerated in Section 2–508. Thus, if the defect is one that could be cured under Section 2–508, the buyer will have waived that defect as a basis for rejecting the goods or revoking acceptance if the buyer fails to state the defect with sufficient particularity to facilitate the seller's exercise of its right to cure as provided in Section 2–508.

Subsection (1) as revised has been extended to include a notice requirement not only as to rejection but also as to revocation of acceptance. This is necessitated by the expansion of the right to cure (Section 2–508) to cover revocation of acceptance in nonconsumer contracts. The application of the subsection to revocation cases is limited in the following ways: 1) because a revocation under Section 2–608(1)(a) does not activate a right to cure under Section 2–508, the revocation does not activate subsection (1); 2) because Section 2–608(1)(b) involves defects that are by definition difficult to discover, there is no waiver under subsection (1) unless the defect justifies the revocation and the buyer has notice of it; and 3) because the right to cure following revocation of acceptance is restricted under Section 2–508 to nonconsumer contracts, this notice requirement does not apply to a consumer who is seeking to revoke acceptance.

2. When the time for cure has passed, subsection (1)(b) provides that a merchant seller is entitled upon request to a final statement of objections by a merchant buyer upon which the seller can rely. What is needed is a clear statement to the buyer of exactly what is being sought. A formal demand

will be sufficient in the case of a merchant-buyer.

3. Subsection (2) has been amended to make clear that a buyer that makes payment upon presentation of the documents to the buyer may waive defects, but that a person that is not the buyer, such as the issuer of a letter of credit that pays as against documents, is not waiving the buyer's right to assert defects in the documents as against the seller.

Subsection (2) applies to documents the same principle contained in Section 2–606(1)(a) for the acceptance of goods; that is, if the buyer accepts documents that have apparent defects, the buyer is presumed to have waived the defects as a basis for rejecting the documents. Subsection (2) is limited to defects which are apparent in the documents. This rule applies to both tangible and electronic documents of title. When payment is required against documents, the documents must be inspected before the payment, and the payment constitutes acceptance of the documents. When the documents are delivered without requiring a contemporary payment by the buyer, the acceptance of the documents by non-objection is postponed until after a reasonable time for the buyer to inspect the documents. In either situation, however, the buyer "waives" only what is apparent in the documents. Moreover, in either case, the acceptance of the documents does not constitute an acceptance of the goods and does not impair any options or remedies of the buyer for improper delivery of the goods. *See* Section 2–512(2).

§ 2–606. What Constitutes Acceptance of Goods

(1) Acceptance of goods occurs when the buyer:

    (a) after a reasonable opportunity to inspect the goods signifies to the seller that the goods are conforming or that ~~he~~ the buyer will take or retain them in spite of their ~~non-conformity~~ nonconformity;

    (b) fails to make an effective rejection ~~(subsection (1) of Section 2–602)~~ under Section 2–602(1), but such acceptance does not occur until the buyer has had a reasonable opportunity to inspect them; or

    (c) Subject to Section 2–608(4), does any act inconsistent with the seller's ownership ~~but if such act is wrongful as against the seller it is an acceptance only if ratified by him~~.

(2) Acceptance of a part of any commercial unit is acceptance of that entire unit.

§ 2–607. Effect of Acceptance; Notice of Breach; Burden of Establishing Breach After Acceptance; Notice of Claim or Litigation to Person Answerable Over

(1) The buyer must pay at the contract rate for any goods accepted.

(2) Acceptance of goods by the buyer precludes rejection of the goods accepted and if made with knowledge of a ~~non-conformity cannot~~ nonconformity may not be revoked because of it unless the acceptance

189

was on the reasonable assumption that the ~~non-conformity~~ nonconformity would be seasonably cured, but acceptance does not of itself impair any other remedy provided by this Article for ~~non-conformity~~ nonconformity.

(3) ~~Where~~ If a tender has been accepted:

    (a) the buyer must within a reasonable time after ~~he~~ the buyer discovers or should have discovered any breach notify the seller ~~of breach or be barred from any remedy.~~, but failure to give timely notice bars the buyer from a remedy only to the extent that the seller is prejudiced by the failure; and

    (b) if the claim is one for infringement or the like ~~(subsection (3) of Section 2–312)~~ under Section 2–312(2) and the buyer is sued as a result of such a breach, ~~he~~ the buyer must so notify the seller within a reasonable time after ~~he~~ the buyer receives notice of the litigation or be barred from any remedy over for liability established by the litigation.

(4) The burden is on the buyer to establish any breach with respect to the goods accepted.

(5) ~~Where~~ If the buyer is sued for indemnity, breach of a warranty, or other obligation for which ~~his seller~~ another party is answerable over:

    (a) ~~he~~ the buyer may give ~~his seller~~ the other party ~~written~~ notice of the ~~litigation. If~~ litigation in a record, and if the notice states that the ~~seller~~ other party may come in and defend and that if the ~~seller~~ other party does not do so ~~he~~ the other party will be bound in any action against ~~him~~ the other party by ~~his~~ the buyer by any determination of fact common to the two litigations, then unless the ~~seller~~ other party after seasonable receipt of the notice does come in and defend ~~he~~ the other party is so bound.

    (b) if the claim is one for infringement or the like ~~(subsection (3) of Section 2–312)~~ under Section 2–312(2), the original seller may demand in ~~writing~~ a record that ~~his~~ its buyer turn over to ~~him~~ it control of the litigation including settlement or else be barred from any remedy over and if ~~he~~ it also agrees to bear all expense and to satisfy any adverse judgment, ~~then~~ the buyer is so barred unless the buyer after seasonable receipt of the demand does turn over control ~~the buyer is so barred~~.

(6) ~~The provisions of subsections~~ Subsections (3), (4), and (5) apply to any obligation of a buyer to hold the seller harmless against infringement or the like ~~(subsection (3) of Section 2–312)~~ under Section 2–312(2).

Official Comment

1. Under subsection (1), once the buyer accepts a tender the seller acquires a right to its price on the contract terms. In cases of partial acceptance, the price of any part accepted is, if possible, to be reasonably apportioned. Usually this is to be determined in terms of "the contract rate," which is the rate determined from the agreement based on the rules and policies of this Article.

2. Under subsection (2) acceptance of goods precludes their subsequent rejection of the goods. Any return of the goods thereafter must be by way of revocation of acceptance under Section 2–608. Revocation is unavailable for a non-conformity known to the buyer at the time of acceptance, except where the buyer has accepted on the reasonable assumption that the non-conformity would be seasonably cured.

3. All other remedies of the buyer remain unimpaired under subsection (2). This is intended to include the buyer's full rights for future installments despite the buyer's acceptance of any earlier non-conforming installment.

4. Subsection (3)(a) provides that the buyer must, within a reasonable time of the discovery, or when the buyer should have discovered any breach, give the seller notification of the breach. A failure to give this notice to the seller bars the buyer from a remedy for breach of contract if the seller suffers prejudice due to the failure to notify. *See* Restatement (Second) of Contracts § 229, which provides for an excuse of a condition where the failure is not material and implementation would result in a disproportionate forfeiture.

The time of notification is to be determined by applying commercial standards to a merchant buyer. "A reasonable time" for notification from a retail consumer is to be judged by different standards so that in that case it could be extended beyond what would be a "commercially" reasonable time' in appropriate circumstances because the requirement of notification is meant to defeat commercial bad faith, not to deprive a good faith consumer of a remedy.

The content of the notification need merely be sufficient to let the seller know that the transaction is still troublesome and must be watched. There is no reason to require that the notification which saves the buyer's rights under this section must include a clear statement of all the objections that will be relied on by the buyer, as is required for statements of defects upon rejection (Section 2–605). Nor is there reason to require the notification to be a claim for damages or of any threatened litigation or other resort to a remedy. The notification which preserves the buyer's rights under this Article need only be one that informs the seller that the transaction is claimed to involve a breach, and thus opens the way for normal settlement through negotiation.

5. Under this Article various beneficiaries are given rights for injuries sustained by them because of the seller's breach of warranty. Such a beneficiary does not fall within the reason of the present section in regard to discovery of defects and the giving of notice within a reasonable time after acceptance, since he has nothing to do with acceptance. However, the reason of this section does extend to requiring the beneficiary to notify the seller that an injury has occurred. What is said above, with regard to the extended time for reasonable notification from the lay consumer after the injury is also applicable here; but even a beneficiary can be properly held to the use of good faith in notifying, once he has

had time to become aware of the legal situation.

6. Subsection (4) unambiguously places the burden of proof to establish breach on the buyer after acceptance. However, this rule becomes one purely of procedure when the tender accepted was non-conforming and the buyer has given the seller notice of breach under subsection (3). For subsection (2) makes it clear that acceptance leaves unimpaired the buyer's right to be made whole, and that right can be exercised by the buyer not only by way of cross-claim for damages, but also by way of recoupment in diminution or extinction of the price.

7. The vouching-in procedure in subsection (5) includes indemnity actions, and it includes any other party that is answerable over, not just the immediate seller.

Vouching-in does not confer on the notified seller a right to intervene, does not confer jurisdiction of any kind on the court over the seller, and does not create a duty to defend on the part of the seller. Those matters continue to be governed by the applicable rules of civil procedure and substantive law outside this section. Vouching in is based upon the principle that the seller is liable for its contractual obligations for quality or title to the goods which the buyer is being forced to defend.

8. Subsections (3)(b) and (5)(b) give a warrantor against infringement an opportunity to defend or compromise third-party claims or be relieved of liability. Subsection (5)(a) codifies for all warranties the practice of voucher to defend. Subsection (6) makes these provisions applicable to the buyer's liability for infringement under Section 2–312.

9. All of the provisions of this section are subject to any explicit reservation of rights. Section 1–308.

§ 2–608. Revocation of Acceptance in Whole or in Part

(1) ~~The~~ A buyer may revoke ~~his~~ acceptance of a lot or commercial unit whose ~~non-conformity~~ nonconformity substantially impairs its value to ~~him~~ the buyer if ~~he~~ the buyer has accepted it:

  (a) on the reasonable assumption that its ~~non-conformity~~ nonconformity would be cured and it has not been seasonably cured; or

  (b) without discovery of ~~such non-conformity~~ the nonconformity if ~~his~~ the buyer's acceptance was reasonably induced either by the difficulty of discovery before acceptance or by the seller's assurances.

(2) Revocation of acceptance must occur within a reasonable time after the buyer discovers or should have discovered the ground for it and before any substantial change in condition of the goods which is not caused by their own defects. ~~It~~ The revocation is not effective until the buyer notifies the seller of it.

(3) A buyer ~~who~~ that so revokes has the same rights and duties with regard to the goods involved as if ~~he~~ the buyer had rejected them.

(4) If a buyer uses the goods after a rightful rejection or justifiable revocation of acceptance, the following rules apply:

(a) Any use by the buyer that is unreasonable under the circumstances is wrongful as against the seller and is an acceptance only if ratified by the seller.

(b) Any use of the goods that is reasonable under the circumstances is not wrongful as against the seller and is not an acceptance, but in an appropriate case the buyer is obligated to the seller for the value of the use to the buyer.

Official Comment

8. Subsection (4) deals with the problem of post-rejection or revocation use of the goods. The courts have developed several alternative approaches. Under original Article 2, a buyer's post-rejection or revocation use of the goods could be treated as an acceptance, thus undoing the rejection or revocation, could be a violation of the buyer's obligation of reasonable care, or could be a reasonable use for which the buyer must compensate the seller. Subsection (4) adopts the third approach.

In general, a buyer that either rejects or revokes acceptance of the goods should not subsequently use the goods in a manner that is inconsistent with the seller's ownership. In some instances, however, the use may be reasonable. For example, a consumer buyer may have incurred an unavoidable obligation to a third-party financier and, if the seller fails to refund the price as required by this Article, the buyer may have no reasonable alternative but to use the goods (e.g., a rejected mobile home that provides needed shelter). Another example might involve a commercial buyer that is unable immediately to obtain cover and must use the goods to fulfill its obligations to third parties. If circumstances change so that the buyer's use after an effective rejection or a justified revocation of acceptance is no longer reasonable, the continued use of the goods is unreasonable and is wrongful against the seller. This gives the seller the option of ratifying the use, thereby treating it as an acceptance, or pursuing a non-Code remedy for conversion.

If the buyer's use is reasonable under the circumstances, the buyer's actions cannot be treated as an acceptance. The buyer must compensate the seller for the value of the use of the goods to the buyer. Determining the appropriate level of compensation requires a consideration of the buyer's particular circumstances and should take into account the defective condition of the goods. There may be circumstances, such as where the use is solely for the purpose of protecting the buyer's security interest in the goods, where no compensation is due the seller under this section. If the seller has a right to compensation under this section that compensation must be netted out against any right of the buyer to damages for the seller's breach of contract.

§ 2–609. Right to Adequate Assurance of Performance

(1) A contract for sale imposes an obligation on each party that the other's expectation of receiving due performance will not be impaired. ~~When~~ If reasonable grounds for insecurity arise with respect to the performance of either party, the other may ~~in writing~~ demand in a record adequate assurance of due performance and until ~~he~~ the party receives the assurance may if commercially reasonable suspend any performance for which ~~he~~ it has not already received the agreed return.

(2) Between merchants, the reasonableness of grounds for insecurity and the adequacy of any assurance offered shall be determined according to commercial standards.

(3) Acceptance of any improper delivery or payment does not prejudice the aggrieved party's right to demand adequate assurance of future performance.

(4) After receipt of a justified demand, failure to provide within a reasonable time not exceeding ~~thirty~~ 30 days such assurance of due performance as is adequate under the circumstances of the particular case is a repudiation of the contract.

§ 2–610. Anticipatory Repudiation

(1) ~~When~~ If either party repudiates the contract with respect to a performance not yet due the loss of which will substantially impair the value of the contract to the other, the aggrieved party may:

    (a) for a commercially reasonable time await performance by the repudiating party; or

    (b) resort to any remedy for breach (Section 2–703 or Section 2–711), even ~~though he~~ if the aggrieved party has notified the repudiating party that ~~he~~ it would await the latter's performance and has urged retraction; and

    (c) in either case suspend ~~his own~~ performance or proceed in accordance with the provisions of this Article on the seller's right to identify goods to the contract notwithstanding breach or to salvage unfinished goods (Section 2–704).

(2) Repudiation includes language that a reasonable person would interpret to mean that the other party will not or cannot make a performance still due under the contract or voluntary, affirmative conduct that would appear to a reasonable person to make a future performance by the other party impossible.

Official Comment

5. Subsection (2) provides guidance on when a party can be considered to have repudiated a performance obligation based upon the Restatement (Second) of Contracts § 250 and does not purport to be an exclusive statement of when a repudiation has occurred. Repudiation centers upon an overt communication of intention, actions which render performance impossible, or a demonstration of a clear determination not to perform. Failure to provide adequate assurance of due performance under Section 2–609 also operates as a repudiation.

§ 2–611. Retraction of Anticipatory Repudiation

(1) Until the repudiating party's next performance is due, ~~he can~~ that party may retract ~~his~~ the repudiation unless the aggrieved party has since the repudiation canceled or materially changed ~~his~~ position or otherwise indicated that ~~he considers~~ the repudiation is final.

(2) Retraction may be by any method ~~which~~ that clearly indicates to the aggrieved party that the repudiating party intends to perform, but must include any assurance justifiably demanded under ~~the provisions of this Article (Section 2–609)~~ Section 2–609.

(3) Retraction reinstates the repudiating party's rights under the contract with due excuse and allowance to the aggrieved party for any delay occasioned by the repudiation.

§ 2–612. "Installment Contract"; Breach

(1) An "installment contract" is one ~~which~~ that requires or authorizes the delivery of goods in separate lots to be separately accepted, even ~~though~~ if the contract contains a clause "each delivery is a separate contract" or its equivalent.

(2) The buyer may reject any installment ~~which~~ that is ~~non-conforming~~ nonconforming if the ~~non-conformity~~ nonconformity substantially impairs the value of that installment ~~and cannot be cured~~ to the buyer or if the ~~non-conformity~~ nonconformity is a defect in the required ~~documents; but~~ documents. However, if the ~~non-conformity~~ nonconformity does not fall within subsection (3) and the seller gives adequate assurance of its cure the buyer must accept that installment.

(3) ~~Whenever non-conformity~~ If nonconformity or default with respect to one or more installments substantially impairs the value of the whole contract, there is a breach of the whole. But the aggrieved party reinstates the contract if ~~he~~ the party accepts a ~~non-conforming~~ nonconforming installment without seasonably notifying of cancellation or if ~~he~~ the party brings an action with respect only to past installments or demands performance as to future installments.

Official Comments

4. One of the requirements for rejection under subsection (2) is nonconformity substantially impairing the value of the installment in question. However, an installment agreement may require accurate conformity in quality as a condition to the right to acceptance if the need for the conformity is made clear either by express provision or by the circumstances. In this case the effect of the agreement is to define explicitly what amounts to substantial impairment of value. A clause that requires accurate compliance as a condition to the right to acceptance must, however, have some basis in reason, must avoid imposing hardship by surprise, and it is subject to waiver or to displacement by practical construction.

5. Substantial impairment of the value of an installment can turn not only on the quality of the goods but also on such factors as time, quantity, assortment, and the like. It must be judged in terms of the normal or specifically known purposes of the contract. The defect in required documents refers to such matters as the absence of insurance documents under a contract that requires these documents, falsity of a bill of lading, or one failing to show shipment within the contract period or to the contract destination. Even in these cases, however, the provisions on cure of tender may

apply if appropriate documents are readily procurable.

8. Subsection (2) makes it clear that the buyer's right in the first instance to reject an installment depends upon whether there has been a substantial impairment of the value of the installment to the buyer and not on the seller's ability to cure the nonconformity. The seller can prevent a rightful rejection by giving adequate assurances of cure. Subsection (2) uses the words "to the buyer" to clarify that the standard for rejecting an installment consistent is the same standard for revoking acceptance under Section 2–608. Therefore, the test is not what the seller had reason to know at the time of contracting; the question is whether the non-conformity is one that will cause a substantial impairment of value to the buyer even though the seller had no knowledge about the buyer's particular circumstances at the time of contracting.

§ 2–613. Casualty to Identified Goods

~~Where~~ If the contract requires for its performance goods identified when the contract is made, and the goods suffer casualty without fault of either party before the risk of loss passes to the buyer, ~~or in a proper case under a "no arrival, no sale" term (Section 2–324)~~ then:

(a) if the loss is total the contract is ~~avoided~~ terminated; and

(b) if the loss is partial or the goods have so deteriorated ~~as~~ that they no longer ~~to~~ conform to the contract, the buyer may nevertheless demand inspection and at ~~his~~ the buyer's option either treat the contract as ~~avoided~~ terminated or accept the goods with due allowance from the contract price for the deterioration or the deficiency in quantity but without further right against the seller.

Official Comment

3. The use of the word "terminated" in paragraph (a) clarifies that pre-termination breaches are preserved. *See* Section 2–106(3).

§ 2–614. Substituted Performance

(1) ~~Where~~ If without fault of either party the agreed berthing, loading, or unloading facilities fail or an agreed type of carrier becomes unavailable or the agreed manner of ~~delivery~~ performance otherwise becomes commercially impracticable but a commercially reasonable substitute is available, ~~such~~ the substitute performance must be tendered and accepted.

(2) If the agreed means or manner of payment fails because of domestic or foreign governmental regulation, the seller may withhold or stop delivery unless the buyer provides a means or manner of payment which is commercially a substantial equivalent. If delivery has already been taken, payment by the means or in the manner provided by the regulation discharges the buyer's obligation unless the regulation is discriminatory, oppressive, or predatory.

Official Comment

1. Subsection (1) requires the tender of a commercially reasonable substituted performance where agreed to facilities have failed or have become commercially impracticable. Under this Article, in the absence of a specific agreement, the normal or usual facilities enter into the agreement either through the circumstances of the transaction, a usage of trade or a prior course of dealing between the parties.

This section appears between Section 2–613 on casualty to identified goods and Section 2–615 on excuse by failure of presupposed conditions. Those two sections deal with excuse and complete avoidance of the contract when the occurrence or non-occurrence of a contingency which was a basic assumption of the contract makes the expected performance impossible. The distinction between the present section and those sections is whether the failure or impossibility of performance arises in connection with an incidental matter or goes to the very heart of the agreement. The differing lines of solution are contrasted in a comparison of *International Paper Co. v. Rockefeller*, 161 App.Div. 180, 146 N.Y.S. 371 (1914), and *Meyer v. Sullivan*, 40 Cal.App. 723, 181 P. 847 (1919). In the former case, a contract for the sale of spruce to be cut from a particular tract of land was involved. When a fire destroyed the trees growing on that tract the seller was held excused since performance was impossible. In the latter case, the contract called for delivery of wheat "f.o.b. Kosmos Steamer at Seattle." The war led to cancellation of that line's sailing schedule after space had been duly engaged and the buyer was held entitled to demand substituted delivery at the warehouse on the line's loading dock. Under this Article, of course, the seller would also be entitled, had the market gone the other way, to make a substituted tender in that manner.

There must, however, be a true commercial impracticability to excuse the agreed to performance and justify a substituted performance. When this is the case, a reasonable substituted performance tendered by either party should excuse that party from strict compliance with the contract terms which do not go to the essence of the agreement.

2. The substitution provided for in this section as between buyer and seller does not carry over into the obligation of a financing agency under a letter of credit, since the financing agency is entitled to performance which is plainly adequate on its face and without need to look into commercial evidence outside of the documents. *See* Article 5, especially Section 5–108.

3. Under subsection (2), when the contract is still executory on both sides, the seller is permitted to withdraw unless the buyer can provide the seller with a commercially equivalent performance despite the governmental regulation. When, however, only the debt for the price remains, a larger leeway is permitted. The buyer may pay in the manner provided by the regulation, even though this may not be a commercially equivalent performance, provided that the regulation is not "discriminatory, oppressive or predatory."

§ 2–615. Excuse By Failure of Presupposed Conditions

Except ~~so far as~~ to the extent that a seller may have assumed a greater obligation and subject to ~~the preceding section on substituted performance~~ Section 2–614:

    (a) Delay in ~~delivery or non-delivery~~ performance or nonperformance in whole or in part by a seller ~~who~~ that complies with paragraphs (b) and (c) is not a breach of ~~his~~ the seller's duty under a contract for sale if performance as agreed has been made impracticable by the occurrence of a contingency the ~~non-occurrence~~ nonoccurrence of which was a basic assumption on which the contract was made or by compliance in good faith with any applicable foreign or domestic governmental regulation or order whether or not it later proves to be invalid.

(b) ~~Where~~ If the causes mentioned in paragraph (a) affect only a part of the seller's capacity to perform, ~~he~~ the seller must allocate production and deliveries among ~~his~~ its customers but may at ~~his~~ its option include regular customers not then under contract as well as ~~his~~ its own requirements for further manufacture. ~~He~~ The seller may so allocate in any manner ~~which~~ that is fair and reasonable.

(c) The seller must notify the buyer seasonably that there will be delay or nonperformance ~~non-delivery~~ and, ~~when~~ if allocation is required under paragraph (b), of the estimated quota thus made available for the buyer.

§ 2–616. Procedure on Notice Claiming Excuse

(1) ~~Where the~~ If a buyer receives notification of a material or indefinite delay or an allocation justified under ~~the preceding section he~~ Section 2–615, the buyer may by ~~written~~ notification in a record to the seller as to any ~~delivery~~ performance concerned, and ~~where~~ if the prospective deficiency substantially impairs the value of the whole contract under ~~the provisions of this Article relating to breach of installment contracts (Section 2–612)~~ Section 2–612, then also as to the ~~whole,~~ whole:

(a) terminate and thereby discharge any unexecuted portion of the contract; or

(b) modify the contract by agreeing to take ~~his~~ the buyer's available quota in substitution.

(2) If after receipt of ~~such~~ notification from the seller the buyer fails ~~so~~ to modify the contract within a reasonable time not exceeding ~~thirty~~ 30 days, the contract ~~lapses~~ is terminated with respect to any ~~deliveries~~ performance affected.

(3) The provisions of this section may not be negated by agreement except in so far as the seller has assumed a greater obligation under ~~the preceding section~~ Section 2–615.

Official Comment

2. In subsection (2), the term "terminated" conforms with Section 2–613(a) to clarify that pre-termination breaches are preserved and the term "performance" conforms with Section 2–615(a) to specify the broad range of obligation that may be included under this provision.

PART 7

REMEDIES

§ 2–701. Remedies for Breach of Collateral Contracts Not Impaired

Remedies for breach of any obligation or promise collateral or ancillary to a contract for sale are not impaired by the provisions of this Article.

§ 2–702. Seller's Remedies on Discovery of Buyer's Insolvency

(1) ~~Where~~ If the seller discovers ~~the buyer to be~~ that the buyer is insolvent, ~~he~~ the seller may refuse delivery except for cash including payment for all goods theretofore delivered under the contract, and stop delivery under ~~this Article (Section 2–705)~~ Section 2–705.

(2) ~~Where~~ If the seller discovers that the buyer has received goods on credit while insolvent, ~~he~~ the seller may reclaim the goods upon demand made within ~~ten days~~ a reasonable time after the buyer's receipt of the goods, ~~but if misrepresentation of solvency has been made to the particular seller in writing within three months before delivery the ten day limitation does not apply~~. Except as provided in this subsection, the seller may not base a right to reclaim goods on the buyer's fraudulent or innocent misrepresentation of solvency or of intent to pay.

(3) The seller's right to reclaim under subsection (2) is subject to the rights of a buyer in ordinary course of business or other good-faith purchaser for value under ~~this Article (Section 2–403)~~ Section 2–403. Successful reclamation of goods excludes all other remedies with respect to them.

Official Comment

1. The seller's right to withhold the goods or to stop delivery except for cash when the seller discovers the buyer's insolvency is made explicit in subsection (1) regardless of the passage of title, and the concept of stoppage has been extended to include goods in the possession of any bailee that has not yet attorned to the buyer.

2. Subsection (2) takes as its base line the proposition that any receipt of goods on credit by an insolvent buyer amounts to a tacit business misrepresentation of solvency and therefore is fraudulent as against the particular seller. This section omits the 10–day limitation and the 3–month exception to the 10–day limitation that was in original Article 2. If the buyer is in bankruptcy at the time of reclamation, the seller will have to comply with Section 546(c) of the Bankruptcy Code of 1978, which includes a 10–day limitation.

199

3. Because the right of the seller to reclaim goods under this section constitutes preferential treatment as against the buyer's other creditors, subsection (3) provides that such reclamation bars all of the seller's other remedies the goods involved.

4. The rights of a seller to reclamation from the buyer under section 2–702 are subordinate to the rights of good faith purchasers from that buyer under Section 2–403. This section takes no position on the seller's claims to proceeds of the goods.

§ 2–703. Seller's Remedies in General

~~Where the buyer wrongfully rejects or revokes acceptance of goods or fails to make a payment due on or before delivery or repudiates with respect to a part or the whole, then with respect to any goods directly affected and, if the breach is of the whole contract (Section 2–612), then also with respect to the whole undelivered balance, the aggrieved seller may~~

> ~~(a) withhold delivery of such goods;~~

> ~~(b) stop delivery by any bailee as hereafter provided (Section 2–705);~~

> ~~(c) proceed under the next section respecting goods still unidentified to the contract;~~

> ~~(d) resell and recover damages as hereafter provided (Section 2–706);~~

> ~~(e) recover damages for non-acceptance (Section 2–708) or in a proper case the price (Section 2–709);~~

> ~~(f) cancel.~~

(1) A breach of contract by the buyer includes the buyer's wrongful rejection or wrongful attempt to revoke acceptance of goods, wrongful failure to perform a contractual obligation, failure to make a payment when due, and repudiation.

(2) If the buyer is in breach of contract the seller, to the extent provided for by this Act or other law, may:

> (a) withhold delivery of the goods under Section 2–703(4);

> (b) stop delivery of the goods under Section 2–705;

> (c) proceed under Section 2–704 with respect to goods unidentified to the contract or unfinished;

> (d) reclaim the goods under Section 2–507(2) or 2–702(2);

> (e) require payment directly from the buyer under Section 2–325(c);

> (f) cancel under Section 2–703(4);

> (g) resell and recover damages under Section 2–706;

> (h) recover damages for nonacceptance or repudiation under Section 2–708(1);

(i) recover lost profits under Section 2–708(2);

(j) recover the price under Section 2–709;

(k) obtain specific performance under Section 2–716;

(*l*) recover liquidated damages under Section 2–718;

(m) in other cases, recover damages in any manner that is reasonable under the circumstances.

(3) If the buyer becomes insolvent, the seller may:

(a) withhold delivery under Section 2–702(1);

(b) stop delivery of the goods under Section 2–705;

(c) reclaim the goods under Section 2–702(2).

(4) If the buyer wrongfully rejects or revokes acceptance of goods, fails to make a payment when due, or repudiates with respect to a part or the whole, with respect to any goods directly affected and, if the breach is of the whole contract (Section 2–612), with respect to the whole undelivered balance, the aggrieved seller may

(a) withhold delivery of such goods; or

(b) cancel.

Official Comment

1. This section is a list of the remedies of the seller available under this Article to remedy any breach by the buyer. It also lists the seller's statutory remedies in the event of the buyer's insolvency. The subsection does not address the extent to which other law provides additional remedies or supplements the statutory remedies in Article 2 (*see* Section 1–103). The remedies available to the seller enumerated in this section may be modified or limited as provided for in Section 2–719.

In addition to the enumerated statutory remedies, the Section also provides for remedies agreed upon by the parties, *see* subsection (2)(*l*). This section does not cover the remedies that become available to the parties upon demand for adequate assurance under Section 2–609.

This Article rejects any doctrine of election of remedy as a fundamental policy and thus the remedies are essentially cumulative in nature and include all of the available remedies for breach. Whether the pursuit of one remedy bars another depends entirely on the facts of the individual case.

2. The buyer's breach which occasions the use of the remedies under this section may involve only one lot or delivery of goods, or may involve all of the goods which are the subject matter of the particular contract. The right of the seller to pursue a remedy as to all the goods when the breach is as to only one or more lots is covered by the section on breach in installment contracts. The present section deals only with remedies available after the goods involved in the breach have been determined by that section.

3. In addition to the typical case of refusal to pay or default in payment, the language in subsection (1), "failure to make a payment when due," is intended to cover the dishonor of a check on due presentment, or the non-acceptance of a draft, and the failure to furnish an agreed letter of credit.

4. It should also be noted that this Act requires its provisions to be lib-

erally administered and provides that any right or obligation which it declares is enforceable by action unless a different effect is specifically prescribed (Section 1–103).

§ 2–704. Seller's Right to Identify Goods to the Contract Notwithstanding Breach or to Salvage Unfinished Goods

(1) An aggrieved seller ~~under the preceding section may,~~ may in an appropriate case involving breach by the buyer:

> (a) identify to the contract conforming goods not already identified if at the time ~~he~~ the seller learned of the breach ~~they~~ the goods are in ~~his~~ the seller's possession or control;
>
> (b) treat as the subject of resale goods ~~which~~ that have demonstrably been intended for the particular contract even ~~though~~ if those goods are unfinished.

(2) ~~Where~~ If the goods are unfinished, an aggrieved seller may in the exercise of reasonable commercial judgment for the purposes of avoiding loss and of effective realization either complete the manufacture and wholly identify the goods to the contract or cease manufacture and resell for scrap or salvage value or proceed in any other reasonable manner.

§ 2–705. Seller's Stoppage of Delivery in Transit or Otherwise

(1) ~~The~~ A seller may stop delivery of goods in the possession of a carrier or other bailee ~~when he~~ if the seller discovers the buyer to be insolvent (Section 2–702) ~~and may stop delivery of carload, truckload, planeload or larger shipments of express or freight~~ or ~~when~~ if the buyer repudiates or fails to make a payment due before delivery or if for any other reason the seller has a right to withhold or reclaim the goods.

(2) As against such buyer the seller may stop delivery until:

> (a) receipt of the goods by the buyer; ~~or~~
>
> (b) acknowledgment to the buyer by any bailee of the goods, except a carrier, that the bailee holds the goods for the buyer; ~~or~~
>
> (c) such acknowledgment to the buyer by a carrier by reshipment or as ~~warehouseman~~ warehouse; or
>
> (d) negotiation to the buyer of any negotiable document of title covering the goods.

(3)(a) To stop delivery the seller must so notify as to enable the bailee by reasonable diligence to prevent delivery of the goods.

> (b) After such notification the bailee must hold and deliver the goods according to the directions of the seller but the seller is liable to the bailee for any ensuing charges or damages.

(c) If a negotiable document of title has been issued for goods, the bailee is not obliged to obey a notification to stop until surrender of <u>possession or control of</u> the document.

(d) A carrier ~~who~~ <u>that</u> has issued a ~~non-negotiable~~ <u>nonnegotiable</u> bill of lading is not obliged to obey a notification to stop received from a person other than the consignor.

Official Comment

1. Subsection (1) applies when goods are in the possession of a carrier or other bailee. It applies, in addition to a buyer's insolvency, also to any case where the buyer repudiates or fails to make a payment due before delivery or for any other reason the seller has the right to withhold or reclaim the goods. Where stoppage occurs for insecurity, it is merely a suspension of performance, and if assurances are duly forthcoming from the buyer the seller is not entitled to resell or divert.

Improper stoppage is a breach by the seller if it effectively interferes with the buyer's right to due tender under the section on manner of tender of delivery. However, if the bailee obeys an unjustified order to stop the bailee may also be liable to the buyer. The measure of the obligation is dependent on the provisions of the Documents of Title Article (Section 7–303). Subsection 3(b) therefore gives the bailee a right of indemnity as against the seller in this case.

2. "Receipt by the buyer" includes receipt by the buyer's designated representative, the subpurchaser, when shipment is made direct to the subpurchaser and the buyer never receives the goods. As between the buyer and the seller, the seller's right to stop the goods at any time until they reach the place of final delivery is recognized by this section.

Under subsection (3)(c) and (d), the carrier is under no duty to recognize the stop order of a person who is a stranger to the carrier's contract. But the seller's right as against the buyer to stop delivery remains, whether or not the carrier is obligated to recognize the stop order. If the carrier does obey it, the buyer cannot complain merely because of that circumstance; and the seller becomes obligated under subsection (3)(b) to pay the carrier any ensuing damages or charges.

3. A diversion of a shipment is not a "reshipment" under subsection (2)(c) when it is merely an incident to the original contract of transportation, nor is the procurement of "exchange bills" of lading which change only the name of the consignee to that of the buyer's local agent but do not alter the destination of a reshipment.

Acknowledgment by the carrier as a "warehouse" within the meaning of this Article requires a contract of a truly different character from the original shipment, a contract not in extension of transit but as a warehouse.

4. Subsection (3)(c) makes the bailee's obedience of a notification to stop conditional upon the surrender of possession or control of any outstanding negotiable document.

5. The seller is responsible for any charges or losses incurred by the carrier in following the seller's orders, whether or not the carrier was obligated to do so.

6. After an effective stoppage under this section the seller's rights in the goods are the same as if the seller had never made a delivery.

§ 2–706. Seller's Resale Including Contract for Resale

(1) ~~Under the conditions stated in Section 2–703 on seller's remedies~~ In an appropriate case involving breach by the buyer, the seller may resell the goods concerned or the undelivered balance thereof. ~~Where~~ If the resale is made in good faith and in a commercially reasonable manner, the seller may recover the difference between the contract price and the resale price ~~and the contract price~~ together with any incidental or consequential damages allowed under ~~the provisions of this Article (Section 2–710)~~ Section 2–710, but less expenses saved in consequence of the buyer's breach.

(2) Except as otherwise provided in subsection (3) or unless otherwise agreed, resale may be at public or private sale including sale by way of one or more contracts to sell or of identification to an existing contract of the seller. Sale may be as a unit or in parcels and at any time and place, and on any terms, but every aspect of the sale including the method, manner, time, place and terms must be commercially reasonable. The resale must be reasonably identified as referring to the broken contract, but it is not necessary that the goods be in existence or that any or all of them have been identified to the contract before the breach.

(3) ~~Where~~ If the resale is at private sale, the seller must give the buyer reasonable notification of ~~his~~ an intention to resell.

(4) ~~Where~~ If the resale is at public sale:

    (a) only identified goods ~~can~~ may be sold ~~except where~~ unless there is a recognized market for a public sale of futures in goods of the kind; ~~and~~

    (b) it must be made at a usual place or market for public sale if one is reasonably available and except in the case of goods which are perishable or threaten to decline in value speedily the seller must give the buyer reasonable notice of the time and place of the resale; ~~and~~

    (c) if the goods are not to be within the view of those attending the sale, the notification of sale must state the place where the goods are located and provide for their reasonable inspection by prospective bidders; and

    (d) the seller may buy.

(5) A purchaser ~~who~~ that buys in good faith at a resale takes the goods free of any rights of the original buyer even ~~though~~ if the seller fails to comply with one or more of the requirements of this section.

(6) The seller is not accountable to the buyer for any profit made on any resale. A person in the position of a seller (Section 2–707) or a buyer ~~who~~ that has rightfully rejected or justifiably revoked acceptance must account for any excess over the amount of ~~his~~ the buyer's security

interest, ~~as hereinafter defined (subsection (3) of Section 2–711)~~ under Section 2–711(3).

(7) Failure of a seller to resell under this section does not bar the seller from any other remedy.

Official Comment

1. Consistent with the revision of Section 2–710, this section now provides for consequential as well as incidental damages. Subsection (7) is new, and parallels the provision for buyer cover in 2–713. Original Section 2–706(1) measured damages by the difference between the resale price and the contract price; amended subsection (1) reverses these terms ("difference between the contract price and the resale price") because the contract price must be the larger number for there to be direct damages.

2. The right of resale under this section arises when a seller reclaims goods under Section 2–507 or a buyer repudiates or makes a wrongful but effective rejection. In addition, there is a right of resale if the buyer unjustifiably attempts to revoke acceptance and the seller takes back the goods. However, the seller may choose to ignore the buyer's unjustifiable attempt to revoke acceptance, in which case the appropriate remedy is an action for the price under Section 2–709. Application of the right of resale to cases of buyer repudiation is supplemented by subsection (2), which authorizes a resale of goods which are not in existence or were not identified to the contract before the breach.

Subsection (1) allows the seller to resell the goods after a buyer's breach of contract if the seller has possession or control of the goods. The seller may have possession or control of the goods at the time of the breach or may have regained possession of the goods upon the buyer's wrongful rejection. If the seller has regained possession of the goods from the buyer pursuant to Arti-cle 9, that Article controls the seller's rights of resale.

3. Under this Article the seller resells by authority of law, on the seller's own behalf, for the seller's own benefit and for the purpose of setting the seller's damages. The theory of a seller's agency is therefore rejected. The question of whether the title to the goods has or has not passed to the buyer is not relevant for the operation of this section.

4. To recover the damages prescribed in subsection (1), the seller must act "in good faith and in a commercially reasonable manner" in making the resale. If the seller complies with the prescribed standards in making the resale, the seller may recover from the buyer the damages provided for in subsection (1). Evidence of market or current prices at any particular time or place is relevant only for the question of whether the seller acted in a commercially reasonable manner in making the resale.

5. Subsection (2) enables the seller to resell in accordance with reasonable commercial practices so as to realize as high a price as possible in the circumstances. A seller may sell at a public sale or a private sale as long as the choice is commercially reasonable. A "public" sale is one to which members of the public are admitted. A public sale is usually a sale by auction, but all auctions are not public auctions. A private sale may be effected by an auction or by solicitation and negotiation conducted either directly or through a broker. In choosing between a public and private sale, the character of the goods must be considered and relevant trade practices and usages must be

observed. A public sale has further requirements stated in subsection (4).

The purpose of subsection (2) is to enable the seller to dispose of the goods to the best advantage, and therefore the seller is permitted in making the resale to depart from the terms and conditions of the original contract for sale to any extent "commercially reasonable" in the circumstances.

As for the place for resale, the focus is on the commercial reasonableness of the seller's choice as to the place for an advantageous resale. This section rejects the theory that the seller should normally resell at the agreed place for delivery and that a resale elsewhere can be permitted only in exceptional cases.

The time for resale is a reasonable time after the buyer's breach. What is a reasonable time depends on the nature of the goods, the condition of the market and the other circumstances of the case; its length cannot be measured by any legal yardstick or divided into degrees. When a seller contemplating resale receives a demand from the buyer for inspection under Section 2–515, the time for resale may be appropriately lengthened.

6. The provision of subsection (2) that the goods need not be in existence to be resold applies when the buyer is guilty of anticipatory repudiation of a contract for future goods before the goods or some of the goods have come into existence. In this case, the seller may exercise the right of resale and fix the damages by "one or more contracts to sell" the quantity of conforming future goods affected by the repudiation.

The companion provision of subsection (2), that resale may be made although the goods were not identified to the contract prior to the buyer's breach, likewise contemplates an anticipatory repudiation by the buyer, but one occurring after the goods are in existence. The seller may identify goods to the contract after the breach, but must identify the goods being sold as pertaining to the breached contract. If the identified goods conform to the contract, their resale will fix the seller's damages as satisfactorily as if the goods had been identified before the breach.

7. If the resale is to be by private sale, subsection (3) requires that reasonable notification of the seller's intention to resell must be given to the buyer. Notification of the time and place of a private resale is not required.

8. Subsection (4) states requirements for a public resale. The requirements of this subsection are in addition to the requirements of subsection (2), which pertain to all resales under this section.

Paragraph (a) of subsection (4) qualifies the last sentence of subsection (2) with respect to resales of unidentified and future goods at public sale. If conforming goods are in existence the seller may identify them to the contract after the buyer's breach and then resell them at public sale. If the goods have not been identified, however, the seller may resell them at public sale only as "future" goods and only if there is a recognized market for public sale of futures in goods of the kind.

Subsection (4)(b) requires that the seller give the buyer reasonable notice of the time and place of a public resale so that the buyer may have an opportunity to bid or to secure the attendance of other bidders. An exception is made in the case of goods "which are perishable or threaten to decline speedily in value."

Since there would be no reasonable prospect of competitive bidding elsewhere, subsection (4)(b) requires that a public resale "must be made at a usual place or market for public sale if one is reasonably available"; *i.e.*, a place or market which prospective bidders may reasonably be expected to attend. The market may still be "reasonably available" under this subsection, although at a considerable distance from the place where the goods are located. In this case, the expense of transporting the goods for resale is recoverable from the buyer as part of the seller's incidental damages under subsection (1). However, the question of availability is one of commercial reasonableness in the circumstances and if such "usual" place or market is not reasonably available, a duly advertised public resale may be held at another place if it is one which prospective bidders may reasonably be expected to attend, as distinguished from a place where there is no demand whatsoever for goods of the kind.

Subsection (4)(c) is designed to permit intelligent bidding. Subsection (4)(d), which permits the seller to bid and, of course, to become the purchaser, benefits the original buyer by tending to increase the resale price and thus decreasing the damages the buyer will have to pay.

9. Subsection (5) allows a purchaser to take the goods free of the rights of the buyer even if the seller has not complied with this section. The policy of resolving any doubts in favor of the resale purchaser operates to the benefit of the buyer by increasing the price the purchaser should be willing to pay.

10. Subsection (6) recognizes that when the seller is entitled to resell under this Article, the goods are the seller's goods and the purpose of resale under this section is to set the seller's damages as against the buyer. However, a person in the position of the seller under Section 2-707 or a buyer asserting a security interest in the goods under Section 2-711(3) has only a limited right in the goods and so must account to the seller for any excess over the limited amount necessary to satisfy that right.

11. Subsection (7) expresses the policy that resale is not a mandatory remedy for the seller. Except as otherwise provided in Section 2-710, the seller is always free to choose between resale and damages for repudiation or nonacceptance under Section 2-708.

Subsection (7) parallels the provision in the cover section, Section 2-712. A seller that fails to comply with the requirements of this section may recover damages under Section 2-708(1). In addition, a seller may recover both incidental and consequential damages under Section 2-710 is the seller's damages have not been liquidated under Section 2-718 or limited under Section 2-719.

§ 2-707. "Person in the Position of a Seller"

(1) A "person in the position of a seller" includes as against a principal an agent ~~who~~ that has paid or become responsible for the price of goods on behalf of ~~his~~ the principal or ~~anyone~~ a person ~~who~~ that otherwise holds a security interest or other right in goods similar to that of a seller.

(2) A person in the position of a seller ~~may as provided in this Article withhold or stop delivery (Section 2-705) and resell (Section 2-706) and recover incidental damages (Section 2-710)~~ has the same remedies as a seller under this Article.

Official Comment

Unlike original Article 2, which gave a limited range of remedies, subsection (2) now provides that a "person in the position of a seller" has the full range of remedies available to a seller.

§ 2–708. Seller's Damages for ~~Non–Acceptance~~ Nonacceptance or Repudiation

(1) Subject to subsection (2) and to ~~the provisions of this Article with respect to proof of market price (Section 2–723)~~ Section 2–723:

(a) the measure of damages for ~~non-acceptance or repudiation~~ nonacceptance by the buyer is the difference between the contract price and the market price at the time and place for tender ~~and the unpaid contract price~~ together with any incidental or consequential damages provided in ~~this Article (Section 2–710)~~ Section 2–710, but less expenses saved in consequence of the buyer's ~~breach.~~ breach; and

(b) the measure of damages for repudiation by the buyer is the difference between the contract price and the market price at the place for tender at the expiration of a commercially reasonable time after the seller learned of the repudiation, but no later than the time stated in paragraph (a), together with any incidental or consequential damages provided in Section 2–710, less expenses saved in consequence of the buyer's breach.

(2) If the measure of damages provided in subsection (1) or in Section 2–706 is inadequate to put the seller in as good a position as performance would have ~~done then~~ done, the measure of damages is the profit (including reasonable overhead) ~~which~~ that the seller would have made from full performance by the buyer, together with any incidental or consequential damages provided in this Article (Section 2–710)~~, due allowance for costs reasonably incurred and due credit for payments or proceeds of resale~~.

Official Comment

1. This section contains the following changes from original Section 2–708:

a) Consistent with the revision of Section 2–710, this section now provides for consequential as well as incidental damages. Subsection (1) has been divided into two paragraphs. The new paragraph clarifies the measure of damages in anticipatory repudiation. The same approach has taken in Section 2–713 for a buyer's market-based damage claims.

b) Original Section 2–708(1) set the measure of damages as the difference between the market price and the unpaid contract price. The word "unpaid" has been deleted as superfluous and misleading. An aggrieved buyer that has already paid a portion of the price is entitled to recover it in restitution under Section 2–718.

c) Original Section 2–708(1) measured damages by the difference between the market price and the contract price. Subsection

(1) reverses the terms ("difference between the contract price and the market price") because the contract price must be the larger number for there to be direct damages. *Compare* Sections 2–712 and 2–713 on buyer's remedies, where the contract price is listed after the cover or market price.

d) Subsection (2) now has the following emphasized language added: "provided in subsection (1) *or in Section 2–706* is inadequate. . . ." Most courts have correctly assumed that original Section 2–708(2) was an alternative to Section 2–706 as well as Section 2–708(1) but still had to ask the question. *See, e.g., R.E. Davis Chemical Corp. v. Diasonics, Inc.,* 826 F.2d 678 (7th Cir. 1987). The change makes this result explicit.

e) In subsection (2), the phrases that appeared in original 2–708(2), "due allowance for costs reasonably incurred" and "due credit for payments or proceeds of resale" have been deleted. As has been noted repeatedly (*see, e.g.,* Harris, A General Theory for Measuring Seller's Damages for Total Breach of Contract, 60 Mich. L. Rev. 577 (1962)), the "due credit" language makes no sense for a seller that has lost a sale not because it ceased manufacture on a buyer's breach but because it has resold a finished product (that was made for its breaching buyer) to one of the seller's existing buyers. When a seller ceases manufacture and resells component parts for scrap or salvage value under Section 2–704(2), a credit for the proceeds is due the buyer to offset the damages under this section. When a seller incurs costs that are not recovered by scrap or salvage, the seller must be given an "allowance" for those costs to measure

its loss accurately. *See* E. Farnsworth Contracts Section 12.9 (3rd ed. 1999) (general measure of damages = loss in value + other loss–cost avoided–loss avoided).

2. The right to damages under this section arises when a seller reclaims goods under Section 2–507 or a buyer repudiates or makes a wrongful but effective rejection. In addition, there is a right to damages under this Section if the buyer unjustifiably attempts to revoke acceptance and the seller takes back the goods. However, if the seller refuses to take the goods back in the face of the buyer's unjustifiable attempt to revoke acceptance, the appropriate remedy is an action for the price under Section 2–709.

3. The market price at the time and place for tender is the standard by which damages for nonacceptance are to be determined. The time and place of tender are determined by Section 2–503 on tender of delivery and by the use of common shipping terms. The provisions of Section 2–723 are relevant to determine the market price.

In the event that there is no evidence available of the current market price at the time and place of tender, proof of a substitute market may be made as provided for in Section 2–723. Section 2–723, which is consistent with the admissibility of market quotations, is intended to ease materially the problem of providing competent evidence.

4. Subsection (1)(b) addresses the question of when the market price should be measured in the case of an anticipatory repudiation by the buyer. This section provides that the market price should be measured in a case of repudiation at the place of tender under the agreement at a commercially reasonable time after the seller learned of the repudiation, but no later than the time of tender under the agreement. This time approximates the

market price at the time the seller would have resold the goods, even though the seller has not done so under Section 2–706. To determine whether the seller has learned of the repudiation, the court should be sensitive to the rights of the aggrieved party when tactical behavior by the buyer has made the determination difficult. *See Louisiana Power and Light v. Allegheny Ludlow*, 517 F. Supp. 1319 (D.C. La. 1981).

5. Subsection (2) is used in the cases of uncompleted goods, jobbers or middlemen, and other lost-volume sellers. This remedy is an alternative to the remedy under subsection (1) or Section 2–706, and it is available when the damages based upon resale of the goods or market price of the goods do not achieve the goal of full compensation for harm caused by the buyer's breach. No effort has been made to state how lost profits should be calculated because of the variety of situations in which this measurement may be appropriate and the variety of ways in which courts have measured lost profits. This subsection permits the recovery of lost profits in all appropriate cases. Since this section deals with the plaintiff's lost profit on a particular sale, and not with cases where a plaintiff is suing for the "lost profits" from an enterprise as consequential damages, it is not necessary to show a history of earnings; all that is necessary is that the plaintiff shows a loss of the marginal benefit to be gained from performance of the broken contract.

To qualify as a "lost volume" seller, the seller needs to show only that it could have supplied both the breaching purchaser and the resale purchaser with the goods. *Islamic Republic of Iran v. Boeing Co.*, 771 F.2d 1279 (9th Cir. 1985). Where an aggrieved seller has sold goods made for the breaching party to another, courts should consider whether the seller could and would have made a profit on an additional sale in addition to the breached sale. If the seller could not or would not have profitably made another sale in the absence of breach, there is no lost volume and the seller would normally be made whole by a recovery of the incidental costs associated with the substitute transaction.

6. Consequential damages are not recoverable under this section unless the seller has made reasonable attempts to minimize the damages in good faith, either by resale under Section 2–706 or by other reasonable means.

7. When an agreement contains provisions for payment of a liquidated sum of money as an alternative to performance, (such as a take-or-pay contract), it must be determined whether the agreement is truly for alternative performances or whether the alternatives are performance or liquidated damages. Recovery under this section is available when a buyer breaches an alternative performance contract. When the "alternative" is truly liquidated damages and when that damage provision complies with Section 2–718, recovery is under the liquidated damage clause. *See Roye Realty & Developing, Inc. v. Arkla, Inc.*, 863 P.2d 1150, 1154, 22 U.C.C. Rep Serv. 2d 183 (Okl. 1993); 5A Corbin, Corbin on Contracts § 1082, at 463–64 (1964).

§ 2–709. Action for the Price

(1) ~~When~~ If the buyer fails to pay the price as it becomes due, the seller may recover, together with any incidental or consequential damages under ~~the next section~~ Section 2–710, the price:

> (a) of goods accepted or of conforming goods lost or damaged within a commercially reasonable time after risk of their loss has passed to the buyer; and

(b) of goods identified to the contract if the seller is unable after reasonable effort to resell them at a reasonable price or the circumstances reasonably indicate that such effort will be unavailing.

(2) ~~Where~~ If the seller sues for the price, ~~he~~ the seller must hold for the buyer any goods ~~which~~ that have been identified to the contract and are still in ~~his~~ the seller's ~~control except that~~ control. However, if resale becomes possible, ~~he~~ the seller may resell them at any time prior to the collection of the judgment. The net proceeds of any such resale must be credited to the buyer, and payment of the judgment entitles ~~him~~ the buyer to any goods not resold.

(3) After the buyer has wrongfully rejected or revoked acceptance of the goods or has failed to make a payment due or has repudiated (Section 2–610), a seller ~~who~~ that is held not entitled to the price under this section shall nevertheless be awarded damages for ~~non-acceptance~~ nonacceptance under ~~the preceding section~~ Section 2–708.

§ 2–710. Seller's Incidental and Consequential Damages

(1) Incidental damages to an aggrieved seller include any commercially reasonable charges, expenses or commissions incurred in stopping delivery, in the transportation, care, and custody of goods after the buyer's breach, in connection with return or resale of the goods or otherwise resulting from the breach.

(2) Consequential damages resulting from the buyer's breach include any loss resulting from general or particular requirements and needs of which the buyer at the time of contracting had reason to know and which could not reasonably be prevented by resale or otherwise.

(3) In a consumer contract, a seller may not recover consequential damages from a consumer.

Official Comment

1. Subsection (1) provides for reimbursement by the seller for the expenses reasonably incurred as a result of the buyer's breach. The section sets forth as examples the usual and normal types of damages that may arise from the breach but the provision is ~~intended~~ intends to provide for all commercially reasonable expenditures made by the seller.

2. Subsection (2) permits an aggrieved seller to recover consequential damages. Under this section the loss must result from general or particular requirements of the seller of which the buyer had reason to know at the time of contracting. As with Section 2–715, the "tacit agreement" test is rejected. (*See* Official Comment 2 to Section 2–715). The buyer is not liable for losses that could have been mitigated.

Sellers rarely suffer compensable consequential damages. A buyer's usual default is failure to pay. In normal circumstances, the disappointed seller will be able to sell to another buyer, borrow to replace the breaching buyer's promised payment, or otherwise adjust the seller's affairs to avoid consequential loss. *cf. Afram Export Corp.*

211

v. Metallurgiki Halyps, S.A., 772 F.2d 1358, 1368 (7th Cir. 1985).

3. Subsection (3) precludes a seller from recovering consequential dam-ages from a consumer. This is a non-waivable provision.

§ 2–711. Buyer's Remedies in General; Buyer's Security Interest in Rejected Goods

~~(1) Where the seller fails to make delivery or repudiates or the buyer rightfully rejects or justifiably revokes acceptance then with respect to any goods involved, and with respect to the whole if the breach goes to the whole contract (Section 2–612), the buyer may cancel and whether or not he has done so may in addition to recovering so much of the price as has been paid~~

> ~~(a) "cover" and have damages under the next section as to all the goods affected whether or not they have been identified to the contract; or~~

> ~~(b) recover damages for non-delivery as provided in this Article (Section 2–713).~~

~~(2) Where the seller fails to deliver or repudiates the buyer may also~~

> ~~(a) if the goods have been identified recover them as provided in this Article (Section 2–502); or~~

> ~~(b) in a proper case obtain specific performance or replevy the goods as provided in this Article (Section 2–716).~~

(1) A breach of contract by the seller includes the seller's wrongful failure to deliver or to perform a contractual obligation, making of a nonconforming tender of delivery or performance, and repudiation.

(2) If the seller is in breach of contract, the buyer, to the extent provided for by this Act or other law, may:

> (a) in the case of rightful cancellation, rightful rejection, or justifiable revocation of acceptance, recover so much of the price as has been paid;

> (b) deduct damages from any part of the price still due under Section 2–717;

> (c) cancel under Section 2–711(4);

> (d) cover and have damages under Section 2–712 as to all goods affected whether or not they have been identified to the contract;

> (e) recover damages for nondelivery or repudiation under Section 2–713;

> (f) recover damages for breach with regard to accepted goods or breach with regard to a remedial promise under Section 2–714;

> (g) recover identified goods under Section 2–502;

(h) obtain specific performance or obtain the goods by replevin or similar remedy under Section 2–716;

(i) recover liquidated damages under Section 2–718;

(j) in other cases, recover damages in any manner that is reasonable under the circumstances.

(3) On rightful rejection or justifiable revocation of acceptance a buyer has a security interest in goods in ~~his~~ the buyer's possession or control for any payments made on their price and any expenses reasonably incurred in their inspection, receipt, transportation, care and custody and may hold such goods and resell them in a like manner as an aggrieved seller (Section 2–706).

(4) If the seller fails to make delivery or repudiates or the buyer rightfully rejects or justifiably revokes acceptance, with respect to any goods involved and with respect to the whole if the breach goes to the whole contract (Section 2–612), the buyer may cancel.

Official Comment

1. Despite the seller's breach proper re-tender of delivery as a cure under Section 2–508 effectively precludes the buyer's remedies under this section except for damages for any delay.

2. Under subsection (3), the buyer may hold and resell rejected goods if the buyer has paid a part of the price or incurred expenses of the type specified. "Paid," as used here, includes acceptance of a draft or other time negotiable instrument or the signing of a negotiable note. The buyer's freedom of resale is coextensive with that of a seller under this Article except that the buyer may not keep any profit resulting from the resale and the buyer is limited to retaining only the amount of the price paid and the costs involved in the inspection and handling of the goods. The buyer's security interest in the goods is intended to be limited to the items listed in subsection (3), and the buyer is not permitted to retain funds that the buyer might believe adequate for the damages. The buyer's right to cover, or to have damages for non-delivery, is not impaired by the buyer's exercise of the right of resale.

3. This Act requires its remedies to be liberally administered and provides that any right or obligation which it declares is enforceable by action unless a different effect is specifically prescribed (Section 1–103).

§ **2–712.** "Cover"; Buyer's Procurement of Substitute Goods

(1) ~~After a breach within the preceding section~~ If the seller wrongfully fails to deliver or repudiates or the buyer rightfully rejects or justifiably revokes acceptance, the buyer may "cover" by making in good faith and without unreasonable delay any reasonable purchase of or contract to purchase goods in substitution for those due from the seller.

(2) ~~The~~ A buyer may recover from the seller as damages the difference between the cost of cover and the contract price together with any incidental or consequential damages ~~as hereinafter defined (Section 2–715)~~ under Section 2–715, but less expenses saved in consequence of the seller's breach.

(3) Failure of the buyer to effect cover within this section does not bar ~~him~~ the buyer from any other remedy.

Official Comment

1. The purpose of this section is to provide the buyer with a remedy to enable the buyer to obtain the goods the buyer is entitled to under the contract with the seller. This remedy is the buyer's equivalent of the seller's right to resell.

The buyer is entitled to this remedy if the seller wrongfully fails to deliver the goods or repudiates the contract or if the buyer rightfully rejects or justifiably revokes acceptance. Cover is not available under this section if the buyer accepts the goods and does not rightfully revoke the acceptance.

2. Subsection (1) clarifies the circumstances in which a buyer is entitled to cover, prior language referred to "breach." The language makes it clear that there is a right to cover "[i]f the seller wrongfully fails to deliver or repudiates or the buyer rightfully rejects or justifiably revokes acceptance."

3. Subsection (2) allows a buyer that has appropriately covered to measure damages by the difference between the cover price and the contract price. In addition, the buyer is entitled to incidental damages, and when appropriate, consequential damages under Section 2–715.

4. The definition of "cover" is necessarily flexible, and therefore cover may include a series of contracts or sales as well as a single contract or sale, goods not identical with those involved but commercially usable as reasonable substitutes under the circumstances, and contracts on credit or delivery terms differing from the contract in breach but reasonable under the circumstances. The test of a proper cover is whether at the time and place of cover the buyer acted in good faith and in a reasonable manner. It is immaterial that hindsight may later prove that the method of cover used was not the cheapest or most effective.

5. The requirement in subsection (1) that the buyer must cover "without unreasonable delay" is not intended to limit the time necessary for the buyer to examine reasonable options and decide how best to effect cover.

6. Subsection (3) expresses the policy that cover is not a mandatory remedy for the buyer. The buyer is always free to choose between cover and damages for nondelivery under Section 2–713. However, this subsection must be read in conjunction with the section 2–715(2)(a), which limits the recovery of consequential damages to those damages that could not reasonably be prevented by cover or otherwise. Moreover, the operation of Section 2–716(3) on replevin and the like must be considered because the inability to cover is made an express condition to the right of the buyer to replevy the goods.

§ 2–713. Buyer's Damages for ~~Non–Delivery~~ Nondelivery or Repudiation

(1) Subject to ~~the provisions of this Article with respect to proof of market price (Section 2–723),~~ Section 2–723, if the seller wrongfully fails to deliver or repudiates or the buyer rightfully rejects or justifiably revokes acceptance:

> (a) the measure of damages ~~for non-delivery or repudiation~~ in the case of wrongful failure to deliver by the seller or

rightful rejection or justifiable revocation of acceptance by the buyer is the difference between the market price at the time ~~when the buyer learned of the breach~~ for tender under the contract and the contract price together with any incidental ~~and~~ or consequential damages ~~provided in this Article (Section 2–715)~~ under Section 2–715, but less expenses saved in consequence of the seller's ~~breach.~~ breach; and

(b) the measure of damages for repudiation by the seller is the difference between the market price at the expiration of a commercially reasonable time after the buyer learned of the repudiation, but no later than the time stated in paragraph (a), and the contract price together with any incidental or consequential damages provided in this Article (Section 2–715), less expenses saved in consequence of the seller's breach.

(2) Market price is to be determined as of the place for tender or, in cases of rejection after arrival or revocation of acceptance, as of the place of arrival.

Official Comment

1. This section provides a rule for anticipatory repudiation cases. This is consistent with the new rule for sellers in Section 2–708(1)(b). In a case not involving repudiation, the buyer's damages will be based on the market price at the time for tender under the agreement. This changes the former rule where the time for measuring damages was at the time the buyer learned of the breach.

2. This section provides for a buyer's expectancy damages when the seller wrongfully fails to deliver the goods or repudiates the contract or the buyer rightfully rejects or justifiably revokes acceptance. This section provides an alternative measure of damages to the cover remedy provided for in Section 2–712.

3. Under subsection (1)(a), the measure of damages for a wrongful failure to deliver the goods by the seller or a rightful rejection or justifiable revocation of acceptance by the buyer is the difference between the market price at the time for tender under the agreement and the contract price.

4. Under subsection (1)(b), in the case of an anticipatory repudiation by the seller the market price should be measured at the place where the buyer would have covered at a commercially reasonable time after the buyer learned of the repudiation, but no later than the time of tender under the agreement. This time approximates the market price at the time the buyer would have covered even though the buyer has not done so under Section 2–712. This subsection is designed to put the buyer in the position the buyer would have been in if the seller had performed by approximating the harm the buyer has suffered without allowing the buyer an unreasonable time to speculate on the market at the seller's expense.

5. The market price to be used in comparison with the contract price under this section is the price for goods of the same kind and in the same branch of trade.

When the market price under this section is difficult to prove, Section 2–723 on the determination and proof of market price is available to permit a showing of a comparable market price. When no market price is available, evidence of spot sale prices may be used to determine damages under this section. When the unavailability of a market price is caused by a scarcity of goods of the type involved, a good case may be made for specific performance under Section 2-716. *See* the Official Comment to that Section.

6. In addition to the damages provides in this section, the buyer is entitled to incidental and consequential damages under Section 2-715.

7. A buyer that has covered under Section 2-712 may not recover the contract price market price difference under this section, but instead must base the damages on those provided in Section 2-712. To award an additional

amount because the buyer could show the market price was higher than the contract price would put the buyer in a better position than performance would have. Of course, the seller would bear the burden of proving that cover had the economic effect of limiting the buyer's actual loss to an amount less than the contract price-market price difference.

An apparent cover, which does not in fact replace the goods contracted for, should not foreclose the use of the contract price-market price measure of damages. If the breaching seller cannot prove that the new purchase is in fact a replacement for the one not delivered under the contract, the "cover" purchase should not foreclose the buyer's recovery under 2-713 of the market contract difference.

§ 2-714. Buyer's Damages for Breach in Regard to Accepted Goods

(1) ~~Where~~ If the buyer has accepted goods and given notification ~~(subsection (3) of Section 2-607)~~ ~~he~~ pursuant to Section 2-607(3), the buyer may recover as damages for any ~~non-conformity~~ nonconformity of tender the loss resulting in the ordinary course of events from the seller's breach as determined in any reasonable manner ~~which is reasonable~~.

(2) The measure of damages for breach of warranty is the difference at the time and place of acceptance between the value of the goods accepted and the value they would have had if they had been as warranted, unless special circumstances show proximate damages of a different amount.

(3) In a proper case any incidental and consequential damages under ~~the next section~~ Section 2-715 may also be recovered.

§ 2-715. Buyer's Incidental and Consequential Damages

(1) Incidental damages resulting from the seller's breach include expenses reasonably incurred in inspection, receipt, transportation and care and custody of goods rightfully rejected, any commercially reasonable charges, expenses or commissions in connection with effecting cover and any other reasonable expense incident to the delay or other breach.

(2) Consequential damages resulting from the seller's breach include

(a) any loss resulting from general or particular requirements and needs of which the seller at the time of contracting had reason to know and which could not reasonably be prevented by cover or otherwise; and

(b) injury to person or property proximately resulting from any breach of warranty.

§ 2–716. ~~Buyer's Right to~~ Specific Performance ~~or;~~ Buyer's Right to Replevin

(1) Specific performance may be decreed ~~where~~ <u>if</u> the goods are unique or in other proper circumstances. <u>In a contract other than a consumer contract, specific performance may be decreed if the parties have agreed to that remedy. However, even if the parties agree to specific performance, specific performance may not be decreed if the breaching party's sole remaining contractual obligation is the payment of money.</u>

(2) The decree for specific performance may include such terms and conditions as to payment of the price, damages, or other relief as the court may deem just.

(3) The buyer has a right of replevin <u>or similar remedy</u> for goods identified to the contract if after reasonable effort ~~he~~ <u>the buyer</u> is unable to effect cover for such goods or the circumstances reasonably indicate that such effort will be unavailing or if the goods have been shipped under reservation and satisfaction of the security interest in them has been made or tendered. ~~In the case of goods bought for personal, family, or household purposes, the buyer's right of replevin vests upon acquisition of a special property, even if the seller had not then repudiated or failed to deliver.~~

(4) <u>The buyer's right under subsection (3) vests upon acquisition of a special property, even if the seller had not then repudiated or failed to deliver.</u>

Official Comment

1. This section contains the following changes from original Section 2–716:

a) The caption has been amended to make it clear that either party may be entitled to specific performance.

b) The second sentence of subsection (1) explicitly permits parties to bind themselves to specific performance even where it would not otherwise be available.

c) In subsection (3), the phrase "or similar remedy" has been added after "replevin" to reflect the fact that under the governing state law the right may be called "detinue," "sequestration," "claim and delivery," or something else.

d) Subsection (4) corresponds with Section 2–502(2), which in turn is derived from (but broader than) the conforming amendments to Article 9. It provides a vesting rule for cases in which there is a right of replevin.

2. Uniqueness should be determined in light of the total circumstances surrounding the contract and is not limited to goods identified when the contract is formed. The typical specific performance situation today involves an output or requirements contract rather than a contract for the sale of an heirloom or priceless work of art. A buyer's inability to cover is evidence of "other proper circumstances."

3. Subsection (1) provides that a court may decree specific performance if the parties have agreed to that remedy. The parties' agreement to specific performance can be enforced even if legal remedies are entirely adequate. Even in a commercial contract, the third sentence of subsection (1) prevents the aggrieved party from obtaining specific performance if the only obligation of the party in breach is the payment of money. Whether a buyer is obligated to pay the price is determined by Section 2-709, not by this section.

Nothing in this section constrains the court's exercise of its equitable discretion to decide whether to enter a decree for specific performance or to determine the conditions or terms of the decree. This section assumes that the decree for specific performance is conditioned on a tender of full performance by the party that seeks the remedy.

4. The legal remedy of replevin or a similar remedy is also available for cases in which cover is unavailable and where the goods have been identified to the contract. This is in addition to the prepaying buyer's right to recover identified goods upon the seller's insolvency or, when the goods have been bought for a consumer purpose, upon the seller's repudiation or failure to deliver (Section 2-502). If a negotiable document of title is outstanding, the buyer's right of replevin relates to the document and does not directly relate to the goods. *See* Article 7, especially Section 7-602.

5. Subsection (4) provides that a buyer's right to replevin or a similar remedy vests upon the buyer's acquisition of a special property in the goods (Section 2-501) even if the seller has not at that time repudiated or failed to make a required delivery. This vesting rule assumes application of a "first in time" priority rule. In other words, if the buyer's rights vest under this rule before a creditor acquires an *in rem* right to the goods, including an Article 9 security interest and a lien created by levy, the buyer should prevail.

§ 2-717. Deduction of Damages from the Price

The buyer on notifying the seller of ~~his~~ the intention to do so may deduct all or any part of the damages resulting from any breach of the contract from any part of the price still due under the same contract.

§ 2-718. Liquidation or Limitation of Damages; Deposits

(1) Damages for breach by either party may be liquidated in the agreement but only at an amount ~~which~~ that is reasonable in the light of the anticipated or actual harm caused by the breach and, in a consumer contract, the difficulties of proof of loss, and the inconvenience or nonfeasibility of otherwise obtaining an adequate remedy. ~~A term fixing unreasonably large liquidated damages is void as a penalty.~~ Section 2-

719 determines the enforceability of a term that limits but does not liquidate damages.

(2) ~~Where~~ If the seller justifiably withholds delivery of goods or stops performance because of the buyer's breach or insolvency, the buyer is entitled to restitution of any amount by which the sum of ~~his~~ the buyer's payments exceeds ~~(a)~~ the amount to which the seller is entitled by virtue of terms liquidating the seller's damages in accordance with subsection (1)~~, or (b) in the absence of such terms, twenty per cent of the value of the total performance for which the buyer is obligated under the contract or $500, whichever is smaller~~.

(3) The buyer's right to restitution under subsection (2) is subject to offset to the extent that the seller establishes:

> (a) a right to recover damages under the provisions of this Article other than subsection ~~(1),~~ (1); and

> (b) the amount or value of any benefits received by the buyer directly or indirectly by reason of the contract.

(4) ~~Where~~ If a seller has received payment in goods, their reasonable value or the proceeds of their resale shall be treated as payments for the purposes of subsection ~~(2); but~~ (2). However, if the seller has notice of the buyer's breach before reselling goods received in part performance, ~~his~~ the resale is subject to the conditions ~~laid down in~~ of this Article on resale by an aggrieved seller (Section 2–706).

Official Comment

1. The last sentence of subsection (1) clarifies the relationship between this section and Section 2–719.

2. A valid liquidated damages term may liquidate the amount of all damages, including consequential and incidental damages. As under former law, liquidated damages clauses should be enforced if the amount is reasonable in light of the factors provided in subsection (1). This section thus respects the parties' ability to contract for damages while providing some control by requiring that the term be reasonable under the circumstances of the particular case.

Under original Section 2–718, a party seeking to enforce a liquidated damages term had to demonstrate the difficulty of proving the loss and the inconvenience or nonfeasibility of obtaining an adequate remedy. These requirement have been eliminated in commercial contracts but are retained in consumer contracts.

3. Original Section 2–718(1) stated that an unreasonably large liquidated damage term was void as a penalty. This language has been eliminated as unnecessary and misleading. If the liquidated damages are reasonable in light of the test of subsection (1), the term should be enforced, thereby rendering the penalty language of the former law redundant. The language was also misleading because of its emphasis on unreasonably large damages. A liquidated damages term that provided for damages that are unreasonably small is likewise unenforceable.

4. If a liquidated damages term is unenforceable, the remedies of this Article become available to the aggrieved party.

5. Under subsection (2), only the buyer's payments that are more than

the amount of an enforceable liquidated damages term need to be returned to the buyer. If the buyer has made payment by virtue of a trade-in or other goods deposited with the seller, subsection (4) provides that the reasonable value of the goods or the goods' resale price should be used to determine what the buyer has paid, not the value the seller allowed the buyer in the trade-in. To assure that the seller obtains a reasonable price for the goods, the seller must comply with the resale provisions of Section 2–706 if the seller knows of the buyer's breach before the seller has otherwise resold them.

Subsection (2) expands the situations in which restitution was available under prior law. Original Section 2–718(2) was limited to circumstances in which the seller justifiably withheld delivery because of the buyer's breach. Subsection (2) extends the right to situations where the seller stops performance because of the buyer's breach or insolvency.

6. Subsection (3) continues the rule from the former law without change. If there is no enforceable liquidated damages term, under subsection (2) the buyer is entitled to restitution subject to a right of set off by the seller for any damages to which the seller is otherwise entitled to under this Article.

§ 2–719. Contractual Modification or Limitation of Remedy

(1) Subject to the provisions of subsections (2) and (3) of this section and of the preceding section on liquidation and limitation of damages,

  (a) the agreement may provide for remedies in addition to or in substitution for those provided in this Article and may limit or alter the measure of damages recoverable under this Article, as by limiting the buyer's remedies to return of the goods and repayment of the price or to repair and replacement of non-conforming goods or parts; and

  (b) resort to a remedy as provided is optional unless the remedy is expressly agreed to be exclusive, in which case it is the sole remedy.

(2) Where circumstances cause an exclusive or limited remedy to fail of its essential purpose, remedy may be had as provided in this Act.

(3) Consequential damages may be limited or excluded unless the limitation or exclusion is unconscionable. Limitation of consequential damages for injury to the person in the case of consumer goods is prima facie unconscionable but limitation of damages where the loss is commercial is not.

§ 2–720. Effect of "Cancellation" or "Rescission" on Claims for Antecedent Breach

Unless the contrary intention clearly appears, expressions of "cancellation" or "rescission" of the contract or the like shall not be construed as a renunciation or discharge of any claim in damages for an antecedent breach.

§ 2–721. Remedies for Fraud

Remedies for material misrepresentation or fraud include all remedies available under this Article for non-fraudulent breach. Neither rescission or a claim for rescission of the contract for sale nor rejection or return of the goods shall bar or be deemed inconsistent with a claim for damages or other remedy.

§ 2–722. Who ~~Can~~ May Sue Third Parties for Injury to Goods

~~Where~~ If a third party so deals with goods ~~which~~ that have been identified to a contract for sale as to cause actionable injury to a party to that contract:

(a) a right of action against the third party is in either party to the contract for sale ~~who~~ that has title to or a security interest or a special property or an insurable interest in the ~~goods;~~ goods, and if the goods have been destroyed or converted, a right of action is also in the party ~~who~~ that either bore the risk of loss under the contract for sale or has since the injury assumed that risk as against the other;

(b) if at the time of the injury the party plaintiff did not bear the risk of loss as against the other party to the contract for sale and there is no arrangement between them for disposition of the recovery, ~~his~~ the party plaintiff's suit or settlement is, subject to ~~his~~ its own interest, as a fiduciary for the other party to the contract; and

(c) either party may with the consent of the other sue for the benefit of whom it may concern.

§ 2–723. Proof of Market: Time and Place

~~(1) If an action based on anticipatory repudiation comes to trial before the time for performance with respect to some or all of the goods, any damages based on market price (Section 2–708 or Section 2–713) shall be determined according to the price of such goods prevailing at the time when the aggrieved party learned of the repudiation.~~

~~(2)~~ (1) If evidence of a price prevailing at the times or places described in this Article is not readily available, the price prevailing within any reasonable time before or after the time described or at any other place ~~which~~ that in commercial judgment or under usage of trade would serve as a reasonable substitute for the one described may be used, making any proper allowance for the cost of transporting the goods to or from ~~such~~ the other place.

~~(3)~~ (2) Evidence of a relevant price prevailing at a time or place other than the one described in this Article offered by one party is not admissible unless and until ~~he~~ the party has given the other party such notice as the court finds sufficient to prevent unfair surprise.

§ 2-724. Admissibility of Market Quotations

~~Whenever~~ If the prevailing price or value of any goods regularly bought and sold in any established commodity market is in issue, reports in official publications or trade journals or in newspapers ~~or periodicals~~ , periodicals or other means of communication in ~~of~~ general circulation published as the reports of ~~such~~ the market ~~shall be~~ are admissible in evidence. The circumstances of the preparation of such a report may be shown to affect its weight but not its admissibility.

§ 2-725. Statute of Limitations in Contracts for Sale

~~(1) An action for breach of any contract for sale must be commenced within four years after the cause of action has accrued. By the original agreement the parties may reduce the period of limitation to not less than one year but may not extend it.~~

~~(2) A cause of action accrues when the breach occurs, regardless of the aggrieved party's lack of knowledge of the breach. A breach of warranty occurs when tender of delivery is made, except that where a warranty explicitly extends to future performance of the goods and discovery of the breach must await the time of such performance the cause of action accrues when the breach is or should have been discovered.~~

(1) Except as otherwise provided in this section, an action for breach of any contract for sale must be commenced within the later of four years after the right of action has accrued under subsection (2) or (3) or one year after the breach was or should have been discovered, but no longer than five years after the right of action accrued. By the original agreement the parties may reduce the period of limitation to not less than one year but may not extend it. However, in a consumer contract, the period of limitation may not be reduced.

(2) Except as otherwise provided in subsection (3), the following rules apply:

    (a) Except as otherwise provided in this subsection, a right of action for breach of a contract accrues when the breach occurs, even if the aggrieved party did not have knowledge of the breach.

    (b) For breach of a contract by repudiation, a right of action accrues at the earlier of when the aggrieved party elects to treat the repudiation as a breach or when a commercially reasonable time for awaiting performance has expired.

    (c) For breach of a remedial promise, a right of action accrues when the remedial promise is not performed when performance is due.

    (d) In an action by a buyer against a person that is answerable over to the buyer for a claim asserted against the buyer, the buyer's right of action against the person answerable over accrues at the time the claim was originally asserted against the buyer.

(3) If a breach of a warranty arising under Section 2–312, 2–313(2), 2–314, or 2–315, or a breach of an obligation, other than a remedial promise, arising under Section 2–313A or 2–313B, is claimed, the following rules apply:

(a) Except as otherwise provided in paragraph (c), a right of action for breach of a warranty arising under Section 2–313(2), 2–314, or 2–315 accrues when the seller has tendered delivery to the immediate buyer, as defined in Section 2–313, and has completed performance of any agreed installation or assembly of the goods.

(b) Except as otherwise provided in paragraph (c), a right of action for breach of an obligation, other than a remedial promise, arising under Section 2–313A or 2–313B accrues when the remote purchaser, as defined in Section 2–313A or 2–313B, receives the goods.

(c) If a warranty arising under Section 2–313(2) or an obligation, other than a remedial promise, arising under Section 2–313A or 2–313B explicitly extends to future performance of the goods and discovery of the breach must await the time for performance, the right of action accrues when the immediate buyer as defined in Section 2–313 or the remote purchaser as defined in Section 2–313A or 2–313B discovers or should have discovered the breach.

(d) A right of action for breach of warranty arising under Section 2–312 accrues when the aggrieved party discovers or should have discovered the breach. However, an action for breach of the warranty of noninfringement may not be commenced more than six years after tender of delivery of the goods to the aggrieved party.

(3) (4) ~~Where~~ If an action commenced within the time limited by subsection (1) is so terminated as to leave available a remedy by another action for the same breach, ~~such~~ the other action may be commenced after the expiration of the time limited and within six months after the termination of the first action unless the termination resulted from voluntary discontinuance or from dismissal for failure or neglect to prosecute.

(4) (5) This section does not alter the law on tolling of the statute of limitations nor does it apply to causes of action ~~which have~~ that accrued before this Act becomes effective.

223

Official Comment

1. Original Section 2–725 has been changed as follows: 1) The basic four-year limitation period in subsection (1) has been supplemented by a discovery rule that permits a cause of action to be brought within one year after the breach was or should have been discovered, although no later than five years after the time the cause would otherwise have accrued; 2) The applicable limitation period cannot be reduced in a consumer contract (subsection (1)); 3) Subsection (2) contains specific rules for cases of repudiation, breach of a remedial promise, and actions where another person is answerable over; 4) Subsection (3)(a) provides that the limitation period for breach of warranty accrues when tender of delivery has occurred and the seller has completed any agreed installation or assembly of the goods; 5) Subsection (3) contains specific rules for breach of an obligation arising under Section 2–313A or 2–313B, for breach of a warranty arising under Section 2–312, and for breach of a warranty against infringement.

2. Subsection (1) continues the four-year limitation period of original Article 2 but provides for a possible one-year extension to accommodate a discovery of the breach late in the four year period after accrual. The four year period under this Article is shorter than many other statutes of limitation for breach of contract and it provides a period which is appropriate given the nature of the contracts under this Article and modern business practices. As under original Article 2, the period of limitation can be reduced to one year by an agreement in a commercial contract, but the amended section does not permit this reduction in consumer contracts.

3. Subsections (2) and (3) provide rules for accrual of the various types of action that this Article allows. Certainty of commercial relationships is advanced when the rules are clearly set forth. Subsection (2) sets out the accrual rules for actions other than for breach of a warranty, which includes actions based on repudiation or breach of a remedial promise and actions where another person is answerable over. Subsection (3) sets out the accrual rules for the various claims based on a warranty, including a warranty of title and a warranty against infringement, or on an obligation other than a remedial promise arising under Section 2–313A or 2–313B.

Subsection (2)(a) states the general rule from prior law that a right of action for breach of contract accrues when the breach occurs without regard to the aggrieved party's knowledge of the breach. This general rule is then subject to the three more explicit rules in subsection (2) and to the rules for breach of warranty stated in subsection (3).

Subsection (2)(b) provides an explicit rule for repudiation. In a repudiation, the aggrieved party may await performance for a commercially reasonable time or resort to any remedy for breach. Section 2–610. The accrual rule for breach of contract in a repudiation case is based on the earlier of those two time periods.

Subsection (2)(c) provides that a cause of action for breach of a remedial promise accrues when the promise is not performed at the time performance is due.

Subsection (2)(d) addresses the problem that has arisen in the cases when an intermediary party is sued for a breach of obligation for which its seller or another person is answerable over, but the limitations period in the upstream lawsuit has already expired. This subsection allows a party four years, or if reduced in the agreement, not less than one year, from when the claim is originally asserted against the buyer for the buyer to sue the person that is answerable over. Whether a party is in fact answerable over to the buyer is not addressed in this section.

4. Subsection (3) addresses the accrual rules for breach of a warranty arising under Section 2–312, 2–313(2), 2–314 or 2–315, or of an obligation other than a remedial promise arising under Section 2–313A or 2–313B. The subsection does not apply to remedial promises arising under Section 2–313(4); the limitation for all remedial promises are governed by subsection 2(c). The accrual rules explicitly incorporate the definitions of "immediate buyer" and "remote purchaser" in Sections 2–313, 2–313A and 2–313B. Any cause of action brought by another person to which the warranty or obligation extends is derivative in nature. Thus, the time period applicable to the immediate buyer or remote purchaser governs even if the action is brought by a person to which the warranty or obligation extends under Section 2–318.

Subsection (3)(a) continues the general rule that an action for breach of warranty accrues in the case of an express or implied warranty to an immediate buyer upon completion of tender of delivery of nonconforming goods to the immediate buyer but makes explicit that accrual is deferred until the completion of any installation or assembly that the seller has agreed to undertake. This extension of the time of accrual in the case of installation or assembly applies only in the case of a seller that promises to install or assemble and not in the case of a third party, independent of the seller, undertaking the action.

Subsection (3)(b) addresses the accrual of a cause of action for breach of an obligation other than a remedial promise arising under Section 2–313A

or 2–313B. In these cases, the cause of action accrues when the remote purchaser (as defined in those sections) receives the goods. This accrual rule balances the rights of the remote buyer or remote lessee to be able to have a cause of action based upon the warranty obligation the seller has created against the rights of the seller to have some limit on the length of time the seller is liable.

Both of these accrual rules are subject to the exception in subsection (3)(c) for a warranty or obligation that explicitly extends to the future performance of the goods and discovery of the breach must await the time for performance. In this case, the cause of action does not accrue until the buyer or remote purchaser discovers or should have discovered the breach.

For a warranty of title or a warranty of non-infringement under Section 2–312, subsection (3)(d) provides that a cause of action accrues when the aggrieved party discovers or should have discovered the breach. In a typical case, the aggrieved party will not discover the breach until it is sued by a party that asserts title to the goods or that asserts an infringement, either event which could be many years after the buyer acquired the goods. This accrual rule allows the aggrieved party appropriate leeway to then bring a claim against the person that made the warranty. In recognition of a need to have a time of repose in an infringement case, a party may not bring an action based upon a warranty of non-infringement more than six years after tender of delivery.

5. Subsection (4) states the saving provision included in many state statutes and permits an additional short period for bringing new actions where suits begun within the four year period have been terminated so as to leave a

remedy still available for the same breach.

6. Subsection (5) makes it clear that this Article does not purport to alter or modify in any respect the law on tolling of the Statute of Limitations as it now prevails in the various jurisdictions.

PART 8

TRANSITIONAL PROVISIONS

§ 2–801. Effective Date

This [Act] takes effect on _____, 20___.

§ 2–802. Amendment of Existing Article 2

This [Act] amends [insert citation to existing Article 2].

§ 2–803. Application to Existing Relations

(1) This [Act] applies to a transaction within its scope that is entered into on or after the effective date of this [Act].

(2) This [Act] does not apply to a transaction that is entered into before the effective date of this [Act] even if the transaction would be subject to this [Act] if it had been entered into after the effective date of this [Act].

(3) This [Act] does not apply to a right of action that accrued before the effective date of this [Act].

(4) Section 2–313B of this [Act] does not apply to an advertisement or similar communication made before the effective date of this [Act].

§ 2–804. Savings Clause

A transaction entered into before the effective date of this [Act], and the rights, obligations, and interests flowing from that transaction, are governed by any statute or other law amended or repealed by this [Act] as if amendment or repeal had not occurred and may be terminated, completed, consummated, or enforced under that statute or other law.

ARTICLE 3.   NEGOTIABLE INSTRUMENTS

Section

3–311.   Accord and Satisfaction by Use of Instrument

§ 3–311.   Accord and Satisfaction by Use of Instrument

(a) If a person against whom a claim is asserted proves that (i) that person in good faith tendered an instrument to the claimant as full satisfaction of the claim, (ii) the amount of the claim was unliquidated or subject to a bona fide dispute, and (iii) the claimant obtained payment of the instrument, the following subsections apply.

(b) Unless subsection (c) applies, the claim is discharged if the person against whom the claim is asserted proves that the instrument or an accompanying written communication contained a conspicuous statement to the effect that the instrument was tendered as full satisfaction of the claim.

(c) Subject to subsection (d), a claim is not discharged under subsection (b) if either of the following applies:

(1) The claimant, if an organization, proves that (i) within a reasonable time before the tender, the claimant sent a conspicuous statement to the person against whom the claim is asserted that communications concerning disputed debts, including an instrument tendered as full satisfaction of a debt, are to be sent to a designated person, office, or place, and (ii) the instrument or accompanying communication was not received by that designated person, office, or place.

(2) The claimant, whether or not an organization, proves that within 90 days after payment of the instrument, the claimant tendered repayment of the amount of the instrument to the person against whom the claim is asserted. This paragraph does not apply if the claimant is an organization that sent a statement complying with paragraph (1)(i).

(d) A claim is discharged if the person against whom the claim is asserted proves that within a reasonable time before collection of the instrument was initiated, the claimant, or an agent of the claimant having direct responsibility with respect to the disputed obligation, knew that the instrument was tendered in full satisfaction of the claim.

UNIFORM ELECTRONIC TRANSACTIONS ACT (UETA)

Table of Contents

---

§ 1. Short Title

This [Act] may be cited as the Uniform Electronic Transactions Act.

§ 2. Definitions

In this [Act]:

(1) "Agreement" means the bargain of the parties in fact, as found in their language or inferred from other circumstances and from rules, regulations, and procedures given the effect of agreements under laws otherwise applicable to a particular transaction.

(2) "Automated transaction" means a transaction conducted or performed, in whole or in part, by electronic means or electronic records, in which the acts or records of one or both parties are not reviewed by an individual in the ordinary course in forming a contract, performing

under an existing contract, or fulfilling an obligation required by the transaction.

(3) "Computer program" means a set of statements or instructions to be used directly or indirectly in an information processing system in order to bring about a certain result.

(4) "Contract" means the total legal obligation resulting from the parties' agreement as affected by this [Act] and other applicable law.

(5) "Electronic" means relating to technology having electrical, digital, magnetic, wireless, optical, electromagnetic, or similar capabilities.

(6) "Electronic agent" means a computer program or an electronic or other automated means used independently to initiate an action or respond to electronic records or performances in whole or in part, without review or action by an individual.

(7) "Electronic record" means a record created, generated, sent, communicated, received, or stored by electronic means.

(8) "Electronic signature" means an electronic sound, symbol, or process attached to or logically associated with a record and executed or adopted by a person with the intent to sign the record.

(9) "Governmental agency" means an executive, legislative, or judicial agency, department, board, commission, authority, institution, or instrumentality of the federal government or of a State or of a county, municipality, or other political subdivision of a State.

(10) "Information" means data, text, images, sounds, codes, computer programs, software, databases, or the like.

(11) "Information processing system" means an electronic system for creating, generating, sending, receiving, storing, displaying, or processing information.

(12) "Person" means an individual, corporation, business trust, estate, trust, partnership, limited liability company, association, joint venture, governmental agency, public corporation, or any other legal or commercial entity.

(13) "Record" means information that is inscribed on a tangible medium or that is stored in an electronic or other medium and is retrievable in perceivable form.

(14) "Security procedure" means a procedure employed for the purpose of verifying that an electronic signature, record, or performance is that of a specific person or for detecting changes or errors in the information in an electronic record. The term includes a procedure that requires the use of algorithms or other codes, identifying words or numbers, encryption, or callback or other acknowledgment procedures.

(15) "State" means a State of the United States, the District of Columbia, Puerto Rico, the United States Virgin Islands, or any territory or insular possession subject to the jurisdiction of the United States. The term includes an Indian tribe or band, or Alaskan native village, which is recognized by federal law or formally acknowledged by a State.

(16) "Transaction" means an action or set of actions occurring between two or more persons relating to the conduct of business, commercial, or governmental affairs

§ 3. Scope

(a) Except as otherwise provided in subsection (b), this [Act] applies to electronic records and electronic signatures relating to a transaction.

(b) This [Act] does not apply to a transaction to the extent it is governed by:

> (1) a law governing the creation and execution of wills, codicils, or testamentary trusts;
>
> (2) [The Uniform Commercial Code other than Sections 1–107 and 1–206, Article 2, and Article 2A];
>
> (3) [the Uniform Computer Information Transactions Act]; and
>
> (4) [other laws, if any, identified by State].

(c) This [Act] applies to an electronic record or electronic signature otherwise excluded from the application of this [Act] under subsection (b) to the extent it is governed by a law other than those specified in subsection (b).

(d) A transaction subject to this [Act] is also subject to other applicable substantive law.

§ 4. Prospective Application

This [Act] applies to any electronic record or electronic signature created, generated, sent, communicated, received, or stored on or after the effective date of this [Act].

§ 5. Use of Electronic Records and Electronic Signatures; Variation By Agreement

(a) This [Act] does not require a record or signature to be created, generated, sent, communicated, received, stored, or otherwise processed or used by electronic means or in electronic form.

(b) This [Act] applies only to transactions between parties each of which has agreed to conduct transactions by electronic means. Whether the parties agree to conduct a transaction by electronic means is determined from the context and surrounding circumstances, including the parties' conduct.

(c) A party that agrees to conduct a transaction by electronic means may refuse to conduct other transactions by electronic means. The right granted by this subsection may not be waived by agreement.

(d) Except as otherwise provided in this [Act], the effect of any of its provisions may be varied by agreement. The presence in certain provisions of this [Act] of the words "unless otherwise agreed", or words of similar import, does not imply that the effect of other provisions may not be varied by agreement.

(e) Whether an electronic record or electronic signature has legal consequences is determined by this [Act] and other applicable law.

§ 6. Construction and Application

This [Act] must be construed and applied:

(1) to facilitate electronic transactions consistent with other applicable law;

(2) to be consistent with reasonable practices concerning electronic transactions and with the continued expansion of those practices; and

(3) to effectuate its general purpose to make uniform the law with respect to the subject of this [Act] among States enacting it.

§ 7. Legal Recognition of Electronic Records, Electronic Signatures, and Electronic Contracts

(a) A record or signature may not be denied legal effect or enforceability solely because it is in electronic form.

(b) A contract may not be denied legal effect or enforceability solely because an electronic record was used in its formation.

(c) If a law requires a record to be in writing, an electronic record satisfies the law.

(d) If a law requires a signature, an electronic signature satisfies the law.

§ 8. Provision of Information in Writing; Presentation of Records

(a) If parties have agreed to conduct a transaction by electronic means and a law requires a person to provide, send, or deliver information in writing to another person, the requirement is satisfied if the information is provided, sent, or delivered, as the case may be, in an electronic record capable of retention by the recipient at the time of receipt. An electronic record is not capable of retention by the recipient if the sender or its information processing system inhibits the ability of the recipient to print or store the electronic record.

(b) If a law other than this [Act] requires a record (i) to be posted or displayed in a certain manner, (ii) to be sent, communicated, or transmitted by a specified method, or (iii) to contain information that is formatted in a certain manner, the following rules apply:

(1) The record must be posted or displayed in the manner specified in the other law.

(2) Except as otherwise provided in subsection (d)(2), the record must be sent, communicated, or transmitted by the method specified in the other law.

(3) The record must contain the information formatted in the manner specified in the other law.

(c) If a sender inhibits the ability of a recipient to store or print an electronic record, the electronic record is not enforceable against the recipient.

(d) The requirements of this section may not be varied by agreement, but:

(1) to the extent a law other than this [Act] requires information to be provided, sent, or delivered in writing but permits that requirement to be varied by agreement, the requirement under subsection (a) that the information be in the form of an electronic record capable of retention may also be varied by agreement; and

(2) a requirement under a law other than this [Act] to send, communicate, or transmit a record by [first-class mail, postage prepaid] [regular United States mail], may be varied by agreement to the extent permitted by the other law.

§ 9. Attribution and Effect of Electronic Record and Electronic Signature

(a) An electronic record or electronic signature is attributable to a person if it was the act of the person. The act of the person may be shown in any manner, including a showing of the efficacy of any security procedure applied to determine the person to which the electronic record or electronic signature was attributable.

(b) The effect of an electronic record or electronic signature attributed to a person under subsection (a) is determined from the context and surrounding circumstances at the time of its creation, execution, or adoption, including the parties' agreement, if any, and otherwise as provided by law.

§ 10. Effect of Change or Error.

If a change or error in an electronic record occurs in a transmission between parties to a transaction, the following rules apply:

(1) If the parties have agreed to use a security procedure to detect changes or errors and one party has conformed to the

procedure, but the other party has not, and the nonconforming party would have detected the change or error had that party also conformed, the conforming party may avoid the effect of the changed or erroneous electronic record.

(2) In an automated transaction involving an individual, the individual may avoid the effect of an electronic record that resulted from an error made by the individual in dealing with the electronic agent of another person if the electronic agent did not provide an opportunity for the prevention or correction of the error and, at the time the individual learns of the error, the individual:

   (A) promptly notifies the other person of the error and that the individual did not intend to be bound by the electronic record received by the other person;

   (B) takes reasonable steps, including steps that conform to the other person's reasonable instructions, to return to the other person or, if instructed by the other person, to destroy the consideration received, if any, as a result of the erroneous electronic record; and (C) has not used or received any benefit or value from the consideration, if any, received from the other person.

(3) If neither paragraph (1) nor paragraph (2) applies, the change or error has the effect provided by other law, including the law of mistake, and the parties' contract, if any.

(4) Paragraphs (2) and (3) may not be varied by agreement.

§ 11. Notarization and Acknowledgment

If a law requires a signature or record to be notarized, acknowledged, verified, or made under oath, the requirement is satisfied if the electronic signature of the person authorized to perform those acts, together with all other information required to be included by other applicable law, is attached to or logically associated with the signature or record.

§ 12. Retention of Electronic Records; Originals

(a) If a law requires that a record be retained, the requirement is satisfied by retaining an electronic record of the information in the record which:

   (1) accurately reflects the information set forth in the record after it was first generated in its final form as an electronic record or otherwise; and

   (2) remains accessible for later reference.

(b) A requirement to retain a record in accordance with subsection (a) does not apply to any information the sole purpose of which is to enable the record to be sent, communicated, or received.

(c) A person may satisfy subsection (a) by using the services of another person if the requirements of that subsection are satisfied.

(d) If a law requires a record to be presented or retained in its original form, or provides consequences if the record is not presented or retained in its original form, that law is satisfied by an electronic record retained in accordance with subsection (a).

(e) If a law requires retention of a check, that requirement is satisfied by retention of an electronic record of the information on the front and back of the check in accordance with subsection (a).

(f) A record retained as an electronic record in accordance with subsection (a) satisfies a law requiring a person to retain a record for evidentiary, audit, or like purposes, unless a law enacted after the effective date of this [Act] specifically prohibits the use of an electronic record for the specified purpose.

(g) This section does not preclude a governmental agency of this State from specifying additional requirements for the retention of a record subject to the agency's jurisdiction.

§ 13. Admissibility in Evidence

In a proceeding, evidence of a record or signature may not be excluded solely because it is in electronic form.

§ 14. Automated Transaction

In an automated transaction, the following rules apply:

(1) A contract may be formed by the interaction of electronic agents of the parties, even if no individual was aware of or reviewed the electronic agents' actions or the resulting terms and agreements.

(2) A contract may be formed by the interaction of an electronic agent and an individual, acting on the individual's own behalf or for another person, including by an interaction in which the individual performs actions that the individual is free to refuse to perform and which the individual knows or has reason to know will cause the electronic agent to complete the transaction or performance.

(3) The terms of the contract are determined by the substantive law applicable to it.

§ 15. Time and Place of Sending and Receipt

(a) Unless otherwise agreed between the sender and the recipient, an electronic record is sent when it:

(1) is addressed properly or otherwise directed properly to an information processing system that the recipient has designated or uses for the purpose of receiving electronic records or information of the type sent and from which the recipient is able to retrieve the electronic record;

(2) is in a form capable of being processed by that system; and

(3) enters an information processing system outside the control of the sender or of a person that sent the electronic record on behalf of the sender or enters a region of the information processing system designated or used by the recipient which is under the control of the recipient.

(b) Unless otherwise agreed between a sender and the recipient, an electronic record is received when:

(1) it enters an information processing system that the recipient has designated or uses for the purpose of receiving electronic records or information of the type sent and from which the recipient is able to retrieve the electronic record; and

(2) it is in a form capable of being processed by that system.

(c) Subsection (b) applies even if the place the information processing system is located is different from the place the electronic record is deemed to be received under subsection (d).

(d) Unless otherwise expressly provided in the electronic record or agreed between the sender and the recipient, an electronic record is deemed to be sent from the sender's place of business and to be received at the recipient's place of business. For purposes of this subsection, the following rules apply:

(1) If the sender or recipient has more than one place of business, the place of business of that person is the place having the closest relationship to the underlying transaction.

(2) If the sender or the recipient does not have a place of business, the place of business is the sender's or recipient's residence, as the case may be.

(e) An electronic record is received under subsection (b) even if no individual is aware of its receipt.

(f) Receipt of an electronic acknowledgment from an information processing system described in subsection (b) establishes that a record was received but, by itself, does not establish that the content sent corresponds to the content received.

(g) If a person is aware that an electronic record purportedly sent under subsection (a), or purportedly received under subsection (b), was not actually sent or received, the legal effect of the sending or receipt is determined by other applicable law. Except to the extent permitted by the other law, the requirements of this subsection may not be varied by agreement.

§ 16. Transferable Records

(a) In this section, "transferable record" means an electronic record that:

> (1) would be a note under [Article 3 of the Uniform Commercial Code] or a document under [Article 7 of the Uniform Commercial Code] if the electronic record were in writing; and
>
> (2) the issuer of the electronic record expressly has agreed is a transferable record.

(b) A person has control of a transferable record if a system employed for evidencing the transfer of interests in the transferable record reliably establishes that person as the person to which the transferable record was issued or transferred.

(c) A system satisfies subsection (b), and a person is deemed to have control of a transferable record, if the transferable record is created, stored, and assigned in such a manner that:

> (1) a single authoritative copy of the transferable record exists which is unique, identifiable, and, except as otherwise provided in paragraphs (4), (5), and (6), unalterable;
>
> (2) the authoritative copy identifies the person asserting control as:
>
> > (A) the person to which the transferable record was issued; or
> >
> > (B) if the authoritative copy indicates that the transferable record has been transferred, the person to which the transferable record was most recently transferred;
>
> (3) the authoritative copy is communicated to and maintained by the person asserting control or its designated custodian;
>
> (4) copies or revisions that add or change an identified assignee of the authoritative copy can be made only with the consent of the person asserting control;
>
> (5) each copy of the authoritative copy and any copy of a copy is readily identifiable as a copy that is not the authoritative copy; and
>
> (6) any revision of the authoritative copy is readily identifiable as authorized or unauthorized.

(d) Except as otherwise agreed, a person having control of a transferable record is the holder, as defined in [Section 1–201(20) of the Uniform Commercial Code], of the transferable record and has the same rights and defenses as a holder of an equivalent record or writing under [the Uniform Commercial Code], including, if the applicable statutory requirements under [Section 3–302(a), 7–501, or 9–308 of the Uniform Commercial Code] are satisfied, the rights and defenses of a holder in due course, a holder to which a negotiable document of title has been duly negotiated, or a purchaser, respectively. Delivery, possession, and indorsement are not required to obtain or exercise any of the rights under this subsection.

(e) Except as otherwise agreed, an obligor under a transferable record has the same rights and defenses as an equivalent obligor under equivalent records or writings under [the Uniform Commercial Code].

(f) If requested by a person against which enforcement is sought, the person seeking to enforce the transferable record shall provide reasonable proof that the person is in control of the transferable record. Proof may include access to the authoritative copy of the transferable record and related business records sufficient to review the terms of the transferable record and to establish the identity of the person having control of the transferable record.

[§ 17. Creation and Retention of Electronic Records and Conversion of Written Records By Governmental Agencies

[Each governmental agency] [The designated state officer] of this State shall determine whether, and the extent to which, [it] [a governmental agency] will create and retain electronic records and convert written records to electronic records.]

[§ 18. Acceptance and Distribution of Electronic Records By Governmental Agencies

(a) Except as otherwise provided in Section 12(f), [each governmental agency] [the [designated state officer]] of this State shall determine whether, and the extent to which, [it] [a governmental agency] will send and accept electronic records and electronic signatures to and from other persons and otherwise create, generate, communicate, store, process, use, and rely upon electronic records and electronic signatures.

(b) To the extent that a governmental agency uses electronic records and electronic signatures under subsection (a), the [governmental agency] [designated state officer], giving due consideration to security, may specify:

    (1) the manner and format in which the electronic records must be created, generated, sent, communicated, received, and stored and the systems established for those purposes;

    (2) if electronic records must be signed by electronic means, the type of electronic signature required, the manner and for-

mat in which the electronic signature must be affixed to the electronic record, and the identity of, or criteria that must be met by, any third party used by a person filing a document to facilitate the process;

(3) control processes and procedures as appropriate to ensure adequate preservation, disposition, integrity, security, confidentiality, and auditability of electronic records; and

(4) any other required attributes for electronic records which are specified for corresponding nonelectronic records or reasonably necessary under the circumstances.

(c) Except as otherwise provided in Section 12(f), this [Act] does not require a governmental agency of this State to use or permit the use of electronic records or electronic signatures.]

[§ 19. Interoperability

The [governmental agency] [designated officer] of this State which adopts standards pursuant to Section 18 may encourage and promote consistency and interoperability with similar requirements adopted by other governmental agencies of this and other States and the federal government and nongovernmental persons interacting with governmental agencies of this State. If appropriate, those standards may specify differing levels of standards from which governmental agencies of this State may choose in implementing the most appropriate standard for a particular application.]

§ 20. Severability Clause

If any provision of this [Act] or its application to any person or circumstance is held invalid, the invalidity does not affect other provisions or applications of this [Act] which can be given effect without the invalid provision or application, and to this end the provisions of this [Act] are severable.

§ 21. Effective Date

This [Act] takes effect _____

ELECTRONIC SIGNATURES IN GLOBAL AND NATIONAL COMMERCE ACT (E–SIGN) (excerpts)

§ 1 (15 U.S.C.A. § 7001 Note). Short Title.

This Act may be cited as the "Electronic Signatures in Global and National Commerce Act".

TITLE I

ELECTRONIC RECORDS AND SIGNATURES IN COMMERCE

§ 101 (15 U.S.C.A. § 7001). General Rule of Validity.

(a) IN GENERAL.—Notwithstanding any statute, regulation, or other rule of law (other than this title and title II), with respect to any transaction in or affecting interstate or foreign commerce—

> (1) a signature, contract, or other record relating to such transaction may not be denied legal effect, validity, or enforceability solely because it is in electronic form; and

> (2) a contract relating to such transaction may not be denied legal effect, validity, or enforceability solely because an electronic signature or electronic record was used in its formation.

(b) PRESERVATION OF RIGHTS AND OBLIGATIONS.—This title does not—

> (1) limit, alter, or otherwise affect any requirement imposed by a statute, regulation, or rule of law relating to the rights and obligations of persons under such statute, regulation, or rule of law other than a requirement that contracts or other records be written, signed, or in nonelectronic form; or

> (2) require any person to agree to use or accept electronic records or electronic signatures, other than a governmental agency with respect to a record other than a contract to which it is a party.

(c) CONSUMER DISCLOSURES.—

> (1) CONSENT TO ELECTRONIC RECORDS.—Notwithstanding subsection (a), if a statute, regulation, or other rule of law requires that information relating to a transaction or transactions in or affecting interstate or foreign commerce be provided or made available to a consumer in writing, the

use of an electronic record to provide or make available (whichever is required) such information satisfies the requirement that such information be in writing if—

(A) the consumer has affirmatively consented to such use and has not withdrawn such consent;

(B) the consumer, prior to consenting, is provided with a clear and conspicuous statement—

(i) informing the consumer of (I) any right or option of the consumer to have the record provided or made available on paper or in nonelectronic form, and (II) the right of the consumer to withdraw the consent to have the record provided or made available in an electronic form and of any conditions, consequences (which may include termination of the parties' relationship), or fees in the event of such withdrawal;

(ii) informing the consumer of whether the consent applies (I) only to the particular transaction which gave rise to the obligation to provide the record, or (II) to identified categories of records that may be provided or made available during the course of the parties' relationship;

(iii) describing the procedures the consumer must use to withdraw consent as provided in clause (i) and to update information needed to contact the consumer electronically; and

(iv) informing the consumer (I) how, after the consent, the consumer may, upon request, obtain a paper copy of an electronic record, and (II) whether any fee will be charged for such copy;

(C) the consumer—

(i) prior to consenting, is provided with a statement of the hardware and software requirements for access to and retention of the electronic records; and

(ii) consents electronically, or confirms his or her consent electronically, in a manner that reasonably demonstrates that the consumer can access information in the electronic form that will be used to provide the information that is the subject of the consent; and

(D) after the consent of a consumer in accordance with subparagraph (A), if a change in the hardware or software requirements needed to access or retain electronic records creates a material risk that the consumer will not be able to access or retain a subsequent electronic record that was the subject of the consent, the person providing the electronic record—

 (i) provides the consumer with a statement of (I) the revised hardware and software requirements for access to and retention of the electronic records, and (II) the right to withdraw consent without the imposition of any fees for such withdrawal and without the imposition of any condition or consequence that was not disclosed under subparagraph (B)(i); and

 (ii) again complies with subparagraph (C).

(2) OTHER RIGHTS.—

 (A) PRESERVATION OF CONSUMER PROTECTIONS.— Nothing in this title affects the content or timing of any disclosure or other record required to be provided or made available to any consumer under any statute, regulation, or other rule of law.

 (B) VERIFICATION OR ACKNOWLEDGMENT.—If a law that was enacted prior to this Act expressly requires a record to be provided or made available by a specified method that requires verification or acknowledgment of receipt, the record may be provided or made available electronically only if the method used provides verification or acknowledgment of receipt (whichever is required).

(3) EFFECT OF FAILURE TO OBTAIN ELECTRONIC CONSENT OR CONFIRMATION OF CONSENT.—The legal effectiveness, validity, or enforceability of any contract executed by a consumer shall not be denied solely because of the failure to obtain electronic consent or confirmation of consent by that consumer in accordance with paragraph (1)(C)(ii).

(4) PROSPECTIVE EFFECT.—Withdrawal of consent by a consumer shall not affect the legal effectiveness, validity, or enforceability of electronic records provided or made available to that consumer in accordance with paragraph (1) prior to implementation of the consumer's withdrawal of consent. A consumer's withdrawal of consent shall be effective within a reasonable period of time after receipt of the withdrawal by the provider of the record. Failure to comply with paragraph (1)(D) may, at the election of the consumer, be treated as a withdrawal of consent for purposes of this paragraph.

(5) PRIOR CONSENT.—This subsection does not apply to any records that are provided or made available to a consumer who has consented prior to the effective date of this title to receive such records in electronic form as permitted by any statute, regulation, or other rule of law.

(6) ORAL COMMUNICATIONS.—An oral communication or a recording of an oral communication shall not qualify as an electronic record for purposes of this subsection except as otherwise provided under applicable law.

(d) RETENTION OF CONTRACTS AND RECORDS.—

(1) ACCURACY AND ACCESSIBILITY.—If a statute, regulation, or other rule of law requires that a contract or other record relating to a transaction in or affecting interstate or foreign commerce be retained, that requirement is met by retaining an electronic record of the information in the contract or other record that—

(A) accurately reflects the information set forth in the contract or other record; and

(B) remains accessible to all persons who are entitled to access by statute, regulation, or rule of law, for the period required by such statute, regulation, or rule of law, in a form that is capable of being accurately reproduced for later reference, whether by transmission, printing, or otherwise.

(2) EXCEPTION.—A requirement to retain a contract or other record in accordance with paragraph (1) does not apply to any information whose sole purpose is to enable the contract or other record to be sent, communicated, or received.

(3) ORIGINALS.—If a statute, regulation, or other rule of law requires a contract or other record relating to a transaction in or affecting interstate or foreign commerce to be provided, available, or retained in its original form, or provides consequences if the contract or other record is not provided, available, or retained in its original form, that statute, regulation, or rule of law is satisfied by an electronic record that complies with paragraph (1).

(4) CHECKS.—If a statute, regulation, or other rule of law requires the retention of a check, that requirement is satisfied by retention of an electronic record of the information on the front and back of the check in accordance with paragraph (1).

(e) ACCURACY AND ABILITY TO RETAIN CONTRACTS AND OTHER RECORDS.—Notwithstanding subsection (a), if a statute, regulation, or other rule of law requires that a contract or other record relating to a transaction in or affecting interstate or foreign commerce be in writing, the legal effect, validity, or enforceability of an electronic record of such contract or other record may be denied if such electronic record is not in a form that is capable of being retained and accurately reproduced for later reference by all parties or persons who are entitled to retain the contract or other record.

(f) PROXIMITY.—Nothing in this title affects the proximity required by any statute, regulation, or other rule of law with respect to any warning, notice, disclosure, or other record required to be posted, displayed, or publicly affixed.

(g) NOTARIZATION AND ACKNOWLEDGMENT.—If a statute, regulation, or other rule of law requires a signature or record relating to a transaction in or affecting interstate or foreign commerce to be notarized, acknowledged, verified, or made under oath, that requirement is satisfied if the electronic signature of the person authorized to perform those acts, together with all other information required to be included by other applicable statute, regulation, or rule of law, is attached to or logically associated with the signature or record.

(h) ELECTRONIC AGENTS.—A contract or other record relating to a transaction in or affecting interstate or foreign commerce may not be denied legal effect, validity, or enforceability solely because its formation, creation, or delivery involved the action of one or more electronic agents so long as the action of any such electronic agent is legally attributable to the person to be bound.

(i) INSURANCE.—It is the specific intent of the Congress that this title and title II apply to the business of insurance.

(j) INSURANCE AGENTS AND BROKERS.—An insurance agent or broker acting under the direction of a party that enters into a contract by means of an electronic record or electronic signature may not be held liable for any deficiency in the electronic procedures agreed to by the parties under that contract if—

> (1) the agent or broker has not engaged in negligent, reckless, or intentional tortious conduct;

> (2) the agent or broker was not involved in the development or establishment of such electronic procedures; and

> (3) the agent or broker did not deviate from such procedures.

§ 102 (15 U.S.C.A. § 7002). Exemption to Preemption.

(a) IN GENERAL.—A State statute, regulation, or other rule of law may modify, limit, or supersede the provisions of section 101 with respect to State law only if such statute, regulation, or rule of law—

> (1) constitutes an enactment or adoption of the Uniform Electronic Transactions Act as approved and recommended for

enactment in all the States by the National Conference of Commissioners on Uniform State Laws in 1999, except that any exception to the scope of such Act enacted by a State under section 3(b)(4) of such Act shall be preempted to the extent such exception is inconsistent with this title or title II, or would not be permitted under paragraph (2)(A)(ii) of this subsection; or

(2)(A) specifies the alternative procedures or requirements for the use or acceptance (or both) of electronic records or electronic signatures to establish the legal effect, validity, or enforceability of contracts or other records, if—

(i) such alternative procedures or requirements are consistent with this title and title II; and

(ii) such alternative procedures or requirements do not require, or accord greater legal status or effect to, the implementation or application of a specific technology or technical specification for performing the functions of creating, storing, generating, receiving, communicating, or authenticating electronic records or electronic signatures; and

(B) if enacted or adopted after the date of the enactment of this Act, makes specific reference to this Act.

(b) EXCEPTIONS FOR ACTIONS BY STATES AS MARKET PARTICIPANTS.—Subsection (a)(2)(A)(ii) shall not apply to the statutes, regulations, or other rules of law governing procurement by any State, or any agency or instrumentality thereof.

(c) PREVENTION OF CIRCUMVENTION.—Subsection (a) does not permit a State to circumvent this title or title II through the imposition of nonelectronic delivery methods under section 8(b)(2) of the Uniform Electronic Transactions Act.

§ 103 (15 U.S.C.A. § 7003). Specific Exceptions.

(a) EXCEPTED REQUIREMENTS.—The provisions of section 101 shall not apply to a contract or other record to the extent it is governed by—

(1) a statute, regulation, or other rule of law governing the creation and execution of wills, codicils, or testamentary trusts;

(2) a State statute, regulation, or other rule of law governing adoption, divorce, or other matters of family law; or

(3) the Uniform Commercial Code, as in effect in any State, other than sections 1–107 and 1–206 and Articles 2 and 2A.

(b) ADDITIONAL EXCEPTIONS.—The provisions of section 101 shall not apply to—

    (1) court orders or notices, or official court documents (including briefs, pleadings, and other writings) required to be executed in connection with court proceedings;

    (2) any notice of—

        (A) the cancellation or termination of utility services (including water, heat, and power);

        (B) default, acceleration, repossession, foreclosure, or eviction, or the right to cure, under a credit agreement secured by, or a rental agreement for, a primary residence of an individual;

        (C) the cancellation or termination of health insurance or benefits or life insurance benefits (excluding annuities); or

        (D) recall of a product, or material failure of a product, that risks endangering health or safety; or

    (3) any document required to accompany any transportation or handling of hazardous materials, pesticides, or other toxic or dangerous materials.

(c) REVIEW OF EXCEPTIONS.—

    (1) EVALUATION REQUIRED.—The Secretary of Commerce, acting through the Assistant Secretary for Communications and Information, shall review the operation of the exceptions in subsections (a) and (b) to evaluate, over a period of 3 years, whether such exceptions continue to be necessary for the protection of consumers. Within 3 years after the date of enactment of this Act, the Assistant Secretary shall submit a report to the Congress on the results of such e valuation.

    (2) DETERMINATIONS.—If a Federal regulatory agency, with respect to matter within its jurisdiction, determines after notice and an opportunity for public comment, and publishes a finding, that one or more such exceptions are no longer necessary for the protection of consumers and eliminating such exceptions will not increase the material risk of harm to consumers, such agency may extend the application of section 101 to the exceptions identified in such finding.

§ **106** (15 U.S.C.A. § 7006). Definitions.

For purposes of this title:

    (1) CONSUMER.—The term "consumer" means an individual who obtains, through a transaction, products or services

which are used primarily for personal, family, or household purposes, and also means the legal representative of such an individual.

(2) ELECTRONIC.—The term "electronic" means relating to technology having electrical, digital, magnetic, wireless, optical, electromagnetic, or similar capabilities.

(3) ELECTRONIC AGENT.—The term "electronic agent" means a computer program or an electronic or other automated means used independently to initiate an action or respond to electronic records or performances in whole or in part without review or action by an individual at the time of the action or response.

(4) ELECTRONIC RECORD.—The term "electronic record" means a contract or other record created, generated, sent, communicated, received, or stored by electronic means.

(5) ELECTRONIC SIGNATURE.—The term "electronic signature" means an electronic sound, symbol, or process, attached to or logically associated with a contract or other record and executed or adopted by a person with the intent to sign the record.

(6) FEDERAL REGULATORY AGENCY.—The term "Federal regulatory agency" means an agency, as that term is defined in section 552(f) of title 5, United States Code.

(7) INFORMATION.—The term "information" means data, text, images, sounds, codes, computer programs, software, databases, or the like.

(8) PERSON.—The term "person" means an individual, corporation, business trust, estate, trust, partnership, limited liability company, association, joint venture, governmental agency, public corporation, or any other legal or commercial entity.

(9) RECORD.—The term "record" means information that is inscribed on a tangible medium or that is stored in an electronic or other medium and is retrievable in perceivable form.

(10) REQUIREMENT.—The term "requirement" includes a prohibition.

(11) SELF–REGULATORY ORGANIZATION.—The term "self-regulatory organization" means an organization or entity that is not a Federal regulatory agency or a State, but that is under the supervision of a Federal regulatory agency and is authorized under Federal law to adopt and administer rules applicable to its members that are enforced by such

organization or entity, by a Federal regulatory agency, or by another self-regulatory organization.

(12) STATE.—The term "State" includes the District of Columbia and the territories and possessions of the United States.

(13) TRANSACTION.—The term "transaction" means an action or set of actions relating to the conduct of business, consumer, or commercial affairs between two or more persons, including any of the following types of conduct—

(A) the sale, lease, exchange, licensing, or other disposition of (i) personal property, including goods and intangibles, (ii) services, and (iii) any combination thereof; and

(B) the sale, lease, exchange, or other disposition of any interest in real property, or any combination thereof.

§ 201 (15 U.S.C.A. § 7021). Transferable Records.

(a) DEFINITIONS.—For purposes of this section:

(1) TRANSFERABLE RECORD.—The term "transferable record" means an electronic record that—

(A) would be a note under Article 3 of the Uniform Commercial Code if the electronic record were in writing;

(B) the issuer of the electronic record expressly has agreed is a transferable record; and

(C) relates to a loan secured by real property.

A transferable record may be executed using an electronic signature.

(2) OTHER DEFINITIONS.—The terms "electronic record", "electronic signature", and "person" have the same meanings provided in section 106 of this Act.

(b) CONTROL.—A person has control of a transferable record if a system employed for evidencing the transfer of interests in the transferable record reliably establishes that person as the person to which the transferable record was issued or transferred.

(c) CONDITIONS.—A system satisfies subsection (b), and a person is deemed to have control of a transferable record, if the transferable record is created, stored, and assigned in such a manner that—

(1) a single authoritative copy of the transferable record exists which is unique, identifiable, and, except as otherwise provided in paragraphs (4), (5), and (6), unalterable;

(2) the authoritative copy identifies the person asserting control as—

(A) the person to which the transferable record was issued; or

(B) if the authoritative copy indicates that the transferable record has been transferred, the person to which the transferable record was most recently transferred;

(3) the authoritative copy is communicated to and maintained by the person asserting control or its designated custodian;

(4) copies or revisions that add or change an identified assignee of the authoritative copy can be made only with the consent of the person asserting control;

(5) each copy of the authoritative copy and any copy of a copy is readily identifiable as a copy that is not the authoritative copy; and

(6) any revision of the authoritative copy is readily identifiable as authorized or unauthorized.

(d) STATUS AS HOLDER.—Except as otherwise agreed, a person having control of a transferable record is the holder, as defined in section 1–201(20) of the Uniform Commercial Code, of the transferable record and has the same rights and defenses as a holder of an equivalent record or writing under the Uniform Commercial Code, including, if the applicable statutory requirements under section 3–302(a), 9–308, or revised section 9–330 of the Uniform Commercial Code are satisfied, the rights and defenses of a holder in due course or a purchaser, respectively. Delivery, possession, and endorsement are not required to obtain or exercise any of the rights under this subsection.

(e) OBLIGOR RIGHTS.—Except as otherwise agreed, an obligor under a transferable record has the same rights and defenses as an equivalent obligor under equivalent records or writings under the Uniform Commercial Code.

(f) PROOF OF CONTROL.—If requested by a person against which enforcement is sought, the person seeking to enforce the transferable record shall provide reasonable proof that the person is in control of the transferable record. Proof may include access to the authoritative copy of the transferable record and related business records sufficient to review the terms of the transferable record and to establish the identity of the person having control of the transferable record.

(g) UCC REFERENCES.—For purposes of this subsection, all references to the Uniform Commercial Code are to the Uniform Commercial Code as in effect in the jurisdiction the law of which governs the transferable record.

RESTATEMENT OF THE LAW, SECOND, OF CONTRACTS

(Selected Sections)

COMPILERS' NOTE

The American Law Institute was formed in 1923 as the outgrowth of a "Committee on the Establishment of a Permanent Organization for the Improvement of the Law." Its members were to be 400 practitioners, judges and law professors; there are now about 4,000. The idea of the Institute, and of "restating" the law, was broached by Professor William Draper Lewis and fostered by Elihu Root and others. The Carnegie Corporation supported work on the original Restatement, comprising nine subjects, which was completed by 1944.

Contracts was one of the first three subjects upon which the Institute began work, and the Restatement of Contracts was completed in 1932. Professor Samuel Williston acted as Reporter, with responsibility for preparing drafts. (Professor Arthur L. Corbin served as Reporter for the Chapter on Remedies.) Other experts in the subject were formed into a Committee of Advisers who conferred with the Reporter over the whole period in producing drafts for submission to the Council of the Institute. The plan was "that the drafts of the different chapters submitted to the Council shall be the product of the committee composed of the Reporter and his advisers; that these drafts after discussion and amendment by the Council and before revision shall be submitted as tentative drafts for criticism and suggestion with a view to their improvement to the annual meetings of the Institute and to bar associations and the profession generally." Restatement of Contracts, Introduction, p. x. Final promulgation depended on approval of the text by both the Council and the full meeting of Institute members. The same procedure was followed in making revisions and in preparing the Restatement Second.

In 1962 the Institute initiated the preparation of the Restatement (Second) of Contracts, parts of which are reproduced here. Professor Robert Braucher served as Reporter until his appointment to the Supreme Judicial Court of Massachusetts in 1971; he was succeeded by Professor E. Allan Farnsworth. The work was completed in 1980.

As originally conceived, the first Restatement was to be accompanied by treatises citing and discussing case authority, but experience proved that group production of such volumes was not feasible. As they stand, the Restatements consist of sections stating rules or principles (the so-called black letter), each followed by one or more comments with illustrations, and in the Restatement Second also by Reporter's Notes in which supporting authorities are collected. (Reproduced here are the black letter of selected sections and in a few instances their comments and illustrations.)

Assaults on the Restatement, along with sympathetic appraisals, have produced a rich literature. An eminent critic of the Restatement of Contracts immediately objected that the American Law Institute "seems constantly to be seeking the force of a statute without statutory enactment." Clark, The Restatement of the Law of Contracts, 42 Yale L.J. 643, 654 (1933).[1] To what measure of authority is the Restatement entitled, then, in the courts?

This general question can have only a general answer. The Supreme Court of Oregon has emphasized the difference between statutory and Restatement texts:[2]

> Although this court frequently quotes sections of the Restatements of the American Law Institute, it does not literally "adopt" them in the manner of a legislature enacting, for instance, a draft prepared by the Commissioners on Uniform State Laws, such as the Residential Landlord and Tenant Act. In the nature of common law, such quotations in opinions are no more than shorthand expressions of the court's view that the analysis summarized in the Restatement corresponds to Oregon law applicable to the facts of the case before the court. They do not enact the exact phrasing of the Restatement rule, complete with comments, illustrations, and caveats. Such quotations should not be relied on in briefs as if they committed his court or lower courts to track every detail of the Restatement analysis in other cases. The Restatements themselves purport to be just that, "restatements" of law found in other sources, although at times they candidly report that the law is in flux and offer a formula preferred on policy grounds.

There is agreement among those who applaud the Restatement and those who deprecate it about the persuasiveness of an ideal restatement of the law. "A restatement, then, can have no other authority than as the product of men learned in the subject who have studied and deliberated over it. It needs no other, and what could be higher?" Clark, op. cit. supra, p. 655. Judge Herbert Goodrich, for many years Director of the Institute, explained:

> If an advocate thinks the Restatement was wrong as applied to his case, he can urge the court not to follow it, but to apply some other

---

1. On occasion a legislature has given statutory backing to the Restatement. The Virgin Islands Code (Title 1, § 4) provides: "The rules of the common law, as expressed in the restatements of the law approved by the American Law Institute ..., shall be the rules of decision ... in cases to which they apply, in the absence of local laws to the contrary."

2. Brewer v. Erwin, 600 P.2d 398, 410 n. 12 (Or.1979).

rule. If the court agrees, it will do so, but it will so do with the knowledge that the rule which it rejects has been written by the people who by training and reputation are supposed to be eminently learned in the particular subject and that the specialist's conclusions have been discussed and defended before a body of very able critics. The presumption is in favor of the Restatement.... Yet it can be overthrown and that fact leaves Restatement acceptance to persuasion. It is common law "persuasive authority" with a high degree of persuasion.

Restatement and Codification, David D. Field Centenary Essays 241, 244–45 (1949).

The Restatement Second. To a substantial extent the Restatement Second reflects the thought of two men in particular: Professor Corbin and Professor Karl Llewellyn, who shared an attitude toward law sometimes described as "legal realism."[3] Professor Corbin prepared a critical review of the original Restatement, which "has been the basis for much of the work on the revision."[4] He served also as consultant for the Restatement Second in its early stages. Professor Llewellyn's efforts affected the revision less directly, largely through the impact of his contributions to the Uniform Commercial Code.

In restating the law of contracts for the second half of the twentieth century, an obvious difficulty arose from the fact that large tracts of the subject had recently been occupied by legislation such as the Code and, to a lesser extent, consumer-protection statutes. Indeed, the worth of the enterprise was questioned on the ground of an apparently diminishing importance of common law doctrine. In response, Professor Braucher made this claim:

The effort to restate the law of contracts in modern terms highlights the reliance of private autonomy in an era of expanding government activity.... Freedom of contract, refined and redefined in response to social change, has power as it always had.[5]

At the beginning of the twenty-first century, work was begun on a Restatement (Third) of Restitution and Unjust Enrichment.

A continuing theme of controversy about the Restatements is the wisdom or unwisdom of departing from rules derived from existing precedents, in the interest of a more just and more convenient regime of law. Professor Herbert Wechsler, when Director of the Institute, proposed "a working formula" that received the unanimous approval of the

---

3. For symposia devoted to the Restatement Second, see 81 Colum.L.Rev. 1 (1981) and 67 Cornell L.Rev. 631 (1982).

4. Braucher, Formation of Contract and the Second Restatement, 78 Yale L.J. 598 (1969). See also Perillo, Twelve Letters from Arthur L.Corbin to Robert Braucher Annotated, 50 Wash. & Lee L. Rev. 755 (1993).

5. Id. at 615–16. For another comment by Professor Braucher, see Offer and Acceptance in the Second Restatement, 74 Yale L.J. 302 (1964)

Council: "we should feel obliged in our deliberations to give weight to all of the considerations that the courts, under a proper view of the judicial function, deem it right to weigh in theirs."[6] An example of creative restating from the first Restatement of Contracts was the formulation of the doctrine of promissory estoppel, in section 90.[7]

6. Wechsler, The Course of the Restatements, 55 A.B.A.J. 147, 150 (1969).

7. The Oregon opinion quoted above refers to a section of the Torts Restatement as a "bold sally." Notwithstanding that, the section has gained widespread adherence.

RESTATEMENT (SECOND)
OF CONTRACTS[1]

Table of Contents

CHAPTER 1. MEANING OF TERMS

CHAPTER 2. FORMATION OF CONTRACTS—
PARTIES AND CAPACITY

CHAPTER 3. FORMATION OF CONTRACTS—MUTUAL ASSENT

TOPIC 1. IN GENERAL

TOPIC 2. MANIFESTATION OF ASSENT IN GENERAL

TOPIC 3. MAKING OF OFFERS

TOPIC 4. DURATION OF THE OFFEREE'S POWER OF ACCEPTANCE

CHAPTER 6. MISTAKE

CHAPTER 7. MISREPRESENTATION, DURESS AND UNDUE INFLUENCE

TOPIC 1. MISREPRESENTATION

TOPIC 2. DURESS AND UNDUE INFLUENCE

CHAPTER 8. UNENFORCEABILITY ON GROUNDS OF PUBLIC POLICY

TOPIC 1. UNENFORCEABILITY IN GENERAL

TOPIC 2. RESTRAINT OF TRADE

TOPIC 4. INTERFERENCE WITH OTHER PROTECTED INTERESTS

TOPIC 5. RESTITUTION

CHAPTER 9. THE SCOPE OF CONTRACTUAL OBLIGATIONS

TOPIC 1. THE MEANING OF AGREEMENTS

CHAPTER 1. MEANING OF TERMS

§ 1. Contract Defined

A contract is a promise or a set of promises for the breach of which the law gives a remedy, or the performance of which the law in some way recognizes as a duty.

CHAPTER 2. FORMATION OF CONTRACTS— PARTIES AND CAPACITY

§ 14. Infants

Unless a statute provides otherwise, a natural person has the capacity to incur only voidable contractual duties until the beginning of the day before the person's eighteenth birthday.

§ 15. Mental Illness or Defect

(1) A person incurs only voidable contractual duties by entering into a transaction if by reason of mental illness or defect

(a) he is unable to understand in a reasonable manner the nature and consequences of the transaction, or

(b) he is unable to act in a reasonable manner in relation to the transaction and the other party has reason to know of his condition.

(2) Where the contract is made on fair terms and the other party is without knowledge of the mental illness or defect, the power of avoidance under Subsection (1) terminates to the extent that the contract has been so performed in whole or in part or the circumstances have so changed that avoidance would be unjust. In such a case a court may grant relief on such equitable terms as justice requires.

CHAPTER 3. FORMATION OF CONTRACTS—MUTUAL ASSENT

TOPIC 1. IN GENERAL

§ 17. Requirement of a Bargain

(1) Except as stated in Subsection (2), the formation of a contract requires a bargain in which there is a manifestation of mutual assent to the exchange and a consideration.

(2) Whether or not there is a bargain a contract may be formed under special rules applicable to formal contracts or under the rules stated in §§ 82–94.

TOPIC 2. MANIFESTATION OF ASSENT IN GENERAL

§ 20. Effect of Misunderstanding

(1) There is no manifestation of mutual assent to an exchange if the parties attach materially different meanings to their manifestations and

(a) neither party knows or has reason to know the meaning attached by the other; or

(b) each party knows or each party has reason to know the meaning attached by the other.

(2) The manifestations of the parties are operative in accordance with the meaning attached to them by one of the parties if

(a) that party does not know of any different meaning attached by the other, and the other knows the meaning attached by the first party; or

(b) that party has no reason to know of any different meaning attached by the other, and the other has reason to know the meaning attached by the first party.

TOPIC 3. MAKING OF OFFERS

§ 24. Offer Defined

An offer is the manifestation of willingness to enter into a bargain, so made as to justify another person in understanding that his assent to that bargain is invited and will conclude it.

§ 26. Preliminary Negotiations

A manifestation of willingness to enter into a bargain is not an offer if the person to whom it is addressed knows or has reason to know that the person making it does not intend to conclude a bargain until he has made a further manifestation of assent.

§ 27. Existence of Contract Where Written Memorial Is Contemplated

Manifestations of assent that are in themselves sufficient to conclude a contract will not be prevented from so operating by the fact that the parties also manifest an intention to prepare and adopt a written memorial thereof; but the circumstances may show that the agreements are preliminary negotiations.

§ 30. Form of Acceptance Invited

(1) An offer may invite or require acceptance to be made by an affirmative answer in words, or by performing or refraining from performing a specified act, or may empower the offeree to make a selection of terms in his acceptance.

(2) Unless otherwise indicated by the language or the circumstances, an offer invites acceptance in any manner and by any medium reasonable in the circumstances.

§ 32. Invitation of Promise or Performance

In case of doubt an offer is interpreted as inviting the offeree to accept either by promising to perform what the offer requests or by rendering the performance, as the offeree chooses.

§ 33. Certainty

(1) Even though a manifestation of intention is intended to be understood as an offer, it cannot be accepted so as to form a contract unless the terms of the contract are reasonably certain.

(2) The terms of a contract are reasonably certain if they provide a basis for determining the existence of a breach and for giving an appropriate remedy.

(3) The fact that one or more terms of a proposed bargain are left open or uncertain may show that a manifestation of intention is not intended to be understood as an offer or as an acceptance.

TOPIC 4. DURATION OF THE OFFEREE'S POWER OF ACCEPTANCE

§ **36.** Methods of Termination of the Power of Acceptance

(1) An offeree's power of acceptance may be terminated by

    (a) rejection or counter-offer by the offeree, or

    (b) lapse of time, or

    (c) revocation by the offeror, or

    (d) death or incapacity of the offeror or offeree.

(2) In addition, an offeree's power of acceptance is terminated by the non-occurrence of any condition of acceptance under the terms of the offer.

§ **37.** Termination of Power of Acceptance Under Option Contract

Notwithstanding §§ 38–49, the power of acceptance under an option contract is not terminated by rejection or counter-offer, by revocation, or by death or incapacity of the offeror, unless the requirements are met for the discharge of a contractual duty.

§ **38.** Rejection

(1) An offeree's power of acceptance is terminated by his rejection of the offer, unless the offeror has manifested a contrary intention.

(2) A manifestation of intention not to accept an offer is a rejection unless the offeree manifests an intention to take it under further advisement.

§ **39.** Counter–Offers

(1) A counter-offer is an offer made by an offeree to his offeror relating to the same matter as the original offer and proposing a substituted bargain differing from that proposed by the original offer.

(2) An offeree's power of acceptance is terminated by his making of a counter-offer, unless the offeror has manifested a contrary intention or unless the counter-offer manifests a contrary intention of the offeree.

§ **40.** Time When Rejection or Counter–Offer Terminates the Power of Acceptance

Rejection or counter-offer by mail or telegram does not terminate the power of acceptance until received by the offeror, but limits the power so that a letter or telegram of acceptance started after the sending of an otherwise effective rejection or counter-offer is only a counter-offer unless the acceptance is received by the offeror before he receives the rejection or counter-offer.

§ 41. Lapse of Time

(1) An offeree's power of acceptance is terminated at the time specified in the offer, or, if no time is specified, at the end of a reasonable time.

(2) What is a reasonable time is a question of fact, depending on all the circumstances existing when the offer and attempted acceptance are made.

(3) Unless otherwise indicated by the language or the circumstances, and subject to the rule stated in § 49, an offer sent by mail is seasonably accepted if an acceptance is mailed at any time before midnight on the day on which the offer is received.

§ 42. Revocation by Communication From Offeror Received by Offeree

An offeree's power of acceptance is terminated when the offeree receives from the offeror a manifestation of an intention not to enter into the proposed contract.

§ 43. Indirect Communication of Revocation

An offeree's power of acceptance is terminated when the offeror takes definite action inconsistent with an intention to enter into the proposed contract and the offeree acquires reliable information to that effect.

§ 45. Option Contract Created by Part Performance or Tender

(1) Where an offer invites an offeree to accept by rendering a performance and does not invite a promissory acceptance, an option contract is created when the offeree tenders or begins the invited performance or tenders a beginning of it.

(2) The offeror's duty of performance under any option contract so created is conditional on completion or tender of the invited performance in accordance with the terms of the offer.

Comment:

a. *Offer limited to acceptance by performance only.* This Section is limited to cases where the offer does not invite a promissory acceptance. Such an offer has often been referred to as an "offer for a unilateral contract." Typical illustrations are found in offers of rewards or prizes and in non-commercial arrangements among relatives and friends. See Comment b to § 32. As to analogous cases arising under offers which give the offeree power to accept either by performing or by promising to perform, as he chooses, see §§ 32, 62.

b. *Manifestation of contrary intention.* The rule of this Section is designed to protect the offeree in justifiable reliance on the offeror's promise, and the rule yields to a manifestation of intention which makes reliance unjustified. A reservation of power to revoke after performance has begun means that as yet there is no promise and no offer. See §§ 2, 24. In particular, if the performance is one which requires the cooperation of both parties, such as the payment of money or the manual delivery of goods, a person who reserves the right to refuse to receive the performance has not made an offer. See § 26.

Illustrations:

1. B owes A $5000 payable in installments over a five-year period. A proposes that B discharge the debt by paying $4,500 cash within one month, but reserves the right to refuse any such payment. A has not made an offer. A tender by B in accordance with the proposal is an offer by B.

2. A, an insurance company, issues a bulletin to its agents, entitled "Extra Earnings Agreement," providing for annual bonus payments to the agents varying according to "monthly premiums in force" and "lapse ratio," but reserving the right to change or discontinue the bonus, individually or collectively, with or without notice, at any time before payment. There is no offer or promise.

c. *Tender of performance.* A proposal to receive a payment of money or a delivery of goods is an offer only if acceptance can be completed without further cooperation by the offeror. If there is an offer, it follows that accep-

tance must be complete at the latest when performance is tendered. A tender of performance, so bargained for and given in exchange for the offer, ordinarily furnishes consideration and creates a contract. See §§ 17, 71, 72.

This is so whether or not the tender carries with it any incidental promises. See §§ 54, 62. If no commitment is made by the offeree, the contract is an option contract. See § 25.

Illustration:

3. A promises B to sell him a specified chattel for $5, stating that B is not to be bound until he pays the money. B tenders $5 within a reasonable time, but A refuses to accept the tender. There is a breach of contract.

d. *Beginning to perform.* If the invited performance takes time, the invitation to perform necessarily includes an invitation to begin performance. In most such cases the beginning of performance carries with it an express or implied promise to complete performance. See § 62. In the less common case where the offer does not contemplate or invite a promise by the offeree, the beginning of performance nevertheless completes the manifestation of mutual assent and furnishes consideration for an option contract. See § 25. If the beginning of performance requires the cooperation of the offeror, tender of part performance has the same effect. Part performance or tender may also create an option contract in a situation where the offeree is invited to take up the option by making a promise, if the offer invites a preliminary performance before the time for the offeree's final commitment.

Illustrations:

4. A offers a reward for the return of lost property. In response to the offer, B searches for the

property and finds it. A then notifies B that the offer is revoked. B makes a tender of the property to A conditional on payment of the reward, and A refuses. There is a breach of contract by A.

5. A, a magazine, offers prizes in a subscription contest. At a time when B has submitted the largest number of subscriptions, A cancels the contest. A has broken its contract with B.

6. A writes to her daughter B, living in another state, an offer to leave A's farm to B if B gives up her home and cares for A during A's life, B remaining free to terminate the arrangement at any time. B gives up her home, moves to A's farm, and begins caring for A. A is bound by an option contract.

7. A offers to sell a piece of land to B, and promises that if B incurs expense in employing experts to appraise the property the offer will be irrevocable for 30 days. B hires experts and pays for their transportation to the land. A is bound by an option contract.

8. In January A, an employer, publishes a notice to his employees, promising a stated Christmas bonus to any employee who is continuously in A's employ from January to Christmas. B, an employee hired by the week, reads the notice and continues at work beyond the expiration of the current week. A is bound by an option contract, and if B is continuously in A's employ until Christmas a notice of revocation of the bonus is ineffective.

e. Completion of performance. Where part performance or tender by the offeree creates an option contract, the offeree is not bound to complete performance. The offeror alone is bound, but his duty of performance is conditional on completion of the offeree's performance. If the offeree abandons performance, the offeror's duty to perform never arises. See § 224, defining "condition," and Illustration 4 to that Section. But the condition may be excused, for example, if the offeror prevents performance, waives it, or repudiates. See Comment b to § 225 and §§ 239, 278.

f. Preparations for performance. What is begun or tendered must be part of the actual performance invited in order to preclude revocation under this Section. Beginning preparations, though they may be essential to carrying out the contract or to accepting the offer, is not enough. Preparations to perform may, however, constitute justifiable reliance sufficient to make the offeror's promise binding under § 87(2).

In many cases what is invited depends on what is a reasonable mode of acceptance. See § 30. The distinction between preparing for performance and beginning performance in such cases may turn on many factors: the extent to which the offeree's conduct is clearly referable to the offer, the definite and substantial character of that conduct, and the extent to which it is of actual or prospective benefit to the offeror rather than the offeree, as well as the terms of the communications between the parties, their prior course of dealing, and any relevant usages of trade.

Illustration:

9. A makes a written promise to pay $5000 to B, a hospital, "to aid B in its humanitarian work." Relying upon this and other like promises, B proceeds in its humanitarian work, expending large sums of money and incurring large liabilities. Performance by B has begun, and A's offer is irrevocable.

g. *Agency contracts.* This Section frequently applies to agency arrangements, particularly offers made to real estate brokers. Sometimes there is a return promise by the agent, particularly if there is an agreement for exclusive dealing, since such an agreement normally imposes an obligation on the agent to use best efforts. See Uniform Commercial Code § 2–306(2); compare Restatement, Second, Agency § 378. In other cases the agent does not promise to act, but the principal must compensate him if he does act. The rules governing the principal's duty of compensation are stated in detail in Chapter 14 of the Restatement, Second, Agency, particularly §§ 443–57.

§ 46. Revocation of General Offer

Where an offer is made by advertisement in a newspaper or other general notification to the public or to a number of persons whose identity is unknown to the offeror, the offeree's power of acceptance is terminated when a notice of termination is given publicity by advertisement or other general notification equal to that given to the offer and no better means of notification is reasonably available.

§ 48. Death or Incapacity of Offeror or Offeree

An offeree's power of acceptance is terminated when the offeree or offeror dies or is deprived of legal capacity to enter into the proposed contract.

TOPIC 5. ACCEPTANCE OF OFFERS

§ 50. Acceptance of Offer Defined; Acceptance by Performance; Acceptance by Promise

(1) Acceptance of an offer is a manifestation of assent to the terms thereof made by the offeree in a manner invited or required by the offer.

(2) Acceptance by performance requires that at least part of what the offer requests be performed or tendered and includes acceptance by a performance which operates as a return promise.

(3) Acceptance by a promise requires that the offeree complete every act essential to the making of the promise.

§ 51. Effect of Part Performance Without Knowledge of Offer

Unless the offeror manifests a contrary intention, an offeree who learns of an offer after he has rendered part of the performance requested by the offer may accept by completing the requested performance.

§ 52. Who May Accept an Offer

An offer can be accepted only by a person whom it invites to furnish the consideration.

§ 53. Acceptance by Performance; Manifestation of Intention Not to Accept

(1) An offer can be accepted by the rendering of a performance only if the offer invites such an acceptance.

(2) Except as stated in § 69, the rendering of a performance does not constitute an acceptance if within a reasonable time the offeree exercises reasonable diligence to notify the offeror of non-acceptance.

(3) Where an offer of a promise invites acceptance by performance and does not invite a promissory acceptance, the rendering of the invited performance does not constitute an acceptance if before the offeror performs his promise the offeree manifests an intention not to accept.

§ 54. Acceptance by Performance; Necessity of Notification to Offeror

(1) Where an offer invites an offeree to accept by rendering a performance, no notification is necessary to make such an acceptance effective unless the offer requests such a notification.

(2) If an offeree who accepts by rendering a performance has reason to know that the offeror has no adequate means of learning of the performance with reasonable promptness and certainty, the contractual duty of the offeror is discharged unless

    (a) the offeree exercises reasonable diligence to notify the offeror of acceptance, or

    (b) the offeror learns of the performance within a reasonable time, or

    (c) the offer indicates that notification of acceptance is not required.

§ 56. Acceptance by Promise; Necessity of Notification to Offeror

Except as stated in § 69 or where the offer manifests a contrary intention, it is essential to an acceptance by promise either that the offeree exercise reasonable diligence to notify the offeror of acceptance or that the offeror receive the acceptance seasonably.

§ 58. Necessity of Acceptance Complying With Terms of Offer

An acceptance must comply with the requirements of the offer as to the promise to be made or the performance to be rendered.

§ 59. Purported Acceptance Which Adds Qualifications

A reply to an offer which purports to accept it but is conditional on the offeror's assent to terms additional to or different from those offered is not an acceptance but is a counter-offer.

§ 60. Acceptance of Offer Which States Place, Time or Manner of Acceptance

If an offer prescribes the place, time or manner of acceptance its terms in this respect must be complied with in order to create a contract. If an offer merely suggests a permitted place, time or manner of acceptance, another method of acceptance is not precluded.

§ 61. Acceptance Which Requests Change of Terms

An acceptance which requests a change or addition to the terms of the offer is not thereby invalidated unless the acceptance is made to depend on an assent to the changed or added terms.

§ 62. Effect of Performance by Offeree Where Offer Invites Either Performance or Promise

(1) Where an offer invites an offeree to choose between acceptance by promise and acceptance by performance, the tender or beginning of the invited performance or a tender of a beginning of it is an acceptance by performance.

(2) Such an acceptance operates as a promise to render complete performance.

§ 63. Time When Acceptance Takes Effect

Unless the offer provides otherwise,

    (a) an acceptance made in a manner and by a medium invited by an offer is operative and completes the manifestation of mutual assent as soon as put out of the offeree's possession, without regard to whether it ever reaches the offeror; but

    (b) an acceptance under an option contract is not operative until received by the offeror.

§ 64. Acceptance By Telephone Or Teletype

Acceptance given by telephone or other medium of substantially instantaneous two-way communication is governed by the principles applicable to acceptances where the parties are in the presence of each other.

§ 69. Acceptance by Silence or Exercise of Dominion

(1) Where an offeree fails to reply to an offer, his silence and inaction operate as an acceptance in the following cases only:

    (a) Where an offeree takes the benefit of offered services with reasonable opportunity to reject them and reason to know that they were offered with the expectation of compensation.

(b) Where the offeror has stated or given the offeree reason to understand that assent may be manifested by silence or inaction, and the offeree in remaining silent and inactive intends to accept the offer.

(c) Where because of previous dealings or otherwise, it is reasonable that the offeree should notify the offeror if he does not intend to accept.

(2) An offeree who does any act inconsistent with the offeror's ownership of offered property is bound in accordance with the offered terms unless they are manifestly unreasonable. But if the act is wrongful as against the offeror it is an acceptance only if ratified by him.

CHAPTER 4. FORMATION OF CONTRACTS—CONSIDERATION

TOPIC 1. THE REQUIREMENT OF CONSIDERATION

§ 71. Requirement of Exchange; Types of Exchange

(1) To constitute consideration, a performance or a return promise must be bargained for.

(2) A performance or return promise is bargained for if it is sought by the promisor in exchange for his promise and is given by the promisee in exchange for that promise.

(3) The performance may consist of

(a) an act other than a promise, or

(b) a forbearance, or

(c) the creation, modification, or destruction of a legal relation.

(4) The performance or return promise may be given to the promisor or to some other person. It may be given by the promisee or by some other person.

Comment:

a. Other meanings of "consideration." The word "consideration" has often been used with meanings different from that given here. It is often used merely to express the legal conclusion that a promise is enforceable. Historically, its primary meaning may have been that the conditions were met under which an action of assumpsit would lie. It was also used as the equivalent of the quid pro quo required in an action of debt. A seal, it has been said, "imports a consideration," although the law was clear that no element of bargain was necessary to enforcement of a promise under seal. On the other hand, consideration has sometimes been used to refer to almost any reason asserted for enforcing a promise, even though the reason was insufficient. In this sense we find references to promises "in consideration of love and affection," to "illegal consideration," to "past consideration," and to consideration furnished by reliance on a gratuitous promise.

Consideration has also been used to refer to the element of exchange without regard to legal consequences. Consistent with that usage has been the use of the phrase "sufficient consideration" to express the legal conclusion that one requirement for an enforceable bargain is met. Here § 17 states the element of exchange required for a contract enforceable as a bargain as "a consideration." Thus "consideration" refers to an element of exchange which is sufficient to satisfy the legal requirement; the word "sufficient" would be redundant and is not used.

b. "Bargained for." In the typical bargain, the consideration and the promise bear a reciprocal relation of motive or inducement: the consideration induces the making of the promise and the promise induces the furnishing of the consideration. Here, as in the matter of mutual assent, the law is concerned with the external manifestation rather than the undisclosed mental state: it is enough that one party manifests an intention to induce the other's response and to be induced by it and that the other responds in accordance with the inducement. See § 81; compare §§ 19, 20. But it is not enough that the promise induces the conduct of the promisee or that the conduct of the promisee induces the making of the promise; both elements must be present, or there is no bargain. Moreover, a mere pretense of bargain does not suffice, as where there is a false recital of consideration or where the purported consideration is merely nominal. In such cases there is no consideration and the promise is enforced, if at all, as a promise binding without consideration under §§ 82–94. See Comments b and c to § 87.

Illustrations:

1. A offers to buy a book owned by B and to pay B $10 in exchange therefor. B accepts the offer and delivers the book to A. The transfer and delivery of the book constitute a performance and are consideration for A's promise. See Uniform Commercial Code §§ 2–106, 2–301. This is so even though A at the time he makes the offer secretly intends to pay B $10 whether or not he gets the book, or even though B at the time he accepts secretly intends not to collect the $10.

2. A receives a gift from B of a book worth $10. Subsequently A promises to pay B the value of the book. There is no consideration for A's promise. This is so even though B at the time he makes the gift secretly hopes that A will pay him for it. As to the enforcement of such promises, see § 86.

3. A promises to make a gift of $10 to B. In reliance on the promise B buys a book from C and promises to pay C $10 for it. There is no consideration for A's promise. As to the enforcement of such promises, see § 90.

4. A desires to make a binding promise to give $1000 to his son B. Being advised that a gratuitous promise is not binding, A writes out and signs a false recital that B has sold him a car for $1000 and a promise to pay that amount. There is no consideration for A's promise.

5. A desires to make a binding promise to give $1000 to his son B. Being advised that a gratuitous promise is not binding, A offers to buy from B for $1000 a book worth less than $1. B accepts the offer knowing that the purchase of the book is a mere pretense. There is no consideration for A's promise to pay $1000.

c. Mixture of bargain and gift. In most commercial bargains there is a rough equivalence between the value promised and the value received as consideration. But the social functions of bargains include the provision of opportunity for free individual action and exercise of judgment and the fixing of values by private action, either generally or for purposes of the particular transaction. Those functions would be impaired by judicial review of the values so fixed. Ordinarily, therefore, courts do not inquire into the adequacy of consideration, particularly where one or both of the values exchanged are difficult to measure. See § 79. Even where both parties know that a transaction is in part a bargain and in part a gift, the element of bargain may nevertheless furnish consideration for the entire transaction.

On the other hand, a gift is not ordinarily treated as a bargain, and a promise to make a gift is not made a bargain by the promise of the prospective donee to accept the gift, or by his acceptance of part of it. This may be true even though the terms of gift impose a burden on the donee as well as the donor. See Illustration 2 to § 24. In such cases the distinction between bargain and gift may be a fine one, depending on the motives manifested by the parties. In some cases there may be no bargain so long as the agreement is entirely executory, but performance may furnish consideration or the agreement may become fully or partly enforceable by virtue of the reliance of one party or the unjust enrichment of the other. Compare § 90.

Illustrations:

6. A offers to buy a book owned by B and to pay B $10 in exchange therefor. B's transfer and delivery of the book are consideration for A's promise even though both parties know that such books regularly sell for $5 and that part of A's

motive in making the offer is to make a gift to B. See §§ 79, 81.

7. A owns land worth $10,000 which is subject to a mortgage to secure a debt of $5,000. A promises to make a gift of the land to his son B and to pay off the mortgage, and later gives B a deed subject to the mortgage. B's acceptance of the deed is not consideration for A's promise to pay the mortgage debt.

8. A and B agree that A will advance $1000 to B as a gratuitous loan. B's promise to accept the loan is not consideration for A's promise to make it. But the loan when made is consideration for B's promise to repay.

d. Types of consideration. Consideration may consist of a performance or of a return promise. Consideration by way of performance may be a specified act of forbearance, or any one of several specified acts or forbearances of which the offeree is given the choice, or such conduct as will produce a specified result. Or either the offeror or the offeree may request as consideration the creation, modification or destruction of a purely intangible legal relation. Not infrequently the consideration bargained for is an act with the added requirement that a certain legal result shall be produced. Consideration by way of return promise requires a promise as defined in § 2. Consideration may consist partly of promise and partly of other acts or forbearances, and the consideration invited may be a performance or a return promise in the alternative. Though a promise is itself an act, it is treated separately from other acts. See § 75.

Illustrations:

9. A promises B, his nephew aged 16, that A will pay B $1000 when B becomes 21 if B does not smoke before then. B's forbear-

ance to smoke is a performance and if bargained for is consideration for A's promise.

10. A says to B, the owner of a garage, "I will pay you $100 if you will make my car run properly." The production of this result is consideration for A's promise.

11. A has B's horse in his possession. B writes to A, "If you will promise me $100 for the horse, he is yours." A promptly replies making the requested promise. The property in the horse at once passes to A. The change in ownership is consideration for A's promise.

12. A promises to pay B $1,000 if B will make an offer to C to sell C certain land for $25,000 and will leave the offer open for 24 hours. B makes the requested offer and forbears to revoke it for 24 hours, but C does not accept. The creation of a power of acceptance in C is consideration for A's promise.

13. A mails a written order to B, offering to buy specified machinery on specified terms. The order provides "Ship at once." B's prompt shipment or promise to ship is consideration for A's promise to pay the price. See § 32; Uniform Commercial Code § 2–206(1)(b).

e. Consideration moving from or to a third person. It matters not from whom the consideration moves or to whom it goes. If it is bargained for and given in exchange for the promise, the promise is not gratuitous.

Illustrations:

14. A promises B to guarantee payment of a bill of goods if B sells the goods to C. Selling the goods to C is consideration for A's promise.

15. A makes a promissory note payable to B in return for a payment by B to C. The payment is consideration for the note.

16. A, at C's request and in exchange for $1 paid by C, promises B to give him a book. The payment is consideration for A's promise.

17. A promises B to pay B $1, in exchange for C's promise to A to give A a book. The promises are consideration for one another.

18. A promises to pay $1,000 to B, a bank, in exchange for the delivery of a car by C to A's son D. The delivery of the car is consideration for A's promise.

§ 73. Performance of Legal Duty

Performance of a legal duty owed to a promisor which is neither doubtful nor the subject of honest dispute is not consideration; but a similar performance is consideration if it differs from what was required by the duty in a way which reflects more than a pretense of bargain.

§ 74. Settlement of Claims

(1) Forbearance to assert or the surrender of a claim or defense which proves to be invalid is not consideration unless

(a) the claim or defense is in fact doubtful because of uncertainty as to the facts or the law, or

(b) the forbearing or surrendering party believes that the claim or defense may be fairly determined to be valid.

(2) The execution of a written instrument surrendering a claim or defense by one who is under no duty to execute it is consideration if the execution of the written instrument is bargained for even though he is not asserting the claim or defense and believes that no valid claim or defense exists.

§ 75. Exchange of Promise for Promise

Except as stated in §§ 76 and 77, a promise which is bargained for is consideration if, but only if, the promised performance would be consideration.

§ 77. Illusory and Alternative Promises

A promise or apparent promise is not consideration if by its terms the promisor or purported promisor reserves a choice of alternative performances unless

> (a) each of the alternative performances would have been consideration if it alone had been bargained for; or

> (b) one of the alternative performances would have been consideration and there is or appears to the parties to be a substantial possibility that before the promisor exercises his choice events may eliminate the alternatives which would not have been consideration.

§ 79. Adequacy of Consideration; Mutuality of Obligation

If the requirement of consideration is met, there is no additional requirement of

> (a) a gain, advantage, or benefit to the promisor or a loss, disadvantage, or detriment to the promisee; or

> (b) equivalence in the values exchanged; or

> (c) "mutuality of obligation."

§ 81. Consideration as Motive or Inducing Cause

(1) The fact that what is bargained for does not of itself induce the making of a promise does not prevent it from being consideration for the promise.

(2) The fact that a promise does not of itself induce a performance or return promise does not prevent the performance or return promise from being consideration for the promise.

TOPIC 2. CONTRACTS WITHOUT CONSIDERATION

§ 82. Promise to Pay Indebtedness; Effect on the Statute of Limitations

(1) A promise to pay all or part of an antecedent contractual or quasi-contractual indebtedness owed by the promisor is binding if the indebtedness is still enforceable or would be except for the effect of a statute of limitations.

(2) The following facts operate as such a promise unless other facts indicate a different intention:

> (a) A voluntary acknowledgment to the obligee, admitting the present existence of the antecedent indebtedness; or

> (b) A voluntary transfer of money, a negotiable instrument, or other thing by the obligor to the obligee, made as interest on or part payment of or collateral security for the antecedent indebtedness; or

> (c) A statement to the obligee that the statute of limitations will not be pleaded as a defense.

§ 83. Promise to Pay Indebtedness Discharged in Bankruptcy

An express promise to pay all or part of an indebtedness of the promisor, discharged or dischargeable in bankruptcy proceedings begun before the promise is made, is binding.

§ 84. Promise to Perform a Duty in Spite of Non-occurrence of a Condition

(1) Except as stated in Subsection (2), a promise to perform all or part of a conditional duty under an antecedent contract in spite of the non-occurrence of the condition is binding, whether the promise is made before or after the time for the condition to occur, unless

> (a) occurrence of the condition was a material part of the agreed exchange for the performance of the duty and the promisee was under no duty that it occur; or

> (b) uncertainty of the occurrence of the condition was an element of the risk assumed by the promisor.

(2) If such a promise is made before the time for the occurrence of the condition has expired and the condition is within the control of the promisee or a beneficiary, the promisor can make his duty again subject to the condition by notifying the promisee or beneficiary of his intention to do so if

(a) the notification is received while there is still a reasonable time to cause the condition to occur under the antecedent terms or an extension given by the promisor; and

(b) reinstatement of the requirement of the condition is not unjust because of a material change of position by the promisee or beneficiary; and

(c) the promise is not binding apart from the rule stated in Subsection (1).

§ 86. Promise for Benefit Received

(1) A promise made in recognition of a benefit previously received by the promisor from the promisee is binding to the extent necessary to prevent injustice.

(2) A promise is not binding under Subsection (1)

(a) if the promisee conferred the benefit as a gift or for other reasons the promisor has not been unjustly enriched; or

(b) to the extent that its value is disproportionate to the benefit.

Comment:

a. "Past consideration"; "moral obligation." Enforcement of promises to pay for benefit received has sometimes been said to rest on "past consideration" or on the "moral obligation" of the promisor, and there are statutes in such terms in a few states. Those terms are not used here: "past consideration" is inconsistent with the meaning of consideration stated in § 71, and there seems to be no consensus as to what constitutes a "moral obligation." The mere fact of promise has been thought to create a moral obligation, but it is clear that not all promises are enforced. Nor are moral obligations based solely on gratitude or sentiment sufficient of themselves to support a subsequent promise.

Illustrations:

1. A gives emergency care to B's adult son while the son is sick and without funds far from home. B subsequently promises to reimburse A for his expenses. The promise is not binding under this Section.

2. A lends money to B, who later dies. B's widow promises to pay the debt. The promise is not binding under this Section.

3. A has immoral relations with B, a woman not his wife, to her injury. A's subsequent promise to reimburse B for her loss is not binding under this Section.

b. Rationale. Although in general a person who has been unjustly enriched at the expense of another is required to make restitution, restitution is denied in many cases in order to protect persons who have had benefits thrust upon them. See Restatement of Restitution §§ 1, 2, 112. In other cases restitution is denied by virtue of rules designed to guard against false claims, stale claims, claims already litigated, and the like. In many such cases a subsequent promise to make restitution removes the reason for the denial of relief, and the policy against unjust enrichment then prevails. Compare Restatement, Second, Agency § 462 on ratification of the acts of a person who officiously purports to act as an agent. Enforcement of the subsequent promise sometimes makes it unnecessary to decide a difficult question as to the limits on quasi-contractual relief.

Many of the cases governed by the rules stated in §§ 82–85 are within the broader principle stated in this Section. But the broader principle is not so firmly established as those rules, and it may not be applied if there is doubt whether the objections to restitution are fully met by the subsequent promise. Facts such as the definite and substantial character of the benefit received, formality in the making of the promise, part performance of the promise, reliance on the promise or the probability of such reliance may be relevant to show that no imposition results from enforcement.

c. Promise to correct a mistake. One who makes a mistake in the conferring of a benefit is commonly entitled to restitution regardless of any promise. But restitution is often denied to avoid prejudice to the recipient of the benefit. Thus restitution of the value of services or of improvements to land or chattels may require a payment which the recipient cannot afford. See Restatement of Restitution §§ 41, 42. Where a subsequent promise shows that the usual protection is not needed in the particular case, restitution is granted to the extent promised.

Illustrations:

4. A is employed by B to repair a vacant house. By mistake A repairs the house next door, which belongs to C. A subsequent promise by C to pay A the value of the repairs is binding.

5. A pays B a debt and gets a signed receipt. Later B obtains a default judgment against A for the amount of the debt, and A pays again. B's subsequent promise to refund the second payment if A has a receipt is binding.

d. Emergency services and necessaries. The law of restitution in the absence of promise severely limits recovery for necessaries furnished to a person under disability and for emergency services. See Restatement of Restitution §§ 113–17, 139. A subsequent promise in such a case may remove doubt as to the reality of the benefit and as to its value, and may negate any danger of imposition or false claim. A positive showing that payment was expected is not then required; an intention to make a gift must be shown to defeat restitution.

Illustrations:

6. A finds B's escaped bull and feeds and cares for it. B's subsequent promise to pay reasonable compensation to A is binding.

7. A saves B's life in an emergency and is totally and permanently disabled in so doing. One month later B promises to pay A $15 every two weeks for the rest of A's life, and B makes the payments for 8 years until he dies. The promise is binding.

e. Benefit conferred as a gift. In the absence of mistake or the like, there is no element of unjust enrichment in the receipt of a gift, and the rule of this Section has no application to a promise to pay for a past gift. Similarly, when a debt is discharged by a binding agreement, the transaction is closed even though full payment is not made. But marginal cases arise in which both parties understand that what is in form a gift is intended to be reimbursed indirectly, or in which a subsequent promise to pay is expressly contemplated. See Illustration 3 to § 83. Enforcement of the subsequent promise is proper in some such cases.

Illustrations:

8. A submits to B at B's request a plan for advertising products manufactured by B, expecting payment only if the plan is adopted. Because of a change in B's selling arrangements, B rejects the plan without giving it fair consideration. B's subsequent promise to reimburse A's expenses in preparing the plan is binding.

9. A contributes capital to B, an insurance company, on the understanding that B is not liable to reimburse A but that A will be reimbursed through salary and commissions. Later A withdraws from the company and B promises to pay him ten percent of premiums received until he is reimbursed. The promise is binding.

f. Benefit conferred pursuant to contract. By virtue of the policy of enforcing bargains, the enrichment of one party as a result of an unequal exchange is not regarded as unjust, and this Section has no application to a promise to pay or perform more or to accept less than is called for by a pre-existing bargain between the same parties. Compare §§ 79, 89. Similarly, if a third person receives a benefit as a result of the performance of a bargain, this Section does not make binding the subsequent promise of the third person to pay extra compensation to the performing party. But a promise to pay in substitution for the return performance called for by the bargain may be binding under this Section.

Illustration:

10. A digs a well on B's land in performance of a bargain with B's tenant C. C is unable to pay as agreed, and B promises to pay A the reasonable value of the well. The promise is binding.

g. Obligation unenforceable under the Statute of Frauds. A promise to pay a debt unenforceable under the Statute of Frauds is very similar to the promises governed by §§ 82–85. But the problem seldom arises. Part performance often renders the Statute inapplicable; if it does not, the contract can be made enforceable by a subsequent memorandum. See § 136. In any event, the Statute does not ordinarily foreclose the remedy of restitution. See § 375. Where the question does arise, the new promise is binding if the policy of the Statute is satisfied.

Illustration:

11. By statute an agreement authorizing a real estate broker to sell land for compensation is void unless the agreement or a memorandum thereof is in writing. A, a real estate broker, procures a purchaser for B's land without any written agreement. In the written sale agreement, signed by B, B promises to pay A $200, the usual commission, "for services rendered." The promise is binding.

h. Obligation unenforceable because usurious. If a promise is unenforceable because it is usurious, an agreement in renewal or substitution for it that provides for a payment including the usurious interest is also unenforceable, even though the interest from the date of renewal or substitution is not usurious. However, a promise to pay the original debt with interest that is not usurious in substitution for the usurious interest is enforceable.

i. Partial enforcement. The rules stated in §§ 82–85 refer to promises to perform all or part of an antecedent duty, and do not make enforceable a promise to do more. Similarly, where a benefit received is a liquidated sum of money, a promise is not enforceable under this Section beyond the amount of the benefit. Where the value of the benefit is uncertain, a promise to pay the value is binding and a promise to pay a liquidated sum may serve to fix the amount due if in all the circumstances it is not disproportionate to the benefit. See Illustration 7. A promise which is excessive may sometimes be enforced to the extent of the value of the benefit, and the remedy may be thought of as quasi-contractual rather than contractual. In other cases a promise of disproportionate value may tend to show unfair pressure or other conduct by the promisee such that justice does not require any enforcement of the promise. Compare Comment c to § 72.

Illustrations:

12. A, a married woman of sixty, has rendered household services without compensation over a period of years for B, a man of eighty living alone and having no close relatives. B has a net worth of three million dollars and has often assured A that she will be well paid for her services, whose reasonable value is not in excess of $6,000. B executes and delivers to A a written promise to pay A $25,000 "to be taken from my estate." The promise is binding.

13. The facts being otherwise as stated in Illustration 12, B's promise is made orally and is to leave A his entire estate. A cannot recover more than the reasonable value of her services.

§ 87. Option Contract

(1) An offer is binding as an option contract if it

(a) is in writing and signed by the offeror, recites a purported consideration for the making of the offer, and proposes an exchange on fair terms within a reasonable time; or

(b) is made irrevocable by statute.

(2) An offer which the offeror should reasonably expect to induce action or forbearance of a substantial character on the part of the offeree before acceptance and which does induce such action or forbearance is binding as an option contract to the extent necessary to avoid injustice.

§ 89. Modification of Executory Contract

A promise modifying a duty under a contract not fully performed on either side is binding

(a) if the modification is fair and equitable in view of circumstances not anticipated by the parties when the contract was made; or

(b) to the extent provided by statute; or

(c) to the extent that justice requires enforcement in view of material change of position in reliance on the promise.

Comment:

a. Rationale. This Section relates primarily to adjustments in on-going transactions. Like offers and guaranties, such adjustments are ancillary to exchanges and have some of the same presumptive utility. See §§ 72, 87, 88. Indeed, paragraph (a) deals with bargains which are without consideration only because of the rule that performance of a legal duty to the promisor is not consideration. See § 73. This Section is also related to § 84 on waiver of conditions: it may apply to cases in which § 84 is inapplicable because a condition is material to the exchange or risk. As in cases governed by § 84, relation to a bargain tends to satisfy the cautionary and channeling functions of legal formalities. See Comment c to § 72. The Statute of Frauds may prevent enforcement in the absence of reliance. See §§ 149–50. Otherwise formal requirements are at a minimum.

b. Performance of legal duty. The rule of § 73 finds its modern justification in cases of promises made by mistake or induced by unfair pressure. Its application to cases where those elements are absent has been much criticized and is avoided if paragraph (a) of this Section is applicable. The limitation to a modification which is "fair and equitable" goes beyond absence of coercion and requires an objectively demonstrable reason for seeking a modification. Compare Uniform Commercial Code § 2–209 Comment. The reason for modification must rest in circumstances not "anticipated" as part of the context in which the contract was made, but a frustrating event may be unanticipated for this purpose if it was not adequately covered, even though it was foreseen as a remote possibility. When such a reason is present, the relative financial strength of the parties, the formality with which the modification is made, the extent to which it is performed or relied on and other circumstances may be relevant to show or negate imposition or unfair surprise.

The same result called for by paragraph (a) is sometimes reached on the ground that the original contract was "rescinded" by mutual agreement and that new promises were then made which furnished consideration for each other. That theory is rejected here because it is fictitious when the "rescission" and new agreement are simultaneous, and because if logically carried out it might uphold unfair and inequitable modifications.

Illustrations:

1. By a written contract A agrees to excavate a cellar for B for a stated price. Solid rock is unexpectedly encountered and A so notifies B. A and B then orally agree that A will remove the rock at a unit price which is reasonable but nine times that used in computing the original price, and A completes the job. B is bound to pay the increased amount.

2. A contracts with B to supply for $300 a laundry chute for a building B has contracted to build for the Government for $150,000. Later A discovers that he made an error as to the type of material to be used and should have bid $1,200. A offers to supply the chute for $1000, eliminating overhead and profit. After ascertaining that other suppliers would charge more, B agrees. The new agreement is binding.

3. A is employed by B as a designer of coats at $90 a week for a year beginning November 1 under a written contract executed September 1. A is offered $115 a week by another employer and so informs B. A and B then agree that A will be paid $100 a week and in October execute a new written contract to that effect, simultaneously tearing up the prior contract. The new contract is binding.

4. A contracts to manufacture and sell to B 2,000 steel roofs for corn cribs at $60. Before A begins manufacture a threat of a nationwide steel strike raises the cost of steel about $10 per roof, and A

and B agree orally to increase the price to $70 per roof. A thereafter manufactures and delivers 1700 of the roofs, and B pays for 1,500 of them at the increased price without protest, increasing the selling price of the corn cribs by $10. The new agreement is binding.

5. A contracts to manufacture and sell to B 100,000 castings for lawn mowers at 50 cents each. After partial delivery and after B has contracted to sell a substantial number of lawn mowers at a fixed price, A notifies B that increased metal costs require that the price be increased to 75 cents. Substitute castings are available at 55 cents, but only after several months delay. B protests but is forced to agree to the new price to keep its plant in operation. The modification is not binding.

c. Statutes. Uniform Commercial Code § 2–209 dispenses with the requirement of consideration for an agreement modifying a contract for the sale of goods. Under that section the original contract can provide against oral modification, and the requirements of the Statute of Frauds must be met if the contract as modified is within its provisions; but an ineffective modification can operate as a waiver. The Comment indicates that extortion of a modification without legitimate commercial reason is ineffective as a violation of the duty of good faith imposed by the Code. A similar limitation may be applicable under statutes which give effect to a signed writing as a substitute for the seal, or under statutes which give effect to acceptance by the promisee of the modified performance. In some States statutes or constitutional provisions flatly forbid the payment of extra compensation to Government contractors.

d. Reliance. Paragraph (c) states the application of § 90 to modification of an executory contract in language adapted from Uniform Commercial Code § 2–209. Even though the promise is not binding when made, it may become binding in whole or in part by reason of action or forbearance by the promisee or third persons in reliance on it. In some cases the result can be viewed as based either on estoppel to contradict a representation of fact or on reliance on a promise. Ordinarily reliance by the promisee is reasonably foreseeable and makes the modification binding with respect to performance by the promisee under it and any return performance owed by the promisor. But as under § 84 the original terms can be reinstated for the future by reasonable notification received by the promisee unless reinstatement would be unjust in view of a change of position on his part. Compare Uniform Commercial Code § 2–209(5).

Illustrations:

6. A defaults in payment of a premium on a life insurance policy issued by B, an insurance company. Pursuant to the terms of the policy, B notifies A of the lapse of the policy and undertakes to continue the insurance until a specified future date, but by mistake specifies a date two months later than the insured would be entitled to under the policy. On inquiry by A two years later, B repeats the mistake, offering A an option to take a cash payment. A fails to do so, and dies one month before the specified date. B is bound to pay the insurance.

7. A is the lessee of an apartment house under a 99–year lease from B at a rent of $10,000 per year. Because of war conditions many of the apartments become vacant, and in order to enable A to stay in business B agrees to reduce the rent to $5,000. The reduced rent is

paid for five years. The war being over, the apartments are then fully rented, and B notifies A that the full rent called for by the lease must be paid. A is bound to pay the full rent only from a reasonable time after the receipt of the notification.

8. A contracts with B to carry a shipment of fish under refrigeration. During the short first leg of the voyage the refrigeration equipment on the ship breaks down, and A offers either to continue under ventilation or to hold the cargo at the first port for later shipment. B agrees to shipment under ventilation but later changes his mind. A receives notification of the change before he has changed his position. A is bound to ship under refrigeration.

§ **90.** Promise Reasonably Inducing Action or Forbearance

(1) A promise which the promisor should reasonably expect to induce action or forbearance on the part of the promisee or a third person and which does induce such action or forbearance is binding if injustice can be avoided only by enforcement of the promise. The remedy granted for breach may be limited as justice requires.

(2) A charitable subscription or a marriage settlement is binding under Subsection (1) without proof that the promise induced action or forbearance.

Comment:

a. Relation to other rules. Obligations and remedies based on reliance are not peculiar to the law of contracts. This Section is often referred to in terms of "promissory estoppel," a phrase suggesting an extension of the doctrine of estoppel. Estoppel prevents a person from showing the truth contrary to a representation of fact made by him after another has relied on the representation. See Restatement, Second, Agency § 8B; Restatement, Second, Torts §§ 872, 894. Reliance is also a significant feature of numerous rules in the law of negligence, deceit and restitution. See, e.g., Restatement, Second, Agency §§ 354, 378; Restatement, Second, Torts §§ 323, 537; Restatement of Restitution § 55. In some cases those rules and this Section overlap; in others they provide analogies useful in determining the extent to which enforcement is necessary to avoid injustice.

It is fairly arguable that the enforcement of informal contracts in the action of assumpsit rested historically on justifiable reliance on a promise. Certainly reliance is one of the main bases for enforcement of the half-completed exchange, and the probability of reliance lends support to the enforcement of the executory exchange. See Comments to §§ 72, 75. This Section thus states a basic principle which often renders inquiry unnecessary as to the precise scope of the policy of enforcing bargains. Sections 87–89 state particular applications of the same principle to promises ancillary to bargains, and it also applies in a wide variety of non-commercial situations. See, e.g., § 94.

Illustration:

1. A, knowing that B is going to college, promises B that A will give him $5,000 on completion of his course. B goes to college, and borrows and spends more than $5,000 for college expenses. When he has nearly completed his course, A notifies him of an intention to revoke the promise. A's promise is bind-

ing and B is entitled to payment on completion of the course without regard to whether his performance was "bargained for" under § 71.

b. Character of reliance protected. The principle of this Section is flexible. The promisor is affected only by reliance which he does or should foresee, and enforcement must be necessary to avoid injustice. Satisfaction of the latter requirement may depend on the reasonableness of the promisee's reliance, on its definite and substantial character in relation to the remedy sought, on the formality with which the promise is made, on the extent to which the evidentiary, cautionary, deterrent and channeling functions of form are met by the commercial setting or otherwise, and on the extent to which such other policies as the enforcement of bargains and the prevention of unjust enrichment are relevant. Compare Comment to § 72. The force of particular factors varies in different types of cases: thus reliance need not be of substantial character in charitable subscription cases, but must in cases of firm offers and guaranties. Compare Subsection (2) with §§ 87, 88.

Illustrations:

2. A promises B not to foreclose, for a specified time, a mortgage which A holds on B's land. B thereafter makes improvements on the land. A's promise is binding and may be enforced by denial of foreclosure before the time has elapsed.

3. A sues B in a municipal court for damages for personal injuries caused by B's negligence. After the one year statute of limitations has run, B requests A to discontinue the action and start again in the superior court where the action can be consolidated with other ac-

tions against B arising out of the same accident. A does so. B's implied promise that no harm to A will result bars B from asserting the statute of limitations as a defense.

4. A has been employed by B for 40 years. B promises to pay A a pension of $200 per month when A retires. A retires and forbears to work elsewhere for several years while B pays the pension. B's promise is binding.

c. Reliance by third persons. If a promise is made to one party for the benefit of another, it is often foreseeable that the beneficiary will rely on the promise. Enforcement of the promise in such cases rests on the same basis and depends on the same factors as in cases of reliance by the promisee. Justifiable reliance by third persons who are not beneficiaries is less likely, but may sometimes reinforce the claim of the promisee or beneficiary.

Illustrations:

5. A holds a mortgage on B's land. To enable B to obtain a loan, A promises B in writing to release part of the land from the mortgage upon payment of a stated sum. As A contemplated, C lends money to B on a second mortgage, relying on A's promise. The promise is binding and may be enforced by C.

6. A executes and delivers a promissory note to B, a bank, to give B a false appearance of assets, deceive the banking authorities, and enable the bank to continue to operate. After several years B fails and is taken over by C, a representative of B's creditors. A's note is enforceable by C.

7. A and B, husband and wife, are tenants by the entirety of a tract of land. They make an oral promise to B's niece C to give her

283

the tract. B, C and C's husband expend money in building a house on the tract and C and her husband take possession and live there for several years until B dies. The expenditures by B and by C's husband are treated like those by C in determining whether justice requires enforcement of the promise against A.

d. Partial enforcement. A promise binding under this section is a contract, and full-scale enforcement by normal remedies is often appropriate. But the same factors which bear on whether any relief should be granted also bear on the character and extent of the remedy. In particular, relief may sometimes be limited to restitution or to damages or specific relief measured by the extent of the promisee's reliance rather than by the terms of the promise. See §§ 84, 89; compare Restatement, Second, Torts § 549 on damages for fraud. Unless there is unjust enrichment of the promisor, damages should not put the promisee in a better position than performance of the promise would have put him. See §§ 344, 349. In the case of a promise to make a gift it would rarely be proper to award consequential damages which would place a greater burden on the promisor than performance would have imposed.

Illustrations:

8. A applies to B, a distributor of radios manufactured by C, for a "dealer franchise" to sell C's products. Such franchises are revocable at will. B erroneously informs A that C has accepted the application and will soon award the franchise, that A can proceed to employ salesmen and solicit orders, and that A will receive an initial delivery of at least 30 radios. A expends $1,150 in preparing to do business, but does not receive the franchise or any radios. B is liable to A for the $1,150 but not for the lost profit on 30 radios. Compare Restatement, Second, Agency § 329.

9. The facts being otherwise as stated in Illustration 8, B gives A the erroneous information deliberately and with C's approval and requires A to buy the assets of a deceased former dealer and thus discharge C's "moral obligation" to the widow. C is liable to A not only for A's expenses but also for the lost profit on 30 radios.

10. A, who owns and operates a bakery, desires to go into the grocery business. He approaches B, a franchisor of supermarkets. B states to A that for $18,000 B will establish A in a store. B also advises A to move to another town and buy a small grocery to gain experience. A does so. Later B advises A to sell the grocery, which A does, taking a capital loss and foregoing expected profits from the summer tourist trade. B also advises A to sell his bakery to raise capital for the supermarket franchise, saying "Everything is ready to go. Get your money together and we are set." A sells the bakery taking a capital loss on this sale as well. Still later, B tells A that considerably more than an $18,000 investment will be needed, and the negotiations between the parties collapse. At the point of collapse many details of the proposed agreement between the parties are unresolved. The assurances from B to A are promises on which B reasonably should have expected A to rely, and A is entitled to his actual losses on the sales of the bakery and grocery and for his moving and temporary living expenses. Since the proposed agreement was never made,

however, A is not entitled to lost profits from the sale of the grocery or to his expectation interest in the proposed franchise from B.

11. A is about to buy a house on a hill. Before buying he obtains a promise from B, who owns adjoining land, that B will not build on a particular portion of his lot, where a building would obstruct the view from the house. A then buys the house in reliance on the promise. B's promise is binding, but will be specifically enforced only so long as A and his successors do not permanently terminate the use of the view.

12. A promises to make a gift of a tract of land to B, his son-in-law. B takes possession and lives on the land for 17 years, making valuable improvements. A then dispossesses B, and specific performance is denied because the proof of the terms of the promise is not sufficiently clear and definite. B is entitled to a lien on the land for the value of the improvements, not exceeding their cost.

e. Gratuitous promises to procure insurance. This Section is to be applied with caution to promises to procure insurance. The appropriate remedy for breach of such a promise makes the promisor an insurer, and thus may result in a liability which is very large in relation to the value of the promised service. Often the promise is properly to be construed merely as a promise to use reasonable efforts to procure the insurance, and reliance by the promisee may be unjustified or may be justified only for a short time. Or it may be doubtful whether he did in fact rely. Such difficulties may be removed if the proof of the promise and the reliance are clear, or if the promise is made with some formality, or if part performance or a commercial setting or a potential benefit to the promisor provide a substitute for formality.

Illustrations:

13. A, a bank, lends money to B on the security of a mortgage on B's new home. The mortgage requires B to insure the property. At the closing of the transaction A promises to arrange for the required insurance, and in reliance on the promise B fails to insure. Six months later the property, still uninsured, is destroyed by fire. The promise is binding.

14. A sells an airplane to B, retaining title to secure payment of the price. After the closing A promises to keep the airplane covered by insurance until B can obtain insurance. B could obtain insurance in three days but makes no effort to do so, and the airplane is destroyed after six days. A is not subject to liability by virtue of the promise.

f. Charitable subscriptions, marriage settlements, and other gifts. One of the functions of the doctrine of consideration is to deny enforcement to a promise to make a gift. Such a promise is ordinarily enforced by virtue of the promisee's reliance only if his conduct is foreseeable and reasonable and involves a definite and substantial change of position which would not have occurred if the promise had not been made. In some cases, however, other policies reinforce the promisee's claim. Thus the promisor might be unjustly enriched if he could reclaim the subject of the promised gift after the promisee has improved it.

Subsection (2) identifies two other classes of cases in which the promisee's claim is similarly reinforced. American courts have traditionally favored charitable subscriptions and marriage settlements, and have found consideration in many cases where the element of exchange was doubtful or nonexistent. Where recovery is rested on reliance in such cases, a probability of reliance is enough, and no effort is made to sort out mixed motives or to consider whether partial enforcement would be appropriate.

Illustrations:

15. A promises B $5000, knowing that B desires that sum for the purchase of a parcel of land. Induced thereby, B secures without any payment an option to buy the parcel. A then tells B that he withdraws his promise. A's promise is not binding.

16. A orally promises to give her son B a tract of land to live on. As A intended, B gives up a homestead elsewhere, takes possession of the land, lives there for a year and makes substantial improvements. A's promise is binding.

17. A orally promises to pay B, a university, $100,000 in five annual installments for the purposes of its fund-raising campaign then in progress. The promise is confirmed in writing by A's agent, and two annual installments are paid before A dies. The continuance of the fund-raising campaign by B is sufficient reliance to make the promise binding on A and his estate.

18. A and B are engaged to be married. In anticipation of the marriage A and his father C enter into a formal written agreement by which C promises to leave certain property to A by will. A's subsequent marriage to B is sufficient reliance to make the promise binding on C and his estate.

CHAPTER 5. THE STATUTE OF FRAUDS

TOPIC 2. THE SURETYSHIP PROVISION

§ 116. Main Purpose; Advantage to Surety

A contract that all or part of a duty of a third person to the promisee shall be satisfied is not within the Statute of Frauds as a promise to answer for the duty of another if the consideration for the promise is in fact or apparently desired by the promisor mainly for his own economic advantage, rather than in order to benefit the third person. If, however, the consideration is merely a premium for insurance, the contract is within the Statute.

TOPIC 6. SATISFACTION OF THE STATUTE BY A MEMORANDUM

§ 131. General Requisites of a Memorandum

Unless additional requirements are prescribed by the particular statute, a contract within the Statute of Frauds is enforceable if it is evidenced by any writing, signed by or on behalf of the party to be charged, which

(a) reasonably identifies the subject matter of the contract,

(b) is sufficient to indicate that a contract with respect thereto has been made between the parties or offered by the signer to the other party, and

(c) states with reasonable certainty the essential terms of the unperformed promises in the contract.

TOPIC 8. CONSEQUENCES OF NON–COMPLIANCE

§ 139. Enforcement by Virtue of Action in Reliance

(1) A promise which the promisor should reasonably expect to induce action or forbearance on the part of the promisee or a third person and which does induce the action or forbearance is enforceable notwithstanding the Statute of Frauds if injustice can be avoided only by enforcement of the promise. The remedy granted for breach is to be limited as justice requires.

(2) In determining whether injustice can be avoided only by enforcement of the promise, the following circumstances are significant:

(a) the availability and adequacy of other remedies, particularly cancellation and restitution;

(b) the definite and substantial character of the action or forbearance in relation to the remedy sought;

(c) the extent to which the action or forbearance corroborates evidence of the making and terms of the promise, or the making and terms are otherwise established by clear and convincing evidence;

(d) the reasonableness of the action or forbearance;

(e) the extent to which the action or forbearance was foreseeable by the promisor.

Comment:

a. Relation to other rules. This Section is complementary to § 90, which dispenses with the requirement of consideration if the same conditions are met, but it also applies to promises supported by consideration. Like § 90, this Section overlaps in some cases with rules based on estoppel or fraud; it states a basic principle which sometimes renders inquiry unnecessary as to the precise scope of other policies. Sections 128 and 129 state particular applications of the same principle to land contracts; §§ 125(3) and 130(2) also rest on it in part. See also Uniform Commercial Code §§ 2–201(3), 8–319(b). Where a promise is made without intention to perform, remedies under this Section may be alternative to remedies for fraud. See Comment b to § 313; Restatement, Second, Torts § 530.

b. Avoidance of injustice. Like § 90 this Section states a flexible principle, but the requirement of consideration is more easily displaced than the requirement of a writing. The reliance must be foreseeable by the promisor, and enforcement must be necessary to avoid injustice. Subsection (2) lists some of the relevant factors in applying the latter requirement. Each factor relates either to the extent to which reliance furnishes a compelling substantive basis for relief in addition to the expectations created by the promise or to the extent to which the circumstances satisfy the evidentiary purpose of the Statute and fulfill any cautionary, deterrent and channeling functions it may serve.

Illustrations:

1. A is lessee of a building for five years at $75 per month and has sublet it for three years at $100 per month. A seeks to induce B to purchase the building, and to that end orally promises to assign to B the lease and sublease and to execute a written assignment as soon as B obtains a deed. B purchases the building in reliance on the promise. B is entitled to the rentals from the sublease.

2. A is a pilot with an established airline having rights to continued employment, and could take up to six months leave without prejudice to those rights. He takes such leave to become general manager of B, a small airline which hopes to expand if a certificate to operate over an important route is granted. When his six months leave is about to expire, A demands definite employment because of that fact, and B orally agrees to employ A for two years and on the granting of the certificate to give A an increase in salary and a written contract. In reliance on this agreement A lets his right to return to his prior employer expire. The certificate is soon granted, but A is discharged in breach of the agreement. The Statute of Frauds does not prevent recovery of damages by A.

c. Particular factors. The force of the factors listed varies in different

types of cases, and additional factors may affect particular types of contracts. Thus reliance of the kinds usual in suretyship transactions is not sufficient to justify enforcement of an oral guaranty, where the evidentiary and cautionary functions performed by the statutory formalities are not fulfilled. See Comment a to § 112. In the case of a contract between prospective spouses made upon consideration of marriage, the policy of the Statute is reinforced by a policy against legal interference in the marriage relation, and reliance incident to the marriage relation does not make the contract enforceable. See Comment d to § 124. Where restitution is an unavailable remedy because to grant it would nullify the statutory purpose, a remedy based on reliance will ordinarily also be denied. See Comment a to § 375.

Illustration:

3. A orally promises to pay B a commission for services in negotiating the sale of a business opportunity, and B finds a purchaser to whom A sells the business opportunity. A statute extends the Statute of Frauds to such promises, and is interpreted to preclude recovery of the reasonable value of such services. The promise is not made enforceable by B's reliance on it.

d. Partial enforcement; particular remedies. The same factors which bear on whether any relief should be granted also bear on the character and extent of the remedy. In particular, the remedy of restitution is not ordinarily affected by the Statute of Frauds (see § 375); where restitution is an adequate remedy, other remedies are not made available by the rule stated in this Section. Again, when specific enforcement is available under the rule stated in § 129, an ordinary action for damages is commonly less satisfactory, and justice then does not require enforcement in such an action. See Comment c to § 129. In some cases it may be appropriate to measure relief by the extent of the promisee's reliance rather than by the terms of the promise. See § 90 Comment e and Illustrations.

Illustration:

4. A renders services to B under an oral contract within the Statute by which B promises to pay for the services. On discharge without cause in breach of the contract, A is entitled to the reasonable value of the services, but in the absence of additional circumstances is not entitled to damages for wrongful discharge.

§ 141. Action for Value of Performance Under Unenforceable Contract

(1) In an action for the value of performance under a contract, except as stated in Subsection (2), the Statute of Frauds does not invalidate any defense which would be available of the contract were enforceable against both parties.

(2) Where a party to a contract which is unenforceable against him refuses either to perform the contract or to sign a sufficient memorandum, the other party is justified in suspending any performance for which he has not already received the agreed return, and such a suspension is not a defense in an action for the value of performance rendered before the suspension.

CHAPTER 6. MISTAKE

§ 151. Mistake Defined

A mistake is a belief that is not in accord with the facts.

§ 152. When Mistake of Both Parties Makes a Contract Voidable

(1) Where a mistake of both parties at the time a contract was made as to a basic assumption on which the contract was made has a material effect on the agreed exchange of performances, the contract is voidable by the adversely affected party unless he bears the risk of the mistake under the rule stated in § 154.

(2) In determining whether the mistake has a material effect on the agreed exchange of performances, account is taken of any relief by way of reformation, restitution, or otherwise.

§ 153. When Mistake of One Party Makes a Contract Voidable

Where a mistake of one party at the time a contract was made as to a basic assumption on which he made the contract has a material effect on the agreed exchange of performances that is adverse to him, the contract is voidable by him if he does not bear the risk of the mistake under the rule stated in § 154, and

    (a) the effect of the mistake is such that enforcement of the contract would be unconscionable, or

    (b) the other party had reason to know of the mistake or his fault caused the mistake.

§ 154. When a Party Bears the Risk of a Mistake

A party bears the risk of a mistake when

    (a) The risk is allocated to him by agreement of the parties, or

    (b) he is aware, at the time the contract is made, that he has only limited knowledge with respect to the facts to which the mistake relates but treats his limited knowledge as sufficient, or

    (c) the risk is allocated to him by the court on the ground that it is reasonable in the circumstances to do so.

§ 157. Effect of Fault of Party Seeking Relief

A mistaken party's fault in failing to know or discover the facts before making the contract does not bar him from avoidance or reformation under the rules stated in this Chapter, unless his fault amounts to a failure to act in good faith and in accordance with reasonable standards of fair dealing.

§ 158. Relief Including Restitution

(1) In any case governed by the rules stated in this Chapter, either party may have a claim for relief including restitution under the rules stated in §§ 240 and 376.

(2) In any case governed by the rules stated in this Chapter, if those rules together with the rules stated in Chapter 16 will not avoid injustice, the court may grant relief on such terms as justice requires including protection of the parties' reliance interest.

CHAPTER 7. MISREPRESENTATION, DURESS AND UNDUE INFLUENCE

TOPIC 1. MISREPRESENTATION

§ 159. Misrepresentation Defined

A misrepresentation is an assertion that is not in accord with the facts.

§ 160. When Action is Equivalent to an Assertion (Concealment)

Action intended or known to be likely to prevent another from learning a fact is equivalent to an assertion that the fact does not exist.

§ **161.** When Non-disclosure Is Equivalent to an Assertion

A person's non-disclosure of a fact known to him is equivalent to an assertion that the fact does not exist in the following cases only:

(a) where he knows that disclosure of the fact is necessary to prevent some previous assertion from being a misrepresentation or from being fraudulent or material.

(b) where he knows that disclosure of the fact would correct a mistake of the other party as to a basic assumption on which that party is making the contract and if non-disclosure of the fact amounts to a failure to act in good faith and in accordance with reasonable standards of fair dealing.

(c) where he knows that disclosure of the fact would correct a mistake of the other party as to the contents or effect of a writing, evidencing or embodying an agreement in whole or in part.

(d) where the other person is entitled to know the fact because of a relation of trust and confidence between them.

§ **162.** When a Misrepresentation Is Fraudulent or Material

(1) A misrepresentation is fraudulent if the maker intends his assertion to induce a party to manifest his assent and the maker

(a) knows or believes that the assertion is not in accord with the facts, or

(b) does not have the confidence that he states or implies in the truth of the assertion, or

(c) knows that he does not have the basis that he states or implies for the assertion.

(2) A misrepresentation is material if it would be likely to induce a reasonable person to manifest his assent, or if the maker knows that it would be likely to induce the recipient to do so.

§ **163.** When a Misrepresentation Prevents Formation of a Contract

If a misrepresentation as to the character or essential terms of a proposed contract induces conduct that appears to be a manifestation of assent by one who neither knows nor has reasonable opportunity to know of the character or essential terms of the proposed contract, his conduct is not effective as a manifestation of assent.

§ **164.** When a Misrepresentation Makes a Contract Voidable

(1) If a party's manifestation of assent is induced by either a fraudulent or a material misrepresentation by the other party upon

which the recipient is justified in relying, the contract is voidable by the recipient.

(2) If a party's manifestation of assent is induced by either a fraudulent or a material misrepresentation by one who is not a party to the transaction upon which the recipient is justified in relying, the contract is voidable by the recipient, unless the other party to the transaction in good faith and without reason to know of the misrepresentation either gives value or relies materially on the transaction.

§ 166. When a Misrepresentation as to a Writing Justifies Reformation

If a party's manifestation of assent is induced by the other party's ·fraudulent misrepresentation as to the contents or effect of a writing evidencing or embodying in whole or in part an agreement, the court at the request of the recipient may reform the writing to express the terms of the agreement as asserted,

> (a) if the recipient was justified in relying on the misrepresentation, and
>
> (b) except to the extent that rights of third parties such as good faith purchasers for value will be unfairly affected.

§ 168. Reliance on Assertions of Opinion

(1) An assertion is one of opinion if it expresses only a belief, without certainty, as to the existence of a fact or expresses only a judgment as to quality, value, authenticity, or similar matters.

(2) If it is reasonable to do so, the recipient of an assertion of a person's opinion as to facts not disclosed and not otherwise known to the recipient may properly interpret it as an assertion

> (a) that the facts known to that person are not incompatible with his opinion, or
>
> (b) that he knows facts sufficient to justify him in forming it.

§ 169. When Reliance on an Assertion of Opinion Is Not Justified

To the extent that an assertion is one of opinion only, the recipient is not justified in relying on it unless the recipient

> (a) stands in such a relation of trust and confidence to the person whose opinion is asserted that the recipient is reasonable in relying on it, or
>
> (b) reasonably believes that, as compared with himself, the person whose opinion is asserted has special skill, judgment or objectivity with respect to the subject matter, or

(c) is for some other special reason particularly susceptible to a misrepresentation of the type involved.

TOPIC 2.   DURESS AND UNDUE INFLUENCE

§ 175. When Duress by Threat Makes a Contract Voidable

(1) If a party's manifestation of assent is induced by an improper threat by the other party that leaves the victim no reasonable alternative, the contract is voidable by the victim.

(2) If a party's manifestation of assent is induced by one who is not a party to the transaction, the contract is voidable by the victim unless the other party to the transaction in good faith and without reason to know of the duress either gives value or relies materially on the transaction.

§ 176. When a Threat Is Improper

(1) A threat is improper if

(a) what is threatened is a crime or a tort, or the threat itself would be a crime or a tort if it resulted in obtaining property,

(b) what is threatened is a criminal prosecution,

(c) what is threatened is the use of civil process and the threat is made in bad faith, or

(d) the threat is a breach of the duty of good faith and fair dealing under a contract with the recipient.

(2) A threat is improper if the resulting exchange is not on fair terms, and

(a) the threatened act would harm the recipient and would not significantly benefit the party making the threat,

(b) the effectiveness of the threat in inducing the manifestation of assent is significantly increased by prior unfair dealing by the party making the threat, or

(c) what is threatened is otherwise a use of power for illegitimate ends.

§ 177. When Undue Influence Makes a Contract Voidable

(1) Undue influence is unfair persuasion of a party who is under the domination of the person exercising the persuasion or who by virtue of the relation between them is justified in assuming that that person will not act in a manner inconsistent with his welfare.

(2) If a party's manifestation of assent is induced by undue influence by the other party, the contract is voidable by the victim.

(3) If a party's manifestation of assent is induced by one who is not a party to the transaction, the contract is voidable by the victim unless the other party to the transaction in good faith and without reason to know of the undue influence either gives value or relies materially on the transaction.

CHAPTER 8.   UNENFORCEABILITY ON GROUNDS OF PUBLIC POLICY

TOPIC 1.   UNENFORCEABILITY IN GENERAL

§ 178.   When a Term Is Unenforceable on Grounds of Public Policy

(1) A promise or other term of an agreement is unenforceable on grounds of public policy if legislation provides that it is unenforceable or the interest in its enforcement is clearly outweighed in the circumstances by a public policy against the enforcement of such terms.

(2) In weighing the interest in the enforcement of a term, account is taken of

 (a) the parties' justified expectations,

 (b) any forfeiture that would result if enforcement were denied, and

 (c) any special public interest in the enforcement of the particular term.

(3) In weighing a public policy against enforcement of a term, account is taken of

 (a) the strength of that policy as manifested by legislation or judicial decisions,

 (b) the likelihood that a refusal to enforce the term will further that policy,

 (c) the seriousness of any misconduct involved and the extent to which it was deliberate, and

 (d) the directness of the connection between that misconduct and the term.

§ 179.   Bases of Public Policies Against Enforcement

A public policy against the enforcement of promises or other terms may be derived by the court from

 (a) legislation relevant to such a policy, or

 (b) the need to protect some aspect of the public welfare, as is the case for the judicial policies against, for example,

  (i) restraint of trade (§§ 186–188),

(ii) impairment of family relations (§§ 189–191), and

(iii) interference with other protected interests (§§ 192–196, 356).

§ 181. Effect of Failure to Comply With Licensing or Similar Requirement

If a party is prohibited from doing an act because of his failure to comply with a licensing, registration or similar requirement, a promise in consideration of his doing that act or of his promise to do it is unenforceable on grounds of public policy if

(a) the requirement has a regulatory purpose, and

(b) the interest in the enforcement of the promise is clearly outweighed by the public policy behind the requirement.

§ 184. When Rest of Agreement is Enforceable

(1) If less than all of an agreement is unenforceable under the rule stated in § 178, a court may nevertheless enforce the rest of the agreement in favor of a party who did not engage in serious misconduct if the performance as to which the agreement is unenforceable is not an essential part of the agreed exchange.

(2) A court may treat only part of a term an unenforceable under the rule stated in Subsection (1) if the party who seeks to enforce the term obtained it in good faith and in accordance with reasonable standards of fair dealing.

§ 185. Excuse of a Condition on Grounds of Public Policy

To the extent that a term requiring the occurrence of a condition is unenforceable under the rule stated in § 178, a court may excuse the non-occurrence of the condition unless its occurrence was an essential part of the agreed exchange.

TOPIC 2. RESTRAINT OF TRADE

§ 186. Promise in Restraint of Trade

(1) A promise is unenforceable on grounds of public policy if it is unreasonably in restraint of trade.

(2) A promise is in restraint of trade if its performance would limit competition in any business or restrict the promisor in the exercise of a gainful occupation.

§ 187. Non-ancillary Restraints on Competition

A promise to refrain from competition that imposes a restraint that is not ancillary to an otherwise valid transaction or relationship is unreasonably in restraint of trade.

§ 188. Ancillary Restraints on Competition

(1) A promise to refrain from competition that imposes a restraint that is ancillary to an otherwise valid transaction or relationship is unreasonably in restraint of trade if

> (a) the restraint is greater than is needed to protect the promisee's legitimate interest, or
>
> (b) the promisee's need is outweighed by the hardship to the promisor and the likely injury to the public.

(2) Promises imposing restraints that are ancillary to a valid transaction or relationship include the following:

> (a) a promise by the seller of a business not to compete with the buyer in such a way as to injure the value of the business sold;
>
> (b) a promise by an employee or other agent not to compete with his employer or other principal;
>
> (c) a promise by a partner not to compete with the partnership.

TOPIC 4. INTERFERENCE WITH OTHER PROTECTED INTERESTS

§ 193. Promise Inducing Violation of Fiduciary Duty

A promise by a fiduciary to violate his fiduciary duty or a promise that tends to induce such a violation is unenforceable on grounds of public policy.

TOPIC 5. RESTITUTION

§ 197. Restitution Generally Unavailable

Except as stated in §§ 198 and 199, a party has no claim in restitution for performance that he has rendered under or in return for a promise that is unenforceable on grounds of public policy unless denial of restitution would cause disproportionate forfeiture.

CHAPTER 9. THE SCOPE OF CONTRACTUAL OBLIGATIONS

TOPIC 1. THE MEANING OF AGREEMENTS

§ 201. Whose Meaning Prevails

(1) Where the parties have attached the same meaning to a promise or agreement or a term thereof, it is interpreted in accordance with that meaning.

(2) Where the parties have attached different meanings to a promise or agreement or a term thereof, it is interpreted in accordance with the meaning attached by one of them if at the time the agreement was made

(a) that party did not know of any different meaning attached by the other, and the other knew the meaning attached by the first party; or

(b) that party had no reason to know of any different meaning attached by the other, and the other had reason to know the meaning attached by the first party.

(3) Except as stated in this Section, neither party is bound by the meaning attached by the other, even though the result may be a failure of mutual assent.

§ 202. Rules in Aid of Interpretation

(1) Words and other conduct are interpreted in the light of all the circumstances, and if the principal purpose of the parties is ascertainable it is given great weight.

(2) A writing is interpreted as a whole, and all writings that are part of the same transaction are interpreted together.

(3) Unless a different intention is manifested,

(a) where language has a generally prevailing meaning, it is interpreted in accordance with that meaning;

(b) technical terms and words of art are given their technical meaning when used in a transaction within their technical field.

(4) Where an agreement involves repeated occasions for performance by either party with knowledge of the nature of the performance and opportunity for objection to it by the other, any course of performance accepted or acquiesced in without objection is given great weight in the interpretation of the agreement.

(5) Wherever reasonable, the manifestations of intention of the parties to a promise or agreement are interpreted as consistent with each other and with any relevant course of performance, course of dealing, or usage of trade.

§ 203. Standards of Preference in Interpretation

In the interpretation of a promise or agreement or a term thereof, the following standards of preference are generally applicable:

(a) an interpretation which gives a reasonable, lawful, and effective meaning to all the terms is preferred to an interpretation which leaves a part unreasonable, unlawful, or of no effect;

(b) express terms are given greater weight than course of performance, course of dealing, and usage of trade, course of performance is given greater weight than course of dealing or usage of trade, and course of dealing is given greater weight than usage of trade;

(c) specific terms and exact terms are given greater weight than general language;

(d) separately negotiated or added terms are given greater weight than standardized terms or other terms not separately negotiated.

§ 204. Supplying an Omitted Essential Term

When the parties to a bargain sufficiently defined to be a contract have not agreed with respect to a term which is essential to a determination of their rights and duties, a term which is reasonable in the circumstances is supplied by the court.

TOPIC 2. CONSIDERATIONS OF FAIRNESS AND THE PUBLIC INTEREST

§ 205. Duty of Good Faith and Fair Dealing

Every contract imposes upon each party a duty of good faith and fair dealing in its performance and its enforcement.

§ 208. Unconscionable Contract or Term

If a contract or term thereof is unconscionable at the time the contract is made a court may refuse to enforce the contract, or may enforce the remainder of the contract without the unconscionable term, or may so limit the application of any unconscionable term as to avoid any unconscionable result.

TOPIC 3. EFFECT OF ADOPTION OF A WRITING

§ 209. Integrated Agreements

(1) An integrated agreement is a writing or writings constituting a final expression of one or more terms of an agreement.

(2) Whether there is an integrated agreement is to be determined by the court as a question preliminary to determination of a question of interpretation or to application of the parol evidence rule.

(3) Where the parties reduce an agreement to a writing which in view of its completeness and specificity reasonably appears to be a complete agreement, it is taken to be an integrated agreement unless it is established by other evidence that the writing did not constitute a final expression.

§ 210. Completely and Partially Integrated Agreements

(1) A completely integrated agreement is an integrated agreement adopted by the parties as a complete and exclusive statement of the terms of the agreement.

(2) A partially integrated agreement is an integrated agreement other than a completely integrated agreement.

(3) Whether an agreement is completely or partially integrated is to be determined by the court as a question preliminary to determination of a question of interpretation or to application of the parol evidence rule.

§ 211. Standardized Agreements

(1) Except as stated in Subsection (3), where a party to an agreement signs or otherwise manifests assent to a writing and has reason to believe that like writings are regularly used to embody terms of agreements of the same type, he adopts the writing as an integrated agreement with respect to the terms included in the writing.

(2) Such a writing is interpreted wherever reasonable as treating alike all those similarly situated, without regard to their knowledge or understanding of the standard terms of the writing.

(3) Where the other party has reason to believe that the party manifesting such assent would not do so if he knew that the writing contained a particular term, the term is not part of the agreement.

§ 213. Effect of Integrated Agreement on Prior Agreements (Parol Evidence Rule)

(1) A binding integrated agreement discharges prior agreements to the extent that it is inconsistent with them.

(2) A binding completely integrated agreement discharges prior agreements to the extent that they are within its scope.

(3) An integrated agreement that is not binding or that is voidable and avoided does not discharge a prior agreement. But an integrated agreement, even though not binding, may be effective to render inoperative a term which would have been part of the agreement if it had not been integrated.

§ 214. Evidence of Prior or Contemporaneous Agreements and Negotiations

Agreements and negotiations prior to or contemporaneous with the adoption of a writing are admissible in evidence to establish

   (a) that the writing is or is not an integrated agreement;

   (b) that the integrated agreement, if any, is completely or partially integrated;

   (c) the meaning of the writing, whether or not integrated;

   (d) illegality, fraud, duress, mistake, lack of consideration, or other invalidating cause;

   (e) ground for granting or denying rescission, reformation, specific performance, or other remedy.

§ 215. Contradiction of Integrated Terms

Except as stated in the preceding Section, where there is a binding agreement, either completely or partially integrated, evidence of prior or contemporaneous agreements or negotiations is not admissible in evidence to contradict a term of the writing.

§ 216. Consistent Additional Terms

(1) Evidence of a consistent additional term is admissible to supplement an integrated agreement unless the court finds that the agreement was completely integrated.

(2) An agreement is not completely integrated if the writing omits a consistent additional agreed term which is

   (a) agreed to for separate consideration, or

   (b) such a term as in the circumstances might naturally be omitted from the writing.

§ 217. Integrated Agreement Subject to Oral Requirement of a Condition

Where the parties to a written agreement agree orally that performance of the agreement is subject to the occurrence of a stated condition, the agreement is not integrated with respect to the oral condition.

TOPIC 5. CONDITIONS AND SIMILAR EVENTS

§ 224. Condition Defined

A condition is an event, not certain to occur, which must occur, unless its non-occurrence is excused, before performance under a contract becomes due.

§ 225. Effects of the Non-occurrence of a Condition

(1) Performance of a duty subject to a condition cannot become due unless the condition occurs or its non-occurrence is excused.

(2) Unless it has been excused, the non-occurrence of a condition discharges the duty when the condition can no longer occur.

(3) Non-occurrence of a condition is not a breach by a party unless he is under a duty that the condition occur.

§ 227. Standards of Preference With Regard to Conditions

(1) In resolving doubts as to whether an event is made a condition of an obligor's duty, and as to the nature of such an event, an interpretation is preferred that will reduce the obligee's risk of forfeiture, unless the event is within the obligee's control or the circumstances indicate that he has assumed the risk.

(2) Unless the contract is of a type under which only one party generally undertakes duties, when it is doubtful whether

    (a) a duty is imposed on an obligee that an event occur, or

    (b) the event is made a condition of the obligor's duty, or

    (c) the event is made a condition of the obligor's duty and a duty is imposed on the obligee that the event occur,

the first interpretation is preferred if the event is within the obligee's control.

(3) In case of doubt, an interpretation under which an event is a condition of an obligor's duty is preferred over an interpretation under which the non-occurrence of the event is a ground for discharge of that duty after it has become a duty to perform.

§ 228. Satisfaction of the Obligor as a Condition

When it is a condition of an obligor's duty that he be satisfied with respect to the obligee's performance or with respect to something else, and it is practicable to determine whether a reasonable person in the position of the obligor would be satisfied, an interpretation is preferred under which the condition occurs if such a reasonable person in the position of the obligor would be satisfied.

§ 229. Excuse of a Condition to Avoid Forfeiture

To the extent that the non-occurrence of a condition would cause disproportionate forfeiture, a court may excuse the non-occurrence of that condition unless its occurrence was a material part of the agreed exchange.

CHAPTER 10. PERFORMANCE AND NON–PERFORMANCE

TOPIC 1. PERFORMANCES TO BE EXCHANGED UNDER AN EXCHANGE OF PROMISES

§ 231. Criterion for Determining When Performances Are to Be Exchanged Under an Exchange of Promises

Performances are to be exchanged under an exchange of promises if each promise is at least part of the consideration for the other and the performance of each promise is to be exchanged at least in part for the performance of the other.

§ 232. When it is Presumed That Performances Are to Be Exchanged Under an Exchange of Promises

Where the consideration given by each party to a contract consists in whole or in part of promises, all the performances to be rendered by each party taken collectively are treated as performances ot be exchanged under an exchange of promises, unless a contrary intention is clearly manifested.

§ 234. Order of Performances

(1) Where all or part of the performances to be exchanged under an exchange of promises can be rendered simultaneously, they are to that extent due simultaneously, unless the language or the circumstances indicate the contrary.

(2) Except to the extent stated in Subsection (1), where the performance of only one party under such an exchange requires a period of time, his performance is due at an earlier time than that of the other party, unless the language or the circumstances indicate the contrary.

TOPIC 2.   EFFECT OF PERFORMANCE AND NON–PERFORMANCE

§ 236. Claims for Damages for Total and for Partial Breach

(1) A claim for damages for total breach is one for damages based on all of the injured party's remaining rights to performance.

(2) A claim for damages for partial breach is one for damages based on only part of the injured party's remaining rights to performance.

§ 237. Effect on Other Party's Duties of a Failure to Render Performance

Except as stated in § 240, it is a condition of each party's remaining duties to render performances to be exchanged under an exchange of promises that there be no uncured material failure by the other party to render any such performance due at an earlier time.

§ 238. Effect on Other Party's Duties of a Failure to Offer Performance

Where all or part of the performances to be exchanged under an exchange of promises are due simultaneously, it is a condition of each party's duties to render such performance that the other party either render or, with manifested present ability to do so, offer performance of his part of the simultaneous exchange.

§ 240. Part Performances as Agreed Equivalents

If the performances to be exchanged under an exchange of promises can be apportioned into corresponding pairs of part performances so that the parts of each pair are properly regarded as agreed equivalents, a party's performance of his part of such a pair has the same effect on the other's duties to render performance of the agreed equivalent as it would have if only that pair of performances had been promised.

§ 241. Circumstances Significant in Determining Whether a Failure Is Material

In determining whether a failure to render or to offer performance is material, the following circumstances are significant:

   (a) the extent to which the injured party will be deprived of the benefit which he reasonably expected;

   (b) the extent to which the injured party can be adequately compensated for the part of that benefit of which he will be deprived;

   (c) the extent to which the party failing to perform or to offer to perform will suffer forfeiture;

   (d) the likelihood that the party failing to perform or to offer to perform will cure his failure, taking account of all the circumstances including any reasonable assurances;

   (e) the extent to which the behavior of the party failing to perform or to offer to perform comports with standards of good faith and fair dealing.

Comment:

a. Nature of significant circumstances. The application of the rules stated in §§ 237 and 238 turns on a standard of materiality that is necessarily imprecise and flexible. (Contrast the situation where the parties have, by their agreement, made an event a condition. See § 226 and Comments a and c thereto and § 229.) The standard of materiality applies to contracts of all types and without regard to whether the whole performance of either party is to be rendered at one time or part performances are to be rendered at different times. See Uniform Commercial Code § 2–612. It also applies to pairs of agreed equivalents under § 240. See Illustration 2. It is to be applied in the light of the facts of each case in such a way as to further the purpose of securing for each party his expectation of an exchange of performances. This Section therefore states circumstances, not rules, which are to be considered in determining whether a particular failure is material. A determination that a failure is not material means only that it does not have the effect of the non-occurrence of a condition under §§ 237 and 238. Even if not material, the failure may be a breach and give rise to a claim for damages for partial breach (§§ 236, 243).

Illustrations:

   1. A, a subcontractor, contracts to do excavation and earth moving on a housing subdivision project

for B, the owner and general contractor, and to do all work "in a workmanlike manner." B is to make monthly progress payments for the work performed during the preceding month less a retainer of ten percent. A negligently damages a building with his bulldozer causing serious damage and denies any liability for B's loss. When B refuses to make further progress payments until A repairs the damage or admits liability, A notifies B that he cancels the contract. If the court determines that A's breach is material, A has no claim against B. B has a claim against A for damages for breach of contract.

2. The facts being otherwise as stated in Illustration 6 to § 240, A completes the part concerned with the excavation and grading of lots and streets but fails in a minor respect to comply with the specifications. If a court determines that the failure is not material, A has a claim against B for $75,000 under the contract for the excavation and grading. B has a claim for damages against A for his failure fully to perform as to excavation and grading and also for his unjustified refusal to make street improvements.

b. Loss of benefit to injured party. Since the purpose of the rules stated in §§ 237 and 238 is to secure the parties' expectation of an exchange of performances, an important circumstance in determining whether a failure is material is the extent to which the injured party will be deprived of the benefit which he reasonably expected from the exchange (Subsection (a)). If the consideration given by either party consists partly of some performance and only partly of a promise (see Comment a to § 232), regard must be had to the entire exchange, including that performance, in applying this criterion.

Although the relationship between the monetary loss to the injured party as a result of the failure and the contract price may be significant, no simple rule based on the ratio of the one to the other can be laid down, and here, as elsewhere under this Section, all relevant circumstances must be considered. In construction contracts, for example, defects affecting structural soundness are ordinarily regarded as particularly significant. In the sale of goods a particularly exacting standard has evolved. There it has long been established that, in the absence of a showing of a contrary intention, a buyer is entitled to expect strict performance of the contract, and Uniform Commercial Code § 2–601 carries forward this expectation by allowing the buyer to reject "if the goods or the tender of delivery fail in any respect to conform to the contract." The Code, however, compensates to some extent for the severity of this standard by extending the seller's right to cure beyond the point when the time for performance has expired in some instances (§ 2–508(2)), by allowing revocation of acceptance only if a nonconformity "substantially impairs" the value of the goods to the buyer (§ 2–608(1)), and by allowing the injured party to treat a nonconformity or default as to one installment under an installment contract as a breach of the whole only if it "substantially impairs" the value of the whole (§ 2–612(3)).

c. Adequacy of compensation for loss. The second circumstance, the extent to which the injured party can be adequately compensated for his loss of benefit (Subsection (b)), is a corollary of the first. Difficulty that he may have in proving with sufficient certainty the amount of that loss will affect the adequacy of compensation. If the failure is a breach, the injured party always has a claim for damages, and the question becomes one of the adequacy of that claim to compensate him for the lost benefit. Where the failure is not a breach, the question becomes one of the adequacy of any claim, such as one in restitution, to which the injured party may be entitled. This is a particularly important circumstance when the party in breach seeks specific performance. Such relief may be granted if damages can adequately compensate the injured party for the defect in performance. See Comment c to § 242.

d. Forfeiture by party who fails. Because a material failure acts as the non-occurrence of a condition, the same risk of forfeiture obtains as in the case of conditions generally if the party who fails to perform or tender has relied substantially on the expectation of the exchange, as through preparation or performance. Therefore a third circumstance is the extent to which the party failing to perform or to make an offer to perform will suffer forfeiture if the failure is treated as material. For this reason a failure is less likely to be regarded as material if it occurs late, after substantial preparation or performance, and more likely to be regarded as material if it occurs early, before such reliance. For the same reason the failure is more likely to be regarded as material if such preparation or performance as has taken place can be returned to and salvaged by the party failing to perform or tender, and less likely to be regarded as material if it cannot. These factors argue against a finding of material failure and in favor of one of substantial performance where a builder has completed performance under a construction contract and, because the building is on the owner's land, can salvage nothing if he is denied recovery of the balance of the price. Even in such a case, however, the potential forfeiture may be mitigated if the builder has a claim in restitution (§§ 370–77, especially § 374) or if he has already received progress payments under a

provision of the contract. The same factors argue for a finding of material failure where a seller tenders goods and can salvage them by resale to others if they are rejected and he is denied recovery of the price. This helps to explain the severity of the rule as applied to the sale of goods. See Comment b. Even in such a case, however, the potential forfeiture may be aggravated if the seller has manufactured the goods specially for the buyer or has spent substantial sums in shipment.

Illustrations:

3. A contracts to sell and B to buy 300 crates of Australian onions, shipment to be from Australia in March. A has 300 crates ready for shipment in March, but government requisitions prevent him from loading more than 240 crates on the only ship available in March. B refuses to accept or pay for the onions when they are tendered. Under the circumstances stated in Subsections (a) and (c), A's failure is material and A has no claim against B. If A's failure is unjustified, B has a claim against A for damages for partial breach because of the delay even if A cures his failure, and has a claim against A for damages for total breach if A does not cure his failure (§ 243).

4. The facts being otherwise as stated in Illustration 2 to § 232, B can have the part of the street in front of his own lot paved for $500, but this will not give him the expected access to his lot because the rest of the street is not paved. Under the circumstances stated in Subsections (a), (b), and (c), the failure of performance is material and A has no claim against B. If A's failure is unjustified, B has a claim against A for damages for partial breach be-

cause of the delay even if A cures his failure, and has a claim against A for damages for total breach if A does not cure his failure (§ 243).

e. Uncertainty. A material failure by one party gives the other party the right to withhold further performance as a means of securing his expectation of an exchange of performances. To the extent that that expectation is already reasonably secure, in spite of the failure, there is less reason to conclude that the failure is material. The likelihood that the failure will be cured is therefore a significant circumstance in determining whether it is material (Subsection (d)). The fact that the injured party already has some security for the other party's performance argues against a determination that the failure is material. So do reasonable assurances of performance given by the other party after his failure. So does a shift in the market that makes performance of the contract more favorable to the other party. On the other hand, defaults by the other party under other contracts or as to other installments under the same contract argue for a determination of materiality. So does such financial weakness of the other party as suggests an inability to cure. This circumstance differs from the notion of reasonable grounds for insecurity (§ 251), in that the former can become relevant only after there has been an actual failure to perform or to tender. On discharge by repudiation, see § 253(2).

Illustration:

5. A contracts to sell and B to buy land for $25,000. B is to make a $5,000 down payment and pay the balance in four annual installments of $5,000 each. A is to proceed immediately to have abstracts of title prepared showing a marketable title and to deliver them prior to the time for pay-

ment of the first annual installment. Without explanation, A fails to have abstracts prepared for delivery prior to the time for payment of the first annual installment. B refuses to pay that installment. Under the circumstances stated in Subsections (a)–(d), the failure of performance is material and A has no claim against B. B has a claim against A for damages for partial breach based on the delay if A cures his failure and a claim for damages for total breach if he does not (§ 243).

f. Absence of good faith or fair dealing. A party's adherence to standards of good faith and fair dealing (§ 205) will not prevent his failure to perform a duty from amounting to a breach (§ 236(2)). Nor will his adherence to such standards necessarily prevent his failure from having the effect of the non-occurrence of a condition (§ 237; cf. § 238). The extent to which the behavior of the party failing to perform or to offer to perform comports with standards of good faith and fair dealing is, however, a significant circumstance in determining whether the failure is material (Subsection (e)). In giving weight to this factor courts have often used such less precise terms as "wilful." Adherence to the standards stated in Subsection (e) is not conclusive, since other circumstances may cause a failure to be material in spite of such adherence. Nor is nonadherence conclusive, and other circumstances may cause a failure not to be material in spite of such non-adherence.

Illustrations:

6. A contracts to build a house for B, using pipe of Reading manufacture. In return, B agrees to pay $75,000, with provision for progress payments. Without B's knowl-

edge, a subcontractor mistakenly uses pipe of Cohoes manufacture which is identical in quality and is distinguishable only by the name of the manufacturer which is stamped on it. The substitution is not discovered until the house is completed, when replacement of the pipe will require destruction of substantial parts of the house. B refuses to pay the unpaid balance of $10,000. Under the circumstances stated in Subsections (a), (c), and (e), the failure of performance is not material and A has a claim against B for the unpaid balance of $10,000, subject to a claim by B against A for damages for A's breach of his duty to use Reading pipe. See Illustration 1 to § 229.

7. A contracts to build a supermarket for B. In return B agrees to pay $250,000, with provision for progress payments. A completes performance except that, angered by a dispute over an unrelated transaction, he refuses to build a cover over a compressor. B can have the cover built by another builder for $300. B refuses to pay the unpaid balance of $40,000. In spite of the circumstances stated in Subsection (e), under the circumstances stated in Subsections (a), (b), and (c), the failure of performance is not material and A has a claim against B for the unpaid balance of $40,000, subject to a claim by B against A for damages for A's breach of his duty to build a cover over the compressor.

§ 242. Circumstances Significant in Determining When Remaining Duties Are Discharged

In determining the time after which a party's uncured material failure to render or to offer performance discharges the other party's remaining duties to render performance under the rules stated in §§ 237 and 238, the following circumstances are significant:

(a) those stated in § 241;

(b) the extent to which it reasonably appears to the injured party that delay may prevent or hinder him in making reasonable substitute arrangements;

(c) the extent to which the agreement provides for performance without delay, but a material failure to perform or to offer to perform on a stated day does not of itself discharge the other party's remaining duties unless the circumstances, including the language of the agreement, indicate that performance or an offer to perform by that day is important.

Comment:

a. Cure. Under §§ 237 and 238, a party's uncured material failure to perform or to offer to perform not only has the effect of suspending the other party's duties (§ 225(1)) but, when it is too late for the performance or the offer to perform to occur, the failure also has the effect of discharging those duties (§ 225(2)). Ordinarily there is some period of time between suspension and discharge, and during this period a party may cure his failure. Even then, since any breach gives rise to a claim, a party who has cured a material breach has still committed a breach, by his delay, for which he is liable in damages. Furthermore, in some instances timely performance is so essential that any delay immediately results in discharge and there is no period of time during which the injured party's duties are merely suspended and the other party can cure his failure.

b. Significant circumstances. This Section states circumstances which are to be considered in determining whether there is still time to cure a particular failure, or whether the period of time for discharge has expired. They are similar to the circumstances stated in the preceding section. The importance of delay to the injured party will depend on the extent to which it will deprive him of the benefit which he reasonably expected (§ 241(a)) and on the extent to which he can be adequately compensated (§ 241(b)). The extent of the forfeiture by the party failing to perform or to offer to perform (§ 241(c)) is also significant in determining the importance of delay. The likelihood that the injured party's withholding of performance will induce the other party to cure his failure is particularly important (§ 241(d)), because the very reason for suspending rather than immediately discharging the injured party's duties is that this will induce cure. The reasonableness of the injured party's conduct in communicating his grievances and in seeking satisfaction is a factor to be considered in this connection. Where performance is to extend over a period of time, as where delivery of goods is to be in installments, so that a continuing relationship between the parties is contemplated, the injured party may be expected to give more opportunity for cure than in the case of an isolated exchange. On discharge by repudiation, see § 253(2). Finally, the nature of the behavior of the party failing to perform or to offer to perform may be considered here as under the preceding section (§ 241(e)).

Illustration:

1. The facts being otherwise as stated in Illustration 1 to § 237, B tenders the progress payment after a two-day delay along with damages for the delay. A refuses to accept the payment and resume work and notifies B that he cancels the contract. B's tender cured his breach before A's remaining duties to render performance were discharged, and B has a claim against A for total breach of contract, subject to a claim by A against B for damages for partial breach because of the delay.

c. Substitute arrangements. It is often said that in commercial transactions, notably those for the sale of goods, prompt performance by a party is essential if he is to be allowed to require the other to perform or, as it is sometimes put, "time is of the essence." The importance of prompt delivery by a seller of goods generally derives from the circumstance that goods, as contrasted for example with land, are particularly likely to be subject to rapid fluctuations in market price. Therefore, even a relatively short delay in a rising market may adversely affect the buyer by causing a sharp increase in the cost of "cover." See Uniform Commercial Code §§ 2–712, 2–713. A less rigid standard applies to contracts for the sale of goods to be delivered in installments or to be specially manufactured for the buyer. On the other hand, considerable delay does not preclude enforcement of a contract for the sale of land if damages are adequate to compensate for the delay and there are no special circumstances indicating that prompt performance was essential and no express provision requiring such performance. But these are all merely particular applications of a more general principle. Subsection (b) states that principle. Under any contract, the extent to which it reasonably appears to the injured party that delay may prevent or hinder him from making reasonable substitute arrangements is a consideration in determining the effect of delay. Cf. § 241(a), (b). As in the case of § 241 (see Comment c), a party in breach who seeks specific performance may be granted relief with compensation for the delay, in circumstances where he would have no claim for damages.

Illustrations:

2. A, a theater manager, contracts with B, an actress, for her performance for six months in a play that A is about to present. B becomes ill during the second month of the performance, and A immediately engages another actress to fill B's place during the remainder of the six months. B recovers at the end of ten days and offers to perform the remainder of the contract, but A refuses. Whether B's failure to render performance due to illness immediately discharges A's remaining duties of performance, instead of merely suspending them, depends on the circumstances stated in Subsection (b) and in § 241(b) and (d), and in particular on the possibility as it reasonably appears to A when B becomes ill of the illness being only temporary and of A's obtaining an adequate temporary substitute.

3. A contracts to sell and B to buy 1,000 shares of stock traded on a national securities exchange, delivery and payment to be on February 1. B offers to pay the price on February 1, but A unjustifiably and without explanation fails to offer to deliver the stock until February 2. B then refuses to accept the stock or pay the price. Under the circumstances stated in Subsection (b) and in § 241(a) and (c), the period of time has passed after which B's remaining duties to render performance are discharged because of A's material breach and A therefore has no claim against B. B has a claim against A for breach.

4. A contracts to sell and B to buy land, the transfer to be on February 1. B tenders the price on February 1, but A does not tender a deed until February 2. B then refuses to accept the deed or pay the price. Under the circumstances stated in Subsections (b) and (c) and in § 241(a), in the absence of special circumstances, the period of time has not passed after which B's remaining duties to render performance are discharged. Although A's breach is material, it has been cured. A has a claim against B for damages for total breach of contract, subject to a claim by B against A for damages for partial breach because of the delay.

5. A agrees to sell and B to buy land, the transfer to be on February 1. A tenders a sufficient deed on February 1, but B explains that although he wants to carry out the contract he would like to have a few weeks more to raise the amount of the price. A replies that unless B tenders the price immediately he will not deliver the deed. On February 15, B sues for specific performance, offering in his pleading to pay the agreed price with interest to compensate A for the delay. In the circumstances stated in Subsection (b) and in § 241(a), (b), and (d), the period of time has not passed after which A's remaining duties to render performance are discharged. Although B's breach is material, the court may decree specific perform-

ance subject to B's tender of the price and payment by B of damages for partial breach to compensate A for the delay.

6. A contracts to sell and B to buy 5,000 tons of iron at a stated price, delivery to be in five monthly installments of 1,000 tons each on the first of each month and payment for each installment to be made on the tenth of that month. A makes the first three deliveries on the first of the month but, although the market price for iron is falling, he delays twelve days in making the fourth delivery, explaining to B that temporary labor troubles have caused the delay. B notifies A that he refuses to take or pay for the fourth delivery and that he cancels the contract. Whether the period of time has passed after which B's remaining duties to render performance are discharged, so that B's notification is not a repudiation, depends on the circumstances stated in Subsection (b) and in § 241(a), (b), (d), and (e). See Uniform Commercial Code § 2–612.

7. A contracts to sell and B to buy 5,000 tons of iron at a stated price, delivery to be in five monthly installments of 1,000 tons each on the first of each month and payment for each installment to be made on the tenth of that month. A makes the first four deliveries on the first of the month, and B makes the first three payments by the tenth but does not make the fourth payment. The market price for iron is falling and B gives no assurances or explanation for the delay. On the twentieth of the month A notifies B that he will make no further deliveries and that he cancels the contract.

Whether the period of time has passed after which A's remaining duties to render performance are discharged, so that A's notification is not a repudiation, depends on the circumstances stated in Subsection (b) and in § 241(a), (b), (d), and (e). See Uniform Commercial Code § 2–612.

d. *Effect of agreement.* The agreement of the parties often contains a provision for the time of performance or tender. It may simply provide for performance on a stated date. In that event, a material breach on that date entitles the injured party to withhold his performance and gives him a claim for damages for delay, but it does not of itself discharge the other party's remaining duties. Only if the circumstances, viewed as of the time of the breach, indicate that performance or tender on that day is of genuine importance are the injured party's remaining duties discharged immediately, with no period of time during which they are merely suspended. It is, of course, open to the parties to make performance or tender by a stated date a condition by their agreement, in which event, absent excuse (see Comment b to § 225 and Comment c to § 229), delay beyond that date results in discharge (§ 225(2)). Such stock phrases as "time is of the essence" do not necessarily have this effect, although under Subsection (c) they are to be considered along with other circumstances in determining the effect of delay.

Illustrations:

8. A contracts to charter a vessel belonging to B and to pay stipulated freight "on condition that the vessel arrive in New York ready for loading by March 1." B promises that the vessel will ar-

rive by that date and carry A's cargo. B unjustifiably fails to have the vessel in New York to be loaded until March 2. A refuses to load the vessel. Whether or not the period of time has passed after which B's uncured material failure would discharge A's remaining duties to render performance, A's duties are discharged under § 225(2) by the non-occurrence of an event that is made a condition by the agreement of the parties. B has no claim against A. A has a claim against B for damages for total breach.

9. The facts being otherwise as stated in Illustration 4, the parties use a printed form contract that provides that "time is of the essence." Absent other circumstances indicating that perform-

ance by February 1 is of genuine importance, A has a claim against B for damages for total breach of contract.

10. The facts being otherwise as stated in Illustration 4, the contract provides that A's rights are "conditional on his tendering a deed on or before February 1." A has no claim against B. But cf. Illustration 4 to § 229.

e. Excuse and reinstatement. Just as a party may under § 84 promise to perform in spite of the complete non-occurrence of a condition, he may under that section promise to perform in spite of a delay in its occurrence. If he places no limit on the delay, his power to impose a time limit by later notification of the other party is subject to the rules on reinstatement stated in § 84(2).

§ 243. Effect of a Breach by Non-performance as Giving Rise to a Claim for Damages for Total Breach

(1) With respect to performances to be exchanged under an exchange of promises, a breach by non-performance gives rise to a claim for damages for total breach only if it discharges the injured party's remaining duties to render such performance, other than a duty to render an agreed equivalent under § 240.

(2) Except as stated in Subsection (3), a breach by nonperformance accompanied or followed by a repudiation gives rise to a claim for damages for total breach.

(3) Where at the time of the breach the only remaining duties of performance are those of the party in breach and are for the payment of money in installments not related to one another, his breach by non-performance as to less than the whole, whether or not accompanied or followed by a repudiation, does not give rise to a claim for damages for total breach.

(4) In any case other than those stated in the preceding subsections, a breach by non-performance gives rise to a claim for total breach only if it so substantially impairs the value of the contract to the injured party at the time of the breach that it is just in the circumstances to allow him to recover damages based on all his remaining rights to performance.

§ 245. Effect of a Breach by Non–Performance as Excusing the Non-occurrence of a Condition

Where a party's breach by non-performance contributes materially to the non-occurrence of a condition of one of his duties, the non-occurrence is excused.

§ 248. Effect of Insufficient Reason for Rejection as Excusing the Non-occurrence of a Condition

Where a party rejecting a defective performance or offer of performance gives an insufficient reason for rejection, the non-occurrence of a condition of his duty is excused only if he knew or had reason to know of that non-occurrence and then only to the extent that the giving of an insufficient reason substantially contributes to a failure by the other party to cure.

TOPIC 3.   EFFECT OF PROSPECTIVE NON–PERFORMANCE

§ 250. When a Statement or an Act Is a Repudiation

A repudiation is

> (a) a statement by the obligor to the obligee indicating that the obligor will commit a breach that would of itself give the obligee a claim for damages for total breach under § 243, or
>
> (b) a voluntary affirmative act which renders the obligor unable or apparently unable to perform without such a breach.

question of fact

§ 251. When a Failure to Give Assurance May Be Treated as a Repudiation

(1) Where reasonable grounds arise to believe that the obligor will commit a breach by non-performance that would of itself give the obligee a claim for damages for total breach under § 243, the obligee may demand adequate assurance of due performance and may, if reasonable, suspend any performance for which he has not already received the agreed exchange until he receives such assurance.

(2) The obligee may treat as a repudiation the obligor's failure to provide within a reasonable time such assurance of due performance as is adequate in the circumstances of the particular case.

§ 253. Effect of a Repudiation as a Breach and on Other Party's Duties

(1) Where an obligor repudiates a duty before he has committed a breach by non-performance and before he has received all of the agreed exchange for it, his repudiation alone gives rise to a claim for damages for total breach.

(2) Where performances are to be exchanged under an exchange of promises, one party's repudiation of a duty to render performance discharges the other party's remaining duties to render performance.

§ 254. Effect of Subsequent Events on Duty to Pay Damages

(1) A party's duty to pay damages for total breach by repudiation is discharged if it appears after the breach that there would have been a total failure by the injured party to perform his return promise.

(2) A party's duty to pay damages for total breach by repudiation is discharged if it appears after the breach that the duty that he repudiated would have been discharged by impracticability or frustration before any breach by non-performance.

§ 256. Nullification of Repudiation or Basis for Repudiation

(1) The effect of a statement as constituting a repudiation under § 250 or the basis for a repudiation under § 251 is nullified by a retraction of the statement if notification of the retraction comes to the attention of the injured party before he materially changes his position in reliance on the repudiation or indicates to the other party that he considers the repudiation to be final.

(2) The effect of events other than a statement as constituting a repudiation under § 250 or the basis for a repudiation under § 251 is nullified if, to the knowledge of the injured party, those events have ceased to exist before he materially changes his position in reliance on the repudiation or indicates to the other party that he considers the repudiation to be final.

§ 257. Effect of Urging Performance in Spite of Repudiation

The injured party does not change the effect of a repudiation by urging the repudiator to perform in spite of his repudiation or to retract his repudiation.

CHAPTER 11. IMPRACTICABILITY OF PERFORMANCE AND FRUSTRATION OF PURPOSE

§ 261. Discharge by Supervening Impracticability

Where, after a contract is made, a party's performance is made impracticable without his fault by the occurrence of an event the non-occurrence of which was a basic assumption on which the contract was made, his duty to render that performance is discharged, unless the language or the circumstances indicate the contrary.

Comment:

a. Scope. Even though a party, in assuming a duty, has not qualified the language of his undertaking, a court may relieve him of that duty if performance has unexpectedly become impracticable as a result of a supervening event (see Introductory Note to this Chapter). This Section states the general principle under which a party's duty may be so discharged. The following three sections deal with the three categories of cases where this general principle has traditionally been applied: supervening death or incapacity of a person necessary for performance (§ 262), supervening destruction of a specific thing necessary for performance (§ 263), and supervening prohibition or prevention by law (§ 264). But, like Uniform Commercial Code § 2–615(a), this Section states a principle broadly applicable to all types of impracticability and it "deliberately refrains from any effort at an exhaustive expression of contingencies" (Comment 2 to Uniform Commercial Code § 2–615). The principle, like others in this Chapter, yields to a contrary agreement by which a party may assume a greater as well as a lesser obligation. By such an agreement, for example, a party may undertake to achieve a result irrespective of supervening events that may render its achievement impossible, and if he does so his non-performance is a breach even if it is caused by such an event. See Comment c. The rule stated in this Section applies only to discharge a duty to render a performance and does not affect a claim for breach that has already arisen. The effect of events subsequent to a breach on the amount of damages recoverable is governed by the rules on remedies stated in Chapter 16. See Comment e to § 347. Their effect on a claim for breach by anticipatory repudiation is governed by the rules on discharge stated in Chapter

12. Cases of existing, as opposed to supervening, impracticability are governed by § 266 rather than this Section.

b. Basic assumption. In order for a supervening event to discharge a duty under this Section, the non-occurrence of that event must have been a "basic assumption" on which both parties made the contract (see Introductory Note to this Chapter). This is the criterion used by Uniform Commercial Code § 2–615(a). Its application is simple enough in the cases of the death of a person or destruction of a specific thing necessary for performance. The continued existence of the person or thing (the non-occurrence of the death of destruction) is ordinarily a basic assumption on which the contract was made, so that death or destruction effects a discharge. Its application is also simple enough in the cases of market shifts or the financial inability of one of the parties. The continuation of existing market conditions and of the financial situation of the parties are ordinarily not such assumptions, so that mere market shifts or financial inability do not usually effect discharge under the rule stated in this Section. In borderline cases this criterion is sufficiently flexible to take account of factors that bear on a just allocation of risk. The fact that the event was foreseeable, or even foreseen, does not necessarily compel a conclusion that its non-occurrence was not a basic assumption. See Comment c to this Section and Comment a to § 265.

Illustrations:

1. On June 1, A agrees to sell and B to buy goods to be delivered in October at a designated port. The port is subsequently closed by quarantine regulations during the entire month of October, no commercially reasonable substitute

performance is available (see Uniform Commercial Code § 2–614(1)), and A fails to deliver the goods. A's duty to deliver the goods is discharged, and A is not liable to B for breach of contract.

2. A contracts to produce a movie for B. As B knows, A's only source of funds is a $100,000 deposit in C bank. C bank fails, and A does not produce the movie. A's duty to produce the movie is not discharged, and A is liable to B for breach of contract.

3. A and B make a contract under which B is to work for A for two years at a salary of $50,000 a year. At the end of one year, A discontinues his business because governmental regulations have made it unprofitable and fires B. A's duty to employ B is not discharged, and A is liable to B for breach of contract.

4. A contracts to sell and B to buy a specific machine owned by A to be delivered on July 30. On July 29, as a result of a creditor's suit against A, a receiver is appointed and takes charge of all of A's assets, and A does not deliver the goods on July 30. A's duty to deliver the goods is not discharged, and A is liable to B for breach of contract.

c. Contrary indication. A party may, by appropriate language, agree to perform in spite of impracticability that would otherwise justify his nonperformance under the rule stated in this Section. He can then be held liable for damages although he cannot perform. Even absent an express agreement, a court may decide, after considering all the circumstances, that a party impliedly assumed such a greater obligation. In this respect the rule stated in this Section parallels that of Uniform Commercial Code § 2–615, which applies "Except so far

as a seller may have assumed a greater obligation...." Circumstances relevant in deciding whether a party has assumed a greater obligation include his ability to have inserted a provision in the contract expressly shifting the risk of impracticability to the other party. This will depend on the extent to which the agreement was standardized (cf. § 211), the degree to which the other party supplied the terms (cf. § 206), and, in the case of a particular trade or other group, the frequency with which language so allocating the risk is used in that trade or group (cf. § 219). The fact that a supplier has not taken advantage of his opportunity expressly to shift the risk of a shortage in his supply by means of contract language may be regarded as more significant where he is middleman, with a variety of sources of supply and an opportunity to spread the risk among many customers on many transactions by slight adjustment of his prices, than where he is a producer with a limited source of supply, few outlets, and no comparable opportunity. A commercial practice under which a party might be expected to insure or otherwise secure himself against a risk also militates against shifting it to the other party. If the supervening event was not reasonably foreseeable when the contract was made, the party claiming discharge can hardly be expected to have provided against its occurrence. However, if it was reasonably foreseeable, or even foreseen, the opposite conclusion does not necessarily follow. Factors such as the practical difficulty of reaching agreement on the myriad of conceivable terms of a complex agreement may excuse a failure to deal with improbable contingencies. See Comment b to this Section and Comment a to § 265.

Illustration:

5. A, who has had many years of experience in the field of salvage,

contracts to raise and float B's boat, which has run aground. The contract, prepared by A, contains no clause limiting A's duty in the case of unfavorable weather, unforeseen circumstances, or otherwise. The boat then slips into deep water and fills with mud, making it impracticable for A to raise it. If the court concludes, on the basis of such circumstances as A's experience and the absence of any limitation in the contract that A prepared, that A assumed an absolute duty, it will decide that A's duty to raise and float the boat is not discharged and that A is liable to B for breach of contract.

d. Impracticability. Events that come within the rule stated in this Section are generally due either to "acts of God" or to acts of third parties. If the event that prevents the obligor's performance is caused by the obligee, it will ordinarily amount to a breach by the latter and the situation will be governed by the rules stated in Chapter 10, without regard to this Section. See Illustrations 4–7 to § 237. If the event is due to the fault of the obligor himself, this Section does not apply. As used here "fault" may include not only "willful" wrongs, but such other types of conduct as that amounting to breach of contract or to negligence. See Comment 1 to Uniform Commercial Code § 2–613. Although the rule stated in this Section is sometimes phrased in terms of "impossibility," it has long been recognized that it may operate to discharge a party's duty even though the event has not made performance absolutely impossible. This Section, therefore, uses "impracticable," the term employed by Uniform Commercial Code § 2–615(a), to describe the required extent of the impediment to performance. Performance may be impracticable because extreme and unreasonable difficulty, expense, injury, or loss to one of the parties will be involved. A severe shortage of raw materials or of supplies due to war, embargo, local crop failure, unforeseen shutdown of major sources of supply, or the like, which either causes a marked increase in cost or prevents performance altogether may bring the case within the rule stated in this Section. Performance may also be impracticable because it will involve a risk of injury to person or to property, of one of the parties or of others, that is disproportionate to the ends to be attained by performance. However, "impracticability" means more than "impracticality." A mere change in the degree of difficulty or expense due to such causes as increased wages, prices of raw materials, or costs of construction, unless well beyond the normal range, does not amount to impracticability since it is this sort of risk that a fixed-price contract is intended to cover. Furthermore, a party is expected to use reasonable efforts to surmount obstacles to performance (see § 205), and a performance is impracticable only if it is so in spite of such efforts.

Illustrations:

6. A contracts to repair B's grain elevator. While A is engaged in making repairs, a fire destroys the elevator without A's fault, and A does not finish the repairs. A's duty to repair the elevator is discharged, and A is not liable to B for breach of contract. See Illustration 3 to § 263.

7. A contracts with B to carry B's goods on his ship to a designated foreign port. A civil war then unexpectedly breaks out in that country and the rebels announce that they will try to sink all vessels bound for that port. A refuses to perform. Although A did not contract to sail on the vessel, the risk of injury to others is sufficient

to make A's performance impracticable. A's duty to carry the goods to the designated port is discharged, and A is not liable to B for breach of contract. Compare Illustration 5 to § 262.

8. The facts being otherwise as stated in Illustration 7, the rebels announce merely that they will confiscate all vessels found in the designated port. The goods can be bought and sold on markets throughout the world. A refuses to perform. Although there is no risk of injury to persons, the court may conclude that the risk of injury to property is disproportionate to the ends to be attained. A's duty to carry the goods to the designated port is then discharged, and A is not liable to B for breach of contract. If, however, B is a health organization and the goods are scarce medical supplies vital to the health of the population of the designated port, the court may conclude that the risk is not disproportionate to the ends to be attained and may reach a contrary decision.

9. Several months after the nationalization of the Suez Canal, during the international crisis resulting from its seizure, A contracts to carry a cargo of B's wheat on A's ship from Galveston, Texas to Bandar Shapur, Iran for a flat rate. The contract does not specify the route, but the voyage would normally be through the Straits of Gibraltar and the Suez Canal, a distance of 10,000 miles. A month later, and several days after the ship has left Galveston, the Suez Canal is closed by an outbreak of hostilities, so that the only route to Bandar Shapur is the longer 13,000 mile voyage around the Cape of Good Hope. A refuses to complete the voyage unless B

pays additional compensation. A's duty to carry B's cargo is not discharged, and A is liable to B for breach of contract.

10. The facts being otherwise as in Illustration 9, the Suez Canal is closed while A's ship is in the Canal, preventing the completion of the voyage. A's duty to carry B's cargo is discharged, and A is not liable to B for breach of contract.

11. A contracts to construct and lease to B a gasoline service station. A valid zoning ordinance is subsequently enacted forbidding the construction of such a station but permitting variances in appropriate cases. A, in breach of his duty of good faith and fair dealing (§ 205), makes no effort to obtain a variance, although variances have been granted in similar cases, and fails to construct the station. A's performance has not been made impracticable. A's duty to construct is not discharged, and A is liable to B for breach of contract.

e. "Subjective" and "objective" impracticability. It is sometimes said that the rule stated in this Section applies only when the performance itself is made impracticable, without regard to the particular party who is to perform. The difference has been described as that between "the thing cannot be done" and "I cannot do it," and the former has been characterized as "objective" and the latter as "subjective." This Section recognizes that if the performance remains practicable and it is merely beyond the party's capacity to render it, he is ordinarily not discharged, but it does not use the terms "objective" and "subjective" to express this. Instead, the rationale is that a party generally assumes the risk of his own inability to perform his duty. Even if a party contracts to render a performance that depends on some act by a third party, he is not ordinarily discharged because of a failure by that party because this is also a risk that is commonly understood to be on the obligor. See Comment c. But see Comment a to § 262.

Illustrations:

12. A, a milkman, and B, a dairy farmer, make a contract under which B is to sell and A to buy all of A's requirements of milk, but not less than 200 quarts a day, for one year. B may deliver milk from any source but expects to deliver milk from his own herd. B's herd is destroyed because of hoof and mouth disease and he fails to deliver any milk. B's duty to deliver milk is not discharged, and B is liable to A for breach of contract. See Illustration 1 to § 263; compare Illustration 7 to § 263.

13. A contracts to sell and B to buy on credit 1,500,000 gallons of molasses "of the usual run from the C sugar refinery." C delivers molasses to others but fails to deliver any to A, and A fails to deliver any to B. A's duty to deliver molasses is not discharged, and A is liable to B for breach of contract. If A has a contract with C, C may be liable to A for breach of contract.

14. A, a general contractor, is bidding on a construction contract with B which gives B the right to disapprove the choice of subcontractors. A makes a contract with C, a subcontractor, under which, if B awards A the contract, A will obtain B's approval of C and C will do the excavation for A. A is awarded the contract by B, but B disapproves A's choice of C, and A has the excavation work done by another subcontractor. A's duty to have C do the excavation is not discharged, and A is liable to C for breach of contract.

f. Alternative performances. A contract may permit a party to choose to perform in one of several different ways, any of which will discharge his duty. Where the duty is to render such an alternative performance, the fact that one or more of the alternatives has become impracticable will not discharge the party's duty to perform if at least one of them remains practicable. The form of the promise is not controlling, however, and not every promise that is expressed in alternative form gives rise to a duty to render an alternative performance. For example, a surety's undertaking that either the principal will perform or the surety will compensate the creditor does not ordinarily impose such a duty. See Restatement of Security § 117. Nor does a promise either to render a performance or pay liquidated damages impose such a duty. Furthermore, a duty that is originally one to render alternative performances ceases to be such a duty if all but one means of performance have been foreclosed, as by the lapse of time or the occurrence of a condition including election by the obligor, or on the grounds of public policy (Chapter 8) or unconscionability (§ 208).

Illustrations:

15. On June 1, A contracts to sell and B to buy whichever of three specified machines A chooses to deliver on October 1. Two of the machines are destroyed by fire on July 1, and A fails to deliver the third on October 1. A's duty to deliver a machine is not discharged, and A is liable to B for breach of contract. If all three machines had been destroyed, A's duty to deliver a machine would have been discharged, and A would not have been liable to B

for breach of contract. See Uniform Commercial Code § 2–613.

16. A contracts to repair B's building. The contract contains a valid provision requiring A to pay liquidated damages if he fails to make any of the repairs. S is surety for A's performance. Before A is able to begin, B's building is destroyed by fire. Neither A's nor S's duty is one to render an alternative performance. A's duty to repair the building is discharged, and A is not liable to B for liquidated damages or otherwise for breach of contract. S's duty as surety for A is also discharged, and S is not liable to B for breach of contract.

§ 265. Discharge by Supervening Frustration

Where, after a contract is made, a party's principal purpose is substantially frustrated without his fault by the occurrence of an event the non-occurrence of which was a basic assumption on which the contract was made, his remaining duties to render performance are discharged, unless the language or the circumstances indicate the contrary.

§ 272. Relief Including Restitution

(1) In any case governed by the rules stated in this Chapter, either party may have a claim for relief including restitution under the rules stated in §§ 240 and 377.

(2) In any case governed by the rules stated in this Chapter, if those rules together with the rules stated in Chapter 16 will not avoid injustice, the court may grant relief on such terms as justice requires including protection of the parties' reliance interests.

CHAPTER 14.   CONTRACT BENEFICIARIES

§ 302. Intended and Incidental Beneficiaries

(1) Unless otherwise agreed between promisor and promisee, a beneficiary of a promise is an intended beneficiary if recognition of a right to performance in the beneficiary is appropriate to effectuate the intention of the parties and either

> (a) the performance of the promise will satisfy an obligation of the promisee to pay money to the beneficiary; or

> (b) the circumstances indicate that the promisee intends to give the beneficiary the benefit of the promised performance.

(2) An incidental beneficiary is a beneficiary who is not an intended beneficiary.

§ 307. Remedy of Specific Performance

Where specific performance is otherwise an appropriate remedy, either the promisee or the beneficiary may maintain a suit for specific enforcement of a duty owed to an intended beneficiary.

§ 309. Defenses Against the Beneficiary

(1) A promise creates no duty to a beneficiary unless a contract is formed between the promisor and the promisee; and if a contract is voidable or unenforceable at the time of its formation the right of any beneficiary is subject to the infirmity.

(2) If a contract ceases to be binding in whole or in part because of impracticability, public policy, non-occurrence of a condition, or present or prospective failure of performance, the right of any beneficiary is to that extent discharged or modified.

(3) Except as stated in Subsections (1) and (2) and in § 311 or as provided by the contract, the right of any beneficiary against the promisor is not subject to the promisor's claims or defenses against the promisee or to the promisee's claims or defenses against the beneficiary.

(4) A beneficiary's right against the promisor is subject to any claim or defense arising from his own conduct or agreement.

§ 311. Variation of a Duty to a Beneficiary

(1) Discharge or modification of a duty to an intended beneficiary by conduct of the promisee or by a subsequent agreement between promisor and promisee is ineffective if a term of the promise creating the duty so provides.

(2) In the absence of such a term, the promisor and promisee retain power to discharge or modify the duty by subsequent agreement.

(3) Such a power terminates when the beneficiary, before he receives notification of the discharge or modification, materially changes his position in justifiable reliance on the promise or brings suit on it or manifests assent to it at the request of the promisor or promisee.

(4) If the promisee receives consideration for an attempted discharge or modification of the promisor's duty which is ineffective against the beneficiary, the beneficiary can assert a right to the consideration so received. The promisor's duty is discharged to the extent of the amount received by the beneficiary.

§ 313. Government Contracts

(1) The rules stated in this Chapter apply to contracts with a government or governmental agency except to the extent that application would contravene the policy of the law authorizing the contract or prescribing remedies for its breach.

(2) In particular, a promisor who contracts with a government or governmental agency to do an act for or render a service to the public is not subject to contractual liability to a member of the public for consequential damages resulting from performance or failure to perform unless

(a) the terms of the promise provide for such liability; or

(b) the promisee is subject to liability to the member of the public for the damages and a direct action against the promisor is consistent with the terms of the contract and with the policy of the law authorizing the contract and prescribing remedies for its breach.

§ 315. Effect of a Promise of Incidental Benefit

An incidental beneficiary acquires by virtue of the promise no right against the promisor or the promisee.

CHAPTER 15. ASSIGNMENT AND DELEGATION

TOPIC 1. WHAT CAN BE ASSIGNED OR DELEGATED

§ 317. Assignment of a Right

(1) An assignment of a right is a manifestation of the assignor's intention to transfer it by virtue of which the assignor's right to performance by the obligor is extinguished in whole or in part and the assignee acquires a right to such performance.

(2) A contractual right can be assigned unless

(a) the substitution of a right of the assignee for the right of the assignor would materially change the duty of the obligor, or materially increase the burden or risk imposed on him by his contract, or materially impair his chance of obtaining return performance, or materially reduce its value to him, or

(b) the assignment is forbidden by statute or is otherwise inoperative on grounds of public policy, or

(c) assignment is validly precluded by contract.

§ 318. Delegation of Performance of Duty

(1) An obligor can properly delegate the performance of his duty to another unless the delegation is contrary to public policy or the terms of his promise.

(2) Unless otherwise agreed, a promise requires performance by a particular person only to the extent that the obligee has a substantial interest in having that person perform or control the acts promised.

(3) Unless the obligee agrees otherwise, neither delegation of performance nor a contract to assume the duty made with the obligor by the person delegated discharges any duty or liability of the delegating obligor.

§ 322. Contractual Prohibition of Assignment

(1) Unless the circumstances indicate the contrary, a contract term prohibiting assignment of "the contract" bars only the delegation to an assignee of the performance by the assignor of a duty or condition.

(2) A contract term prohibiting assignment of rights under the contract, unless a different intention is manifested,

    (a) does not forbid assignment of a right to damages for breach of the whole contract or a right arising out of the assignor's due performance of his entire obligation;

    (b) gives the obligor a right to damages for breach of the terms forbidding assignment but does not render the assignment ineffective;

    (c) is for the benefit of the obligor, and does not prevent the assignee from acquiring rights against the assignor or the obligor from discharging his duty as if there were no such prohibition.

TOPIC 2. MODE OF ASSIGNMENT OR DELEGATION

§ 324. Mode of Assignment in General

It is essential to an assignment of a right that the obligee manifest an intention to transfer the right to another person without further action or manifestation of intention by the obligee. The manifestation may be made to the other or to a third person on his behalf and, except as provided by statute or by contract, may be made either orally or by a writing.

§ 326. Partial Assignment

(1) Except as stated in Subsection (2), an assignment of a part of a right, whether the part is specified as a fraction, as an amount, or otherwise, is operative as to that part to the same extent and in the same manner as if the part had been a separate right.

(2) If the obligor has not contracted to perform separately the assigned part of a right, no legal proceeding can be maintained by the assignor or assignee against the obligor over his objection, unless all the persons entitled to the promised performance are joined in the proceeding, or unless joinder is not feasible and it is equitable to proceed without joinder.

§ 328. Interpretation of Words of Assignment; Effect of Acceptance of Assignment

(1) Unless the language or the circumstances indicate the contrary, as in an assignment for security, an assignment of "the contract" or of "all my rights under the contract" or an assignment in similar general

terms is an assignment of the assignor's rights and a delegation of his unperformed duties under the contract.

(2) Unless the language or the circumstances indicate the contrary, the acceptance by an assignee of such an assignment operates as a promise to the assignor to perform the assignor's unperformed duties, and the obligor of the assigned rights is an intended beneficiary of the promise.

Caveat: The Institute expresses no opinion as to whether the rule stated in Subsection (2) applies to an assignment by a purchaser of his rights under a contract for the sale of land.

TOPIC 3. EFFECT BETWEEN ASSIGNOR AND ASSIGNEE

§ 332. Revocability Of Gratuitous Assignments

(1) Unless a contrary intention is manifested, a gratuitous assignment is irrevocable if

(a) the assignment is in a writing either signed or under seal that is delivered by the assignor; or

(b) the assignment is accompanied by delivery of a writing of a type customarily accepted as a symbol or as evidence of the right assigned.

(2) Except as stated in this Section, a gratuitous assignment is revocable and the right of the assignee is terminated by the assignor's death or incapacity, by a subsequent assignment by the assignor, or by notification from the assignor received by the assignee or by the obligor.

(3) A gratuitous assignment ceases to be revocable to the extent that before the assignee's right is terminated he obtains

(a) payment or satisfaction of the obligation, or

(b) judgment against the obligor, or

(c) a new contract of the obligor by novation.

(4) A gratuitous assignment is irrevocable to the extent necessary to avoid injustice where the assignor should reasonably expect the assignment to induce action or forbearance by the assignee or a subassignee and the assignment does induce such action or forbearance.

(5) An assignment is gratuitous unless it is given or taken

(a) in exchange for a performance or return promise that would be consideration for a promise; or

(b) as security for or in total or partial satisfaction of a pre-existing debt or other obligation.

TOPIC 4. EFFECT ON THE OBLIGOR'S DUTY

§ 336. Defenses Against an Assignee

(1) By an assignment the assignee acquires a right against the obligor only to the extent that the obligor is under a duty to the assignor; and if the right of the assignor would be voidable by the obligor or unenforceable against him if no assignment had been made, the right of the assignee is subject to the infirmity.

(2) The right of an assignee is subject to any defense or claim of the obligor which accrues before the obligor receives notification of the assignment, but not to defenses or claims which accrue thereafter except as stated in this Section or as provided by statute.

(3) Where the right of an assignor is subject to discharge or modification in whole or in part by impossibility, illegality, non-occurrence of a condition, or present or prospective failure of performance by an obligee, the right of the assignee is to that extent subject to discharge or modification even after the obligor receives notification of the assignment.

(4) An assignee's right against the obligor is subject to any defense or claim arising from his conduct or to which he was subject as a party or a prior assignee because he had notice.

TOPIC 5. PRIORITIES BETWEEN ASSIGNEE AND ADVERSE CLAIMANTS

§ 342. SUCCESSIVE ASSIGNEES FROM THE SAME ASSIGNOR

Except as otherwise provided by statute, the right of an assignee is superior to that of a subsequent assignee of the same right from the same assignor, unless

> (a) the first assignment is ineffective or revocable or is voidable by the assignor or by the subsequent assignee; or
>
> (b) the subsequent assignee in good faith and without knowledge or reason to know of the prior assignment gives value and obtains
>
> > (i) payment or satisfaction of the obligation,
> >
> > (ii) judgment against the obligor,
> >
> > (iii) a new contract with the obligor by novation, or
> >
> > (iv) possession of a writing of a type customarily accepted as a symbol or as evidence of the right assigned.

CHAPTER 16.   REMEDIES

TOPIC 1. IN GENERAL

§ 344.   Purposes of Remedies

Judicial remedies under the rules stated in this Restatement serve to protect one or more of the following interests of a promisee:

> (a) his "expectation interest," which is his interest in having the benefit of his bargain by being put in as good a position as he would have been in had the contract been performed,
>
> (b) his "reliance interest," which is his interest in being reimbursed for loss caused by reliance on the contract by being put in as good a position as he would have been in had the contract not been made, or
>
> (c) his "restitution interest," which is his interest in having restored to him any benefit that he has conferred on the other party.

TOPIC 2.   ENFORCEMENT BY AWARD OF DAMAGES

§ 347.   Measure of Damages in General

Subject to the limitations stated in §§ 350–53, the injured party has a right to damages based on his expectation interest as measured by

> (a) the loss in the value to him of the other party's performance caused by its failure or deficiency, plus
>
> (b) any other loss, including incidental or consequential loss, caused by the breach, less
>
> (c) any cost or other loss that he has avoided by not having to perform.

§ 348.   Alternatives to Loss in Value of Performance

(1) If a breach delays the use of property and the loss in value to the injured party is not proved with reasonable certainty, he may recover damages based on the rental value of the property or on interest on the value of the property.

(2) If a breach results in defective or unfinished construction and the loss in value to the injured party is not proved with sufficient certainty, he may recover damages based on

> (a) the diminution in the market price of the property caused by the breach, or
>
> (b) the reasonable cost of completing performance or of remedying the defects if that cost is not clearly disproportionate to the probable loss in value to him.

325

(3) If a breach is of a promise conditioned on a fortuitous event and it is uncertain whether the event would have occurred had there been no breach, the injured party may recover damages based on the value of the conditional right at the time of breach.

§ 349. Damages Based on Reliance Interest

As an alternative to the measure of damages stated in § 347, the injured party has a right to damages based on his reliance interest, including expenditures made in preparation for performance or in performance, less any loss that the party in breach can prove with reasonable certainty the injured party would have suffered had the contract been performed.

§ 350. Avoidability as a Limitation on Damages

(1) Except as stated in Subsection (2), damages are not recoverable for loss that the injured party could have avoided without undue risk, burden or humiliation.

(2) The injured party is not precluded from recovery by the rule stated in Subsection (1) to the extent that he has made reasonable but unsuccessful efforts to avoid loss.

§ 351. Unforeseeability and Related Limitations on Damages

(1) Damages are not recoverable for loss that the party in breach did not have reason to foresee as a probable result of the breach when the contract was made.

(2) Loss may be foreseeable as a probable result of a breach because it follows from the breach

  (a) in the ordinary course of events, or

  (b) as a result of special circumstances beyond the ordinary course of events, that the party in breach had reason to know.

(3) A court may limit damages for foreseeable loss by excluding recovery for loss of profits, by allowing recovery only for loss incurred in reliance, or otherwise if it concludes that in the circumstances justice so requires in order to avoid disproportionate compensation.

Comment:

a. Requirement of foreseeability. A contracting party is generally expected to take account of those risks that are foreseeable at the time he makes the contract. He is not, however, liable in the event of breach for loss that he did not at the time of contracting have reason to foresee as a probable result of such a breach. The mere circumstance that some loss was foreseeable, or even that some loss of the same general kind was foreseeable, will not suffice if the loss that actually occurred was not foreseeable. It is enough, however, that the loss was foreseeable as a probable, as distinguished from a necessary, result of his breach. Furthermore, the party in breach need not have made a "tacit agreement" to be liable for the loss. Nor must he have had the loss in mind when making the contract, for the test is an objective one based on what he had reason to foresee. There is no requirement of foreseeability with respect to the injured party. In spite of these qualifications, the requirement of foreseeability is a more severe limitation of liability than is the requirement of substantial or "proximate" cause in the case of an action in tort or for breach of warranty. Compare Restatement, Second, Torts § 431; Uniform Commercial Code § 2–715(2)(b). Although the recovery that is precluded by the limitation of foreseeability is usually based on the expectation interest and takes the form of lost profits (see Illustration 1), the limitation may also preclude recovery based on the reliance interest (see Illustration 2).

Illustrations:

1. A, a carrier, contracts with B, a miller, to carry B's broken crankshaft to its manufacturer for repair. B tells A when they make the contract that the crankshaft is part of B's milling machine and that it must be sent at once, but not that the mill is stopped because B has no replacement. Because A delays in carrying the crankshaft, B loses profit during an additional period while the mill is stopped because of the delay. A is not liable for B's loss of profit. That loss was not foreseeable by A as a probable result of the breach at the time the contract was made because A did not know that the broken crankshaft was necessary for the operation of the mill.

2. A contracts to sell land to B and to give B possession on a stated date. Because A delays a short time in giving B possession, B incurs unusual expenses in providing for cattle that he had already purchased to stock the land as a ranch. A had no reason to know when they made the contract that B had planned to purchase cattle for this purpose. A is not liable for B's expenses in providing for the cattle because that loss was not foreseeable by A as a probable result of the breach at the time the contract was made.

b. *"General" and "special" damages.* Loss that results from a breach in the ordinary course of events is foreseeable as the probable result of the breach. See Uniform Commercial Code § 2–714(1). Such loss is sometimes said to be the "natural" result of the breach, in the sense that its occurrence accords with the common experience of ordinary persons. For example, a seller of a commodity to a wholesaler usually has reason to foresee that his failure to deliver the commodity as agreed will probably cause the wholesaler to lose a reasonable profit on it. See Illustrations 3 and 4. Similarly, a seller of a machine to a manufacturer usually has reason to foresee that his delay in delivering the machine as agreed will probably cause the manufacturer to lose a reasonable profit from its use, although courts have been somewhat more cautious in allowing the manufacturer recovery for loss of such profits than in allowing a middleman recovery for loss of profits on an intended resale. See Illustration 5. The damages recoverable for such loss that results in the ordinary course of events are sometimes called "general" damages.

If loss results other than in the ordinary course of events, there can be no recovery for it unless it was foreseeable by the party in breach because of special circumstances that he had reason to know when he made the contract. See Uniform Commercial Code § 2–715(2)(a). For example, a seller who fails to deliver a commodity to a wholesaler is not liable for the wholesaler's loss of profit to the extent that it is extraordinary nor for his loss due to unusual terms in his resale contracts unless the seller had reason to know of these special circumstances. See Illustration 6. Similarly, a seller who delays in delivering a machine to a manufacturer is not liable for the manufacturer's loss of profit to the extent that it results from an intended use that was abnormal unless the seller had reason to know of this special circumstance. See Illustration 7. In the case of a written agreement, foreseeability is sometimes established by the use of recitals in the agreement itself. The parol evidence rule (§ 213) does not, however, preclude the use of negotiations prior to the making of the contract to show for this purpose circumstances that were then known to a party. The damages recoverable for loss that results other than in the ordinary course of events are sometimes called "special" or "consequential" damages. These terms are often misleading, however, and it is not necessary to distinguish between "general" and "special" or "consequential" damages for the purpose of the rule stated in this Section.

Illustrations:

    3. A and B make a written contract under which A is to recondition by a stated date a used machine owned by B so that it will be suitable for sale by B to C. A knows when they make the contract that B has contracted to sell the machine to C but knows nothing of the terms of B's contract with C. Because A delays in returning the machine to B, B is unable to sell it to C and loses the profit that he would have made on that sale. B's loss of reasonable

profit was foreseeable by A as a probable result of the breach at the time the contract was made.

    4. A, a manufacturer of machines, contracts to make B his exclusive selling agent in a specified area for the period of a year. Because A fails to deliver any machines, B loses the profit on contracts that he would have made for their resale. B's loss of reasonable profit was foreseeable by A as a probable result of the breach at the time the contract was made.

    5. A and B make a contract under which A is to recondition by a stated date a used machine owned by B so that it will be suitable for use in B's canning factory. A knows that the machine must be reconditioned by that date if B's factory is to operate at full capacity during the canning season, but nothing is said of this in the written contract. Because A delays in returning the machine to B, B loses its use for the entire canning season and loses the profit that he would have made had his factory operated at full capacity. B's loss of reasonable profit was foreseeable by A as a probable result of the breach at the time the contract was made.

    6. The facts being otherwise as stated in Illustration 3, the profit that B would have made under his contract with A was extraordinarily large because C promised to pay an exceptionally high price as a result of a special need for the machine of which A was unaware. A is not liable for B's loss of profit to the extent that it exceeds what would ordinarily result from such a contract. To that extent the loss was not foreseeable by A as a probable result of the breach at the time the contract was made.

7. The facts being otherwise as stated in Illustration 5, the profit that B would have made from the use of the machine was unusually large because of an abnormal use to which he planned to put it of which A was unaware. A is not liable for B's loss of profit to the extent that it exceeds what would ordinarily result from the use of such a machine. To that extent the loss was not foreseeable by A at the time the contract was made as a probable result of the breach.

c. Litigation or settlement caused by breach. Sometimes a breach of contract results in claims by third persons against the injured party. The party in breach is liable for the amount of any judgment against the injured party together with his reasonable expenditures in the litigation, if the party in breach had reason to foresee such expenditures as the probable result of his breach at the time he made the contract. See Illustrations 8, 10, 11 and 12. This is so even if the judgment in the litigation is based on a liquidated damage clause in the injured party's contract with the third party. See Illustration 8. A failure to notify the party in breach in advance of the litigation may prevent the result of the litigation from being conclusive as to him. But to the extent that the injured party's loss resulting from litigation is reasonable, the fact that the party in breach was not notified does not prevent the inclusion of that loss in the damages assessed against him. In furtherance of the policy favoring private settlement of disputes, the injured party is also allowed to recover the reasonable amount of any settlement made to avoid litigation, together with the costs of settlement. See Illustration 9.

Illustrations:

8. The facts being otherwise as stated in Illustration 3, B not only loses the profit that he would have made on sale of the machine to C, but is held liable for damages in an action brought by C for breach of contract. The damages paid to C and B's reasonable expenses in defending the action were also foreseeable by A as a probable result of the breach at the time he made the contract with B. The result is the same even though they were based on a liquidated damage clause in the contract between B and C if A knew of the clause or if the use of such a clause in the contract between B and C was foreseeable by A at the time he made the contract with B.

9. The facts being otherwise as stated in Illustration 3, B not only loses the profit that he would have made on sale of the machine to C, but settles with C by paying C a reasonable sum of money to avoid litigation. The amount of the settlement paid to C and B's reasonable expenses in settling were also foreseeable by A at the time he made the contract with B as a probable result of the breach.

10. A contracts to supply B with machinery for unloading cargo. A, in breach of contract, furnishes defective machinery, and C, an employee of B, is injured. C sues B and gets a judgment, which B pays. The amount of the judgment and B's reasonable expenditures in defending the action were foreseeable by A at the time the contract was made as a probable result of the breach.

11. A contracts to procure a right of way for B, for a railroad. Because A, in breach of contract, fails to do this, B has to acquire the right of way by condemnation proceedings. B's reasonable expenditures in those proceedings were

foreseeable by A at the time the contract was made as a probable result of the breach.

12. A leases land to B with a covenant for quiet enjoyment. C brings an action of ejectment against B and gets judgment. B's reasonable expenditures in defending the action were foreseeable by A as the probable result of the breach at the time the contract was made.

d. *Unavailability of substitute.* If several circumstances have contributed to cause a loss, the party in breach is not liable for it unless he had reason to foresee all of them. Sometimes a loss would not have occurred if the injured party had been able to make substitute arrangements after breach, as, for example, by "cover" through purchase of substitute goods in the case of a buyer of goods (see Uniform Commercial Code § 2–712). If the inability of the injured party to make such arrangements was foreseeable by the party in breach at the time he made the contract, the resulting loss was foreseeable. See Illustration 13. On the impact of this principle on contracts to lend money, see Comment e.

Illustration:

13. A contracts with B, a farmer, to lease B a machine to be used harvesting B's crop, delivery to be made on July 30. A knows when he makes the contract that B's crop will be ready on that date and that B cannot obtain another machine elsewhere. Because A delays delivery until August 10, B's crop is damaged and he loses profit. B's loss of profit was foreseeable by A at the time the contract was made as a probable result of the breach.

e. *Breach of contract to lend money.* The limitation of foreseeability is often applied in actions for damages for breach of contracts to lend money. Be-

cause credit is so widely available, a lender often has no reason to foresee at the time the contract is made that the borrower will be unable to make substitute arrangements in the event of breach. See Comment d. In most cases, then, the lender's liability will be limited to the relatively small additional amount that it would ordinarily cost to get a similar loan from another lender. However, in the less common situation in which the lender has reason to foresee that the borrower will be unable to borrow elsewhere or will be delayed in borrowing elsewhere, the lender may be liable for much heavier damages based on the borrower's inability to take advantage of a specific opportunity (see Illustration 14), his having to postpone or abandon a profitable project (see Illustration 15), or his forfeiture of security for failure to make prompt payment (see Illustration 16).

Illustrations:

14. A contracts to lend B $100,000 for one year at eight percent interest for the stated purpose of buying a specific lot of goods for resale. B can resell the goods at a $20,000 profit. A delays in making the loan, and although B can borrow money on the market at ten percent interest, he is unable to do so in time and loses the opportunity to buy the goods. Unless A had reason to foresee at the time that he made the contract that such a delay in making the loan would probably cause B to lose the opportunity, B can only recover damages based on two percent of the amount of the loan.

15. A contracts to lend $1,000,000 to B for the stated purpose of enabling B to build a building and takes property of B as security. After construction is begun, A refuses to make the loan or

release the security. Because B lacks further security, he is unable to complete the building, which becomes a total loss. B's loss incurred in partial construction of the building was foreseeable by A at the time of the contract as a probable result of the breach.

16. A, who holds B's land as security for a loan, contracts to lend B a sum of money sufficient to pay off other liens on the land at the current rate of interest. A repudiates and informs B in time to obtain money elsewhere on the market, but B is unable to do so. The liens are foreclosed and the land sold at a loss. Unless A knew when he made the contract that B would probably be unable to borrow the money elsewhere, B's loss on the foreclosure sale was not foreseeable as a probable result of A's breach.

f. Other limitations on damages. It is not always in the interest of justice to require the party in breach to pay damages for all of the foreseeable loss that he has caused. There are unusual instances in which it appears from the circumstances either that the parties assumed that one of them would not bear the risk of a particular loss or that, although there was no such assumption, it would be unjust to put the risk on that party. One such circumstance is an extreme disproportion between the loss and the price charged by the party whose liability for that loss is in question. The fact that the price is relatively small suggests that it was not intended to cover the risk of such liability. Another such circumstance is an informality of dealing, including the absence of a detailed written contract, which indicates that there was no careful attempt to allocate all of the risks. The fact that the parties did not attempt to delineate with precision all of the risks justifies

a court in attempting to allocate them fairly. The limitations dealt with in this Section are more likely to be imposed in connection with contracts that do not arise in a commercial setting. Typical examples of limitations imposed on damages under this discretionary power involve the denial of recovery for loss of profits and the restriction of damages to loss incurred in reliance on the contract. Sometimes these limits are covertly imposed, by means of an especially demanding requirement of foreseeability or of certainty. The rule stated in this Section recognizes that what is done in such cases is the imposition of a limitation in the interests of justice.

Illustrations:

17. A, a private trucker, contracts with B to deliver to B's factory a machine that has just been repaired and without which B's factory, as A knows, cannot re-open. Delivery is delayed because A's truck breaks down. In an action by B against A for breach of contract the court may, after taking into consideration such factors as the absence of an elaborate written contract and the extreme disproportion between B's loss of profits during the delay and the price of the trucker's services, exclude recovery for loss of profits.

18. A, a retail hardware dealer, contracts to sell B an inexpensive lighting attachment, which, as A knows, B needs in order to use his tractor at night on his farm. A is delayed in obtaining the attachment and, since no substitute is available, B is unable to use the tractor at night during the delay. In an action by B against A for breach of contract, the court may, after taking into consideration such factors as the absence of an elaborate written contract and the

extreme disproportion between B's loss of profits during the delay and the price of the attachment, exclude recovery for loss of profits.

19. A, a plastic surgeon, makes a contract with B, a professional entertainer, to perform plastic surgery on her face in order to improve her appearance. The result of the surgery is, however, to disfigure her face and to require a second operation. In an action by B against A for breach of contract, the court may limit damages by allowing recovery only for loss incurred by B in reliance on the contract, including the fees paid by B and expenses for hospitalization, nursing care and medicine for both operations, together with any damages for the worsening of B's appearance if these can be proved with reasonable certainty, but not including any loss resulting from the failure to improve her appearance.

§ 352. Uncertainty as a Limitation on Damages

Damages are not recoverable for loss beyond an amount that the evidence permits to be established with reasonable certainty.

§ 353. Loss Due to Emotional Disturbance

Recovery for emotional disturbance will be excluded unless the breach also caused bodily harm or the contract or the breach is of such a kind that serious emotional disturbance was a particularly likely result.

§ 355. Punitive Damages

Punitive damages are not recoverable for a breach of contract unless the conduct constituting the breach is also a tort for which punitive damages are recoverable.

§ 356. Liquidated Damages and Penalties

(1) Damages for breach by either party may be liquidated in the agreement but only at an amount that is reasonable in the light of the anticipated or actual loss caused by the breach and the difficulties of proof of loss. A term fixing unreasonably large liquidated damages is unenforceable on grounds of public policy.

(2) A term in a bond providing for an amount of money as a penalty for non-occurrence of the condition of the bond is unenforceable on grounds of public policy to the extent that the amount exceeds the loss caused by such non-occurrence.

TOPIC 3. ENFORCEMENT BY SPECIFIC PERFORM- ANCE AND INJUNCTION

§ 358. Form of Order and Other Relief

(1) An order of specific performance or an injunction will be so drawn as best to effectuate the purposes for which the contract was

made and on such terms as justice requires. It need not be absolute in form and the performance that it requires need not be identical with that due under the contract.

(2) If specific performance or an injunction is denied as to part of the performance that is due, it may nevertheless be granted as to the remainder.

(3) In addition to specific performance or an injunction, damages and other relief may be awarded in the same proceeding and an indemnity against future harm may be required.

§ 359. Effect of Adequacy of Damages

(1) Specific performance or an injunction will not be ordered if damages would be adequate to protect the expectation interest of the injured party.

(2) The adequacy of the damage remedy for failure to render one part of the performance due does not preclude specific performance or injunction as to the contract as a whole.

(3) Specific performance or an injunction will not be refused merely because there is a remedy for breach other than damages, but such a remedy may be considered in exercising discretion under the rule stated in § 357.

§ 360. Factors Affecting Adequacy of Damages

In determining whether the remedy in damages would be adequate, the following circumstances are significant:

> (a) the difficulty of proving damages with reasonable certainty,
>
> (b) the difficulty of procuring a suitable substitute performance by means of money awarded as damages, and
>
> (c) the likelihood that an award of damages could not be collected.

TOPIC 4. RESTITUTION

§ 370. Requirement That Benefit Be Conferred

A party is entitled to restitution under the rules stated in this Restatement only to the extent that he has conferred a benefit on the other party by way of part performance or reliance.

§ 371. Measure of Restitution Interest

If a sum of money is awarded to protect a party's restitution interest, it may as justice requires be measured by either

> (a) the reasonable value to the other party of what he received in terms of what it would have cost him to obtain it from a person in the claimant's position, or

(b) the extent to which the other party's property has been increased in value or his other interests advanced.

§ 373. Restitution When Other Party Is in Breach

(1) Subject to the rule stated in Subsection (2), on a breach by nonperformance that gives rise to a claim for damages for total breach or on a repudiation, the injured party is entitled to restitution for any benefit that he has conferred on the other party by way of part performance or reliance.

(2) The injured party has no right to restitution if he has performed all of his duties under the contract and no performance by the other party remains due other than payment of a definite sum of money for that performance.

§ 374. Restitution in Favor of Party in Breach

(1) Subject to the rule stated in Subsection (2), if a party justifiably refuses to perform on the ground that his remaining duties of performance have been discharged by the other party's breach, the party in breach is entitled to restitution for any benefit that he has conferred by way of part performance or reliance in excess of the loss that he has caused by his own breach.

(2) To the extent that, under the manifested assent of the parties, a party's performance is to be retained in the case of breach, that party is not entitled to restitution if the value of the performance as liquidated damages is reasonable in the light of the anticipated or actual loss caused by the breach and the difficulties of proof of loss.

§ 375. Restitution When Contract Is Within Statute of Frauds

A party who would otherwise have a claim in restitution under a contract is not barred from restitution for the reason that the contract is unenforceable by him because of the Statute of Frauds unless the Statute provides otherwise or its purpose would be frustrated by allowing restitution.

§ 376. Restitution When Contract Is Voidable

A party who has avoided a contract on the ground of lack of capacity, mistake, misrepresentation, duress, undue influence or abuse of a fiduciary relation is entitled to restitution for any benefit that he has conferred on the other party by way of part performance or reliance.

§ 377. Restitution in Cases of Impracticability, Frustration, Non-occurrence of Condition or Disclaimer by Beneficiary

A party whose duty of performance does not arise or is discharged as a result of impracticability of performance, frustration of purpose, non-occurrence of a condition or disclaimer by a beneficiary is entitled to restitution for any benefit that he has conferred on the other party by way of part performance or reliance.

UNITED NATIONS CONVENTION ON CONTRACTS FOR THE INTERNATIONAL SALE OF GOODS

COMPILERS' NOTE

Since January 1, 1988 American exporters and importers have been subject to the Convention on Contracts for the International Sale of Goods (CISG). With respect to transactions within its scope, it displaces much of Article 2, Sales, of the Uniform Commercial Code—including, for example, the requirements of the statute of frauds (CISG 11).[1]

The Convention "applies to contracts for the sale of goods between parties whose places of business are in different States ... when the States are Contracting States" (CISG 1).[2] The Convention preserves the autonomy of the parties by allowing them to "exclude the application of this Convention or ... derogate from or vary the effect of any of its provisions" (CISG 6). The Convention does not displace rules of national law that relate to "the validity of the contract or of any of its provisions or of any usages." (CISG 4(a)).[3]

Work on the Convention began in the 1930s when the Institute for the Unification of Private Law in Rome, then under the auspices of the League of Nations, set up a drafting committee of European scholars to work on a uniform law for international sales. By the outbreak of the Second World War, the committee had prepared a first draft, solicited comments from governments, and prepared a revised draft taking account of these comments.

After the War the Dutch Government appointed a commission to do further work, solicited comments from governments and, in 1964, convened a diplomatic conference at The Hague. The conference approved a uniform law on the international sale of goods (ULIS) and a shorter companion uniform law on the formation of contracts for the international sale of goods.

1. The United States did not make the declaration described in CISG 12.

2. In this context "States" means nations and "Contracting" means adopting. The United States did not accept CISG 1(b), which would have given the Convention a broader application.

3. For a definitive treatment of the Convention, see J. Honnold, Uniform Law for International Sales under the 1980 U.N. Convention (3d ed. 1999). See also C. Bianca, M. Bonell et al., Commentary on the International Sales Law: The 1980 Vienna Convention (1987); P. Schlechtriem et al., Commentary on the UN Convention on the International Sale of Goods (CISG) (G. Thomas trans. 2d ed. 1998).

Although the United States had quickly put together a delegation to The Hague to consider a draft prepared by a group of exclusively European scholars, that delegation's influence was not pervasive enough to produce a final text that justified United States ratification.[4] Nevertheless, ULIS did receive eight adoptions by other countries, enough for it to take effect.

Even before ULIS had taken effect, however, efforts were afoot under United Nations auspices to produce a revised international sales law that would be more widely acceptable. In 1966, the United Nations General Assembly established the United Nations Commission on International Trade Law (UNCITRAL). The Commission has "for its object the promotion of the progressive harmonization and unification of the law of international trade." Its thirty-six members include common law as well as civil law countries, developing as well as industrialized countries, and countries with centrally planned economics as well as those with free-market economies.

In 1969, UNCITRAL appointed a fourteen-member Working Group on Sales to consider what changes in ULIS would make it more acceptable to countries of varied legal, social, and economic systems. The United States was an active member of this Working Group from its inception. In 1977 UNCITRAL revised and approved a text of CISG prepared by the Working Group on Sales, and in 1978 it integrated into CISG additional provisions on formation and interpretation. In 1980, the United Nations held in Vienna a diplomatic conference to propose a final text of CISG. After five weeks of intensive effort by the sixty-two countries represented, CISG—often referred to as "the Vienna Convention"—was adopted.

The final product of this half-century of work consists of eighty-eight substantive articles (what we in the United States would call "sections") plus thirteen more articles on effective date, reservations, and the like. Only the eighty-eight substantive articles are set out below. CISG took effect following adoption by ten countries. It has now be adopted by about sixty.[5]

4. The traditional scheme for international unification results in a multilateral treaty, put in final form at a diplomatic conference and then adopted by ratification or accession. One important difference between this scheme and that used for unification within the United States is that a country ratifying or acceding to a treaty cannot make changes in its text, except for a few variations that the diplomatic conference has allowed countries to make by means of reservations.

5. Countries that have ratified the Convention include Argentina, Australia, Austria, Belgium, Bulgaria, Belarus, Canada, Chile, China, Cuba, Czechoslovakia, Denmark, Equador, Egypt, Finland, France, Germany, Greece, Guinea, Hungary, Iraq, Italy, Mexico, Netherlands, New Zealand, Norway, Poland, Romania, Russian Federation, Singapore, Spain, Syrian Arab Republic, Sweden, Switzerland, Ukraine, United States, Uruguay, Yugoslavia, Zambia.

CONVENTION ON CONTRACTS FOR THE INTERNATIONAL SALE OF GOODS

THE STATES PARTIES TO THIS CONVENTION,

Bearing in mind the broad objectives in the resolutions adopted by the sixth special session of the General Assembly of the United Nations on the establishment of a New International Economic Order,

Considering that the development of international trade on the basis of equality and mutual benefit is an important element in promoting friendly relations among States,

Being of the opinion that the adoption of uniform rules which govern contracts for the international sale of goods and take into account the different social, economic and legal systems would contribute to the removal of legal barriers in international trade and promote the development of international trade,

Have agreed as follows:

Part I. Sphere of application and general provisions

CHAPTER I. SPHERE OF APPLICATION

Article 1

(1) This Convention applies to contracts of sale of goods between parties whose places of business are in different States:

  (a) When the States are Contracting States; or

  (b) When the rules of private international law lead to the application of the law of a Contracting State.

(2) The fact that the parties have their places of business in different States is to be disregarded whenever this fact does not appear either from the contract or from any dealings between, or from information disclosed by, the parties at any time before or at the conclusion of the contract.

(3) Neither the nationality of the parties nor the civil or commercial character of the parties or of the contract is to be taken into consideration in determining the application of this Convention.

Article 2

This Convention does not apply to sales:

    (a) Of goods bought for personal, family or household use, unless the seller, at any time before or at the conclusion of the contract, neither knew nor ought to have known that the goods were bought for any such use;

    (b) By auction;

    (c) On execution or otherwise by authority of law;

    (d) Of stocks, shares, investment securities, negotiable instruments or money;

    (e) Of ships, vessels, hovercraft or aircraft;

    (f) Of electricity.

Article 3

(1) Contracts for the supply of goods to be manufactured or produced are to be considered sales unless the party who order the goods undertakes to supply a substantial part of the materials necessary for such manufacture or production.

(2) This Convention does not apply to contracts in which the preponderant part of the obligations of the party who furnishes the goods consists in the supply of labour or other services.

Article 4

This Convention governs only the formation of the contract of sale and the rights and obligations of the seller and the buyer arising from such a contract. In particular, except as otherwise expressly provided in this Convention, it is not concerned with:

    (a) The validity of the contract or of any of its provisions or of any usage;

    (b) The effect which the contract may have on the property in the goods sold.

Article 5

This Convention does not apply to the liability of the seller for death or personal injury caused by the goods to any person.

Article 6

The parties may exclude the application of this Convention or, subject to article 12, derogate from or vary the effect of any of its provisions.

CHAPTER II. GENERAL PROVISIONS

Article 7

(1) In the interpretation of this Convention, regard is to be had to its international character and to the need to promote uniformity in its application and the observance of good faith in international trade.

(2) Questions concerning matters governed by this Convention which are not expressly settled in it are to be settled in conformity with the general principles on which it is based or, in the absence of such principles, in conformity with the law applicable by virtue of the rules of private international law.

Article 8

(1) For the purposes of this Convention statements made by and other conduct of a party are to be interpreted according to his intent where the other party knew or could not have been unaware what that intent was.

(2) If the preceding paragraph is not applicable, statements made by and other conduct of a party are to be interpreted according to the understanding that a reasonable person of the same kind as the other party would have had in the same circumstances.

(3) In determining the intent of a party or the understanding a reasonable person would have had, due consideration is to be given to all relevant circumstances of the case including the negotiations, any practices which the parties have established between themselves, usages and any subsequent conduct of the parties.

Article 9

(1) The parties are bound by any usages to which they have agreed and by any practices which they have established between themselves.

(2) The parties are considered, unless otherwise agreed, to have impliedly made applicable to their contract or its formation a usage of which the parties knew or ought to have known and which in international trade is widely known to, and regularly observed by, parties to contracts of the type involved in the particular trade concerned.

Article 10

For the purposes of this Convention:

(a) If a party has more than one place of business, the place of business is that which has the closest relationship to the contract and its performance, having regard to the circumstances known to or contemplated by the parties at any time before or at the conclusion of the contract;

(b) If a party does not have a place of business, reference is to be made to his habitual residence.

Article 11

A Contract of sale need not be concluded in or evidenced by writing and is not subject to any other requirement as to form. It may be proved by any means, including witnesses.

Article 12

Any provision of article 11, article 29 or Part II of this Convention that allows a contract of sale or its modification or termination by agreement or any offer, acceptance or other indication of intention to be made in any form other than in writing does not apply where any party has his place of business in a Contracting State which has made a declaration under article 96 of this Convention. The parties may not derogate from or vary the effect of this article.

Article 13

For the purposes of this Convention "writing" includes telegram and telex.

Part II. Formation of the contract

Article 14

(1) A proposal for concluding a contract addressed to one or more specific persons constitutes an offer if it is sufficiently definite and indicates the intention of the offeror to be bound in case of acceptance. A proposal is sufficiently definite if it indicates the goods and expressly or implicitly fixes or makes provision for determining the quantity and the price.

(2) A proposal other than one addressed to one or more specific persons is to be considered merely as an invitation to make offers, unless the contrary is clearly indicated by the person making the proposal.

Article 15

(1) An offer becomes effective when it reaches the offeree.

(2) An offer, even if it is irrevocable, may be withdrawn if the withdrawal reaches the offeree before or at the same time as the offer.

Article 16

(1) Until a contract is concluded an offer may be revoked if the revocation reaches the offeree before he has dispatched an acceptance.

(2) However, an offer cannot be revoked:

(a) If it indicates, whether by stating a fixed time for acceptance or otherwise, that it is irrevocable; or

(b) If it was reasonable for the offeree to rely on the offer as being irrevocable and the offeree has acted in reliance on the offer.

Article 17

An offer, even if it is irrevocable, is terminated when a rejection reaches the offeror.

Article 18

(1) A statement made by or other conduct of the offeree indicating assent to an offer is an acceptance. Silence or inactivity does not in itself amount to acceptance.

(2) An acceptance of an offer becomes effective at the moment the indication of assent reaches the offeror. An acceptance is not effective if the indication of assent does not reach the offeror within the time he has fixed or, if no time is fixed, within a reasonable time, due account being taken of the circumstances of the transaction, including the rapidity of the means of communication employed by the offeror. An oral offer must be accepted immediately unless the circumstances indicate otherwise.

(3) However, if, by virtue of the offer or as a result of practices which the parties have established between themselves or of usage, the offeree may indicate assent by performing an act, such as one relating to the dispatch of the goods or payment of the price, without notice to the offeror, the acceptance is effective at the moment the act is performed, provided that the act is performed within the period of time laid down in the preceding paragraph.

Article 19

(1) A reply to an offer which purports to be an acceptance but contains additions, limitations or other modifications is a rejection of the offer and constitutes a counter-offer.

(2) However, a reply to an offer which purports to be an acceptance but contains additional or different terms which do not materially alter the terms of the offer constitutes an acceptance, unless the offeror, without undue delay, objects orally to the discrepancy or dispatches a notice to that effect. If he does not so object, the terms of the contract are the terms of the offer with the modifications contained in the acceptance.

(3) Additional or different terms relating, among other things, to the price, payment, quality and quantity of the goods, place and time of delivery, extent of one party's liability to the other or the settlement of disputes are considered to alter the terms of the offer materially.

Article 20

(1) A period of time for acceptance fixed by the offeror in a telegram or a letter begins to run from the moment the telegram is handed in for dispatch or from the date shown on the letter or, if no such date is shown, from the date shown on the envelope. A period of time for acceptance fixed by the offeror by telephone, telex or other means of instantaneous communication, begins to run from the moment that the offer reaches the offeree.

(2) Official holidays or non-business days occurring during the period for acceptance are included in calculating the period. However, if a notice of acceptance cannot be delivered at the address of the offeror on the last day of the period because that day falls on an official holiday or a non-business day at the place of business of the offeror, the period is extended until the first business day which follows.

Article 21

(1) A late acceptance is nevertheless effective as an acceptance if without delay the offeror orally so informs the offeree or dispatches a notice to that effect.

(2) If a letter or other writing containing a late acceptance shows that it has been sent in such circumstances that if its transmission had been normal it would have reached the offeror in due time, the late acceptance is effective as an acceptance unless, without delay, the offeror orally informs the offeree that he considers his offer as having lapsed or dispatches a notice to that effect.

Article 22

An acceptance may be withdrawn if the withdrawal reaches the offeror before or at the same time as the acceptance would have become effective.

Article 23

A contract is concluded at the moment when an acceptance of an offer becomes effective in accordance with the provisions of this Convention.

Article 24

For the purposes of this Part of the Convention, an offer, declaration of acceptance or any other indication of intention "reaches" the addressee when it is made orally to him or delivered by any other means to him personally, to his place of business or mailing address or, if he does not have a place of business or mailing address, to his habitual residence.

Part III. Sale of goods

CHAPTER I. GENERAL PROVISIONS

Article 25

A breach of contract committed by one of the parties is fundamental if it results in such detriment to the other party as substantially to deprive him of what he is entitled to expect under the contract, unless the party in breach did not foresee, and a reasonable person of the same kind in the same circumstances would not have foreseen, such a result.

Article 26

A declaration of avoidance of the contract is effective only if made by notice to the other party.

Article 27

Unless otherwise expressly provided in this Part of the Convention, if any notice, request or other communication is given or made by a party in accordance with this Part, and by means appropriate in the circumstances, a delay or error in the transmission of the communication or its failure to arrive does not deprive that party of the right to rely on the communication.

Article 28

If, in accordance with the provisions of this Convention, one party is entitled to require performance of any obligation by the other party, a court is not bound to enter a judgment for specific performance unless the court would do so under its own law in respect of similar contracts of sale not governed by this Convention.

Article 29

(1) A contract may be modified or terminated by the mere agreement of the parties.

(2) A contract in writing which contains a provision requiring any modification or termination by agreement to be in writing may not be otherwise modified or terminated by agreement. However, a party may be precluded by his conduct from asserting such a provision to the extent that the other party has relied on that conduct.

CHAPTER II. OBLIGATIONS OF THE SELLER

Article 30

The seller must deliver the goods, hand over any documents relating to them and transfer the property in the goods, as required by the contract and this Convention.

Section I. Delivery of the goods and handing over of documents

Article 31

If the seller is not bound to deliver the goods at any other particular place, his obligation to deliver consists:

(a) If the contract of sale involves carriage of the goods—in handing the goods over to the first carrier for transmission to the buyer;

(b) If, in cases not within the preceding subparagraph, the contract relates to specific goods, or unidentified goods to be drawn from a specific stock or to be manufactured or produced, and at the time of the conclusion of the contract the parties knew that the goods were at, or were to be manufactured or produced at, a particular place—in placing the goods at the buyer's disposal at that place;

(c) In other cases—in placing the goods at the buyer's disposal at the place where the seller had his place of business at the time of the conclusion of the contract.

Article 32

(1) If the seller, in accordance with the contract or this Convention, hands the goods over to a carrier and if the goods are not clearly identified to the contract by markings on the goods, by shipping documents or otherwise, the seller must give the buyer notice of the consignment specifying the goods.

(2) If the seller is bound to arrange for carriage of the goods, he must make such contracts as are necessary for carriage to the place fixed by means of transportation appropriate in the circumstances and according to the usual terms for such transportation.

(3) If the seller is not bound to effect insurance in respect of the carriage of the goods, he must, at the buyer's request, provide him with all available information necessary to enable him to effect such insurance.

Article 33

The seller must deliver the goods:

(a) If a date is fixed by or determinable from the contract, on that date;

(b) If a period of time is fixed by or determinable from the contract, at any time within that period unless circumstances indicate that the buyer is to choose a date; or

(c) In any other case, within a reasonable time after the conclusion of the contract.

Article 34

If the seller is bound to hand over documents relating to the goods, he must hand them over at the time and place and in the form required by the contract. If the seller has handed over documents before that time, he may, up to that time, cure any lack of conformity in the documents, if the exercise of this right does not cause the buyer unreasonable inconvenience or unreasonable expense. However, the buyer retains any right to claim damages as provided for in this Convention.

Section II.   Conformity of the goods and third party claims

Article 35

(1) The seller must deliver goods which are of the quantity, quality and description required by the contract and which are contained or packaged in the manner required by the contract.

(2) Except where the parties have agreed otherwise, the goods do not conform with the contract unless they:

> (a) Are fit for the purposes for which goods of the same description would ordinarily be used;
>
> (b) Are fit for any particular purpose expressly or impliedly made known to the seller at the time of the conclusion of the contract, except where the circumstances show that the buyer did not rely, or that it was unreasonable for him to rely, on the seller's skill and judgment;
>
> (c) Possess the qualities of goods which the seller has held out to the buyer as a sample or model;
>
> (d) Are contained or packaged in the manner usual for such goods or, where there is no such manner, in a manner adequate to preserve and protect the goods.

(3) The seller is not liable under subparagraphs (a) to (d) of the preceding paragraph for any lack of conformity of the goods if at the time of the conclusion of the contract the buyer knew or could not have been unaware of such lack of conformity.

Article 36

(1) The seller is liable in accordance with the contract and this Convention for any lack of conformity which exists at the time when the risk passes to the buyer, even though the lack of conformity becomes apparent only after that time.

(2) The seller is also liable for any lack of conformity which occurs after the time indicated in the preceding paragraph and which is due to a breach of any of his obligations, including a breach of any guarantee that for a period of time the goods will remain fit for their ordinary purpose or for some particular purpose or will retain specified qualities or characteristics.

Article 37

If the seller has delivered goods before the date for delivery, he may, up to that date, deliver any missing part or make up any deficiency in the quantity of the goods delivered, or deliver goods in replacement of any nonconforming goods delivered or remedy any lack of conformity in the goods delivered, provided that the exercise of this right does not cause the buyer unreasonable inconvenience or unreasonable expense.

However, the buyer retains any right to claim damages as provided for in this Convention.

Article 38

(1) The buyer must examine the goods, or cause them to be examined, within as short a period as is practicable in the circumstances.

(2) If the contract involves carriage of the goods, examination may be deferred until after the goods have arrived at their destination.

(3) If the goods are redirected in transit or redispatched by the buyer without a reasonable opportunity for examination by him and at the time of the conclusion of the contract the seller knew or ought to have known of the possibility of such redirection or redispatch, examination may be deferred until after the goods have arrived at the new destination.

Article 39

(1) The buyer loses the right to rely on a lack of conformity of the goods if he does not give notice to the seller specifying the nature of the lack of conformity within a reasonable time after he has discovered it or ought to have discovered it.

(2) In any event, the buyer loses the right to rely on a lack of conformity of the goods if he does not give the seller notice thereof at the latest within a period of two years from the date on which the goods were actually handed over to the buyer, unless this time-limit is inconsistent with a contractual period of guarantee.

Article 40

The seller is not entitled to rely on the provisions of articles 38 and 39 if the lack of conformity relates to facts of which he knew or could not have been unaware and which he did not disclose to the buyer.

Article 41

The seller must deliver goods which are free from any right or claim of a third party, unless the buyer agreed to take the goods subject to that right or claim. However, if such right or claim is based on industrial property or other intellectual property, the seller's obligation is governed by article 42.

Article 42

(1) The seller must deliver goods which are free from any right or claim of a third party based on industrial property or other intellectual property, of which at the time of the conclusion of the contract the seller knew or could not have been unaware, provided that the right or claim is based on industrial property or other intellectual property:

(a) Under the law of the State where the goods will be resold or otherwise used, if it was contemplated by the parties at the time of the conclusion of the contract that the goods would be resold or otherwise used in that State; or

(b) In any other case, under the law of the State where the buyer has his place of business.

(2) The obligation of the seller under the preceding paragraph does not extend to cases where:

(a) At the time of the conclusion of the contract the buyer knew or could not have been unaware of the right or claim; or

(b) The right or claim results from the seller's compliance with technical drawings, designs, formulae or other such specifications furnished by the buyer.

Article 43

(1) The buyer loses the right to rely on the provisions of article 41 or article 42 if he does not give notice to the seller specifying the nature of the right or claim of the third party within a reasonable time after he has become aware or ought to have become aware of the right or claim.

(2) The seller is not entitled to rely on the provisions of the preceding paragraph if he knew of the right or claim of the third party and the nature of it.

Article 44

Notwithstanding the provisions of paragraph (1) of article 39 and paragraph (1) of article 43, the buyer may reduce the price in accordance with article 50 or claim damages, except for loss of profit, if he has a reasonable excuse for his failure to give the required notice.

Section III.   Remedies for breach of contract by the seller

Article 45

(1) If the seller fails to perform any of his obligations under the contract or this Convention, the buyer may:

(a) Exercise the rights provided in articles 46 to 52;

(b) Claim damages as provided in articles 74 to 77.

(2) The buyer is not deprived of any right he may have to claim damages by exercising his right to other remedies.

(3) No period of grace may be granted to the seller by a court or arbitral tribunal when the buyer resorts to a remedy for breach of contract.

Article 46

(1) The buyer may require performance by the seller of his obligations unless the buyer has resorted to a remedy which is inconsistent with this requirement.

(2) If the goods do not conform with the contract, the buyer may require delivery of substitute goods only if the lack of conformity constitutes a fundamental breach of contract and a request for substitute goods is made either in conjunction with notice given under article 39 or within a reasonable time thereafter.

(3) If the goods do not conform with the contract, the buyer may require the seller to remedy the lack of conformity by repair, unless this is unreasonable having regard to all the circumstances. A request for repair must be made either in conjunction with notice given under article 39 or within a reasonable time thereafter.

Article 47

(1) The buyer may fix an additional period of time of reasonable length for performance by the seller of his obligations.

(2) Unless the buyer has received notice from the seller that he will not perform within the period so fixed, the buyer may not, during that period, resort to any remedy for breach of contract. However, the buyer is not deprived thereby of any right he may have to claim damages for delay in performance.

Article 48

(1) Subject to article 49, the seller may, even after the date for delivery, remedy at his own expense any failure to perform his obligations, if he can do so without unreasonable delay and without causing the buyer unreasonable inconvenience or uncertainty of reimbursement by the seller of expenses advanced by the buyer. However, the buyer retains any right to claim damages as provided for in this Convention.

(2) If the seller requests the buyer to make known whether he will accept performance and the buyer does not comply with the request within a reasonable time, the seller may perform within the time indicated in his request. The buyer may not, during that period of time, resort to any remedy which is inconsistent with performance by the seller.

(3) A notice by the seller that he will perform within a specified period of time is assumed to include a request, under the preceding paragraph, that the buyer make known his decision.

(4) A request or notice by the seller under paragraph (2) or (3) of this article is not effective unless received by the buyer.

350

Article 49

(1) The buyer may declare the contract avoided:

    (a) If the failure by the seller to perform any of his obligations under the contract or this Convention amounts to a fundamental breach of contract; or

    (b) In case of non-delivery, if the seller does not deliver the goods within the additional period of time fixed by the buyer in accordance with paragraph (1) of article 47 or declares that he will not deliver within the period so fixed.

(2) However, in cases where the seller has delivered the goods, the buyer loses the right to declare the contract avoided unless he does so:

    (a) In respect of late delivery, within a reasonable time after he has become aware that delivery has been made;

    (b) In respect of any breach other than late delivery, within a reasonable time:

        (i) After he knew or ought to have known of the breach;

        (ii) After the expiration of any additional period of time fixed by the buyer in accordance with paragraph (1) of article 47, or after the seller has declared that he will not perform his obligations within such an additional period; or

        (iii) After the expiration of any additional period of time indicated by the seller in accordance with paragraph (2) of article 48, or after the buyer has declared that he will not accept performance.

Article 50

If the goods do not conform with the contract and whether or not the price has already been paid, the buyer may reduce the price in the same proportion as the value that the goods actually delivered had at the time of the delivery bears to the value that conforming goods would have had at that time. However, if the seller remedies any failure to perform his obligations in accordance with article 37 or article 48 or if the buyer refuses to accept performance by the seller in accordance with those articles, the buyer may not reduce the price.

Article 51

(1) If the seller delivers only a part of the goods or if only a part of the goods delivered is in conformity with the contract, articles 46 to 50 apply in respect of the part which is missing or which does not conform.

(2) The buyer may declare the contract avoided in its entirety only if the failure to make delivery completely or in conformity with the contract amounts to a fundamental breach of the contract.

Article 52

(1) If the seller delivers the goods before the date fixed, the buyer may take delivery or refuse to take delivery.

(2) If the seller delivers a quantity of goods greater than that provided for in the contract, the buyer may take delivery or refuse to take delivery of the excess quantity. If the buyer takes delivery of all or part of the excess quantity, he must pay for it at the contract rate.

CHAPTER III. OBLIGATIONS OF THE BUYER

Article 53

The buyer must pay the price for the goods and take delivery of them as required by the contract and this Convention.

Section I. Payment of the price

Article 54

The buyer's obligation to pay the price includes taking such steps and complying with such formalities as may be required under the contract or any laws and regulations to enable payment to be made.

Article 55

Where a contract has been validly concluded but does not expressly or implicitly fix or make provision for determining the price, the parties are considered, in the absence of any indication to the contrary, to have impliedly made reference to the price generally charged at the time of the conclusion of the contract for such goods sold under comparable circumstances in the trade concerned.

Article 56

If the price is fixed according to the weight of the goods, in case of doubt it is to be determined by the net weight.

Article 57

(1) If the buyer is not bound to pay the price at any other particular place, he must pay it to the seller:

    (a) At the seller's place of business; or

    (b) If the payment is to be made against the handing over of the goods or of documents, at the place where the handing over takes place.

(2) The seller must bear any increase in the expenses incidental to payment which is caused by a change in his place of business subsequent to the conclusion of the contract.

Article 58

(1) If the buyer is not bound to pay the price at any other specific time, he must pay it when the seller places either the goods or documents controlling their disposition at the buyer's disposal in accordance with the contract and this Convention. The seller may make such payment a condition for handing over the goods or documents.

(2) If the contract involves carriage of the goods, the seller may dispatch the goods on terms whereby the goods, or documents controlling their disposition, will not be handed over to the buyer except against payment of the price.

(3) The buyer is not bound to pay the price until he has had an opportunity to examine the goods, unless the procedures for delivery or payment agreed upon by the parties are inconsistent with his having such an opportunity.

Article 59

The buyer must pay the price on the date fixed by or determinable from the contract and this Convention without the need for any request or compliance with any formality on the part of the seller.

Section II. Taking delivery

Article 60

The buyer's obligation to take delivery consists:

(a) In doing all the acts which could reasonably be expected of him in order to enable the seller to make delivery; and

(b) In taking over the goods.

Section III. Remedies for breach of contract by the buyer

Article 61

(1) If the buyer fails to perform any of his obligations under the contract or this Convention, the seller may:

(a) Exercise the rights provided in articles 62 to 65;

(b) Claim damages as provided in articles 74 to 77.

(2) The seller is not deprived of any right he may have to claim damages by exercising his right to other remedies.

(3) No period of grace may be granted to the buyer by a court or arbitral tribunal when the seller resorts to a remedy for breach of contract.

Article 62

The seller may require the buyer to pay the price, take delivery or perform his other obligations, unless the seller has resorted to a remedy which is inconsistent with this requirement.

Article 63

(1) The seller may fix an additional period of time of reasonable length for performance by the buyer of his obligations.

(2) Unless the seller has received notice from the buyer that he will not perform within the period so fixed, the seller may not, during that period, resort to any remedy for breach of contract. However, the seller is not deprived thereby of any right he may have to claim damages for delay in performance.

Article 64

(1) The seller may declare the contract avoided:

    (a) If the failure by the buyer to perform any of his obligations under the contract or this Convention amounts to a fundamental breach of contract; or

    (b) If the buyer does not, within the additional period of time fixed by the seller in accordance with paragraph (1) of article 63, perform his obligation to pay the price or take delivery of the goods, or declares that he will not do so within the period so fixed.

(2) However, in cases where the buyer has paid the price, the seller loses the right to declare the contract avoided unless he does so:

    (a) In respect of late performance by the buyer, before the seller has become aware that performance has been rendered; or

    (b) In respect of any breach other than late performance by the buyer, within a reasonable time:

        (i) After the seller knew or ought to have known of the breach; or

        (ii) After the expiration of any additional period of time fixed by the seller in accordance with paragraph (1) of article 63, or after the buyer has declared that he will not perform his obligations within such an additional period.

Article 65

(1) If under the contract the buyer is to specify the form, measurement or other features of the goods and he fails to make such specification either on the date agreed upon or within a reasonable time after receipt of a request from the seller, the seller may, without prejudice to any other rights he may have, make the specification himself in accordance with the requirements of the buyer that may be known to him.

(2) If the seller makes the specification himself, he must inform the buyer of the details thereof and must fix a reasonable time within which the buyer may make a different specification. If, after receipt of such a

communication, the buyer fails to do so within the time so fixed, the specification made by the seller is binding.

CHAPTER IV. PASSING OF RISK
Article 66

Loss of or damage to the goods after the risk has passed to the buyer does not discharge him from his obligation to pay the price, unless the loss or damage is due to an act or omission of the seller.

Article 67

(1) If the contract of sale involves carriage of the goods and the seller is not bound to hand them over at a particular place, the risk passes to the buyer when the goods are handed over to the first carrier for transmission to the buyer in accordance with the contract of sale. If the seller is bound to hand the goods over to a carrier at a particular place, the risk does not pass to the buyer until the goods are handed over to the carrier at that place. The fact that the seller is authorized to retain documents controlling the disposition of the goods does not affect the passage of the risk.

(2) Nevertheless, the risk does not pass to the buyer until the goods are clearly identified to the contract, whether by markings on the goods, by shipping documents, by notice given to the buyer or otherwise.

Article 68

The risk in respect of goods sold in transit passes to the buyer from the time of the conclusion of the contract. However, if the circumstances so indicate, the risk is assumed by the buyer from the time the goods were handed over to the carrier who issued the documents embodying the contract of carriage. Nevertheless, if at the time of the conclusion of the contract of sale the seller knew or ought to have known that the goods had been lost or damaged and did not disclose this to the buyer, the loss or damage is at the risk of the seller.

Article 69

(1) In cases not within articles 67 and 68, the risk passes to the buyer when he takes over the goods or, if he does not do so in due time, from the time when the goods are placed at his disposal he commits a breach of contract by failing to take delivery.

(2) However, if the buyer is bound to take over the goods at a place other than a place of business of the seller, the risk passes when delivery is due and the buyer is aware of the fact that the goods are placed at his disposal at that place.

(3) If the contract relates to goods not then identified, the goods are considered not to be placed at the disposal of the buyer until they are clearly identified to the contract.

Article 70

If the seller has committed a fundamental breach of contract, articles 67, 68, and 69 do not impair the remedies available to the buyer on account of the breach.

CHAPTER V.   PROVISIONS COMMON TO THE OBLIGATIONS OF THE SELLER AND OF THE BUYER

Section I.   Anticipatory breach and installment contracts

Article 71

(1) A party may suspend the performance of his obligations if, after the conclusion of the contract, it becomes apparent that the other party will not perform a substantial part of his obligations as a result of:

(a) A serious deficiency in his ability to perform or in his creditworthiness; or

(b) His conduct in preparing to perform or in performing the contract.

(2) If the seller has already dispatched the goods before the grounds described in the preceding paragraph become evident, he may prevent the handing over of the goods to the buyer even though the buyer holds a document which entitles him to obtain them. The present paragraph relates only to the rights in the goods as between the buyer and the seller.

(3) A party suspending performance, whether before or after dispatch of the goods, must immediately give notice of the suspension to the other party and must continue with performance if the other party provides adequate assurance of his performance.

Article 72

(1) If prior to the date for performance of the contract it is clear that one of the parties will commit a fundamental breach of contract, the other party may declare the contract avoided.

(2) If time allows, the party intending to declare the contract avoided must give reasonable notice to the other party in order to permit him to provide adequate assurance of his performance.

(3) The requirements of the preceding paragraph do not apply if the other party has declared that he will not perform his obligations.

Article 73

(1) In the case of a contract for delivery of goods by instalments, if the failure of one party to perform any of his obligations in respect of any instalment constitutes a fundamental breach of contract with re-

spect to that instalment, the other party may declare the contract avoided with respect to that instalment.

(2) If one party's failure to perform any of his obligations in respect of any instalment gives the other party good grounds to conclude that a fundamental breach of contract will occur with respect to future instalments, he may declare the contract avoided for the future, provided that he does so within a reasonable time.

(3) A buyer who declares the contract avoided in respect of any delivery may, at the same time, declare it avoided in respect of deliveries already made or of future deliveries if, by reason of their interdependence, those deliveries could not be used for the purpose contemplated by the parties at the time of the conclusion of the contract.

Section II. Damages

Article 74

Damages for breach of contract by one party consist of a sum equal to the loss, including loss of profit, suffered by the other party as a consequence of the breach. Such damages may not exceed the loss which the party in breach foresaw or ought to have foreseen at the time of the conclusion of the contract, in the light of the facts and matters of which he then knew or ought to have known, as a possible consequence of the breach of contract.

Article 75

If the contract is avoided and if, in a reasonable manner and within a reasonable time after avoidance, the buyer has bought goods in replacement or the seller has resold the goods, the party claiming damages may recover the difference between the contract price and the price in the substitute transaction as well as any further damages recoverable under article 74.

Article 76

(1) If the contract is avoided and there is a current price for the goods, the party claiming damages may, if he has not made a purchase or resale under article 75, recover the difference between the price fixed by the contract and the current price at the time of avoidance as well as any further damages recoverable under article 74. If, however, the party claiming damages has avoided the contract after taking over the goods, the current price at the time of such taking over shall be applied instead of the current price at the time of avoidance.

(2) For the purposes of the preceding paragraph, the current price is the price prevailing at the place where delivery of the goods should have been made or, if there is no current price at that place, the price at such other place as serves as a reasonable substitute, making due allowance for differences in the cost of transporting the goods.

Article 77

A party who relies on a breach of contract must take such measures as are reasonable in the circumstances to mitigate the loss, including loss of profit, resulting from the breach. If he fails to take such measures, the party in breach may claim a reduction in the damages in the amount by which the loss should have been mitigated.

Section III.   Interest

Article 78

If a party fails to pay the price or any other sum that is in arrears, the other party is entitled to interest on it, without prejudice to any claim for damages recoverable under article 74.

Section IV.   Exemptions

Article 79

(1) A party is not liable for a failure to perform any of his obligations if he proves that the failure was due to an impediment beyond his control and that he could not reasonably be expected to have taken the impediment into account at the time of the conclusion of the contract or to have avoided or overcome it or its consequences.

(2) If the party's failure is due to the failure by a third person whom he has engaged to perform the whole or a party of the contract, that party is exempt from liability only if:

  (a) He is exempt under the preceding paragraph; and

  (b) The person whom he has so engaged would be so exempt if the provisions of that paragraph were applied to him.

(3) The exemption provided by this article has effect for the period during which the impediment exists.

(4) The party who fails to perform must give notice to the other party of the impediment and its effect on his ability to perform. If the notice is not received by the other party within a reasonable time after the party who fails to perform knew or ought to have known of the impediment, he is liable for damages resulting from such non-receipt.

(5) Nothing in this article prevents either party from exercising any right other than to claim damages under this Convention.

Article 80

A party may not rely on a failure of the other party to perform, to the extent that such failure was caused by the first party's act or omission.

Section V.   Effects of avoidance

Article 81

(1) Avoidance of the contract releases both parties from their obligations under it, subject to any damages which may be due.   Avoidance does not affect any provision of the contract for the settlement of disputes or any other provision of the contract governing the rights and obligations of the parties consequent upon the avoidance of the contract.

(2) A party who has performed the contract either wholly or in part may claim restitution from the other party of whatever the first party has supplied or paid under the contract.   If both parties are bound to make restitution, they must do so concurrently.

Article 82

(1) The buyer loses the right to declare the contract avoided or to require the seller to deliver substitute goods if it is impossible for him to make restitution of the goods substantially in the condition in which he received them.

(2) The preceding paragraph does not apply:

    (a) If the impossibility of making restitution of the goods or of making restitution of the goods substantially in the condition in which the buyer received them is not due to his act or omission;

    (b) If the goods or part of the goods have perished or deteriorated as a result of the examination provided for in article 38; or

    (c) If the goods or part of the goods have been sold in the normal course of business or have been consumed or transformed by the buyer in the course of normal use before he discovered or ought to have discovered the lack of conformity.

Article 83

A buyer who has lost the right to declare the contract avoided or to require the seller to deliver substitute goods in accordance with article 82 retains all other remedies under the contract and this Convention.

Article 84

(1) If the seller is bound to refund the price, he must also pay interest on it, from the date on which the price was paid.

(2) The buyer must account to the seller for all benefits which he has derived from the goods or part of them:

    (a) If he must make restitution of the goods or part of them; or

(b) If it is impossible for him to make restitution of all or part of the goods or to make restitution of all or part of the goods substantially in the condition in which he received them, but he has nevertheless declared the contract avoided or required the seller to deliver substitute goods.

Section VI.   Preservation of the goods

Article 85

If the buyer is in delay in taking delivery of the goods or, where payment of the price and delivery of the goods are to be made concurrently, if he fails to pay the price, and the seller is either in possession of the goods or otherwise able to control their disposition, the seller must take such steps as are reasonable in the circumstances to preserve them. He is entitled to retain them until he has been reimbursed his reasonable expenses by the buyer.

Article 86

(1) If the buyer has received the goods and intends to exercise any right under the contract or this Convention to reject them, he must take such steps to preserve them as are reasonable in the circumstances.   He is entitled to retain them until he has been reimbursed his reasonable expenses by the seller.

(2) If goods dispatched to the buyer have been placed at his disposal at their destination and he exercises the right to reject them, he must take possession of them on behalf of the seller, provided that this can be done without payment of the price and without unreasonable inconvenience or unreasonable expense.   This provision does not apply if the seller or a person authorized to take charge of the goods on his behalf is present at the destination.   If the buyer takes possession of the goods under this paragraph, his rights and obligations are governed by the preceding paragraph.

Article 87

A party who is bound to take steps to preserve the goods may deposit them in a warehouse of a third person at the expense of the other party provided that the expense incurred is not unreasonable.

Article 88

(1) A party who is bound to preserve the goods in accordance with article 85 or 86 may sell them by any appropriate means if there has been an unreasonable delay by the other party in taking possession of the goods or in taking them back or in paying the price or the cost of preservation, provided that reasonable notice of the intention to sell has been given to the other party.

(2) If the goods are subject to rapid deterioration or their preservation would involve unreasonable expense, a party who is bound to preserve the goods in accordance with article 85 or 86 must take reasonable measures to sell them. To the extent possible he must give notice to the other party of this intention to sell.

(3) A party selling the goods has the right to retain out of the proceeds of sale an amount equal to the reasonable expenses of preserving the goods and of selling them. He must account to the other party for the balance.

UNIDROIT PRINCIPLES OF INTERNATIONAL COMMERCIAL CONTRACTS

COMPILERS' NOTE[1]

In 1994, there appeared an important body of rules for international contracts, the UNIDROIT Principles of International Commercial Contracts.[2] Like the Restatements, the Principles are not designed for legislative enactment. What is the source of these Principles? "For the most part," their Introduction explains, they "reflect concepts to be found in many, if not all, legal systems," though "they also embody what are perceived to be the best solutions, even if still not yet generally adopted." These concepts are drawn from a variety of sources such as the United Nations Convention on Contracts for the International Sale of Goods (CISG), generally recognized principles of civil law systems, and generally recognized principles of common law systems—including the Uniform Commercial Code and the Restatement (Second) of Contracts.

Since the Principles have not been enacted by a legislature, parties that want them to apply should incorporate them, either by name or generally. According to their Preamble, they "set forth general rules for international commercial contracts" to be applied "when the parties have agreed that their contract be governed by [them or by] 'general principles of law,' the 'lex mercatoria' or the like." It is likely that their impact will be largely in international arbitration, and their Preamble suggests that arbitrators apply them if "it proves impossible to establish the relevant rule of the applicable law." This might be the case if it is uncertain what law is applicable or if, though this is certain, that law lacks a clear rule. Because CISG covers international sales of goods, it is likely that the Principles will be significant in disputes arising under other types of contracts, notably contracts for services.

The Principles are the product of the same organization that began the work on the unification of the law of international sales, the International Institute for the Unification of Private Law (UNIDROIT) in Rome. Founded in 1926 under the auspices of the League of Nations,

---

1. Copyright by E. Farnsworth. This Note is adapted from Farnsworth on Contracts § 1.8a (2d ed. 1998) and is used with permission.

2. For discussion by the chair of the working group that drafted the Principles, see M. Bonell, An International Restatement of Contract Law: The UNIDROIT Principles of International Commercial Contracts (2d ed.1997) (includes bibliography and the text in eight languages). See generally Perillo, UNIDROIT Principles of International Commercial Contracts: The Black Letter Text and a Review, 63 Fordham L.Rev. 281 (1994); Symposium, 69 Tul. L.Rev. 1121 (1995); Symposium, 3 Tul. J.Intl. & Comp.L. 45 (1995); Symposium, 40 Am.J.Comp.L. 541 (1992).

it has continued as an independent governmental organization of which the United States is a member. The idea of drafting the Principles dates back to 1971, when the topic was put on the Institute's work program, but it was not until 1980 that the Institute set up a working group, which the United States joined toward the end of that decade. After more than a decade of semiannual meetings of the working group, the Institute's Governing Council approved publication of the Principles in 1994. Like the Restatement and the Uniform Commercial Code, they are accompanied by comments, illustrations, and section captions. Their initial success was such that an expanded set of Principles is now in preparation. A similar effort, under different auspices, has prepared a set of Principles of European Contract Law.[3]

The Principles contain some hundred and twenty articles and deal with such matters as contract formation, performance, excuse from performance, and remedies. As to many of these matters they track the provisions of CISG. On some matters, however, the Principles break fresh ground. These include precontractual liability, hardship as an excuse for nonperformance, specific performance, and stipulated damages.

The Principles also break fresh ground by stating a number of general principles. One is freedom of contract: "parties are free to enter into a contract and to determine its contents"[4] and "may exclude the application of these Principles ... or vary [their] effect."[5] A second is *pacta sunt servanda* (agreements are to be observed): if "performance becomes more onerous for one of the parties, that party is nevertheless bound to perform its obligations."[6] A third is fairness: a party may avoid a contract or term "if, at the time of the conclusion of the contract, the contract or term unjustifiably gave the other party an excessive advantage,"[7] and a term "contained in standard terms" that "is of such a character that the other party could not reasonably have expected it" is not effective unless expressly accepted by that party.[8] A fourth is good faith and fair dealing: a "party must act in accordance with good faith and fair dealing in international trade."[9]

The Principles raise troublesome questions concerning mandatory rules—rules that the parties are not free to change by agreement. Given that the Principles are generally applicable only as a result of agreement of the parties, one might make two assumptions as to mandatory rules. The first is that the parties would be completely free to exclude or modify the Principles, an assumption that seems to be confirmed by the

---

3. Principles of European Contract Law (Parts I & II) (2000) (includes comments, illustrations, and citations to largely European national sources).

4. Art. 1.1 ("Freedom of contract").

5. Art. 1.5 ("Exclusion or modification by the parties").

6. Art. 6.2.1 ("Contract to be observed").

7. Art. 3.10 ("Gross disparity").

8. Art. 2.20 ("Surprising terms").

9. Art. 1.7 ("Good faith and fair dealing").

principle of freedom of contract mentioned above. The second is that the parties could not themselves exclude or modify mandatory rules of the applicable law, an assumption that seems to be confirmed by a provision that the Principles do not "restrict the application of mandatory rules . . . which are applicable in accordance with the relevant rules of private international law."[10]

Perhaps surprisingly, the Principles qualify both assumptions. As to the first assumption, despite the general principle of freedom of contract, the Principles subject their declaration that they may be excluded or varied by the parties to an exception where "otherwise provided in the Principles."[11] These exceptions include the rules on good faith and fair dealing[12] and on gross disparity.[13] It is, to be sure, unlikely that parties would include in their contracts explicit provisions derogating from either of these rules, but if they were to do so it might be difficult explain why such provisions should not be given effect. As to the second assumption, despite the statement that the Principles cannot affect mandatory rules, the Principles seem to contemplate exceptions as to the requirement of a writing, the requirement for modification of an agreement, the availability of specific performance, and the enforceability of a provision for stipulated damages. As to all of these, the Principles state rules that change common law rules that the parties cannot change by agreement—common law mandatory rules.

At its 83rd session in 2004 the Governing Council of UNIDROIT adopted the new edition of the UNIDROIT Principles.* As compared to the 1994 edition, the new edition contains 5 additional chapters as well as an expanded Preamble and new provisions on Inconsistent Behaviour and on Release by Agreement. In addition, wherever appropriate the 1994 edition of the Principles has been adapted to meet the needs of electronic contracting.

The UNIDROIT Principles 2004 consist of the Preamble (1994 version, with the addition of paragraphs 4 and 6 as well as the footnote) and 185 articles divided into ten chapters, namely Chapter 1: "General Provisions" (1994 version, with the addition of Arts. 1.8 and 1.12); Chapter 2, Section 1: "Formation" (1994 version) and Section 2: "Authority of Agents" (new); Chapter 3: "Validity" (1994 version); Chapter 4: "Interpretation" (1994 version); Chapter 5, Section 1: "Content" (1994 version, with the addition of Art. 5.1.9) and Section 2: "Third

10. Art. 1.4 ("Mandatory rules").

11. Art. 1.5.

12. Art. 1.7.

13. Art. 3.10

* This material is reprinted from The International Institute for the Unification of Private Law, UNIDROIT PRINCIPLES OF INTERNATIONAL COMMERCIAL CONTRACTS, available at http://www.unidroit.org/english/principles/contracts/main.htm.

Party Rights" (new); Chapter 6, Section 1: "Performance in General" (1994 version) and Section 2: "Hardship" (1994 version); Chapter 7, Section 1: "Non-performance in General" (1994 version), Section 2: "Right to Performance" (1994 version), Section 3: "Termination" (1994 version) and Section 4: "Damages" (1994 version); Chapter 8: "Set-off" (new); Chapter 9, Section 1: "Assignment of Rights" (new), Section 2: "Transfer of Obligations" (new) and Section 3: "Assignment of Contracts" (new); Chapter 10: "Limitation Periods" (new).

UNIDROIT PRINCIPLES OF INTERNATIONAL COMMERCIAL CONTRACTS 2004*

Table of Contents

PREAMBLE

(Purpose of the Principles)

* For a collection of international case law and bibliography on the UNIDROIT Principles of International Commercial Contracts see http://www.unilex.info.

Section 2.   Third Party Rights

CHAPTER 6. PERFORMANCE

Section 1.   Performance in General

Section 2.   Hardship

CHAPTER 7. NON–PERFORMANCE

Section 1.   Non-performance in General

Section 2. Right to Performance

Section 3. Termination

Section 4. Damages

CHAPTER 8. SET–OFF

CHAPTER 9. ASSIGNMENT OF RIGHTS, TRANSFER OF OBLIGATIONS, ASSIGNMENT OF CONTRACTS

Section 1. Assignment of Rights

PREAMBLE

(Purpose of the Principles)

These Principles set forth general rules for international commercial contracts.

They shall be applied when the parties have agreed that their contract be governed by them.(*)

They may be applied when the parties have agreed that their contract be governed by general principles of law, the *lex mercatoria* or the like.

They may be applied when the parties have not chosen any law to govern their contract.

They may be used to interpret or supplement international uniform law instruments.

They may be used to interpret or supplement domestic law.

They may serve as a model for national and international legislators.

Chapter 1—General Provisions

Article 1.1

(Freedom of contract)

The parties are free to enter into a contract and to determine its content.

Article 1.2

(No form required)

Nothing in these Principles requires a contract, statement or any other act to be made in or evidenced by a particular form. It may be proved by any means, including witnesses.

Article 1.3

(Binding character of contract)

A contract validly entered into is binding upon the parties. It can only be modified or terminated in accordance with its terms or by agreement or as otherwise provided in these Principles.

Article 1.4

(Mandatory rules)

Nothing in these Principles shall restrict the application of mandatory rules, whether of national, international or supranational origin, which are applicable in accordance with the relevant rules of private international law.

Article 1.5

(Exclusion or modification by the parties)

The parties may exclude the application of these Principles or derogate from or vary the effect of any of their provisions, except as otherwise provided in the Principles.

Article 1.6

(Interpretation and supplementation of the Principles)

(1) In the interpretation of these Principles, regard is to be had to their international character and to their purposes including the need to promote uniformity in their application.

(2) Issues within the scope of these Principles but not expressly settled by them are as far as possible to be settled in accordance with their underlying general principles.

Article 1.7

(Good faith and fair dealing)

(1) Each party must act in accordance with good faith and fair dealing in international trade.

(2) The parties may not exclude or limit this duty.

Official Comment

1. "Good faith and fair dealing" as a fundamental idea underlying the Principles

There are a number of provisions throughout the different chapters of the Principles which constitute a direct or indirect application of the principle of good faith and fair dealing. See above all Art. 1.8, but see also for instance, Arts. 1.9(2); 2.1.4(2)(b), 2.1.15, 2.1.16, 2.1.18, and 2.1.20; 2.2.4(2), 2.2.5(2), 2.2.7 and 2.2.10; 3.5, 3.8 and 3.10; 4.1(2), 4.2(2), 4.6 and 4.8; 5.1.2 and 5.1.3; 5.2.5; 6.1.3, 6.1.5, 6.1.16(2) and 6.1.17(1); 6.2.3(3)(4); 7.1.2, 7.1.6 and 7.1.7; 7.2.2(b)(c); 7.4.8 and 7.4.13; 9.1.3, 9.1.4 and 9.1.10(1). This means that good faith and fair dealing may be considered to be one of the fundamental ideas underlying the Principles. By stating in general terms that each party must act in accordance with good faith and fair dealing, para. (1) of this article makes it clear that even in the absence of special provisions in the Principles the parties' behaviour throughout the life of the contract, including the negotiation process, must conform to good faith and fair dealing.

Illustrations

1. A grants B forty-eight hours as the time within which B may accept its offer. When B, shortly before the expiry of the deadline, decides to accept, it is unable to do so: it is the weekend, the fax at A's office is disconnected and there is no telephone answering machine which can take the message. When on the following Monday A refuses B's acceptance A acts contrary to good faith since when it fixed the time-limit for acceptance it was for A to ensure that messages could be received at its office throughout the forty-eight hour period.

2. A contract for the supply and installation of a special production line contains a provision according to which A, the seller, is obliged to communicate to B, the purchaser, any improvements made by A to the technology of that line. After a year B learns of an important improvement of which it had not been informed. A is not excused by the fact that the production of that particular type of production line is no longer its responsibility but that of C, a wholly-owned affiliated company of A. It would be against good faith for A to invoke the separate entity of C, which was specifically set up to take over this production in order to avoid A's contractual obligations vis-à-vis B.

3. A, an agent, undertakes on behalf of B, the principal, to promote the sale of B's goods in a given area. Under the contract A's right to compensation arises only after B's approval of the contracts pro-

cured by A. While B is free to decide whether or not to approve the contracts procured by A, a systematic and unjustified refusal to approve any contract procured by A would be against good faith.

4. Under a line of credit agreement between A, a bank, and B, a customer, A suddenly and inexplicably refuses to make further advances to B whose business suffers heavy losses as a consequence. Notwithstanding the fact that the agreement contains a term permitting A to accelerate payment "at will", A's demand for payment in full without prior warning and with no justification would be against good faith.

2. *Abuse of rights*

A typical example of behaviour contrary to the principle of good faith and fair dealing is what in some legal systems is known as "abuse of rights". It is characterised by a party's malicious behaviour which occurs for instance when a party exercises a right merely to damage the other party or for a purpose other than the one for which it had been granted, or when the exercise of a right is disproportionate to the originally intended result.

Illustrations

5. A rents premises from B for the purpose of setting up a retail business. The rental contract is for five years, but when three years later A realises that business in the area is very poor, it decides to close the business and informs B that is no longer interested in renting the premises. A's breach of contract would normally lead to B's having the choice of either terminating the contract and claiming damages or requesting specific performance. However, under the circumstances B would be abusing its right if it required A to pay the rent for the remaining two years of the contract instead of terminating the contract and claiming damages from A for the rent it has lost for the length of time necessary to find a new tenant.

6. A rents premises from B for the purpose of opening a restaurant. During the summer months A sets up a few tables out of doors, but still on the owner's property. On account of the noise caused by the restaurant's customers late at night, B has increasing difficulties finding tenants for apartments in the same building. B would be abusing its right if, instead of requesting A to desist from serving out of doors late at night, it required A not to serve out of doors at all.

3. *"Good faith and fair dealing in international trade"*

The reference to "good faith and fair dealing in international trade" first makes it clear that in the context of the Principles the two concepts are not to be applied according to the standards ordinarily adopted within the different national legal systems. In other words, such domestic standards may be taken into account only to the extent that they are shown to be generally accepted among the various legal systems. A further implication of the formula used is that good faith and fair dealing must be construed in the light of the special conditions of international trade. Standards of business practice may indeed vary considerably from one trade sector to another, and even within a given trade sector they may be more or less stringent depending on the socio-economic environment in which the enterprises operate, their size and technical skill, etc.

It should be noted that the provisions of the Principles and/or the comments thereto at times refer only to "good faith" or to "good faith and fair dealing". Such references should always be understood as a reference to "good faith and fair dealing in international trade" as specified in this article.

Illustrations

7. Under a contract for the sale of high-technology equipment the purchaser loses the right to rely on any defect in the goods if it does not give notice to the seller specifying the nature of the defect without undue delay after it has discovered or ought to have discovered the defect. A, a buyer operating in a country where such equipment is commonly used, discovers a defect in the equipment after having put it into operation, but in its notice to B, the seller of the equipment, A gives misleading indications as to the nature of the defect. A loses its right to rely on the defect since a more careful examination of the defect would have permitted it to give B the necessary specifications.

8. The facts are the same as in Illustration 7, the difference being that A operates in a country where this type of equipment is so far almost unknown. A does not lose its right to rely on the defect because B, being aware of A's lack of technical knowledge, could not reasonably have expected A properly to identify the nature of the defect.

4. The mandatory nature of the principle of good faith and fair dealing

The parties' duty to act in accordance with good faith and fair dealing is of such a fundamental nature that the parties may not contractually exclude or limit it (para. (2)). As to specific applications of the general prohibition to exclude or limit the principle of good faith and fair dealing between the parties, see Arts. 3.19, 7.1.6 and 7.4.13.

On the other hand, nothing prevents parties from providing in their contract for a duty to observe more stringent standards of behaviour.

Article 1.8

(Inconsistent Behaviour)

A party cannot act inconsistently with an understanding it has caused the other party to have and upon which that other party reasonably has acted in reliance to its detriment.

Article 1.9

(Usages and practices)

(1) The parties are bound by any usage to which they have agreed and by any practices which they have established between themselves.

(2) The parties are bound by a usage that is widely known to and regularly observed in international trade by parties in the particular trade concerned except where the application of such a usage would be unreasonable.

Article 1.10

(Notice)

(1) Where notice is required it may be given by any means appropriate to the circumstances.

(2) A notice is effective when it reaches the person to whom it is given.

(3) For the purpose of paragraph (2) a notice "reaches" a person when given to that person orally or delivered at that person's place of business or mailing address.

(4) For the purpose of this article "notice" includes a declaration, demand, request or any other communication of intention.

Article 1.11

(Definitions)

In these Principles

— "court" includes an arbitral tribunal;

— where a party has more than one place of business the relevant "place of business" is that which has the closest relationship to the contract and its performance, having regard to the circumstances known to or contemplated by the parties at any time before or at the conclusion of the contract;

— "obligor" refers to the party who is to perform an obligation and "obligee" refers to the party who is entitled to performance of that obligation.

— "writing" means any mode of communication that preserves a record of the information contained therein and is capable of being reproduced in tangible form.

Article 1.12

(Computation of time set by parties)

(1) Official holidays or non-business days occurring during a period set by parties for an act to be performed are included in calculating the period.

(2) However, if the last day of the period is an official holiday or a non-business day at the place of business of the party to perform the act, the period is extended until the first business day which follows, unless the circumstances indicate otherwise.

(3) The relevant time zone is that of the place of business of the party setting the time, unless the circumstances indicate otherwise.

CHAPTER 2—FORMATION AND AUTHORITY OF AGENTS
SECTION 1: FORMATION
Article 2.1.1

(Manner of formation)

A contract may be concluded either by the acceptance of an offer or by conduct of the parties that is sufficient to show agreement.

Article 2.1.2

(Definition of offer)

A proposal for concluding a contract constitutes an offer if it is sufficiently definite and indicates the intention of the offeror to be bound in case of acceptance.

Article 2.1.3

(Withdrawal of offer)

(1) An offer becomes effective when it reaches the offeree.

(2) An offer, even if it is irrevocable, may be withdrawn if the withdrawal reaches the offeree before or at the same time as the offer.

Article 2.1.4

(Revocation of offer)

(1) Until a contract is concluded an offer may be revoked if the revocation reaches the offeree before it has dispatched an acceptance.

(2) However, an offer cannot be revoked

    (a) if it indicates, whether by stating a fixed time for acceptance or otherwise, that it is irrevocable; or

    (b) if it was reasonable for the offeree to rely on the offer as being irrevocable and the offeree has acted in reliance on the offer.

Article 2.1.5

(Rejection of offer)

An offer is terminated when a rejection reaches the offeror.

Article 2.1.6

(Mode of acceptance)

(1) A statement made by or other conduct of the offeree indicating assent to an offer is an acceptance. Silence or inactivity does not in itself amount to acceptance.

(2) An acceptance of an offer becomes effective when the indication of assent reaches the offeror.

(3) However, if, by virtue of the offer or as a result of practices which the parties have established between themselves or of usage, the offeree may indicate assent by performing an act without notice to the offeror, the acceptance is effective when the act is performed.

Article 2.1.7

(Time of acceptance)

An offer must be accepted within the time the offeror has fixed or, if no time is fixed, within a reasonable time having regard to the circumstances, including the rapidity of the means of communication employed by the offeror. An oral offer must be accepted immediately unless the circumstances indicate otherwise.

Article 2.1.8

(Acceptance within a fixed period of time)

A period of acceptance fixed by the offeror begins to run from the time that the offer is dispatched. A time indicated in the offer is deemed to be the time of dispatch unless the circumstances indicate otherwise.

Article 2.1.9

(Late acceptance. Delay in transmission)

(1) A late acceptance is nevertheless effective as an acceptance if without undue delay the offeror so informs the offeree or gives notice to that effect.

(2) If a communication containing a late acceptance shows that it has been sent in such circumstances that if its transmission had been normal it would have reached the offeror in due time, the late acceptance is effective as an acceptance unless, without undue delay, the offeror informs the offeree that it considers the offer as having lapsed.

Article 2.1.10

(Withdrawal of acceptance)

An acceptance may be withdrawn if the withdrawal reaches the offeror before or at the same time as the acceptance would have become effective.

Article 2.1.11

(Modified acceptance)

(1) A reply to an offer which purports to be an acceptance but contains additions, limitations or other modifications is a rejection of the offer and constitutes a counter-offer.

(2) However, a reply to an offer which purports to be an acceptance but contains additional or different terms which do not materially alter the terms of the offer constitutes an acceptance, unless the offeror, without undue delay, objects to the discrepancy. If the offeror does not object, the terms of the contract are the terms of the offer with the modifications contained in the acceptance.

Article 2.1.12

(Writings in confirmation)

If a writing which is sent within a reasonable time after the conclusion of the contract and which purports to be a confirmation of the contract contains additional or different terms, such terms become part of the contract, unless they materially alter the contract or the recipient, without undue delay, objects to the discrepancy.

Article 2.1.13

(Conclusion of contract dependent on agreement on specific matters or in a particular form)

Where in the course of negotiations one of the parties insists that the contract is not concluded until there is agreement on specific matters or in a particular form, no contract is concluded before agreement is reached on those matters or in that form.

Article 2.1.14

(Contract with terms deliberately left open)

(1) If the parties intend to conclude a contract, the fact that they intentionally leave a term to be agreed upon in further negotiations or to be determined by a third person does not prevent a contract from coming into existence.

(2) The existence of the contract is not affected by the fact that subsequently

 (a) the parties reach no agreement on the term; or

 (b) the third person does not determine the term,

provided that there is an alternative means of rendering the term definite that is reasonable in the circumstances, having regard to the intention of the parties.

Article 2.1.15

(Negotiations in bad faith)

(1) A party is free to negotiate and is not liable for failure to reach an agreement.

(2) However, a party who negotiates or breaks off negotiations in bad faith is liable for the losses caused to the other party.

(3) It is bad faith, in particular, for a party to enter into or continue negotiations when intending not to reach an agreement with the other party.

Official Comment

1. Freedom of negotiation

As a rule, parties are not only free to decide when and with whom to enter

379

into negotiations with a view to concluding a contract, but also if, how and for how long to proceed with their efforts to reach an agreement. This follows from the basic principle of freedom of contract enunciated in Art. 1.1, and is essential in order to guarantee healthy competition among business people engaged in international trade.

2. *Liability for negotiating in bad faith*

A party's right freely to enter into negotiations and to decide on the terms to be negotiated is, however, not unlimited, and must not conflict with the principle of good faith and fair dealing laid down in Art. 1.7. One particular instance of negotiating in bad faith which is expressly indicated in para. (3) of this article is that where a party enters into negotiations or continues to negotiate without any intention of concluding an agreement with the other party. Other instances are where one party has deliberately or by negligence misled the other party as to the nature or terms of the proposed contract, either by actually misrepresenting facts, or by not disclosing facts which, given the nature of the parties and/or the contract, should have been disclosed. As to the duty of confidentiality, see Art. 2.1.16.

A party's liability for negotiating in bad faith is limited to the losses caused to the other party (para. (2)). In other words, the aggrieved party may recover the expenses incurred in the negotiations and may also be compensated for the lost opportunity to conclude another contract with a third person (so-called reliance or negative interest), but may generally not recover the profit which would have resulted had the original contract been concluded (so-called expectation or positive interest).

Only if the parties have expressly agreed on a duty to negotiate in good faith, will all the remedies for breach of contract be available to them, including the remedy of the right of performance.

Illustrations

1. A learns of B's intention to sell its restaurant. A, who has no intention whatsoever of buying the restaurant, nevertheless enters into lengthy negotiations with B for the sole purpose of preventing B from selling the restaurant to C, a competitor of A's. A, who breaks off negotiations when C has bought another restaurant, is liable to B, who ultimately succeeds in selling the restaurant at a lower price than that offered by C, for the difference in price.

2. A, who is negotiating with B for the promotion of the purchase of military equipment by the armed forces of B's country, learns that B will not receive the necessary export licence from its own governmental authorities, a prerequisite for permission to pay B's fees. A does not reveal this fact to B and finally concludes the contract, which, however, cannot be enforced by reason of the missing licences. A is liable to B for the costs incurred after A had learned of the impossibility of obtaining the required licences.

3. A enters into lengthy negotiations for a bank loan from B's branch office. At the last minute the branch office discloses that it had no authority to sign and that its head office has decided not to approve the draft agreement. A, who could in the meantime have obtained the loan from another bank, is entitled to recover the expenses entailed by the negotiations and the profits it would have made during the delay before ob-

taining the loan from the other bank.

3. *Liability for breaking off negotiations in bad faith*

The right to break off negotiations also is subject to the principle of good faith and fair dealing. Once an offer has been made, it may be revoked only within the limits provided for in Art. 2.1.4. Yet even before this stage is reached, or in a negotiation process with no ascertainable sequence of offer and acceptance, a party may no longer be free to break off negotiations abruptly and without justification. When such a point of no return is reached depends of course on the circumstances of the case, in particular the extent to which the other party, as a result of the conduct of the first party, had reason to rely on the positive outcome of the negotiations, and on the number of issues relating to the future contract on which the parties have already reached agreement.

Illustration

4. A assures B of the grant of a franchise if B takes steps to gain experience and is prepared to invest US$150,000. During the next two years B makes extensive preparations with a view to concluding the contract, always with A's assurance that B will be granted the franchise. When all is ready for the signing of the agreement, A informs B that the latter must invest a substantially higher sum. B, who refuses, is entitled to recover from A the expenses incurred with a view to the conclusion of the contract.

Article 2.1.16

(Duty of confidentiality)

Where information is given as confidential by one party in the course of negotiations, the other party is under a duty not to disclose that information or to use it improperly for its own purposes, whether or not a contract is subsequently concluded. Where appropriate, the remedy for breach of that duty may include compensation based on the benefit received by the other party.

Article 2.1.17

(Merger clauses)

A contract in writing which contains a clause indicating that the writing completely embodies the terms on which the parties have agreed cannot be contradicted or supplemented by evidence of prior statements or agreements. However, such statements or agreements may be used to interpret the writing.

Article 2.1.18

(Modification in a particular form)

A contract in writing which contains a clause requiring any modification or termination by agreement to be in a particular form may not be otherwise modified or terminated. However, a party may be precluded by its conduct from asserting such a clause to the extent that the other party has reasonably acted in reliance on that conduct.

Article 2.1.19

(Contracting under standard terms)

(1) Where one party or both parties use standard terms in concluding a contract, the general rules on formation apply, subject to Articles 2.1.20–2.1.22.

(2) Standard terms are provisions which are prepared in advance for general and repeated use by one party and which are actually used without negotiation with the other party.

Article 2.1.20

(Surprising terms)

(1) No term contained in standard terms which is of such a character that the other party could not reasonably have expected it, is effective unless it has been expressly accepted by that party.

(2) In determining whether a term is of such a character regard shall be had to its content, language and presentation.

Article 2.1.21

(Conflict between standard terms and non-standard terms)

In case of conflict between a standard term and a term which is not a standard term the latter prevails.

Article 2.1.22

(Battle of forms)

Where both parties use standard terms and reach agreement except on those terms, a contract is concluded on the basis of the agreed terms and of any standard terms which are common in substance unless one party clearly indicates in advance, or later and without undue delay informs the other party, that it does not intend to be bound by such a contract.

SECTION 2: AUTHORITY OF AGENTS

Article 2.2.1

(Scope of the Section)

(1) This Section governs the authority of a person ("the agent"), to affect the legal relations of another person ("the principal"), by or with respect to a contract with a third party, whether the agent acts in its own name or in that of the principal.

(2) It governs only the relations between the principal or the agent on the one hand, and the third party on the other.

(3) It does not govern an agent's authority conferred by law or the authority of an agent appointed by a public or judicial authority.

Article 2.2.2

(Establishment and scope of the authority of the agent)

(1) The principal's grant of authority to an agent may be express or implied.

(2) The agent has authority to perform all acts necessary in the circumstances to achieve the purposes for which the authority was granted.

Article 2.2.3

(Agency disclosed)

(1) Where an agent acts within the scope of its authority and the third party knew or ought to have known that the agent was acting as an agent, the acts of the agent shall directly affect the legal relations between the principal and the third party and no legal relation is created between the agent and the third party.

(2) However, the acts of the agent shall affect only the relations between the agent and the third party, where the agent with the consent of the principal undertakes to become the party to the contract.

Article 2.2.4

(Agency undisclosed)

(1) Where an agent acts within the scope of its authority and the third party neither knew nor ought to have known that the agent was acting as an agent, the acts of the agent shall affect only the relations between the agent and the third party.

(2) However, where such an agent, when contracting with the third party on behalf of a business, represents itself to be the owner of that business, the third party, upon discovery of the real owner of the business, may exercise also against the latter the rights it has against the agent.

Article 2.2.5

(Agent acting without or exceeding its authority)

(1) Where an agent acts without authority or exceeds its authority, its acts do not affect the legal relations between the principal and the third party.

(2) However, where the principal causes the third party reasonably to believe that the agent has authority to act on behalf of the principal and that the agent is acting within the scope of that authority, the principal may not invoke against the third party the lack of authority of the agent.

Article 2.2.6

(Liability of agent acting without or exceeding its authority)

(1) An agent that acts without authority or exceeds its authority is, failing ratification by the principal, liable for damages that will place the third party in the same position as if the agent had acted with authority and not exceeded its authority.

(2) However, the agent is not liable if the third party knew or ought to have known that the agent had no authority or was exceeding its authority.

Article 2.2.7

(Conflict of interests)

(1) If a contract concluded by an agent involves the agent in a conflict of interests with the principal of which the third party knew or ought to have known, the principal may avoid the contract. The right to avoid is subject to Articles 3.12 and 3.14 to 3.17.

(2) However, the principal may not avoid the contract

(a) if the principal had consented to, or knew or ought to have known of, the agent's involvement in the conflict of interests; or

(b) if the agent had disclosed the conflict of interests to the principal and the latter had not objected within a reasonable time.

Article 2.2.8

(Sub-agency)

An agent has implied authority to appoint a sub-agent to perform acts which it is not reasonable to expect the agent to perform itself. The rules of this Section apply to the sub-agency.

Article 2.2.9

(Ratification)

(1) An act by an agent that acts without authority or exceeds its authority may be ratified by the principal. On ratification the act produces the same effects as if it had initially been carried out with authority.

(2) The third party may by notice to the principal specify a reasonable period of time for ratification. If the principal does not ratify within that period of time it can no longer do so.

(3) If, at the time of the agent's act, the third party neither knew nor ought to have known of the lack of authority, it may, at any time

before ratification, by notice to the principal indicate its refusal to become bound by a ratification.

Article 2.2.10

(Termination of authority)

(1) Termination of authority is not effective in relation to the third party unless the third party knew or ought to have known of it.

(2) Notwithstanding the termination of its authority, an agent remains authorised to perform the acts that are necessary to prevent harm to the principal's interests.

CHAPTER 3—VALIDITY

Article 3.1

(Matters not covered)

These Principles do not deal with invalidity arising from

(a) lack of capacity;

(b) immorality or illegality.

Article 3.2

(Validity of mere agreement)

A contract is concluded, modified or terminated by the mere agreement of the parties, without any further requirement.

Article 3.3

(Initial impossibility)

(1) The mere fact that at the time of the conclusion of the contract the performance of the obligation assumed was impossible does not affect the validity of the contract.

(2) The mere fact that at the time of the conclusion of the contract a party was not entitled to dispose of the assets to which the contract relates does not affect the validity of the contract.

Article 3.4

(Definition of mistake)

Mistake is an erroneous assumption relating to facts or to law existing when the contract was concluded.

Article 3.5

(Relevant mistake)

(1) A party may only avoid the contract for mistake if, when the contract was concluded, the mistake was of such importance that a reasonable person in the same situation as the party in error would only

have concluded the contract on materially different terms or would not have concluded it at all if the true state of affairs had been known, and

(a) the other party made the same mistake, or caused the mistake, or knew or ought to have known of the mistake and it was contrary to reasonable commercial standards of fair dealing to leave the mistaken party in error; or

(b) the other party had not at the time of avoidance reasonably acted in reliance on the contract.

(2) However, a party may not avoid the contract if

(a) it was grossly negligent in committing the mistake; or

(b) the mistake relates to a matter in regard to which the risk of mistake was assumed or, having regard to the circumstances, should be borne by the mistaken party.

Article 3.6

(Error in expression or transmission)

An error occurring in the expression or transmission of a declaration is considered to be a mistake of the person from whom the declaration emanated.

Article 3.7

(Remedies for non-performance)

A party is not entitled to avoid the contract on the ground of mistake if the circumstances on which that party relies afford, or could have afforded, a remedy for non-performance.

Article 3.8

(Fraud)

A party may avoid the contract when it has been led to conclude the contract by the other party's fraudulent representation, including language or practices, or fraudulent non-disclosure of circumstances which, according to reasonable commercial standards of fair dealing, the latter party should have disclosed.

Article 3.9

(Threat)

A party may avoid the contract when it has been led to conclude the contract by the other party's unjustified threat which, having regard to the circumstances, is so imminent and serious as to leave the first party no reasonable alternative. In particular, a threat is unjustified if the act or omission with which a party has been threatened is wrongful in itself, or it is wrongful to use it as a means to obtain the conclusion of the contract.

Article 3.10

(Gross disparity)

(1) A party may avoid the contract or an individual term of it if, at the time of the conclusion of the contract, the contract or term unjustifiably gave the other party an excessive advantage. Regard is to be had, among other factors, to

> (a) the fact that the other party has taken unfair advantage of the first party's dependence, economic distress or urgent needs, or of its improvidence, ignorance, inexperience or lack of bargaining skill, and

> (b) the nature and purpose of the contract.

(2) Upon the request of the party entitled to avoidance, a court may adapt the contract or term in order to make it accord with reasonable commercial standards of fair dealing.

(3) A court may also adapt the contract or term upon the request of the party receiving notice of avoidance, provided that that party informs the other party of its request promptly after receiving such notice and before the other party has reasonably acted in reliance on it. The provisions of Article 3.13(2) apply accordingly.

Article 3.11

(Third persons)

(1) Where fraud, threat, gross disparity or a party's mistake is imputable to, or is known or ought to be known by, a third person for whose acts the other party is responsible, the contract may be avoided under the same conditions as if the behaviour or knowledge had been that of the party itself.

(2) Where fraud, threat or gross disparity is imputable to a third person for whose acts the other party is not responsible, the contract may be avoided if that party knew or ought to have known of the fraud, threat or disparity, or has not at the time of avoidance reasonably acted in reliance on the contract.

Article 3.12

(Confirmation)

If the party entitled to avoid the contract expressly or impliedly confirms the contract after the period of time for giving notice of avoidance has begun to run, avoidance of the contract is excluded.

Article 3.13

(Loss of right to avoid)

(1) If a party is entitled to avoid the contract for mistake but the other party declares itself willing to perform or performs the contract as

it was understood by the party entitled to avoidance, the contract is considered to have been concluded as the latter party understood it. The other party must make such a declaration or render such performance promptly after having been informed of the manner in which the party entitled to avoidance had understood the contract and before that party has reasonably acted in reliance on a notice of avoidance.

(2) After such a declaration or performance the right to avoidance is lost and any earlier notice of avoidance is ineffective.

Article 3.14

(Notice of avoidance)

The right of a party to avoid the contract is exercised by notice to the other party.

Article 3.15

(Time limits)

(1) Notice of avoidance shall be given within a reasonable time, having regard to the circumstances, after the avoiding party knew or could not have been unaware of the relevant facts or became capable of acting freely.

(2) Where an individual term of the contract may be avoided by a party under Article 3.10, the period of time for giving notice of avoidance begins to run when that term is asserted by the other party.

Article 3.16

(Partial avoidance)

Where a ground of avoidance affects only individual terms of the contract, the effect of avoidance is limited to those terms unless, having regard to the circumstances, it is unreasonable to uphold the remaining contract.

Article 3.17

(Retroactive effect of avoidance)

(1) Avoidance takes effect retroactively.

(2) On avoidance either party may claim restitution of whatever it has supplied under the contract or the part of it avoided, provided that it concurrently makes restitution of whatever it has received under the contract or the part of it avoided or, if it cannot make restitution in kind, it makes an allowance for what it has received.

Article 3.18

(Damages)

Irrespective of whether or not the contract has been avoided, the party who knew or ought to have known of the ground for avoidance is liable for damages so as to put the other party in the same position in which it would have been if it had not concluded the contract.

Article 3.19

(Mandatory character of the provisions)

The provisions of this Chapter are mandatory, except insofar as they relate to the binding force of mere agreement, initial impossibility or mistake.

Article 3.20

(Unilateral declarations)

The provisions of this Chapter apply with appropriate adaptations to any communication of intention addressed by one party to the other.

CHAPTER 4—INTERPRETATION

Article 4.1

(Intention of the parties)

(1) A contract shall be interpreted according to the common intention of the parties.

(2) If such an intention cannot be established, the contract shall be interpreted according to the meaning that reasonable persons of the same kind as the parties would give to it in the same circumstances.

Article 4.2

(Interpretation of statements and other conduct)

(1) The statements and other conduct of a party shall be interpreted according to that party's intention if the other party knew or could not have been unaware of that intention.

(2) If the preceding paragraph is not applicable, such statements and other conduct shall be interpreted according to the meaning that a reasonable person of the same kind as the other party would give to it in the same circumstances.

Article 4.3

(Relevant circumstances)

In applying Articles 4.1 and 4.2, regard shall be had to all the circumstances, including

    (a) preliminary negotiations between the parties;

    (b) practices which the parties have established between themselves;

    (c) the conduct of the parties subsequent to the conclusion of the contract;

(d) the nature and purpose of the contract;

(e) the meaning commonly given to terms and expressions in the trade concerned;

(f) usages.

Article 4.4

(Reference to contract or statement as a whole)

Terms and expressions shall be interpreted in the light of the whole contract or statement in which they appear.

Article 4.5

(All terms to be given effect)

Contract terms shall be interpreted so as to give effect to all the terms rather than to deprive some of them of effect.

Article 4.6

(Contra proferentem rule)

If contract terms supplied by one party are unclear, an interpretation against that party is preferred.

Article 4.7

(Linguistic discrepancies)

Where a contract is drawn up in two or more language versions which are equally authoritative there is, in case of discrepancy between the versions, a preference for the interpretation according to a version in which the contract was originally drawn up.

Article 4.8

(Supplying an omitted term)

(1) Where the parties to a contract have not agreed with respect to a term which is important for a determination of their rights and duties, a term which is appropriate in the circumstances shall be supplied.

(2) In determining what is an appropriate term regard shall be had, among other factors, to

(a) the intention of the parties;

(b) the nature and purpose of the contract;

(c) good faith and fair dealing;

(d) reasonableness.

CHAPTER 5—CONTENT AND THIRD PARTY RIGHTS
SECTION 1: CONTENT
Article 5.1.1
(Express and implied obligations)

The contractual obligations of the parties may be express or implied.

Article 5.1.2
(Implied obligations)

Implied obligations stem from

    (a) the nature and purpose of the contract;

    (b) practices established between the parties and usages;

    (c) good faith and fair dealing;

    (d) reasonableness.

Article 5.1.3
(Co-operation between the parties)

Each party shall cooperate with the other party when such co-operation may reasonably be expected for the performance of that party's obligations.

Article 5.1.4
(Duty to achieve a specific result. Duty of best efforts)

(1) To the extent that an obligation of a party involves a duty to achieve a specific result, that party is bound to achieve that result.

(2) To the extent that an obligation of a party involves a duty of best efforts in the performance of an activity, that party is bound to make such efforts as would be made by a reasonable person of the same kind in the same circumstances.

Article 5.1.5
(Determination of kind of duty involved)

In determining the extent to which an obligation of a party involves a duty of best efforts in the performance of an activity or a duty to achieve a specific result, regard shall be had, among other factors, to

    (a) the way in which the obligation is expressed in the contract;

    (b) the contractual price and other terms of the contract;

    (c) the degree of risk normally involved in achieving the expected result;

    (d) the ability of the other party to influence the performance of the obligation.

Article 5.1.6

(Determination of quality of performance)

Where the quality of performance is neither fixed by, nor determinable from, the contract a party is bound to render a performance of a quality that is reasonable and not less than average in the circumstances.

Article 5.1.7

(Price determination)

(1) Where a contract does not fix or make provision for determining the price, the parties are considered, in the absence of any indication to the contrary, to have made reference to the price generally charged at the time of the conclusion of the contract for such performance in comparable circumstances in the trade concerned or, if no such price is available, to a reasonable price.

(2) Where the price is to be determined by one party and that determination is manifestly unreasonable, a reasonable price shall be substituted notwithstanding any contract term to the contrary.

(3) Where the price is to be fixed by a third person, and that person cannot or will not do so, the price shall be a reasonable price.

(4) Where the price is to be fixed by reference to factors which do not exist or have ceased to exist or to be accessible, the nearest equivalent factor shall be treated as a substitute.

Article 5.1.8

(Contract for an indefinite period)

A contract for an indefinite period may be ended by either party by giving notice a reasonable time in advance.

Article 5.1.9

(Release by agreement)

(1) An obligee may release its right by agreement with the obligor.

(2) An offer to release a right gratuitously shall be deemed accepted if the obligor does not reject the offer without delay after having become aware of it.

SECTION 2: THIRD PARTY RIGHTS

Article 5.2.1

(Contracts in favour of third parties)

(1) The parties (the "promisor" and the "promisee") may confer by express or implied agreement a right on a third party (the "beneficiary").

(2) The existence and content of the beneficiary's right against the promisor are determined by the agreement of the parties and are subject to any conditions or other limitations under the agreement.

Article 5.2.2

(Third party identifiable)

The beneficiary must be identifiable with adequate certainty by the contract but need not be in existence at the time the contract is made.

Article 5.2.3

(Exclusion and limitation clauses)

The conferment of rights in the beneficiary includes the right to invoke a clause in the contract which excludes or limits the liability of the beneficiary.

Article 5.2.4

(Defences)

The promisor may assert against the beneficiary all defences which the promisor could assert against the promisee.

Article 5.2.5

(Revocation)

The parties may modify or revoke the rights conferred by the contract on the beneficiary until the beneficiary has accepted them or reasonably acted in reliance on them.

Article 5.2.6

(Renunciation)

The beneficiary may renounce a right conferred on it.

CHAPTER 6—PERFORMANCE

SECTION 1: PERFORMANCE IN GENERAL

Article 6.1.1

(Time of performance)

A party must perform its obligations:

  (a) if a time is fixed by or determinable from the contract, at that time;

  (b) if a period of time is fixed by or determinable from the contract, at any time within that period unless circumstances indicate that the other party is to choose a time;

(c) in any other case, within a reasonable time after the conclusion of the contract.

Article 6.1.2

(Performance at one time or in instalments)

In cases under Article 6.1.1(b) or (c), a party must perform its obligations at one time if that performance can be rendered at one time and the circumstances do not indicate otherwise.

Article 6.1.3

(Partial performance)

(1) The obligee may reject an offer to perform in part at the time performance is due, whether or not such offer is coupled with an assurance as to the balance of the performance, unless the obligee has no legitimate interest in so doing.

(2) Additional expenses caused to the obligee by partial performance are to be borne by the obligor without prejudice to any other remedy.

Article 6.1.4

(Order of performance)

(1) To the extent that the performances of the parties can be rendered simultaneously, the parties are bound to render them simultaneously unless the circumstances indicate otherwise.

(2) To the extent that the performance of only one party requires a period of time, that party is bound to render its performance first, unless the circumstances indicate otherwise.

Article 6.1.5

(Earlier performance)

(1) The obligee may reject an earlier performance unless it has no legitimate interest in so doing.

(2) Acceptance by a party of an earlier performance does not affect the time for the performance of its own obligations if that time has been fixed irrespective of the performance of the other party's obligations.

(3) Additional expenses caused to the obligee by earlier performance are to be borne by the obligor, without prejudice to any other remedy.

Article 6.1.6

(Place of performance)

(1) If the place of performance is neither fixed by, nor determinable from, the contract, a party is to perform:

(a) a monetary obligation, at the obligee's place of business;

(b) any other obligation, at its own place of business.

(2) A party must bear any increase in the expenses incidental to performance which is caused by a change in its place of business subsequent to the conclusion of the contract.

Article 6.1.7

(Payment by cheque or other instrument)

(1) Payment may be made in any form used in the ordinary course of business at the place for payment.

(2) However, an obligee who accepts, either by virtue of paragraph (1) or voluntarily, a cheque, any other order to pay or a promise to pay, is presumed to do so only on condition that it will be honoured.

Article 6.1.8

(Payment by funds transfer)

(1) Unless the obligee has indicated a particular account, payment may be made by a transfer to any of the financial institutions in which the obligee has made it known that it has an account.

(2) In case of payment by a transfer the obligation of the obligor is discharged when the transfer to the obligee's financial institution becomes effective.

Article 6.1.9

(Currency of payment)

(1) If a monetary obligation is expressed in a currency other than that of the place for payment, it may be paid by the obligor in the currency of the place for payment unless

    (a) that currency is not freely convertible; or

    (b) the parties have agreed that payment should be made only in the currency in which the monetary obligation is expressed.

(2) If it is impossible for the obligor to make payment in the currency in which the monetary obligation is expressed, the obligee may require payment in the currency of the place for payment, even in the case referred to in paragraph (1)(b).

(3) Payment in the currency of the place for payment is to be made according to the applicable rate of exchange prevailing there when payment is due.

(4) However, if the obligor has not paid at the time when payment is due, the obligee may require payment according to the applicable rate of exchange prevailing either when payment is due or at the time of actual payment.

Article 6.1.10

(Currency not expressed)

Where a monetary obligation is not expressed in a particular currency, payment must be made in the currency of the place where payment is to be made.

Article 6.1.11

(Costs of performance)

Each party shall bear the costs of performance of its obligations.

Article 6.1.12

(Imputation of payments)

(1) An obligor owing several monetary obligations to the same obligee may specify at the time of payment the debt to which it intends the payment to be applied. However, the payment discharges first any expenses, then interest due and finally the principal.

(2) If the obligor makes no such specification, the obligee may, within a reasonable time after payment, declare to the obligor the obligation to which it imputes the payment, provided that the obligation is due and undisputed.

(3) In the absence of imputation under paragraphs (1) or (2), payment is imputed to that obligation which satisfies one of the following criteria in the order indicated:

    (a) an obligation which is due or which is the first to fall due;

    (b) the obligation for which the obligee has least security;

    (c) the obligation which is the most burdensome for the obligor;

    (d) the obligation which has arisen first.

If none of the preceding criteria applies, payment is imputed to all the obligations proportionally.

Article 6.1.13

(Imputation of non-monetary obligations)

Article 6.1.12 applies with appropriate adaptations to the imputation of performance of non-monetary obligations.

Article 6.1.14

(Application for public permission)

Where the law of a State requires a public permission affecting the validity of the contract or its performance and neither that law nor the circumstances indicate otherwise

(a) if only one party has its place of business in that State, that party shall take the measures necessary to obtain the permission;

(b) in any other case the party whose performance requires permission shall take the necessary measures.

Article 6.1.15

(Procedure in applying for permission)

(1) The party required to take the measures necessary to obtain the permission shall do so without undue delay and shall bear any expenses incurred.

(2) That party shall whenever appropriate give the other party notice of the grant or refusal of such permission without undue delay.

Article 6.1.16

(Permission neither granted nor refused)

(1) If, notwithstanding the fact that the party responsible has taken all measures required, permission is neither granted nor refused within an agreed period or, where no period has been agreed, within a reasonable time from the conclusion of the contract, either party is entitled to terminate the contract.

(2) Where the permission affects some terms only, paragraph (1) does not apply if, having regard to the circumstances, it is reasonable to uphold the remaining contract even if the permission is refused.

Article 6.1.17

(Permission refused)

(1) The refusal of a permission affecting the validity of the contract renders the contract void. If the refusal affects the validity of some terms only, only such terms are void if, having regard to the circumstances, it is reasonable to uphold the remaining contract.

(2) Where the refusal of a permission renders the performance of the contract impossible in whole or in part, the rules on non-performance apply.

SECTION 2: HARDSHIP

Article 6.2.1

(Contract to be observed)

Where the performance of a contract becomes more onerous for one of the parties, that party is nevertheless bound to perform its obligations subject to the following provisions on hardship.

Article 6.2.2

(Definition of hardship)

There is hardship where the occurrence of events fundamentally alters the equilibrium of the contract either because the cost of a party's performance has increased or because the value of the performance a party receives has diminished, and

    (a) the events occur or become known to the disadvantaged party after the conclusion of the contract;

    (b) the events could not reasonably have been taken into account by the disadvantaged party at the time of the conclusion of the contract;

    (c) the events are beyond the control of the disadvantaged party; and

    (d) the risk of the events was not assumed by the disadvantaged party.

Official Comment

1. Hardship defined

This article defines hardship as a situation where the occurrence of events fundamentally alters the equilibrium of the contract, provided that those events meet the requirements which are laid down in sub-paras. (a) to (d).

2. Fundamental alteration of equilibrium of the contract

Since the general principle is that a change in circumstances does not affect the obligation to perform (see Art. 6.2.1), it follows that hardship may not be invoked unless the alteration of the equilibrium of the contract is fundamental. Whether an alteration is "fundamental" in a given case will of course depend upon the circumstances.

Illustration

1. In September 1989 A, a dealer in electronic goods situated in the former German Democratic Republic, purchases stocks from B, situated in country X, also a former socialist country. The goods are to be delivered by B in December 1990. In November 1990, A informs B that the goods are no longer of any use to it, claiming that after the unification of the German Democratic Republic and the Federal Republic of Germany there is no longer any market for such goods imported from country X. Unless the circumstances indicate otherwise, A is entitled to invoke hardship.

a. Increase in cost of performance

In practice a fundamental alteration in the equilibrium of the contract may manifest itself in two different but related ways. The first is characterised by a substantial increase in the cost for one party of performing its obligation. This party will normally be the one who is to perform the non-monetary obligation. The substantial increase in the cost may, for instance, be due to a dramatic rise in the price of the raw materials necessary for the production of the goods or the rendering of the services, or to the introduction of new safety regulations requiring far more expensive production procedures.

b. Decrease in value of the performance received by one party

The second manifestation of hardship is characterised by a substantial decrease in the value of the performance received by one party, including cases where the performance no longer has any value at all for the receiving party. The performance may be that either of a monetary or of a non-monetary obligation. The substantial decrease in the value or the total loss of any value of the performance may be due either to drastic changes in market conditions (e.g. the effect of a dramatic increase in inflation on a contractually agreed price) or the frustration of the purpose for which the performance was required (e.g. the effect of a prohibition to build on a plot of land acquired for building purposes or the effect of an export embargo on goods acquired with a view to their subsequent export).

Naturally the decrease in value of the performance must be capable of objective measurement: a mere change in the personal opinion of the receiving party as to the value of the performance is of no relevance. As to the frustration of the purpose of the performance, this can only be taken into account when the purpose in question was known or at least ought to have been known to both parties.

3. Additional requirements for hardship to arise

a. Events occur or become known after conclusion of the contract

According to sub-para. (a) of this article, the events causing hardship must take place or become known to the disadvantaged party after the conclusion of the contract. If that party had known of those events when entering into the contract, it would have been able to take them into account at that time and may not subsequently rely on hardship.

b. Events could not reasonably have been taken into account by disadvantaged party

Even if the change in circumstances occurs after the conclusion of the contract, sub-para. (b) of this article makes it clear that such circumstances cannot cause hardship if they could reasonably have been taken into account by the disadvantaged party at the time the contract was concluded.

Illustration

2. A agrees to supply B with crude oil from country X at a fixed price for the next five years, notwithstanding the acute political tensions in the region. Two years after the conclusion of the contract, a war erupts between contending factions in neighbouring countries. The war results in a world energy crisis and oil prices increase drastically. A is not entitled to invoke hardship because such a rise in the price of crude oil was not unforeseeable.

Sometimes the change in circumstances is gradual, but the final result of those gradual changes may constitute a case of hardship. If the change began before the contract was concluded, hardship will not arise unless the pace of change increases dramatically during the life of the contract.

Illustration

3. In a sales contract between A and B the price is expressed in the currency of country X, a currency whose value was already depreciating slowly against other major currencies before the conclusion of the contract. One month afterwards a political crisis in country X leads to a massive devaluation

of the order of 80% of its currency. Unless the circumstances indicate otherwise, this constitutes a case of hardship, since such a dramatic acceleration of the loss of value of the currency of country X was not foreseeable.

c. Events beyond the control of disadvantaged party

Under sub-para. (c) of this article a case of hardship can only arise if the events causing the hardship are beyond the control of the disadvantaged party.

d. Risks must not have been assumed by disadvantaged party

Under sub-para. (d) there can be no hardship if the disadvantaged party had assumed the risk of the change in circumstances. The word "assumption" makes it clear that the risks need not have been taken over expressly, but that this may follow from the very nature of the contract. A party who enters into a speculative transaction is deemed to accept a certain degree of risk, even though it may not have been fully aware of that risk at the time it entered into the contract.

Illustration

4. A, an insurance company specialised in the insurance of shipping risks, requests an additional premium from those of its customers who have contracts which include the risks of war and civil insurrection, so as to meet the substantially greater risk to which it is exposed following upon the simultaneous outbreak of war and civil insurrection in three countries in the same region. A is not entitled to such an adaptation of the contract, since by the war and civil insurrection clause insurance companies assume these risks even if three countries are affected at the same time.

4. Hardship relevant only to performance not yet rendered

By its very nature hardship can only become of relevance with respect to performances still to be rendered: once a party has performed, it is no longer entitled to invoke a substantial increase in the costs of its performance or a substantial decrease in the value of the performance it receives as a consequence of a change in circumstances which occurs after such performance.

If the fundamental alteration in the equilibrium of the contract occurs at a time when performance has been only partially rendered, hardship can be of relevance only to the parts of the performance still to be rendered.

Illustration

5. A enters into a contract with B, a waste disposal company in country X, for the purpose of arranging the storage of its waste. The contract provides for a four-year term and a fixed price per ton of waste. Two years after the conclusion of the contract, the environmental movement in country X gains ground and the Government of country X prescribes prices for storing waste which are ten times higher than before. B may successfully invoke hardship only with respect to the two remaining years of the life of the contract.

5. Hardship normally relevant to long-term contracts

Although this article does not expressly exclude the possibility of hardship being invoked in respect of other kinds of contracts, hardship will normally be of relevance to long-term contracts, i.e. those where the performance of at least one party extends over a certain period of time.

6. Hardship and force majeure

In view of the respective definitions of hardship and force majeure (see Art. 7.1.7) under these Principles there may be factual situations which can at the same time be considered as cases of hardship and of force majeure. If this is the case, it is for the party affected by these events to decide which remedy to pursue. If it invokes force majeure, it is with a view to its non-performance being excused. If, on the other hand, a party invokes hardship, this is in the first instance for the purpose of renegotiating the terms of the contract so as to allow the contract to be kept alive although on revised terms.

7. Hardship and contract practice

The definition of hardship in this article is necessarily of a rather general character. International commercial contracts often contain much more precise and elaborate provisions in this regard. The parties may therefore find it appropriate to adapt the content of this article so as to take account of the particular features of the specific transaction.

Article 6.2.3

(Effects of hardship)

(1) In case of hardship the disadvantaged party is entitled to request renegotiations. The request shall be made without undue delay and shall indicate the grounds on which it is based.

(2) The request for renegotiation does not in itself entitle the disadvantaged party to withhold performance.

(3) Upon failure to reach agreement within a reasonable time either party may resort to the court.

(4) If the court finds hardship it may, if reasonable,

(a) terminate the contract at a date and on terms to be fixed, or

(b) adapt the contract with a view to restoring its equilibrium.

Official Comment

1. Disadvantaged party entitled to request renegotiations

Since hardship consists in a fundamental alteration of the equilibrium of the contract, para. (1) of this article in the first instance entitles the disadvantaged party to request the other party to enter into renegotiation of the original terms of the contract with a view to adapting them to the changed circumstances.

Illustration

1. A, a construction company situated in country X, enters into a lump sum contract with B, a governmental agency, for the erection of a plant in country Y. Most of the sophisticated machinery has to be imported from abroad. Due to an unexpected devaluation of the currency of country Y, which is the currency of payment, the cost of the machinery increases by more than 50%. A is entitled to request B to renegotiate the original contract price so as to adapt it to the changed circumstances.

A request for renegotiations is not admissible where the contract itself already incorporates a clause providing for the automatic adaptation of the contract (e.g. a clause providing for automatic indexation of the price if certain events occur).

Illustration

2. The facts are the same as in Illustration 1, the difference being that the contract contains a price indexation clause relating to variations in the cost of materials and labour. A is not entitled to request a renegotiation of the price.

However, even in such a case renegotiation on account of hardship would not be precluded if the adaptation clause incorporated in the contract did not contemplate the events giving rise to hardship.

Illustration

3. The facts are the same as in Illustration 2, the difference being that the substantial increase in A's costs is due to the adoption of new safety regulations in country Y. A is entitled to request B to renegotiate the original contract price so as to adapt it to the changed circumstances.

2. Request for renegotiations without undue delay

The request for renegotiations must be made as quickly as possible after the time at which hardship is alleged to have occurred (para. (1)). The precise time for requesting renegotiations will depend upon the circumstances of the case: it may, for instance, be longer when the change in circumstances takes place gradually (see comment 3(b) on Art. 6.2.2).

The disadvantaged party does not lose its right to request renegotiations simply because it fails to act without undue delay. The delay in making the request may however affect the finding as to whether hardship actually existed and, if so, its consequences for the contract.

3. Grounds for request for renegotiations

Para. (1) of this article also imposes on the disadvantaged party a duty to indicate the grounds on which the request for renegotiations is based so as to permit the other party better to assess whether or not the request for renegotiations is justified. An incomplete request is to be considered as not being raised in time, unless the grounds of the alleged hardship are so obvious that they need not be spelt out in the request.

Failure to set forth the grounds on which the request for renegotiations is based may have similar effects to those resulting from undue delay in making the request (see comment 2 on this article).

4. Request for renegotiations and withholding of performance

Para. (2) of this article provides that the request for renegotiations does not of itself entitle the disadvantaged party to withhold performance. The reason for this lies in the exceptional character of hardship and in the risk of possible abuses of the remedy. Withholding performance may be justified only in extraordinary circumstances.

Illustration

4. A enters into a contract with B for the construction of a plant. The plant is to be built in country X, which adopts new safety regulations after the conclusion of the contract. The new regulations require additional apparatus and thereby fundamentally alter the equilibrium of the contract making A's performance substantially more onerous. A is entitled to request renegotiations and may withhold performance in view of the time it needs to implement the new safety regulations, but it may also withhold the delivery of the additional apparatus, for as long as the corresponding price adaptation is not agreed.

5. Renegotiations in good faith

Although nothing is said in this article to that effect, both the request for renegotiations by the disadvantaged party and the conduct of both parties during the renegotiation process are subject to the general principle of good faith (Art. 1.7) and to the duty of co-operation (Art. 5.1.3). Thus the disadvantaged party must honestly believe that a case of hardship actually exists and not request renegotiations as a purely tactical manoeuvre. Similarly, once the request has been made, both parties must conduct the renegotiations in a constructive manner, in particular by refraining from any form of obstruction and by providing all the necessary information.

6. Resort to the court upon failure to reach an agreement

If the parties fail to reach agreement on the adaptation of the contract to the changed circumstances within a reasonable time, para. (3) of the present article authorises either party to resort to the court. Such a situation may arise either because the non-disadvantaged party completely ignored the request for renegotiations or because the renegotiations, although conducted by both parties in good faith, did not achieve a positive outcome.

How long a party must wait before resorting to the court will depend on the complexity of the issues to be settled and the particular circumstances of the case.

7. Court measures in case of hardship

According to para. (4) of this article a court which finds that a hardship situation exists may react in a number of different ways.

A first possibility is for it to terminate the contract. However, since termination in this case does not depend on a non-performance by one of the parties, its effects on the performances already rendered might be different from those provided for by the rules governing termination in general (Arts. 7.3.1. et seq.). Accordingly, para. (4)(a) provides that termination shall take place "at a date and on terms to be fixed" by the court.

Another possibility would be for a court to adapt the contract with a view to restoring its equilibrium (para. (4)(b)). In so doing the court will seek to make a fair distribution of the losses between the parties. This may or may not, depending on the nature of the hardship, involve a price adaptation. However, if it does, the adaptation will not necessarily reflect in full the loss entailed by the change in circumstances, since the court will, for instance, have to consider the extent to which one of the parties has taken a risk and the extent to which the party entitled to receive a performance may still benefit from that performance.

Para. (4) of this article expressly states that the court may terminate or adapt the contract only when this is reasonable. The circumstances may even be such that neither termination nor adaptation is appropriate and in consequence the only reasonable solution will be for the court either to direct the parties to resume negotiations with a view to reaching agreement on the adaptation of the contract, or to confirm the terms of the contract as they stand.

Illustration

5. A, an exporter, undertakes to supply B, an importer in country X, with beer for three years. Two years after the conclusion of the contract new legislation is introduced in country X prohibiting the sale and consumption of alcoholic drinks. B immediately invokes hardship and requests A to renegotiate the contract. A recognises that hardship has occurred, but

refuses to accept the modifications of the contract proposed by B. After one month of fruitless discussions B resorts to the court.

If B has the possibility to sell the beer in a neighbouring country, although at a substantially lower price, the court may decide to uphold the contract but to reduce the agreed price.

If on the contrary B has no such possibility, it may be reasonable for the court to terminate the contract, at the same time however requiring B to pay A for the last consignment still en route.

CHAPTER 7—NON–PERFORMANCE

SECTION 1: NON–PERFORMANCE IN GENERAL

Article 7.1.1

(Non-performance defined)

Non-performance is failure by a party to perform any of its obligations under the contract, including defective performance or late performance.

Article 7.1.2

(Interference by the other party)

A party may not rely on the non-performance of the other party to the extent that such non-performance was caused by the first party's act or omission or by another event as to which the first party bears the risk.

Article 7.1.3

(Withholding performance)

(1) Where the parties are to perform simultaneously, either party may withhold performance until the other party tenders its performance.

(2) Where the parties are to perform consecutively, the party that is to perform later may withhold its performance until the first party has performed.

Article 7.1.4

(Cure by non-performing party)

(1) The non-performing party may, at its own expense, cure any non-performance, provided that

    (a) without undue delay, it gives notice indicating the proposed manner and timing of the cure;

    (b) cure is appropriate in the circumstances;

    (c) the aggrieved party has no legitimate interest in refusing cure; and

    (d) cure is effected promptly.

(2) The right to cure is not precluded by notice of termination.

(3) Upon effective notice of cure, rights of the aggrieved party that are inconsistent with the non-performing party's performance are suspended until the time for cure has expired.

(4) The aggrieved party may withhold performance pending cure.

(5) Notwithstanding cure, the aggrieved party retains the right to claim damages for delay as well as for any harm caused or not prevented by the cure.

Article 7.1.5

(Additional period for performance)

(1) In a case of non-performance the aggrieved party may by notice to the other party allow an additional period of time for performance.

(2) During the additional period the aggrieved party may withhold performance of its own reciprocal obligations and may claim damages but may not resort to any other remedy. If it receives notice from the other party that the latter will not perform within that period, or if upon expiry of that period due performance has not been made, the aggrieved party may resort to any of the remedies that may be available under this Chapter.

(3) Where in a case of delay in performance which is not fundamental the aggrieved party has given notice allowing an additional period of time of reasonable length, it may terminate the contract at the end of that period. If the additional period allowed is not of reasonable length it shall be extended to a reasonable length. The aggrieved party may in its notice provide that if the other party fails to perform within the period allowed by the notice the contract shall automatically terminate.

(4) Paragraph (3) does not apply where the obligation which has not been performed is only a minor part of the contractual obligation of the non-performing party.

Article 7.1.6

(Exemption clauses)

A clause which limits or excludes one party's liability for non-performance or which permits one party to render performance substantially different from what the other party reasonably expected may not be invoked if it would be grossly unfair to do so, having regard to the purpose of the contract.

Article 7.1.7

(Force majeure)

(1) Non-performance by a party is excused if that party proves that the non-performance was due to an impediment beyond its control and

that it could not reasonably be expected to have taken the impediment into account at the time of the conclusion of the contract or to have avoided or overcome it or its consequences.

(2) When the impediment is only temporary, the excuse shall have effect for such period as is reasonable having regard to the effect of the impediment on the performance of the contract.

(3) The party who fails to perform must give notice to the other party of the impediment and its effect on its ability to perform. If the notice is not received by the other party within a reasonable time after the party who fails to perform knew or ought to have known of the impediment, it is liable for damages resulting from such non-receipt.

(4) Nothing in this article prevents a party from exercising a right to terminate the contract or to withhold performance or request interest on money due.

SECTION 2: RIGHT TO PERFORMANCE

Article 7.2.1

(Performance of monetary obligation)

Where a party who is obliged to pay money does not do so, the other party may require payment.

Article 7.2.2

(Performance of non-monetary obligation)

Where a party who owes an obligation other than one to pay money does not perform, the other party may require performance, unless

    (a) performance is impossible in law or in fact;

    (b) performance or, where relevant, enforcement is unreasonably burdensome or expensive;

    (c) the party entitled to performance may reasonably obtain performance from another source;

    (d) performance is of an exclusively personal character; or

    (e) the party entitled to performance does not require performance within a reasonable time after it has, or ought to have, become aware of the non-performance.

Article 7.2.3

(Repair and replacement of defective performance)

The right to performance includes in appropriate cases the right to require repair, replacement, or other cure of defective performance. The provisions of Articles 7.2.1 and 7.2.2 apply accordingly.

Article 7.2.4

(Judicial penalty)

(1) Where the court orders a party to perform, it may also direct that this party pay a penalty if it does not comply with the order.

(2) The penalty shall be paid to the aggrieved party unless mandatory provisions of the law of the forum provide otherwise. Payment of the penalty to the aggrieved party does not exclude any claim for damages.

Article 7.2.5

(Change of remedy)

(1) An aggrieved party who has required performance of a non-monetary obligation and who has not received performance within a period fixed or otherwise within a reasonable period of time may invoke any other remedy.

(2) Where the decision of a court for performance of a non-monetary obligation cannot be enforced, the aggrieved party may invoke any other remedy.

SECTION 3: TERMINATION

Article 7.3.1

(Right to terminate the contract)

(1) A party may terminate the contract where the failure of the other party to perform an obligation under the contract amounts to a fundamental non-performance.

(2) In determining whether a failure to perform an obligation amounts to a fundamental non-performance regard shall be had, in particular, to whether

    (a) the non-performance substantially deprives the aggrieved party of what it was entitled to expect under the contract unless the other party did not foresee and could not reasonably have foreseen such result;

    (b) strict compliance with the obligation which has not been performed is of essence under the contract;

    (c) the non-performance is intentional or reckless;

    (d) the non-performance gives the aggrieved party reason to believe that it cannot rely on the other party's future performance;

    (e) the non-performing party will suffer disproportionate loss as a result of the preparation or performance if the contract is terminated.

(3) In the case of delay the aggrieved party may also terminate the contract if the other party fails to perform before the time allowed it under Article 7.1.5 has expired.

Article 7.3.2

(Notice of termination)

(1) The right of a party to terminate the contract is exercised by notice to the other party.

(2) If performance has been offered late or otherwise does not conform to the contract the aggrieved party will lose its right to terminate the contract unless it gives notice to the other party within a reasonable time after it has or ought to have become aware of the offer or of the non-conforming performance.

Article 7.3.3

(Anticipatory non-performance)

Where prior to the date for performance by one of the parties it is clear that there will be a fundamental non-performance by that party, the other party may terminate the contract.

Article 7.3.4

(Adequate assurance of due performance)

A party who reasonably believes that there will be a fundamental non-performance by the other party may demand adequate assurance of due performance and may meanwhile withhold its own performance. Where this assurance is not provided within a reasonable time the party demanding it may terminate the contract.

Article 7.3.5

(Effects of termination in general)

(1) Termination of the contract releases both parties from their obligation to effect and to receive future performance.

(2) Termination does not preclude a claim for damages for non-performance.

(3) Termination does not affect any provision in the contract for the settlement of disputes or any other term of the contract which is to operate even after termination.

Article 7.3.6

(Restitution)

(1) On termination of the contract either party may claim restitution of whatever it has supplied, provided that such party concurrently makes restitution of whatever it has received. If restitution in kind is not

possible or appropriate allowance should be made in money whenever reasonable.

(2) However, if performance of the contract has extended over a period of time and the contract is divisible, such restitution can only be claimed for the period after termination has taken effect.

SECTION 4: DAMAGES

Article 7.4.1

(Right to damages)

Any non-performance gives the aggrieved party a right to damages either exclusively or in conjunction with any other remedies except where the non-performance is excused under these Principles.

Article 7.4.2

(Full compensation)

(1) The aggrieved party is entitled to full compensation for harm sustained as a result of the non-performance. Such harm includes both any loss which it suffered and any gain of which it was deprived, taking into account any gain to the aggrieved party resulting from its avoidance of cost or harm.

(2) Such harm may be non-pecuniary and includes, for instance, physical suffering or emotional distress.

Article 7.4.3

(Certainty of harm)

(1) Compensation is due only for harm, including future harm, that is established with a reasonable degree of certainty.

(2) Compensation may be due for the loss of a chance in proportion to the probability of its occurrence.

(3) Where the amount of damages cannot be established with a sufficient degree of certainty, the assessment is at the discretion of the court.

Article 7.4.4

(Foreseeability of harm)

The non-performing party is liable only for harm which it foresaw or could reasonably have foreseen at the time of the conclusion of the contract as being likely to result from its non-performance.

Article 7.4.5

(Proof of harm in case of replacement transaction)

Where the aggrieved party has terminated the contract and has made a replacement transaction within a reasonable time and in a reasonable manner it may recover the difference between the contract price and the price of the replacement transaction as well as damages for any further harm.

Article 7.4.6

(Proof of harm by current price)

(1) Where the aggrieved party has terminated the contract and has not made a replacement transaction but there is a current price for the performance contracted for, it may recover the difference between the contract price and the price current at the time the contract is terminated as well as damages for any further harm.

(2) Current price is the price generally charged for goods delivered or services rendered in comparable circumstances at the place where the contract should have been performed or, if there is no current price at that place, the current price at such other place that appears reasonable to take as a reference.

Article 7.4.7

(Harm due in part to aggrieved party)

Where the harm is due in part to an act or omission of the aggrieved party or to another event as to which that party bears the risk, the amount of damages shall be reduced to the extent that these factors have contributed to the harm, having regard to the conduct of each of the parties.

Article 7.4.8

(Mitigation of harm)

(1) The non-performing party is not liable for harm suffered by the aggrieved party to the extent that the harm could have been reduced by the latter party's taking reasonable steps.

(2) The aggrieved party is entitled to recover any expenses reasonably incurred in attempting to reduce the harm.

Article 7.4.9

(Interest for failure to pay money)

(1) If a party does not pay a sum of money when it falls due the aggrieved party is entitled to interest upon that sum from the time when payment is due to the time of payment whether or not the non-payment is excused.

(2) The rate of interest shall be the average bank short-term lending rate to prime borrowers prevailing for the currency of payment at the place for payment, or where no such rate exists at that place, then the same rate in the State of the currency of payment. In the absence of

such a rate at either place the rate of interest shall be the appropriate rate fixed by the law of the State of the currency of payment.

(3) The aggrieved party is entitled to additional damages if the non-payment caused it a greater harm.

Article 7.4.10

(Interest on damages)

Unless otherwise agreed, interest on damages for non-performance of non-monetary obligations accrues as from the time of non-performance.

Article 7.4.11

(Manner of monetary redress)

(1) Damages are to be paid in a lump sum. However, they may be payable in instalments where the nature of the harm makes this appropriate.

(2) Damages to be paid in instalments may be indexed.

Article 7.4.12

(Currency in which to assess damages)

Damages are to be assessed either in the currency in which the monetary obligation was expressed or in the currency in which the harm was suffered, whichever is more appropriate.

Article 7.4.13

(Agreed payment for non-performance)

(1) Where the contract provides that a party who does not perform is to pay a specified sum to the aggrieved party for such non-performance, the aggrieved party is entitled to that sum irrespective of its actual harm.

(2) However, notwithstanding any agreement to the contrary the specified sum may be reduced to a reasonable amount where it is grossly excessive in relation to the harm resulting from the non-performance and to the other circumstances.

CHAPTER 8—SET–OFF

Article 8.1

(Conditions of set-off)

(1) Where two parties owe each other money or other performances of the same kind, either of them ("the first party") may set off its obligation against that of its obligee ("the other party") if at the time of set-off,

411

(a) the first party is entitled to perform its obligation;

(b) the other party's obligation is ascertained as to its existence and amount and performance is due.

(2) If the obligations of both parties arise from the same contract, the first party may also set off its obligation against an obligation of the other party which is not ascertained as to its existence or to its amount.

Article 8.2

(Foreign currency set-off)

Where the obligations are to pay money in different currencies, the right of set-off may be exercised, provided that both currencies are freely convertible and the parties have not agreed that the first party shall pay only in a specified currency.

Article 8.3

(Set-off by notice)

The right of set-off is exercised by notice to the other party.

Article 8.4

(Content of notice)

(1) The notice must specify the obligations to which it relates.

(2) If the notice does not specify the obligation against which set-off is exercised, the other party may, within a reasonable time, declare to the first party the obligation to which set-off relates. If no such declaration is made, the set-off will relate to all the obligations proportionally.

Article 8.5

(Effect of set-off)

(1) Set-off discharges the obligations.

(2) If obligations differ in amount, set-off discharges the obligations up to the amount of the lesser obligation.

(3) Set-off takes effect as from the time of notice.

CHAPTER 9—ASSIGNMENT OF RIGHTS, TRANSFER OF OBLIGATIONS, ASSIGNMENT OF CONTRACTS

SECTION 1: ASSIGNMENT OF RIGHTS

Article 9.1.1

(Definitions)

"Assignment of a right" means the transfer by agreement from one person (the "assignor") to another person (the "assignee"), including transfer by way of security, of the assignor's right to payment of a monetary sum or other performance from a third person ("the obligor").

Article 9.1.2

(Exclusions)

This Section does not apply to transfers made under the special rules governing the transfers:

(a) of instruments such as negotiable instruments, documents of title or financial instruments, or—

(b) of rights in the course of transferring a business.

Article 9.1.3

(Assignability of non-monetary rights)

A right to non-monetary performance may be assigned only if the assignment does not render the obligation significantly more burdensome.

Article 9.1.4

(Partial assignment)

(1) A right to the payment of a monetary sum may be assigned partially.

(2) A right to other performance may be assigned partially only if it is divisible, and the assignment does not render the obligation significantly more burdensome.

Article 9.1.5

(Future rights)

A future right is deemed to be transferred at the time of the agreement, provided the right, when it comes into existence, can be identified as the right to which the assignment relates.

Article 9.1.6

(Rights assigned without individual specification)

A number of rights may be assigned without individual specification, provided such rights can be identified as rights to which the assignment relates at the time of the assignment or when they come into existence.

Article 9.1.7

(Agreement between assignor and assignee sufficient)

(1) A right is assigned by mere agreement between the assignor and the assignee, without notice to the obligor.

(2) The consent of the obligor is not required unless the obligation in the circumstances is of an essentially personal character.

Article 9.1.8

(Obligor's additional costs)

The obligor has a right to be compensated by the assignor or the assignee for any additional costs caused by the assignment.

Article 9.1.9

(Non-assignment clauses)

(1) The assignment of a right to the payment of a monetary sum is effective notwithstanding an agreement between the assignor and the obligor limiting or prohibiting such an assignment. However, the assignor may be liable to the obligor for breach of contract.

(2) The assignment of a right to other performance is ineffective if it is contrary to an agreement between the assignor and the obligor limiting or prohibiting the assignment. Nevertheless, the assignment is effective if the assignee, at the time of the assignment, neither knew nor ought to have known of the agreement. The assignor may then be liable to the obligor for breach of contract.

Article 9.1.10

(Notice to the obligor)

(1) Until the obligor receives a notice of the assignment from either the assignor or the assignee, it is discharged by paying the assignor.

(2) After the obligor receives such a notice, it is discharged only by paying the assignee.

Article 9.1.11

(Successive assignments)

If the same right has been assigned by the same assignor to two or more successive assignees, the obligor is discharged by paying according to the order in which the notices were received.

Article 9.1.12

(Adequate proof of assignment)

(1) If notice of the assignment is given by the assignee, the obligor may request the assignee to provide within a reasonable time adequate proof that the assignment has been made.

(2) Until adequate proof is provided, the obligor may withhold payment.

(3) Unless adequate proof is provided, notice is not effective.

(4) Adequate proof includes, but is not limited to, any writing emanating from the assignor and indicating that the assignment has taken place.

Article 9.1.13

(Defences and rights of set-off)

(1) The obligor may assert against the assignee all defences that the obligor could assert against the assignor.

(2) The obligor may exercise against the assignee any right of set-off available to the obligor against the assignor up to the time notice of assignment was received.

Article 9.1.14

(Rights related to the right assigned)

The assignment of a right transfers to the assignee:

  (a) all the assignor's rights to payment or other performance under the contract in respect of the right assigned, and

  (b) all rights securing performance of the right assigned.

Article 9.1.15

(Undertakings of the assignor)

The assignor undertakes towards the assignee, except as otherwise disclosed to the assignee, that:

  (a) the assigned right exists at the time of the assignment, unless the right is a future right;

  (b) the assignor is entitled to assign the right;

  (c) the right has not been previously assigned to another assignee, and it is free from any right or claim from a third party;

  (d) the obligor does not have any defences;

  (e) neither the obligor nor the assignor has given notice of set-off concerning the assigned right and will not give any such notice;

  (f) the assignor will reimburse the assignee for any payment received from the obligor before notice of the assignment was given.

SECTION 2: TRANSFER OF OBLIGATIONS
Article 9.2.1

(Modes of transfer)

An obligation to pay money or render other performance may be transferred from one person (the "original obligor") to another person (the "new obligor") either

(a) by an agreement between the original obligor and the new obligor subject to Article 9.2.3, or

(b) by an agreement between the obligee and the new obligor, by which the new obligor assumes the obligation.

Article 9.2.2

(Exclusion)

This Section does not apply to transfers of obligations made under the special rules governing transfers of obligations in the course of transferring a business.

Article 9.2.3

(Requirement of obligee's consent to transfer)

The transfer of an obligation by an agreement between the original obligor and the new obligor requires the consent of the obligee.

Article 9.2.4

(Advance consent of obligee)

(1) The obligee may give its consent in advance.

(2) If the obligee has given its consent in advance, the transfer of the obligation becomes effective when a notice of the transfer is given to the obligee or when the obligee acknowledges it.

Article 9.2.5

(Discharge of original obligor)

(1) The obligee may discharge the original obligor.

(2) The obligee may also retain the original obligor as an obligor in case the new obligor does not perform properly.

(3) Otherwise the original obligor and the new obligor are jointly and severally liable.

Article 9.2.6

(Third party performance)

(1) Without the obligee's consent, the obligor may contract with another person that this person will perform the obligation in place of the obligor, unless the obligation in the circumstances has an essentially personal character.

(2) The obligee retains its claim against the obligor.

Article 9.2.7

(Defences and rights of set-off)

(1) The new obligor may assert against the obligee all defences which the original obligor could assert against the obligee.

(2) The new obligor may not exercise against the obligee any right of set-off available to the original obligor against the obligee.

Article 9.2.8

(Rights related to the obligation transferred)

(1) The obligee may assert against the new obligor all its rights to payment or other performance under the contract in respect of the obligation transferred.

(2) If the original obligor is discharged under Article 9.2.5(1), a security granted by any person other than the new obligor for the performance of the obligation is discharged, unless that other person agrees that it should continue to be available to the obligee.

(3) Discharge of the original obligor also extends to any security of the original obligor given to the obligee for the performance of the obligation, unless the security is over an asset which is transferred as part of a transaction between the original obligor and the new obligor.

SECTION 3: ASSIGNMENT OF CONTRACTS

Article 9.3.1

(Definitions)

"Assignment of a contract" means the transfer by agreement from one person (the "assignor") to another person (the "assignee") of the assignor's rights and obligations arising out of a contract with another person (the "other party").

Article 9.3.2

(Exclusion)

This Section does not apply to the assignment of contracts made under the special rules governing transfers of contracts in the course of transferring a business.

Article 9.3.3

(Requirement of consent of the other party)

The assignment of a contract requires the consent of the other party.

Article 9.3.4

(Advance consent of the other party)

(1) The other party may give its consent in advance.

(2) If the other party has given its consent in advance, the assignment of the contract becomes effective when a notice of the assignment is given to the other party or when the other party acknowledges it.

Article 9.3.5

(Discharge of the assignor)

(1) The other party may discharge the assignor.

(2) The other party may also retain the assignor as an obligor in case the assignee does not perform properly.

(3) Otherwise the assignor and the assignee are jointly and severally liable.

Article 9.3.6

(Defences and rights of set-off)

(1) To the extent that the assignment of a contract involves an assignment of rights, Article 9.1.13 applies accordingly.

(2) To the extent that the assignment of a contract involves a transfer of obligations, Article 9.2.7 applies accordingly.

Article 9.3.7

(Rights transferred with the contract)

(1) To the extent that the assignment of a contract involves an assignment of rights, Article 9.1.14 applies accordingly.

(2) To the extent that the assignment of a contract involves a transfer of obligations, Article 9.2.8 applies accordingly.

CHAPTER 10—LIMITATION PERIODS

Article 10.1

(Scope of the Chapter)

(1) The exercise of rights governed by these Principles is barred by the expiration of a period of time, referred to as "limitation period", according to the rules of this Chapter.

(2) This Chapter does not govern the time within which one party is required under these Principles, as a condition for the acquisition or exercise of its right, to give notice to the other party or to perform any act other than the institution of legal proceedings.

Article 10.2

(Limitation periods)

(1) The general limitation period is three years beginning on the day after the day the obligee knows or ought to know the facts as a result of which the obligee's right can be exercised.

(2) In any event, the maximum limitation period is ten years beginning on the day after the day the right can be exercised.

Article 10.3

(Modification of limitation periods by the parties)

(1) The parties may modify the limitation periods.

(2) However they may not

(a) shorten the general limitation period to less than one year;

(b) shorten the maximum limitation period to less than four years;

(c) extend the maximum limitation period to more than fifteen years.

Article 10.4

(New limitation period by acknowledgement)

(1) Where the obligor before the expiration of the general limitation period acknowledges the right of the obligee, a new general limitation period begins on the day after the day of the acknowledgement.

(2) The maximum limitation period does not begin to run again, but may be exceeded by the beginning of a new general limitation period under Art. 10.2(1).

Article 10.5

(Suspension by judicial proceedings)

(1) The running of the limitation period is suspended

(a) when the obligee performs any act, by commencing judicial proceedings or in judicial proceedings already instituted, that is recognised by the law of the court as asserting the obligee's right against the obligor;

(b) in the case of the obligor's insolvency when the obligee has asserted its rights in the insolvency proceedings; or

(c) in the case of proceedings for dissolution of the entity which is the obligor when the obligee has asserted its rights in the dissolution proceedings.

(2) Suspension lasts until a final decision has been issued or until the proceedings have been otherwise terminated.

Article 10.6

(Suspension by arbitral proceedings)

(1) The running of the limitation period is suspended when the obligee performs any act, by commencing arbitral proceedings or in arbitral proceedings already instituted, that is recognised by the law of the arbitral tribunal as asserting the obligee's right against the obligor. In the absence of regulations for arbitral proceedings or provisions

determining the exact date of the commencement of arbitral proceedings, the proceedings are deemed to commence on the date on which a request that the right in dispute should be adjudicated reaches the obligor.

(2) Suspension lasts until a binding decision has been issued or until the proceedings have been otherwise terminated.

Article 10.7
(Alternative dispute resolution)

The provisions of Articles 10.5 and 10.6 apply with appropriate modifications to other proceedings whereby the parties request a third person to assist them in their attempt to reach an amicable settlement of their dispute.

Article 10.8
(Suspension in case of force majeure, death or incapacity)

(1) Where the obligee has been prevented by an impediment that is beyond its control and that it could neither avoid nor overcome, from causing a limitation period to cease to run under the preceding articles, the general limitation period is suspended so as not to expire before one year after the relevant impediment has ceased to exist.

(2) Where the impediment consists of the incapacity or death of the obligee or obligor, suspension ceases when a representative for the incapacitated or deceased party or its estate has been appointed or a successor has inherited the respective party's position. The additional one-year period under paragraph (1) applies accordingly.

Article 10.9
(The effects of expiration of limitation period)

(1) The expiration of the limitation period does not extinguish the right.

(2) For the expiration of the limitation period to have effect, the obligor must assert it as a defence.

(3) A right may still be relied on as a defence even though the expiration of the limitation period for that right has been asserted.

Article 10.10
(Right of set-off)

The obligee may exercise the right of set-off until the obligor has asserted the expiration of the limitation period.

Article 10.11
(Restitution)

Where there has been performance in order to discharge an obligation, there is no right of restitution merely because the limitation period has expired.

SELECTED CONTRACTS AND STANDARD FORM AGREEMENTS

COMPILERS' NOTE

This section offers the complete contracts that underlie the disputes in a series of well known cases. The cases, presented in chronological order, are: *Wood v. Lucy*, *Peevyhouse v. Garland Coal & Mining Co.*, *Bloor v. Falstaff Brewing Corp.*, *In the Matter of Baby M.*, and *Dalton v. Educational Testing Service*.

We also include three standard form agreements. The first is the 2007–08 SAT Service Terms and Conditions regarding Cancellation of Scores; this makes an interesting comparison with the 1991 Registration Bulletin used in *Dalton*. The second is the Standard Consent Agreement signed by participants in connection with the 2006 *Borat* movie. Finally, we include a standard form agreement with which some readers may be familiar: Google's Terms of Service.

CONTRACT IN *WOOD v. LUCY**

"Whereas, the said Lucy, Lady Duff–Gordon, occupies a unique and high position as a creator of fashions in America, England and France,

"And whereas, her personal approval and endorsement over her own name of certain articles and fabrics used not only in the manufacture of dresses, millinery and other adjuncts of fashion, but also divers other articles of use to people of taste has a distinct monetary value to the manufacturers of such articles,

"And whereas, the said Otis F. Wood possesses a business organization adapted to the placing such endorsements as the said Lucy, Lady Duff–Gordon, has approved,

"It is agreed by the said Lucy, Lady Duff–Gordon, that the said Otis F. Wood is hereby granted the exclusive right to place such endorsements on such terms and conditions as may in his judgment, and also in the judgment of the said Lucy, Lady Duff–Gordon, or A. Merritt, her personal business adviser, be most advantageous to the said Lucy, Lady Duff–Gordon, and the said Otis. F. Wood.

"And whereas, the said Lucy, Lady Duff–Gordon's approval and selection of certain articles and fabrics used in the manufacture of her model gowns, millinery and other adjuncts of fashion which she designs, has a distinct monetary value to the manufacturers of such articles used,

"It is agreed, that the said Otis F. Wood shall have the exclusive right to make such terms, under the same conditions as set forth in this agreement, but it is expressly understood and agreed by both parties that no such arrangement can be entered into before such goods have been personally passed upon and approved by the said Lucy, Lady Duff–Gordon, and also that nothing in this limits the right of the said Lucy, Lady Duff–Gordon, to select and use any fabrics or other articles whatsoever in her business, provided the said Lucy, Lady Duff–Gordon, does not allow her endorsement to be used for said goods.

"And whereas, the said Lucy, Lady Duff–Gordon, creates from time to time different articles, such as parasols, belts, handbags, garters, etc., etc., and these also have a distinct monetary value independent of their specific use in her own dress creations sold at her own houses of 'Lucile,'

"It is agreed, that the said Otis F. Wood shall have the exclusive right of placing these articles on sale or licensing the rights to others to manufacture and market of such articles.

* 118 N.E. 214 (N.Y. 1914). The contract is taken from the Amended Complaint, Read in Support of Motion. Thanks to Victor Goldberg for providing this material. For more on the contract, see *Reading Wood v. Lucy, Lady Duff Gordon with Help from the Kewpie Dolls* in Professor Goldberg's FRAMING CONTRACT LAW: AN ECONOMIC ANALYSIS (2007), also available at http://papers.ssrn.com/sol3/papers.cfm?abstract_id=870474.

"It is expressly understood and agreed by both parties that nothing in this agreement shall apply to any other executed or pending contract made by the said Lucy, Lady Duff–Gordon, prior to this date, nor does this agreement include any rights to moving pictures, theatrical performances and lectures, the distribution of photographs of her gowns or publication of signed articles by the said Lucy, Lady Duff–Gordon, or any articles or books which may be hereafter written by her, or the sale of portraits of dresses unless said permission be expressly granted by the said Lucy, Lady Duff–Gordon, or by the said A. Merritt, from time to time, as such permission may be asked by the said Otis F. Wood.

"It is agreed, that in the event any arrangement is made with the third party running longer than the time stated in this agreement, that the said Otis F. Wood is to share in the returns from same during his lifetime of such agreement, and the said Otis F. Wood's rights thereunder are not to cease at the expiration of this agreement.

"It is understood, that the Fashion Portfolio Service, suggested by the said Otis F. Wood, is covered under the terms of this agreement.

"It is agreed, that all profits and revenues derived under and contracts made with third persons hereunder are to be paid over and collected by the said Otis F. Wood, and that all said profits and royalties are to be divided equally between the parties hereto, it being expressly understood, however, that the cost of securing such profits and royalties shall be directed toward this half share of Otis F. Wood, the said Lucy, Lady Duff–Gordon, receiving a full half share of all said profits and royalties without any expense whatsoever being directed against it; and it is further expressly understood that the said Otis F. Wood shall account monthly, to wit, on the first day of each month, to the said Lucy, Lady Duff–Gordon, for all such moneys received by him. The said Otis F. Wood agrees to take out and procure such patents, copyrights or trade-marks as may in his judgment be necessary to protect such names, ideas, or articles as are affected hereby and to carry out such actions or proceedings as may, in his judgment, be necessary in order to protect such patents, copyrights or trade-marks. And it is further understood that such patents, copyrights or trade-marks shall be held in the name of the said Lucy, Lady Duff–Gordon, and that the expense of obtaining such patents, copyrights, or trade-marks and of protecting the same from infringement, shall be shared equally by parties hereto. But it is expressly understood and agreed that no such suit or action can be begun by the said Otis F. Wood without the consent of the said Lucy, Lady Duff–Gordon, or of the said A. Merritt.

"It is agreed, that this contract shall cover a period of one year from the signing hereof, and that at the expiration of the said period it shall automatically renew itself for another year, and thereafter from year to year, unless either party shall give notice in writing to the other party of his or her intention to terminate this agreement not less than ninety (90) days preceding the expiration of the said term of one year or the expiration of any succeeding term thereafter."

CONTRACT IN *BLOOR v. FALSTAFF BREWING CORP.**

Purchase Agreement dated as of March 3, 1972 between P. BAL-LANTINE & SONS, a New Jersey corporation (hereinafter called the Seller), and FALSTAFF BREWING CORPORATION, a Delaware corporation (hereinafter called the Buyer).

The Seller desires to sell, and the Buyer desires to purchase, the Ballantine Assets (as defined in Section 1 hereof) of the seller for the cash payments, referred to in Section 2 hereof and the assumption by the Buyer of certain obligations of the Seller as specified in Section 3 hereof, all upon the terms and subjects to the conditions hereinafter set forth.

NOW, THEREFORE, in consideration of the promises and of the mutual agreements hereinafter set forth, the parties hereto agree as follows:

1. **Sale of Ballantine Assets**. On the terms and subject to the conditions set forth in this Agreement, the Seller hereby agrees to sell, convey, assign, transfer and deliver to the Buyer on the Closing Date, and the Buyer hereby agrees to purchase from the Seller on the Closing Date the following assets, properties, and rights of the Seller relating to or used in connection with the production, bottling, packaging, storage and distribution of malt alcoholic beverage by the Seller, all as the same shall exist on the Closing Date except as such assets, properties and rights may have been disposed of, adjusted or supplemented prior to the Closing Date in the ordinary course of business or in accordance with the provisions of this Agreement (hereinafter called the "Ballantine Assets"):

(a) all right, title and interest of the Seller in and to the brand names, trademarks, trade names, copyrights and other proprietary rights owned by or registered in the name of the Seller and listed and described in Exhibit A hereto (hereinafter called the "Proprietary Rights");

(b) all right, title and interest of the Seller in and to the inventory and supplies held and used by the Seller generally described in Exhibit B hereto;

(c) all right, title and interest of the Seller in and to (i) the vehicles and auxiliary equipment and cooperage in hand or in the trade and related component parts listed or generally described in Exhibit C hereto and (ii) all cases, bottles and pallets on hand or in the trade of similar character to the items referred to in paragraph (a) above returnable to the Seller;

(d) all right, title and interest of the Seller in and to the (i) the leases or other agreements under which the Seller is lessee of or holds or operates personal property owned by any third party and

* 601 F2d 413 (2d Cir.1979). Thanks to Professor Victor Goldberg for providing this contract from the case file. The contract has been retyped for clarity.

which are listed in Exhibit D hereto and (ii) the contracts, orders agreements, commitments and other instruments, including without limitation, supply and requirements contracts and collective bargaining agreements to which the Seller is a party relating to the items of personal property referred to in Exhibits B–D hereto or to the sale and delivery by the Seller of its malt alcoholic beverage directly to retail sellers and which are listed in Exhibit E hereto;

(e) all right, title and interest of the seller in the advertising and promotional signs and materials used or for use by the Seller in connection with the Proprietary Rights; and

(f) provided that such purchase is not precluded by an order of a court of competent jurisdiction issued at the request of a governmental authority and effective on the Closing Date, all right, title and interest of the Seller in and to each retail account receivable of the Seller and each account receivable of the Seller confirmed in writing to either party hereto prior to May 1, 1972 (hereinafter called the "Buyer's Receivable"), excluding those accounts receivable listed in Exhibit F hereto (hereinafter called the "Seller's Receivable").

2. **Purchase Price and payment**. (a) Upon the terms and subject to the conditions set forth in this Agreement, the Buyer agrees to pay to the Seller as the Purchase Price for the Ballantine Assets (in addition to the assumption of certain obligations as provided herein),

i) On the date hereof, $2,000,000 in respect of the Ballantine Assets referred to in paragraphs (a) and (c)–(e) of Section 1 hereof, the receipt of which is hereby acknowledge

(ii) On March 15, 1972, $1,000,000 in respect of the Ballantine Assets referred to in paragraphs (a) and (c)–(e) of Section 1 hereof;

(iii) On the Closing Date, $1,000,000 in respect of the Ballantine Assets referred to in paragraphs (a) and (c)–(e) of Section 1 hereof;

(iv) On the Closing Date, a sum in cash equal to the cost, as determined by the Seller in accordance with the books and records of the Seller, of the inventory and supplies described in Exhibit B hereto, in respect of the Ballantine Assets referred to in paragraph (b) of Section 1 hereof; provided, however, that at the time that the Buyer shall take possession of any such Ballantine Assets pursuant to Section 5 (c) hereof prior to the Closing Date, it shall pay to the Seller the pro rata cost of such Ballantine Assets;

(v) on the 7th day of each month, commencing May 7, 1972, and terminating April 7, 1978 (the "Royalty Period"), a sum in cash computed at the rate of $.50 per barrel for each barrel of 31 U. S. gallons sold by the Buyer during the preceding calendar month under any of the Proprietary Rights, as royalties in respect of the use of such Proprietary Rights; provided that the Royalty Period will be extended by the duration of any restraining order, if lifted, issued by a court of competent jurisdiction, and the obligation to make royalty payments hereunder will recommence immediately following the lifting of such order; and provided, however, that if during the Royalty Period the Buyer substantially discontinues the distribution of beer under the brand name "Ballantine" (except as the result of a restraining order in effect for 30 days issued by a court of competent jurisdiction at the request of a governmental authority), it will pay to the Seller a cash sum equal to the years and fraction thereof remaining in the Royalty Period times $1,100,000, payable in equal monthly installments on the first day of each month commencing with the first month following the month in which such discontinuation occurs;

(vi) On the Closing Date, a sum in cash equal to 75% of the aggregate amount of the Buyer's Receivables as of the Closing Data (hereinafter called the "First Receivables Payment"), in respect of part of the Ballantine Assets referred to in paragraph (f) of Section 1 hereof; and

(vii) (1) On May 7, 1972, a sum in cash equal to 75% of the aggregate amount of the Buyer's Receivables as of April 30, 1972, in addition to those referred to in subparagraph (vi) above (hereinafter called the "Second Receivables payment") and (2) on the seventh day of each month commencing May 7, 1972, a sum, if any, in cash equal to 75% of that portion collected by the Buyer during the previous month of the difference between the aggregate of the First and Second Receivables Payments and the aggregate amount in excess thereof the total of all Buyer's Receivables collected up to and including the last day of the previous month.

(b) The aggregate of the First and Second Receivables Payments shall not exceed $7,125,000. For purposes of the computation of payments pursuant to clause (2) of subparagraph (vii) of paragraph (a) above, any amounts which may be paid to the Buyer by an obligor in satisfaction of any obligation distinct from the Buyer's Receivables relating to such obligor shall be treated by the Buyer as a collection of Buyer's Receivables, and the Buyer waives any right which it may have to make any claim, offset or counterclaim against such amounts received. Upon the termination of contractual or customer relations with any distributor, the Buyer will promptly pay to the Seller an amount equal to 75% of any Buyer's Receivables then due in respect of such distributor.

(c) Those portions of the Purchase Price referred to in subparagraphs (ii)–(iv) and (vi) of paragraph (a) above shall be paid by delivery to the Seller on the dates referred to therein of a certified or official bank check payable to the order of the Seller in the amounts specified therein. Payments of that portion of the Purchase Price referred to in subparagraphs (i), (v), and (vii) of paragraph (a) above shall be paid on the dates referred to therein by delivery to the Seller on such dates of checks, subject to collection, payable to the order of the Seller.

(d) If the Buyer shall apply for or consent to the appointment of a receiver, trustee or liquidator, of the Buyer or its assets, make a general assignment for the benefit of creditors, become insolvent, file a voluntary petition in bankruptcy or be adjudicated a bankrupt, file a petition or an answer seeking reorganization or an arrangement with creditors or take advantage of any bankruptcy, insolvency, dissolution or liquidation law or statute, then each of the payments or installments provided for in subparagraph (v) of paragraph (a) above shall immediately become forthwith due any payable without demand or other notice of any kind.

3. **Assumption of Certain obligations by the Buyer and Indemnity**. (a) Upon the terms and subject to the conditions set forth in this Agreement, the Buyer will assume on and as of the Closing Date and agrees to pay, perform and discharge in accordance with their terms:

(i) all obligations and liabilities of the Seller (1) under the leases and other agreements listed in Exhibit D hereto, (2) under the contracts, orders, commitments and other agreements listed in Exhibit E hereto, (3) for all premium payments under insurance contracts and binders covering or relating to the items generally described in Exhibits B and C hereto and (4) under relevant collective bargaining agreements, commitments or otherwise, including, without limitation, all obligations relating to severance and vacation pay, regarding all delivery, sales, marketing, clerical and administrative personnel; provided however, that the Buyer shall not assume any accounts payable under or in respect of the instruments set forth in (1) and (2) above, including; without limitation, liabilities for taxes, incurred by the Seller and due during or in respect of the period prior to the Closing Date; and

(ii) the obligations and liabilities of the Seller in respect of the advertising contracts, orders, commitments and other agreements set forth in Exhibit G hereto.

(b) All obligations and liabilities of the Seller not assumed by the Buyer pursuant to paragraph (a) above shall remain the sole responsibility of the Seller. The Seller will indemnify and save the Buyer harmless from and against any and all claims, liabilities or obligations whatsoever, to the extent the same shall arise our of or result from (i) the ownership of the Ballantine Assets prior to Closing Date and shall not have been assumed by the Buyer pursuant to a paragraph (a) above. The Buyer will indemnify and save the Seller harmless from and against any and all claims, liabilities or obligations on account of obligations and liabilities of the Seller assumed by the Buyer pursuant to paragraph (a) above or arising out of or resulting from the ownership by the Buyer of the Ballantine Assets on and after Closing Date.

(c) Each party shall promptly notify the other of the assertion of any claim against such party to be indemnified against hereunder, and will give to the indemnifying party an opportunity to participate, at its own expense, in the conduct of any proceedings instituted by any third party or in the settlement of such claim.

4. **Information**. From and after the date of this Agreement until June 30, 1973, pursuant to the reasonable requests of the Buyer, the Seller shall give the Buyer access to the Ballantine Assets, shall furnish information relating thereto and permit the Buyer to make extracts from, or copies of the books and records of the Buyer relating thereto. The Buyer shall use its best efforts to keep confidential all information respecting the business and operations of the Seller which it may have obtained in the course of its investigations and which is not public information.

5. **The Closing.** (a) The purchase and sale provided for in this Agreement shall take place at the offices of Investors Funding Corporation of New York, 630 Fifth Avenue, New York, NY at 10:00 a.m., Eastern Standard Time, on March 31, 1972, or such other date as the Seller and the Buyer may mutually agree upon (herein called the "Closing Date").

(b) The sale, conveyance, transfer, assignment and delivery of the Ballantine Assets as provided in this Agreement shall be effected by bills of sale, endorsements, assignments and other instruments of transfer and conveyance as the Buyer shall reasonably request and shall be sufficient to convey all of the title of the Seller to the Ballantine Assets. The Seller agrees that it will at anytime on or after the Closing Date, upon the reasonable request of the Buyer, execute, acknowledge, and deliver, or will cause to be done, executed, acknowledged and delivered, all such further acts, deeds, assignments, transfers, conveyances, powers of attorney and assurances as may be required for the better assigning, transferring, granting conveying, assuring and confirming such title to the Buyer.

(c) The Buyer at its expense shall take possession of the Ballantine Assets and remove them from the premises of the Seller as soon as possible after the date hereof. The Seller agrees to make delivery to the Buyer to such locations the Buyer may designate within a radius of 17 miles of Seller's premises of all finished goods included in Exhibit B hereto. The Buyer shall pay the Seller for such deliveries delivery charges at the rate of $.06 per case and $.50 per half-barrel. The Seller agrees to cooperate with the Buyer in assembling and removing the other Ballantine Assets from its premises.

6. **Assignment and Collection of Receivables**. (a) Nothing contained in this Agreement shall be construed as an attempt to assign (i) any contract, right, lease, license, commitment or agreement, including, without limitation, any sales or purchase order, which is in law non-assignable without the consent of the other party or parties thereto unless consent shall have been given or (ii) any such instrument or right as to which all the remedies for the enforcement thereof enjoyed by the Seller would not, as a matter of law, pass to the Buyer as an incident of the assignment provided for by this Agreement. The Seller agrees to use its best efforts to obtain the consent of the other party to any contract, right, lease, license, commitment or agreement to the assignment thereof to the Buyer in all cases where such consent is required for assignment.

(b) The Seller agrees that the Buyer shall have the right and authority to collect as the agent of the Seller, and the Buyer agrees to use its best efforts to collect, for the account of the Seller, all Seller's Receivables. The Buyer agrees that it will promptly transfer and deliver to the Seller any and all checks, cash or other property that the Buyer may receive in respect of Seller's Receivables or any and all checks or cash which it may receive from any party which is at the time of receipt an obligor of both the Buyer and Seller up to the amount of the outstanding Seller's Receivables due the Seller in respect of such party, and until so transferred and delivered the same shall be deemed to be held in trust for the Seller (it being the intention of both parties hereto that all such payments received by the Buyer shall be applied first on account of the customer's indebtedness to the Seller, and not to such customer's indebtedness to the Buyer, if any, until all such indebtedness to the Seller has been paid in full). The Buyer waives any right which it may have to make any claim, offset or counterclaim against such payments received. Upon termination of contractual or customer relations with any distributor with respect to which a Seller's Receivables are due, the Buyer will promptly pay to the Seller the aggregate amount of such Seller's Receivables and agrees to assume any obligation for the payment of any amounts which may become refundable to such distributor as a result of such termination. The Seller and the Buyer will cooperate, and will use their best efforts to have their officers, directors and other employees cooperate, at the request of either party, on and after the Closing Date; in endeavoring to effect the collection of all receivables and other items owing to the Seller and in furnishing information, evidence, testimony and other assistance in connection with any actions, proceedings, arrangements, or disputes involving the Seller or the Buyer based upon contracts, arrangements or acts of the Seller which were in effect or occurred on or prior to the Closing Date.

7. **Certain Other Covenants of Seller**. (a) After the Closing Date the Seller will cease and desist from using in its corporate name or that of any of its subsidiaries or affiliates or otherwise (i) the word or name "Ballantine", (ii) any trademark or trade name included in Ballantine Assets or (iii) any other words, initials or expressions so closely resembling such words or name or any of them as to be likely to be confused therewith by the general public. The Seller will execute such consents and other documents as the Buyer may reasonably request in writing in order to enable the Buyer to use as it may desire such words, or any one or more of them, or any similar words, names, initials or expressions.

(b) The Seller will reimburse the Buyer for all liabilities and obligations assumed by the Buyer pursuant to subparagraph (ii) of Section 3(a) hereof for all advertising payments made by the Buyer in respect thereof exceeding an aggregate amount of $389,885.00. Any such reimbursement shall be made by the Seller by way of set-off against monthly royalty payments due from the Buyer to the Seller pursuant to subparagraph (v) of Section 2(a) hereof, and the Seller hereby authorizes the Buyer to credit such advertising payments made in any particular month against the royalty payments due to the Seller in respect of such month.

(c) The Seller will repurchase after the Closing Date the Buyer's Receivables then uncollected by the Seller at the purchase price paid therefor by the Buyer pursuant to subparagraph (vi) of Section 2(a) hereof in the event a court of competent jurisdiction issues an order at the request of a governmental authority effective for a period of 30 days during the period from the Closing Date through May 30, 1972, restraining the use by the Buyer of the Proprietary Rights.

8. **Certain Other Covenants of Buyer**. (a) After the Closing Date the Seller will use its best efforts to promote and maintain a high volume of sales under the Proprietary Rights.

(b) The Buyer agrees to deliver to the Seller on the Closing Data a pledge of the Buyer to the Seller, dated the Closing Date and in form and substance satisfactory to the Seller, of the Proprietary Rights as security for the payments set forth in subparagraph (v) of Section 3 (a) hereof, and the Buyer agrees to execute and deliver to the Seller such financing statement or amendment thereto as the Seller may reasonably request so as to better to perfect in the Seller the security interest created thereby; provided, however, that if such a pledge would be in violation of any of the terms, conditions or covenants of any other agreement of the Buyer currently in full force and effect, the Buyer will in good faith attempt to obtain prior to the Closing Date any consents to such pledge which maybe required; and if any required consent is unobtainable or obtainable only upon conditions detrimental to the Buyer, such pledge will not be deliverable as aforesaid. In such event, the Buyer will furnish the Seller with such evidence as it may reasonably request to ascertain the reasons therefor.

(c) The Buyer agrees that it shall pay and shall hold the Seller harmless against the payment of any sales or use tax, if any, which may be imposed in connection with the purchase and sale contemplated hereby or the possession by the Buyer of any of the Ballantine Assets.

(d) The Buyer agrees that it will use its best efforts to retain as its own employees those personnel described in clause (4) of subparagraph (i) of Section 3(a) hereof.

(e) The Buyer agrees that it will not sell, assign or otherwise transfer the Proprietary Rights during the Royalty Period without the written consent of the Seller.

(f) From and after the date hereof, the Buyer will afford to the officers, attorney, accountants and other authorized representatives of the Seller access to the offices, properties, books and records of the Buyer relating to or used in connection with the use by the Buyer of the Proprietary Rights and the collection by the Buyer of the Buyer's and Seller's Receivables, in order that the Seller may have full opportunity to make such reasonable investigation and verification as it shall desire to confirm the amounts of royalty payments due pursuant to subsection (v) of Section 2(a) hereof, and the Seller shall be permitted to make extracts from, or copies of, such books and records. The Buyer shall also furnish to the Buyer such information relating thereto as the Seller may from time to time reasonably request.

(g) The Buyer shall in good faith use its best efforts to collect all Buyer's Receivables.

9. **Representations and Warranties of the Seller**. The Seller hereby represents and warrants to the Buyer as follows:

(a) The Seller is a corporation duly organized, validly existing and in good standing under the laws of the State of New Jersey and has the corporate power to own or lease its properties and to carry on its business as now being conducted.

(b) Except as stated in Exhibits D and E, each of the instruments described therein is to its knowledge in full force and effect and constitute a legal, valid and binding obligation of the respective parties thereto enforceable in accordance with its terms.

(c) Except as stated in Exhibits B and C, the Seller owns outright all the items and equipment referred to therein other than properties sold or otherwise disposed of in the ordinary course of business subsequent to the date hereof, in each case free and clear of all mortgages, liens, encumbrances or charges of any kind or nature whatsoever, except as stated herein or in the Exhibits hereto.

(d) The Seller has no knowledge and has received no notice, except as stated in Exhibit B hereto, that any of the items listed in Exhibit C hereto, or the sale or use thereof, infringe any trademark, trade name or copyright of another.

(e) The Board of Directors of the Seller has approved this Agreement and the transactions contemplated herein and has authorized the execution and delivery of this Agreement by the Seller, and the Seller has full power, authority and legal right under its certificate of incorporation, by-laws and the laws of the State of New Jersey to sell and transfer the Ballantine Assets as herein provided.

(f) The items generally described in Exhibits B and C are useable or marketable by the Seller in accordance with its customary standards, and all finished malt alcoholic beverage products sold to the Buyer hereunder shall be produced under a high degree of quality control.

10. **Representation and Warranties of the Buyer**. The Buyer hereby represents and warrants to the Seller as follows:

(a) The Buyer is a corporation duly organized and existing and in good standing under the laws of the State of Delaware and has the corporate power to own its properties and to carry on its business now being conducted.

(b) The Board of Directors of the Buyer has approved this Agreement and the transaction contemplated herein and has authorized the execution and delivery of this Agreement by the Buyer, and the Buyer has full power, authority and legal right under its certificate of incorporation, by-laws and the laws of the State of Delaware and Missouri to carry out the transactions to be carried out on its part hereunder.

11. **Conditions to Obligations of the Buyer**. The Obligations of the Buyer hereunder are, at the option of the Buyer, subject to the conditions that on or before the Closing Date:

(a) The Seller shall have performed and complied with in all material respects all of the terms, covenants and conditions contained herein to be performed and complied with by it on or prior to the Closing Date.

(b) The Seller shall have furnished to the Buyer a copy, certified by its Secretary, of resolution duly adopted by its Board of Directors which constitute necessary corporate authorization for the consummation by the Seller of the transactions contemplated herein.

(c) All actions, proceedings, instruments and documents required to carry out this Agreement or incidental thereto and all other related legal matters shall have been approved by Messrs. Willson, Cunningham and McClellan, counsel for the Buyer, which approval shall not be unreasonably withheld.

(d) The Buyer shall have received an opinion, dated the Closing Date, or Messrs, Carro, Spanbeck and Londin, counsel for the Seller, in form and substance satisfactory to the Buyer, to the effect that the Seller is a corporation duly organized and existing and in good standing under the laws of the State of New Jersey and has the corporate power to own or lease its properties and to carry on its business as now being conducted; that no provision of the Articles of Incorporation or the By-laws of the Seller, or of any contract or other instrument to which the Seller is a party listed in any Exhibits hereto, requires the consent or authorization of any other person, firm or corporation as a condition precedent to the consummation of this Agreement or the transactions contemplated herein, or if such consent or authorization is required, that such consent or authorization has been duly given in a proper manner and form; that the Seller has full power and authority to sell, convey, assign, transfer and deliver the Ballantine Assets to the Buyer as herein provided; that all corporate acts and other proceedings required to be taken by or on the part of the Seller or its shareholders to authorize the Seller to carry out this Agreement and the transactions contemplated hereby and to sell, convey, assign, transfer and deliver the Ballantine Assets have been duly and properly taken; and that the instruments of conveyance, transfer and assignment from the Seller to the Buyer of the Ballantine Assets have been duly authorized, executed and delivered, are legally effective in accordance with their respective terms and vest in the Buyer all right, title and interest of the Seller in and to the Ballantine Assets. In rendering the foregoing option, Messrs. Carro, Spanbeck & Londin.

(e) The representatives and warranties made by the Seller herein shall be substantially correct, as of the Closing Date, with the same force and effect as though such representations and warranties had been made on and as of the Closing Date, except to the extent that such representations and warranties shall be incorrect as of the Closing Date because of events or changes occurring or arising after the date hereof in the ordinary course of business of the Seller or in fulfillment of the express provisions of this Agreement.

13. **Conditions to Obligations of the Seller**. The Obligations of the Seller under this Agreement are, at the option of the Seller, subject to the conditions that on or before the Closing Date:

(a) The Buyer shall have performed and complied with in all material respects all of the terms, covenants and conditions-con-

433

tained herein to be performed and complied with by it on or prior to the Closing Date.

(b) All actions, proceedings, instruments and documents required to carry out this Agreement or incidental thereto and all other related legal matters shall have been approved by Messrs. Carro, Spanbeck, and Londin, counsel for the Seller, which approval shall not be unreasonably withheld.

(c) The Seller shall have received an opinion dated the Closing Date, of Messrs. Willson, Cunningham, and McClellan to the effect that the Buyer is a corporation duly organized, validly existing and in good standing under the laws of the State of Delaware and that all corporate acts and proceedings to be taken by the Buyer to authorize the carrying out of this Agreement and the transactions contemplated hereby shall have been duly and properly taken.

14. **Termination of Covenants**. All representations, warranties and covenants in or pursuant to this Agreement (other than the obligations set forth in subparagraphs (v) and (vii) of Section 2 (a) and Sections 2(b)–(d), 3, 4, 5 (b) and (c) and 6–8 and 9 (f) hereof) shall be deemed to be conditions to the purchase and sale contemplated hereby and shall not survive the Closing Date.

15. **Brokerage Commissions**. Each party hereto represents and warrants that there are no claims for brokerage commissions or finders' fees in connection with the transactions contemplated by this Agreement resulting from any action taken by it. Each party hereto will indemnify the other party and hold harmless against and in respect of any claim for brokerage or other commissions relative to this Agreement or to the transactions contemplated hereby, based in any way on agreements, arrangements, or understandings claimed to have been made by such former party with any other party or parties whatsoever.

16. **No Warranty as to Condition**. Except as set forth in paragraph (f) of Section 9 hereof, Ballantine Assets will be sold by the seller hereunder "as is" and that the Seller makes no representations or warranties of any kind with respect to the description, condition, merchantability or fitness for any particular purpose of any of the Ballantine Assets.

17. **Bulk Sales Law.** The Buyer hereby waives compliance by the Seller with the provisions of the so-called Bulk Sales Law of any State.

18. **Expenses:** Whether or not the transactions contemplated hereby shall be consummated, each party hereto shall pay to costs and expenses incurred by it or on its behalf incident to the preparation of and entering into this Agreement and the consummation of said transactions.

19. **Assignment and Amendment**. (a) This Agreement shall be binding upon and inure to the benefit of the parties hereto and their

respective successors and assigns, provided that neither party shall assign this Agreement or any of its rights, privileges or obligations hereunder without this prior written consent of the other.

(b) This Agreement cannot be altered or otherwise amended except pursuant to an instrument in writing signed by each of the parties hereto.

20.   **Notices.** Any notices, requests, instruction or other document to be given hereunder by either party to the other shall be in writing and delivered personally or sent by registered or certified mail, postage paid, (a) if to the Buyer, addressed to it at 5050 Oakland Avenue, St. Louis, Missouri 63166, attention of Robert T. Colson or such other persona as the Buyer shall designate, and (b) if to the Seller addressed to it at 57 Freeman St., Newark, New Jersey 07101, attention of Stephen D. Haymes. Copies thereof shall be delivered or sent to counsel referred to in Section 10 hereof.

21.   Entire Agreement. This Agreement, together with the Exhibits hereto, contains the entire agreement between the parties hereto with respect to the transactions contemplated herein and supersedes all previous negotiations, commitments, and writings.

22.   Counterparts. This Agreement shall be executed in one or more counterparts, each of which shall be deemed an original and all of which together shall constitute one and the same instrument.

CONTRACT IN *PEEVYHOUSE v. GARLAND COAL & MINING CO.**

COAL LEASE

THIS LEASE executed this 23rd day of November 1954 by and between Willie Peevyhouse and Lucille Peevyhouse, husband and wife, hereinafter called Lessors, and Garland Coal and Mining Company, hereinafter called Lessee;

WITNESSETH

WHEREAS, the Lessors are the owners of, or have the right to mine and remove ~~the coal~~ underlying and the right to take all or any part of the ~~surface~~ of the following described lands in Haskell County, State of Oklahoma, to-wit:

The Southwest Quarter of the Southwest Quarter of Section 7, Township 8 North and Range 21 East, and, the South Half of the Northeast Quarter of the Southeast Quarter of Section 12, Township 8 North and Range 20 East,

WHEREAS, Lessee desires to mine and remove the coal underlying said premises and Lessors desire to lease the same to Lessee for that purpose;

NOW, THEREFORE, in consideration of the sum of One Dollar ($1.00) cash in hand paid by Lessee to Lessors, receipt whereof is hereby acknowledged, and in consideration of the performance by each party of the conditions hereinafter set forth, Lessors grant and lease to the Lessee the exclusive right to slope, shaft, deep mine or strip and remove coal underlying the above described property, together with the right to use and/or remove any and/all the surface of said lands necessarily incidental thereto, subject to the following terms and conditions:

—1—

This lease shall be in full force and effect for a term and period of 5 years from and after the date hereof, unless terminated sooner under its provisions. ~~[illegible]~~ the minimum royalty ~~[illegible]~~.

—2—

~~2. The Lessee agrees to commence operations on said land within one year from date hereof or in lieu thereof will pay to the Lessor an advance royalty on any part or portion of within described land Lessee shall determine needed in Lessee's operation at any time during the life of this lease the sum of 50 cents per acre the second year; 75 cents per acre the third year; and One Dollar ($1.00) per acre the fourth and all subsequent years during the term of this Lease as minimum royalty on coal to be mined from said lands, these payments to begin one year from the date hereof and to be credited on any royalty due for coal thereafter mined from said lands by said Lessee, his heirs, successors, and assigns.~~

—3—

Lessee agrees to pay to the Lessors upon all coal mined, removed and sold from these premises a royalty of ~~15~~ 20 cents per ton of 2000 pounds, railroad weights to govern if shipped by rail, truck scale weights if loaded on trucks, such royalty to be paid not later than the 10th day of each month succeeding the month in which the same be mined, removed and sold, provided that minimum royalties which may have been advanced at the rates per acre herein set forth shall be credited on royalty due for coal mined and sold. And Lessee will furnish to the Lessors on or before said date a statement showing the amount of coal mined and removed and sold during the preceding month; the Lessors shall have the right at reasonable times to inspect Lessee's books for the purpose of verifying the amount of coal so mined and Lessors shall have the right at reasonable times to inspect Lessee's operations.

—4—

Lessee shall have the exclusive right to enter upon same and prospect for coal, drill holes and make any necessary excavations and if it determines coal be present in paying quantities, then to dig, mine or strip, remove, sell and dispose of all the mineable and marketable coal that in the opinion of the Lessee can be profitably mined and removed therefrom, together with all incidental mining rights necessary to the success of such operation, and the right of ingress and egress in, to and across said property, ~~or any other property owned by Lessors~~ for the purpose of entering upon said premises in connection with the production and transportation of coal from said premises on adjacent lands.

—5—

After commencement, such operations shall be carried on in a miner-like and workmanlike manner, as usually conducted in similar operations. Lessee may strip the overburden from such coal as shall be profitably mineable and marketable and will pay all taxes arising from the mining operation, and Lessors agree that they will pay and keep paid all taxes upon the premises herein leased. Lessee shall pay for damages, caused by Lessee's prospecting operations, to growing crops on said lands.

—6—

It is understood that in the mining operations hereunder the surface of said land may be excavated and the Lessors agree to furnish Lessee, in consideration of said royalty, all surface as may be necessary to be used by Lessee in the operation of strip pits, and may be used by Lessee for drainage ditches, haulage roads, spoil banks, tipples, tracks, and any other structures that Lessee finds necessary in the operation of said strip pit or pits or coal mine and the Lessee agrees that all such structures shall be located consistent with good operating practice so as to cause the least damage or inconvenience to the owner or user of such surface; Lessee agrees that he will save Lessors harmless from claims arising out of the actual mining and removing of said coal and Lessors agree that they will save harmless and indemnify the Lessee from any claim or liability arising from any damage to the surface of these lands caused by such operations; it is further recognized the Lessee shall have the right without liability to the Lessor, wherever it may be necessary in conducting such operations, to change the course of any streams or water courses and to erect and maintain such drainage ditches as it shall deem advisable having due regard for the successful operation of said strip pit and damage to the remainder of the property.

—7—

It is understood and agreed that in the type of operation contemplated by Lessee it is necessary to procure leases of other property from which coal can be mined or stripped so as to justify the investment to be made by Lessee and in consideration of the royalty herein paid, Lessors grant to the Lessee the right to haul over and across said premises and through said pits coal from adjacent lands free from any charge.

* 382 P.2d 109 (Okla.1962). Thanks to Professor Judith L. Maute for unearthing this contract. Prof. Maute describes the lease as "a preprinted form lease containing some handwritten modifications and one typed page defining the remedial and other specific duties." Maute, Peevyhouse v. Garland Coal and Mining Co. Revisited: The Ballad of Willie and Lucille, 89 Northwestern L. Rev. 1341 (1995). We include a copy of the original lease followed by a more legible, retyped version.

- 7a -

Lessors hereby acknowledges receipt of the sum of $2,000.00 as advanced royalty which is to be credited on any royalty due for coal thereafter mined from said lands by said Lessee from the first coal produced.

- 7b -

Lessee agrees to make fills in the pits dug on said premises on the property lines in such manner that fences can be placed thereon and access had to opposite sides of the pits.

- 7c -

Lessee agrees to smooth off the top of the spoils banks on the above premises.

- 7d -

Lessee agrees to leave the creek crossing the above premises in such a condition that it will not interfere with the crossings to be made in pits as set out in 7b.

- 7e -

Lessee agrees to build and maintain a cattle guard in the south fence of SW¼ SW¼ of Section 7 if an access road is made through said fence.

- 7f -

Lessee further agrees to leave no shale or dirt on the high wall of said pits.

- 7g -

It is further agreed between the parties hereto that this lease is not to be assigned, transferred or sub-let without the written permission of the lessors. Provided however, that an assignment of this lease to the Canadian Mining Company shall not require such written permission.

- 7h -

Lessee agrees to have the above described premises surveyed and the boundary lines on said premises established prior to commencement of digging coal.

—8—

The right is hereby conferred upon Lessee to cancel this Lease upon thirty (30) days' written notice when the operation of removal of coal therefrom shall in his judgment become unprofitable and Lessee shall be the sole judge as to when same is unprofitable.

—9—

In case Lessee fails to pay the royalty when due or fails to comply with any one of the other terms of this Lease, the Lessors shall give the Lessee fifteen (15) days' written notice, calling attention to the default by Lessee, specifying wherein the Lessee has failed to comply with the terms of this agreement, and, if at the end of said period, Lessee is still in default, the Lessors shall have the right to take immediate possession of the leased premises without let or hindrance, and the Lessee shall not have the right to remove any of its property, machinery, tools or supplies from the demised premises until all amounts due the Lessors have been paid in full.

In the event this Lease expires by operation of its own terms, or the Lessee elects to cancel the same under the provisions hereinabove set out, the Lessee shall have, provided it is not in default, six (6) months from said termination or cancellation within which to remove all of its property, machinery, tools, supplies or equipment that it might have upon said demised premises. All structures built or erected upon said premises shall be and remain the sole and separate property of the Lessee.

—10—

It is mutually understood and agreed that the right, privileges and obligations herein conferred on the parties shall be binding on the executors, administrators, heirs, successors or assigns of the parties hereto whether so specifically stated herein or not; in the event that the Lessors shall own less than the fee of the premises and coal herein demised Lessee shall pay royalty to them as their respective interests shall appear. If the property is encumbered by a mortgage or other liens, Lessee shall have the right to pay said liens and deduct from royalty due Lessors.

IN WITNESS WHEREOF, the parties have set their hands this_____23rd_____day of_____November_____, 19__54__

Willie Peevyhouse

Lucille Peevyhouse
                                          Lessors
Garland Coal & Mining Company

By *Bernard Compton*
                                          Lessee

STATE OF___Oklahoma___
                                          } ss.
COUNTY OF___Haskell___

Before me, the undersigned, a Notary Public, in and for the said County and State, on this_____23rd_____day of_____November_____, 19__54__ personally appeared __Willie Peevyhouse and Lucille Peevyhouse, his wife__ to me known to be the identical persons who executed the within and foregoing instrument and acknowledged to me that they executed the same as their free and voluntary act and deed for the uses and purposes therein set forth.

IN WITNESS WHEREOF, I have hereunto set my hand and official seal the day and year last above written.

My Commission Expires___9-24-1957___   *J. F. Hudson*
                                                          Notary Public

STATE OF_____
                                          } ss.
COUNTY OF_____

Before me, the undersigned, a Notary Public, in and for the said County and State, on this_____day of_____, 19_____ personally appeared_____ to me known to be the identical person who executed the within and foregoing instrument and acknowledged to me that he executed the same as his free and voluntary act and deed for the uses and purposes therein set forth.

IN WITNESS WHEREOF, I have hereunto set my hand and official seal the day and year last above written.

                                                          Notary Public

My Commission Expires_____

State of Oklahoma,
      ss:
County of Haskell,

    Before me, the undersigned, a Notary Public in and for said State, on this 23rd day of November, 1954, personally appeared Burrow Cumpton, to me known to be the identical person who executed the within and foregoing instrument as attorney in fact of Garland Coal & Mining Company, and acknowledged to me that he executed the same as his free and voluntary act and deed and as the free and voluntary act and deed of Garland Coal and Mining Company, for the uses and purposes therein set forth.

    Witness my hand and official seal the day and year last above written.

                                _____
                                   Notary Public

My commission expires:

    9-24-1957

CONTRACT IN *PEEVYHOUSE v. GARLAND COAL & MINING CO*
(Retyped)

Whereas, Lessee desires to mine and remove the coal underlying said premises and Lessors desire to lease the same to Lessee for that purpose:

Now, therefore, in consideration of the sum of One Dollar ($1.00) cash in hand paid by Lessee to Lessors, receipt whereof is hereby acknowledged and in consideration of the performance by each party of the conditions hereinafter set forth, Lessors grant and lease to the Lessee the exclusive right to slope, shaft, deep mine or strip and remove coal underlying the above described property, together with the right to use and/or remove any and/all the surface of said lands necessarily incidental thereto, subject to the following terms and conditions:

–1–

This lease shall be in full force and effect for a term and period of 3 years from and after the date hereof unless terminated sooner under its provisions. The xxxxxxxxxx xxxxxxxxxx xxxxxxxxxx xxxxxxxx xxxxxxxxxx to the Lessor xxx xxxxxxxxxx xxxxxxxxxx xxxxxxxxxx lessee for xxxxxxxxx xxxxxxxxxx xxxxxxxxxx xxxxxxxxxx xxxxxxxxxx xxxxxxxx xxxxxxxxx xxxxxxxxx xxxxxxxx the minimum royalty xxxxxxxxxx xxxxxxxxxx xxxxx.

–2–

The Lessee agrees to common operations on said land within one year from date hereof or in xxxx thereof will pay to the Lessor an advance royalty on any part or portion of within described land Lessee shall determine needed in Lessees operation of any time during the life of this lease the sum of 50 xxxx xxx xxxx the second year 75 xxxx xxx xxxx the third year, and One Dollar ($1.00) per acre the fourth and all subsequent years during the term of this Lease as minimum royalty on coal to be mined from said lands these payments to begin one year from the date hereof and to be credited xx xxx royalty due for coal these after mined from said lands by said Lessee, his heirs, successors, and assigns.

–3–

Lessee agrees to pay the Lessors upon all coal mined, removed and sold from these premises a royalty of 16 XX 20 cents per ton of 2000 pounds, railroad weights to govern if shipped by rail, truck scale weights if loaded on trucks, such royalty to be paid not later that the 20th day of each month succeeding the month in which the same to be mined, removed and sold, provided that minimum royalties which may have been advanced at the rates per acre herein set forth shall be credited on royalty due for coal mined and sold. And Lessee will furnish to the

Lessors on or before said date a statement showing the amount of coal mined and removed and sold during the preceding month: the Lessors shall have the right at reasonable times to inspect Lessee's books for the purpose of verifying the amount of coal so mined and Lessors shall have the right at reasonable times to inspect Lessee's operations.

–4–

Lessee shall have the exclusive right to enter upon same and prospect for coal, drill holes and make any necessary excavations and if it determines coal be present in paying quantities, then to dig, mine or strip, remove, sell and dispose of all the mineable and marketable coal that in the opinion of the Lessee can be profitably mined and removed therefrom, together with all incidental mining rights necessary to the success of such operation, and the right of ingress and egress in, to and across said property. Or xxx the property owned by Lessors for the purpose of entering upon said premises in connection with the production and transportation of coal from said premises on adjacent lands.

–5–

After commencement, such operations shall be carried on in a miner-like and workmanlike manner, as usually conducted in similar operations. Lessee may strip the overburden from such coal as shall be profitably mineable and marketable and will pay all taxes arising from the mining operation, and Lessors agree that they will pay and keep paid all said taxes upon the premises herein leased. Lessee shall pay for damages, caused by Lessee's prospecting operations, to growing crops on said lands.

–6–

It is understood that in the mining operations hereunder the surface of said land may be excavated and the Lessors agree to furnish Lessee, in consideration of said royalty, all surface as may be necessary to be used by Lessee in the operation of strip pits, and may be used by Lessee for drainage ditches, haulage roads, spoil banks, tipples, tracks, and any other structures that Lessee finds necessary in the operation of said strip pit or pits or coal mine and the Lessee agrees that all such structures will be located consistent with good operating practice so as to cause the least damage or inconvenience to the owner or user of such surface: Lessee agrees that he will save Lessors harmless from claims arising out of the actual mining and removing of said coal and Lessors agree that they will save harmless and indemnity the Lessee from any claim or liability arising from any damage to the surface of these lands caused by such operations: it is further recognized that the Lessee shall have the right without liability to the Lessor, wherever it may be necessary in conducting such operations, to change the course of any streams or water courses and to erect and maintain such drainage ditches as it shall deem advisable having due regard for the successful operation of said strip pit and damage to the remainder of the property.

–7–

It is understood and agreed that in the type of operation contemplated by the Lessee it is necessary to procure leases of other property from which coal can be mined or stripped so as to justify the investment to be made by the Lessee and in consideration of the royalty herein paid, Lessors grant to the lessee the right to haul over and across said premises and through said pits coal from adjacent lands free from any charge.

–7a–

Lessors hereby acknowledges receipt of the sum of $2,000.00 as advanced royalty which is to be credited on any royalty due for coal thereafter mined from said lands by said Lessee from the first coal produced.

–7b–

Lessee agrees to make fills in the pits dug on said premises on the property lines in such manner that fences can be place thereon and access had to opposite sides of the pits.

–7c–

Lessee agrees to smooth off the top of the spoils banks on the above premises.

–7d–

Lessee agrees to leave the creek crossing the above premises in such a condition that it will not interfere with the crossings to be made in pits as set out in 7b.

–7e–

Lessee agrees to build and maintain a cattle guard in the south fence of SWL SWL of Section 7 if an access road is made through said fence.

–7f–

Lessee further agrees to leave no shale or dirt on the high wall of said pits.

–7g–

It is further agreed between the parties hereto that this lease is not to be assigned, transferred, or sub-let without the written permission of the lessors. Provided however, that an assignment of this lease to the Canadian Mining Company shall not require such written permission.

–7h–

Lessee agrees to have the above described premises surveyed and the boundary lines on said premises established prior to commencement of digging coal.

–8–

The right is hereby conferred upon Lessee to cancel this Lease upon thirty (30) days' written notice when the operation of removal of coal therefrom shall in his judgment become unprofitable and Lessee shall be the sole judge as to when same is unprofitable

–9–

In case Lessee fails to pay the royalty when due or fails to comply with any one of the other terms of this lease, the Lessors shall give the Lessee fifteen (15) days' written notice, calling attention to the default by Lessee, specifying wherein the Lessee has failed to comply with the terms of this agreement, and if at the end of said period, Lessee is still in default, the Lessors shall have the right to take immediate possession of the leased premises without let or hindrance, and the Lessee shall not have the right to remove any of its property, machinery, tools, or supplies from the demised premises until all amounts due the Lessors have been paid in full.

In the event this lease expires by operation of its own terms, or the Lessee elects to cancel the same under the provisions hereinabove set out, the Lessee shall have, provided it is not in default, six (6) months from said termination or cancellation within which to remove all of its property, machinery, tools, supplies, or equipment that it might have upon said demised premises. All structures built or erected upon said premises shall be and remain the sole and separate property of the Lessee.

–10–

It is mutually understood and agreed that the right, privileges and obligations herein conferred on the parties shall be binding on the executors, administrators, heirs, successors, or assigns of the parties hereto whether so specifically stated herein or not: ~~in the event that the Lessors shall own less than the fee of the premises and coal herein xxxxxxx Lessee shall pay royalty to them as their respective interests shall appear.~~ If the property is encumbered by a mortgage or other liens, lessee shall have to the right to pay said liens and deduct from royalty due Lessors.

In witness whereof, the parties have set their hands this <u>23rd</u> day of <u>November</u> 19<u>54.</u>

<u>Willie Peevyhouse (signature)</u>

<u>Lucille Peevyhouse (signature)</u>

Lessors

Garland Coal and Mining Company

<u>By xxxxxxxx Compton (signature)</u>

CONTRACT IN *IN THE MATTER OF BABY M**

SURROGATE PARENTING AGREEMENT

THIS AGREEMENT is made this 6th day of February, 1985, by and between MARY BETH WHITEHEAD, a married woman (herein referred to as "Surrogate"), RICHARD WHITEHEAD, her husband (herein referred to a "Husband"), and WILLIAM STERN, (herein referred to as "Natural Father").

RECITALS

THIS AGREEMENT is made with reference to the following facts:

(1) WILLIAM STERN, Natural Father, is an individual over the age of eighteen (18) years who is desirous of entering into this Agreement.

(2) The sole purpose of this Agreement is to enable WILLIAM STERN and his infertile wife to have a child which is biologically related to WILLIAM STERN.

(3) MARY BETH WHITEHEAD, Surrogate, and RICHARD WHITE-HEAD, her husband, are over the age of eighteen (18) years and desirous of entering into this Agreement in consideration of the following:

NOW THEREFORE, in consideration of the mutual promises contained Herein and the intentions of being legally bound hereby, the parties agree as follows:

1. MARY BETH WHITEHEAD, Surrogate, represents that she is capable of conceiving children. MARY BETH WHITEHEAD understands and agrees that in the best interest of the child, she will not form or attempt to form a parent-child relationship with any child or children she may conceive, carry to term and give birth to, pursuant to the provisions of this Agreement, and shall freely surrender custody to WILLIAM STERN, Natural Father, immediately upon birth of the child; and terminate all parental rights to said child pursuant to this Agreement.

2. MARY BETH WHITEHEAD, Surrogate, and RICHARD WHITE-HEAD, her husband, have been married since 12/2/73, and RICHARD WHITEHEAD is in agreement with the purposes, intents and provisions of this Agreement and acknowledges that his wife, MARY BETH WHITEHEAD, Surrogate, shall be artificially inseminated pursuant to the provisions of this Agreement. RICHARD WHITEHEAD agrees that in the best interest of the child, he will not form or attempt to form a parent-child relationship with any child or children MARY BETH WHITEHEAD, Surrogate, may conceive by artificial insemination as described herein, and agrees to freely and readily surrender immediate custody of the child to WILLIAM STERN, Natural Father; and terminate his parental rights; RICHARD WHITEHEAD further acknowledges he will do all acts necessary to rebut the presumption of paternity of any

* Appendix A, 537 A2d 1227, 1265 (N.J. 1988).

offspring conceived and born pursuant to aforementioned agreement as provided by law, including blood testing and/or HLA testing.

3. WILLIAM STERN, Natural Father, does hereby enter into this written contractual Agreement with MARY BETH WHITEHEAD, Surrogate, where MARY BETH WHITEHEAD shall be artificially inseminated with the semen of WILLIAM STERN by a physician. MARY BETH WHITEHEAD, Surrogate, upon becoming pregnant, acknowledges that she will carry said embryo/fetus(s) until delivery. MARY BETH WHITE-HEAD, Surrogate, and RICHARD WHITEHEAD, her husband, agree that they will cooperate with any background investigation into the Surrogate's medical, family and personal history and warrants the information to be accurate to the best of their knowledge. MARY BETH WHITEHEAD, Surrogate, and RICHARD WHITEHEAD, her husband, agree to surrender custody of the child to WILLIAM STERN, Natural Father, immediately upon birth, acknowledging that it is the intent of this Agreement in the best interests of the child to do so; as well as institute and cooperate in proceedings to terminate their respective parental rights to said child, and sign any and all necessary affidavits, documents, and the like, in order to further the intent and purposes of this Agreement. It is understood by MARY BETH WHITEHEAD, and RICHARD WHITEHEAD, that the child to be conceived is being done so for the sole purpose of giving said child to WILLIAM STERN, its natural and biological father. MARY BETH WHITEHEAD and RICHARD WHITEHEAD agree to sign all necessary affidavits prior to and after the birth of the child and voluntarily participate in any paternity proceedings necessary to have WILLIAM STERN'S name entered on said child's birth certificate as the natural or biological father.

4. That the consideration for this Agreement, which is compensation for services and expenses, and in no way is to be construed as a fee for termination of parental rights or a payment in exchange for a consent to surrender the child for adoption, in addition to other provisions contained herein, shall be as follows:

(A) $10,000 shall be paid to MARY BETH WHITEHEAD, Surrogate, upon surrender of custody to WILLIAM STERN, the natural and biological father of the child born pursuant to the provisions of this Agreement for surrogate services and expenses in carrying out her obligations under this Agreement;

(B) The consideration to be paid to MARY BETH WHITEHEAD, Surrogate, shall be deposited with the Infertility Center of New York (hereinafter ICNY), the representative of WILLIAM STERN, at the time of the signing of this Agreement, and held in escrow until completion of the duties and obligations of MARY BETH WHITEHEAD, Surrogate, (see Exhibit "A" for a copy of the Escrow Agreement), as herein described.

(C) WILLIAM STERN, Natural Father, shall pay the expenses incurred by MARY BETH WHITEHEAD, Surrogate, pursuant to her pregnancy, more specifically defined as follows:

(1) All medical, hospitalization, and pharmaceutical, laboratory and therapy expenses incurred as a result of MARY BETH WHITEHEAD'S pregnancy, not covered or allowed by her present health and major medical insurance, including all extraordinary medical expenses and all reasonable expenses for treatment of any emotional or mental conditions or problems related to said pregnancy, but in no case shall any such expenses be paid or reimbursed after a period of six (6) months have elapsed since the date of the termination of the pregnancy, and this Agreement specifically excludes any expenses for lost wages or other non-itemized incidentals (see Exhibit "B") related to said pregnancy.

(2) WILLIAM STERN, Natural Father, shall not be responsible for any latent medical expenses occurring six (6) weeks subsequent to the birth of the child, unless the medical problem or abnormality incident thereto was known and treated by a physician prior to the expiration of said six (6) week period and in written notice of the same sent to ICNY, as representative of WILLIAM STERN by certified mail, return receipt requested, advising of this treatment.

(3) WILLIAM STERN, Natural Father, shall be responsible for the total costs of all paternity testing. Such paternity testing may, at the option of WILLIAM STERN, Natural Father, be required prior to release of the surrogate fee from escrow. In the event WILLIAM STERN, Natural Father, is conclusively determined not to be the biological father of the child as a result of an HLA test, this Agreement will be deemed breached and MARY BETH WHITEHEAD, Surrogate, shall not be entitled to any fee. WILLIAM STERN, Natural Father, shall be entitled to reimbursement of all medical and related expenses from MARY BETH WHITE-HEAD, Surrogate, and RICHARD WHITEHEAD, her husband.

(4) MARY BETH WHITEHEAD'S reasonable travel expenses incurred at the request of WILLIAM STERN, pursuant to this Agreement.

5. MARY BETH WHITEHEAD, Surrogate, and RICHARD WHITE-HEAD, her husband, understand and agree to assume all risks, including the risk of death, which are incidental to conception, pregnancy, child-birth, including but not limited to, postpartum complications. A copy of said possible risks and/or complications is attached hereto and made a part hereof (see Exhibit "C").

6. MARY BETH WHITEHEAD, Surrogate, and RICHARD WHITE-HEAD, her husband, hereby agree to undergo psychiatric evaluation by JOAN EINWOHNER, a psychiatrist as designated by WILLIAM STERN or an agent thereof. WILLIAM STERN shall pay for the cost of said psychiatric evaluation. MARY BETH WHITEHEAD and RICHARD WHITEHEAD shall sign, prior to their evaluations, a medical release

permitting dissemination of the report prepared as a result of said psychiatric evaluations to ICNY or WILLIAM STERN and his wife.

7. MARY BETH WHITEHEAD, Surrogate, and RICHARD WHITE-HEAD, her husband, hereby agree that it is the exclusive and sole right of WILLIAM STERN, Natural Father, to name said child.

8. "Child" as referred to in this Agreement shall include all children born simultaneously pursuant to the inseminations contemplated herein.

9. In the event of the death of WILLIAM STERN, prior or subsequent to the birth of said child, it is hereby understood and agreed by MARY BETH WHITEHEAD, Surrogate, and RICHARD WHITEHEAD, her husband, that the child will be placed in the custody of WILLIAM STERN'S wife.

10. In the event that the child is miscarried prior to the fifth (5th) month of pregnancy, no compensation, as enumerated in paragraph 4(A), shall be paid to MARY BETH WHITEHEAD, Surrogate. However, the expenses enumerated in paragraph 4(C) shall be paid or reimbursed to MARY BETH WHITEHEAD, Surrogate. In the event the child is miscarried, dies or is stillborn subsequent to the fourth (4th) month of pregnancy and said child does not survive, the Surrogate shall receive $1,000.00 in lieu of the compensation enumerated in paragraph 4(A). In the event of a miscarriage or stillbirth as described above, this Agreement shall terminate and neither MARY BETH WHITEHEAD, Surrogate, nor WILLIAM STERN, Natural Father, shall be under any further obligation under this Agreement.

11. MARY BETH WHITEHEAD, Surrogate, and WILLIAM STERN, Natural Father, shall have undergone complete physical and genetic evaluation, under the direction and supervision of a licensed physician, to determine whether the physical health and well-being of each is satisfactory. Said physical examination shall include testing for venereal diseases, specifically including but not limited to, syphilis, herpes and gonorrhea. Said venereal diseases testing shall be done prior to, but not limited to, each series of inseminations.

12. In the event that pregnancy has not occurred within a reasonable time, in the opinion of WILLIAM STERN, Natural Father, this Agreement shall terminate by written notice to MARY BETH WHITEHEAD, Surrogate, at the residence provided to the ICNY by the Surrogate, from ICNY, as representative of WILLIAM STERN, Natural Father.

13. MARY BETH WHITEHEAD, Surrogate, agrees that she will not abort the children conceived except, if in the professional medical opinion of the inseminating physician, such action is necessary for the physical health of MARY BETH WHITEHEAD or the child has been determined by said physician to be physiologically abnormal. MARY BETH WHITEHEAD further agrees, upon the request of said physician to undergo amniocentesis (see Exhibit "D") or similar tests to detect

genetic and congenital defects. In the event said test reveals that the fetus is genetically or congenitally abnormal, MARY BETH WHITE-HEAD, Surrogate, agrees to abort the fetus upon demand of WILLIAM STERN, Natural Father, in which event, the fee paid to the Surrogate will be in accordance to Paragraph 10. If MARY BETH WHITEHEAD refuses to abort the fetus upon demand of WILLIAM STERN, his obligations as stated in this Agreement shall cease forthwith, except as to obligation of paternity imposed by statute.

14. Despite the provisions of Paragraph 13, WILLIAM STERN, Natural Father, recognizes that some genetic and congenital abnormalities may not be detected by amniocentesis or other tests, and therefore, if proven to be the biological father of the child, assumes the legal responsibility for any child who may possess genetic or congenital abnormalities. (See Exhibits "E" and "F").

15. MARY BETH WHITEHEAD, Surrogate, further agrees to adhere to all medical instructions given to her by the inseminating physician as well as her independent obstetrician. MARY BETH WHITEHEAD also agrees not to smoke cigarettes, drink alcoholic beverages, use illegal drugs, or take non-prescription medications or prescribed medications without written consent from her physician. MARY BETH WHITE-HEAD agrees to follow a prenatal medical examination schedule to consist of no fewer visits then: one visit per month during the first seven (7) months of pregnancy, two visits (each to occur at two-week intervals) during the eighth and ninth month of pregnancy.

16. MARY BETH WHITEHEAD, Surrogate, agrees to cause RICHARD WHITEHEAD, her husband, to execute a refusal of consent form as annexed hereto as Exhibit "G".

17. Each party acknowledges that he or she fully understands this Agreement and its legal effect, and that they are signing the same freely and voluntarily and that neither party has any reason to believe that the other(s) did not freely and voluntarily execute said Agreement.

18. In the event any of the provisions of this Agreement are deemed to be invalid or unenforceable, the same shall be deemed severable from the remainder of this Agreement and shall not cause the invalidity or unenforceability of the remainder of this Agreement. If such provision shall be deemed invalid due to its scope or breadth, then said provision shall be deemed valid to the extent of the scope or breadth permitted by law.

19. The original of this Agreement, upon execution, shall be retained by the Infertility Center of New York, with photocopies being distributed to MARY BETH WHITEHEAD, Surrogate and WILLIAM STERN, Natural Father, having the same legal effect as the original.

WILLIAM STERN, Natural Father

DATE 2/6/85

STATE OF NEW YORK

SS.:

COUNTY OF NEW YORK

On the 6th day of February, 1985, before me personally came WILLIAM STERN, known to me, and to me known, to be the individual described in the foregoing instrument and he acknowledged to me that he executed the same as his free and voluntary act.

NOTARY PUBLIC

APPENDIX B

We have read the foregoing five pages of this Agreement, and it is our collective intention by affixing our signatures below, to enter into a binding legal obligation.

MARY BETH WHITEHEAD, Surrogate

DATE 1–30–85

RICHARD WHITEHEAD, Surrogate's Husband

DATE 1–30–85

STATE OF NEW YORK

SS.:

COUNTY OF NEW YORK

On the 6th day of February, 1985, before as personally came MARY BETH WHITEHEAD, known to me, and to me known to be the individual described in the foregoing instrument and she acknowledged to me that she executed the same as her free and voluntary act.

NOTARY PUBLIC

STATE OF NEW YORK

SS.:

COUNTY OF NEW YORK

On the 6th day of February, 1985, before as personally came RICHARD WHITEHEAD, known to me, and to me known to be the individual described in the foregoing instrument and he acknowledged to me that he executed the same me his free and voluntary act.

NOTARY PUBLIC

CONTRACT IN *DALTON v. EDUCATIONAL TESTING SERVICE**

* 63 N.E.2d 289 (N.Y. 1995). Many thanks to Vincent Nicolosi, Esq., for providing this material. Copyright © 1991 The College Board. Reprinted with permission.

You can request services and information 24 hours,* 7 days a week,* if you call from a TouchTone™ phone

CALL: 609-771-7600 (Princeton, NJ) ● 510-653-1564 (Bay Area, CA)

- To speed your call, try to avoid the busiest day (Monday) and the busiest hours daily (3:00 to 5:00 p.m. Eastern time)
- If you call from a rotary phone, or if you need information or services not listed here, please hold. You will be connected with one of our customer service representatives, who are on duty 8:30 a.m. – 9:30 p.m. ET Monday-Friday.

To change your test choice, test date, or test center
You must call by Wednesday, two and one-half weeks before the test date. If you can't call by the Wednesday deadline, on the test day take your ticket to the test center where you want to be tested. If space and materials are available, you will be admitted ahead of standby candidates. The fee for changing your test choice, test date, or test center is $15.00. You will be billed for this service.
If you change your test date, you are not entitled to an absentee refund for the original date.

To re-register
If you are currently in high school and have previously submitted a Registration Form for either the SAT or Achievement Tests, you don't have to fill out another Registration Form to register for another test date. Just call.
You'll be billed $6.00 for each test date you request, plus the test fees and fees for any additional services you request. See the back cover for registration deadlines.

To send additional score reports
If you have already received scores and want to send them to additional colleges and scholarship programs, scores will be mailed three to five weeks after you call.
You will be billed $3.00 per call, plus $6.00 for each report.

To rush scores
It takes about three weeks to score the tests and another two weeks to send out scores. However, if you want colleges to get your scores faster, you can call to request Rush Reporting. When you order Rush Reporting, your scores are sent within two working days after your test has been scored; your test is not scored faster. If you request scores for a future test date your request will be held until those scores are available.
When you request Rush Reporting, we will send to the colleges and scholarship programs an interim report containing all your SAT and Achievement Test scores plus identification information. You will receive a copy confirming where reports have been sent. You will be billed $20.00 for this service plus $6.00 for each report. Full reports will be sent to the institutions you specified during the next scheduled processing of reports.
There is only one $20.00 service fee regardless of the number of calls you make in one day. If you order more than eight reports, you'll have to place a second call.

Call 609-771-7600 ☎
for recorded information
(A recap of the *Bulletin*)
- Registration deadlines for each test date
- Standby testing
- Admission tickets and correction form
- Acceptable ID
- Score reports — general information
- SAT Question and Answer Service — how to order

You'll need:
- Your 7-digit registration number (you'll find it on your score report or ticket) and the test date that matches it (you're assigned a different registration number for each test date). We need this information to retrieve your file.
- The 5-digit code for the test center you want (when you re-register or change test center or test date). See page 12 for codes.
- The 4-digit codes for colleges or scholarship programs (when you send or rush scores or re-register). See page 17 for codes.

* Occasionally, the database may not be available because it is being updated. Please call again.

TDD for hearing impaired:
609-771-7150
(must call from a TDD)

Call 609-771-7600 ☎
to request publications
To request the *Registration Bulletin, Taking the SAT, Taking the Achievement Tests*, Additional Report Request Forms, and information on College Board publications and software, leave your name and address.

2

452

Scholastic Aptitude Test (SAT)

The SAT is a three-hour, multiple-choice test that measures the verbal and mathematical abilities you have developed over many years both in and out of school. Each test book contains:

- two 30-minute sections that test your vocabulary, verbal reasoning, and reading comprehension
- two 30-minute sections that test your ability to solve problems involving arithmetic, algebra, and geometry
- one 30-minute Test of Standard Written English (TSWE) that measures your ability to recognize and use standard written English. Your TSWE score can help the college you attend place you in an English course appropriate to your abilities.

The test also includes a 30-minute section of equating questions (verbal, mathematical, or TSWE). Answers to these questions do not count toward your score.

Your SAT scores, course grades, and other information about your academic background help college admission officers evaluate how well prepared you are to do college-level work. Because courses and grading standards vary widely from school to school, scores on standardized tests, such as the SAT, help colleges compare the ability of students from different schools.

Taking the SAT is a free booklet available from your school guidance office that explains how the test is organized, timed, and scored, and the types of questions used. Take the complete practice test in that booklet to get a good idea of what to expect. You will also find the test-taking tips helpful.

You may have heard that changes to the SAT are planned. However, most of the changes will not be implemented for several years. The information about the test contained in this 1991-92 *Bulletin* and in *Taking the SAT* reflects the content of the test to be administered in 1991-92.

Achievement Tests

The Achievement Tests are one-hour, multiple-choice tests in specific subjects. Unlike the SAT, which measures more general abilities, Achievement Tests measure your knowledge of particular subjects and your ability to apply that knowledge. Some colleges require one or more Achievement Tests for admission or placement purposes.

Some require various combinations of tests; others permit students to choose. Check the requirements of the colleges where you might apply before deciding which tests to take.

Taking the Achievement Tests, a free booklet available from your school guidance office, has detailed descriptions and sample questions for each test. Sixteen Achievement Tests are offered on the dates indicated below.

Achievement Tests[1]	Nov. 2, 1991	Dec. 7, 1991	Jan. 25, 1992	May 2, 1992	June 6, 1992
English Composition[2]					
All-multiple-choice[3]	●		●	●	●
With Essay		●			
Literature	●	●		●	●
American History and Social Studies	●	●	●	●	●
European History and World Cultures					●
Mathematics Level I[3]	●	●	●	●	●
Mathematics Level II[3]	●	●		●	●
Mathematics Level IIC (Calculator)[4]					●
French	●	●	●	●	●
German		●			●
Modern Hebrew					●
Italian[5]		●			
Latin		●			●
Spanish	●	●		●	●
Biology	●	●		●	●
Chemistry	●	●		●	●
Physics	●	●		●	●

[1] For Sunday administrations see page 4. The June 1992 Sunday administration will be held on May 31, 1992.

[2] The English Composition Test comes in two versions: one has only multiple-choice questions; the other, English Composition with Essay, has an essay question (20 minutes) and multiple-choice questions (40 minutes). Please note that English Composition with Essay is offered only in the first hour of testing and only in December; the all-multiple-choice English Composition Test is given on all other Achievement test dates except December.

[3] In Texas only, English Composition (multiple-choice only), Mathematics Level I, and Mathematics Level II will be offered on April 4, 1992.

[4] A new Achievement Test, Mathematics Level IIC, was introduced in June 1991. It can be taken only during the first hour of testing. A calculator is required for this test. See your math teacher or guidance counselor for an updated list of approved calculators.

[5] Beginning in 1991, the Italian Test will be offered in December only.

You Can Re-Register by Phone . . .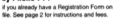

if you already have a Registration Form on file. See page 2 for instructions and fees.

To Fill Out the Registration Form . . .

refer to the instructions here and on the form.

Items 1-3: Your name, date of birth, and sex are required to establish your file and match your records. Fill in these items **exactly** the same way each time you register, on answer sheets, and any time you request ATP services. If you don't, your scores and other services will be delayed.

Item 4: Your **social security number** is used to help identify your record and add scores to it if you test at other times. It will appear on score reports you request to be sent to your school and to colleges and scholarship programs. With your social security number, your records can be matched more readily. If you participate in the Student Search Service (see Item 8), it will also be made available to participating institutions.

Item 7: Write in the **year you expect to graduate** from high school, and fill in the corresponding ovals and the oval for the **month you expect to graduate.**

Item 8: The Student Search Service is a free information service for students who take the SAT. Fill in the "Yes" oval to participate.

Use Item 8 to give the College Board permission to let colleges and government-sponsored scholarship programs know that you are interested in receiving information about educational and financial aid opportunities they offer.

The Student Search Service will send colleges the following information about you: name, address, sex, birth date, school, social security number (if you give it), and intended college major.

Colleges and government-sponsored scholarship programs that use the Student Search Service receive your name because of certain characteristics you have such as a specific grade average, score range,

3

intended college major, state or zip code, or ethnic background (if you provide it). The Student Search Service does not report your scores to them.

Item 10: If you live more than 75 miles from the nearest test center (see list, page 12), it may be possible to test closer to your home. Enter the number 02-000 as your first-choice test center, enclose a letter describing your situation, and mail the Registration Form and letter before the regular registration deadline. (See the calendar on the back cover.) Requests from outside the United States must be received by the special requests deadline.

Item 11: To have **score reports sent to colleges or scholarship programs,** write in their code numbers and fill in the corresponding ovals. Codes are listed on pages 17-23. (If a college or program is not listed, see *Code Lists: Test Centers and Test Score Recipients* in your school guidance office.)

Your fee for the SAT or Achievement Tests covers the cost of sending reports to any four colleges or scholarship programs that you request at the time you register, or on the Correction Form (see page 5), provided the form is received by College Board ATP by the day of the test. You may enter up to four more score recipients in item 11b of the Registration Form or if you re-register by telephone, for a fee of $6.00 for each additional score report. Additional reports may also be requested at any time by telephone (page 6), or on the Additional Report Request Form (page 6), or through telephone Rush Reporting (page 6).

Item 13: Use the following abbreviations for street addresses.

Apartment	APT	Park	PK
Avenue	AVE	Parkway	PKY
Boulevard	BLVD	Pike	PI
Box	BX	Place	PL
Broadway	BDWY	Point	PT
Circle	CI	Port	PRT
Court	CT	Post Office	PO
Drive	DR	Road	RD
East	E	Route	RT
Fort	FT	South	S
Garden	GDN	Square	SQ
Headquarters	HQ	Street	ST
Heights	HTS	Terrace	TER
Highway	HWY	Trail	TRL
Lake	LK	Trailer	TRLR
Lane	LN	Turnpike	TPKE
Mount	MT	Way	WY
Mountain	MTN	West	W
North	N		

If your street address has a fraction, leave a blank box after the whole number, then enter the numerator in the next box, a slash in the next, and the denominator in the next. Fill in the corresponding ovals (the oval for the slash is at the bottom of the column of ovals). For example, you would enter the address 24½ as follows:

Use the following abbreviations for states and U. S. territories.

Alabama	AL	Missouri	MO
Alaska	AK	Montana	MT
American Samoa	AS	Nebraska	NE
Arizona	AZ	Nevada	NV
Arkansas	AR	New Hampshire	NH
California	CA	New Jersey	NJ
Colorado	CO	New Mexico	NM
Connecticut	CT	New York	NY
Delaware	DE	North Carolina	NC
District of Columbia	DC	North Dakota	ND
Federated States		Northern Mariana Islands	MP
of Micronesia	FM	Ohio	OH
Florida	FL	Oklahoma	OK
Georgia	GA	Oregon	OR
Guam	GU	Palau Island	PW
Hawaii	HI	Pennsylvania	PA
Idaho	ID	Puerto Rico	PR
Illinois	IL	Rhode Island	RI
Indiana	IN	South Carolina	SC
Iowa	IA	South Dakota	SD
Kansas	KS	Tennessee	TN
Kentucky	KY	Texas	TX
Louisiana	LA	Utah	UT
Maine	ME	Vermont	VT
Marshall Islands	MH	Virginia	VA
Maryland	MD	Virgin Islands	VI
Massachusetts	MA	Washington	WA
Michigan	MI	West Virginia	WV
Minnesota	MN	Wisconsin	WI
Mississippi	MS	Wyoming	WY

If You Need a Fee Waiver

If you cannot afford the test fee, you may apply for a fee waiver through your guidance counselor. Eligible seniors or juniors may receive only one fee waiver for the SAT and one for the Achievement Tests which may be used in **either** the senior **or** junior year only. The waiver covers the test fee and the fee for the SAT Question-and-Answer Service or SAT Score Verification Service (see pages 6 and 7). It does not cover any other fees. Fee waivers are available only to students testing in the United States, Puerto Rico, or U.S. territories. For more information, ask your counselor or consult the 1991-92 *Guidelines and Procedures for Distributing ATP Fee Waivers* or to call the College Board Regional Office that serves your state.

Note: Your registration cannot be processed unless the appropriate fee-waiver card is enclosed. *A letter from your counselor is not acceptable.* If you do not enclose a fee-waiver card, *your Registration Form will be returned,* and you may miss the registration deadline.

To Register Late

If you miss the regular registration deadline, you can still register by the late registration deadline. (See calendar, back cover.) However, Registration Forms postmarked after the regular registration deadline **must be accompanied** by an additional $15.00 late registration fee. Registration Forms postmarked after the late registration deadline will be returned. Students registering late through Easy Re-Registration will be billed the late fee.

Late registration is not available to students who test outside the United States and Puerto Rico or to students who test through ATP Services for Handicapped Students.

Testing as a Standby

If you miss the late registration deadline, you may still be able to take the test as a standby. However, **there is no guarantee:** test centers accept standbys — on a first-come, first-served basis — *only* if they have suffi-

cient space, testing materials, and staff. Don't try to make arrangements with test supervisors in advance because they will not know if you can be admitted.

If you are a standby, arrive at a test center by 8:00 a.m., although you will not be admitted until all pre-registered candidates have been seated. Take with you:

- a *completed* Registration Form, sealed in its registration envelope along with a check or money order (no cash), payable to Admissions Testing Program, for the appropriate test fee and the additional $30.00 standby fee; and
- acceptable ID. You will not be admitted without it.

If your fee is not enclosed, your Registration Form will be returned to you and your scores will be delayed.

Sunday Testing

Sunday testing is available **only** for students who cannot take a test on Saturday because of religious convictions. To be eligible:

- enter 01-000 in item 10 (under First Choice) on your Registration Form; do not enter a second choice;
- include with your Registration Form a letter of explanation on your cleric's letterhead stationery, signed by your cleric; and
- send the Registration Form and letter together before the regular registration deadline (or in time to be received by the special requests deadline if testing outside the United States or Puerto Rico). If you miss the late registration deadline and wish to test on a Sunday as a standby, you must take with you the letter from your cleric. See "Testing as a Standby," above.

Candidates re-registering by telephone (see page 2) will be assigned to a Sunday center only if they tested on a Sunday previously.

Sunday administrations follow each Saturday test date except for the June 6 Saturday test date, for which the Sunday administration will be May 31. In 1991-92, Sunday administrations will be on November 3, December 8, January 26, April 5, May 3, and May 31. In states where the SAT is given in October, the Sunday test date will be October 13. (Students testing in New York State should consult the schedule in the *New York State* edition of the *Bulletin*.) May 3 is the only Sunday administration for which the SAT Question-and-Answer Service is available.

Testing on both Saturday and Sunday is not permitted, and scores from both days will not be reported.

If You Need a Sign-Language Interpreter

Students who are deaf or hard of hearing may bring an interpreter to sign the introductory instructions to the SAT or Achievement Tests. Following the instructions, the signer **must** leave the test room. Additional testing

4

time is **not** available under this option. Score reports will **not** indicate that the student took the test at a "nonstandard administration." To be eligible, the student or guidance counselor must notify the test center supervisor several days before the test. Also, the student and signer should arrive early at the center.

Students with Disabilities

Eligibility requirements and accommodations are explained in *Information for Students with Special Needs* and in registration materials available in your guidance office, or ask your counselor to write ATP Services for Handicapped Students, P.O. Box 6226, Princeton, NJ 08541-6226. Two options are available.

Plan A (Special Accommodations). Students with documented visual, hearing, physical, or learning disabilities may register for special editions of the SAT (in regular type, large type, braille, or cassette versions) and are permitted use of certain aids (reader, recorder, magnifying glass) and extended testing time. Achievement Tests are available in regular and large type. For Achievement Tests eligible students may use magnifying devices and extended time. Eligible students may take these tests at their home school at times arranged by the student and counselor.

Plan B (Extended Time Only). This plan is more limited than Plan A: (1) only students with documented learning disabilities may participate, (2) only the SAT is available, (3) a regular-type SAT and machine-scannable answer sheet must be used, (4) no accommodation is offered except 90 minutes of additional testing time, (5) only two dates are available (November 2, 1991, and May 2, 1992), and (6) the test must be taken at a test center listed in this *Bulletin*. The SAT Question-and-Answer Service is available (see page 6).

A **Registration Form** and the additional form required by ATP Services for Handicapped Students must be postmarked six weeks prior to administration of Plan A and by regular registration deadlines for Plan B (September 27, 1991, for November and March 27, 1992, for May).

Practice materials for Plan A are: a descriptive booklet with sample questions, sample SAT (regular type, large type, braille, or cassette), and sample answer sheet. Be sure to ask your counselor to order practice materials in plenty of time to allow for shipping and practice. For Plan B, *Taking the SAT* is available from your guidance office.

Score reports for any student who tests through ATP Services for Handicapped Students will indicate that the student took the SAT or the Achievement Tests at a "nonstandard administration." If your disability requires neither special arrangements nor extended testing time, you should register for the regular national program.

Students with **temporary disabilities** — a broken arm, for instance — should register for a later date in the regular national program. However, if you need to meet an application deadline, ask your counselor to contact ATP Services for Handicapped Students.

Your Admission Ticket/ Correction Form

You will receive an admission packet at your mailing address before the test date. It will contain your Admission Ticket with attached Correction Form and an Additional Report Request Form (see page 6). **If your packet does not arrive by the Wednesday before the test, call 609-771-7600.**

If you lose your Admission Ticket, call 609-771-7600 for your registration number and the name and address of your assigned test center. When you arrive at the test center, explain to the test center supervisor. If you have acceptable identification (see examples below), you will be admitted.

Changing Your Test Choice, Test Date, or Test Center

To change your test choice (from SAT to Achievements or vice versa), **test date, or test center,** call 609-771-7600 by Wednesday two and one-half weeks before the test date. See page 2 for instructions.

On the Test Day

Arrive at the test center between 8:00 and 8:15 a.m. Take with you:

- **Your Admission Ticket**
- **Two No. 2 (soft-lead) pencils** and a good eraser
- **Acceptable identification** (required for admission and may also be checked anytime during the test session), which must include (1) **a photograph or a written physical description,** (2) your **name,** and (3) your **signature.** Examples of acceptable ID include:
  - Your driver's license
  - School identification card
  - Current passport
  - Talent Search identification card (grades 7 and 8)
  - A brief description of yourself on school stationery or on a school ID form that you have signed in the presence of your principal or guidance counselor, who must also sign it. Your school can prepare an ID form using the example illustrated above. Your name, physical description, and signature must be included. You may be asked to sign the document again at the test center.

Examples of **unacceptable** ID include a social security card, parent's driver's license, or a birth certificate (including wallet-size birth certificates available in some states).

IF YOU DON'T TAKE ACCEPTABLE ID WITH YOU TO THE TEST CENTER, YOU WILL NOT BE PERMITTED TO TAKE THE TEST.

```
(on school letterhead)
Name of Student
Height            Weight
Eye Color         Hair Color
Age               Sex
To the ATP Test Center Supervisor:
The test taker described above is a student at this
school and has signed this document in my presence.
Signature of Student        Date
Signature of Counselor
   or Principal             Date

I am the person whose description and signature
appear above. I am signing this document in the
presence of test center staff on the day of the test.
Signature of Student        Date
```

A watch might be helpful, but you cannot take a watch with an alarm or a calculator, or a watch that beeps. Other things you may NOT take into the test room include:

- food or drink
- scratch paper
- notes, books, dictionaries
- calculators of any kind (except for the Level IIC Mathematics Achievement Test. See *Taking the Achievement Tests* for the list of approved calculators.)
- compasses, protractors, rulers, or any other aids
- portable listening or recording devices of any kind (with or without earphones) or photographic equipment

Taking the Test

The test administration starts at 8:30 a.m. and ends at about 12:30 p.m. You will get a short break at the end of each hour of testing time. You must work within each section of the test only for the time allotted to it. You will not be permitted to go back to a section once that section has ended. Your supervisor will keep track of testing time. Proctors may walk about the room during the test to check on students' progress.

Before the test starts, the test supervisor will give you all the necessary instructions. First you will be asked to fill in identifying information on your answer sheet. Make sure you give the identical information that you gave on your Registration Form or your Correction Form. **Any differences between the identifying information on your answer sheet and your registration record will delay your scores.**

When you take the test, be sure that you mark your answers only on the answer sheet. You may use the test book for scratch work, but you will not receive credit for any responses written in it.

To prevent any student from gaining an unfair advantage over others, certain procedures or regulations are enforced by ETS that allow students an equal opportunity to do their best on the test. Students may be dismissed from the testing room or may have

5

their scores canceled if they fail to follow any of the testing instructions given by the test supervisor, or

- attempt to remove from the test room any part of a test book or any notes relating to the test
- attempt to take the test for someone else
- give or receive assistance during the test
- create a disturbance
- read or work on one section of the test during time allowed for another or continue to work after time is called
- look through the test book before the start of the test
- leave the test room without permission
- use any of the prohibited aids
- take food or drink into the test room

Score Reports

You will receive your College Planning Report, which includes your scores, at your home address about five weeks after the test. Some scores may take longer to report, however, because of problems such as inconsistent identification information. In any case, you should receive your score report **no later than ten weeks** after the test. **In order to keep your scores confidential, they will not be given on the telephone. Please do not call to ask for your scores.**

If you requested that your scores be sent to colleges or scholarship programs, a report will be sent to each, usually within four weeks after the test. Your high school will also receive a score report if you provided your high school code number.

These reports are cumulative: they include information you gave on the Student Descriptive Questionnaire, and scores for up to six SAT and six Achievement Test administrations. **You cannot send only your latest or highest scores, or separate scores for the SAT, TSWE, or Achievement Tests.** Under current procedures, your scores are kept indefinitely. However, scores more than five years old will be accompanied by a message explaining that they may be less valid predictors of college academic performance than more recent scores would be.

Your College Planning Report will also list all the colleges and scholarship programs you designated to receive score reports, with descriptive and deadline information about each of the colleges listed. (The list of colleges does not appear on reports sent to colleges.)

To Send Additional Score Reports

- If you have already received scores ☎ and want to send them to additional colleges call 609-771-7600. See page 2 for instructions and fees.
  OR
- Send in an Additional Report Request Form. You received one with your admission packet. Additional forms are available from your guidance counselor. The fee for

each report is $6.00. Make your request at least five weeks before the date you want colleges and scholarship programs to receive your report. **Once received, the request cannot be canceled.**

To Rush Scores ☎

It takes about three weeks to score all the tests, and another two weeks to send out all the scores. However, if you want colleges to get your scores faster, you can call to request Rush Reporting. When you order Rush Reporting, your scores are sent within two working days after your test has been scored; **your test is not scored faster.** See page 2 for instructions and fees.

Stopping Automatic Reporting of Scores

Your test scores and the information you give about yourself are confidential. Except for certain state scholarship and guidance programs, your scores are sent only to the institutions you have specifically designated. If you are from one of the states listed below, your scores will be routinely sent to the state's scholarship program unless you tell us otherwise. Scores are sent for all juniors in Pennsylvania and for all juniors in Illinois who take the test between September 1, 1991, and June 30, 1992. In New Jersey, Rhode Island, and Maryland, scores are sent following the junior year and again in the middle of the senior year. In Washington state, scores are sent for all juniors who take the test between September 1, 1991 and June 7, 1992. If you attend school or live in one of these states and do *not* want your scores sent to the state scholarship or guidance program, write College Board ATP, P.O. Box 6200, Princeton, NJ 08541-6200, by the following deadlines: Rhode Island and New Jersey (seniors), January 31, 1992; Maryland, February 15, 1992; Pennsylvania, May 31, 1992; Illinois, Rhode Island, and New Jersey (juniors), August 1, 1992; Washington juniors, June 15, 1992.

Cancellation of Scores by the College Board

The College Board is obligated to report scores that accurately reflect your performance. For this reason, ETS maintains, on behalf of the College Board, test administration and test security standards designed to assure that all test takers are given the same opportunity to demonstrate their abilities and to prevent any student from gaining an unfair advantage over others because of testing irregularities or misconduct. ETS routinely reviews irregularities and test scores believed to be earned under unusual or questionable circumstances.

ETS reserves the right to cancel any test score if the student engages in misconduct, if there is an administration irregularity, or if

ETS believes there is reason to question the score's validity. Before test scores are canceled for misconduct, the student is notified and given an opportunity to provide additional information. When test scores are canceled because of administrative irregularities, such as improper timing or defective materials, the student is given an opportunity to take the test again as soon as possible at the College Board's expense.

When the validity of a test score is questioned because it may have been obtained unfairly, ETS notifies the test taker of the reasons for questioning the score and gives him or her an opportunity to provide additional information, to confirm the questioned score by taking the test again, or to authorize ETS to cancel the score and receive a refund of all test fees.

In addition, the test taker can request third-party review of the matter by asking any institution to review the information and make its own decision about accepting a score that may be invalid or by asking that a member of the American Arbitration Association arbitrate ETS's action in accordance with ETS procedures established for this purpose. Special exceptions and additional details of the procedures for questioning scores and for third-party reviews are available upon request.

Archived Scores

There is an additional $5.00 fee to report scores more than one year after your high school graduation. In addition to your current name and address, please provide your name and address at the time you tested.

Missing Scores

If previous scores are missing from your College Planning Report, call 609-771-7600 or write to College Board ATP, Attention: Unreported Scores, P.O. Box 6200, Princeton, NJ 08541-6200. Please provide identification information, test dates for the unreported scores, and previous score recipients to which you want updated reports sent (they will be sent at no charge).

If you have taken more than six SATs, or Achievement Tests on more than six test dates, or have been out of high school more than two years, your entire record cannot be combined, but reproductions from microfiche of your unreported scores will be sent. If you test in the seventh or eighth grade, these scores are removed from your files at the end of that testing year.

SAT Question-and-Answer Service

You can get a copy of the verbal and mathematical sections of the SAT you took, and a copy of your answer sheet, the correct answers, and scoring instructions, if you order the SAT Question-and-Answer Service. This service is available only for the SAT taken on the following dates:

6

Saturday, November 2, 1991
Saturday, January 25, 1992
Saturday, April 4, 1992
Saturday, May 2, 1992
Sunday, May 3, 1992

The fee for the SAT Question-and-Answer Service is $10.00. You may order it when you register for the test or up to five months after the test date. Fill in the appropriate oval in item 18 of the Registration Form, request it when you call in for Easy Re-Registration, or complete the order form in the booklet *Using Your College Planning Report*, which accompanies your score report. If you request the service when you register, materials will be mailed about eight weeks after your scores are available. If you use the order form in *Using Your College Planning Report*, material will be mailed about eight weeks after your request is received.

This service does not include the TSWE, the equating section of the SAT, the Achievement Tests, or an SAT given on any other date or under Plan A for students with disabilities.

SAT Score Verification Service

You can check the scoring of your SAT answer sheet by requesting the SAT Score Verification Service. You will receive a copy of your answer sheet, the correct answers, and instructions for scoring, but you will not receive the test questions. The service is available for all SAT test dates except those for which the SAT Question-and-Answer Service is available. (See above.) Students with disabilities who test under Plan A are not eligible. You may order this service after you receive your score report and up to five months after the test date. Complete the order form in the booklet *Using Your College Planning Report*. The fee is $8.00. You will receive the materials about eight weeks after your request is received.

Hand Scoring Service

In addition to machine scoring, you can request that your answer sheet be hand scored by a hand-scoring specialist. Hand scoring is available for all test dates for all tests — SAT, TSWE, and the Achievement Tests. (For the English Composition Achievement Test with Essay, only the multiple-choice portion will be hand scored. The essays are routinely read by a minimum of two expert readers.)

You will receive a letter showing the computation of your scores. If an error in the original scoring of the answer sheet is found, the hand scoring fee will be refunded. In the unlikely event that scores differ, the hand scores will prevail, and the recipients of your scores will be notified by letter.

You may order hand scoring after you receive your score report and up to five months after the test date. Complete the order form in the booklet *Using your College Planning Report* or send a letter to College

Board ATP, P. O. Box 6203, Princeton, NJ 08541-6203. Include your test date and your name, birth date, sex, registration number, street, city, state, and zip code, the name, city, and state of your test center, and your signature. The fee for the Hand Scoring Service is $25.00 for all tests taken on the same date. Requests received without a signature or fee will be returned. You will receive the letter about eight weeks after your request is received.

To Question a Test Question

If you find an error or ambiguity in a test question, please report it to the test supervisor on the test day or notify ETS **by the Wednesday after the test date**. (See the chart, right, for instructions.)

Include the test date, the name and address of the test center, the name of the test, the test section, the test question (as well as you can remember), and an explanation of your concern.

ETS will send you a written response after your inquiry has been reviewed by subject-matter specialists. If the response does not resolve your concern, you can request that the Director of Test Development initiate further reviews of your inquiry. If you still have concerns, you can request a formal review of your inquiry by an independent review panel. Copies of ETS's procedures for resolving inquiries about test questions can be obtained by writing to College Board Test Development, Educational Testing Service, P.O. Box 6656, Princeton, NJ 08541-6656.

If your inquiry concerns a test for which the SAT Question-and-Answer Service is available, ETS will retain your letter (with your identification deleted) along with other letters concerning the tests. You can obtain copies of this correspondence for a nominal fee by writing to the above address.

To Complain about the Test Center

If you have a complaint about the test center or the conditions under which you were tested, contact ETS **by the Wednesday after the test date** with the name of the test, the test date, the name and address of the test center, and an explanation of the problem. (See the chart, right, for instructions.)

To Cancel Your Scores

After the test, you may decide that you do not want your test scores reported. To cancel your scores, ask the test supervisor for a Request to Cancel Test Scores Form, complete it immediately, and return it to the supervisor before you leave the room.

You must cancel *all* scores for that test date. If you took the SAT, you may not cancel only your SAT-verbal, or SAT-math, or TSWE score. If you took Achievement Tests, you may not cancel scores from individual tests. If you erase all responses to an individual Achievement Test, it will be considered a

request for cancellation, and scores from all Achievement Tests taken on that date will be canceled. You cannot get a refund if you cancel your SAT or Achievement Test scores.

If you decide to cancel your scores after you leave the test center, you must notify ETS **by the Wednesday after the test date**. (See the chart above.) Include your test date, your test center number, the test you want to cancel (SAT or Achievement Tests), your last name, first name, and middle initial, address, sex, birth date, social security number, and registration number. **Once your request for canceling scores has been received, your scores cannot be reinstated and will not be reported to you or your designated institutions.**

If You're Absent from a Test

If you were absent from a test for which you had registered and want to test on another date, call 609-771-7600. You will be charged the $15.00 test date change fee.

If you were absent and do not want to test on another date, you can get a **partial** refund. Sign the back of the Admission Ticket and return it within two months after the test date to College Board ATP, Candidate Refunds, P.O. Box 6200, Princeton, NJ 08541-6200. If you were absent from the test, no score reports will be sent. If you lost your Admission Ticket, write a letter to the above address requesting a refund. Indicate the test for which you registered and include identification information. (See page 2.) No refunds will be processed until about six weeks after the test.

You will receive a refund of $4.00 for the SAT and $8.00 for the Achievement Tests. The test service fee and late registration fee are not refundable. However, you will automatically receive a refund for any additional paid score reports and other services you requested when you registered for that test date.

Contact ETS **by the Wednesday after the test date**			
To:	Complain about a Test Center	Question a Test Question	Cancel Your Scores
Label inquiries:	Attention: ATP Test Centers	Attention: ATP Test Development	Attention: ATP Score Cancellation
FAX:	609-520-1092	609-734-5410	609-771-7681 609-771-7906
Telex:	843420 EDUTESTSV PRIN		
TWX:	510-685-9592 EDUCTEST SVC		
Cable:	EDUCTESTSVS		
Overnight Mail:	U. S. Postal Service Express Mail: P.O. Box 6228, Princeton, NJ 08541-6228		
	Other overnight mail service: Document Processing, 1440 Lower Ferry Rd. Trenton, NJ 08618		
First-class mail:	(can only be used to query a test question) College Board Test Development, Educational Testing Service, P.O. Box 6656, Princeton, NJ 08541-6656		

7

457

Special Information for Students Testing in New York State

This section contains information about test dates, fees, and special procedures that apply to students who register to take the SAT and Achievement Tests in New York State. These modifications have been adopted by the College Board in order to comply with the New York State Standardized Testing Law as enacted in 1979 and amended in 1980, 1981, 1983, 1986, and 1987. The information in this section and on the back cover is subject to change if additional amendments are passed by the New York State Legislature and become law. All schools and colleges in New York State will be notified as promptly as possible of any such changes.

Test Dates

During 1991-92, the SAT and Achievement Tests will be offered in New York State on the following dates.

November 2, 1991	SAT and Achievement Tests
December 7, 1991	*SAT and Achievement Tests
January 25, 1992	SAT and Achievement Tests
April 4, 1992	SAT only
May 2, 1992	SAT and Achievement Tests
June 6, 1992	*SAT and Achievement Tests

---

*Notice

The SAT Question-and-Answer Service is not offered for the December or June test dates. Therefore, students who take the SATs administered on December 7, 1991, and June 6, 1992, will not be entitled to receive a copy of the test questions, answer key, and their answer sheets. However, students will be entitled to receive a copy of the answer key and their answer sheets through the SAT Score Verification Service.

See "Procedures for Requesting Your SAT Questions" on this page for further information about the SAT Question-and-Answer Service, which is offered following five test dates. See also information about the Score Verification Service on page 7 in this *Bulletin*.

Check the calendar on the back cover for registration deadlines and other information about the test offerings.

Fees

The following fees are for all students who register to take the SAT or the Achievement Tests in New York State in 1991-92.

$17.00	SAT Test Fee
$ 1.00	New York State SAT Surcharge*
$18.00	Total SAT Fee (NY State)
$21.00	Achievement Test Fee
$ 1.00	New York State Achievement Test Surcharge*
$22.00	Total Achievement Test Fee (NY State)

* These surcharges, which apply to all SAT and Achievement Test administrations in New York State, have been set to recover some of the costs of compliance with the New York State Standardized Testing Law.

Other fees are listed on the back cover. Fee waivers used in New York State will cover the New York State surcharges as well as the test fees.

Note that the total fees for standby candidates (see page 4) in New York State test centers are $48.00 for the SAT ($18.00 New York test fee plus $30.00 standby fee) and $52.00 for the Achievement Tests ($22.00 New York test fee plus $30.00 standby fee).

Students who registered to take the SAT or Achievement Tests in New York State and who request refunds because they were absent from the test (see page 7) will get a refund of $5.00 for the SAT; $9.00 for the Achievement Tests.

Registering for the Test

- Use the special New York State Registration Form enclosed in this *New York State Edition* of the *Bulletin*.

- Check the calendars on the back cover and page 3 to be sure that the test you are planning to take is offered on the date for which you are registering.

- Be sure you include the correct fee (SAT-$18.00; Achievement Tests-$22.00).

Releasing Your Scores to the New York State Scholarship Program

---

As this edition goes to press, the New York State Legislature is considering the discontinuation of the New York State Scholarship Program. It is not known if these scholarships will be continued, or whether SAT scores will be a basis for consideration for these scholarships during 1991-92. If SAT scores are used, the information provided below describes the procedures that will be followed. In the event that SAT scores are not used for scholarship purposes, none of the information given below will be applicable. Final details about the basis for 1991-92 New York State Scholarships will be sent in the fall of 1991 to all secondary schools in the state by the Division of Educational Testing of the New York State Education Department.

The New York State Scholarship Program requires that students who wish to be considered for the scholarship awards on the basis of their SAT scores take this test before November 5 of their final high school year. The latest SAT administration that meets this deadline is November 2, 1991.

The New York State Standardized Testing Law requires that you specifically authorize the sending of all reports. Your SAT scores and other information from your ATP record will be sent to the New York State Scholarship Program if you authorize the release of your scores on the New York State Scholarship application form. To do that, you must answer "yes" and sign the score release statement on page 4 of the scholarship application. New York State Scholarship application forms are sent by the State Education Department to principals of all high schools in New York State in early September. If you follow the procedures described above, there is no fee for sending reports to the New York State Scholarship Program.

The College Board will release to the New York State Scholarship Program the names, addresses, and other identifying information of all seniors who registered to take the SAT prior to November 5, 1991, and who are New York State residents or who attend school in New York State. This procedure will facilitate the matching of student files so that scores for all students who authorized their release are sent to the New York State Scholarship Program. If you do not want your name and address released for this purpose, notify College Board ATP, P.O. Box 6200, Princeton, NJ 08541-6200 by November 8, 1991.

Procedures for Requesting Your SAT Questions, the Correct Answers, and a Copy of Your Answer Sheet after You Have Taken the Test

If you take the SAT on any of the five dates listed below, you may obtain the SAT Question-and-Answer Service, which includes the following:

- A copy of the questions from the two verbal and two mathematical sections that are the basis of the SAT scores

- A list of corresponding correct answers

- The raw scores used to calculate the reported scores

- A table to convert your raw scores to the College Board scale

- A copy of your answer sheet

This service is available only for national administrations of the SAT on the following dates:

> Saturday, November 2, 1991
> Saturday, January 25, 1992
> Saturday, April 4, 1992
> Saturday, May 2, 1992
> Sunday, May 3, 1992

You may order this service when you register for one of the above SAT dates or up to five months after the test date. Beginning 30 days after scores have been released, materials will be sent to students who request them and who submit the $10 fee. Your request must be made within 120 days after the date that scores are released. You will receive materials eight weeks after we receive your order.

To order the service, either fill in the oval for the SAT Question-and-Answer Service in item 18 on the Registration Form and include the appropriate fee or complete the order form on the back cover of *Using Your College Planning Report*, a booklet that you receive with your score report. (The fee for this service will be waived for SAT fee-waiver recipients who wish to receive this information.)

The SAT Question-and-Answer Service is available only for regular administrations of the SAT on the dates listed above. It does not include the Test of Standard Written English (TSWE), the equating section of the SAT, the Achievement Tests, or an SAT given on any other date or at special administrations.

The SAT Score Verification Service (see page 7) will be offered for every SAT administration *except* those for which the SAT Question-and-Answer Service is available.

The Score Verification Service is not available to students who use ATP Services for Handicapped Students.

Procedures for Reviewing Challenges to the Keying, Scoring, Wording, or Other Aspects of Test Questions

If you have any concerns regarding the questions on the test you took or the accuracy of the scoring, you should write to:

College Board Test Development
Educational Testing Service
P.O. Box 6656
Princeton, New Jersey 08541-6656

Further information on the procedures for inquiries about a test question is included on page 7 of this *Bulletin.*

In compliance with the New York State Standardized Testing Law, a file of correspondence is maintained related to test questions used in calculating scores for which the SAT Question-and-Answer Service is available. Copies of this file can be obtained for a nominal fee by writing to the above address.

Information Requirements of the New York State Standardized Testing Law

A provision of this law is that certain information concerning the purposes of the test, property rights of the test subject and test agency to the test scores, test fairness and equity, procedures for releasing score reports and for reviewing challenges about test questions, and score interpretation is to be provided to test candidates along with the Registration Form or score report. This information is furnished in this *Bulletin* and in other ATP publications routinely provided to test takers.

Your Scores

Each time you take an ATP test, the scores are added to your permanent ATP record, which is stored at Educational Testing Service for the College Board, and a copy of this record is sent to you. If you provide your high school code on the Registration Form, a copy of your record is sent to your high school and, if you provide the appropriate codes, to the colleges and scholarship programs you choose.

Your ATP score report contains *all* your ATP scores; you cannot choose to send only selected scores or to have certain scores removed from your record. (If you do not want your test scored at all, see "To Cancel Your Scores" on page 7.)

You alone determine whether any person or institution receives your report. The College Board may use scores and information you provide for research purposes, but no information that can be identified with you is released without your consent. Under present procedures, your scores are retained indefinitely.

ATP scores assist admissions officers in estimating your current readiness to do college work. Scores more than five years old will be sent to institutions at your request, but

they will be accompanied by a message explaining that they may be less valid predictors of college academic performance than are more recent scores.

The report you receive and the reports received by colleges and your high school contain scores that have been converted to the College Board 200 to 800 scale. The College Board does not use either your raw score or your reported scaled score by itself or in combination with any other information to predict in any way your future academic performance in any postsecondary institution. However, the College Board does provide assistance to individual colleges and universities to help them use ATP scores, high school record, and other relevant information in making appropriate admissions and placement decisions.

Relationship of Test Scores to Grades in College

The basic purpose of the SAT is to assist admissions officers in evaluating applications for admission to college. Studies have shown that the use of SAT scores combined with the high school record (class rank or grade point average) increases the accuracy of forecasting college freshman grades over the use of either SAT scores or high school record alone. For all 685 colleges that have used the College Board's Validity Study Service to find out how well SAT scores and high school record predicted freshman grade point average (GPA), the median correlation* for forecasting freshman GPA was +.36 for the SAT-verbal score (that is, for half the colleges studied, the correlation was higher than +.36 and for the other half it was lower), +.35 for the SAT-mathematical score, +.42 for the two scores combined,** and +.48 for high school record. When the two SAT scores and high school record were combined to forecast freshman GPA, the median correlation increased to +.55. Willingham, Lewis, Morgan, and Ramist (1990) show that SAT scores are most useful in adding information over high school record for students in the bottom third of their freshman class, where critical admissions decisions are typically made.

Still greater accuracy in the forecast of freshman grades can be obtained by the addition of Achievement Test scores. Studies done for 133 colleges have shown that the median correlation would increase to about +.58 if Achievement Test scores were added to high school record and SAT scores.

The TSWE is used by some colleges to assist in placing students in appropriate course levels in English. Studies of the effectiveness of the TSWE score in predicting

---

* Correlation is the tendency for two scores or measures, such as height and weight, to vary together or be related for individuals in a group. If, as in the case of height and weight, people who are high on one measure (height) tend to be high on the other (weight), the correlation is said to be positive. When a high measure on one characteristic is associated with a low measure on another, the correlation is said to be negative. Months of training and length of time to run a mile would have negative correlation, because as training increases, running time usually decreases. Correlation is stated as a coefficient; +1.00 shows perfect positive correlation, 0.00 indicates no relationship, and −1.00 indicates perfect negative correlation.

** The two scores are weighted statistically to result in the best possible prediction of freshman GPA.

the grades of students in freshman English courses at 25 colleges show a median correlation of +.39. The median correlation between SAT-mathematical scores and grades in freshman mathematics courses at 29 colleges studied was +.33.

Although most validity studies focus on the prediction of freshman grades, other studies use other educational indicators. Wilson (1983) shows that both SAT scores and high school record are as valid for predicting long-term grade point average as for freshman grade point average. Astin (1977), Willingham and Breland (1982), Manski and Wise (1983), and other analyses by the ATP Summary Reporting Service confirm the effectiveness of SAT scores, high school grades, and high school rank for predicting persistence beyond the freshman year. Willingham, Lewis, Morgan, and Ramist (1990) find that if the prediction is for individual course grades instead of freshman GPA, average correlations are higher for SAT scores than for high school record.

Relationship of SAT Scores to Family Income

Many valid measures of educational achievement are found to be correlated with family income level. This is a reflection of the fact that students from families with average or above-average income level often have educational advantages that students from low-income families do not have. A 1976 study by K. R. White of the University of Colorado found that the average correlation between different indicators of educational achievement and family income was .32.

The correlation of SAT scores and student-reported family income for two recent years was found to be about .23 and .29, which is consistent with general research findings on the relationship of educational achievement and family income level. Although average SAT scores tend to be higher for students from higher-income families, students from every income level, as reported on the Student Descriptive Questionnaire, obtain the full range of SAT scores. Furthermore, many students from low-income families do well on the test. For seniors graduating in 1990, one-third of the students with reported family income below $20,000 obtained scores above the national average.

Procedures to Ensure Fairness and Equity

All new SAT, TSWE, and Achievement Test questions, as well as complete new editions of the tests, are reviewed by many individuals, including ETS staff and external committees. One of the purposes of these reviews is to identify and eliminate any wording or content that might be offensive or inappropriate for particular groups of students, such as racial or ethnic groups of students or men or women. In addition, care is taken to assure that the test as a whole includes references to both men and women and individuals from a variety of racial, ethnic, and cultural backgrounds. Statistics are also used to identify questions that are harder for a group of students to answer correctly than would be expected from their performance on the test.

16

2007–08 SAT TERMS AND CONDITIONS*

2007–08 IMPORTANT INFORMATION FOR TEST–TAKERS

Cancellation of Scores

Test Security Issues

The College Board and Educational Testing Service (ETS) strive to report scores that accurately reflect the performance of every test-taker. Accordingly, ETS standards and procedures for administering tests have two primary goals: give all test-takers equivalent opportunities to demonstrate their abilities, and prevent any test-taker from gaining an unfair advantage over others. To promote these objectives, ETS reserves the right to cancel any test scores when, in its judgment, a testing irregularity occurs, there is an apparent discrepancy in a test-taker's identification, a test-taker engages in misconduct or plagiarism, or the score is invalid for another reason. Review of scores by ETS is confidential. When, for any of these reasons, ETS cancels a test score that has already been reported, it notifies score recipients that the score was canceled, but it does not disclose the reason for cancellation unless authorized to do so by the test-taker, and in certain group cases.

Testing irregularities refer to problems with the administration of a test. When they occur, they may affect an individual or groups of test-takers. Such problems include, without limitation, administrative errors (e.g., improper timing, improper seating, defective materials, and defective equipment); improper access to test content; and other disruptions of test administrations (e.g., natural disasters and other emergencies). When testing irregularities occur, ETS may decline to score the test, or cancel the test score. When it is appropriate to do so, ETS gives affected test-takers the opportunity to take the test again as soon as possible, without charge.

Identification Discrepancies. When, in, ETS's or test center personnel's judgment, there is a discrepancy in a test-taker's identification, the test-taker may be dismissed from the test center; in addition, ETS may decline to score the test, or cancel the test score.

Misconduct. When ETS or test center personnel find that there is misconduct in connection with a test, the test-taker may be dismissed from the test center, or ETS may decline to score the test or cancel the test score. Repeated minor infractions may result in score cancellation. Misconduct includes, but is not limited to,

- taking any test questions or essay topics from the testing room, giving them to anyone else, or discussing them with anyone else through any means, including, but not limited to, e-mail, text messages, or the Internet

- obtaining improper access to the test, a part of the test, or information about the test
- referring to, looking through, or working on any test, or test section, other than during the testing period for that test or test section
- using any prohibited aids in connection with the test, including during breaks
- consuming food or drink in the test room
- leaving the test room without permission
- leaving the building at any time during the test administration, including during breaks
- attempting in any manner to remove from the test room any part of a test book or any notes relating to the test
- attempting to give or receive assistance. Discussion or sharing of test content during the test administration, during breaks or after the test is prohibited. Communication with other test-takers in any form during the test administration.
- attempting to take the test for someone else
- using a telephone or cell phone without permission of the test center staff
- using a telephone or cell phone without permission of the test center staff
- failing to follow any of the test administration regulations contained in the *SAT Registration Booklet*, on **www. collegeboard.com**, given by the test supervisor, or specified in any materials

Cheating. Although tests are administered under strict supervision and security measures, testing irregularities may sometimes occur. To report any unusual behavior or suspicion of cheating (for example, someone copying from another test-taker, taking a test for someone else, having access to test questions before the exam, or using notes or unauthorized aids), please contact us by phone at 609 406–5430 between 7:30 a.m. and 5:30 p.m. eastern/New York time, by fax at 609 406–9709, or by e-mail at testsecurity@info.collegeboard.org as soon as possible. All information will be held strictly confidential.

Invalid Scores. ETS may also cancel scores if it judges that there is substantial evidence that they are invalid for any other reason. Evidence of invalid scores may include, without limitation, plagiarism, discrepant handwriting, unusual answer patterns, inconsistent performance on different parts of the test, text that is similar to that in other essays, paraphrasing of text from published sources, and essays that do not reflect the independent composition the test is seeking to measure. Before canceling scores pursuant to this paragraph, ETS notifies the test-taker in writing about its concerns, gives the test-taker an opportunity to submit information that addresses the concerns, considers any such information submitted, and offers the test-taker a choice of options. The options include voluntary score cancellation, a free retest, or arbitration in accordance with ETS's standard Arbitration Agreement. In addition, the test-taker is sent a copy of the booklet *Why and How Educational Testing Service Questions Test Scores* that explains this process in greater detail. (Any test-taker may request a copy of this booklet at any time.)

Note: *The retest option is not available outside the United States and Canada. The arbitration option is available only for tests administered in the United States.*

Score Reporting

General Information. Each time you take an SAT Program test, the scores are added to your permanent SAT Program record; a copy of this record is sent to you. If you provide your high school information at the time of registration, a copy of your record is sent to your high school and to the colleges and scholarship programs you choose. Your score report contains the six most recent SAT Reasoning Test and six most recent SAT Subject Test reportable scores; you cannot choose to have certain scores removed from your record. (If you do not want your test scored at all, see "Score Cancellation" in Section 3.) The report you receive and the reports received by colleges and your high school contain scores that have been converted to the College Board 200–800 scale for all SAT Program tests except the ELPT™ (English Language Profi ciency Test™), which is reported on a scale of 901–999 (this test was last administered in January 2005 and is no longer offered).

The College Board does not use either your raw score or your reported scaled score by itself or in combination with any other information to predict in any way your future academic performance in any postsecondary institution. However, the College Board does provide assistance to individual colleges and universities to help them use SAT Program test scores, high school record, and other relevant information in making appropriate admission and placement decisions.

Test scores are the property of the College Board. The College Board may use scores and information you provide for research purposes, but other than as indicated below or unless legally compelled (for example, subject to a subpoena), no personally identifying information is released without your consent.

Scholarships. Most of the scholarships available from the college and scholarship programs listed in this *SAT Registration Booklet* are restricted to U.S. residents or children of employees of the scholarship sponsors. For more information, contact the colleges and scholarship programs in which you are interested.

If you are a citizen of the United States and a resident of Illinois, Kentucky, Maryland, Massachusetts, Missouri, New Jersey, Pennsylvania, Rhode Island, or West Virginia but your current mailing address is outside the United States or you are using an APO/FPO address, contact scholarship and guidance programs or government-sponsored agencies in these states directly for information on how to be included for scholarship selection.

You can stop the automatic reporting of your test scores. If you do not want your scores released to the U.S. government or if you attend school or live in one of these states and do not want your scores sent to the state scholarship or guidance program, write to College Board SAT Program, Attention: Confidentiality, P.O. Box 025505, Miami, FL 33102 by no later than the 15th day after the test date, or by January 2, 2008, for Massachusetts (or by the 15th day after the test date if testing after January).

State Scholarship Programs. If you are from one of the states listed below, your scores will be routinely sent to the state's scholarship program unless you tell us otherwise. Scores are sent for all test-takers (except 7th and 8th graders and Missouri 9th graders) in Kentucky and Missouri who test between September 1, 2007, and June 30, 2008; for all juniors in Pennsylvania, Illinois, and Washington who take the test between September 1, 2007, and June 30, 2008; and for all seniors in Washington who test between September and December 2007. In Georgia, Maryland, New Jersey, and Rhode Island, scores are sent following the junior year and again in the middle of the senior year. In Texas, scores are sent for all seniors who test in October 2007. In West Virginia and Tennessee, scores are sent for all seniors who tested during high school through January 2008.

Releasing Your Scores to the New York State Scholarship Program. The New York State Scholarship Program requires that New York State students who wish to be considered for the Robert C. Byrd Honors Scholarships and Regents Scholarships in Cornell University on the basis of their SAT scores take this test before November 1, 2007. The latest SAT administration that meets this deadline is October 6, 2007.

The New York State Standardized Testing Law requires that you specifically authorize the sending of all reports. Your SAT scores and other information from your record will be sent to the Scholarship Program if you authorize the release of your scores at the time that you apply for a scholarship. To do that, you must answer "yes" and sign the score release statement on page 4 of the scholarship application. Scholarship application forms are sent by the State Education Department to principals of all high schools in New York State in December or January. If you follow these procedures, there is no fee for sending reports to the New York State Scholarship Program.

The College Board releases to the New York State Scholarship Program the names, addresses, and other identifying information of seniors who registered to take the SAT prior to November 1, 2007, who are New York State residents, and who apply for scholarship(s). This procedure facilitates the matching of student files so that scores for all students who authorized their release are sent to the New York State Scholarship Program. If you do not want your name and address released for this purpose, notify College Board SAT Program, NYS Scholarship Program, P. O. Box 025505, Miami, FL 33102.

Research and Reporting. Your test scores and the background information you provide about yourself (not including your name, street address, social security number, or email address) may be used in research or in aggregate reports about groups of students. In some cases—for example, if a validity study is done for the college in which you have enrolled—all your scores and background information may be included in the study even if you did not request that the SAT Program send your scores to the college. Your individual scores may be reported to your district or state for educational purposes. For more information about the guidelines on the uses of College Board test scores and related data, ask your counselor or visit www.collegeboard.com/research.

Procedures for Keeping Scores on File. Your scores are kept indefinitely, unless you tested before entering the 9th grade. If you test in the 7th or 8th grade, your scores are removed from your file at the end of the year that you tested. If you don't want your scores removed, you must let us know before the end of June of the year you tested. Talent Search Program candidates: see "Scores Earned Before High School" in Section 4 for more information.

Your test scores and your responses to the SAT Questionnaire are maintained on active file by the SAT Program until June, one year after your class graduates from high school. (If you tested after high school, this information is kept on active file for a full year beyond the year in which you tested.) After that time, these data are placed in an archival file. Test scores can be obtained from the archival file indefinitely.

Reporting Scores More Than One Year After Your High School Graduation. Scores are usually archived one year after high school graduation or any account activity. To report archived scores provide your current name and address, sex, date of birth, and the year you tested, along with your name and address at that time. See back cover for fee information. Scores from tests taken before 1996 are subject to additional charges. The fee covers the cost of looking up your scores and will be charged whether or not scores can be located.

Official score reports sent to colleges five or more years after a test date are accompanied by a message explaining that they may be less valid predictors of college academic performance than more recent scores would be. This message also notifies colleges that for Subject Tests, knowledge of the subject may change given additional study in the area, and scores may become less valid predictors within a shorter time period.

Special Information for Students Testing in California and New York State

The California Education Code requires that you be given certain information concerning the purposes of the tests, property rights of the test subject and test agency to the test scores, procedures for releasing score reports, and score interpretation.

Statistical information related to the use of test scores in predicting future grade point averages (GPAs) must be provided to test-takers prior to the administration of the test or coinciding with the initial reporting of test scores.

The New York State Standardized Testing Law requires that certain information concerning the purposes of the test, property rights of the test-taker and test agency to the test scores, test fairness and equity, procedures for releasing score reports and for reviewing challenges about test questions, and score interpretation be provided to test-takers along with the Registration Form or score report.

The information for both California and New York State test-takers is furnished in the *SAT Registration Booklet* and in the material included with score reports. Complete descriptions of the content of the tests, along with information on test preparation and sample questions, are provided in the *SAT Preparation Booklet* and *SAT Subject Tests Preparation Booklet*, which are available without charge from school offices for students who plan to register for these tests.

Scores and Score Reports. Each time you take an SAT Program test, the scores are added to your permanent SAT Program record; a copy of this record is sent to you. If you provide the appropriate codes on the Registration Form, a copy of your record is sent to your high school and to the colleges and scholarship programs you choose.

Your score report contains all your scores; you cannot choose to have certain scores removed from your record. (If you do not want your test scored at all, see Score Cancellation.)

You alone determine whether or not any person or institution receives your score report. The College Board may use scores and information you provide for research purposes, but no information that can be identified with you is released without your consent.

The report you receive and the reports received by colleges and your high school contain scores that have been converted to the College Board 200–800 scale for all SAT Program tests except the ELPT (English Language Proficiency Test), which is reported on a scale of 901–999 (no longer administered). The College Board does not use either your raw

465

score or your reported scaled score by itself or in combination with any other information to predict in any way your future academic performance in any postsecondary institution. However, the College Board does provide assistance to individual colleges and universities to help them use SAT Program test scores, high school record, and other relevant information in making appropriate admission and placement decisions.

Test scores are the property of the College Board. The College Board may use scores and information you provide for research purposes, but other than as indicated below or unless legally compelled (for example, subject to a subpoena), no personally identifying information is released without your consent.

Predicting College Grades. The basic purpose of the SAT is to provide information to college admissions staff that will help them to evaluate a student's application. Results of research conducted using data from 26 colleges show that SAT test scores, in combination with a student's high school grade point average, predict college freshman GPA more accurately than either SAT scores or high school GPA alone.

For all college freshmen in the study (N=110,468), the predictive validity of an optimally weighted combination of SAT scores and high school record is .65. The correlation between the critical reading score and freshman GPA is .50; between the math score and freshman GPA is .52; between combined critical reading and math scores and freshman GPA is .55; and between high school GPA and freshman GPA is .58. Typically, the correlation for high school GPA is slightly higher than for combined SAT scores.

The combination of scores and high school GPA raised the correlation .10 over scores alone, and .07 over high school record. For males, the correlation between the combination of scores and high school GPA with freshman GPA is .63, an increase of .09 over scores alone and .07 over high school GPA. For females, the correlation between the combination of scores and high school GPA with freshman GPA is .68, an increase of .07 over scores alone and .09 over high school GPA.

All correlations are adjusted for restriction of range so that the full range of scores and high school GPA are the same as for the national college-bound seniors cohort. See how to request SAT Answer–Reporting Services at http://www.collegeboard.com/student/testing/sat/reg/services. html. In addition, students who took the SAT in California in December 2007 can review the test questions under secure conditions at the ETS Western Field Office in Concord by calling 925 808–2000.

Procedures to Ensure Fairness and Equity. All new SAT Program test questions and complete new editions of the tests are reviewed by many individuals, including committees whose members are drawn from all regions of the United States. These reviews help identify and eliminate any wording or content that might be offensive or inappropriate for particular groups of students, such as racial or ethnic groups or men or women. Assessment staff ensure that the test as a whole includes references to men and women and individuals from varied racial, ethnic, and cultural backgrounds. Statistical procedures are used to identify questions that are harder for a group of students to answer correctly than would be expected from their performance on the test.

Relationship of SAT Scores to Family Income. The correlation of SAT scores and student reported family income for two recent years was found to be about .23 and .29, which is consistent with general research findings on the relationship of educational achievement and family income level. Although average SAT scores tend to be higher for students from higher-income families, students from every income level, as reported on the SAT Questionnaire, obtain the full range of SAT scores. Furthermore, many students from low-income families do well on the test. For seniors graduating in 2000, one-third of the students with reported family income at or below $30,000 obtained scores above the national average.

Releasing Your Scores to the New York State Scholarship Program. The New York State Scholarship Program requires that New York State students who wish to be considered for the Robert C. Byrd Honors Scholarships and Regents Scholarships in Cornell University on the basis of their SAT scores take this test before November 1, 2007. The latest SAT administration that meets this deadline is October 14, 2007.

The New York State Standardized Testing Law requires that you specifically authorize the sending of all reports. Your SAT scores and other information from your record will be sent to the Scholarship Program if you authorize the release of your scores at the time that you apply for a scholarship. To do that, you must answer "yes" and sign the score release statement on page 4 of the scholarship application. Scholarship application forms are sent by the State Education Department to principals of all high schools in New York State in December or January. If you follow these procedures, there is no fee for sending reports to the New York State Scholarship Program.

The College Board releases to the New York State Scholarship Program the names, addresses, and other identifying information of seniors who registered to take the SAT prior to November 1, 2007, who are New York State residents, and who apply for scholarship(s). This procedure facilitates the matching of student files so that scores for all students who authorized their release are sent to the New York State Scholarship Program. If you do not want your name and address released for this purpose, notify College Board SAT Program, P.O. Box, Miami, FL 33102, by November 1, 2007.

BORAT RELEASE*

STANDARD CONSENT AGREEMENT

This is an agreement between Springland Films (the "Producer") and the undersigned participant (the "Participant"). In exchange for the Producer's obligation to pay a participation fee in the amount of $ 2.00 (receipt of which is acknowledged by the Participant) and the opportunity for the Participant to appear in a motion picture, the Participant agrees as follows:

1. The Participant agrees to be filmed and audiotaped by the Producer for a documentary-style film (the "Film"). It is understood that the Producer hopes to reach a young adult audience by using entertaining content and formats.

2. The Participant agrees that any rights that the Participant may have in the Film or the Participant's contribution to the Film are hereby assigned to the Producer, and that the Producer shall be exclusively entitled to use, or to assign or license to others the right to use, the Film and any recorded material that includes the Participant without restriction in any media throughout the universe in perpetuity and without liability to the Participant, and the Participant hereby grants any consents required for those purposes. The Participant also agrees to allow the Producer, and any of its assignees or licensees, to use the Participant's contribution, photograph, film footage, and biographical material in connection not only with the Film, but also in any advertising, marketing or publicity for the Film and in connection with any ancillary products associated with the Film.

3. The Participant understands that the Producer and its assignees or licensees are relying upon this consent agreement in spending time, money and effort on the Film and the Participant's participation in it, and that the consent agreement, for this and other reasons, shall be irrevocable.

4. The Participant specifically, but without limitation, waives, and agrees not to bring at any time in the future, any claims against the Producer, or against any of its assignees or licensees or anyone associated with the Film, that include assertions of (a) infringement of rights of publicity or misappropriation (such as any allegedly improper or unauthorized use of the Participant's name or likeness or image), (b) damages caused by "acts of God" (such as, but not limited to, injuries from natural disasters), (c) damages caused by acts of terrorism or war, (d) intrusion (such as any allegedly offensive behavior or questioning or any invasion of privacy), (e) false light (such as any allegedly false or misleading portrayal of the Participant), (f) infliction of emotional distress (whether allegedly intentional or negligent), (g) trespass (to property or person), (h) breach of any alleged contract (whether the alleged contract is verbal or in writing), (i) allegedly deceptive business or trade practices, (j) copyright or trademark infringement, (k) defamation (such as any allegedly false statements made on the Film), (l) violations of Section 43(a) of the Lanham Act (such as allegedly false or misleading statements or suggestions about the Participant in relation to the Film or the Film in relation to the Participant), (m) prima facie tort (such as alleged intentional harm to the Participant), (n) fraud (such as any alleged deception or surprise about the Film or this consent agreement), (o) breach of alleged moral rights, or (p) tortious or wrongful interference with any contracts or business of the Participant, or any claim arising out of the Participant's viewing of any sexually-oriented materials or activities.

5. This is the entire agreement between the Participant and the Producer or anyone else in relation to the Film, and the Participant acknowledges that in entering into it, the Participant is not relying upon any promises or statements made by anyone about the nature of the Film or the identity of any other Participants or persons involved in the Film.

6. Although the Participant agrees not to bring any claim in connection with the Film or its production, if any claim nevertheless is made, the Participant agrees that any such claim must be brought

Exhibit 1

---

* This release underlies a lawsuit for fraud, rescission, and negligent infliction of emotional distress (among other claims) brought by two men who appeared in the movie *Borat: Cultural Learning of America for Make Benefit Glorious Nation of Kazakhstan*. The agreement is appended to a Movie Defendant's Special Motion to Strike Plaintiffs' Complaint. The case was dismissed on February 23, 2007. We thank Olivier Taillieu, Esq. for making this material available to us.

before, and adjudicated by, only a competent court located in the State of New York and County of New York, under the laws of the State of New York.

AGREED AND ACCEPTED:

_____
[please sign above line and print name below]

Dated: __10/28/05__
[date to be filled in by Participant]

Springland Films

By: _____

[please sign above line and print name below]

Description: Shirt_____ Height_____ Age_____

Hair_____ Sex_____

Other_____

Name: _____

Address: _____

Phone Number: _____

Social Security Number: _____

GOOGLE TERMS OF SERVICE*

.

Google Terms of Service	United States

Home

About Google

Privacy Highlights

Privacy Policy

Privacy FAQ

Terms of Service

Terms of Service Highlights

More privacy info:
- Desktop
- Gmail
- Groups
- Orkut
- Personalized Homepage
- Personalized Search
- Store
- Talk
- Toolbar
- Web Accelerator

Find on this site:

[   ]

Search

Google Terms of Service*

Welcome to Google!

1. Your relationship with Google

1.1 Your use of Google's products, software, services and web sites (referred to collectively as the "Services" in this document and excluding any services provided to you by Google under a separate written agreement) is subject to the terms of a legal agreement between you and Google. "Google" means Google Inc., whose principal place of business is at 1600 Amphitheatre Parkway, Mountain View, CA 94043, United States. This document explains how the agreement is made up, and sets out some of the terms of that agreement.

1.2 Unless otherwise agreed in writing with Google, your agreement with Google will always include, at a minimum, the terms and conditions set out in this document. These are referred to below as the "Universal Terms".

1.3 Your agreement with Google will also include the terms of any Legal Notices applicable to the Services, in addition to the Universal Terms. All of these are referred to below as the "Additional Terms". Where Additional Terms apply to a Service, these will be accessible for you to read either within, or through your use of, that Service.

1.4 The Universal Terms, together with the Additional Terms, form a legally binding agreement between you and Google in relation to your use of the Services. It is important that you take the time to read them carefully. Collectively, this legal agreement is referred to below as the "Terms".

1.5 If there is any contradiction between what the Additional Terms say and what the Universal Terms say, then the Additional Terms shall take precedence in relation to that Service.

* Reprinted with the permission of Google.

2. Accepting the Terms

2.1 In order to use the Services, you must first agree to the Terms. You may not use the Services if you do not accept the Terms.

2.2 You can accept the Terms by:

(A) clicking to accept or agree to the Terms, where this option is made available to you by Google in the user interface for any Service; or

(B) by actually using the Services. In this case, you understand and agree that Google will treat your use of the Services as acceptance of the Terms from that point onwards.

2.3 You may not use the Services and may not accept the Terms if (a) you are not of legal age to form a binding contract with Google, or (b) you are a person barred from receiving the Services under the laws of the United States or other countries including the country in which you are resident or from which you use the Services.

2.4 Before you continue, you should print off or save a local copy of the Universal Terms for your records.

3. Language of the Terms

3.1 Where Google has provided you with a translation of the English language version of the Terms, then you agree that the translation is provided for your convenience only and that the English language versions of the Terms will govern your relationship with Google.

3.2 If there is any contradiction between what the English language version of the Terms says and what a translation says, then the English language version shall take precedence.

4. Provision of the Services by Google

4.1 Google has subsidiaries and affiliated legal entities around the world ("Subsidiaries and Affiliates").

471

Sometimes, these companies will be providing the Services to you on behalf of Google itself. You acknowledge and agree that Subsidiaries and Affiliates will be entitled to provide the Services to you.

4.2 Google is constantly innovating in order to provide the best possible experience for its users. You acknowledge and agree that the form and nature of the Services which Google provides may change from time to time without prior notice to you.

4.3 As part of this continuing innovation, you acknowledge and agree that Google may stop (permanently or temporarily) providing the Services (or any features within the Services) to you or to users generally at Google's sole discretion, without prior notice to you. You may stop using the Services at any time. You do not need to specifically inform Google when you stop using the Services.

4.4 You acknowledge and agree that if Google disables access to your account, you may be prevented from accessing the Services, your account details or any files or other content which is contained in your account.

4.5 You acknowledge and agree that while Google may not currently have set a fixed upper limit on the number of transmissions you may send or receive through the Services or on the amount of storage space used for the provision of any Service, such fixed upper limits may be set by Google at any time, at Google's discretion.

5. Use of the Services by you

5.1 In order to access certain Services, you may be required to provide information about yourself (such as identification or contact details) as part of the registration process for the Service, or as part of your continued use of the Services. You agree that any registration information you give to Google will always be accurate, correct and up to date.

5.2 You agree to use the Services only for purposes that are permitted by (a) the Terms and (b) any applicable law, regulation or generally accepted practices or guidelines in the relevant jurisdictions (including any laws regarding the export of data or software to and from the United States or other relevant countries).

5.3 You agree not to access (or attempt to access) any of the Services by any means other than through the interface that is provided by Google, unless you have been specifically allowed to do so in a separate agreement with Google. You specifically agree not to access (or attempt to access) any of the Services through any automated means (including use of scripts or web crawlers) and shall ensure that you comply with the instructions set out in any robots.txt file present on the Services.

5.4 You agree that you will not engage in any activity that interferes with or disrupts the Services (or the servers and networks which are connected to the Services).

5.5 Unless you have been specifically permitted to do so in a separate agreement with Google, you agree that you will not reproduce, duplicate, copy, sell, trade or resell the Services for any purpose.

5.6 You agree that you are solely responsible for (and that Google has no responsibility to you or to any third party for) any breach of your obligations under the Terms and for the consequences (including any loss or damage which Google may suffer) of any such breach.

6. Your passwords and account security

6.1 You agree and understand that you are responsible for maintaining the confidentiality of passwords associated with any account you use to access the Services.

6.2 Accordingly, you agree that you will be solely responsible to Google for all activities that occur under your account.

6.3 If you become aware of any unauthorized use of your password or of your account, you agree to notify Google immediately at http://www.google.com/support/accounts/bin/answer.py?answer=48601.

7. Privacy and your personal information

7.1 For information about Google's data protection practices, please read Google's privacy policy at http://www.google.com/privacy.html. This policy explains how

Google treats your personal information, and protects your privacy, when you use the Services.

7.2 You agree to the use of your data in accordance with Google's privacy policies.

8. Content in the Services

8.1 You understand that all information (such as data files, written text, computer software, music, audio files or other sounds, photographs, videos or other images) which you may have access to as part of, or through your use of, the Services are the sole responsibility of the person from which such content originated. All such information is referred to below as the "Content".

8.2 You should be aware that Content presented to you as part of the Services, including but not limited to advertisements in the Services and sponsored Content within the Services may be protected by intellectual property rights which are owned by the sponsors or advertisers who provide that Content to Google (or by other persons or companies on their behalf). You may not modify, rent, lease, loan, sell, distribute or create derivative works based on this Content (either in whole or in part) unless you have been specifically told that you may do so by Google or by the owners of that Content, in a separate agreement.

8.3 Google reserves the right (but shall have no obligation) to pre-screen, review, flag, filter, modify, refuse or remove any or all Content from any Service. For some of the Services, Google may provide tools to filter out explicit sexual content. These tools include the SafeSearch preference settings (see http://www.google.com/help/customize.html#safe). In addition, there are commercially available services and software to limit access to material that you may find objectionable.

8.4 You understand that by using the Services you may be exposed to Content that you may find offensive, indecent or objectionable and that, in this respect, you use the Services at your own risk.

8.5 You agree that you are solely responsible for (and that Google has no responsibility to you or to any third party for) any Content that you create, transmit or display while using the Services and for the consequences of your actions (including any loss or damage which Google may suffer) by doing so.

9. Proprietary rights

9.1 You acknowledge and agree that Google (or Google's licensors) own all legal right, title and interest in and to the Services, including any intellectual property rights which subsist in the Services (whether those rights happen to be registered or not, and wherever in the world those rights may exist). You further acknowledge that the Services may contain information which is designated confidential by Google and that you shall not disclose such information without Google's prior written consent.

9.2 Unless you have agreed otherwise in writing with Google, nothing in the Terms gives you a right to use any of Google's trade names, trade marks, service marks, logos, domain names, and other distinctive brand features.

9.3 If you have been given an explicit right to use any of these brand features in a separate written agreement with Google, then you agree that your use of such features shall be in compliance with that agreement, any applicable provisions of the Terms, and Google's brand feature use guidelines as updated from time to time. These guidelines can be viewed online at http://www.google.com/permissions/guidelines.html (or such other URL as Google may provide for this purpose from time to time).

9.4 Other than the limited license set forth in Section 11, Google acknowledges and agrees that it obtains no right, title or interest from you (or your licensors) under these Terms in or to any Content that you submit, post, transmit or display on, or through, the Services, including any intellectual property rights which subsist in that Content (whether those rights happen to be registered or not, and wherever in the world those rights may exist). Unless you have agreed otherwise in writing with Google, you agree that you are responsible for protecting and enforcing those rights and that Google has no obligation to do so on your behalf.

9.5 You agree that you shall not remove, obscure, or alter any proprietary rights notices (including copyright and trade mark notices) which may be affixed to or contained within the Services.

9.6 Unless you have been expressly authorized to do so in writing by Google, you agree that in using the Services, you will not use any trade mark, service mark, trade name, logo of any company or organization in a way that is likely or intended to cause confusion about the owner or authorized user of such marks, names or logos.

10. License from Google

10.1 Google gives you a personal, worldwide, royalty-free, non-assignable and non-exclusive licence to use the software provided to you by Google as part of the Services as provided to you by Google (referred to as the "Software" below). This licence is for the sole purpose of enabling you to use and enjoy the benefit of the Services as provided by Google, in the manner permitted by the Terms.

10.2 You may not (and you may not permit anyone else to) copy, modify, create a derivative work of, reverse engineer, decompile or otherwise attempt to extract the source code of the Software or any part thereof, unless this is expressly permitted or required by law, or unless you have been specifically told that you may do so by Google, in writing.

10.3 Unless Google has given you specific written permission to do so, you may not assign (or grant a sub-licence of) your rights to use the Software, grant a security interest in or over your rights to use the Software, or otherwise transfer any part of your rights to use the Software.

11. Content licence from you

11.1 You retain copyright and any other rights you already hold in Content which you submit, post or display on or through, the Services. By submitting, posting or displaying the content you give Google a perpetual, irrevocable, worldwide, royalty-free, and non-exclusive licence to reproduce, adapt, modify, translate, publish, publicly perform, publicly display and distribute any Content which you submit, post or display on or through, the Services. This licence is for the sole purpose of enabling Google to display, distribute and promote the Services and may be revoked for certain Services as defined in the Additional Terms of those Services.

11.2 You agree that this licence includes a right for Google to make such Content available to other companies, organizations or individuals with whom Google has relationships for the provision of syndicated services, and to use such Content in connection with the provision of those services.

11.3 You understand that Google, in performing the required technical steps to provide the Services to our users, may (a) transmit or distribute your Content over various public networks and in various media; and (b) make such changes to your Content as are necessary to conform and adapt that Content to the technical requirements of connecting networks, devices, services or media. You agree that this licence shall permit Google to take these actions.

11.4 You confirm and warrant to Google that you have all the rights, power and authority necessary to grant the above licence.

12. Software updates

12.1 The Software which you use may automatically download and install updates from time to time from Google. These updates are designed to improve, enhance and further develop the Services and may take the form of bug fixes, enhanced functions, new software modules and completely new versions. You agree to receive such updates (and permit Google to deliver these to you) as part of your use of the Services.

13. Ending your relationship with Google

13.1 The Terms will continue to apply until terminated by either you or Google as set out below.

13.2 If you want to terminate your legal agreement with Google, you may do so by (a) notifying Google at any time and (b) closing your accounts for all of the Services which you use, where Google has made this option available to you. Your notice should be sent, in writing, to Google's address which is set out at the beginning of these Terms.

13.3 Google may at any time, terminate its legal agreement with you if:

(A) you have breached any provision of the Terms (or have acted in manner which clearly shows that you do not intend to, or are unable to comply with the provisions of the Terms); or

(B) Google is required to do so by law (for example, where the provision of the Services to you is, or becomes, unlawful); or

(C) the partner with whom Google offered the Services to you has terminated its relationship with Google or ceased to offer the Services to you; or

(D) Google is transitioning to no longer providing the Services to users in the country in which you are resident or from which you use the service; or

(E) the provision of the Services to you by Google is, in Google's opinion, no longer commercially viable.

13.4 Nothing in this Section shall affect Google's rights regarding provision of Services under Section 4 of the Terms.

13.5 When these Terms come to an end, all of the legal rights, obligations and liabilities that you and Google have benefited from, been subject to (or which have accrued over time whilst the Terms have been in force) or which are expressed to continue indefinitely, shall be unaffected by this cessation, and the provisions of paragraph 20.7 shall continue to apply to such rights, obligations and liabilities indefinitely.

14. EXCLUSION OF WARRANTIES

14.1 NOTHING IN THESE TERMS, INCLUDING SECTIONS 14 AND 15, SHALL EXCLUDE OR LIMIT GOOGLE'S WARRANTY OR LIABILITY FOR LOSSES WHICH MAY NOT BE LAWFULLY EXCLUDED OR LIMITED BY APPLICABLE LAW. SOME JURISDICTIONS

DO NOT ALLOW THE EXCLUSION OF CERTAIN WARRANTIES OR CONDITIONS OR THE LIMITATION OR EXCLUSION OF LIABILITY FOR LOSS OR DAMAGE CAUSED BY NEGLIGENCE, BREACH OF CONTRACT OR BREACH OF IMPLIED TERMS, OR INCIDENTAL OR CONSEQUENTIAL DAMAGES. ACCORDINGLY, ONLY THE LIMITATIONS WHICH ARE LAWFUL IN YOUR JURISDICTION WILL APPLY TO YOU AND OUR LIABILITY WILL BE LIMITED TO THE MAXIMUM EXTENT PERMITTED BY LAW.

14.2 YOU EXPRESSLY UNDERSTAND AND AGREE THAT YOUR USE OF THE SERVICES IS AT YOUR SOLE RISK AND THAT THE SERVICES ARE PROVIDED "AS IS" AND "AS AVAILABLE."

14.3 IN PARTICULAR, GOOGLE, ITS SUBSIDIARIES AND AFFILIATES, AND ITS LICENSORS DO NOT REPRESENT OR WARRANT TO YOU THAT:

(A) YOUR USE OF THE SERVICES WILL MEET YOUR REQUIREMENTS,

(B) YOUR USE OF THE SERVICES WILL BE UNINTERRUPTED, TIMELY, SECURE OR FREE FROM ERROR,

(C) ANY INFORMATION OBTAINED BY YOU AS A RESULT OF YOUR USE OF THE SERVICES WILL BE ACCURATE OR RELIABLE, AND

(D) THAT DEFECTS IN THE OPERATION OR FUNCTIONALITY OF ANY SOFTWARE PROVIDED TO YOU AS PART OF THE SERVICES WILL BE CORRECTED.

14.4 ANY MATERIAL DOWNLOADED OR OTHERWISE OBTAINED THROUGH THE USE OF THE SERVICES IS DONE AT YOUR OWN DISCRETION AND RISK AND THAT YOU WILL BE SOLELY RESPONSIBLE FOR ANY DAMAGE TO YOUR COMPUTER SYSTEM OR OTHER DEVICE OR LOSS OF DATA THAT RESULTS FROM THE DOWNLOAD OF ANY SUCH MATERIAL.

14.5 NO ADVICE OR INFORMATION, WHETHER ORAL OR WRITTEN, OBTAINED BY YOU FROM GOOGLE OR

THROUGH OR FROM THE SERVICES SHALL CREATE ANY WARRANTY NOT EXPRESSLY STATED IN THE TERMS.

14.6 GOOGLE FURTHER EXPRESSLY DISCLAIMS ALL WARRANTIES AND CONDITIONS OF ANY KIND, WHETHER EXPRESS OR IMPLIED, INCLUDING, BUT NOT LIMITED TO THE IMPLIED WARRANTIES AND CONDITIONS OF MERCHANTABILITY, FITNESS FOR A PARTICULAR PURPOSE AND NON-INFRINGEMENT.

15. LIMITATION OF LIABILITY

15.1 SUBJECT TO OVERALL PROVISION IN PARAGRAPH 14.1 ABOVE, YOU EXPRESSLY UNDERSTAND AND AGREE THAT GOOGLE, ITS SUBSIDIARIES AND AFFILIATES, AND ITS LICENSORS SHALL NOT BE LIABLE TO YOU FOR:

(A) ANY DIRECT, INDIRECT, INCIDENTAL, SPECIAL CONSEQUENTIAL OR EXEMPLARY DAMAGES WHICH MAY BE INCURRED BY YOU, HOWEVER CAUSED AND UNDER ANY THEORY OF LIABILITY.. THIS SHALL INCLUDE, BUT NOT BE LIMITED TO, ANY LOSS OF PROFIT (WHETHER INCURRED DIRECTLY OR INDIRECTLY), ANY LOSS OF GOODWILL OR BUSINESS REPUTATION, ANY LOSS OF DATA SUFFERED, COST OF PROCUREMENT OF SUBSTITUTE GOODS OR SERVICES, OR OTHER INTANGIBLE LOSS;

(B) ANY LOSS OR DAMAGE WHICH MAY BE INCURRED BY YOU, INCLUDING BUT NOT LIMITED TO LOSS OR DAMAGE AS A RESULT OF:

(I) ANY RELIANCE PLACED BY YOU ON THE COMPLETENESS, ACCURACY OR EXISTENCE OF ANY ADVERTISING, OR AS A RESULT OF ANY RELATIONSHIP OR TRANSACTION BETWEEN

YOU AND ANY ADVERTISER OR SPONSOR WHOSE ADVERTISING APPEARS ON THE SERVICES;

(II) ANY CHANGES WHICH GOOGLE MAY MAKE TO THE SERVICES, OR FOR ANY PERMANENT OR TEMPORARY CESSATION IN THE PROVISION OF THE SERVICES (OR ANY FEATURES WITHIN THE SERVICES);

(III) THE DELETION OF, CORRUPTION OF, OR FAILURE TO STORE, ANY CONTENT AND OTHER COMMUNICATIONS DATA MAINTAINED OR TRANSMITTED BY OR THROUGH YOUR USE OF THE SERVICES;

(III) YOUR FAILURE TO PROVIDE GOOGLE WITH ACCURATE ACCOUNT INFORMATION;

(IV) YOUR FAILURE TO KEEP YOUR PASSWORD OR ACCOUNT DETAILS SECURE AND CONFIDENTIAL;

15.2 THE LIMITATIONS ON GOOGLE'S LIABILITY TO YOU IN PARAGRAPH 15.1 ABOVE SHALL APPLY WHETHER OR NOT GOOGLE HAS BEEN ADVISED OF OR SHOULD HAVE BEEN AWARE OF THE POSSIBILITY OF ANY SUCH LOSSES ARISING.

16. Copyright and trade mark policies

16.1 It is Google's policy to respond to notices of alleged copyright infringement that comply with applicable international intellectual property law (including, in the

United States, the Digital Millennium Copyright Act) and to terminating the accounts of repeat infringers. Details of Google's policy can be found at http://www.google.com/ dmca.html.

16.2 Google operates a trade mark complaints procedure in respect of Google's advertising business, details of which can be found at http://www.google.com/ tm_complaint.html.

17. Advertisements

17.1 Some of the Services are supported by advertising revenue and may display advertisements and promotions. These advertisements may be targeted to the content of information stored on the Services, queries made through the Services or other information.

17.2 The manner, mode and extent of advertising by Google on the Services are subject to change without specific notice to you.

17.3 In consideration for Google granting you access to and use of the Services, you agree that Google may place such advertising on the Services.

18. Other content

18.1 The Services may include hyperlinks to other web sites or content or resources. Google may have no control over any web sites or resources which are provided by companies or persons other than Google.

18.2 You acknowledge and agree that Google is not responsible for the availability of any such external sites or resources, and does not endorse any advertising, products or other materials on or available from such web sites or resources.

18.3 You acknowledge and agree that Google is not liable for any loss or damage which may be incurred by you as a result of the availability of those external sites or resources, or as a result of any reliance placed by you on the completeness, accuracy or existence of any advertising, products or other materials on, or available from, such web sites or resources.

19. Changes to the Terms

19.1 Google may make changes to the Universal Terms or Additional Terms from time to time. When these changes are made, Google will make a new copy of the Universal Terms available at http://www.google.com/accounts/TOS?loc=us&hl=en and any new Additional Terms will be made available to you from within, or through, the affected Services.

19.2 You understand and agree that if you use the Services after the date on which the Universal Terms or Additional Terms have changed, Google will treat your use as acceptance of the updated Universal Terms or Additional Terms.

20. General legal terms

20.1 Sometimes when you use the Services, you may (as a result of, or through your use of the Services) use a service or download a piece of software, or purchase goods, which are provided by another person or company. Your use of these other services, software or goods may be subject to separate terms between you and the company or person concerned. If so, the Terms do not affect your legal relationship with these other companies or individuals.

20.2 The Terms constitute the whole legal agreement between you and Google and govern your use of the Services (but excluding any services which Google may provide to you under a separate written agreement), and completely replace any prior agreements between you and Google in relation to the Services.

20.3 You agree that Google may provide you with notices, including those regarding changes to the Terms, by email, regular mail, or postings on the Services.

20.4 You agree that if Google does not exercise or enforce any legal right or remedy which is contained in the Terms (or which Google has the benefit of under any applicable law), this will not be taken to be a formal waiver of Google's rights and that those rights or remedies will still be available to Google.

Google Terms of Service

20.5 If any court of law, having the jurisdiction to decide on this matter, rules that any provision of these Terms is invalid, then that provision will be removed from the Terms without affecting the rest of the Terms. The remaining provisions of the Terms will continue to be valid and enforceable.

20.6 You acknowledge and agree that each member of the group of companies of which Google is the parent shall be third party beneficiaries to the Terms and that such other companies shall be entitled to directly enforce, and rely upon, any provision of the Terms which confers a benefit on (or rights in favor of) them. Other than this, no other person or company shall be third party beneficiaries to the Terms.

20.7 The Terms, and your relationship with Google under the Terms, shall be governed by the laws of the State of California without regard to its conflict of laws provisions. You and Google agree to submit to the exclusive jurisdiction of the courts located within the county of Santa Clara, California to resolve any legal matter arising from the Terms. Notwithstanding this, you agree that Google shall still be allowed to apply for injunctive remedies (or an equivalent type of urgent legal relief) in any jurisdiction.

April 16, 2007

©2007 Google - <u>Home</u> - <u>About Google</u> - <u>Privacy Policy</u> - <u>Terms of Service</u>

†